"Abraham Kuruvilla's commentary set on the Psalter is unique and helpful. He clearly explains the text of each Psalm, laying out its meaning as well as aspects of divine demand, calling its readers to Christlikeness. I thank him for his faithful ministry in helping students bring and use God's word to push believers toward Christlikeness."

—**Michael A. Grisanti**, distinguished research professor of Old Testament, The Master's Seminary

"With keen appreciation for literary and rhetorical features of each psalm, Kuruvilla keeps his finger on the text. He resists a 'homiletical hermeneutic' that is driven by what one wants to preach *out of the text* rather than what the psalmists tried to communicate *with the text*. Although he is an authority on preaching, Kuruvilla does not prescribe how to preach individual psalms, but teachers of Scripture will be inspired by his commentary and find the 'sermon maps' that conclude the commentary on each psalm helpful."

—**Daniel I. Block**, professor emeritus of Old Testament, Wheaton College

"What an extraordinary study! Abraham Kuruvilla has applied himself with resolution and enthusiasm to all 150 psalms, and here he shares the results with us. He thus takes us through the entire Psalter with careful and suggestive outlines of the Psalms for preachers, and with judicious comments on their theological significance. It will be wonderful if pastors make them a resource for preaching. Indeed, any student of the Psalms will learn from them."

—**John Goldingay**, senior professor of Old Testament, Fuller Theological Seminary

"What a delightful surprise this series of commentaries on the Psalms is. Working with proper regard for the newest academic insights, Abraham Kuruvilla makes an innovative synthesis of the meaning of each psalm, building a bridge between its theological essence and practical application of the text in various situations. This series will be extremely useful for anyone who preaches, teaches, or studies the Bible seriously."

—**Philippus (Phil) J. Botha**, professor emeritus of ancient and modern languages and cultures, University of Pretoria, Pretoria, South Africa

"Whenever my friend and former colleague Abe Kuruvilla speaks about preaching, I'm all ears. If you've read his books on preaching or listened to his sermons, you understand why. His hermeneutical approach is carefully crafted, producing penetrating insights and proposals worthy of consideration. This commentary is wonderful and, crafted in the crucible of Abe's personal suffering, will be immensely helpful to those who love the Psalms and the God who inspired ancient authors to compose them."

—**Robert B. Chisholm Jr.**, chair and senior professor of Old Testament studies, Dallas Theological Seminary

"Why is it that we don't hear more excellent sermons on the Psalms that engage the text in deep and serious ways? Abe Kuruvilla has written a monumental three-volume work to help address this shortcoming. He recognizes that the Psalms, as captivating as they may be, are not necessarily easy to interpret and many of their contexts and occasions remain in the shadows. Nevertheless, through close attention to each psalm, Kuruvilla shows that their theology can result in preaching that engages both the heart and the mind."

—**Stanley E. Porter**, president, dean, and professor of New Testament, McMaster Divinity College

"Although preaching from the Psalter was a regular practice in the early church, nowadays Christians might sing and pray the Psalms, but rarely listen to a sermon on one of them. Abraham Kuruvilla's commentary skillfully reverses this trend. He takes seriously each psalm in its poetic Hebrew medium, then applies its theological message, however difficult, to Christian discipleship today. No minister now has an excuse for avoiding preaching from the book of Psalms."

—**Susan Gillingham**, professor emeritus of Hebrew Bible, University of Oxford

"This three-volume series on preaching the Psalms is a masterful work, combining exegesis, hermeneutics, biblical theology, and homiletics. Abraham Kuruvilla astutely guides the preacher through the most difficult step of sermon development in the Psalms. In my opinion, this is the best work on preaching the Psalms that is available today, and it should be on the shelf of all preachers who aspire to proclaim the wonderful message of the Psalms to their congregations."

—**J. Daniel Hays**, senior professor of Old Testament, Southwestern Baptist Theological Seminary

"Abraham Kuruvilla has provided the kind of theological exegesis preachers need to engage in sermon preparation. His thorough exploration draws on his own attention to the literary complexities of the text and his engagement with the best of scholarship. A literal translation, structural analysis, theological focus statement, discerning commentary, and sermon map for each psalm efficiently guide the preacher through the essential steps of sermon development. This will be my go-to commentary on the Psalms."

—**Timothy S. Warren**, senior professor emeritus of pastoral ministries, Dallas Theological Seminary

"In his commentary, Abe Kuruvilla approaches the Psalms with the eye and the heart of a preacher/pastor. He draws deeply from the scholarly literature, but he focuses on the needs of the expositor. His primary emphasis is upon how Christians are to align their lives to what God reveals in the various songs in the Psalter, and how the Psalms guide the people of God in their spiritual transformation toward Christlikeness. What he has written will both stretch the mind and warm the heart of the reader. I highly recommend it!"

—**Daniel Estes**, distinguished professor of Old Testament, Cedarville University

"Abraham Kuruvilla has produced another helpful commentary to guide faithful preaching of God's word. Although best known as a leading scholar in homiletics, he proves himself to be a competent Hebrew exegete as well. His Christiconic hermeneutic allows the Psalms to fully speak their multidimensional message for spiritual formation today."

—**John W. Hilber**, professor of Old Testament, McMaster Divinity College

"This is a valuable addition to Abraham Kuruvilla's existing work on Christian preaching of Scripture. He knows the issues, provides a fresh translation of the Hebrew text to ponder, and offers theologically robust content. Though it is oriented to those who would preach the Psalms, it also has value for those who pray them."

—**Walter Moberly**, professor emeritus of theology and biblical interpretation, Durham University

Psalms 101–150

PSALMS 101–150

A Theological Commentary for Preachers

Abraham Kuruvilla

CASCADE *Books* • Eugene, Oregon

PSALMS 101–150
A Theological Commentary for Preachers

Copyright © 2024 Abraham Kuruvilla. All rights reserved. Except for brief quotations in critical publications or reviews, no part of this book may be reproduced in any manner without prior written permission from the publisher. Write: Permissions, Wipf and Stock Publishers, 199 W. 8th Ave., Suite 3, Eugene, OR 97401.

Cascade Books
An Imprint of Wipf and Stock Publishers
199 W. 8th Ave., Suite 3
Eugene, OR 97401

www.wipfandstock.com

PAPERBACK ISBN: 978-1-6667-5173-4
HARDCOVER ISBN: 978-1-6667-5174-1
EBOOK ISBN: 978-1-6667-5175-8

Cataloguing-in-Publication data:

Names: Kuruvilla, Abraham, author.

Title: Psalms 101–150 : a theological commentary for preachers / by Abraham Kuruvilla.

Description: Eugene, OR: Cascade Books, 2024. | Includes bibliographical references and index.

Identifiers: ISBN 978-1-6667-5173-4 (paperback). | ISBN 978-1-6667-5174-1 (hardcover). | ISBN 978-1-6667-5175-8 (ebook).

Subjects: LCSH: Bible—Psalms CI–CL. | Homiletics.

Classification: BS 1430.3 K87 2024 (print). | BS 1430.3 (epub).

VERSION NUMBER 05/20/24

To
Johann Sebastian Bach (1685–1750)
for the rapture of his *œuvre*

Christ lag in Todes Banden
für unsre Sünd gegeben,
er ist wieder erstanden
und hat uns bracht das Leben;
des wir sollen fröhlich sein,
Gott loben und ihm dankbar sein;
und singen Halleluja!

and

Muthampackal Kochukunju Upadesi (1883–1945)
for the hope of his hymnody

പിതാവില്ലാത്തോർക്കവൻ നല്ലൊരു താതനും,
പെറ്റമ്മയെ കവിഞ്ഞാർദ്രവാനും,
വിധവയ്ക്കു കാന്തനും സാധുവിനപ്പവും,
എല്ലാർക്കും എല്ലാം എൻ കർത്താവത്രേ!

Contents

Abbreviations | ix

Psalm 101:1–8	*The Integrity of God's Leaders*	1
Psalm 102:1–28	*Evanescent Ones Find Security in the Eternal One*	7
Psalm 103:1–22	*Blessing Yahweh for His Lovingkindness*	15
Psalm 104:1–35	*God: Creator and Conservator*	22
Psalm 105:1–45	*Praise for God's Faithfulness in the Past*	32
Psalm 106:1–48	*God's Lovingkindness Forgives and Delivers*	43
Psalm 107:1–43	*Thanksgiving for Deliverances in Lovingkindness*	52
Psalm 108:1–13	*Confidence in, and Praise for, Deliverance*	60
Psalm 109:1–31	*God's Lovingkindness Protects from Persecutors*	65
Psalm 110:1–7	*God's King-Priest*	73
Psalm 111:1–10	*God's Deeds and Directives*	80
Psalm 112:1–10	*Blessing of the God-Fearer*	86
Psalm 113:1–9	*Praising the High One Who Lifts the Lowly*	91
Psalm 114:1–8	*Reverence for the Creator and Redeemer*	95
Psalm 115:1–18	*God vs. Idols*	99
Psalm 116:1–19	*Commitment, Preservation, and Thanksgiving*	104
Psalm 117:1–2	*Nations Praise God's Lovingkindness and Truth*	111
Psalm 118:1–29	*Leader's Thanksgiving for Divine Deliverance*	114
Psalm 119:1–176	*God's Servant and God's Word*	122
Psalm 120:1–7	*Life Among Enemies*	167
Psalm 121:1–8	*Journeying with the Divine Keeper*	172
Psalm 122:1–9	*The City of God at Peace*	177
Psalm 123:1–4	*Utter Dependance of Servant upon Master*	182
Psalm 124:1–8	*But for God . . .*	186
Psalm 125:1–5	*Trust, Don't Totter*	191
Psalm 126:1–6	*The Joy of Divine Restoration*	195
Psalm 127:1–5	*Worthlessness without God; Blessing with God*	199
Psalm 128:1–6	*Blessing upon God-Fearers*	206

Psalm 129:1–8	*Unblessedness of Enemies*	210
Psalm 130:1–8	*The Lovingkindness of Being Forgiven*	214
Psalm 131:1–3	*Resting Humbly and Contentedly in God*	221
Psalm 132:1–18	*Worship, Faithful Obedience, and the Presence of God*	226
Psalm 133:1–3	*Human Worship and Divine Blessing*	236
Psalm 134:1–3	*Blessers Blessed*	240
Psalm 135:1–21	*Praising the Sovereign and Unique God*	244
Psalm 136:1–26	*Lovingkindness unto Forever*	253
Psalm 137:1–9	*Justice for the Infliction of Terror*	259
Psalm 138:1–8	*Thanksgiving to the One on High Who Delivers the Lowly*	269
Psalm 139:1–24	*God's Attributes and God's Aid*	274
Psalm 140:1–13	*Prayer for Preservation*	283
Psalm 141:1–10	*Maintaining Integrity in Distressing Times*	289
Psalm 142:1–7	*Revived, Restored, Recompensed*	295
Psalm 143:1–12	*Spiritual Pursuit of God by His Servants in Distress*	301
Psalm 144:1–15	*Prosperity Under the Hand of God Who Does It All*	308
Psalm 145:1–21	*Praise of the God-King by All Flesh*	315
Psalm 146:1–10	*Trusting in God, the Patron and Ruler*	325
Psalm 147:1–20	*Pleasing God by Obedience*	330
Psalm 148:1–14	*Joining Praise with All Creation*	337
Psalm 149:1–9	*Praise for Justice Executed*	342
Psalm 150:1–6	*Self-Abandoning Praise*	348

Conclusion | 353

Bibliography | 358
Index of Keywords and Selected Topics | 365
Index of Authors | 381
Index of Scripture and Apocrypha | 383

Abbreviations

ANET *Ancient Near Eastern Texts Relating to the Old Testament,*
        edited by James B. Pritchard
LXX   Septuagint
MT   Masoretic Text
NPNF¹ *Nicene and Post-Nicene Fathers, Series 1,*
        edited by Philip Schaff
NT   New Testament
OT   Old Testament

PSALM 101:1–8

Psalm of Orientation

The Integrity of God's Leaders

THE CONTENTS OF PSALM 101 indicate its original use as a manifesto of a leader (king? governor?) pledging before God to maintain integrity himself, and to not tolerate any lack of integrity amongst his subordinates. In that sense, it is a commitment that needs to be made by all of God's people.[1]

Translation

101:1 Of lovingkindness and justice I will sing,
        to You, Yahweh, I will make music.

101:2 I will attend to the way of integrity.
        When will You come to me?
      I will walk in the integrity of my heart
        within my house.

101:3 I will not set before my eyes [any] worthless thing;
        the work of deviants I hated;
        it will not cleave to me.

101:4 A perverse heart will go away from me;
        evil I will not know.

101:5 The one who covertly slanders his neighbor,
        him I will destroy;
      [the one with] haughty eyes and arrogant heart—
        him I will not tolerate.

101:6 My eyes [are] on the faithful of the land,
        to dwell with me.

---

1. For, as go the leaders, so go the people. All God's requirements of leaders in Scripture are ultimately requirements for his people. All translations of Scripture in this work are my own.

> The one who walks in the way of integrity,
>> he will serve me.
> 101:7 He will not dwell within my house,
>> the one working deceit.
> The one speaking falsehood,
>> he will not stand before my eyes.
> 101:8 Morning after morning I will destroy
>> all the wicked of the land,
> to cut off from the city of Yahweh
>> all those doing iniquity.

Structure

Psalm 101 comprises the *Leader's Individual Standard* (101:1–5) and the *Leader's Incorporate Standard* (101:6–8). Each section begins with a positive utterance, followed by a negative one:[2]

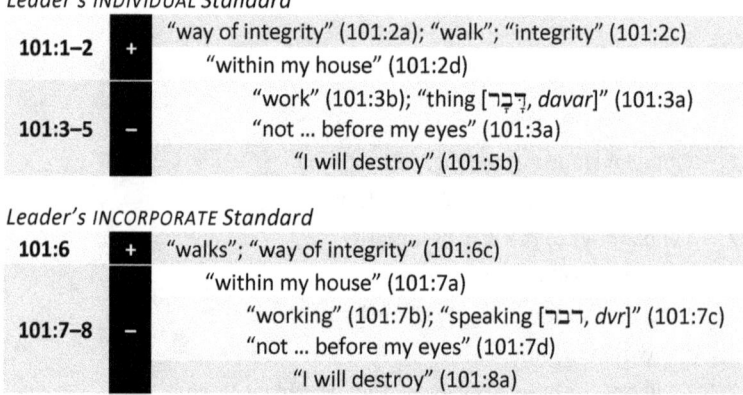

Also notable, the entire psalm is bookended by "Yahweh" (101:1b, 8c), the only two instances of the name in the poem, thus emphasizing that the leader's responsibilities are ultimately grounded in a relationship to God. In all of this, the concern is how the leader discharges his entrusted responsibility over "house" (101:2d, 7a)—his individual standard—and "city" (101:8c) and "land" (101:6a, 8b)—his incorporate standard. "It transpires that Psalm 101 is about choices of association and disassociation in one's personal life and in the public sphere .... These choices are made on the basis of the speaker's dedication to Yahweh."[3]

---

2. Modified from Girard, *Les Psaumes Redécouverts*, 16; and Botha, "Psalm 101," 4. The second section is, itself, bookended by "faithful of the land" (101:6a) and "wicked of the land" (101:8a).

3. Botha, "Psalm 101," 4.

Theological Focus

Loyalty to God that results in his praise and the manifestation of his attributes is reflected in his leaders' intense individual commitment to living in God's way of integrity and in their insistence upon such integrity being manifest in the lives of those whom they incorporately oversee.

Commentary

Leader's Individual Standard (101:1–5)

In the psalm, only 101:1–2b addresses Yahweh directly, in the second person. And the parallels in 101:1 are striking: "lovingkindness and justice" in 101:1a are equated to "You, Yahweh" in 101:1b (and both deity and attributes are sung about or are the objects to whom music is made; 101:1), thereby providing the theme of the psalm. The one who would serve Yahweh and who has been called by him to lead his people must demonstrate these characteristics of deity. But there is implicitly another relationship in the psalm: not just that between deity and leader, but also between leader and community, in whose presence these words are uttered. "The declaration of integrity then expresses before the community and before Yhwh a categorical and total commitment to Yhwh."[4] There is thus a keen sense of accountability on the part of the leader to those he represents, and reciprocally, those people are being taught to hold their leaders accountable and, ultimately, to be like them in their walk with God.

There may be a subtle hint of a leader in distress perhaps, as he asks Yahweh: "When [מָתַי, *mati*] will You come to me?" (101:2b). Of the eleven instances of מָתַי in the Psalter that are directed to God, ten of them arise from a distressed supplicant. Perhaps that might be the case here, as well. If that is so, then the supplicant may be asking God to intervene in some difficult situation on the grounds that he, the leader, has been faithful to his vocation and to his deity.[5] For, if one wants Yahweh to "come," then one's life and living space—"heart," "house" (101:2cd), "city" (101:8c), and "land" (101:6a, 8b)—must be readied for deity's arrival, "so that Yahweh will feel at home, so to speak."[6]

In any case, the "way of *integrity*" (101:2a), i.e., Yahweh's way of integrity, is what the leader promises to walk in: "I will walk in the *integrity* of my heart" (101:2c). God's way will be in the supplicant's heart, and his life will take its course along that path.[7] The mention of both "heart" and "house" (101:2cd) underscores the importance of integrity in private life, often unseen and unsung. Clearly, this is the leader's *Individual Standard* of integrity.

Corresponding to the positive assertion of 101:2, there is a negative assertion in 101:3–5: the items, attitudes, and entities with which the leader will have no truck, particularly those

---

4. Goldingay, *Psalms*, 3:140.

5. The specifics of this hypothetical issue of distress do not affect the thrust of the text, though it needs to be said that a commitment to God such as is demonstrated by the supplicant is vital for a relationship with God, thus increasing the likelihood of God's gracious deliverance from such situations of stress.

6. Botha, "Psalm 101," 4. This is akin to the increasing, and progressively more extensive, dwelling of Christ in the life of the believer—an annexation, so to speak (e.g., Eph 3:14–21).

7. If the one praying was a king, this would be congruent to God's requirement for rulers in Deut 17:18–20.

that are "worthless," which translates בְּלִיַּעַל, *bliyya'al*, "Belial." Later in Christian history this word would become descriptive of things satanic (Βελιάρ, *Beliar*, "Beliar," a variant; in 2 Cor 6:15). Therefore, "hatred is an important spiritual and moral virtue."[8]

Indeed, even those living/working in the presence of the leader, if they practiced these kinds of wickedness, would not be tolerated; they would be destroyed (Ps 101:5).[9] The emphatic use of the pronoun אֹתוֹ/אוֹתוֹ, *'oto*, "him," in 101:5b, 5d, emphasizes his resolve.

> The commitment means not only avoiding crooked action, crooked attitudes, and crooked people, but taking action against crooked peoples. The suppliant speaks again about secret actions and inner attitudes, but now these are the secrets and attitudes of other people. Speaking against . . . one's neighbor in secret implies not merely gossip but the lies that can imperil someone's life [101:5ab].[10]

So also eyes that are haughty and hearts that are arrogant (101:5c).

There are seven verbs in 101:3–5 indicating the leader's dissociation from evil, with alternate verbs negated by the particle, לֹא, *lo'*, "not":[11]

101:3a	"will *not* set"
101:3b	"hated"
101:3c	"will *not* cleave"
101:4a	"will go away"
101:4b	"will *not* know"
101:5b	"will destroy"
101:5d	"will *not* tolerate"

While not precisely corresponding with these verbs, there are also seven items that are disavowed in 101:3–5: "worthless thing," "work of deviants," "perverse heart," "evil," "the one who covertly slanders his neighbor," "[the one with] haughty eyes," and those with an "arrogant heart."[12] It is likely that the number seven is carefully chosen: this is a total renunciation of evil, and a commitment to comprehensive individual purity. Unlike those with "perverse hearts" (101:4a) and "arrogant hearts" (101:5c), this leader's "heart" is one of "integrity" (101:2c).

How would the leader be able to pick out those sinning in their hearts (101:5c)? While those evil attitudes may have become manifest visibly, it seems that only God would be able to identify such offenders accurately. So there seems to be a conflation of leader and deity in the psalm, which may not be accidental: what God sees, the leader sees; God's way of integrity becomes the leader's own. "This overlap in their profiles is by design and serves to emphasise the close association between them."[13]

---

8. Goldingay, *Psalms*, 3:143.

9. While this sounds like the leader's standard for the corporate body, here in the first section (101:1–5) it simply reflects that person's utmost determination to disassociate with anything and anyone ungodly. In the second section, these evildoers stand alone, not lumped with things, doings ("work"), or people, as in 101:3–5.

10. Goldingay, *Psalms*, 3:143.

11. Kselman, "Psalm 101," 48.

12. The imprecision is because in 101:3bc, a single noun becomes the subject of two verbs; and in 101:5cd, two nouns are qualified by a single verb.

13. Botha, "Psalm 101," 3. Conceivably, this could be the reason for the request to Yahweh to "come to

Leader's Incorporate Standard (101:6–8)

As with the first section, this one, too, begins with a positive statement—of association. The leader promises not to set anything from "Belial" (or any "worthless thing") before his "eyes" (101:3a) and not to tolerate those with haughty "eyes" (101:5c); rather, his "eyes" will be upon the faithful, the people of God (101:6a); all others would not be allowed before his "eyes" (101:7d). The commitment of the leader to God's "way of integrity" (101:2a) is so intense, only those equally committed to that "way of integrity" (101:6c) will be his co-laborers. And the leader intends to maintain integrity "within my house" (101:2d), which also involves ostracizing evildoers from "within my house" (101:7a). Just as the leader "walks in . . . integrity" (101:2c), so he wants his reports to "walk in . . . integrity" (101:6c). Thus, not only is the leader committed to integrity as an individual, in his incorporate role also his associates and subordinates are to be likeminded persons of integrity.

On the other hand, workers of deceit[14] and speakers of falsehood will not stand before his "eyes" (101:7d). Thus we have a sequence of "eyes" that focus (!) alternately between godly leader and evildoers:

101:3a	"I will not set before my *eyes*"	Subject: godly leader
101:5c	"eyes"	of evildoers
101:6a	"eyes"	of godly leader
101:7d	"not stand before my *eyes*"	Subject: evildoer

While the faithful will "dwell" with the leader (101:6ab), evildoers will "not dwell" in his presence (101:7a). Not only will they not inhabit space in his "house," such malefactors will be wiped off the face of the "land" (101:8b) and from the "city" of Yahweh (101:8c): excommunication and exile. And this commitment, the leader determines, will not be a one-time cleanup but an ongoing purge, "morning after morning" (101:8a), perhaps the first thing the leader does daily—purification.[15] The contrasting fates of the "faithful of the *land*" (101:6a) and the "wicked of the *land*" (101:8b) are sharp and clear.

Underlying the entire psalm is the leader's awareness of duty and obligation to God, the ruler of his people. Such a commitment is particularly necessary in a day and age where leadership failures are rife, even among the people of God. Goldingay's comment on secular leadership is incisive: "Democracy has made the problem worse, because now the rulers are people who wanted power rather than people who were born into it by accident of birth."[16] May the leaders of God's people in Christ's Church model for the world's leaders (and for their own flock) "a more excellent way" as they serve in God's way of integrity.

---

me" (101:2b), to aid the speaker in upright living.

14. The leader had declared that he hated the "work" of deviants (101:3b); now he asserts that those "working" deceit will be excommunicated from his house (101:7ab).

15. See Goldingay, *Psalms*, 3:144.

16. Goldingay, *Psalms*, 3:145. In other words, a hereditary monarchy has a 50 percent chance of the incumbent not being particularly eager for the job of ruling. Not so in a democracy, where almost everyone who runs for elected office wants the position, power, and privileges appertaining thereunto.

Sermon Map

I. Leader's Individual Standards
   Commitment to personal integrity, the way of God (101:1–5)
   Move-to-relevance: Our toleration of lax standards
II. Leader's Incorporate Standards
   Commitment to integrity in co-workers and subordinates (101:6–8)
   Move-to-relevance: Our lack of responsibility for associates
III. *Character of the Chief!*
   Specifics on developing individual and incorporate integrity

PSALM 102:1–28

Psalm of Disorientation

Evanescent Ones Find Security in the Eternal One

PSALM 102 IS ONE of the seven traditional "Penitential Psalms," the others being Psalms 6; 32; 38; 51; 130; and 143.

Translation

102:1	Yahweh, hear my prayer.	
	My cry for help, may it come before You.	
102:2	Do not hide Your face from me	
	in the day of my distress.	
	Incline Your ear to me;	
	in the day when I call, answer me quickly.	
102:3	For they have been consumed in smoke—my days,	
	and my bones like a furnace have been scorched;	
102:4	my heart has been crushed like grass and has withered.	
	For I forget to eat my bread	
102:5	with the sound of my groaning;	
	my bone clings to my flesh.	
102:6	I have come to resemble a tawny owl of the wilderness;	
	I have become like a screech owl among ruins.	
102:7	I have remained awake;	
	I have become like a lone bird on a housetop.	
102:8	All day long they have reproached me, my enemies;	
	those deriding me swear by me.	
102:9	For I have eaten ashes like bread,	
	and I have mixed my drink with weeping	

102:10 in the face of Your indignation and Your rage,
     for You have lifted me and thrown me away.
102:11 My days are like an extended shadow,
     and I—like grass I wither.
102:12 But You, Yahweh, forever You dwell,
     and Your memory from generation to generation.
102:13 You—You will arise, You will have compassion on Zion;
     for it is time to be gracious to her,
     for the appointed season has come.
102:14 For Your servants have taken delight in her stones,
     and they are gracious to her dust.
102:15 And the nations will fear the name of Yahweh,
     and all the kings of the earth Your glory.
102:16 For Yahweh has built up Zion;
     He has appeared in His glory.
102:17 He has turned to the prayer of the destitute,
     and has not despised their prayer.
102:18 This will be written for the generation to come,
     and a people [yet] to be created will praise Yah.
102:19 For He has looked down from His holy height;
     Yahweh, from heaven, has watched the earth,
102:20 to hear the groaning of the prisoner,
     to liberate the children of death,
102:21 [for them] to recount in Zion the name of Yahweh
     and His praise in Jerusalem,
102:22 in the gathering of peoples together,
     and the kingdoms, to serve Yahweh.
102:23 He has weakened my strength in the way;
     He has shortened my days.
102:24   I say, "My God, do not take me up in the midst of my days."
Your years are from generation to generation.
102:25   [Long] before, You founded the earth,
     and the heavens are the work of Your hands.
102:26 They—they will perish, but You—You will endure;
     and all of them like a garment will wear out;
     like clothing You will make them pass away, and they will pass away.
102:27 But You are the [same] One,
     and Your years will not finish.
102:28 The children of Your servants will abide,
     and their descendants will be established before You.

Structure

This psalm has a *Petition 1*, a *Profession 1* declaring confidence in God, and concludes with a précis that summarizes the preceding petition and the profession (*Petition 2* and *Profession 2*) and borrowing words and phrases from them:[1]

Petition 1 (102:1–11)
  Plea (**102:1–2**)
  Plaint (**102:3–11**)
    "hear"; "prayer" (102:1a)
    "face [פָּנֶה, *paneh*]" (102:2a); "groaning [אֲנָחָה, *'anachah*]" (102:5a)
      "my days" (102:3a, 11a); "not" (102:2a); "answer [ענה, *'nh*]" (102:2d)

Profession 1 (102:12–22)
  Prospect of divine action (**102:12–17**)
  Praise for divine action (**102:18–22**)
    "hear" (102:20a); "prayer" (102:17a, 17b)
    "turned [פנה, *pnh*]" (102:17a); "groaning [אֲנָקָה, *'anaqah*]" (102:20a)
      "and You" (102:12a); "You—You" (102:13a)
      "heaven" (102:19b); "generation to generation" (102:12b)
      "Your servants" (102:14a)

PRÉCIS *(102:23–28)*
Petition 2 (102:23–24a) [= Petition 1]
    "my days" (102:23b, 24a); "not" (102:24a); "weaken [ענה]" (102:23a)

Profession 2 (102:24b–28) [= Profession 1]
      "and You" (102:26a, 27a); "You—You" (102:26a)
      "heavens" (102:25b); "generation to generation" (102:24b)
      "Your servants" (102:28a)

Theological Focus

God's people, in desperate circumstances, boldly plead for God's interventional aid and beseech him to relent from his anger, particularly in light of the temporality of human life that is in contrast to the eternality of divine existence, while emphasizing their own faithfulness to God and anticipating his reciprocal faithfulness to them, the outcome of which will be universal praise of deity and long-lasting stability of the people of God in his presence.

---

1. From deClaissé-Walford et al., *Book of Psalms*, 748–49, 752–53; Girard, *Les Psaumes Redécouverts*, 31; and Allen, *Psalms 101–150*, 14.

Commentary

Petition 1 (102:1–11)

This first petition section of the psalm comprises a plea to Yahweh (102:1–2) and the plaint of the psalmist (102:3–11). The latter section is held together by a number of verbal repeats at its either end (as well as by seven similes employing כְּ, *k*, "like," 102:3b, 4a, 6b, 7b, 9a, 11a, 11b)—all which give a plangent tone to *Petition 1*:[2]

102:3a, 4a	"my days"; "like grass … withered"
102:4b	"eat"; "bread"
102:9a	"eaten"; "bread"
102:11	"my days"; "like grass … wither"

There is no clear description of what exactly the agonies were that the supplicant was facing, but the plea calls upon God not to hide his face from him "in the day" of his distress, and to incline his ear "in the day" that he calls (102:2b, 2d). Help he certainly needed—and that "quickly" (102:2d)!

The plaint bemoans the situation of the psalmist, pointing a finger not only at enemies (102:8) but also at God and his wrath (102:9–11). There is a description of the psalmist's own physical state of attenuation (the "I," 102:3–7), his social state in alienation ("they," 102:8), and his theological state under accusation ("You," 102:9–11). Physically, his organs are "scorched," "crushed," and "withered" (102:3–4a: a tricolon). He goes hungry, he groans, he suffers weight loss (102:4b–5: another tricolon). He is like an owl that is awake at night, but unlike the bird, his is true insomnia—he is unable to sleep (102:6–7). Socially, he has been reproached by his foes (who may have been responsible for this crisis, or are, at least, taking advantage of thereof) (102:8). That they "swear by me" likely means that they use the supplicant as an extreme example: "If I break this oath, may I be miserable and wretched like him." Theologically, he suspects that God himself is aggravating the situation, so much so, in the face of divine anger (against some unspecified—and unrefuted—sin[s] of the psalmist/ the people) that has caused him to be accused and rejected (102:10), his food tastes like ashes and his drink like tears (102:9).

All in all, "my days" (also in 102:3a) are but a shadow,[3] and the sufferer "withers" "like grass" (102:11; also in 102:4a). This impermanence of humanity aggravates an already tenuous situation and is emphasized by the "and I" of the psalmist (102:11b). But it is immediately contrasted in the next section by the permanence of deity emphasized by the "but You" (102:12a).[4]

---

2. From Girard, *Les Psaumes Redécouverts*, 22–24.

3. The "extended shadow," an indication of approaching night and darkness, signals the imminent termination of his life of misery and woe. Indeed, the seven instances of "day(s)" in the psalm (102:2b, 2d, 3a, 8a, 11a, 23b, 24a) all point to the supplicant's time of suffering and the transience of his life.

4. "But You" is also found in 102:26a, 27a; all these instances of the conjunction וְ + second-person pronoun deal with longevity of divine existence; the only instance of the conjunction + first-person pronoun ("and I"; 102:11b) deals with the brevity of the supplicant's.

Profession 1 (102:12–22)

In *Profession 1*, first there is a prospect of divine activity (102:12–17) and then praise for divine activity (102:18–22). It is likely that the prospect and praise are jointly intended to motivate Yahweh to intervene in the current crisis of the psalmist.

This second section (and its two component parts: prospect and praise for divine action), like the first, is united by linguistic bookends, focusing on God's compassionate condescension upon mortal humans despite (or because of) deity's enduring essence:[5]

    "**generation**" (×2; 102:12b)
        "servants" (102:14a)
            "nations"; "name of Yahweh" (102:15a); "kings" (102:15b)
                "earth" (102:15b); "prayer of the destitute" (102:17a)

    "**generation**" (102:18a)
                "heaven"; "earth" (102:19b); "groaning of the prisoner" (102:20a)
            "peoples" (102:22a); "name of Yahweh" (102:21a); "kingdoms" (102:22b)
    "serve" (102:22b)

"Yahweh" and "Yah" are also found seven times (102:12a, 15a, 16a, 18b, 19b, 21a, 22b) in this section, in sync with the seven similes in *Petition 1*, making the argument that the supplicant is . . . , but Yahweh is . . . .

The lament of the psalmist in *Petition 1* (102:1–11) had concluded with exceptional poignancy, a mournful reminder of the impermanence of the suffering people of God (102:11). But then *Profession 1* (102:12–22) immediately commences with an acclamatory reference to the permanence of God (102:12). The brief "days" of the psalmist (102:3a, 11a) are contrasted with the longstanding existence of God. And this remembrance, it is hoped, will sustain the flock "from generation to generation" (102:12b), as the solidity and stability of deity is clung to by his people who are being tossed here and there in a fluid and unstable life.

In fact, if this "forever" God's memory is to be passed along to future generations, his people of the current generation need to survive all their woes and miseries. And they are confident they will, because this eternally "dwelling" Yahweh (102:12a; the verb יֹשֵׁב, *yshv*, can also mean to "sit") is about to "arise" to act on behalf of his own (102:13a), emphatically asserted with the redundant pronoun: "You—You will arise." The forwardness of the psalmist is visible here: he declares that the "time" and "season" for God to take action is *now* (102:13bc), in a sense challenging God to discharge his responsibility by attending to his people.

---

5. From Girard, *Les Psaumes Redécouverts*, 22–24. The second half of *Profession 1*, praise for divine action (102:18–22), is itself bookended by "people(s)" (102:18b, 22a); "praise" (102:18b, 21b); and "written" and "recount" (102:18a, 21a).

The supplicant goes on to provide a reason for divine action, remarkably stated in the parallel structure of 102:13a, 14:

102:13a	"You—You	will arise,	
		You will have compassion	on Zion."
102:14	"Your servants	have taken delight	in her stones,
		and they are gracious	to her dust."

Notice the reciprocity: Yahweh needed to be compassionate to "Zion" (synecdoche for the people of the city—God's flock), because they had been "gracious" to Zion (the actual city, the dwelling of God), even to its very stones and dust (102:14). Yahweh is thereby reminded, in no uncertain terms that, in return, "it is time" for *him* to be "gracious" to them, and that the "season had come" for God to act (102:13bc). The faithfulness of the people to their God, proclaims the supplicant boldly, putting pressure on deity, should prompt him to be faithful to them. If his people have shown graciousness even to the muck and goo of Zion, should not Yahweh then be gracious to them, in return?[6] And when that happens, the result of that divine graciousness would be that even the nations would fear Yahweh, with a reverential awe at his loyalty and commitment to his own (102:15). God would thus be glorified!

The prospect of divine activity then takes a decisive turn employing perfect verbs and expressing the certainty of God's intervention in the future as if it has already happened (102:16–17). That these verses are connected with what preceded is clear from the repetition of "glory" (102:15b, 16b), and from the similar sounding words, "fear," ירא, *yr'*, of Yahweh (102:15a) that is experienced when he "appears," ראה, *r'h* (102:16b): "appearing leads to revering."[7] It is as if a theophany has just taken place (in between 102:15 and 102:16?) and God has answered the "*prayer* of the destitute" (102:17a),[8] i.e., what the psalmist had petitioned for earlier in the psalm: "hear my *prayer* (102:1a). Indeed, in his care for his own, God has "not despised their *prayer*" (102:17b). In the use of his verbs, the psalmist is indicating that Yahweh's "building up [בנה, *bnh*]" of Zion/the people (102:16a) is equivalent to his "turning [פנה]" to his people's prayer (102:17a). God's city, it seems, is built when God's people are blessed.

Therefore, deity's praise is to resound for a "generation to come," voiced by "a people [yet] to be created" (102:18). And those who had once been "derided [הלל, *hll*]" (102:8b) are the ones now going to be indulging in Yahweh's "praise [הלל]" (102:18b, 21b) in that (re)built city, Zion/Jerusalem (120:16a, 21). A new age has dawned, for Yahweh who had[9] "turned to the prayer of the destitute" and "not despised their prayer" (102:17), has also heard "the groaning of the prisoner" and he has liberated his children once doomed to perish (102:20a). That the prayers of the psalmist have been heard is again depicted by the parallels between this section and *Petition 1* earlier in the psalm (see structure of the psalm for the similarities). What God had done would be "written" (102:18a) and what God did would be "recounted," and thus,

---

6. "We look on these fallen stones and this dirt with love, says the psalm, challenging Yhwh to behave the same way" to his people who are themselves falling apart like stones and crumbling like dust (Goldingay, *Psalms*, 3:155–56). The wordplay of "ashes [אֵפֶר, *'epher*]" (102:9a), indicating the food of the sufferer, and "dust [עָפָר, *'aphar*]" (102:14b), indicating the loyalty of the sufferer, further demands of God a reciprocation.

7. Goldingay, *Psalms*, 3:156.

8. The noun עַרְעָר, *'ar'ar*, "destitute," also means "naked/stripped," thus weak, pitiable, helpless.

9. "Had," i.e., from the psalmist's "already, but not yet" vantage point.

the name of Yahweh would be praised (102:21), and he would be served by all in a worldwide conversion to faith (likely in the eschaton; 102:22). The trio of infinitives tells the story: "to liberate" (102:20b), "to recount" (102:21a), and "to serve" (102:22b). God liberates, his children recount, and his world serves.

Précis: Petition 2; Profession 2 (102:23–28)

The précis summarizes the psalm, reprising *Petition 1* (in *Petition 2*, 102:23–24a) and *Profession 1* (in *Profession 2*, 102:24b–28)—the verbal similarities between these sections were noted earlier.[10] *Profession 2* is also bookended by a declaration of the permanence of Yahweh:[11]

> "Your years" (102:24b)
> "before [לְפָנִים, *lphanim*]" (102:25a)
>
> "Your years" (102:27b)
> "before [לְפָנֶיךָ, *lphaneka*]" (102:28b)

In fact, the most explicit plea in the psalm shows up in 102:24a (besides those petitions urging God to listen): Would that this eternal, merciful deity sustain evanescent, mortal humanity. Earlier the psalmist had pled with God to "answer [ענה]" him (102:2d); now he points to God as the one who had "weakened [ענה]" him (102:23a).[12] Surely deity should respond to this dreadful crisis! Once again, a contrast is created between the "days" of the psalmist that have been "shortened" (102:23b) and the "years" of God that are from "generation to generation" (102:24b). After all, this deity will outlive even the earth and the heavens: they will wear out and pass away (102:25–26), but the years of God "will not finish" (102:27). The strong emphasis of this disparity cannot be mistaken, employing a fronted (and redundant) pronoun: "They—they will perish, but You—You will endure" (102:26a).

And with that "re-petition" and "re-profession" in the précis, the psalmist seeks to persuade an everlasting deity to ensure his people will leave a lasting legacy so that "the children of Your servants will settle" (in stability in their land on earth) and that "their descendants will be established" (102:28). "Your servants" who were faithful to you (102:14a) will thus have been rewarded as "Your servants" are kept safe and secure from all alarms (102:28). The "children of death" (102:20b) will then have become the established and entrenched "children of Your servants" (102:28a). And all of this "before You [לְפָנֶיךָ, *lphaneka*]" (102:28b), i.e., before God's face, in his presence—blessed!

> The point of these important theological statements lies in the link between the Yhwh who has no end and the people of Yhwh who seem to have had a very definite end. . . . Living before their master is what servants do, standing there to wait on their master to do his will, and they enjoy there his protection and provision.

10. In addition, the double כְּ, "like," in 102:26bc reflects the sevenfold כְּ in 102:3–11.

11. "Before" (preposition פָּנֶה + לְ, *l + paneh*) in 102:25a, 28b, also refracts "face [פָּנֶה]" in 102:2a, and "turned [פָּנָה]" in 102:17a.

12. What the cause of divine weakening of strength and shortening of days was we are not told, though 102:10 suggests an unspecified sin as the issue. The result, particularly in light of God's own length of days (102:12, 24b–27), is the languishing of the psalmist in the brevity of his (102:11, 23–24a).

It is therefore a great privilege to be a servant of a great master and it is a position of security.[13]

In sum, the entire psalm is a bold entreaty, almost a demand, that this timeless God come to the aid of his suffering people, in time, *now*!

Sermon Map

I. Petition
    Desperate circumstances of the people of God (102:1–11)
    Move-to-relevance: Our desperate circumstances

II. Praise
    Daring persuasion in prayer (102:12–22)
    Move-to-relevance: Our lack of bold prayer

III. *Boldly Beseech When Blitzed!*
    Specifics on developing boldness in prayer

---

13. Goldingay, *Psalms*, 3:161.

PSALM 103:1–22

Psalm of Orientation

Blessing Yahweh for His Lovingkindness

THIS BELOVED PSALM HAS a far-reaching scope that addresses the supplicant (103:1–5), sinners (103:6–13), short-lived ones, i.e., all humanity (103:14–18), and sundry—a number of entities, including angels and God's armies, and even deeds and places (103:19–22). It touches issues of health, age, oppression, forgiveness, transience, and obedience to divine demand. "Given the nearly universal scope of the psalm's praise, one might well consider it the most soaring lyric in the Psalter. The poem has a wingspan that nearly seems to outreach the capacity of any one poem."[1] However, what it focuses upon are not the vicissitudes and exigencies of human existence, but on the commitment and faithfulness of a great God, and the need for his people, in turn, to be committed and faithful to him in obedience.[2]

Translation

103:1   Bless Yahweh, my soul,
             and all that is within me—His holy name.
103:2   Bless Yahweh, my soul,
             and do not forget all His bestowments—
103:3   the One who pardons all your iniquities,
             the One who heals all your diseases,
103:4   the One who redeems your life from the grave,
             the One who crowns you with lovingkindness and compassion,
103:5   the One who satiates your life with good:
             your youth is renewed like an eagle.
103:6   Yahweh does righteousness
             and judgments for all who are oppressed.

---

1. deClaissé-Walford et al., *Book of Psalms*, 759.
2. For the notion of "faithful obedience," see Kuruvilla, *Privilege the Text!*, 195–209.

103:7	He makes known His ways to Moses,
	to the children of Israel, His actions.
103:8	Compassionate and gracious is Yahweh,
	slow to anger and abundant in lovingkindness.
103:9	He does not strive [with us] for perpetuity,
	and He does not maintain [His anger] forever.
103:10	Not in accordance with our sins has He has done to us,
	and not in accordance with our iniquities has He bestowed upon us.
103:11	For in accordance with the height of the heavens above the earth,
	[so] great has been His lovingkindness upon those who fear Him.
103:12	In accordance with the distance of the east from the west,
	[so] He has distanced our rebellions from us.
103:13	In accordance with the compassion of a father upon children,
	[so] Yahweh has had compassion upon those who fear Him.
103:14	For He—He has known our shaping;
	He is mindful that we are dust.
103:15	A mortal—like grass [are] his days;
	like a flower of the field, so he blossoms.
103:16	For the wind has passed over it, and it is no more;
	and its place does not acknowledge it again.
103:17	And the lovingkindness of Yahweh is from forever unto forever,
	upon those who fear Him,
	and His righteousness to the children of children,
103:18	to those who keep His covenant
	and those who remember His precepts to do them.
103:19	Yahweh—in the heavens He has established His throne,
	and His Kingship—over all it rules.
103:20	Bless Yahweh, His angels,
	mighty in strength, those doing His word,
	to obey the voice of His word.
103:21	Bless Yahweh, all His armies,
	those serving Him, those doing what He accepts.
103:22	Bless Yahweh, all His works,
	in all places of His rule.
	Bless Yahweh, my soul.

Structure

Psalm 103 essentially begins and ends with exhortations that sandwich a central explanation section:

103:1–5	**Exhortation 1**	"Bless Yahweh, my soul" (103:1a) "all" (×4; 103:1b, 2b, 3a, 3b) "lovingkindness" (103:4b)
103:6–18	**Explanation**	103:6–13: "lovingkindness" (103:8b, 11b) 103:14–18: "lovingkindness" (103:17a)
103:19–22	**Exhortation 2**	"Bless Yahweh, my soul" (103:22c) "all" (×4; 103:19b, 21a, 22a, 22b) [no "lovingkindness"]

Theological Focus

God is worthy of blessing, he whose bestowments are abundant in lovingkindness to entities both individual and incorporate—all frail humans—as he forgives, heals, rejuvenates, and protects, expecting his faithfulness to be reciprocated in faithful obedience, for God is the supreme ruler over all.

Commentary

Exhortation 1 (103:1–5)

The first exhortation section is a self-address by the psalmist urging his own "soul" (103:1a)[3] to "bless Yahweh," i.e., to declare God as the blessed source of all good things which, in this poem, is primarily his "lovingkindness" (103:4b, 8b, 11b, 17a). "Yahweh" (signifying deity's immanence and his relationship to his people) is parallel to "His holy name" (signifying deity's transcendence and his otherness with relation to creation) (103:1a, 1b). This great God is the one who gives beneficences to his people. Therefore, no one should forget Yahweh's "bestowments" (103:2b).

Each of the following tricola, 103:3–4a and 103:4b–5, deals with a specific bestowment: the first (negative) that has Yahweh sparing the supplicant from the bane of sin, diseases, and death;[4] and the second (positive) about Yahweh satiating the supplicant with the blessing of his goodness.[5] The first tricolon (103:3–4a) describes "God's action of meeting the human

---

3. Every imperative verb and second-person pronominal suffix in 103:1–5 points to the psalmist's soul, as he engages in reflective speech.
4. Perhaps the psalmist is linking these three: sin leading to disease and to death.
5. The Hebrew of 103:5a reads "the one who satiates with the good of your ornaments [עֶדְיֵךְ, *'edyek*]." An

creature in our 'deficit situation,' so to speak—of mending our fallibility, frailty, and finitude. In these clauses, the Lord brings the fallen creation back to a 'zero-sum position.'" The second tricolon (103:4b–5) describes "God's action of blessing, in which the Lord builds the human being up to a surplus position."[6] Thus the elements of the tricola are set in parallel:

103:3–4a	103:4b–5
Sparing: Deficit Reduction	Satiating: Surplus Production
pardoning of "iniquities"	"lovingkindness," "compassion"
healing of "diseases"	"life [satiated] with good"
redemption from the "grave" (= death)	"youth ... renewed"

Since God alone is the source of these "bestowments," to him alone is due worship that is comprehensive and intensive, involving "*all* that is within me," so as not to forget any of "*all* His bestowments," from the hand of the one who pardons "*all* your iniquities" and heals "*all* your diseases" (103:1b, 2b, 3a, 3b).

Explanation (103:6–18)

In this *Explanation* section, the address is to sinners (103:6–13) and to the short-lived (103:14–18). It is linked to the previous section, *Exhortation 1*, by a number of parallels, indicating a continuation of the list of bestowments from Yahweh that began earlier:[7]

103:2b	"bestowments [גְּמוּל, *gmul*]"
103:3a	"iniquities"
103:4bα	"lovingkindness"
103:4bβ	"compassion"
103:8a	"compassion"
103:8b	"lovingkindness"
103:10bα	"iniquities"
103:10bβ	"bestowed [גמל, *gml*]"

Besides, a number of triads ties up the *Explanation* together: "lovingkindness," 103:8b, 11b, 17a; "compassion," 103:8a, 13a, 13b; "upon those who fear Him," 103:11b, 13b, 17b; and "sins," "iniquities," and "rebellions," 103:10a, 10b, 12b.[8]

---

emendation of the last word to עֶדְכִי, *'odeki* ("duration," i.e., life) makes better sense. Five of the six lines of these two tricola (103:3–4a and 103:4b–5) are structured similarly, each commencing with a definite article + participle ("the One who ...").

6. deClaissé-Walford et al., *Book of Psalms*, 764.

7. From Girard, *Les Psaumes Redécouverts*, 38–40.

8. There is also the preposition כְּ, *k*, "in accordance with/like," that resounds seven times: 103:10a, 10b, 11a, 12a, 13a, 15a, 15b; as well as the particle conjunction כִּי, *ki*, "for/that," in 103:11a, 14a, 14b, 16a.

The section as a whole is bookended and carefully structured:[9]

> "Yahweh *does*" (103:6aα)
>   "righteousness" (103:6aβ); "to the children" (103:7b)
>   "lovingkindness"; "upon those who fear Him" (103:11b)
>   "compassion"; "upon those who fear Him" (103:13b)
>   "lovingkindness"; "upon those who fear Him" (103:17ab)
>   "righteousness"; "to the children of children" (103:17c)
> "those who remember His precepts to *do* them" (103:18b)

It is obvious from the recurrence of "upon those who fear Him" (103:11b, 13b, 17b) that there is a shift in this section to the responsibility of God's people who are in relationship to him. Also notice that while the section begins with a statement of what Yahweh "does" (103:6a), it ends with blessing upon those who "do" his precepts (103:18b). Clearly, the obedience of faith, a human doing in response to divine doing, is a key issue of this section.

This *Explanation* section reflects (or better, refracts) Exodus 32–34, with the mention of "know His ways" from Exod 33:13 (in Ps 103:7), "Moses," and with the "creed" of Exod 34:6 (in Ps 103:7–8): note the perfect verbs in 103:10a, 10b, 11b, 12b, 13b, 14a, giving it a historical flavor. Thus 103:6–14 deals with the lovingkindness of God exhibited to sinners of the exodus generation, a grace that he has extended to all his people even to the present. Yet, though the acclamation of God of Exod 34:6 shows up in this psalm, unlike in 34:7 that warned of the iniquity of the "fathers" being visited on their "children," in Ps 103:9–13 it is the compassion of the divine "father" that is exhibited to his people, his "children" (103:13a). Throughout, the "lovingkindness" and "compassion" of God are "upon those who fear Him" (103:11b, 13b, 17): commensurate with the height of the heavens "above [עַל, *'al*]" the earth (103:11a) is the abundance of his lovingkindness "upon [עַל]" God fearers (103:11b).

The negatives of 103:9–10 (akin to the "sparing: deficit reduction" of *Exhortation 1*) are balanced by the positive expressions of God's lovingkindness in 103:11–13 (akin to the "satiating: surplus production" of the previous section). At any rate, this section moves away from the individualistic focus of 103:1–5 to a more corporate view—evident in the first-person plurals in 103:10a, 10b, 12b, 14a, 14b—and deals with God's bestowment of forgiveness (in his "lovingkindness") upon sinners in his flock. "For the ancient reader, the height of sky over earth and the span of east from west suggests the greatest imaginable distance. For the modern reader, the comparison is even more striking because we know that the distance between heavens and earth and between east and west is actually infinity."[10] And besides, the lovingkindness of God is "from forever until forever" (103:17a), overcoming his anger which had been declared not to last "forever" (103:9b). All that to say, an infinity of space and an infinity of time are encompassed in this section: God's lovingkindness extends everywhere and endures always!

That God remembers the finitude of humanity (103:14–18) adds poignancy to his eternal lovingkindness extended towards these short-lived mortals. Thus God will *never* fail his people, but there is a qualification to who might experience his blessings: "those who fear

---

9. Note also that 103:9a, 9b, 10a, 10b in Hebrew begin with the negative particle לֹא, *lo'*; and 103:10a, 10b, 11a, have the preposition כְּ as the second word of the line, while 103:12a, 13a start with it.

10. Goldingay, *Psalms*, 3:172.

Him" (103:17b), "those who keep His covenant" (103:18a), and "those who remember his precepts to do them" (103:18b). God makes his ways known to his "children" (103:7), he has compassion on his "children" (103:13a), and in return his "children," and even their "children," are to remain faithful to him in obedience (103:17c–18). There is thus an unequivocal conditionality expressed if one is to experience the blessings of God: they are for the ones who walk with him, for the ones who obey him. And to extend this motif, the psalm turns to its final section.

Exhortation 2 (103:19–22)

This section is held together by the rulership of Yahweh bookending *Exhortation 2* in 103:19b (מָשַׁל, *mshl*; verb: "rule") and 103:22b (מֶמְשָׁלָה, *memshalah*; noun: "rule"). Thus, after the *Explanation* that moves towards the obedience of faith as the condition for experiencing divine blessing, *Exhortation 2* makes that its prime emphasis, grounded on the supreme "kingship" (103:19b) and dominion of Yahweh, the God-King. Earlier, the psalmist had asserted the transience of humans—their short-livedness (103:15); then he had contrasted the "long-lived-ness" of divine lovingkindness (103:17). Here it is Yahweh's sovereign rulership that is in sharp antithesis to the powerlessness of humanity. Indeed, the syntax of 103:15a and 103:19a are similar:[11]

	Subject	Prepositional Phrase	Predicate
103:15a	"A mortal—	like grass	[are] his days."
103:19a	"Yahweh—	in the heavens	He has established His throne."

Of note, therefore, is the absence of divine lovingkindness that echoed in all the other sections of the psalm (103:4b, 8b, 11b, 17a). That may be deliberate, as the responsibility for obeying God in faith takes on a brighter hue in this section. The emphasis is less on God's grace and more on the duty of the people of God (and the rest of the addressees of the psalm: all and sundry) to serve him. Notice the use of "do [עשׂה, *'sh*]" in the psalm: in 103:6a, it is Yahweh who "does" righteousness; in 103:10a, he "does" to us not according to our sins; therefore we, too, are called to remember his precepts and "do" them (103:18b);[12] even his angels are "doing" his will (103:20b), and his armies are "doing" what He wants (103:21b); and so thus is Yahweh blessed, by all his "works" (103:22a; all these terms are derived from the same root, עשׂה). All that to say, everyone *does* (or *should do*) the will of God!

No wonder this God is deemed blessed by all who obey him—and the psalmist proceeds to list those entities in 103:20–22a): angels, mighty ones, divine armies, those serving God, those doing what is acceptable to him, and even all his deeds, and this in "all places of His rule" (103:22b). Everything, everywhere, in every time, does God's will, submitting to this great deity and obeying him. Just as there were four instances of "all" in *Exhortation 1* (103:1b, 2b, 3a, 3b), there is a balancing quartet of "all" in *Exhortation 2* (103:19b, 21a, 22a, 22b).[13]

11. Also, 103:15a and 103:19a are the only verses in the composition that begin with a noun.

12. God's people are to "remember [זכר, *zkr*]" to obey the precepts of a God who "is mindful [זָכוּר, *zakur*]" of the frailty of his people (103:14b).

13. Yahweh is mentioned in all four verses of *Exhortation 2* (for a total of five times).

Even in structure, the emphasis is unmistakable:

103:19b	"all"; "rules"
103:20ab	"His angels"; "mighty in strength" "those *doing* His word"
103:20c	**"to obey the voice of His word"**
103:21	"His armies"; "those serving Him" "those *doing* what He accepts"
103:22ab	"all" (×2); "rule"

And so the psalmist closes, "Bless Yahweh, my soul!" (103:22c), as if asking himself: "If all of these parties, performances, and places can serve Yahweh and call him blessed, should I not be part of this contingent too, obeying him and proclaiming his blessedness? I should, so, 'Bless Yahweh!'"

This psalm subtly negotiates the tension between deity's faithfulness ("lovingkindness") to his people and his people's faithfulness (obedience) to their God.[14] While the conditionality of divine blessing to people based upon human service to God does not imply a contract, there is no question but that a covenantal, mutual, reciprocal relationship between the two parties is envisaged here (as it is elsewhere in Scripture). God extends lovingkindness to his people unconditionally, but the experience thereof by God's people is conditional upon faithful obedience. Goldingay is right: "Wonder is therefore appropriate," as is also the undertaking to bless this awesome God![15] "Bless Yahweh, my soul!"

Sermon Map

I. The Faithfulness of God

    God's abundant lovingkindness (103:1–16)

    Move-to-relevance: God's grace towards us

II. The Faithfulness of the People of God

    God's expectation of faithfulness in obedience (103:17–22)

    Move-to-relevance: Our failure to reciprocate faithfulness unto God

III. *Be Faithful to the Faithful One!*

    Specifics on faithful obedience as a response to God's grace

---

14. Note that the faithfulness to God (responsibility) is required only of those who are in relationship to him: relationship precedes responsibility. But lest we forget: relationship also mandates responsibility. See Kuruvilla, *Privilege the Text!*, 189–95, 252–58.

15. Goldingay, *Psalms*, 3:177.

PSALM 104:1–35

Psalm of Orientation

God: Creator and Conservator

PSALM 104 IS THE second of the only two psalms in the Psalter that are framed with "Bless Yahweh, my soul!" (104:1a, 35c; also see 103:1a, 22c). It deals in its entirety with the relationship of Yahweh to his creation, both animate and inanimate, both heavenly and earthly.

Translation

104:1	Bless Yahweh, my soul.
	Yahweh, my God, You are very great;
	[with] splendor and majesty You clothed [yourself],
104:2	donning light as with a mantle,
	stretching out the heavens like a tent curtain,
104:3	the One laying beams of His upper chambers in the waters,
	setting clouds as His chariot,
	going about upon the wings of the wind,
104:4	making the winds His messengers,
	flaming fire, His ministers.
104:5	He established the earth upon its supports,
	so that it will not totter forever and always.
104:6	You covered it with the deep as with clothing,
	the waters standing above the mountains.
104:7	From Your rebuke they were fleeing,
	from the sound of Your thunder they were hurrying away.
104:8	They were rising up mountains, they were sinking down valleys—
	to this place that You established for them.
104:9	A boundary You set so that they will not pass over,
	so that they will not return to cover the earth.

104:10 [You are] the One sending forth springs in the riverbeds—
           they go about between the mountains;
104:11 they water every beast of the field;
           the wild donkeys break their thirst.
104:12 By them the birds of the heavens abide;
           between the branches they give sound.
104:13 [You are] the One watering the mountains from His upper chambers;
           with the fruit of Your works the earth is satiated.
104:14 [You are] the One growing the grass for cattle,
           and vegetation for humankind to labor,
        to bring forth food from the earth
104:15   and wine which rejoices a mortal's heart,
        to make faces glisten with oil,
           and food which sustains a mortal's heart.
104:16 The trees of Yahweh are satiated,
           the cedars of Lebanon which He planted,
104:17 there the birds make a nest,
           the heron [makes] the junipers its home.
104:18 The high mountains for the wild goats;
           the cliffs, a refuge for the rock badgers.
104:19 He made the moon for appointed times;
           the sun knows its setting.
104:20 You order darkness and it becomes night,
           in it every beast of the forest swarms.
104:21 The young lions roar for prey
           and to seek from God their sustenance.
104:22 The sun rises, they withdraw,
           and in their dens they lie down.
104:23 Humankind goes forth to its task,
           and to its labor until evening.
104:24 How Your works have abounded, Yahweh.
           All of them in wisdom You have made—
        the earth is full of Your possessions:
104:25   here is the sea, great and wide in reach;
        there are swarms without number,
           animals, small with great.
104:26 There, ships go about;
           Leviathan—this You shaped to play in it.
104:27 All of them, they wait for You
           to give their sustenance at its time.

104:28 You give to them, they gather;
> You open Your hand, they are satiated with good.

104:29 You hide Your face, they are terrified;
> You take away their spirit, they expire
> and to their dust they return.

104:30 You send forth Your Spirit, they are created;
> and You renew the face of the ground.

104:31 May the glory of Yahweh be forever;
> may Yahweh rejoice in His works.

104:32 [He is] looking at the earth, and it trembles;
> He touches the mountains, and they smoke.

104:33 I will sing to Yahweh in [all] my life;
> I will make music to my God for always.

104:34 May my musing be pleasing to Him;
> I—I will rejoice in Yahweh.

104:35 May sinners be consumed from the earth,
> and may the wicked be nonexistent for always.
> Bless Yahweh, my soul.

Structure

The structure demonstrates four cycles of God's acts of *Creation* and *Conservation* (or sustenance of creation) bookended by the *Celebration* of these divine doings:

104:1a	**Celebration 1**	"bless Yahweh, my soul" / "Yahweh, my God"
104:1b–9	*Creation 1*	
104:10–18	*Conservation 1*	
104:19–20		Creation 2
104:21–23		Conservation 2
104:24–26		*Creation 3*
104:27–29		*Conservation 3*
104:30a		Creation 4
104:30b		Conservation 4
104:31–35	**Celebration 2**	"Yahweh … my God" (104:33) / "bless Yahweh, my soul" (104:35c)

"Surely no text of Scripture speaks more directly and in detail about the creation and about what God did and does in creation and in the sustaining of creation than does this psalm."[1] But unlike the liturgical art of Genesis 1 (or the narrative style of Genesis 2), Psalm 104 waxes

---

1. Miller, "Poetry of Creation," 96.

eloquent in the poetic register, at the same time asserting God's order, purpose, and delight in the beauty of his creation and the stability of his conservation.[2]

Theological Focus

God, the Creator and Conservator of all things, is deserving of praise, because of his marvelous acts of creation, precisely balanced and perfected, and his astute, ongoing acts of conservation of creation—his gracious provision of all things for all beings, upon which they are totally dependent—the perfection of which creation and conservation will be consummated one day when evil will be forever removed from the cosmos.

Commentary

Celebration; Creation 1; Conservation 1 (104:1–18)

After the self-exhortation in 104:1a (*Celebration 1*),[3] the first cycle, *Creation 1* and *Conservation 1*, commences (104:1b–18). It is the longest of four such cycles and deals primarily with divine provision of food and water. Six participles (translated here as gerunds) describe God in 104:2a, 2b, 3a, 3b, 3c, 4a. Though the activities describe a past creation, the participles render them present events, vivid and visible. In and through his creation, the attributes of God's "greatness," "splendor," "majesty," and brilliance (104:1b–2a) are manifested in what he made: even the elements, clouds, wind, and fire, are God's vehicles, assistants, and servants (104:3–4). The hymn goes on to describe the establishment of the earth, the setting forth of the oceans, and particularly the "fleeing" and "hurrying away" of the waters above the mountains (104:7), thereby unveiling the dry land, as these fluid entities were settled in their respective loci by Yahweh, delimited and controlled by this God-King (104:8–9). In fact, the waters (104:7) he literally bounded by the mountains (104:6b, 8a), thus establishing, controlling, and organizing his creation according to his sovereign purposes:[4]

---

2. There are a number of correspondences with Genesis 1, including vocabulary and the general sequence of creation: light, waters, vegetation, sun and moon, sea creatures, and provision of food. Incidentally, resemblances have also been noted with the fourteenth century BCE "Hymn to the Aton of Pharaoh Akh-en-Aton" (Amen-hotep IV) perhaps indicating commonalities in the sharing of creation themes in contemporary literature (see *ANET* 369–71).

3. The other self-exhortation in the psalm occurs in the closing *Celebration 2*, 104:35cd; indeed 104:1ab, 33–35 are the only lines the psalm that have self-references with first-person pronouns.

4. From Girard, *Les Psaumes Redécouverts*, 57; and Auffret, *Hymnes d'Égypte*, 145.

104:5–6a	"established"; "earth" "so that it will not [בַּל, *bal*] …"; "covered"
104:6b	"mountains"
104:7a	"from Your rebuke they were fleeing"
104:7b	"from … Your thunder they were hurrying away"
104:8a	"mountains"
104:8b–9	"established"; "earth" "so that they will not [בַּל] …" (×2); "cover"

The one who "sets" clouds as his transportation (104:3b) also "sets" boundaries for the waters of the earth to be constrained (104:9a). The "waters," mentioned in 104:3a, 6b (and the "deep" in 104:6a) are the focus of every line in 104:7–9, yet they are not explicitly named there—they rhetorically disappear, even as they are commanded to subside—yet another case of the text painting a picture.[5] There can hardly be any doubt that the one doing all this creating is totally sovereign over the universe.

Then comes *Conservation 1* (104:10–18) that depicts God's sustenance and upholding of his creation and all therein. That this part and the preceding one, *Creation*, are linked is clear; though conceptually distinct, they form an interwoven double chiasm:[6]

"rising up [עָלָה, *'lh*]" (104:8aα)
"mountains" (104:8aβ)

        "mountains" (104:10b)
        "birds" (104:12a)

"mountains" (104:13aα)
"upper chambers [עֲלִיָּה], *'aliyyah*]" (104:13aβ)

        "birds" (104:17a)
        "mountains" (104:18a)

The rising waters of 104:6b–9 threatening to overwhelm "mountains" (104:8a; likely a representation of the pre-creation "chaos")[7] are no match for God who makes springs go between "mountains" and who also waters the "mountains" from his upper chambers (104:10b, 13a). And in the tender care of this divine conservator the beasts and birds rest carefree and worriless, making their homes (104:10–12, 17–18), even upon those very "mountains" that were once threatened to be overrun by riotous waters (104:18a). This heavenly caretaker provisions all the living (104:14–15). Indeed, the all-encompassing character of God's conservation of both inanimate and animate nature is also structurally emphasized, with deity's provision for humanity taking center stage in 104:14bβ–15 (see below).[8]

---

5. Goldingay, *Psalms*, 3:186.

6. Modified from Girard, *Les Psaumes Redécouverts*, 69. "Earth" shows up in 104:5a, 9b, 13b, 14c; as also do the synonymous terms: "abide" (104:12a), "nest" (104:17a), "home" (104:17b), and "refuge" (104:18b).

7. Or perhaps from the Noachic flood?

8. Modified from Whitekettle, "Communion of Subjects," 186; and Girard, *Les Psaumes Redécouverts*, 59. "By them" in 104:12a refers back to the "springs" in 104:10a, beside which the birds settle and thrive.

104:10–11	wild land ("riverbeds," *"mountains,"* "field")
	wild animals ("every beast," "wild donkeys")
104:12	*"birds"*
104:13b–14abα	*"satiated"*; "grass" and "vegetation"
104:14bβ–15	humans: "food …," "a mortal's heart" (×2)
104:16	*"satiated"*; "trees" and "cedars"
104:17	*"birds"*
104:18	wild land ("high *mountains*"; "cliffs")
	wild animals ("wild goats"; "rock badgers")

God provides for everything and everyone—especially humans: it is *he* who gives them food, wine, and oil, the staples of life in those days (104:14c–15). In fact, God even sees fit to appoint "labor" for humanity to engage in gainfully for food production (104:14bc; also see 104:23).

Creation 2; Conservation 2 (104:19–23)

The scene shifts back to divine creation again, commencing the *Creation 2-Conservation 2* cycle, dealing primarily with times of the day and the activities appointed to beasts and humankind during them.[9] The Creator ordained the moon and the sun in their respective cycles (104:19); he bids it be dark and so it becomes, and every forest animal "swarms" (רמשׂ, *rms*; 104:20b), a verb that echoes throughout the creation account (Gen 1:21, 24, 25, 26, 28, 30). "Here [in Psalm 104, as opposed to Genesis 1] God is actively involved each evening, effecting that transition from day to night. Further, in Gen 1 darkness is at best of neutral significance; it is not God's positive achievement, like light. Here night has positive significance, again for the animal world."[10] It is all divinely planned and purposed—God's conservation for the good and prospering of God's creation.[11] And this deity is closely involved with his creation, every aspect of it, in an ongoing fashion. As opposed to Genesis 1–3,

> the psalm speaks not of a task of creation that could be completed over a week, . . . but of a job of work that continues as long as the world exits. It does not describe this work as something definable and divisible into six or eight discrete acts but pictures God more randomly moving from one task to another, giving a selective picture and letting individual concrete acts stand for the whole.[12]

---

9. However, the pattern of a creation term ("works," מַעֲשֶׂה, *ma'aseh*, 104:13b; and "made," עשׂה, *'sh*, 104:19a) + provision ("food," 104:14c, 15c; and "sustenance," 104:21b) + place of rest ("nest," 104:17a; "home," 104:17b; "refuge," 104:18b; and "den," 104:22b) links both sections (from Girard, *Les Psaumes Redécouverts*, 70).

10. Goldingay, *Psalms*, 3:190.

11. And this involves even "nature, red in tooth and claw"—bloodied by the "lions" in 104:21—at least until the eschaton (Alfred, Lord Tennyson, "In Memoriam A. H. H." [1850], Canto 56).

12. Goldingay, *Psalms*, 3:198.

Creation 3; Conservation 3 (104:24–29)

The third cycle, *Creation 3-Conservation 3*, commences with an exclamation of praise: the abundance of God's "works [מַעֲשֶׂה]" and the incredible wisdom—a new motif—with which he "made [עשׂה]" it all (Ps 104:24ab). And because he created and because he continues to conserve his creation, superintending and governing it, all creation is rightly God's possession (104:24c). With that, there is a focus upon the sea and its denizens (and craft that ply the waters).[13] Once again "swarms [רמשׂ]" is employed (104:25b; as in 104:20b). And there is the "Leviathan," usually a fear-inspiring beast (Isa 27:1; Ps 74:14; Job 3:8; 41:1–34). But here, it was apparently created to "play" in the sea (Ps 104:26b), just another innocent specimen of fauna. This, even as ships "go about" (104:26a). The juxtaposition of a small human vessel with a huge oceanic beast underscores that in the Creator's wisdom, acclaimed earlier in 104:24b, all things and all beings were made to exist in peace and safety together. The fearsome animal (in ancient Near Eastern mythology the Leviathan was a primeval sea dragon/monster, perhaps a whale?) is simply "God's rubber duck in the great ocean bathtub," a tamed and demythologized creature that disports in the breakers![14] Indeed, even the text seems to be joining in the games, with a word*play*: "here" is the sea, and "there" are its denizens; "there" are the ships, and "this" is the Leviathan![15]

104:25a	"here [זֶה, *zeh*]"
104:25b	"there [שָׁם, *sham*]"
104:26a	"there [שָׁם]"
104:26b	"this [זֶה]"

All of this is stated as matter of fact, as if it were but a moment's work by the hand of God (and it probably was, at least the sea and the animals).[16]

The conservation of creation, *Conservation 3*, as in prior similar sections, is focused on the "sustenance" God provides for his creatures (104:27–28). Notice the connection with the prior sections, *Creation 2* and *Conservation 2* (and the following one: *Creation 4* and *Conservation 4*), below.[17]

---

13. The "very great" God (104:1b) created the "great" sea with "great" animals (104:25a, 25c).

14. Miller, "Poetry of Creation," 98.

15. I have kept 104:26 as part of *Creation 3*, because of the verb "shaped [יצר, *ytsr*]" in 104:26b. This shows up in the creation account of Genesis 2 (2:7, 8, 19). Yes, the ships plying the waters do not fit the creation motif; it might simply be an artistic addition to emphasize the harmlessness of the Leviathan that God had made.

16. Akin to the creation of the heavens, "the work of Your fingers" (8:3).

17. From Girard, *Les Psaumes Redécouverts*, 72–73.

Creation 2; Conservation 2
- **104:19a**   "made [עשׂה, *'sh*]"
- **104:20b**   "beast [חַיָּה, *chayyah*]"; "swarms"
- **104:21b**   "their sustenance"

Creation 3; Conservation 3
- **104:24**   "works [מַעֲשֶׂה]"; "made [עשׂה]"
- **104:25bc**   "animal [חַיָּה]"; "swarms"
- **104:27b**   "their sustenance"

Creation 4; Conservation 4
- **104:31b**   "works [מַעֲשֶׂה]"
- **104:33a**   "life [חַי, *chay*]"

That the recipients of God's bounty are "satiated" is emphasized throughout the psalm: in 104:13b, it was the inanimate earth that was "satiated"; in 104:16a, it is the botanical flora that is; here in 104:28b, it is all the rest of animalia that are "satiated *with good*," for the Creator and divine conservator is a *good* God![18] And in a sparkling cascade of more wordplays, the dependence of creatures upon Creator/conservator is underscored:[19]

- **104:27a**   "they wait for You [יְשַׂבֵּרוּן, *ysabberun*]"
- **104:27b**   "to give their sustenance [לָתֵת אָכְלָם, *latet 'aklam*]"
- **104:28a**   "You give to them [תִּתֵּן לָהֶם, *titten lahem*]"
- **104:28b**   "they are satiated [יִשְׂבְּעוּן, *yisb'un*]"

God is, indeed, the fount of all goodness, so much so his turning away his face (with the accompanying retraction of his goodness) is absolutely terrifying to the beneficiaries of God's bounty (104:29a). Besides, life itself is at deity's disposal, unable to exist independently of him (104:29bc). Therefore this good God is one we must consciously be dependent upon always, for he is not a disinterested clockmaker who wound up his instruments at creation and let them run their own courses. Rather this is a deity who is deeply involved with his creation to the point of continuously sustaining (conserving) lives at every moment:[20]

- **104:24b**   "You have made"
- **104:25a**   "reach [יָד, *yad*]" of the sea
- **104:28b**   "hand [יָד]" of deity
- **104:30a**   "they are created"

---

18. A consistent asyndetic syntactical pattern marks 104:28a, 28b, 29a, 29b, and 30a: second-person singular verb (God's action) + third-person plural verb (creatures' responses), all discretely laid out without conjunctions.

19. Auffret, *Hymnes d'Égypte*, 161.

20. From Girard, *Les Psaumes Redécouverts*, 52.

If the "reach" of the sea is vast, then the "hand"/"reach" of the Creator must be more so (implied); that is why all of creation is dependent on that divine conservator's "hand."

Creation 4; Conservation 4; Celebration (104:30–35)

The last of these cycles, *Creation 4-Conservation 4*, serves as a summary, in a single verse (104:30), of all that preceded. Interestingly enough, unlike the consequence of the fall following the creation account in Genesis, when the ground was "cursed" (Gen 3:17), here the ground is "renewed" (Ps 104:30b). While Psalm 104 does not deny that it views the universe in an eschatological and post-fall era, it also asserts that God is doing something even right now to set things straight, pointing to the ultimate fate of fallen nature—renewal, one day. Linking 104:30 with the last verse of the previous section, 104:29, we see the contrast between the fallen world and the new world that God is putting into place:

104:29a	"Your *face*"; "terrified"
104:29bc	"their *spirit*"; "expire"
104:30a	"Your *Spirit*"; "created"
104:30b	"the *face* of the ground"

What a day that will be—a new *Spirit*ual creation set in place! So, appropriately enough, there is *Celebration 4* that closes out the psalm (104:31–35). What is striking is that on that jubilant day, it is not only the humans who "rejoice" (104:34b); *God* himself "rejoices" (104:31b).[21] The cause for rejoicing appears to be twofold—for the judgment of wickedness on one hand, and for the removal of wickedness on the other:[22]

Joy of God	
104:31b	"rejoice"
104:32a	"earth" [judgment of wickedness]
Joy of God's People	
104:34b	"rejoice"
104:35a	"earth" [removal of wickedness]

"Trembling" (104:32a) is always a negative emotion elsewhere in Scripture (Exod 15:15; Ezra 10:9; Ps 55:5; Dan 10:11). "Mountains" and "smoke" are associated with divine judgment also in Ps 144:5.[23] Again, it is likely that the "rejoicing" of both deity and his people indicates not only the delights of creation and conservation now, but extends to the joys of a future state when wickedness will be no more. So, suddenly this psalm, thus far peaceful and blissful, jerks the reader's attention with the notification that evil is still with us and

---

21. Goldingay notes that this is the only place in Scripture with Yahweh as the subject of the verb "rejoice" (Isa 9:17 uses the *negated* verb with "Lord" as subject) (*Psalms*, 3:194n48). This verse, Ps 104:31, is a wish, of course, but one that is almost a reality, or soon will be reality.

22. From Girard, *Les Psaumes Redécouverts*, 64.

23. Also see Exod 19:18; Pss 18:8–9; 37:20; 68:2; 74:1; 80:4.

that God's peace and blessedness have not been consummated yet. But one day it will. Evil banished, good established. Forever! Then the people of God can say with unreserved and unalloyed joy: "Bless Yahweh, my soul. Praise Yah!"[24] (104:35c).

Sermon Map

I. The Creator God
    God's greatness (104:1b–9, 19–20, 30a)
    God's wisdom (104:24–26)
    Move-to-relevance: Our acclamation of God's greatness (104:1a)

II. The Conservator God
    God's goodness (104:10–18, 21–23, 30b)
    God's delight (104:27–29, 31)
    Move-to-relevance: Our acclamation of God's goodness (104:35cd)

III. The Consuming God
    God's justice (104:32–35b)
    Move-to-relevance: The ongoing presence of evil

IV. *Praise the Producer and Provider and Purifier*
    Specifics on praising God for his creation and conservation

---

24. I.e., "Hallelu-Yah!"

PSALM 105:1–45

Psalm of Orientation

Praise for God's Faithfulness in the Past

THIS IS ANOTHER PSALM with bookended exhortations to praise, with an explanation for praise in the middle, that forms the bulk of the composition. However, unlike other similarly organized songs, the explanation of praise in Psalm 105 is entirely a recitation of Israel's history.

Translation

105:1 Give thanks to Yahweh, call upon His name;
    make known His actions among the peoples.
105:2 Sing to Him, make music to Him;
    muse about all His wonders.
105:3 Make praise to His holy name;
    let it rejoice, the heart of those who look to Yahweh.
105:4 Seek Yahweh and His strength;
    look to His face continually.
105:5 Remember His wonders which He has done,
    His portents and the judgments of His mouth,
105:6 seed of Abraham, His servant,
    children of Jacob, His chosen ones.
105:7 He is Yahweh our God;
    His judgments are in all the land.
105:8 He has remembered forever His covenant,
    the word He commanded to a thousand generations,
105:9 which He made with Abraham,
    and His oath to Isaac.
105:10 And He designated it to Jacob as a statute,
    to Israel as a covenant forever,

105:11	saying, "To you I will give the land of Canaan
	the share of your inheritance,"
105:12	when they were men—in number few—
	and sojourners in it.
105:13	And they went about from nation to nation,
	from [one] kingdom to another people;
105:14	He did not let any person to oppress them,
	and He reproved kings for their sakes:
105:15	"Do not touch My anointed ones,
	and to My prophets [do] no harm."
105:16	And He called famine upon the land;
	all the supply of bread He destroyed.
105:17	He sent before them a man,
	sold as a slave—Joseph.
105:18	They afflicted his feet with fetters,
	into iron [collars] came his neck.
105:19	Until the time that his word came [to pass],
	the utterance of Yahweh refined him.
105:20	The king sent and released him—
	the one ruling the peoples even set him free.
105:21	He set him lord of his house,
	and the one ruling over all his possessions,
105:22	to imprison his princes at his desire,
	and to teach wisdom to his elders.
105:23	And Israel came into Egypt;
	and Jacob sojourned in the land of Ham.
105:24	And He made His people very fruitful,
	and made them stronger than their adversaries.
105:25	He turned their heart to hate His people,
	to act deceitfully with His servants.
105:26	He sent Moses His servant,
	Aaron, whom He had chosen.
105:27	They set the word of His signs among them,
	and portents in the land of Ham.
105:28	He sent darkness and it made [it] dark;
	and they did not defy His words.
105:29	He turned their waters to blood,
	and their fish He caused to die.
105:30	Their land teemed with frogs
	[even] in the rooms of their kings.

105:31	He spoke, and a swarm [of flies] came—
	gnats in all their territory.
105:32	He gave them rains of hail,
	flaming fire in their land.
105:33	And He struck their vine and their fig tree,
	and destroyed the tree [in] their territory.
105:34	He spoke, and the locust came—
	and the young locust—and without number,
105:35	and it ate up all vegetation in their land,
	and it ate up the fruit of their ground.
105:36	And He struck all the firstborn in their land,
	the first fruits of all their [generative] vigor.
105:37	And He brought them out with silver and gold,
	and no one among His tribes was stumbling.
105:38	Egypt rejoiced when they went out,
	for the terror of them had fallen upon them.
105:39	He spread a cloud for covering,
	and fire to give light by night.
105:40	They asked, and He caused quail to come,
	and with bread of heaven He satiated them.
105:41	He opened the rock and waters flowed;
	it went about in the dry places [as] a river.
105:42	For He remembered His holy word
	with Abraham, His servant,
105:43	and He brought out His people with gladness,
	with a joyful exclamation, His chosen ones.
105:44	And He gave to them the lands of the nations,
	and [the product of] the peoples' toil, they took possession of,
105:45	so that they might keep His statutes
	and observe His laws.
	Praise Yah.

Structure

Psalm 105 is structured with a core giving historical explanations for praise. It implicitly asserts that what God has done in the past, he will do in the present, and therefore he is worthy of praise![1]

---

1. From deClaissé-Walford et al., *Book of Psalms*, 783; Ceresko, "Poetic Analysis," 21–27; Martin, "Embedded Chiasm," 8; and Girard, *Les Psaumes Redécouverts*, 98. The faithfulness of God is what is sung about, perhaps explaining the lack of mention of the people's rebellions in the wilderness.

EXHORTATION TO PRAISE 1 (105:1–6)
  God's faithfulness: "make praise" (105:3a)

EXPLANATION FOR PRAISE (105:7–45b)
  God's faithfulness in history 1: Abraham, Isaac, Jacob **(105:7–15)**
    "He has remembered"; "word [דָּבָר, *davar*]" (105:8)
    "with Abraham" (105:9a); "statute" (105:10a)
    "give"; "land of Canaan" (105:11a); "went about" (105:13a)

  God's faithfulness in history 2: Joseph (Jacob) **(105:16–23)**
    "sent" (105:17a, 20a); "word [דְּבַר]" (105:19a)
    "set" (105:21a); "in the land of Ham" (105:23b)
    "his princes [שָׂרָיו, *sarayw*]" (105:22a); "king" (105:20a)

  God's faithfulness in history 3: Moses, Aaron **(105:24–38)**
    "sent" (105:26a, 28a); "acts/words" (both דָּבָר; 105:27a, 28b)
    "set" (105:27a); "in the land of Ham" (105:27b)
    "their adversaries [צָרָיו, *tsarayw*]" (105:24b); "kings" (105:30b)

  God's faithfulness in history 4: Wilderness, Canaan, Law **(105:39–45b)**
    "He remembered"; "word [דְּבַר]" (105:42a)
    "with Abraham" (105:42b); "statutes" (105:45a)
    "gave"; "lands of the nations" (105:44a); "went about" (105:41b)

EXHORTATION TO PRAISE 2 (105:45c)
  God's faithfulness: "praise"

Theological Focus

The constant and consistent faithfulness of a God who keeps his word to his people, protecting them, providing for them, performing wonders for them, preparing leaders for them, and punishing their enemies, makes deity worthy of praise and his divine demand worthy of practice.

Commentary

Exhortation to Praise 1 (105:1–6)

All the imperatives directed to the praising of God are plural (105:1aα, 1aβ, 1b, 2aα, 2aβ, 2b, 3a, 4a, 4b, 5a):[2] "the congregation is to become a corporate witness [to the peoples] to what God has done and to the character of the Lord as a faithful God."[3] That this is for the benefit of the peoples is explicitly stated in 105:1b, emphasized in the assonance of הוֹדוּ, *hodu*, "give thanks," and הוֹדִיעוּ, *hodi'u*, "make known" (105:1).

---

2. There is a singular jussive in 105:3b: "let it rejoice."
3. deClaissé-Walford et al., *Book of Psalms*, 787.

The focus on vocal praise in 105:2a is surrounded by "Yahweh," "His name," and "His actions/wonders," thus already priming the reader for the explanations for praise that will follow:[4]

105:1aα	"Yahweh"	
105:1aβ	"His name"	
105:1b	"His actions"	
105:2aα		"sing to Him"
105:2aβ		"make music to Him"
105:2b		"His wonders"
105:3a	"His ... name"	
105:3b	"Yahweh"	

The ones rejoicing, we find out in 105:6, are the people of God, synonymously labeled "seed of Abraham," "children of Jacob," and "His chosen ones"; these are also the ones "who look to Yahweh," "seek" him and his strength, and "look to his face" (105:3b, 4a, 4b). Having experienced the faithfulness of God, they are now called to "remember" his mighty acts (105:5a) and praise him with hearts of rejoicing (105:3). Therefore the call to praise is not for the benefit of the "peoples" alone (105:1b), it is also for God's own people—their faith in God's faithfulness is amplified thereby. All this keeps the focus on God, as another artistic textual layout depicts:[5]

105:2b	"His wonders"	
105:3bα	"look to"	
105:3bβ		**"Yahweh"**
105:4a		**"Yahweh"**
105:4b	"look to"	
105:5a	"His wonders"	

Yahweh is indeed the one who must be praised!

Explanation: God's faithfulness in history 1 (105:7–15)

God's "judgments" are in all the earth (105:7b), visible, apparent, obvious. In 105:5, God's people had been urged to "remember" those "judgments"; now it turns out that such mindfulness is but a response to God's own "remembering" of his covenant with his people, wherein he delivered to them his judgments in the form of his "word" (105:8b) and his "statute" (105:10a).[6]

---

4. Auffret, *Essai sur la structure littéraire du Psaume 105*, 16.

5. From Auffret, *Essai sur la structure littéraire du Psaume 105*, 18.

6. While God's remembrance is still ongoing—and will be, for the conceivable future of "forever" and "a thousand generations"—the *qatal* verb, "He has remembered," underscores that God will certainly be mindful and never forgetful: the future is as good as done! Later it is noted that God "remembered" his word to his people (105:42).

This covenanting of deity with humanity, his people, is also emphatically depicted:[7]

105:8aα	"forever"		
105:8aβ		*"covenant"*	
105:8b			"word"
105:9–10aα			"made" with the patriarchs
105:10aβ		"statute"	
105:10bα		*"covenant"*	
105:10bβ	"forever"		

The historical covenant—forever!—with the patriarchs was God's "word" (also designated as a "statute") that Israel would possess the promised land (105:8b, 10–11). This was an utterance directed to one individual, Abraham ("you" is singular in 105:11a), but also implicating his seed in the naming of Isaac and Jacob. It is, no doubt, also applicable to the plurality of God's people at the time of the psalmist ("your" is plural in 105:11b). And for those of us in a different dispensation, this assertion continues to emphasize the irrevocability of God's promises.[8]

All in all, this is the first of four historical exigencies that demonstrate divine faithfulness despite the dire circumstances that the protagonists in these recitals found themselves in. God's people were merely "sojourners" and "in number few,"[9] "going about from nation to nation" (105:12–13), yet God protected them, despite that impermanence and insubstantiality. "Prophets" and "anointed ones" in 105:15 designate the leaders and God's people in general during those ages. These terms make a sharp contrast with "sojourners" and "in number few" (105:12): though in the eyes of the world they were insignificant, they were special to God, his chosen ones and his spokespersons. And, what is more, the protection of his special people is stated in an imperative uttered by deity himself (105:15). Surely, God will be equally faithful to his people now.

Explanation: God's faithfulness in history 2 (105:16–23)

The theme of this section continues that begun in the previous one: the divine protection of God's people in ruinous situations proves deity's faithfulness.

Joseph is the protagonist for the most part in this section (but, as in Genesis, Jacob shows up at the end of the Joseph story, 105:23). The "word" of the afflicted Joseph (105:19a) indicates his prophecy (regarding the famine) coming to pass; his "refining" by Yahweh's utterance (105:19b) likely reflects the patriarch's testing/temptation by Potiphar's wife and his subsequent imprisonment (by divine ordination). Whereas iron collars had once been on Joseph's "neck [נֶפֶשׁ, *nephesh*]" (105:18b), after his exaltation by God it was Joseph's "desire [נֶפֶשׁ]" that reciprocally imprisoned his foes, the princes (105:22a). The falsely jailed one now jails the true culprits. Thus "*the one ruling* the peoples" (the Pharaoh, 105:20b) makes Joseph "*the one ruling*

---

7. The verb "make" (כרת, *krt*) is frequently used in conjunction with "covenant" (see 50:5; 83:5; 89:4).

8. The actual possession of the land by Jewish believers will likely take place in the eschaton, because it is their "inheritance," and "forever" (105:10–11). For the people of God in the present day and in the future, such land promises are not applicable; instead the rewards in the eschaton become their similarly hoped-for blessing in the future (taking a different form, of course).

9. "Men" in 105:12a is מַת, *mat*, specifically designating a male.

over all his possessions" (105:21b).¹⁰ Once again the faithfulness of God is substantiated in the protection and care of his people even in a foreign land.

Explanation: God's faithfulness in history 3 (105:24–38)

The third round of recounting the history of God's faithfulness deals with Moses and Aaron, i.e., when God's people were enslaved and he rescued them—the exodus. The bulk of this section comprises a poetic accounting of the "signs" and "portents"—the plagues that came upon Egypt (105:27).¹¹ The sovereign work of God in "turning" the Egyptians' hearts to hate his people and be deceptive towards them (105:25) is inscrutable from a human point of view. That mystery should not be glibly solved; the tension must be permitted to exist, even as it is in the Pentateuch, with the depiction both of God hardening the heart of the Pharaoh and of Pharaoh hardening his own heart. But through it all God is sovereign, an incontrovertible truth, as even the chiastic sequence of divine actions affirms:¹²

105:25a	"He turned"	
105:26a	"He sent"	
105:27		God's "sign-acts," "portents"
105:28a	"He sent"	
105:29a	"He turned"	

Even the fish, 105:29b tells us, "He *caused* to die," the direct hand of God in operation. Notice again, the structural emphasis given to God's performances:¹³

105:31a	"He spoke, and a swarm [of flies] came"
105:32b	"in their land"
105:33a	"and He struck"
105:34a	"He spoke, and the locust came"
105:35a	"in their land"
105:36a	"and He struck"

It is remarkable that the order of plagues in the psalm differs from that in the exodus account, especially in the placement of the ninth plague (darkness) first (105:28; Exod 10:21–29). This is followed by the first plague (turning of water into blood; Ps 105:29; Exod 7:14–25),

---

10. "He/his" in 105:21a, 21b, 22aα, 22b indicate the Pharaoh; in 105:22aβ, it refers to Joseph. It was his prophetic words that Pharaoh and his servants found acceptable (Gen 41:37)—Joseph's impartation of "wisdom" (Ps 105:22b).

11. Moses and Aaron are said to have "set the words of His signs [דִּבְרֵי אֹתוֹתָיו, *divre 'ototayw*]" in Egypt, i.e., they were instrumental in bringing about the word of God regarding the plagues.

12. "They" in 105:28b could refer to Moses and Aaron, the deputies of deity, who obediently carried out his orders without defying God's "words." Or the pronoun suffix to the verb might be a singular (as in the Greek of the Codex Sinaiticus): "and it [i.e., darkness, the nearest antecedent] did not defy His words." See Booij, "Role of Darkness," 211–12. Either way, the sovereignty of God is unquestionable!

13. From Girard, *Les Psaumes Redécouverts*, 91.

the second (frog invasion; Ps 105:30; Exod 8:1–15), the fourth (fly infestation; Ps 105:31a; Exod 8:20–32); the third (gnat pestilence; Ps 105:31b; Exod 8:16–19); the seventh (plague of hail; Ps 105:32; Exod 9:13–35); and the eighth (locust onslaught; Ps 105:34–35; Exod 10:1–20).[14] The oddity of the plague of darkness coming first is solved if we compare the sequence of banes in the psalm with that of the blessings of creation in Genesis 1: the latter decrees order, while the former disrupts order:[15]

DAYS	Genesis 1 *Decreeing Order*	Psalm 105 *Disrupting Order*
1 & 4 HEAVENS	light, luminaries	darkness (105:28)
2 & 5 WATERS	water life in waters	water becomes blood (105:29a) life (fish) die (105:29b)
3 & 6 EARTH	dry land vegetation life on dry land	land teems with pests (105:30–31) vegetation destroyed (105:32–35) human firstborn dies (105:36)

"The same movement from heaven, to waters, to earth is clearly discerned. . . . Both the creation and the Plagues are demonstrations of the might and power of Yahweh in nature and on earth."[16] Besides, whereas the first act of God against Egypt is the plague of darkness, his first act for his people, Israel, is the giving of light to them (Ps 105:39b).[17] "Light is used as a sign of divine presence. The converse appears true as well. . . . darkness is the chief sign of God's displeasure."[18] God was mighty displeased with the Egyptians for troubling his people and he would take a firm stance against their enemies, resulting in the devastation of their land and destruction of their firstborn—notice the wordplay: "and it ate up" is וַיֹּאכַל, *wayyo'kal* (105:35a, 35b); "and He struck all" is וַיַּךְ כָּל, *wayyak kal* (105:36a). As God was then, so he will be for us, the psalmist is implicitly asserting. God *is* faithful to his own!

There is pungent irony in the "coming [בוֹא, *bw'*]" of collars on the neck of Joseph (105:18b) and the "bringing out" and "going out" (both יצא, *yts'*, in 105:37a, 38a) of the Israelites in the exodus. Besides the antonyms that these verbs are ("coming" vs. "going"), both 105:18 and 105:37–38 mention metals—"iron" in the first, "silver and gold" in the second. The former has a stumbling slave desperate in subjection; the latter has successful

---

14. The omitted fifth and sixth plagues (pestilence on animals and boils on both animals and humans, Exod 9:1–7 and 9:8–12)—i.e., devastation on the denizens of dry land—perhaps is represented in the destruction of the human firstborn. Tucker ("Revisiting the Plagues," 407) notes that these two plagues are the only ones in which "land" is not mentioned in their respective summative statements (Exod 9:6, 10; as opposed to those digests of the other plagues: Exod 7:21; 8:6, 16, 24; 9:23; 10:14–15, 22). And here in Psalm 105, "land" is prominent in all the historical accounts of divine faithfulness ("land" alone is mentioned as part of the Abrahamic blessing in 105:11), and remains the focus in this section (105:24–38) as well: see instances of "land" (105: 23b, 27b, 30a, 32b, 35a, 36a); "territory" (105:31b, 33b); and "ground" (105:35b). The other mentions of "land(s)" are in 105:7b, 11a, 16a, 44a. The switching of the sequence of the third and fourth plagues in Psalm 105 is inexplicable, at least to me.

15. From Lee, "Genesis I," 259.

16. Lee, "Genesis I," 259–60.

17. Clifford, "Style and Purpose," 426.

18. Tucker, "Revisiting the Plagues," 408.

sojourners decamping with spoil. Look, says the psalmist, this is what our faithful God can do—turn things around totally![19]

Explanation: God's faithfulness in history 4 (105:39–45b)

The final section evidencing God's faithfulness in history commences with God providing shade and light to his people as they exit Egypt to enter the promised land (105:39). Unlike the previous sections, the people of God face no explicit danger or deprivation in this portion of the psalm.[20]

It appears that the psalmist took some effort to parallel this section with the previous one: the bane upon the Egyptians (105:24–38) vs. the blessing upon the Israelites (105:39–45) creates an extended chiasm:[21]

105:24a, 25a	"His people" (×2)	
105:25b, 26a	"His servant(s)" (×2)	
105:28b	"His words"	
105:29a		"waters"
105:31a		"came"
105:32b		"fire"
105:39b		"fire"
105:40a		"came"
105:41a		"waters"
105:42a	"His ... word"	
105:42b	"His servant"	
105:43a	"His people"	

The "waters" were bloodied (105:29a) for the Egyptians; but "waters" flowed to abate the thirst of the Israelites (105:41a). The swarm of pestilential insects "came" upon the Egyptians (105:31a; as well, a plague of locusts "came" [105:34a]); but a flock of quail "came" upon the Israelites to satiate them (105:40a). "Fire" flamed in the Egyptians' land (105:32b); but divine "fire" led the Israelites in safety (105:39b).[22] And this contrasting structure is surrounded on either side by God's "people" (105:24a, 25a, and 43a), God's "servant(s)" (105:25b, 26a, and 42b), and God's "words" (105:28b and 42a).

---

19. Ceresko, "Poetic Analysis," 35–36.

20. Unless one considers an implied lack of food and drink, which God faithfully remedied in abundance (105:40–41), or the smiting by the sun and the blindness in the dark, neutralized by the divine cloud and fire, respectively (105:39).

21. Modified from Auffret, *Essai sur la structure littéraire du Psaume 105*, 88–89n9.

22. The assonance is also worth noticing: "flaming fire" is אֵשׁ לֶהָבוֹת, *'esh lehavot*; "fire to give light" is אֵשׁ לְהָאִיר, *'esh lha'ir*.

And 105:42 restates 105:5–7 and 105:8–11 in the same sequence, signaling an end to this composition:[23]

105:5a	"remember"	
105:6a	"Abraham, His servant"	
105:6b–7		"Jacob"; "chosen ones"; "land"
105:8	"remembered"; "word"	
105:9a	"Abraham"	
105:10–11		"Jacob"; "statute"; "give … land"
105:42a	"remembered"; "word"	
105:42b	"Abraham, His servant"	
105:43–45		"His people"; chosen ones"; "statutes"; "gave … lands"

A faithful God's faithful words to his people are fulfilled, as he takes care of all their needs and delivers them . . . with delight and pleasure (105:43). God's own "gladness" and "joyful exclamation" had hitherto not been mentioned—deity's exhilaration in shepherding his flock! But in the middle of all this joy, the reader is rapidly brought down to earth in 105:45ab.

> Sinai was omitted from the story the psalm narrated [though "covenant," "word," "oath," and "statute" were mentioned in 105:8–10], but at its close it becomes all-important. The problem with Israel's occupation of the land is that keeping Yhwh's statutes and observing Yhwh's teachings is exactly what Israel did not do, and this is the basis of the promise that they will come into possession of the nations; hence their [subsequent] loss of the land. . . . It would be an exaggeration to say that the psalm reaches its object in . . . [105:45ab]. But whereas the psalm can put 95 percent of its stress on the grace of God, it has to make clear that a response to that grace is required.[24]

Therefore, the keeping of God's law is not forgotten in Psalm 105. Yes, the people of God can trust their faithful deity, but this is a God who makes divine demands upon his flock, for relationship with him mandates responsibility to him.[25] This responsibility of God's people to obey their God is not an abrogation of grace that continues to operate both in the forgiveness of his people's failures and in his empowerment of them for obedience through his Spirit. But neither does grace nullify responsibility. That tension, too, must be upheld without negating one aspect or the other.

---

23. From Girard, *Les Psaumes Redécouverts*, 95.

24. Goldingay, *Psalms*, 3:216–17.

25. The sequence should not be forgotten: relationship first, responsibility later. See Kuruvilla, *Privilege the Text!*, 189–95, 252–58.

Exhortation to Praise 2 (105:45c)

That irresolution notwithstanding, this psalm overwhelmingly focuses upon the praise of a sovereign God who has always been faithful to his people in history. And so the psalm appropriately concludes with "Praise Yah!"[26] (105:45c).

Sermon Map

I. The Past: Faithfulness Pictured
   Remembering of God's faithfulness (105:7–43)
   Move-to-relevance: Remembering God's faithfulness

II. The Present: Faithfulness Praised
   Rejoicing in God's faithfulness (105:1–6, 45c)
   Move-to-relevance: Our praise of God's faithfulness

III. The Future: Faithfulness Practiced
   Response to God's faithfulness (105:44–45b)
   Move-to-relevance: Our failure to obey

IV. *Praise to Praxis!*
   Specifics on praise of God and practice of his divine demand

---

26. I.e., "Hallelu-Yah!"

PSALM 106:1–48

Psalm of Disorientation

God's Lovingkindness Forgives and Delivers

PSALM 106 HAS SIMILARITIES with Psalm 105: both recount Israel's history, but the latter makes no mention of the iniquities of the people and the former focuses exclusively upon them. Both, however, deal with deity's rescue of his people—in Psalm 105 from distress and danger (peril from without), and in Psalm 106 from the consequences of their rebellion and recidivism (peril from within). "Psalm 105 majors in the 'God side' of the covenantal relationship, testifying to the Lord as one who initiates the covenant and proves faithful to it. . . . Psalm 106, on the other hand, majors in the 'human side' of the covenantal relationship, confessing that the humans whom God chose are in bondage to sin."[1] Yet their God is shown to be faithful and steadfastly loving: necessarily, then, the psalm begins and ends with God's "lovingkindness" (106:1c, 45b).

Translation

106:1 Praise Yah.
Give thanks to Yahweh, for He is good;
for His lovingkindness is forever.
106:2 Who can declare the mighty deeds of Yahweh,
[and] cause all His praise to be heard?
106:3 Blessing [upon] those keeping justice,
the one doing righteousness at all times.
106:4 Remember me, Yahweh, in [Your] favor to Your people;
visit me with Your deliverance,
106:5 that I may see the good things of Your chosen ones,
that I may rejoice in the joy of Your nation,
that I may praise with Your inheritance.

---

1. DeClaissé-Walford et al., *Book of Psalms*, 796.

106:6 We have sinned with our fathers;
    we have committed iniquity; we have acted wickedly.
106:7 Our fathers in Egypt did not understand Your wonders;
    they did not remember Your abundant lovingkindnesses,
    and they rebelled by the sea, at the Reed Sea.
106:8 And He delivered them for the sake of His name,
    that He might make His mighty deeds known.
106:9 And He rebuked the Reed Sea and it dried up,
    and He led them in the deeps, as through the wilderness.
106:10 And He delivered them from the hand of the one hating [them],
    and redeemed them from the hand of the enemy.
106:11 And the waters covered their adversaries;
    not one of them was left.
106:12 And they believed His words;
    they were singing His praise.
106:13 They hastened [and] they forgot His works;
    they did not long for His counsel.
106:14 And they craved deeply in the wilderness,
    and tested God in the desert.
106:15 And He gave to them their request,
    and sent wasting in[to] their being.
106:16 And they became jealous of Moses in the camp,
    [and] of Aaron, the holy one of Yahweh.
106:17 The earth opened and swallowed Dathan,
    and covered over the company of Abiram.
106:18 And a fire blazed up in their company;
    the flame, it was devouring the wicked.
106:19 They made a calf in Horeb
    and worshiped a metal image.
106:20 And they exchanged their glory
    for the form of a bull that eats grass.
106:21 They forgot God their deliverer,
    the One doing great things in Egypt,
106:22 wonders in the land of Ham,
    awesome things at the Reed Sea.
106:23 And He said He would exterminate them,
    except that Moses, His chosen one,
stood in the breach before His face,
    to turn back His wrath from destroying.
106:24 And they rejected the pleasant land;
    they did not believe in His word.
106:25 And they grumbled in their tents;
    [and] they did not hear the voice of Yahweh.

106:26	And He lifted His hand [to swear] to them,
	to make them fall in the wilderness,
106:27	and to cause their seed to fall among the nations,
	and to scatter them in the lands.
106:28	And they joined themselves to Baal of Peor,
	and ate sacrifices [offered] for the dead.
106:29	And they provoked [Him] with their actions,
	and the plague breached out among them.
106:30	Then Phinehas stood up and intervened,
	and so the plague was stopped.
106:31	And it was considered to him for righteousness,
	to generation after generation unto forever.
106:32	And they provoked [Him] at the waters of Meribah,
	and it was harmful to Moses on their account,
106:33	for they rebelled against His Spirit,
	and he spoke rashly with his lips.
106:34	They did not exterminate the peoples,
	as Yahweh said to them,
106:35	and they mixed with the nations,
	and they learned their works
106:36	and they served their idols,
	and they became to them a snare.
106:37	And they sacrificed their sons
	and their daughters to demons,
106:38	and they shed innocent blood,
	the blood of their sons and their daughters,
	whom they sacrificed to the idols of Canaan:
	and the land was defiled with the blood.
106:39	And they became unclean in their works,
	and prostituted themselves in their actions.
106:40	And the anger of Yahweh was kindled against His people,
	and He loathed His inheritance.
106:41	And He gave them into the hand of the nations,
	and the ones who hated them ruled over them.
106:42	And their enemies oppressed them,
	and they were subdued under their hand.
106:43	Many times He would rescue them;
	and they—they rebelled in their counsel,
	and they sank in their iniquity.
106:44	And He saw the distress upon them
	when He heard their lament;
106:45	and He remembered His covenant for their sake,
	and He relented according to His abundant lovingkindness.

106:46 And He gave them [as objects] of compassion
        before the face of all their captors.
106:47 Deliver us, Yahweh our God,
        and gather us from among the nations,
    to give thanks to Your holy name
    and to laud Your praise.
106:48 Blessed be Yahweh, the God of Israel,
        from forever even unto forever.
    And all the people say, "Amen."
    Praise Yah.

Structure

Psalm 106 is introduced and concluded with praise and prayer, with a prosecution section (and a brief protection section) in the middle, forming the bulk of the composition.[2]

106:1–5	**Praise 1 and Prayer 1** "Praise Yah!" (106:1a); "deliverance" (106:4b) "praise" (106:1a, 2b, 5c); "give thanks" (106:1b) "blessed" people of Yahweh (106:3a)

106:6–46	**Prosecution (106:6–39)**
	  Heading: Confession (106:6)
	  Egypt
	    106:7–12 Unbelief (Exod 7:1—15:21)
	  Desert, Horeb
	    106:13–15 Craving (Exod 15:22–25; 16:1—17:1; Numbers 11)
	    106:16–18 Jealousy (Numbers 16–17)
	    106:19–23 Idolatry (Deut 9:7–29)
	  Horeb, Promised Land
	    106:24–27 Unbelief (Num 13:25–29; 14:3)
	    106:28–31 Sacrilege (Num 25:3–9)
	    106:32–33 Rebellion (Num 20:8–13)
	  Promised Land
	    106:34–39 Failure (Jdg 1:18–36; 2:1–3, 16–19)
	Protection (106:40–46)
	  106:40–43 Judgment (Jdg 2:18–19)
	  106:44–46 Compassion (Jdg 3:9)

106:47–48	**Prayer 2 and Praise 2** "Praise Yah!" (106:48d); "deliver" (106:47a) "praise" (106:47d, 48d); "give thanks" (106:47c) "blessed" Yahweh (106:48a)

---

2. See deClaissé-Walford et al., *Book of Psalms*, 797; Ross, *Psalms*, 3:289–92; and Martin, "Chiastic Structure," 507, 509.

There is no doubt the poem is carefully constructed:[3]

Psalm 106:1–5
- **A** "Praise Yah!" (106:1a)
  - **B** "forever" (106:1c)
    - **C** "praise" (106:2b); "blessing" (106:3a)
      - **D** prayer for "deliverance" (106:4b)

Psalm 106:6–46
- **E** "did not remember" God's lovingkindness (106:7b)
  - **F** "rebelled" (106:7c)
    - **G** "enemy" (106:10b)
      - **H** "forgot His [God's] works" (106:13a)
        - **I** jealous "of Moses [לְמֹשֶׁה, lmosheh]" (106:16a)
          - **J** "Moses stood" (106:23bcα)
            - **K** "breach" (106:23cβ)
              - **L** rejected the "land" (106:24a)
              - **L'** scattered in the "lands" (106:27b)
            - **K'** "breached out" (106:29b)
          - **J'** "Phinehas stood up" (106:30a)
        - **I'** harmful "to Moses [לְמֹשֶׁה]" (106:32b)
      - **H'** "learned their [Canaanites'] works" (106:35b)
    - **G'** "enemies" (106:42a)
  - **F'** "rebelled" (106:43b)
- **E'** God "remembered His covenant" (106:45a)

Psalm 106:47–48
- **D'** prayer to "deliver" (106:47a)
- **C'** "praise" (106:47d); "blessed" (106:48a)
- **B'** "forever" (×2; 106:48b)
- **A'** "Praise Yah!" (106:48d)

Thus the psalm begins and ends with *Praise and Prayer*, presuming that the pattern of *Prosecution* followed by *Protection* in the past (106:6–39, 40–46) will repeat itself in the present/near future: the people of God praised him then; they hope they will get to praise him again now after a similar sequence of events.

Theological Focus

The lovingkindness of a good God makes it possible for him to be approached with repentance, and yet with confidence, for deity has, in the past, demonstrated his grace upon being supplicated (despite their utter infidelity to him), forgiving and delivering his people from their predicaments and punishments, which results in his praise forever.

---

3. Modified from Martin, "Chiastic Structure," 510; and Girard, *Les Psaumes Redécouverts*, 114.

Commentary

Praise 1 and Prayer 1 (106:1–5)

This is the first psalm in the Psalter to commence with "Praise Yah!" (106:1a).[4] Immediately, praise and thanks are exhorted, but "who" would declare the mighty deeds of Yahweh and praise him (106:2a)? The answer is forthcoming in 106:3–5: it is those who follow after God, his justice and his righteousness, "at all times" (106:3b), and those who—the psalmist prays—will be, in turn, remembered by God as he shows "favor" to his people by saving them (106:4). Perhaps there was some sort of distress being experienced by the psalmist (and/or the people of God),[5] for the request of 106:4–5 for deliverance is earnest and entreating, as the trifold yearning demonstrates:

106:4b	"Visit me with Your deliverance,		
106:5a	that I may see	the good things	of Your chosen ones,
106:5b	that I may rejoice	in the joy	of Your nation,
106:5c	that I may praise		with Your inheritance."

These are the "blessed"—those who "see the good things" of God (106:3a, 5a) from a "good" God (106:1b),[6] who "rejoice" and "praise" Yahweh (106:5bc). And these are the ones who can "declare the mighty deeds of Yahweh" (106:2). Unfortunately, as the bulk of the psalm goes on to demonstrate, God's people failed to recognize the mighty deeds of God, to keep justice, or to do righteousness (106:3).

Prosecution (106:6–39)

Then comes the voluminous *Prosecution* of the failure of the "fathers," the ancient generation of God's people. But it is actually part of a confession (a self-prosecution) that is explicit in 106:6; this verse acts like a heading to the section, piling on the *mea culpa*: "*we* have sinned," "*we* have committed iniquity," "*we* have acted wickedly." Their penitence is not because they have sinned *like* their fathers; no, they have sinned "with" their fathers (106:6a). What follows is a litany of indictments covering the historical days of God's people in Egypt, in the desert, at Horeb, and in the promised land.[7] But, again, if the current generation sinned "with" the fathers, the immoral attitudes and actions of the latter are shared by the former too.

For all the "wonders" performed by God, the fathers "did not understand," and they "did not remember" divine lovingkindness; instead, they rebelled (106:7). God might have worked miracles to deliver his own (106:8–11) and the beneficiaries may have initially "believed His

---

4. The others are Psalms 107; 108; and 136.

5. The *Prayer 2 and Praise 2* at the conclusion of the psalm (106:47–48) validates the sense of an ongoing distress in the life of the psalmist and his cohort. There is the first-person singular, "me," in 106:4–5a, but the addition of "Your people," "Your chosen ones," "Your nation," and "Your inheritance" (likely the land of blessing) in 106:5 makes the transition to the first-person plural, "we," in 106:6 smooth (also see the first-person plural in 106:47ab).

6. Thus "good" effectively bookends this opening *Praise 1 and Prayer 1* section of the psalm.

7. See the outline of the psalm for historical references.

words" and "sung His praise" (106:12),[8] but it did not take them long—"they hastened"—to forget God's works (106:13). And their cravings tempted God (106:14). The waters "covered" is וַיְכַסּוּ, *waykassu* (106:11a)—the work of God in decimating their enemies. But in response, all the people do is provoke God: "tested" is וַיְנַסּוּ, *waynassu* (106:14b). In the end, these recalcitrant ones were punished (106:15). Here, too, the wordplay is pungent: rather than divine "favor [רָצוֹן, *ratson*]" (106:4a), they got divine "wasting [רָזוֹן, *razon*]" (106:15). Tit for tat, indeed!

But that did not stop the unfaithful: their arrogance impelled them to jealousy of their leader, so they were punished again, "wicked" as they were (106:16–18). Once the waters had "covered" Israel's adversaries (106:11a); now the earth opens up and "covers" the sinners among God's own people (106:17). The screed continues: in Horeb they cared more for idols than for their Creator who had delivered them from Egypt (106:19–22).[9] Notice how the primary accusation at either end of the structure below (in 106:13 and in 106:21–22) is the forgetfulness of the people of God as they lapse into idolatry (106:19–20):[10]

106:13	"they forgot" (106:13a)
106:14–15	"wilderness," "desert" (106:14)
106:16–18	**Provocation and punishment**
106:19–20	"Horeb" (106:19)
106:21–22	"they forgot" (106:21a)

Yet a reassuring note of positivity is struck: divine anger turned away as a result of intercession (106:23). Thus there is a hint that in the contemporaneous situation of distress also, this psalm might itself serve as the prayer that turns away divine wrath. The intercession by an ancient protagonist and the warding off of the severe hand of God is repeated in history (106:28–31). When the ones who had once "believed" God's "words" (106:12a) chose, later, *not* to "believe" his "word" (106:24b) and fell into iniquity, suffering the wrath of God, this time it was Phinehas who, like Moses earlier, "stood" (106:23c, 30a). The latter stood in the "breach" (106:23c), and the result of the intervention of the former was that the "breaching" plague was stopped (106:29b–30). Nonetheless, the consequences were severe—even the intercessor of yore, Moses, suffered in the fallout (106:32–33).

These accounts of Moses and Phinehas (J, K, and K′, J′; see structure above) surround the chiastic center of the psalm that deals with the rejection by the people of the "land" promised to them by God (L; 106:24); in turn, God scattered them in the "lands" of foreigners (L′; 106:27b). The "good things of Your chosen ones," the "joy of Your nation," and "Your inheritance" (106:5) had been rejected by God's people; the only land they now had was the despair-ridden land of their exile and diaspora![11]

---

8. Notice the co-occurrence of "lovingkindness" (106:1c, 7b), "mighty deeds" (106:2a, 8b), and "praise" (106:2b, 12b).

9. "Their glory" in 106:20 is a euphemism for the splendor of their God (the Targum has "majesty of their Lord").

10. From Girard, *Les Psaumes Redécouverts*, 113.

11. Rebellion brackets the *Prosecution* section (see chiastic structure, F and F′; also see 106:33a).

The failure to take over the land is detailed in 106:34–39, with the result that Israel became "Canaanized" and partook of the abominable cultic activities of the surrounding peoples (106:35–39): those vile undertakings take center stage again in a chiastic structure:[12]

106:34b	"Yahweh"
106:35b	"their works"
106:36a	"idols"
106:37aα	"and they sacrificed"
106:37aβ–b	"their sons and their daughters"
106:38a	"blood"
106:38bα	"blood"
106:38bβ	"their sons and their daughters"
106:38cα	"whom they sacrificed"
106:38cβ	"idols"
106:39a	"their works"
106:40a	"Yahweh"

They learned the "works" of the pagans (root: עשׂה, ʿsh; 106:35b) and became unclean in their own "works" (עשׂה; 106:39a), all the while disdaining and disregarding the "works" of God (עשׂה; 106:13a), the one who had been "doing" great things for them (עשׂה; 106:21b), and imitating the ungodly by "making" idols (also from עשׂה; 106:19a).

As expected, the ramifications of such infidelity to Yahweh were severe (106:40–42). Once God had liberated them from the "hand" of those "hating" them (106:10a); now he delivers (!) them into the "hands" of those who "hated" them (106:41). Once they had been rescued from their "enemy" (106:10b); now they are oppressed by the "enemy" (106:42). Those who venerated the idols of "Canaan [כנען, knʿn]" (106:38c) are now "subdued [כנע, knʿ]" under the hand of those Canaanites (106:42b).

This was a repeated cycle of iniquity followed by repentance (on the part of the Israelites), and forgiveness followed by their rescue (on the part of their God) (106:43–44), because he remembered his covenant, because of his lovingkindness, because of his compassion (106:45–46). Once God had "given" them their wanton request for more, resulting in their punishment (106:15a), and once he had "given" them over to the hand of the nations (106:41a); but now, in divine grace and mercy, he "gives" them as objects of compassion before all peoples (106:46a). The sinful crowd may not have "heard" God's voice (106:25b), but God "heard" their cry (106:44b): thus 106:43–46 forms the *Protection* section.

Prayer 2 and Praise 2 (106:47–48)

Since the current generation of God's people confessed to having sinned "with" their fathers of yesteryear (106:6a), it is appropriate that the psalm ends with a prayer for their own deliverance (106:47). If God could protect and rescue his people in the past, surely he would do so again (106:47ab). When he does so, praise is promised him (106:47cd). The psalmist had averred that God's "lovingkindness" was forever" (106:1c), but the ancestors had not remembered his "*abundant* lovingkindnesses" (106:7b), despite which God had mercy on them because of his

---

12. From Girard, *Les Psaumes Redécouverts*, 109; and Auffret, *Que seulement de tes yeux*, 340.

"*abundant* lovingkindness" (106:45). Would that that same lavish lovingkindness be bestowed on the people of God again today! So the psalmist pleads for God to "remember me" (106:4a). Though the fathers "did not remember" God's grace (106:7b), *God* did "remember" his covenant with them (106:45a). Perhaps he would remember his own again now. God had delivered his people a number of times (the root "deliver" occurs in 106:8a, 10a, 21a); no wonder the psalm commences and concludes with a plea for "deliverance" at the current moment (106:4b, 47a) and with a benediction and a vocalization of "Praise Yah!"—exactly as it had begun.[13]

Sermon Map

I. Failure of God's People Expressed
    Perversity (106:6–18, 24–27, 32–42)
    Move-to-relevance: Our failure

II. Faithfulness of God to His People Exhibited
    Petition (106:19–23, 28–31)
    Pardon (106:43–46)
    Move-to-relevance: Are we praying?

III. Faithfulness of God to His People Expected
    Pleading (106:4–5, 47)
    Praise (106:1–3, 48)
    Move-to-relevance: Our failure to obey

IV. *Petition for Pardon, Then Praise!*
    Specifics on intercessory supplication in distress

---

13. Psalm 106:48 also concludes Book IV of the Psalter.

PSALM 107:1–43

Psalm of Orientation

Thanksgiving for Deliverances in Lovingkindness

PSALM 107 COMMENCES BY answering the plea of the psalmist in 106:47 to be "delivered" and "gathered" from among the nations: correspondingly, here the people are "redeemed" and "gathered" from the lands (107:2–3).

Translation

107:1 Give thanks to Yahweh, for He is good,
    for His lovingkindness is forever.
107:2 Let the redeemed of Yahweh say [so],
    whom He has redeemed from the hand of the adversary.
107:3 And from the lands He has gathered them,
    from the east and from the west,
    from the north and from the sea.
107:4 They wandered in the wilderness, in the desert;
    the way to an inhabited city they did not find.
107:5 Hungry, also thirsty,
    their soul within them faints.
107:6 And they wailed to Yahweh in their distress;
    from their constraints He rescues them.
107:7 And He led the way for them by a straight way,
    to get to an inhabited city.
107:8 Let them give thanks to Yahweh [for] His lovingkindness,
    and [for] His wonders to the children of humanity.
107:9 For He has satiated the desiccated soul,
    and the hungry soul He has filled with good things.

107:10	The ones who inhabited darkness and the death-shadow,
	those bound in affliction and iron[s]—
107:11	because they rebelled against the utterances of God
	and the counsel of the Most High they spurned—
107:12	He also humbled, with misfortune, their heart;
	they stumbled and there was none helping.
107:13	And they wailed to Yahweh in their distress;
	from their constraints He delivers them.
107:14	He brings them out of darkness and the death-shadow,
	and their bonds He breaks.
107:15	Let them give thanks to Yahweh [for] His lovingkindness,
	and [for] His wonders to the children of humanity.
107:16	For He has broken down doors of bronze,
	and bars of iron He has shattered.
107:17	Fools, because of their way of rebellion,
	and because of their iniquities, are afflicted.
107:18	All foods their soul loathes,
	and they reached unto the gates of death.
107:19	And they wailed to Yahweh in their distress;
	from their constraints He delivers them.
107:20	He sends His word to heal them,
	and to liberate [them] from their pits.
107:21	Let them give thanks to Yahweh [for] His lovingkindness,
	and [for] His wonders to the children of humanity.
107:22	And let them offer sacrifices of thanksgiving,
	and let them recount His works with a joyful exclamation.
107:23	Those going down to the sea in ships,
	those doing business on great waters;
107:24	they—they have seen the works of Yahweh,
	and His wonders in the deep.
107:25	And He spoke, and He raised a windstorm,
	and it lifted its waves.
107:26	They go up to the heavens, they go down to the depths;
	their soul—in evil it melts away.
107:27	They reel and they stagger like a drunk,
	and all their wisdom is confused.
107:28	And they wailed to Yahweh in their distress,
	and from their constraints He brings them out.
107:29	He stands down the windstorm to stillness,
	and the waves of the sea were silent.

107:30 And they rejoiced because they are calm,
        and He led them to their desired haven.
107:31 Let them give thanks to Yahweh [for] His lovingkindness,
        and [for] His wonders to the children of humanity.
107:32 And let them exalt Him in the congregation of the people,
        and at the seat of the elders let them praise Him.
107:33 He makes rivers into wilderness,
        and springs of water into thirsty ground,
107:34 fruitful land into salt marsh,
        because of the evil of those dwelling in it.
107:35 He makes wilderness into a pool of water,
        and dry land into springs of water.
107:36 And there He caused the hungry to dwell,
        and they establish an inhabited city,
107:37 and they sowed fields and planted vineyards,
        and produced a harvest of fruit.
107:38 And He blessed them and they increased greatly,
        and their cattle He does not let diminish.
107:39 And they were diminished and bowed down
        through oppression, evil, and sorrow.
107:40 [He is] the One pouring out contempt upon nobles,
        and He caused them to wander in a wasteland without a way.
107:41 And He secured on high the needy from affliction,
        and made families like a flock.
107:42 The upright see it and they rejoice;
        and all unrighteousness has stopped its mouth.
107:43 Who is the wise [who] also attends to these things?
        And they understand the lovingkindnesses of Yahweh.

Structure

The psalm as a whole may be conveniently divided into *Invitation* (107:1–3), *Instantiation* (107:4–32), and *Instruction* sections (107:33–43). The deeds of Yahweh are explicated in four parallel scenes within *Instantiation* (107:4–32; columns below) and are intended to give God's people insight and understanding (107:33–43)—*Instruction* (see commentary below). The psalm closes with a rally, endorsing the wisdom of the instruction.[1]

1. Modified from Jarick, "Four Corners," 274; and Allen, *Psalms 101–150*, 63. Repetitions within the *Instantiation* delineate the seams of the scenes. East: "way"; "inhabited city" (107:4b, 7ab); "hungry" (107:5a, 9b); "darkness and the death-shadow" (107:10a, 14a); West: "bound," "bonds" (from the same root; 107:10b, 14b); "iron" (107:10b, 16b); and Sea: "go down" (107:23a, 26a); "lift," "exalt" (רום, *rum*; 107:25b, 32a); "waves" (107:25b, 29b). See Allen, *Psalms 101–150*, 63.

Invitation (107:1–3)				
Instantiation (107:4–32)				
	"East"	"West"	"North"	"Sea"
	107:4–9	**107:10–16**	**107:17–22**	**107:23–32**
	Wanderers (Desert)	Prisoners (Darkness)	Sufferers (Illness)	Sailors (Ocean)
Risk	107:4–5	107:10–12	107:17–18	107:23–27
Refrain 1	107:6	107:13	107:19	107:28
Rescue	107:7	107:14	107:20	107:29–30
Refrain 2	107:8	107:15	107:21	107:31
Result	107:9	107:16	107:22	107:32

Instruction (107:33–43)		
	− (enemies)	+ (upright)
Rehearsal	107:33–34	107:35–38
	107:39–40	107:41
Rally		107:42–43

The four scenes in the *Instantiation* section derive their organization from the cardinal points of the compass in 107:3, with the scenes themselves carefully arranged:[2]

107:4–9 "East"	*Desert* (dangers of travel) undeserved suffering: chaos "wailed" (107:6a); "rescues" (107:6b); "for" (107:9a)
107:10–16 "West"	*Darkness* (conditions of threat) deserved suffering: sin "wailed" (107:13a); "delivers" (107:13b); "for" (107:16)
107:17–22 "North"	*Illness* (conditions of threat) deserved suffering: sin "wailed" (107:19a); "delivers" (107:19b); worship (107:22)
107:23–32 "Sea"	*Ocean* (dangers of travel) undeserved suffering: chaos "wailed" (107:28a); "bring out" (107:28b); worship (107:32)

---

2. Modified from Martin, "'Oh Give Thanks,'" 370; and Allen, *Psalms 101–150*, 63. The fourfold categorization is apparently not original: Weinfeld has shown how the Mesopotamian Šamaš Hymn has the same four groups, with its last category of seafarers also, as in Psalm 107, being the longest (Weinfeld, "Comparison," 275–79).

Theological Focus

> The people of God, experiencing, reflecting upon, and recounting the abundant lovingkindnesses of their God in his deliverance of them from all manner of distresses—including the consequence of their own iniquities—give exuberant thanks to their savior, learning from the past to anticipate future reversal of dire circumstances.

Commentary

Invitation (107:1–3)

As was noted, the *Invitation* section appears to answer the plea of 106:47, perhaps referencing the return of God's people ("the redeemed of Yahweh," 107:2a) from exile. Notice also the cardinal points of the compass in 107:3bc that give structure to the *Instantiation* section that follows.[3] This section thus urges thanksgiving be rendered to Yahweh for his lovingkindness and his redemption, specifically for those situations described in each of the *Instantiation* scenes.[4]

Instantiation: Desert (107:4–9)

"East" of Israel lies an arid desert, hardly crossable even by hardy travelers. But far out there in the wilderness and desert, distant from civilization, were these wanderers, suffering the travails of travel—they were lost (107:4).[5] Their provisions had run out; they cried out to God; Yahweh rescued them (107:5–6).[6] There is now reason to thank God for his lovingkindness (107:8)—fulfilling the *Invitation* of 107:1-2—because their deity is a "good" God (107:1a) who gives "good" things to the needy (107:9b).

Instantiation: Darkness (107:10–16)

Perhaps the label "west" (107:3b) was chosen to indicate the "darkness" described (107:10a, 14a), "the place where the sun sets, the deathly place of darkness in which the sun dies every night as it makes its journey over the earthly realm."[7] The "binding [אָסִיר, *'asir*]" and "bonds

---

3. "Sea" likely stands for the "south" (or the "right," when facing east in Israel)—i.e., the Red Sea or the southeast part of the Mediterranean.

4. Where the deliverance of God is instantiated, actualized, "real-ized."

5. Allen suspects these wayfarers were part of the Israelite peoples returning from exile (*Psalms 101–150*, 64). The careful structuring of verses is noticeable in the chiasms therein: 107:4 (verb / location // location / verb); 107:6 (verb / situation // situation / verb); and 107:9 (verb of provision / state of "soul" // state of "soul" / verb of provision).

6. "Rescue" is also used to refer to the exodus and surrounding events (Exod 3:8; 5:23; Ps 106:43).

7. deClaissé-Walford et al., *Book of Psalms*, 818. Again there are chiasms in 107:11 (verb of rejection / "speaking" of God // "counsel" of God / verb of rejection); 107:13 (verb / situation // situation / verb); 107:14 (verb of liberation / situation // situation / verb of liberation); and 107:16 (verb of destruction / metal // metal / verb of destruction). Note, too, the wordplays: in 107:13b, "He delivers them" is יוֹשִׁיעֵם; *yoshi'em*; in

[מוֹסֵרָה, moserah]" (107:10b, 14b), as well as the mention of "iron[s]" (107:10b, 16b), point to the sufferers being prisoners. It appears their incarceration was just deserts for their rebellion against God's word and the spurning of his counsel (107:11). Now, humbled by God, they were languishing helpless, stumbling with no aid in sight (107:12). They, too, cried out to God; Yahweh rescued them (107:13–14).[8] Here, then, is another reason to thank God for his lovingkindness (107:15–16).

Instantiation: Illness (107:17–22)

The reason for linking "north" (107:3c) with illness is unclear, though it seems that "prophets often depict the north, the third direction mentioned in 107:3, as the direction from which the punishment of God came to the ancient Israelites."[9] In any case, the affliction was related to sin of these "fools" who are marked by the utter imprudence of their "rebellion" and "iniquities" (107:17). Yet, these sinful invalids, weighed down by the hand of God, were rescued by the same hand of deity, who healed them with his "word" and liberated them (107:20). Once again, there is cause for thanksgiving to God for his lovingkindness (107:21). The response of the healed and liberated gets an expansion here: they are to offer sacrifices of thanksgiving and joyful shouts of worship (107:22).

Instantiation: Ocean (107:23–32)

Like the first instantiation, the fourth also deals with dangers of travel.[10] To the Israelites, on the whole a non-nautical and sea-averse people, how the ocean farers managed to get around was a matter of divine miracles: sailors saw firsthand the "works of Yahweh and His wonders in the deep" (107:24).[11] In a dangerous storm—also an act of God—these mariners reeled and staggered, all their naval intelligence availing for naught (107:27). So they, too, cried out to God; Yahweh rescued them, stilling the storm and silencing the waves (107:28–29).[12] The shipmates rejoiced to get to their port safe and sound (107:30)—yet another reason to thank God for his lovingkindness (107:31). As in the previous scene, the rescued ones are exhorted to exalt God in the assembly and praise him in public (107:32). The one who "lifted" the waves is surely worthy of being "exalted" himself (both from the root רוּם, 107:25b, 32a).

107:14a, "He brings them out" is יוֹצִיאֵם, yotsi'em; the two verbs are adjacent to each other, too. Then there is paronomasia in 107:11a: כִּי־הִמְרוּ אִמְרֵי־אֵל, ki-himru 'imre-'el, "because they rebelled against the speaking of God." Their "rebellion" was nothing short of sacrilege, the rejection of God's "speaking."

8. Perhaps the "deliverance" (107:19b) is an allusion to the exodus (Exod 14:30; Ps 106:8, 10).

9. deClaissé-Walford et al., Book of Psalms, 818. See Jer 1:13–14; Ezek 9:2. A chiasm is present in this section as well, in Ps 107:19 (verb / situation // situation / verb).

10. Again, chiasms are found in 107:28 (verb / situation // situation / verb); and 107:32 (verb exhorting praise / location // location / verb exhorting praise).

11. The "they" in 107:26a, no doubt, refers to the "they" of 107:23–24, those maritime folks.

12. The verb used for the deliverance in 107:28b is "bring out," a standard term referring to the exodus (Exod 3:10–12; 6:6–7, 13, 26–27; Pss 78:16; 105:37–38, 43, etc.). As well, the verb "lead" (107:30b), for which, see Exod 13:21; 15:13; Ps 78:14, 53, 72.

Instruction (107:33–43)

In the final *Instruction* section, there is first a rehearsal of the events already described, reusing vocabulary from the earlier scenes, including the motif of "lovingkindness" (107:43b), carried over from the refrains in each of the four scenes of the *Instantiation* section: in 107:8a, 15a, 21a, 31a). The closing use of the word in this last section of the psalm is in the plural ("lovingkindnesses"; 107:43b), while the bracketing employment in the first section of the psalm, in 107:1b, was in the singular.

The rehearsal of past events (107:33–41) shifts back and forth between God's negative actions against enemies (107:33–34, 39–40), and his positive actions on behalf of his people (107:35–38, 41). To his own, deity provides fruitfulness of land, sustenance for life, and habitation for dwelling, altogether blessing them so that they increase greatly—both humans and their domesticated animals (107:35–38). The needy among them he protects, and he guards his people as a shepherd would his flock (107:41). But against the enemies God turns their fruitful land into sterile ground (107:33–34), and subjugates the evil ones with further evil, oppression, and sorrows of all kinds, diminishing their leaders and making them wander in a pathless wasteland (107:39–40).[13] The contrast between these negative and positive actions of God is exemplified in the double use of "diminish": God does not let even the animals of his people "diminish" (107:38b), but the enemies are "diminished" (107:39a). And notice that the rivers of the evildoers' lands are "made" into "wilderness" (107:33a), whereas God "makes" the "wilderness" of his people into pools of water (107:35); likewise, "springs of water" are converted into thirsty ground for the nefarious (107:33b), but for the faithful, dry land is transformed into "springs of water" (107:35b).[14] There is also the unfruitfulness of the wicked who "dwell" in a sterile land (107:34b), whereas God causes the needy to "dwell" in a fertile and "inhabited" city (both "dwell" and "inhabit" are derived from ישב, *yshv*; 107:36).

The psalm ends with a rallying cry, the culmination of the *Instruction*, intended by the author to be taken to heart by readers: the upright will see the works of God and rejoice, whereas "unrighteousness" (i.e., those who do unrighteousness) will be stunned into silence (107:42b). It is the wise one who digests and assimilates all these things, the psalmist declares, for they are the ones who have understood all the "lovingkindnesses of Yahweh" as detailed in the *Instantiation* sections of this psalm (hence the plural: "lovingkindnesses"; 107:43b). Thankfully contemplate, urges the psalm and its author!

---

13. Once it was his people who were "wandering," lost in the "way," and God had rescued them (107:4b). Now it is the enemies who "wander" in a wasteland without a "way" (107:40b), and it was God who had afflicted them so. The "thirsty" ones of his people were helped by God (107:5a), but even the very land of the enemies would remain "thirsty" (107:33b).

14. Also, "fruitful land" becomes a salt marsh for enemies (107:34a); for the faithful it is the other way round: dry "land" becomes water laden (107:35b), producing an abundance of "fruit" (107:37b).

PSALM 107:1–43

Sermon Map

I. Lethalities Experienced by the People of God
   Desert, darkness, illness, ocean (107:4–5, 10–12, 17–18, 23–27)
   Move-to-relevance: The lethalities we face
II. Lovingkindnesses Extended by God
   Desert, darkness, illness, ocean (107:6–7, 13–14, 19–20, 28–30)
   Move-to-relevance: The lovingkindnesses of God we experience
III. Lauding Expressed to God
   Desert, darkness, illness, ocean (107:8–9, 15–16, 21–22, 31–32)
IV. *Learn from and Laud God's Lovingkindnesses!*
   Specifics on thanksgiving (and/or remembering for the future)

PSALM 108:1–13

Psalm of Disorientation

Confidence in, and Praise for, Deliverance

THIS PSALM SHARES SEVERAL verses with two other compositions in the psalter: Ps 108:2–6 = 57:8–12; and 108:7–13 = 60:6–12. Thereby, Psalm 108 becomes a "new" composition with a "new" composite text.

Translation

108:1	My heart is steadfast, God, I will sing;
	I will make music, even [with] my inner being.
108:2	Awake, harp and lyre;
	I will wake the dawn.
108:3	I will give You thanks among the peoples, Yahweh,
	and I will make music to You among the nations.
108:4	For great above the heavens is Your lovingkindness,
	and unto the clouds, Your truth.
108:5	Be exalted above the heavens, God,
	and above all the earth, Your glory.
108:6	That Your beloved ones may be liberated,
	deliver with Your right hand and answer me.
108:7	God—He has spoken in His holiness:
	"I will exult, I will apportion Shechem,
	and measure out the valley of Succoth.
108:8	Mine is Gilead, Mine is Manasseh;
	and Ephraim, the stronghold of My head;
	Judah, My scepter.

108:9   Moab [is] My washbasin;
          over Edom I will throw My sandal;
          over Philistia I will shout triumphantly.
108:10 Who will bring Me to the fortified city?
          Who has led Me unto Edom?"
108:11 Have You, God, not rejected us—
          and You, God, do not go forth with our armies?
108:12 Grant to us help against the adversary,
          for worthless is deliverance [from] a human.
108:13 Through God we will do powerfully,
          and He—He will trample our adversaries.

Structure

Psalm 108 comprises two stanzas, 108:1–6 and 108:7–13, each culminating in an entreaty for deliverance (108:6, 12). These stanzas may be further divided thus, with their components organized chiastically:

STANZA 1 (108:1–6)
108:1–5   Eulogy 1
108:6   Entreaty 1 ["deliver"]

STANZA 2 (108:7–13)
108:7–10 Enquiry 1 (God's)
108:11   Enquiry 2 (people's)
108:12   Entreaty 2 ["deliverance"]
108:13   Eulogy 2

Eulogy 1 and *Eulogy 2* (108:1–5, 13) make assertions about God (his lovingkindness and truth; his power) and the people's response to those assertions (celebrating God; conquering enemies). *Entreaty 1* and *Entreaty 2* (108:6, 12) urge God to deliver on those expectations ("liberation," "deliver"; "help" and "deliverance"). God's *Enquiry 1* (including his oracle of dominance; 108:7–10) and the people's *Enquiry 2* in response to God's (108:11) create the centerpiece of the psalm, dealing with the perplexity of God's apparent failure to grant aid to his people.

Theological Focus

Confident in their expectation of a hearing from God, whose gracious love is illimitable, and whose sovereignty and supremacy are unmatched—for all of which they loyally, thankfully, and enthusiastically exalt him publicly—the people of God, beloved by him, seek his deliverance from their dire circumstances.

Commentary

Stanza 1 (108:1–6)

The opening *Eulogy* of *Stanza 1* extends for five verses (108:1–5), declaring God's lovingkindness, exalting him and his glory (108:4–5), and affirming God's people's response to those proclamations: singing, making music, giving thanks (108:1–3).[1] This is an enthusiastic praising of God, visible in the chiastic structure of 108:1–3:[2]

108:1b	"make music"
108:2a	"awake"
108:2b	"wake"
108:3b	"make music"

As was noted, *Eulogy 1* is followed by *Entreaty 1* based on what preceded: "Since you are so great, God, and we've sung your praises, would you not deliver us?" (108:6). After all, the psalmist asserts, "we are your 'beloved ones'" (108:6a).[3] There is a striking assonance between יְדִידֶיךָ, *ydideka*, "Your beloved ones" (108:6a) and אוֹדְךָ, *'odka*, "I will give You thanks" (108:3a): the beloved ones are loyal and faithful, acknowledging and giving thanks to their deity. All that to say, the "lovingkindness" and "truth" of God (108:4) lead God's people to expect deliverance from his hand (108:6), especially as they have been loyal to him in their ascription of praise (108:1–2, 4–5), even "among the peoples" and "among the nations" (108:3). Would that that human loyalty be repaid by divine loyalty!

Stanza 2 (108:7–13)

The logic of *Stanza 2* is different, approaching the whole issue of petitioning for deliverance from another angle. It begins with the psalmist citing an oracle of God that asserts his absolute supremacy over all nations (108:7–9). He it is who allocates the land (108:7bc), for they belong to him, and it is his prerogative to do so.[4] He it is who also owns the land of Israel (108:8).[5] His dominance over surrounding nations is total: he washes off with Moab, pelts Edom with his footwear, and is flush with victory over Philistia (108:9). The tribes of Israel are his cephalic "stronghold" (helmet) and badge of regency ("scepter," 108:8bc; and he exults over and possesses his people, 108:7–8a); their enemies are relegated to being "washbasins" and target practice for the divine "sandal" (108:9ab; and he voices triumph over Philistia, 108:9c). In other words, the people of God are right to assume the sovereignty of their deity will serve them well in the war with their enemies.

---

1. "Inner being" in 108:1b translates כְּבֵדִי, *kvedi* (literally, "my liver"), which emends the MT's כְּבוֹדִי, *kvodi*, "my glory" (as also in 16:9; 30:12; 57:8).

2. Besides, "I will sing" is אָשִׁירָה, *'ashirah* (108:1a), and "I will awaken" is אָעִירָה, *'a'irah* (108:2b).

3. That it is an individual addressing God ("answer *me*," 108:6b) on behalf of the rest of God's people may suggest that the psalmist is a leader of some sort (priest? king? other?) in the divine community.

4. Shechem is west of the Jordan river, and Succoth is to its east.

5. This includes the land east of the Jordan ("Gilead" is the location, and "Manasseh," the largest tribe there) and west of it ("Ephraim" and "Judah," the dominant tribes).

But then God seems to ask, in 108:10, who would bring him and lead him to the cities that he would subjugate, as if to say it was the fault of his people that the enemies were not conquered, not his. The scouts are missing; how can the commander advance?

This is countered by *Enquiry 2* of the people of God (108:11): "Wait, isn't it *You* who have rejected us?" The note of incredulity is hard to miss, twice mentioning "God" in the vocative. Deity, however, does not deign to reply.

The closing *Entreaty 2* for "help" and "deliverance" (108:12) then makes the point that since God is sovereign over all those nations and all those lands that he talked about in his oracle (his *Enquiry 1*), his people are right in expecting victory in their battles aided by this supreme overlord and suzerain! In combination with *Eulogy 2* that closes the psalm (108:13), the preeminence of divine power is asserted and the expectation of help affirmed (108:12–13), emphasized with a stark contrast that should not be missed:

108:12a	"adversary"
108:12bα	"worthless"
108:12bβ	"[from] a human"
108:13aα	"through God"
108:13aβ	"powerfully"
108:13b	"adversaries"

This is to assert that the psalmist and the people were relying only upon their God, their mighty deity, and he—and he alone (notice the emphatic use of the pronoun in 108:13b)—would be able to overcome their adversaries. That Yahweh would "trample" them is suggestive: earlier we had God using his adversaries as a washbasin (for his *feet*?) and heaving *foot*wear at them (108:9ab); now he treads his enemies under*foot*!

It seemed, in God's oracle, that he was asking for help to bring him to the "fortified city [מִבְצָר, *mivtsar*]" (108:10a). Here, in the people's *Entreaty 2*, they want *his* help "against the adversary [מִצָּר, *mitstsar*]" (108:12a): the wordplay is obvious. Likewise, "Edom [אֱדוֹם, *'edom*]" the enemy (108:9b, 10b) is being compared to the "worthlessness" that is characteristic of a "human [אָדָם, *'adam*]" (108:12b). Surely the God who could subjugate אֱדוֹם could "do powerfully" more than any אָדָם. The psalmist's confident expectation of divine might being extended on behalf of his people thus concludes this unique composition.

Sermon Map

I. Reason to Expect Deliverance–1
   God's lovingkindness and love (108:4, 6)
   Move-to-relevance: God's love in our lives

II. Reason to Expect Deliverance–2
   God's sovereignty and supremacy (108:7–10, 13)
   Move-to-relevance: God's power in our lives

III. Response to Expected Deliverance
   Pleading (108:6, 11–12)
   Praise (108:1–3)

IV. *Praying and Praising for Preservation!*
   Specifics on prayer and praise in distress

PSALM 109:1–31

Psalm of Disorientation

God's Lovingkindness Protects from Persecutors

PSALM 109 IS CONSIDERED one of the imprecatory psalms in the Psalter. But the debated question has been who is doing the imprecation. Is 109:6–19, the imprecatory section, made up of the psalmist's own words or is it the psalmist's citation of his persecutors' words?

Excursus

Imprecation—Persecutors' or Psalmist's?

In favor of 109:6–19 being the psalmist's utterance are the following: no verb of speaking announces the shift of speaker from the psalmist in 109:1–5 to another in 109:6;[1] neither would the inconsistency of number ("they" in 109:1–5, followed by a shift to "him" in 109:6) indicate a change of voice;[2] and 109:6–7 could be seen as *lex talionis* against accusers for their treatment of the supplicant described in 109:2–3.

However, there is considerably more evidence in favor of 109:6–19 being a quote of the persecutors (as I have indicated in the translation): there are no imprecations uttered by the psalmist of this length elsewhere in the Psalter; there is a hint that the speaker has shifted from psalmist to adversary in 109:6 (the psalmist's plurality of "accusers" in 109:4a becomes the singular "accuser" the foes appoint against the him, in 109:6b; and references to accusers' words and speech in 109:2, 3a, 4a prime the reader for what comes in 109:6 and following); a number of terms bracket the quotation, setting it apart: "evil" in 109:5a, 20b; "words/speak [דבר, *dvr*]" in 109:3a,[3] 20b; "accuse" in 109:4a, 20a; and "mouth" in 109:2a (×2), 30a;[4] the quotation's "accuser" prosecuting the psalmist at his "right hand" (109:6) is transformed into Yahweh protecting the psalmist at his "right hand" (109:31a); the shift in

---

1. As there is in Pss 2:2–3; 3:2; 13:4; 35:21, 25; 40:15; 41:5, 7–8; etc.

2. For other examples of such a shift, see Pss 17:10–11 vs. 12–13; and 35:3–7, 11–13, 15–17, 19–21, 24–26 vs. 8, 10; among others.

3. In fact, 109:3a has the psalmist lamenting: "[with] words of hatred they have *surrounded* me"; and "words/speaking" textually and literarily surround the extended quotation of the persecutors' angry utterances against him (109:3a, 20b).

4. As also do: "and [. . .] I [וַאֲנִי, *wa'ani*]," 109:4b, 25a; and "against/for me [אִתִּי, *'itti*]," 109:2b, 21a.

number between the plurality of accusers in 109:1–5, 20 and the singularity in 109:6–19 is precisely demarcated;[5] the first person of 109:1 disappears until 109:21; God is addressed in 109:1–5 and 109:21 onward, but deity is almost missing in 109:6–19;[6] in 109:28, the psalmist refers to the accusers cursing, an indictment that would not make sense were the psalmist himself imprecating curses in 109:6–19; the "judging" of the psalmist by evildoers in 109:7a is reflected in 109:31b where Yahweh protects the psalmist from those "judging" him; the psalmist's "I am [in] prayer" in 109:4b becomes the accusers' "his prayer" in 109:7b; the psalmist's "against me" in 109:5a becomes the foes' "against him" in 109:6a; the disjunctive וְאַתָּה, w'attah, "but You," in 109:21 indicates a shift that is also found elsewhere after laments about the speech and actions of enemies (22:19; 41:10; 55:23; 59:8; 86:15); citations without an introductory formula are not uncommon in the Psalms (e.g., 32:8; 46:10; 50:7–15; 89:3–4; 105:15);[7] there seems to be reasonable evidence to read מֵאֵת יְהוָה, me'et yhwh, "from Yahweh," in 109:20a, as אֵת יְהוָה, 'et yhwh, "before Yahweh"—as in my translation—evidenced by the LXX's reading of παρὰ κυρίῳ, para kyriō,[8] which, along with the nominal sentence of that verse commencing with "this," indicates a statement of fact[9]—pointing to what the accusers were saying/doing in 109:6–19;[10] and the emphatic declaration of the psalmist that *he* was the afflicted one, "... [am] I [אָנֹכִי, 'anoki]" (109:22a), suggests a contrast being made between the allegation that the psalmist was a persecutor of the afflicted (109:16b). If 109:6–19 were the words of the protagonist, the psalmist, the psalm as a whole would "narratively be a communication blunder," for it would be he who is wicked and not another: he would be the one hating, accusing, attacking, plotting, and cursing others.[11]

In light of 109:22–25, these vile accusations against the psalmist may have been occasioned by some illness on the part of the supplicant that opened a door to the nefarious workings and sayings of his enemies "without cause" (109:3b). In any case, courtroom language is being employed in this psalm, with 109:6–7 likely being the adversaries' deliberations to prosecute the hapless psalmist, and 109:8–19 being the explicit imprecations of those foes against that unfortunate one, perhaps actually uttered in a forensic setting (specific allegations against the psalmist are found in 109:16–19). Altogether, 109:6–19 comprise the "words of hatred" (109:3a) and the "cursing" (109:28a) of these plotters. The psalmist summarizes these utterances in 109:20, before commencing his prayer for vindication (109:21–31). Thus, the entire psalm, including the citation of his enemies, is the supplicant's marshaled evidence of his tribulation, as adduced before God.[12]

---

5. The only plurals in 109:6–19 are in 109:13–15 (dealing with "posterity"). Also, the plurality of the "accusers"/"those accusing me" (109:4a, 20a, 29a) stands in relation to the singular "accuser" in 109:6b, the one appointed by those enemies to represent them in legal proceedings. Indeed, this singularity is pre-empted in the singular "mouth" (109:2a [×2]). Besides, if 109:6–19 were the psalmist's own imprecation, his asking for a "wicked" accuser for his enemies (109:6), though it would make for poetic justice, would certainly not be lawful (see Jenkins, "Quotation in Psalm 109," 124).

6. Except in 109:14–15 that are more oblique and indirect than are the invocations elsewhere; in any case there are no second person references to God in 109:6–19, as there are in 109:1–5, 21–31.

7. Though all of those verses listed contain the words of God and not of humans.

8. See Codex Sinaiticus, Codex Alexandrinus, Codex Turicensis, and a number of versions (see Booij, "Psalm 109:6–19," 98–99).

9. As in Job 20:29; Ps 49:13.

10. The noun פְּעֻלָּה, p'ullah, in 109:20a is best translated as "doing" (or "work," rather than "reward"), as in 17:4; 28:5; 2 Chr 15:7.

11. Egwim, *Contextual and Cross-Cultural Study of Psalm 109*, 316–17.

12. See Jenkins, "Quotation in Psalm 109," 124, 134–35.

PSALM 109:1–31

Translation

109:1   God of my praise,
    do not be deaf.
109:2   For a wicked mouth and deceitful mouth
    they have opened against me;
    they have spoken against me [with] a false tongue.
109:3   And [with] words of hatred they have surrounded me,
    and fought me without cause.
109:4   In return for my love they act as my accusers;
    and [so] I am [in] prayer.
109:5   And they set against me evil in return for good
    and hatred in return for my love.
109:6   "Appoint against him a wicked one,
    and may an accuser stand at his right hand.
109:7   When he is judged, may he come out as wicked,
    and his prayer, may it become sin.
109:8   May his days be few;
    his appointment may another take.
109:9   May his children be orphans,
    and his wife a widow.
109:10 And roaming, may his children roam about and beg,
    and may they seek [sustenance] from places of ruin.
109:11 May the creditor lay snares for all that he has,
    and may strangers plunder the produce of his labor.
109:12 May there be none extending lovingkindness to him,
    and may there be none being gracious to his orphans.
109:13 May it be that his posterity is cut off;
    in the generation following may it be blotted out—their name.
109:14 May it be remembered—the iniquity of his fathers, before Yahweh,
    and the sin of his mother—may it not be blotted out.
109:15 May they be before Yahweh continually,
    and may He cut off from the earth their memory;
109:16 because [he was] the one who did not remember to do lovingkindness,
    and persecuted the afflicted and needy person,
    and the despondent in heart to be killed.
109:17 And he loved cursing, and it came to him,
    and he did not delight in blessing, and it was far from him.
109:18 And he put on cursing like his garment,
    and it came like water into his inside,
    and like oil into his bones.

109:19	May it be to him like a garment he wraps himself [in],
	and as a belt he continually girds himself [with]."
109:20	This [is] the doing of those accusing me before Yahweh,
	and of those speaking evil against my soul.
109:21	But You, Yahweh, Lord—You do for me, for the sake of Your name,
	for good is Your lovingkindness: rescue me.
109:22	For afflicted and needy [am] I,
	and my heart has been wounded inside me.
109:23	Like a shadow as it lengthens, I am gone;
	I am shaken off like a locust.
109:24	My knees have weakened from fasting,
	and my flesh has become lean, without fatness.
109:25	And I—I have become a reproach to them;
	when they see me, they shake their head.
109:26	Help me, Yahweh my God;
	deliver me according to Your lovingkindness.
109:27	And they will know that this is Your hand,
	[that] You, Yahweh—You have done it.
109:28	They curse—they; but You—You bless;
	they will have arisen and they will be shamed,
	and Your servant will rejoice.
109:29	Those accusing me will put on ignominy,
	and they will wrap on their shame like a robe.
109:30	I will give thanks to Yahweh greatly with my mouth;
	and in the midst of many I will praise Him.
109:31	For He stands at the right hand of the needy,
	to deliver him from those judging his soul.

Structure

With the imprecations being placed in the persecutors' mouths, the composition may be structured thus:

109:1–5	Plaint of Psalmist
109:6–19	***Plot of Persecutors***
109:20–29	Petition of Psalmist
109:30–31	Promise of Psalmist

PSALM 109:1–31

Theological Focus

The person of God, when in the dire circumstance of being assaulted by wicked oppressors with utterly vile and false charges bearing life-threatening consequences, remains so confident in God's lovingkindness, his intervention, and his deliverance that praise is promised for the future.

Commentary

Plaint of Psalmist (109:1–5)

As was noted, the psalmist is apparently on trial at a court of some sort. Firstly, he appeals to God to hear him (109:1). Then he laments about the enemies' speech (109:2–4a), explains that that is why he is praying (109:4b), and describes what those foes are doing (109:5). That the supplicant is operating under some intense emotion is clear, from the repetition of "hatred [...] in return for my love" (109:3–4a, 5), as well as from the chiastic structuring of those verses:[13]

109:2aα	"For a wicked *mouth*
109:2aβ	and a deceitful *mouth*
109:2b	they have opened against me;
109:2c	they have *spoken* [דבר] against me ….
109:3a	And [with] *words* [דָּבָר, *davar*] of hatred …."

Plot of Persecutors (109:6–19)

After all the plaints about "mouth" (×2) being opened, lying "tongue" being employed to "speak" (109:2), "words of hatred" enveloping the defendant (109:3), and the role of the foes as "accusers" (109:4), that the psalmist would actually cite these opponents in 109:6–19 makes sense.

Whom these enemies are addressing in 109:6–7 is unclear; the likely possibility is that it is an *in camera* session of plotting amongst themselves to get rid of the pestilential psalmist. What exactly they say against this individual—their imprecation against him—is recorded for us in 109:8–21, but the veracity of their accusations is to be taken with a big pinch of salt.

The first part of the persecutors' malediction, 109:8–15, employing imperfect verbs, details the financial (and resulting familial) ruin they desire to see befall the psalmist. His life is to be short, his wealth appropriated by others (109:8, 11),[14] his family rendered fatherless and husbandless (109:9), his dependents starving (109:10), and ultimately his posterity cut off (109:13). If that were not enough, they also hope that Yahweh will keep even the sins of

---

13. Besides, 109:2c–3a is also chiastic: verb / noun phrase // noun phrase / verb.
14. "Appointment," פְּקֻדָּה, *pquddah* (109:8b), likely indicates "property/wealth," as in Isa 15:7.

his parents unforgiven, and that he will wipe off even their memories for ever (109:14–15). "The accusers want the implications of his guilt to work backward [in time: parents] as well as forward [in time: posterity]. Their wishes are now even more over the top."[15] The careful structuring of 109:13–14 accentuates the seriousness of these vituperations, with a contrast between an utter eradication of the psalmist's descendants, and a non-eradication—perpetual remembrance—of the sins of the psalmist's ancestors:

> **109:13**
> "May it be that his **posterity**
>   is cut off;
>   in the **generation following**
>   may it be blotted out—
> **their name.**"
>
> **109:14**
> "May it be remembered—
>   the iniquity of his **fathers**,
>   before Yahweh
>   and the sin of his **mother**—
> may it not be blotted out."

The reasons for these imprecations are found in 109:16–18 (providing a short break from the barrage of curses): according to his persecutors, the psalmist failed to demonstrate lovingkindness, instead oppressing—and even causing the death—of the needy (109:16); he was enamored with cursing and wore it like a "garment," and did not bless (109:17–18). In the estimation of his enemies, the psalmist's ongoing woes were a direct result of his own evildoing: he is clothing himself with vile speech (109:18), thus he alone is responsible for his dire situation/punishment.[16] To conclude the litany of imprecations, the foes return to the curse formula: the "garment" of cursing that the psalmist is clothed in (109:18), they hope, will enshroud him in the future as well (the notion of "garment" is repeated for good measure [109:19]). Altogether, the anathemas uttered by the opponents build up to a crescendo of vile wishes!

Petition of the Psalmist (109:20–29)

The imprecations of the previous *Plot of the Persecutors* are summarized by the psalmist in 109:20, as he commences *Petition of the Psalmist* to Yahweh: "This is the work—the denunciations of me that I cited in 109:6–19—of those mobsters accusing me before you, Yahweh!" The structure of 109:20–27 literarily places the "afflicted and needy" psalmist at the center (109:22–25; see 109:22a, below). On the outside are "those accusing me" (109:20a, 27a), but the psalmist is calling upon God to liberate him (109:21bβ, 109:26bα) and, in the chiasm created, it appears that God *does* protect him: Yahweh and his lovingkindness (109:21abα; 109:26bβ–27) form a literary and textual cocoon around the psalmist (and his pleas for aid;

---

15. Goldingay, *Psalms*, 3:282.
16. See Kitz, "Oath, Its Curse," 320.

109:21bβ–26bα), keeping him from those venomous malefactors who are, in the structure, restricted outside, away from the supplicant:

109:20a	"those accusing me"
109:21a	"You, **Yahweh** …—You *do* for me"
109:21bα	"Your *lovingkindness*"
109:21bβ	"rescue me"
109:22–25	**Psalmist: "afflicted and needy"** (109:22a)
109:26bα	"deliver me"
109:26bβ	"Your *lovingkindness*"
109:27b	"You, **Yahweh**—You have *done* it"
109:29a	"those accusing me"

Indeed, the central self-description of the psalmist and his doleful situation (109:22–25) is itself carefully constructed, focusing on his abject helplessness and utter defeat:[17]

109:22aα	"afflicted and needy"
109:22aβ	"I [אָנֹכִי]"
109:22b	"heart"; "inside me"
109:23aα	"like [כְּ, *k*] a shadow"; "as [כְּ] it lengthens"
109:23aβ	**"I am gone"**
109:23bα	**"I am shaken off"**
109:23bβ	"like [כְּ] a locust"
109:24	"knees"; "flesh"
109:25aα	"I [אֲנִי, *'ani*]"
109:25aβ–b	"reproach"; "they shake their head"

So desperate is his condition, that only a miracle from God would liberate the sufferer: "You, Yahweh, Lord—You *do* for me" (109:21a), and when he "did," those enemies would discover that "You, Yahweh—You have *done* it" (109:27). The emphatic pronouns in both cases make the petition and its response powerful.

The psalmist was accused of lacking "lovingkindness" towards the "afflicted and needy" (109:16ab); he now throws himself upon God's "lovingkindness" (109:21b, 26b), claiming that it is he, himself, who is the "afflicted and needy" one (109:22).[18] The adversaries described the supplicant as one wrapped with cursing who had "put on" vituperation like a garment (109:18a); the latter now wishes the former will be the ones ending up "wrapped" with shame, "putting on" ignominy like a robe (109:29). The evil ones cursed, and they would yet continue "cursing," but for the psalmist it would be Yahweh and his blessing that would enable him to "rejoice" and render his foes shamed, as God "blesses" the supplicant (109:28).

---

17. From Auffret, "Et toi, tu béniras," 341.

18. And he, who was accused of crushing the despondent in "heart" (109:16c), claims that it is *he* who is wounded in "heart" (109:22b) by all the false allegations. The nefarious ones alleged that the psalmist so loved cursing it came into his bones like "oil [שֶׁמֶן, *shemen*]" (109:18c); in his adverse condition, he claims his flesh was lean and devoid of "fatness [שֶׁמֶן]" (109:24b).

Promise of the Psalmist (109:30–31)

The psalmist concludes his plangent defense by promising to praise God upon being delivered, an event that he is certain will transpire: the evildoers wanted "an accuser" to "stand at his right hand" (109:6b), to cause him more trouble, but the psalmist is confident that it is "Yahweh" who "stands at the right hand of the needy, to deliver him" (109:31b—the answer to the *Petition of the Psalmist* for "deliverance," 109:26b).

And so what began with "praise" performed (109:1a) ends with "praise" promised (109:30b); what commenced with the wicked one's "mouth" (2×; 109:2a) concludes with vindicated psalmist's "mouth" thanking God (109:30a). All will be well that ends well, and end well, they certainly will, in God's lovingkindness and grace!

Sermon Map

  I. Allegations
   Peril (109:6–19)
   Move-to-relevance: Peril in our lives
  II. Appeal
   Petition (109:1b–5, 20–29)
   Move-to-relevance: God's lovingkindness in our lives
  III. Assurance
   Praise (109:1a, 30–31)
  IV. *Plots: Petition When Perturbed and Praise When Preserved!*
   Specifics on prayer and praise in distress

PSALM 110:1–7

Psalm of Orientation

God's King-Priest

PSALM 110 IS THE most cited text of the Psalter in the NT.[1] Whether David spoke (Matt 22:43–44; Mark 12:36; Luke 20:42–44; Acts 2:34–35) or wrote the psalm (as the superscription to the psalm, "David's," seems to indicate),[2] it is likely that the words are those of a leader announcing the utterance of Yahweh to "my lord" (Ps 110:1) and to "a priest" (110:4), perhaps during a coronation liturgy, for both "lord" and "priest" seem to refer to the same royal-religious individual.

Translation

110:1   The declaration of Yahweh to my lord:
      "Sit [enthroned] at My right hand
      until I make your enemies a footstool for your feet."
110:2   Your strong scepter Yahweh will send from Zion;
      rule in the midst of your enemies.
110:3   Your people [are] free-will [self-]offerings in the day of your power;
      in holy majesty, from the womb of the dawn,
      to you [is] the dew of your youth[s].
110:4   Yahweh has sworn and will not relent:
      "You are a priest forever
      after the manner of Melchizedek."
110:5   The Lord—by your right hand—
      He has smitten, in the day of His wrath, kings.

---

1. It is cited in Matt 22:44; 26:64; Mark 12:36; 14:62; Luke 20:42–43; 22:69; Acts 2:34–35; Heb 1:13; 5:6; 7:17, 21; and possibly alluded to in Mark 16:19; John 12:34; Rom 8:34; 1 Cor 15:25; Eph 1:20; Col 3:1; Heb 1:3; 5:10; 6:20; 7:3; 8:1; 10:12–13; 12:2. All these references and allusions are to Ps 110:1, 4 only (see Aloisi, "Who Is David's Lord?," 103n2).

2. Untranslated here. On superscriptions, particularly those relating to David, see Introduction (in the first volume of this set, *Psalms 1–44*).

110:6	He will execute justice among the nations;
	He has filled [them] with corpses,
	He has smitten a head over the broadness of the earth.
110:7	From the torrent by the way he will drink;
	therefore he will lift up [his] head.

Structure

Following the introductions to each section (each bearing the words of God), the rest of the psalm comprises amplifications of those divine pronouncements:[3]

> **To the Royal Leader** (110:1–3): king, enemies, defeat
>
> *Introduction* (110:1a): "the declaration of Yahweh"
> *Words of God* (110:1bc): static preparation for battle
> *Amplification of God's Words* (110:2–3)
>
>> "lord ... right hand" (110:1ab); "in the day" (110:3a)
>> "your enemies" (×2; 110:1c, 2b); "feet" (110:1c)
>
> **To the Religious Leader** (110:4–7): kings, enemies, defeat
>
> *Introduction* (110:4a): "Yahweh has sworn"
> *Words of God* (110:4bc): dynamic action of battle
> *Amplification of God's Words* (110:5–7)
>
>> "Lord ... right hand" (110:5a); "in the day" (110:5b)
>> "kings" and "nations" (110:5b, 6a); "head" (110:6c, 7b)

While the structure suggests a division between the royal and religious (i.e., priestly) function of the king, the entire psalm is simultaneously royal *and* religious (religious references to "Zion," "free-will offerings," a quasi-cultic "scepter" [see below], and "holy majesty"[4] are found in the royal section, 110:1–3; royal references to "kings," "nations," and "executing justice," with martial imagery, are seen in the religious section, 110:4–7).

Excursus

King-Priest

Even without the NT references, there are good reasons to suspect that there is more to the identity of the royal leader of 110:1–3 and the religious priest of 110:4–7 than what appears on

---

3. Modified from Allen, *Psalms 101–150*, 85; Barbiero, "Non-Violent Messiah," 5; deClaissé-Walford et al., *Book of Psalms*, 834; and Girard, *Les Psaumes Redécouverts*, 163.

4. "Holy majesty" is descriptive of the "worship" of Yahweh elsewhere in the psalter (Pss 29:2; 96:9; also see 1 Chr 16:29; 20:21).

the surface. Though perhaps composed with a Davidic regent in mind, the implications of the psalm extend far beyond what is expected of a human ruler.

That this individual is a *king* is clear: the title "lord" (110:1a); his "scepter" (110:2a);[5] his enemies reduced to a footstool for his feet (110:1c); his "rule" (110:2b) that extends over "the broadness of the earth" (110:6c); the reference to his power (110:3a); the wrathful smiting of "enemies," "kings," and "nations" (110:1c, 2b, 5b, 6a); and the label "your people," i.e., those who submit to the call of the king in the "day of your power" (110:3).

That this individual is also a *priest* is explicitly affirmed (110:4b); besides, his is an office "after the manner of Melchizedek," who was both king and priest (110:4c; Gen 14:18); his scepter comes "from Zion" "sent" by Yahweh (Ps 110:2a); "footstool" (110:1c) is linked with ark traditions of the cult (99:5; 132:7); his people are described as "free-will offerings" apparently clothed "in holy majesty" (110:3ab)[6]—both priestly notions; and the "priest" being "forever" (110:4b) parallels the Psalter's promise of a perpetual Davidic reign (72:17; 89:36–37; 132:11–12).[7]

That the royal section (110:1–3) and the religious section (110:4–7) contain aspects of both kingship *and* priesthood, as was noted earlier, make the division of the psalm somewhat artificial: the entirety of the composition is *simultaneously* royal and religious, pointing to the same individual possessing both offices and performing both roles.[8]

The coalescence of this king-priest's royal and religious functions and the scope and overwhelming power of his reign (110:3, 5–6) suggests that the referent is one greater than any human king. Even more convincing is the strong and intimate affiliation of this individual with Yahweh rendering him quite divine: Yahweh enthrones him at his own right hand (110:1b); later, Yahweh is reciprocally located at the right hand of this regent-cleric (110:5a); "footstool" (110:1c) elsewhere in the OT refers to Yahweh's personal piece of furniture (1 Chr 28:2; Pss 99:5; 132:7; Isa 66:1; Lam 2:1); the Zion-sourced scepter and a commission to rule is given to this king-priest by Yahweh himself (Ps 110:2); incredibly devastating power is exerted by Yahweh on behalf of this person against his enemies, with deity's (and,

---

5. "Scepter" employs מַטֶּה, *matteh*, a rarer word than the usual שֵׁבֶט, *shevet*; perhaps the former was chosen to convey a priestly connotation—that is the term for the "rod" employed by Aaron (Num 17:21, 22, 23, 24, 25), he of the perpetual priesthood (Num 25:13).

6. As was noted, "holy majesty" is redolent of worship.

7. The assertion of this person's permanent priesthood is made emphatic with the pronoun אַתָּה, *'attah*, "you" (110:4b).

8. There is also the mention of "Zion" in 110:2a and the implication of Salem in 110:4c with the mention of Melchizedek who was the king of that district (Gen 14:18). Since David and his line were not of the tribe of Levi (or specifically, not the descendants of Aaron), the priesthood adduced in Ps 110:4 is, of necessity, of a different category—a distinctive "king-priest" kind, "after the manner of Melchizedek," the original king-priest. The reference to this ancient religious royal therefore symbolizes the unique class of the individual of Psalm 110. Nonetheless, "the notion of royal priesthood was not foreign to Israel's ideology" (Merrill, "Royal Priesthood," 59–60): 2 Sam 8:18 references David's sons as "priests"; the entire narrative of the return of the ark from Kiriath-jearim to Jerusalem (2 Samuel 6; 1 Chronicles 15) depicts the royal David as a religious leader, clothed in priestly attire, offering sacrifices, and uttering benedictions; the inauguration of Solomon's reign has this king offering sacrifice (1 Kgs 3:3–4; 2 Chr 1:3, 6; also see Solomon's quasi-priestly role at the establishment of the ark in the temple and at the dedication of that edifice: 1 Kgs 8:5, 55, 62–63); the priestly actions of King Uzziah in the temple were implicitly recognized as appropriate, except, of course, for his burning of incense that illegitimately arrogated to himself the task of the Aaronic priesthood (2 Chr 26:16–23; see Num 16:40). In addition, period "iconographic data demonstrate that Ps 110's constellation of imagery portraying the king as priest alongside the king and deity at war makes sense within both a larger ancient Near Eastern context and a more limited Syro-Palestinian setting" (Purcell, "King as Priest?," 300).

by extension, the king-priest's) preeminence and puissance extending "over the broadness of the earth" (110:6c); Yahweh's prerogative to receive worship of his people "in holy majesty" (29:2; 96:9) is now shared with this king-priest (110:3b); the conflation of Yahweh with this unique character (110:5b–7), with God working "by your right hand" (110:5a); the nomen אָדוֹן, *'adon*, "L/lord," belongs to both (110:1a, 5a); "your [the king-priest's] enemies" (×2; 110:1c, 2b) are identified with God's enemies ("kings," "nations," 110:5b, 6a) whom deity smites and judges; "*the day* of your [the king-priest's] power" (110:3a) becomes coterminous with "*the day* of His [Yahweh's] wrath" (110:5b); the individual addressed in 110:4b is a religious functionary with a mandate "forever"; elsewhere only the Davidic royal leadership is assured permanence (as was noted; see 72:17; 89:36–37; 132:11–12).[9] All things considered, this king-priest is likely to be the Messiah (thus he is the God-King-Priest).[10]

Theological Focus

God's representative, the messianic king-priest, religiously mediating the power of God for his royal reign over all the world and forever, subjugating enemies and executing justice, motivates the people of God to increased fidelity towards him, and raises their confidence for a glorious future.

Commentary

To the Royal One (110:1–3)

The psalm commences without any ado to announce a divine declaration of the enthronement of the king at the right hand of Yahweh and the relegation of the regent's foes to a footstool for him (110:1). Zion, being the place where Yahweh is and where the king is located (at Yahweh's right hand), is the locus from where the ruler's authoritative mark of his reign, his scepter, will be "sent" by Yahweh—i.e., the authorization, initiation, and transactions of the power of the king (his "*strong* scepter";[11] 110:2a)—and, that might is to be

---

9. Barbiero makes the intriguing suggestion that the psalmist, in Psalm 110, followed the ideology of the books of Chronicles in positing a non-belligerent Messiah. According to the chronicler, David was not permitted to build the temple because, as the word of Yahweh declared to him, "much blood you have shed on the earth before Me" (1 Chr 22:8). Curiously, in the context of wars fought by Abraham, Melchizedek, the original king-priest of Genesis 14, is not said to bear any weapon but his blessing. So also in Psalm 110: Yahweh is the one who subjugates the enemies of this king-priest (110:1c), and he is the one who smites kings, executes justice, fills fields with corpses, and utterly defeats the adversary (110:5b–6). God's representative, the king-priest, on the other hand, remains relatively uninvolved, seemingly disengaged from all the martial smiting and slaughtering. Of course, this king-priest is involved in those bellicose engagements, suggested by "day of *your* power" and by the volunteer force he musters (110:3a), not to mention by Yahweh's going to battle "by *your* [the royal-priest's] right hand" (110:5a); besides, this chieftain-cleric's "way" (110:7a) is, in context, related to that military campaign (as in 2 Chr 6:34 that employs "way" in a martial context). See Barbiero, "Non-Violent Messiah," 7n14, 12–15.

10. Yet, to keep the explicit reference to Yahweh as "Lord" intact and distinguishable (110:5a), I have not capitalized "lord" (110:1a); for the same reason, to distinguish between these personages, neither have I capitalized pronouns referring to this unique individual, the God-King-Priest of Psalm 110.

11. And see "day of your *power*," in 110:3a.

manifest in the subjugation of enemies (110:2b).[12] But, as was already noted, it seems to be solely Yahweh who is wielding authority (110:1b, 1c, 2a, 2b; and later, 110:5–6), this despite the mustering of a volunteer human army for the king (110:3). The subsequent description of these free-will self-offerings of humans in 110:3bc is not entirely clear, but an allusion to the priestly context of the rest of the psalm is apparent here: if the king is a priest, then his people donning "holy majesty" and making "offerings" is quite appropriate. In any case, they give of themselves freely as "free-will [self-]offerings" to the king from the beginning ("womb") of dawn (110:3b); and they are, in quantity, as plentiful as the dew at that hour and, in quality, the best of the land's young ones ("youth[s]"; 110:3c):

110:3aα	"Your people"	Identity
110:3aβ	"free-will [self-]offerings"	Fidelity
110:3aγ	"in the day of your power"	Opportunity
110:3bα	"in holy majesty"	
110:3bβ	"from the womb of the dawn"	Opportunity
110:3cα	"to you [is] the dew"	Quantity
110:3cβ	"of your youth[s]"	Quality

And this voluntary conscription into the regent's army will ostensibly bring about the "day of [the king's] power" (110:3a), as he manifests his authority to subdue enemies, through the agency of Yahweh.[13]

To the Religious Leader (110:4–7)

Quite abruptly, the psalmist switches gears to another divine oracle, this time accompanied by God's oath, about the priesthood of this king.[14] Thus, while 110:1 and 110:4 are parallel, the oath of God and an explicit statement that this is an unrelenting affirmation by deity (110:4a) intensifies the solemnity of the utterance here. God declares, in this gravitas-laden announcement, that the king is a priest, and that forever (110:4b). But the cleric is not one from the Levitical or Aaronic order: this is a different priesthood that is being envisaged and recognized (on its non-novelty, see above): the priesthood of Melchizedek (110:4c). There is also an unexpected transposition of seats: in 110:1a the king-priest ("my lord") was at Yahweh's right hand; here in 110:5a, Yahweh ("the Lord") has relocated to the king-priest's right hand!

Perhaps not accidentally, the first half of the name *Melchizedek* (מַלְכִּי־צֶדֶק, *malki-tsedeq*) literally means "my king" (110:4c), and precisely balances אֲדֹנָי, *'adonay*, "my lord" (110:1a). Notably, this also distinguishes this unique king-priest ("*my* king") from other earthly rulers, who are merely "kings" (110:5b). Likewise, "*your* people" (110:3a) distinguishes the subjects of this inimitable king-priest from the citizens of those other kings, collectively disposed as "nations" (110:6a).[15]

---

12. Thus, the scepter-sending of 110:2a by Yahweh is the cause of the enemy defeat in 110:1c.
13. Such "free-will" warrior volunteers are also found in Jdg 5:2, 9; 1 Chr 29:5–6, 17; 2 Chr 17:16.
14. God's "swearing" regarding the Davidic kingship (but not his priesthood) is found in 89:3, 35, 49.
15. Barbiero, "Non-Violent Messiah," 17.

Once again, the destruction of the king's enemies is detailed, and here, too, it is God wreaking all the havoc among them (albeit "by your [the king-priest's] right hand," 110:5a): "He has smitten" occurs twice (110:5b, 6b).[16] The smitten ones are a plural body of "kings" (110:5b) and a singular "head" (110:6c). There is a sense of utter finality with the total demolition of opposition forces, whether plural or singular; so much so, the nations are filled with corpses, and the "head" is smitten over the breadth of the earth (110:6bc).[17] This absolute destruction is depicted literarily:[18]

110:5aα	"The Lord"
110:5aβ	"by [עַל, *'al*]"
110:5aγ	"your right hand"
110:5bα	"He has smitten"
110:5bγ	"wrath"; "**kings**"
110:6a	"justice"; "**nations**"
110:6cα	"He has smitten"
110:6cβ	"a head"
110:6cγ	"over [עַל] the broadness of the earth."

That this defeat occurs "over the broadness of the earth" also demarcates the scope and extent of the reign of Yahweh and of his king-priest—vast indeed, and encompassing all peoples in all places.

There is likely to be a switch in protagonists between 110:5–6 ("He" = Yahweh) and 110:7 ("he" = the king-priest): the mundanity of the activity of imbibing suggests a return to the religious royal. The only instances of this latter individual being referred to in the third person in the entire psalm are in 110:1a ("my lord") and here in 110:7ab ("he"). Thus, those two references form an *inclusio* for the psalm.[19] In any case, the equation of "my lord" of 110:1 with the "he" of 110:7 seems likely.

In light of Zion being mentioned in 110:2, the "torrent" of 110:7a may well be alluding to a cascade of water gushing out of the temple (Ezek 47:5–14; Joel 3:18; Zech 14:8).[20] At any rate, it is this imbibing that results in the king-priest lifting up his head ("therefore" in Ps 110:7b), perhaps indicating the victory that this individual has won over all his foes,[21] with his power for victory coming from the torrent, from the temple, from God himself. Another reason to read it in this fashion is the pattern of the preposition עַל (as noted above): it is from his location "by [עַל]" the king-priest's right hand (110:5a) that Yahweh defeats enemies "over [עַל]"

---

16. The perfect verbs, "has smitten" (110:5b, 6c) and "has filled" (110:6b), are likely to be prophetic and predictive, as the imperfect verbs in 110:6a, 7a, 7b indicate.

17. Whether the singular "head" (110:6c) depicts a collection of heads—i.e., every "head"—or a single leader is unclear, though the smiting over a large area (110:6c) suggests a multiplicity of these cephalic body parts.

18. From Auffret, "Il est seigneur sur les nations," 68.

19. One could also see "feet" in 110:1c forming an *inclusio* with "head" in 110:7b. Or "feet" (110:1c) may be linking with the "way" (110:7a) that is generally traversed by deploying one's lower extremities.

20. See Barbiero, "Non-Violent Messiah," 18. Or it could be an allusion to the anointing of Solomon as king by the Gihon spring outside Jerusalem (1 Kgs 1:38–40).

21. As in 27:6: "And now my *head will be lifted high* above my enemies."

the breadth of the earth (110:6c). The regent-cleric consumes divine waters, and "therefore [עַל־כֵּן, 'al-ken]," in the power of God, he lifts his head in triumph (110:7b).

All in all, the notion of the Davidic king is, in Psalm 110, expanded to include for this one the role of a priest, those joint portfolios borne by a single individual intimately related to God himself. Clearly, this person is more than what he seems to be on the surface, certainly more than just another human Davidide. The NT gives credence to that suspicion and confirms his identity as Jesus the Messiah.

Sermon Map

I. The Royal One
   Kingship (110:1–2)
   Move-to-relevance: Our need for God's leader
II. The Sacerdotal One
   Priesthood (110:4–7)
   Move-to-relevance: Our need for God's mediator
III. *Sign Up with the Sacerdotal Sovereign!*
   Loyalty of the king-priest's people towards him (110:3)
   Specifics on loyalty to the king-priest

PSALM 111:1–10

Psalm of Orientation

God's Deeds and Directives

THE ENTIRETY OF PSALM 111 is a proclamation of the greatness of Yahweh, conveying an explicit mandate to the people of God who sing the praise of God: they are to obey the word of God. Except for the opening "Praise Yah!" (111:1a), the composition is directed not to deity, but to the community of God's people about Yahweh. This wisdom-orientation of Psalm 111 is reflected in the psalm's acrostic construction and particularly in the wisdom-related statement in 111:10 about wisdom and the fear of Yahweh. The psalm also rehearses the origins of God's people: the exodus (111:4), desert and divine provision (110:5), and Canaan and the granting of land (111:6).

Translation

111:1		Praise Yah.
	[א ALEPH]	I will give thanks to Yahweh with all [my] heart,
	[ב BETH]	in the council of the upright and [in] the assembly.
111:2	[ג GIMEL]	Great are the works of Yahweh,
	[ד DALETH]	being sought out by all who delight in them.
111:3	[ה HE]	Splendid and majestic is His deed,
	[ו WAW]	and His righteousness stands for always.
111:4	[ז ZAYIN]	[As a] remembrance He has worked His wonders;
	[ח CHETH]	gracious and compassionate [is] Yahweh.
111:5	[ט TETH]	Food He has given to those who fear Him;
	[י YODH]	He will remember His covenant forever.
111:6	[כ KAPH]	The power of His works He has announced to His people
	[ל LAMED]	in giving them the inheritance of the nations.
111:7	[מ MEM]	The works of His hands are truth and justice;
	[נ NUN]	faithful are all His precepts,

111:8	[ס SAMEKH]	being upheld for always and forever,
	[ע AYIN]	being worked [out] in truth and uprightness.
111:9	[פ PE]	Redemption He has sent to His people;
	[צ TSADE]	He has commanded His covenant forever;
	[ק QOPH]	holy and awesome [is] His name.
111:10	[ר RESH]	The beginning of wisdom [is] the fear of Yahweh;
	[ש SHIN]	good insight have all those who do them;
	[ת TAW]	His praise stands for always.

Structure

In general, the psalm may be seen as addressing *God's Deeds* and *God's Directives* for his people:[1]

> **Introduction** (111:1a): "praise"
>
> **God's Deeds** (111:1b–6): "upright" (111:1c)
> Nominal sentence in 111:4b:
> "gracious and compassionate" + "Yahweh": *Divine immanence*
> Reference to God's directives: 111:5b ("covenant")
>
> **God's Directives** (111:7–10b): "uprightness" (111:8b)
> Nominal sentence in 111:9b:
> "holy and awesome" + "name": *Divine transcendence*
> Reference to God's deeds: 111:9a ("redemption")
>
> **Conclusion** (111:10c): "praise"

Yet, this is not a watertight division: there is a reference to God's directives in the discussion of *God's Deeds* ("His covenant," 111:5b) and, vice versa, there is a mention of God's deeds in the section on *God's Directives* ("redemption," wrought during the exodus, 111:9a).[2]

---

1. See Goldingay, *Psalms*, 3:302; and Girard, *Les Psaumes Redécouverts*, 176.
2. The "work of His hands" in 111:7a does not necessarily refer to God's deeds; notice that it parallels "His precepts" in 111:7b, i.e., the phrase refers to God's directives. Barbiero notes that "truth and justice" (111:7a) occur together elsewhere only in Jer 4:2 and Zech 8:16, both times referring to speech. That suggests that "work of His hands" might well be the two tables of the law personally inscribed by God's own upper limbs (see Barbiero, "Structure of Psalm 111," 331, 331n35).

In any case, the psalm is constructed carefully, centered upon the permanence of God's word and its working out in the lives of God's people:[3]

111:3b	"stands for always"
111:4a	"worked [עשׂה, 'sh]"
111:4b	"Yahweh"
111:5a	"fear [יָרֵא, yare']"
111:5b	"His covenant forever"
111:6a	"to His people"
111:7a	"works"; "truth"
111:8aα	"always"
111:8aβ	"forever"
111:8b	"worked"; "truth"
111:9a	"to His people"
111:9b	"His covenant forever"
111:9c–10aα	"awesome [יָרֵא, yr']"; "fear [יִרְאַת, yir'at]"
111:10aβ	"Yahweh"
111:10b	"do [עשׂה]"
111:10c	"stands for always"

A number of third-person pronominal suffixes on nouns and adjectives keep the focus on God: "His deed," 111:3a; "His righteousness," 111:3b; "His wonders," 111:4a; "to those who fear Him," 111:5a; "His covenant," 111:5b; "His works," 111:6aα; "His people," 111:6aβ; "His hands," 111:7a; "His precepts," 111:7b; "His people," 111:9a; "His covenant," 111:9b; "His name," 111:9c; and "His praise," 111:10c.[4]

Theological Focus

> With praise and thanksgiving, people in relationship with deity—who have directly and indirectly been beneficiaries of the gracious deeds of an immanent God—acknowledge their responsibility to follow the eternal directives of a transcendent God with reverence, thus growing in wisdom and insight.

---

3. From Allen, *Psalms 101–150*, 92; Girard, *Les Psaumes Redécouverts*, 172; and Auffret, "Grandes sont les œuvres," 186.

4. The many word pairs in the composition also point to deity: "splendid and majestic," 111:3a; "gracious and compassionate," 111:4b; "truth and justice," 111:7a; "for always and forever," 111:8a; and "holy and awesome," 111:9c. Two other pairs relate to the people of God: "the council of the upright and ... the assembly," 113:1c; and "truth and uprightness," 111:8b (see below).

Commentary

Introduction; God's Deeds (111:1–6)

The psalm commences with a plural exhortation, "Praise Yah!" (111:1a). However, the subsequent resolution to give thanks is in the singular voice of the psalmist, though it is being planned for the occasion of a corporate assembly (111:1bc). The reasons for the corporate thanksgiving follow: the deeds of deity for his chosen people (111:2–6), centering upon the creedal affirmation of the graciousness and compassion of Yahweh (111:4b),[5] and emphasizing his immanence and his solicitude for his people:[6]

111:3b–4a	"for always"; "remembrance"; "worked"
111:4b	"gracious and compassionate is Yahweh"
111:5b–6a	"forever"; "remember"; "works"

God's Deeds are marked by "splendor" and "majesty" and in his actions his "righteousness" is demonstrated in his deeds and works (111:3).[7] Those divine actions are then spelled out in the next few verses: 111:4 deals with God's deeds during the exodus, 111:5 with his deeds in the desert (and a reference to God's directive: "His covenant"),[8] and 111:6 with his deeds in the promised land—the three verses are patterned (with the first line of each verse being a perfect verb clause) and linked with repetitions:[9]

111:4	Exodus	111:4a, *perfect verb clause*	"worked" (111:4a)
		111:4b, *nominal statement*	"remembrance" (111:4a)
111:5	Desert	111:5a, *perfect verb clause*	"has given" (111:5a)
		111:5b, *imperfect verb clause*	"remember" (111:5b)
111:6	Canaan	111:6a, *perfect verb clause*	"works" (111:6a)
		111:6b, *infinitive verb clause*	"giving" (111:6b)

What the "remembrance" in 111:4a is, is not clear; perhaps it his wondrous works that are to be etched into his people's memory.[10] In any case, the first section, *God's Deeds* directed to his people, establishes his relationship to them, a relationship that mandates a responsibility on the part of God's people towards him. And that is the focus of the next section of Psalm 111.

---

5. The order of Exod 34:6, "compassionate and gracious," is inverted in Ps 111:4b to satisfy the acrostic.

6. From Auffret, "Grandes sont les œuvres," 190.

7. Or, God's righteousness moves him to perform those marvelous deeds for his people.

8. "Covenant," here and in 111:9b, is employed as a synonym for divine directives/commandments, as in Deut 4:13.

9. From Barbiero, "Structure of Psalm 111," 329.

10. It is also possible, in light of God's people "seeking out" the works of Yahweh (111:2), that the remembrancer is the word of God, particularly considering the focus on divine directives in the second half of the psalm. Indeed, 119:27 refers to God's word as "wonders."

God's Directives; Conclusion (111:7–10)

As was noted above, "the works [מַעֲשֵׂה, ma'aseh] of His hands" (111:7a) paralleling "His precepts" (111:7b) likely refers to God's manual inscription of the law. Besides, עשׂה is used of the ordaining of divine law in Num 28:6. Thus this section moves from *God's Deeds* in the previous section ("works," Ps 111:6a) to *God's Directives* in the current section (also "works," 111:7a). *God's Deeds* beget certain obligations on the part of God's people to their God—responsibilities that are to be discharged in accord with *God's Directives*: they are to be "upheld" and "worked [out]" (111:8). And such a working out of divine demand will be characterized by "truth and uprightness."

In other words, a relationship with God, inaugurated and sustained by the deeds of God (including creation and redemption), mandates a responsibility towards God by alignment to his word, guided and oriented by the directives of God (as in Exod 20:2–3; Deut 5:6–7; 24:18).[11] The "works" of God—that are characterized by "truth" Ps 111:6a, 7a—are to be reciprocated by the obedience of God's people: their "working [out]" of divine directives (111:8b), also in "truth" (and "uprightness," 111:8b).[12] And this deity is not only mindful of "His covenant forever" (111:5b)—deity's role in the relationship, his faithful commitment to his people—he also commands "His covenant forever" (111:9b)[13] for his people to keep—humanity's role in the relationship, their faithful commitment to their God.

And keep his directives and demands they must, for "holy and awesome [from ירא] is His name" (111:9c).[14] No wonder then, that "the fear [also from ירא] of Yahweh" is reckoned as the "beginning of wisdom" (111:10a) and the "doing" of God's word is the mark of the insightful (111:10b). To obey the directives of this great God who has performed wondrous deeds for them is the responsibility of those who participate in the relationship God has forged between himself and his people. "The 'fear of God' and 'his praise' [111:10a, 10c] are made concrete in the observance of his commandments, just as, *vice versa*, the observance of his commandments is not something impersonal, but a loving relationship with God."[15]

Appropriately, 111:10 has "the beginning" as its first word, and "always" as its last. Earlier it was God's righteousness that was acclaimed to "stand for always" (111:3b), that interminability giving rise to his wondrous deeds on behalf his own. Now God's directives and its wisdom result in his people's praise of him—and it is that praise that "stands for always" (111:10c). A God who is perpetually righteous deserves perpetual praise! Those who delight in the "works of Yahweh" (111:2) and who have experienced the wonders of his "working" (111:4a) and the power of "His works" (his deeds; 111:6a), as well as the "works of His hands" (his directives; 111:7a), are called to their duty to "work [out]" God's law in

---

11. See Kuruvilla, *Vision for Preaching*, 123–26. This is well attested in the NT, too: John 14:15, 21, 23; 1 John 2:3; 3:24; 5:2–3; 2 John 6; etc.

12. God's law is regarded as "upright" in 19:8; 119:128, 137. No doubt, the "council of the *upright*" (111:1c) comprises those devout who are working out God's law in "uprightness" (111:8b).

13. Such an "ordaining/commanding [צוה, tswh]" is related to the giving of God's law in Exod 19:7 (also employing צוה).

14. This is the element of divine transcendence (111:9c); divine immanence was in view in 111:4b.

15. Barbiero, "Structure of Psalm 111," 335. It is worth attending to the thesis of Levenson in his magisterial work *The Love of God*; he convincingly argues that commitment/loyalty manifest as faithful obedience is the primary meaning of the term "love" in the literature of the ancient Near East (though not neglecting the affect thereof). "Covenantally conceived, love is defined, first and foremost, by a set of deeds. The deeds are not dependent on emotion: whether or not individuals feel a sentiment that they name as 'love,' they are always obligated to serve their lord" (*Love of God*, 60).

their lives (111:8b), to "do" it (111:10b; both "work" and "do" share the same root עשׂה). "All who delight in *them*," i.e., in the deeds of deity (111:2b), are "all those who do *them*," i.e., the directives of deity (111:10b). "Alongside the praise that claps and dances is the reverence that bows before Yhwh's holiness. And in that submission lies insight for life. Worship and wisdom . . . are part of true humanity and of the true life of God's people."[16]

In sum, those who "fear" God (111:5a) are the beneficiaries of the deeds of God; and those who "fear" him (111:10a) respond by obeying the directives of God. And so the psalm ends as it began: with "praise" (111:1a, 10c).

Sermon Map

I. The Relationship with God
   Deeds of an immanent God (111:1–6)
   Move-to-relevance: Our relationship with God/his deeds
II. The Responsibility towards God
   Directives of a transcendent God (111:7–10)
   Move-to-relevance: Our responsibility to God/his directives
III. *Respect the Responsibility in the Relationship!*
   Specifics on discharging the responsibility of obedience

---

16. Goldingay, *Psalms*, 3:307.

PSALM 112:1–10

Psalm of Orientation

Blessing of the God-Fearer

PSALMS 111 AND 112 form an adjacent pair of acrostic psalms with a number of shared words/roots.[1] Not only do the first and last lines of Psalm 112 begin with א and ת, respectively—as acrostics do—but the first (after "Praise Yah," 112:1a, that is excluded from the acrostic) and the last words of the composition also begin with א and ת, respectively, one being the antithesis of the other: אַשְׁרֵי, *'ashrey* ("blessing," 112:1a) and תֹּאבֵד, *to'ved* ("will perish," 112:10c). Prinsloo notes that the beginning + end of Psalm 111 ("praise," "delight," "fear . . . Yahweh," in 111:1–2, 10) are reflected in the beginning of Psalm 112 (see 112:1). "In this way, Ps 112 encapsulates everything that is said about the מעשי יהוה [*m'sy yhwh*, 'works of Yahweh,' 111:2a] in Ps 111 and becomes a continuation of its predecessor's praise of YHWH. Psalm 112 becomes a midrash on Ps 111."[2] That we have here a "blessing [upon] . . ." formula (112:1b), as well as a contrast between the righteous and wicked (112:1–9 and 112:10), makes Psalm 112 a wisdom psalm.

---

1. They include: "praise Yah," 111:1a and 112:1a; "heart," 111:1b and 112:7b, 8a; "upright[ness]," 111:1c, 8b and 112:2b, 4a; "delight," 111:2b and 112:1c; "righteous[ness]," 111:3b and 112:3b, 4b, 6b, 9b; "stands for always," 111:3b, 10c and 112:3b, 9b; "always," 111:3b, 8a, 10c and 112:3b, 9b; "remembrance/remember," 111:4a, 5b and 112:6b; "gracious," 111:4b and 112:4b, 5a; "compassionate," 111:4b and 112:4b; "give," 111:5a, 6b and 112:9a; "fear," 111:5a, 10a and 112:1b, 7a, 8a; "forever," 111:5b, 8a, 9b and 112:6a, 6b; "justice," 111:7a and 112:5b; "upheld," 111:8a and 112:8a; and "good," 111:10b and 112:5a. Goldingay, *Psalms*, 3:309, calls Psalm 112 a "niece or nephew" (not "twin") of Psalm 111. Prinsloo adds that the focus of Psalm 111 is "theology" and of Psalm 112 "anthropology": in the former the works of Yahweh are "great" (111:2a) and in the latter it is the God-fearer who is "mighty" (112:2a); the ones who have "sought out" (דְּרוּשִׁים, *drushim*; 111:2b) become the "generation of the upright" (דּוֹר יְשָׁרִים, *dor ysharim*; 112:2b); in Psalm 111, the "righteousness" of Yahweh "stands for always" (111:3b), and in Psalm 112 it is the "righteousness" of the God-fearer that "stands for always" (112:3b); in 111:4b it is Yahweh who is "gracious and compassionate," but in 112:4b, those qualities are predicated of the Yahweh-fearer; Yahweh is the "giver" of food to those who fear him (111:5a), and in 112:9a it is the latter who "give" freely to the needy; Yahweh is faithful, and his precepts are "upheld" forever (111:7b–8a), and so is the heart of the one devoted to him (112:7b–8a); Yahweh is considered holy and awesome (111:9c), and the one who fears him is exalted in honor (112:9c). The subject of the verbs in the first psalm is God, and that in the second psalm, the God-fearer; thus, "the YHWH-fearer becomes a mirror image of his deity" (Prinsloo, Gert T. M., "Reading Psalm 112," 663).

2. Prinsloo, Gert T. M., "Reading Psalm 112," 661–62.

Translation

112:1		Praise Yah.
	[א ALEPH]	Blessing [upon] the person who fears Yahweh;
	[ב BETH]	in His commandments he delights greatly.
112:2	[ג GIMEL]	Mighty on earth will be his descendant;
	[ד DALETH]	the generation of the upright will be blessed.
112:3	[ה HE]	Wealth and riches [are] in his house,
	[ו WAW]	and his righteousness stands for always.
112:4	[ז ZAYIN]	Light shone in the darkness for the upright—
	[ח CHETH]	[those who are] gracious and compassionate and righteous.
112:5	[ט TETH]	Good is the person who is gracious and the one who lends;
	[י YODH]	he will manage his affairs in justice.
112:6	[כ KAPH]	For he will not totter forever;
	[ל LAMED]	the righteous will be remembered forever.
112:7	[מ MEM]	Evil tidings he will not fear;
	[נ NUN]	his heart is steadfast, trusting in Yahweh.
112:8	[ס SAMEKH]	His heart is upheld; he will not fear,
	[ע AYIN]	until he looks [triumphantly] upon his adversaries.
112:9	[פ PE]	He has scattered, he has given freely to the needy;
	[צ TSADE]	his righteousness stands for always;
	[ק QOPH]	his horn will be exalted in honor.
112:10	[ר RESH]	The wicked will see it and he will be angered;
	[ש SHIN]	he will gnash his teeth and become weak;
	[ת TAW]	the desire of the wicked will perish.

Structure

The predominant focus of the psalm is upon the everlasting blessedness of the upright, as is obvious from its structure (below).[3]

---

3. See Allen, *Psalms 101–150*, 96.

Blessedness of the Upright

112:1–2	"blessing [אַשְׁרֵי, *'ashre*]"; "blessed [בּרך, *brk*]" (112:1b, 2b)
112:3a	"wealth and riches"
112:3b	"his righteousness stands for always"
112:5a	"good"
112:6a	"forever"
112:6b	"forever"
112:7a	"evil"
112:9b	"his righteousness stands for always"
112:9c	"horn ... exalted in honor"

Bane of the Wicked

112:10c	"perish"

Theological Focus

The God-fearing upright, who enthusiastically keep divine demand, are abundantly blessed (and their generations and descendants, too), because they manifest the very attributes of God—righteousness, graciousness, compassion—thus rendering these who trust in God lit-up and long-lasting, stable and steadfast, renowned and respected, in contrast to the wicked who are in despair, and are debilitated, and whose desires are destroyed.

Commentary

Blessedness of the Upright (112:1–9)

After a "Hallelujah" ("Praise Yah," 112:1a), the acrostic psalm proceeds to describe the *Blessing of the Upright*, the God-fearer, the one who delights in divine commandments (112:1bc). The composition subsequently provides "a kaleidoscopic definition of the incentives and life style" of the blessed God-fearer.[4] Fearing Yahweh and delighting in his commands are not merely affective responses on the part of the blessed individual. Both are attitudes that express themselves in actions of submission and obedience; thus these attitudes and actions are mutually non-exclusive.[5] The descendants of such persons will be "mighty" and the generation of these will be "blessed" (112:2b). Thus 112:1b–2 begins and ends with the words "blessing" and "blessed," respectively (the roots of each are different). Thereby this wisdom song is convinced that "virtue brings tangible results into the lives of the virtuous and their families."[6]

---

4. Allen, *Psalms 101–150*, 97.
5. Goldingay, *Psalms*, 3:310.
6. Allen, *Psalms 101–150*, 97.

The longevity of the Yahweh-reverer is indicated by repetitions of "for always" (of this one's righteousness; 112:3b, 9b)[7] and "forever" (of this one's stability and remembrance; 112:6a, 6b). Besides, in the here and now, the house of the devout is visited with "wealth and riches" (112:3a). The reason for the abundance of these blessings overtaking these God-fearers is that, like their God (111:4b), these "upright" are "gracious and compassionate and righteous"—with divine light illuminating their darkness (112:4). No wonder they are blessed: they reflect and image deity himself! The "graciousness" and compassion of these who are righteous (112:4b)—their "good[ness]" (112:5a)—are manifest in their actions: they lend with "graciousness" and run their affairs with justice (112:5a). Later, we are told that they broadcast their resources, giving freely to the needy (112:9a)—yet another characteristic of God (111:5a). In other words, their generous and charitable treatment of their fellow-humans gives evidence of these individuals' devotion to God and manifest the very attributes of God. The structure of 112:1–5 emphasizes the exemplary character of these God-fearers, the fame of whose righteousness will eternally be before God:[8]

112:1bc	"the person"; "in [בְּ, b] His commandments"
112:2b	"upright"
112:3a	"wealth and riches [are] in [בְּ] his house"
112:3b	**"his righteousness stands for always"**
112:4aα	"light shone in [בְּ] the darkness"
112:4aβ	"upright"
112:5	"the person"; "in [בְּ] justice"

In sum, these righteous ones will be stable and unshakable "forever," and remembered and renowned "forever" (112:6a, 6b). So much so, they who "fear Yahweh" (112:1b; and trust him, 112:7b) will themselves know no "fear" of anyone or anything (112:7a, 8a):[9]

112:7a	"He will not fear"
112:7bα	"His *heart* is steadfast"
112:7bβ	**"trusting in Yahweh"**
112:8aα	"His *heart* is upheld"
112:8aβ	"He will not fear"

Bane of the Wicked (112:10)

In stark contrast to the *Blessedness of the Upright* (112:1–9) is the *Bane of the Wicked*. The upright "looks [רָאָה, r'h]" in triumph upon the wicked (112:8b), and reciprocally, the wicked "sees [רָאָה]" the honoring of the upright (112:10a). The "hearts" (body parts) of the upright are steadfast; these persons totter not forever, and they are remembered forever (112:6, 7b–8a).

---

7. Likely meaning that this person's righteousness is noted by God for eternity.
8. From Auffret, "En mémoire éternelle," 8; and Girard, *Les Psaumes Redécouverts*, 177.
9. From Auffret, "En mémoire éternelle," 5.

The wicked on the other hand are irate at the exaltation of the righteous, "gnashing their teeth" (body parts), and they become enfeebled (112:10ab). While the upright have "wealth and riches," enough to give away and to lend (112:3a, 5a, 9a), the "desires"[10] and ambitions of the wicked are thwarted—they perish (112:10c), unlike the righteous and upright who obtain "blessing" and remain "blessed" (112:1b, 2b), along with their descendants and their generations (112:2). Yes, there is wisdom in being righteous!

Sermon Map

I. The Blessing of the Upright
    Blessed, God-like, stable, renowned, fearless (112:1–9)
    Move-to-relevance: The blessing of God on the upright

II. The Bane of the Wicked
    Angry, frustrated, weakened, thwarted (112:10)
    Move-to-relevance: The lack of blessing by God of the wicked

III. *Reverence for God, Reward from God!*
    Specifics on revering God

---

10. The word "desire" can indicate appetite for food, as in 78:29–30; 106:14.

PSALM 113:1–9

Psalm of Orientation

Praising the High One Who Lifts the Lowly

PSALM 113 IS UNIQUE, since it engages in the praise of Yahweh exclusively in the third person: it has no direct address to deity.

Translation

113:1	Praise Yah.
	Praise, servants of Yahweh;
	praise the name of Yahweh.
113:2	May the name of Yahweh be blessed
	from now unto forever.
113:3	From the rising of the sun unto its setting
	[may it] be praised, the name of Yahweh.
113:4	Raised above all nations is Yahweh;
	above the heavens is His glory.
113:5	Who is like Yahweh our God—
	the One who becomes high to sit [enthroned],
113:6	the One who becomes low to see—
	in the heavens and in the earth?
113:7	[He is] One who lifts the poor from the dust,
	[and] from the ash heap raises the needy,
113:8	to make [them] sit with nobles,
	with the nobles of His people,
113:9	One who seats the barren woman in the house
	[as] a joyful mother of children.
	Praise Yah.

Structure

Bounded by *Exclamations of Praise* ("Praise Yah!" 113:1a, 9c), an *Exhortation to Praise* Yahweh is followed by an *Explanation for Praise*. The ground of praise is who Yahweh is (113:1b–3; he is the extolled one) and what Yahweh has done (113:4–9b; he is the exalted one and the exalting one).[1] Somewhat surprisingly, the latter, the deeds of Yahweh, do not detail God's mighty historical acts as creator of the cosmos or as deliverer of his people, but rather they focus on "God's everyday activity in lifting up the poor and giving children to the childless."[2] An immanent God, indeed!

> **Exclamation of Praise 1 (113:1a)**
>
> **Exhortation to Praise (113:1b–3)**
> *Yahweh the Extolled One* (113:1–3)
> Inarticular *pual* participles: "be blessed," "be praised" (113:2a, 3b)
>
> **Explanation for Praise (113:4–9b)**
> *Yahweh the Exalted One* (113:4–6)
> Articular *hiphil* participles: "the one who becomes …" (×2; 113:5b, 6a)
> "raised" (113:4a); "sit" (113:5b)
> *Yahweh the Exalting One* (113:7–9)
> Inarticular *hiphil* participles: "one who …" (×2; 113:7a, 9a)
> "raises" (113:7b); "sit," "seats" (113:8a, 9a)
>
> **Exclamation of Praise 2 (113:9c)**

Theological Focus

> God, the exalted one above all powers in all spaces, is to be extolled for all time, because this divine King, the exalted one, condescends to see the plight of his people, exalting them—the afflicted to positions of superiority, and the downtrodden into places of sufficiency, their needs met, their desires fulfilled.

Commentary

Exhortation to Praise: Yahweh the Extolled One (113:1–3)

After the introduction of 113:1a, the exhortation to praise is expressed with two imperatives, the first linked to the subjects doing the praising, "servants of Yahweh" (113:1b), and the

---

1. In all three subsections, Yahweh as extolled one, exalted one, and exalting one, the pair of participles employed within each of these constituent parts share grammatical forms as shown.
2. Goldingay, *Psalms*, 3:316.

second linked to the object of the praising, "the name of Yahweh" (113:1c). This is followed by an artistic structure in 113:2–3 (below) uttering a wish that Yahweh be blessed and be praised (113:2–3) in all times ("from now unto forever," 113:2b) and in all spaces ("from the rising of the sun unto its setting," 113:3a, denoting the location of those solar activities: east and west):[3]

	"the name of Yahweh"	
113:2	"be blessed"	Pual *participle*
	"from ... unto ..."	*Extent of time*
	"from ... unto ..."	*Extent of space*
113:3	"[may it] be praised"	Pual *participle*
	"the name of Yahweh"	

All that to say, all peoples (and all things?) at all times and in all places are to worship this God, Yahweh! And why are they to do so?

Explanation of Praise: Yahweh the Exalted One (113:4–6)

This exalted deity ("raised," 113:4a) is greater than any power. Whether on earth ("all nations," 113:4a) or in the "heavens" (ostensibly indicating the powers dwelling therein, 113:4b), Yahweh is "above" them all (×2; 113:4a, 4b). "Imperial nations, imposing and often menacing to little Israel, are nothing compared with the great Lord of history.... Their gods cannot match his omnipotence."[4] Thus, Yahweh is at the center of 113:4:

"raised"
"above all nations"
"Yahweh"
"above the heavens"
"His glory"

The explanation of praise continues with two similar participial descriptions of Yahweh as "the one who becomes high to sit [enthroned]" and "the one who becomes low to see" (the situation of his people) (113:5b, 6a). That is to say, there is no one like "Yahweh our God ... in the heavens and in the earth" (113:5a, 6b).

"Who is like Yahweh our God—
the one who becomes high to sit [enthroned],
the one who becomes low to see—
in the heavens and in the earth?"

---

3. It is less likely to be indicating time, sunrise and sunset, since the praise of God continues "forever" (113:2), even in the nights.

4. Allen, *Psalms 101–150*, 101.

The one "*above* all nations" and "*above* the heavens" (113:4) has no comparable entity "*in* the heavens" or "*in* the earth" (113:6b). Therefore, God is to be extolled because he is the exalted one. But at the same time, this exalted one remains "Yahweh *our* God" (113:5a), the personal deity of his people, because this "high" one becomes "low" and is concerned about his people (113:5b, 6a). And how does he manifest his concern for them?

Explanation of Praise: Yahweh, the Exalting One (113:7–9)

The "high" one who became "low" is the exalting one who, in turn, "lifts" the low and "raises" them high (113:7): the "raised" Yahweh (113:4a) "raises" the needy (113:7b). And this enthroned, "seated" Yahweh (113:5b) also makes the downtrodden "sit" with the nobles (113:8a) and "seats" the barren woman in a house full of children (113:9a). No matter if his people are penurious and hungry ("the poor" and "the needy," 113:7), or degraded and shamed ("the barren woman," 113:9a); this exalting one remedies their subjugation and reverses their disenfranchisement.

So, uniquely, in this psalm, the reason for extolling God is not simply because he is exalted by his cosmic marvels and wonders or even by his earthly creation and deliverance. Rather, he is to be extolled because of his "transformative interventions in the lives of the powerless. The definition of God is as one who lifts the literal poor from the literal rubbish heap and turns the literal infertile woman into a literal mother. Perhaps if we want to see Yhwh at work we have to hang around rubbish heaps and keep the company of women weeping in the night because they cannot conceive."[5] Indeed, it takes God and God alone to set right these unfairnesses, to fix these discriminations, to correct these inequities—restitutions and recoveries that only the exalted God can accomplish![6] And here, in Psalm 113, God is described as doing exactly that, exercising his power on behalf of his dispossessed, deprived, and distressed people to transform their status into exalted, endowed, and exhilarated ones. Praise Yah!

Sermon Map

I. The Exalted One

   God is worthy of praise because he is the exalted one (113:4–6)

   Move-to-relevance: The greatness of God

II. The Exalting One

   God is worthy of praise because he is the exalting one (113:7–9)

   Move-to-relevance: The grace of God

III. *Extol the Exalted and Exalting One!*

   The praise of God in every time and every space (113:1–3)

   Specifics on praising God

---

5. Goldingay, *Psalms*, 3:319.

6. "Ps 112 emphasized that human beings need to care for the poor, but Ps 113 warns against the temptation to reckon that everything depends on us" (Goldingay, *Psalms*, 3:319).

PSALM 114:1–8

Psalm of Disorientation

Reverence for the Creator and Redeemer

PSALM 114 IS AN unusual praise psalm, for it has no bidding to the community of God's people to engage in praise. And "Yahweh" is not mentioned at all, though "Lord" and "God of Jacob" are (114:7). Also odd is the out-of-sequence chronology: 114:2 evokes the entry into Canaan *before* the crossing of the sea (114:3); as well, the provision of water in the desert wanderings of the Hebrew children (114:8) shows up *after* the crossing of the Jordan (114:3b, 5b) which is, itself, anachronously conjoined to the parting of the sea (114:3a, 5a).[1] "Idiosyncratic," Goldingay labels Psalm 114.[2] But then again, it is poetry, intended to be artistically interpreted rather than scientifically dissected.

Translation

114:1	When Israel came out from Egypt,	
	the house of Jacob from a people of foreign speech,	
114:2	Judah became a holy place for him,	
	Israel, his dominions.	
114:3	The sea saw and it fled;	
	the Jordan turned back.	
114:4	The mountains skipped like rams,	
	hills, like lambs.	
114:5	What is with you, sea, that you flee,	
	Jordan, that you turn back?	
114:6	Mountains, that you skip like rams,	
	hills, like lambs?	

---

1. There is also considerable hyperbole, anthropomorphizing, and the rhetorical employment of apostrophe (addressing inanimate objects) in the poetic descriptions of the activities of the sea, Jordan, mountains, and hills (114:3–6), not to mention in the account of the divine act of transforming a solid object into a liquid (114:8).

2. Goldingay, *Psalms*, 3:321.

114:7	Before the face of the Lord, tremble, earth,
	before the face of the God of Jacob,
114:8	the One who transformed the rock to a pool of water,
	the flint into a spring of water.

Structure

Despite the anachronisms noted above, the construction of the song is deliberate, with *Event* and *Effect* (in the past; 114:1–4), and *Examination* and *Explanation* (in the present; 114:5–8). Within this structure, the *Event* and the *Explanation* are closely linked (114:1–2, 7–8), as also are the *Effect* and the *Examination* (114:3–4, 5–6), giving the whole a chiastic shape:[3]

PAST
Event (114:1–2)
 "Jacob" (114:1b)
 "from" (מִן, *min*, ×2; 114:1); לְ, *l* ("of," 114:1b; "for," 114:2a)

   Effect (114:3–4)
    "sea"; "fled"; "Jordan"; "turned back" (114:3)
    "mountains"; "skipped like rams"; "hills"; "like lambs" (114:4)

PRESENT
   Examination (114:5–6)
    "sea"; "flee"; "Jordan"; "turn back" (114:5)
    "mountains"; "skip like rams"; "hills"; "like lambs" (114:6)

Explanation (114:7–8)
 "Jacob" (114:7b)
 "before" (מִן ×2, 114:7); לְ ("of," 114:7a, 7b; "into," 114:8b)

Theological Focus

The God who works wonders for his people, liberating them and providing for them, thus accomplishing a re-creation of sorts, is in turn revered by them.

---

3. Notably, every verse contains two pairs of parallel concepts: "Israel" and "house of Jacob"; "Egypt" and "people of foreign speech" (114:1); "Judah" and "Israel"; "holy place" and "dominions" (114:2); "sea" and "Jordan"; "fled/flee" and "turn[ed] back" (114:3 and 114:5); "mountains" and "hills"; "rams" and "lambs" (114:4 and 114:6); "before the face" (×2); "Lord" and "God of Jacob" (114:7); "rock" and "flint"; and "pool of water" and "spring of water" (114:8). In sum, the poem is carefully and deliberately created, oddities and anachronisms and all.

Commentary

Past: Event; Effect (114:1–4)

The originating event of the exodus of the Israelites from Egypt opens the psalm (114:1); it immediately moves to the establishment of the nation in the promised land (114:2), wherein "Judah"/"Israel" became the "holy place"/"dominions" for the house of Jacob.[4] Not only is Canaan the sanctuary ("holy place") for Jacob, it is also the Israelites' political realm ("dominion"). Thus both cult and state are set up in the land granted to the house of Jacob by God, and the promise of Exod 19:6 is fulfilled (cult and state: "kingdom of priests" and "holy nation")—all in all, a momentous series of events, the effects of which are then poetically described.

Once again, a dischronological juxtaposition is detailed, with the sea of the exodus fleeing and the river of the Jordan-crossing turning back (Ps 114:3).[5] Even the mountains and hills are in turmoil at what God has done, quaking and trembling like cavorting animals (114:4).[6] Thus the response of the waters is a metaphor built on story, while the response of the ground is pure metaphor.[7] At any rate, even hints of the creation event are apparent[8]—the creation of Israel is the re-creation of the world!

> The psalm achieves a nexus between exodus and creation by combining the motif of creation with the motif of the exodus and its aftermath. Common imagery drawn from both is melded together, so that creation and exodus become fused. The sea that was restrained in the exodus is the sea that God restrained in the creation of the world. The mountains that react to the exodus are the mountains that signify the created world as fixed in place by God.... By equating the creation and the exodus, the psalm makes its point that the exodus is a (re-)creation of the world. Israel's birth as a nation and its settlement in its land has changed the world order.[9]

Thus what has happened to one peoples has become an event of universal effect and significance.

> It is not for Israel alone that this event is momentous; in fact, the psalm says little about the effect on Israel. Rather, the entire physical world is affected by it. In this psalm's perspective the exodus is not merely an event in Israel's past; it is a cosmic event.... The exodus thereby transcends national history and assumes cosmic proportions; it becomes timeless and universal, just like creation.[10]

The liberation of the people of God is significant for the entirety of the cosmos, for it is through his chosen ones that the plan of God to consummate all things in the heavens and the earth

---

4. The pronominal suffixes in 114:2 ("him" and "his") most likely refer to the "house of Jacob" rather than to God who has not been mentioned yet. Besides, Judah is never described in Scripture as the "holy place" of Yahweh (Goldingay, *Psalms*, 3:322).

5. Though there is a *wayyiqtol* (וַיָּנֹס, *wayyanos*, "and it fled") and a *yiqtol* (יִסֹּב, *yissov*, "turned back") in 114:3, they denote the past, in line with the *qatal* (רָאָה, *ra'ah*, "saw") that precedes them.

6. The phrase in 114:4b, 6b is "sons of sheep," i.e., lambs.

7. Goldingay, *Psalms*, 3:323.

8. See 77:17–19; 97:5; 98:7–8, for the tectonic and oceanic cataclysms, akin to those in 114:4–7, linked to creation.

9. Berlin, "Message of Psalm 114," 352. There may also be an allusion to the primeval "river" in the reference to the Jordan (114:5b; see 24:2; 72:8; 89:25).

10. Berlin, "Myth and Meaning," 69–70.

in Christ—the remaking and reworking of a sin-filled cosmos to a better and brighter world (Eph 1:8–10)—will begin to be accomplished![11]

Present: Examination; Explanation (114:5–8)

To accentuate the effect of the dramatic description in Ps 114:3–4, the psalmist revisits the topographical turbulence, reverting to the figures of 114:3–4, but in interrogative form. "He revels in these past events, pretending not to know, so that its wonder may shine out afresh. . . . The psalmist puts himself into the past and makes the worshipers feel themselves there, as if it had all just happened. He addresses the participants rhetorically in mock astonishment to discover the secret of their consternation."[12] But without waiting for an answer from his subjects to his *Examination*, the poet continues, providing an *Explanation* himself (114:7–8).

God had not shown up directly so far in the recital, but now it is revealed that it was he who was instrumental in all the upheaval described. "The curtains are swept back, as it were, to reveal Yahweh as the divine hero, the victorious warrior whose impact has been measured obliquely by his enemies' reactions."[13] And with this explanation, the verb forms become omnitemporal: imperative ("tremble," 114:7a) and participle ("the one who transformed," 114:8a). This timeless God who works wonders can do so again, and the fearful and worshipful response of the earth to this deity must be that of all peoples of all nations in all times and all spaces! God liberates his people; he provides for his people.[14] May they always hold him in reverential awe!

Sermon Map

I. Redemption

    Redemption of the people of God (114:1–2, 8)

    Move-to-relevance: Our liberation as a momentous event

II. Response

    Response of the cosmos (114:3–6)

    Response of the people (114:7)

III. *Revere the Redeemer!*

    Specifics on demonstrating reverential awe towards God

---

11. This involves *all* the people of God, in all dispensations, but the beginning thereof, the choice of a nation through which the Messiah of God and the oracles of God would come, was manifest through Israel. I call this a consummative-theological interpretation of the metanarrative of Scripture, that includes creation, fall, and redemption, and justification, sanctification, and glorification: God's grand design and purpose.

12. Allen, *Psalms 101–150*, 105.

13. Allen, *Psalms 101–150*, 105.

14. Beyond that fact that God provided water for his people from a rock (Exod 17:1–5: Num 20:1–13), there is also a more specific and proximal sense that the "rock" and "flint" of Ps 114:8 reflect the "mountains" and "hills" of 114:4, 6, and the "pool of water" and "spring of water" of 114:8 reflect the "sea" and "Jordan" of 114:3, 5. Of note, "God" in 114:7b is the unusual אֱלוֹהַּ, *'eloah*, the singular form of אֱלֹהִים, *'elohim*.

PSALM 115:1–18

Psalm of Orientation

God vs. Idols

WHILE THE BEGINNING AND end of Psalm 115 signify that this is a praise psalm (115:1–3, 16–18), there may be more to the composition than that. We have, in 115:2, a question (asked by the psalmist) with another question within it (asked by the nations regarding the absence of God) followed, in 115:4–8, by a philippic on idols and their worshipers. That indicates that this song may also be a prayer psalm, one that declares Yahweh as the true deity, and that affirms the certainty of God blessing his people (115:9–15). "The psalm implies a situation of vulnerability, and a need for Yhwh to bless, but not a situation of desperate need."[1] Nonetheless, I categorize it a psalm of orientation because the bulk of its verses does not address any apparent disorientation.

Translation

115:1	Not to us, Yahweh, not to us,
	but to Your name give glory,
	because of Your lovingkindness, because of Your truth.
115:2	Why should the nations say,
	"Where, now, is their God?"?
115:3	But our God is in the heavens;
	all that He pleases, He has done.
115:4	Their idols are silver and gold,
	the work of human hands.
115:5	They have a mouth, but they cannot speak;
	they have eyes, but they cannot see;
115:6	they have ears, but they cannot hear;
	they have a nose, but they cannot smell;

---

1. Goldingay, *Psalms*, 3:327.

115:7	[they have] their hands, but they cannot feel;
	their feet, but they cannot walk;
	they cannot make a sound with their throat.
115:8	They will become like them—those who make them,
	all who trust in them.
115:9	Israel, trust in Yahweh;
	their help and their shield is He.
115:10	House of Aaron, trust in Yahweh;
	their help and their shield is He.
115:11	The ones who fear Yahweh, trust in Yahweh;
	their help and their shield is He.
115:12	Yahweh—He has remembered us; He will bless;
	He will bless the house of Israel;
	He will bless the house of Aaron.
115:13	He will bless the ones who fear Yahweh,
	the small with the great.
115:14	May Yahweh add to you,
	to you and to your children.
115:15	May you be blessed of Yahweh,
	the One who made the heavens and the earth.
115:16	The heavens are the heavens of Yahweh,
	but the earth He has given to humans.
115:17	The dead do not praise Yah,
	nor all who go down into silence.
115:18	But we—we will bless Yah
	from now unto forever.
	Praise Yah.

Structure

The structure of the psalm is rather opaque. Though the four divisions shown below function sufficiently well, one notices that the sections are chain linked by contrast or repetition (indicated by the vertical gray lines, below).[2] In other words, the demarcations are hardly watertight.

---

2. One could also subdivide the psalm based on who is uttering its words: congregation (115:1–8; "us" [×2], 115:1a); leader and congregation alternating in antiphony (115:9–11); congregation (115:12–13; "us," 115:12a); leader (115:14–15; "you," 115:14a, 14b, 15a; "your children," 115:14b); and congregation (115:16–18; "we" [×2], 115:18a).

> **Yahweh Glorified 1 (115:1–3)**
>   "but our God" (115:3a)
>
> **Idolaters Pilloried (115:4–8)**
>   "their idols" (115:4a)
>   "trust" (115:8b)
>
> **Devout Prospered (115:9–15)**
>   "trust" (115:9a, 10a, 11a)
>   "heavens," "earth" (115:15b)
>
> **Yahweh Glorified 2 (115:16–18)**
>   "heavens" (×2), "earth" (115:16)

Theological Focus

God, the sovereign Creator of the cosmos, manifesting lovingkindness and truth, deserves the praise of his people who trust and fear him—unlike idolaters who are no better than their creations, idols that are insensible and lifeless—because he abundantly blesses all his devout, helping and protecting them.

Commentary

Yahweh Glorified (115:1–3)

There is no appeal to God in the psalm, but there might be an indirect exhortation to Yahweh in 115:1 to act on the behalf of his people, so that his name may be glorified: "May You be glorified, not on account of us, but because of your divine attributes (which we anticipate will be working for us)." The poetic structure of 115:1 emphasizes both "Yahweh"/"Your name"/"glory" and the reason for this glorification, "Your lovingkindness"/"Your truth":[3]

> "Not [לֹא, *loʾ*] to us,   **Yahweh**,   not [לֹא] to us,
>   but to Your *name*
>   give *glory*,
> because of [עַל, *ʿal*]   Your *lovingkindness*,   because of [עַל]
>   Your *truth*."

Perhaps the question asked by God's people in 115:2 is in response to some historical assault on them, possibly verbal, judging by the taunt cited in 115:2b (likely originating from the

---

3. Modified from Auffret, *Merveilles à nos yeux*, 149.

idolaters mentioned in the following section).[4] That question of where God is, his people answer in 115:3: He—"*our* God"—reigns in the heavens, sovereign, unthwartable, untouchable.

Idolaters Pilloried (115:4–8)

In contrast with "*our* God" of 115:3a are "*their* idols" in 115:4a. There is also the contrast between God "doing [עשׂה, 'sh]" all he pleases (115:3b) and those idols being the "work" (also from עשׂה) of human hands (115:4b). Neatly framed (in the structure shown below), by these "idols" that are human "works" (at one end; 115:4a, 4b) and their "makers [מַעֲשֵׂה, *ma'aseh*]" (again from עשׂה) and "those who trust in them" (at the other end; 115:8a, 8b), are seven body parts/faculties of these false gods that are utterly non-functional:[5]

115:4a	"idols"	
115:4b	"work" (מַעֲשֵׂה)	
115:5a	"mouth"; "cannot speak"	Singular
115:5b	"eyes"; "cannot see"	Plural (pairs)
115:6a	"ears"; "cannot hear"	
115:6b	"nose"; "cannot smell"	Singular
115:7a	"hands"; "cannot feel"	Plural (pairs)
115:7b	"feet"; "cannot walk"	
115:7c	"throat"; "cannot make a sound"	Singular
115:8a	"make" (עשׂה)	
115:8b	"those who trust in them" (idolaters)	

Thus idolaters are ridiculed and scorned for their trust in what they have "made" (115:8a; and "work," 115:4b), unlike God-fearers worshiping the God in the heavens who sovereignly "does" as he pleases (115:3b; all three words are derived from עשׂה). No one and nothing can compare with him, and idolaters who trust and worship dumb, blind, deaf, insensate, immovable, silent idols are themselves insensible and devoid of life (115:8).[6]

Devout Prospered (115:9–15)

On the other hand are the devout who "trust" (115:9a, 10a, 11a) Yahweh and "fear" him (115:11a, 13a). Unlike lifeless idols, this God, Yahweh, is the "help" and "shield" (protection) for his peoples (115:11b). And he is also a beatifying God (who will "bless": 115:12a, 12b, 12c, 13a, 15a) to those who fear him—all of them, "the small with the great" (115:13b). The

---

4. That snub was perhaps because the God of the Israelites was invisible, in an iconic or imagistic sense, unlike false gods/idols. And perhaps even because Yahweh was not showing up to defend his people.

5. Alden, "Chiastic Psalms (III)," 205–6. Notice that the body parts alternate between the singular (mouth, nose, and throat) and pairs of the plural (eyes and ears, hands and feet).

6. Idolaters use their "human *hands*" to fashion idols (115:4b) that themselves "have *hands*, but . . . cannot feel" (115:7a), and thus these manufacturers become like their products (115:8a). But this also means that the "human *hands*" of the idolaters are, in the first place, dysfunctional, and thus their creations, idols, are equally effete and inutile. A vicious cycle, indeed!

numerous repetitions underscore the certainty that this God is a blesser of people. Deity reciprocates their trust and fear by prospering them.

Besides the generality of being the protection for his people (115:10–12) and of his remembering them (115:12a), how exactly God blesses them (115:12bc, 13–15) is not detailed. Perhaps that is not necessary. The fact of divine blessing upon God-fearers is indubitable; the manner thereof is left to the sovereignty and providence of deity.

Yahweh Glorified (115:16–18)

The psalm then draws to close with a reprise of God being glorified—"praised" and "blessed" (115:17a, 18a, 18c)—this time by his people. Yahweh is the one who made "the heavens and the earth" (115:15b); and in "the heavens" that are "the heavens of Yahweh" (115:16a), deity does as he pleases (thus there is a clear link between 115:15–16 and 115:3, both having "do"/"made" [עשׂה], and "heavens").

But what about the earth? This planet God has given to humans (115:16b). And in this location on earth what will humans do? The answer is in 115:18: "we—we will bless Yah from now unto forever." The contrast is clear: the dead do not praise Yah, they remain silent (115:17)—no doubt indicating idolaters who, like their idols, are dead and silent. On the other hand, "we—we will" (with an emphatic repetition of the pronoun) praise and bless deity. That is, indeed, an appropriate response to this great and sovereign God of lovingkindness and truth. And the people of God proceed to bless God forever, as they have resolved to do (115:18ab): "Praise Yah!" (115:15c).

Sermon Map

I. Potentate God
  The unthwartable Sovereign, of love and truth (115:1–3)
  Move-to-relevance: God's sovereignty discerned

II. Pathetic Idols; Paralyzed Idolaters
  Defunct idols (115:4–7)
  Dead idolaters (115:8)

III. Prospering God; Praising God-fearers
  God blesses (115:9b, 10b, 11b, 12–15)
  God is blessed (115:16–18)

IV. *Piety for the Potentate!*
  Fearing God and trusting God (115:9a, 10a, 11a)
  Specifics on fearing the Sovereign

PSALM 116:1–19

Psalm of Orientation

Commitment, Preservation, and Thanksgiving

THIS PSALM OF THANKSGIVING (see 116:17) addresses Yahweh (in 116:8, 16–17a), the psalmist himself (116:7), and the community of God (in the rest of the composition).[1]

Translation

116:1	I loved [Yahweh], for Yahweh heard
	my voice—my supplications [for grace].
116:2	For He has inclined His ear to me,
	and through[out] my days I called [upon Him].
116:3	The ropes of death encompassed me,
	and the distresses of Sheol found me;
	distress and sorrow I found.
116:4	And upon the name of Yahweh I called:
	"O Yahweh, liberate my soul."
116:5	Gracious is Yahweh, and righteous;
	and our God is One who is compassionate.
116:6	The One keeping the simple is Yahweh;
	I was brought low, and He delivered me.
116:7	Return, my soul, to your rests,
	for Yahweh has dealt beneficently unto you.
116:8	For You have rescued my soul from death,
	my eyes from tears, my feet from stumbling.

---

1. It appears that the psalmist is recounting a historical experience of distress, as the *qatal* verbs indicate (116:1aα, 2a, 3a, 3b, 6bα, 7b, 8a, 10aα, 10b, 11a). Though there are *yiqtol* verbs interspersed among them (116:1aβ, 2b, 3c, 4a, 6bβ), these bear the perfective force of the *qatals* (the *yiqtol* in 116:9 is considered an imperfect).

116:9	I will walk before the face of Yahweh
	in the lands of the living.
116:10	I believed [Yahweh] for I would speak,
	"I—I have been greatly afflicted."
116:11	I—I said in my apprehension,
	"All humans are ones who lie."
116:12	What shall I return to Yahweh
	[for] all His benefits unto me?
116:13	The cup of deliverance I will lift up,
	and upon the name of Yahweh I will call.
116:14	My vows to Yahweh I will fulfill—
	indeed, before all His people.
116:15	Precious in the eyes of Yahweh
	is the death of His devout ones.
116:16	O Yahweh, indeed I am Your servant;
	I am Your servant, the son of Your maid;
	You have loosed my chains.
116:17	To You I will sacrifice a sacrifice of thanksgiving,
	and upon the name of Yahweh I call.
116:18	My vows to Yahweh I will fulfill—
	indeed, before all His people,
116:19	in the courts of the house of Yahweh,
	in the midst of you, Jerusalem.
	Praise Yah.

Structure

Broadly, the composition may be divided into two parts, 116:1–9 and 116:10–19, each with similarities to the other.[2] *Predicament and Preservation* deals with the threat of death faced by the psalmist and his rescue by Yahweh; it ends with the poet in the "lands of the living" (116:9b).

---

2. Indeed, in the LXX, Ps 116:1–19 is Psalm 114, and 116:10–19 is Psalm 115.

Piety and Praise considers the faith of the psalmist and his promise of praise to his rescuer, Yahweh; it ends with the supplicant in "Jerusalem":[3]

> **Predicament and Preservation** (116:1–9)
>   *Predicament* (116:1–4)
>   *Preservation* (116:5–9) [direct address to Yahweh, 116:8]
>
>> Yahweh's "ear" (116:2a); "O Yahweh" (116:4b)
>> Restrained by "ropes" (116:3a); "death" (116:3a, 8a)
>> בְּאַרְצוֹת, *b'artsoth* ("in the lands," 116:9b)
>> "lands of the living" (116:9b)
>>
>>> "I loved [Yahweh],   for   Yahweh heard" (116:1a)
>>> *qatal* + *implied object* + כִּי (*ki*) + *yiqtol*
>
> **Piety and Praise** (116:10–19)
>   *Piety* (116:10–11)
>   *Praise* (116:12–19) [direct address to Yahweh, 116:16–17]
>
>> Yahweh's "face," "eyes" (116:9a, 15a); "O Yahweh" (116:16a)
>> Released from "chains" (116:16c); "death" (116:15b)
>> בְּחַצְרוֹת, *bchatsrot* ("in the courts," 116:19a)
>> "Jerusalem" (116:19b)
>>
>>> "I believed [Yahweh]   for   I would speak" (116:10a)
>>> *qatal* + *implied object* + כִּי + *yiqtol*

Yahweh is more in focus in the first half; the psalmist, more in the second. Correspondingly, most of the latter's actions in the first section deal with his predicament (he "calls," upon God, 116:2b, 4a; he "finds" distress, 116:3c; and he is "brought low," 116:6b). Following his preservation, the psalmist, whose feet were "stumbling" (116:8b), now "walks" in steadiness (116:9a). The rest of the psalm depicts the supplicant acting with vigor and initiative, as he engages in cultic activity (he "believes" Yahweh and he "speaks"/"says," 116:10a, 11a; he "lifts up" the cup of deliverance, 116:13a; he promises to "fulfill" his vows, 116:14a, 18a; and to "sacrifice," 116:17a). Thus there is a clear movement of the drama of the psalm from its first part to its second.[4]

---

3. Modified from Barré, "Psalm 116," 66–68, 77.
4. See Barré, "Psalm 116," 76.

In any case, there is no question that the psalm is carefully structured, with the center depicting the shift from "death" to "lands of the living":[5]

16:1	*Psalmist's voice calling for help*
116:2b	"I call [upon Him]"
116:3a	"ropes of death"
116:4a	"upon the name of Yahweh I called"
111:6b	"He delivered"
116:7	"return"; "Yahweh … beneficently unto you"
116:8a	"death"
116:9b	**"lands of the living"**
116:12	"return"; "all His benefits unto me"
116:13a	"cup of deliverance"
116:13b	"upon the name of Yahweh I will call"
116:15b, 16c	"death"; "chains"
116:17b	"upon the name of Yahweh I will call"
116:18–19	*Psalmist's vows being fulfilled*

Theological Focus

The people of God, his devout ones, love him and have faith in him because of his compassionate attention to their predicament and their preservation from it in an act of divine grace and beneficence that enables them to walk with God in piety and return their promised thanks to him in public.

Commentary

Predicament and Preservation (116:1–9)

The psalm commences with a declaration of the psalmist's love (i.e., loyalty and commitment) to Yahweh (116:1) because deity had heard his plea (116:2).[6] The reference here is to some past predicament that was fraught with danger to life (116:3; also see 116:8, 15—all mention "death"). "Distresses" "find" the psalmist (116:3b) and the psalmist "finds" "distress" (116:3c)—the psalmist is on a collision course with pain! In his desperate situation, the supplicant was sorrowful (116:3c) and he called upon Yahweh for liberation from his woe (116:2b, 4a).

116:2b	"I called"
116:3b	"distresses … found me"
116:3c	"distress … I found"
116:4a	"I called"

---

5. From Alden, "Chiastic Psalms (III)," 206; and Auffret, "'Je marcherai à la face de YHWH,'" 174.
6. For the OT notion of "love" as loyalty and commitment, involving obedience, see Levenson, *Love of God*.

Then comes his preservation by Yahweh. The "gracious [חַנּוּן, *channun*]," "righteous," and "compassionate" God that he is, he delivered this afflicted one, the "simple" soul[7] (116:5–6), by attending to his "supplications [for grace] [תַּחֲנוּן, *tachanun*]" (116:1b). Not only does the psalmist then speak to himself, exhorting his soul to rest in the beneficent blessings bestowed by Yahweh (116:7), he also addresses Yahweh directly, restating the liberation accomplished earlier by deity: the "soul" rescued from "death" by Yahweh (116:8a) was the same "soul" that was once in danger of "death" (116:3a, 4b). The section ends with a joyous resolution by the psalmist, that he "will walk before the face of Yahweh" (116:9a)—not in "Sheol" (116:3b), where God is not, but in "the lands of the living" (116:9b), no longer trammeled by "the ropes of death" (116:3a). The dramatic turnaround is depicted in 116:8–9:[8]

> "death"
> "eyes"
> "feet"
> "walk"
> "face"
> "living"

"Death means separation from Yhwh . . . . Life means being in Yhwh's presence. The whole of life is lived before Yhwh, literally to the face of Yhwh, under Yhwh's caring and beneficent gaze."[9] That is what has happened to the psalmist: from predicament to preservation. Therefore the people of God love their deity (116:1a)!

Piety and Promise (116:10–19)

The psalmist reprises his predicament as the second half of the psalm commences: He had had faith in Yahweh and had appealed to deity during his self-confessed situation of being "greatly afflicted" (116:10b). He had put no faith in humanity—"ones who lie" and who are undependable—in the midst of his "apprehension" (116:11). The contrast is straightforward: deity alone was trustworthy during the poet's past predicament. And deity alone will be trustworthy during the future predicaments of all God's people.

And for this grace extended to the psalmist that preserved him from his predicament, what "return" or repayment could he make towards his divine benefactor (116:12a)? Whereas earlier he had exhorted his soul to "return" to its rest because "Yahweh" had "dealt beneficently [גָּמַל, *gamal*] unto [עַל, *'al*]" him (116:7b), here he wonders what he could "return" to "Yahweh" for all the "benefits [תַּגְמוּל, *tagmul*] unto [עַל]" him (116:12).[10] "The unpayable nature of the debt does not absolve him from making what contribution he can."[11] And what he can is offer thanks in the cult (116:13–14; and again, 116:17–19; note that 116:14 and

---

7. One who is less experienced in matters of wisdom and understanding (see 19:7), and an unsuspecting and innocent victim of those distresses.
8. From Barré, "Psalm 116," 68.
9. Goldingay, *Psalms*, 3:343.
10. These are the only two instances of the preposition עַל in the psalm.
11. Allen, *Psalms 101–150*, 115.

116:18 are identical). In return for being "delivered" (116:6b), the psalmist would lift up the "cup of deliverance" (116:13a).[12] Whereas earlier, the psalmist had "called" upon "the name of Yahweh" for help in his predicament (116:4a),[13] here he "calls" upon "the name of Yahweh" in his promise of thanksgiving (116:13b; also in 116:17b).[14]

In an aside (116:15–16) that splits the psalmist's promise of thanksgiving into two (116:13–14 and 116:17–19), the composer again reflects on his preservation, the ground of his piety and promise. That the death of Yahweh's devout ones is "precious" to him (116:15a) does not mean that deity finds satisfaction in their demise, but that their death (i.e., their lives, or their blood) is greatly valued by him and not taken trivially; so much so, death/bloodshed would be prevented in God's sovereign way. This is akin to what 72:14 asserts: "From oppression and from violence he will redeem their soul [i.e., of the weak and needy], and their blood will be precious in his eyes."[15] The proof of this value is testified to by the psalmist in 116:16: as "Your servant" (×2) and "the son of Your maid," he was one of the devout whose life was of value to Yahweh, and whose "chains" (116:16c; equivalent to the "ropes of death" in 116:3a) Yahweh had loosed.[16]

116:15–16
"death"
    "His devout ones"
        "Your servant"; "the son of Your maid"
"chains"

With that the psalmist resumes his promises of cultic thanksgiving to Yahweh for his rescue (116:17–19). Whereas the first half of the psalm had ended with mention of "lands of the living" (116:9b), the second half concludes with "Jerusalem" (116:19b), presumably equivalent terms.[17] And thus is the faith of the people of God in their God (116:10a) manifested! Goldingay's conclusion is appropriate:

> The two parts of the psalm suggest that love [116:1a] and trust ["belief," 116:10a] are the two bases for life with Yhwh. Giving our testimony is a gesture of love to

---

12. Perhaps a drink offering of thanks for the "deliverance."

13. Also see 116:2b, for a similar use of "call."

14. Curiously, a structural element relating to this invocation of God is repeated in both halves of the psalm: אֶקְרָא ... ־בְ, *uv- ... 'eqra'*, shows up translated as "and through[out] ... I called" (116:2b) and "and upon ... I called" (116:4a, 13b, 17b), bespeaking a ceaseless dependence upon deity.

15. "Prosaically put, the life of the people committed to him is valuable to Yhwh; or the people in danger of death who are committed to Yhwh are valuable to him. The implication is that Yhwh would therefore not let their death come about; and this is what the worshipper has proved" by his deliverance (Goldingay, *Psalms*, 3:346).

16. Whereas the exclamation "O Yahweh" once appealed to deity to preserve the supplicant (116:4b), here the same expression asserts to deity that the supplicant is, indeed, one of the faithful who has already been preserved (116:16a). "There is a paradox there. One might call the relationship of servant to master a form of bondage, but the positive side to it, especially in the context of the attempted imposition of ropes and restraints by another would-be master [116:3] ... makes it more like a form of freedom" (Goldingay, *Psalms*, 3:347).

17. "Lands," plural (בְּאַרְצוֹת), is likely being employed for the sake of assonance with בְּחַצְרוֹת, "courts," in 116:19a. Also, אֲשַׁלֵּם, *'ashallem*, "I will fulfill" (116:14a, 18a) is assonant with יְרוּשָׁלִַם, *yrushalaim*, "Jerusalem" (116:19b).

Yhwh—not a gesture of emotional love (or not only that) but an expression of the commitment of our whole life. It is the beginning of a confession that will keep recurring in our lives. It is based on the fact that Yhwh listened to us when we cried out because death was overwhelming us and there was no way for us to find an escape. In that context we were once again driven to trust in Yhwh because there was no one else to trust; specifically, we were powerless and human help could get us nowhere. It involves a renewed acknowledgment of Yhwh's grace, faithfulness, and compassion, which have been evidenced in this experience as Yhwh has watched over us. Once again we proved the privilege of being Yhwh's servants, of being committed people, and found that the master was also committed to us. It involves a confession that takes public, outward, sacrificial, sacramental form as well as private, inner, and verbal form. We can now return to that relaxed rest that is the natural habitat of God's people and walk before Yhwh in the breadth and the depth of the place of freedom where we are.[18]

Amen!

Sermon Map

I. Predicament and Preservation: Love towards God
    Predicament (116:3)
    Preservation (116:1–2, 4–9)
    Move-to-relevance: God's gracious preservation of us

II. Piety and Promise: Faith towards God
    Piety (116:10–11, 15–16)
    Promise (116:12–13, 17–19)
    Move-to-relevance: Our faith (and love) towards him

III. *Praise the Preserver!*
    Praise as manifestation of our faith and love towards God
    Specifics on praising God for his gracious preservation

---

18. Goldingay, *Psalms*, 3:348.

PSALM 117:1–2

Psalm of Orientation

Nations Praise God's Lovingkindness and Truth

PSALM 117 IS THE shortest psalm in the psalter. It appears to be a doxology of sorts to Psalms 111–116, all of which (including Psalm 117, but excluding Psalm 114) have "Praise Yah!"

Translation

117:1 Praise Yahweh, all nations;
    laud Him, all peoples.
117:2 For great toward us is His lovingkindness,
    and the truth of Yahweh is forever.
Praise Yah.

Structure

The song is a typical praise psalm, with 117:1 the exhortation to praise, and 117:2 the explanation for praise. The psalm may also be considered chiastic in structure:

Exhortation to Praise (117:1)
"Praise Yahweh" (117:1aα)
  "all nations" (117:1aβ)
  "all peoples" (117:1b)

Explanation for Praise (117:2)
  "His lovingkindness" (117:2a)
  "the truth of Yahweh" (117:2b)
"Praise Yah" (117:2c)

Theological Focus

The people of God, recollecting his lovingkindness and truth from days past and anticipating them for days future, invite all peoples to join in praise of this great God with them.

Commentary

Exhortation to Praise (117:1)

The imperative to praise and laud Yahweh commences this brief composition (117:1), but it is not directed to God's people: "all nations" and "all peoples" are urged to extol deity.[1] "While other psalms have commissioned the proclaiming of Yhwh's glory among the nations and have urged the whole world to sing for, shout for, and serve Yhwh (e.g., Pss 96; 100 [both addressing the "earth"]), only here are the nations themselves urged to do so."[2] Of course, it was unlikely that the "nations" and "peoples" would have seen (or heard) this composition to be moved thereby to praise Yahweh, but the fact remains that the praise of God is the responsibility of all peoples in all nations, and in every place in every time.

Explanation for Praise (117:2)

The reason for praise is the lovingkindness of Yahweh towards his people and his truth that endures forever (117:2):[3]

> "for great toward us [כִּי עָלֵינוּ, *ki 'alenu*]"
> "His lovingkindness"
> "the truth of Yahweh"
> "forever [לְעוֹלָם, *l'olam*]"

Strikingly, though the psalm seems to be addressed to "all nations" and "all peoples," the reason for getting them to praise Yahweh is his treatment of deity's own people—"great toward *us*...."

> The psalm actually declares that Yhwh's faithfulness to Israel is indeed reason for the nations' worship, and explicitly for their enthusiastic praise.... These attitudes and stances of Yhwh to Israel constitute good news for the nations and peoples themselves.... Yhwh's committed truthfulness to Israel shows who Yhwh is and

---

1. Focusing on the consonants, 117:1 begins with ה + ל + ל (*h* + *l* + *l*) in הַלְלוּ, *hallu*, "praise"; it ends with ה + מ + מ (*h* + *m* + *m*) in הָאֻמִּים, *ha'ummim*, "peoples," a neat assonant pattern.
2. Goldingay, *Psalms*, 3:350.
3. Auffret, "Louez YHWH," 6.

draws other people to Yhwh on the assumption that this committed truthfulness is not exclusive but inclusive.[4]

Besides, it is through the blessing of the nation of Israel (the Abrahamic peoples) that the rest of the world is also blessed, primarily in the person of the Lord Jesus Christ and his consummative work, and secondarily by God's devout ones (whether part of Israel or part of the church) who serve to bless the world with their own presence and their lives.

> The perspective of the psalm starts with the present, moves to the past and then to the future. . . . The focus of the psalm on Yahweh is remarkable, it is his *[c]hesed* and *'emet* ["lovingkindness" and "truth"] that are the cause for the call to the praise and nothing else. The people of the Lord have only been the passive receivers of Yahweh's *[c]hesed* and *'emet*. While they are passive receivers of Yahweh's *[c]hesed* and *'emet*, they are also called upon to be active reflectors of Yahweh's *[c]hesed* and *'emet*, so much so that it will bring foreign nations to praise Yahweh.[5]

Thus the psalm also indirectly exhorts God's own people not to neglect his praise and lauding, and to engage in activities such as this in order to attract and draw "all nations" and "all peoples" to this great God (117:1). In lauding their deity, the people of God in days present are urged to reflect upon his lovingkindness in days past, and upon his truth which extends into days future ("forever," 117:2ab), encompassing all time.

A small psalm it might be, but Psalm 117 is ambitious in its reach and scope, seeking to draw all humanity of all time into its fold.

Sermon Map[6]

I. The Present

    Move-to-relevance: current situation of God's people

II. The Past

    God's lovingkindness (117:2a)

    Move-to-relevance: God's lovingkindness in the past

III. The Future

    God's truth (117:2b)

    Move-to-relevance: God's truth forever

IV. *Praise, Peoples, Perpetually!*

    Specifics on praising God

---

4. Goldingay, *Psalms*, 3:351.
5. Snyman, "Reading Psalm 117," 118.
6. Because of its brevity, this psalm is best preached in conjunction with another that mentions praise being offered by the "nations," such as Psalm 47; 57; 67; 68; 96; 99; 100; and 150.

PSALM 118:1–29

Psalm of Orientation

Leader's Thanksgiving for Divine Deliverance

ESSENTIALLY, PSALM 118 IS a communal giving of thanks (118:1, 19, 21, 28–29) for deliverance from some severe crisis (118:5–6, 12–13, 17–18), though there are lines that appear to have been uttered by a king or leader (the first-person singular is found in 118:5–7, 10–14, 17–19, 21, 28).[1] Yahweh remains in the third person for most of the psalm (he is directly addressed only in 118:21, 25, 28).[2]

Translation

118:1	Give thanks to Yahweh, for He [is] good,	
	for forever [is] His lovingkindness.	
118:2	Let Israel indeed say,	
	"For forever [is] His lovingkindness."	
118:3	Let the house of Aaron indeed say,	
	"For forever [is] His lovingkindness."	
118:4	Let those who fear Yahweh indeed say,	
	"For forever [is] His lovingkindness."	
118:5	From distress I called upon Yah;	
	Yah answered me with a broad place.	
118:6	Yahweh is for me; I do not fear.	
	What can he do to me—a human?	

---

1. The first-person plural shows up in 118:23–24, 26–27. Psalm 118:22–26 (or parts thereof) is cited in all four Gospels: Matt 21:9, 42; 23:39; Mark 11:9–10; 12:10; Luke 13:35; 19:38; 20:17; John 12:13. This appropriation of words relating to a leader of God's people by characters in the NT—crowds and Jesus himself (though never by a narrator)—does not necessarily make this psalm prophetic, for there is no indication in this composition that the leader was anything other than human. However, the notions expressed in this OT text are applicable to God's leaders and were, no doubt, considered to be applicable to the Messiah, too.

2. Incidentally, the enemies are addressed directly in 118:13.

118:7	Yahweh is for me as one helping me;
	and I—I look upon the ones hating me.
118:8	It is better to take refuge in Yahweh
	than to trust in a human.
118:9	It is better to take refuge in Yahweh
	than to trust in nobles.
118:10	All the nations surrounded me;
	in the name of Yahweh, indeed, I cut them off.
118:11	They surrounded me, yes, they surrounded me;
	in the name of Yahweh, indeed, I cut them off.
118:12	They surrounded me like bees;
	they were extinguished as a fire of thorns;
	in the name of Yahweh, indeed, I cut them off.
118:13	You pushed me aggressively to fell [me],
	but Yahweh—He helped me.
118:14	My strength and song is Yah,
	and He has become for me deliverance.
118:15	The sound of joyful exclamation and deliverance
	is in the tents of the righteous;
	the right hand of Yahweh does powerfully.
118:16	The right hand of Yahweh is exalted;
	the right hand of Yahweh does powerfully.
118:17	I will not die, but I will live
	and recount the works of Yah.
118:18	Yah has disciplined me severely,
	but unto death He has not given me over.
118:19	Open to me the gates of righteousness;
	I will enter through them, I will give thanks to Yah.
118:20	This is the gate of Yahweh;
	the righteous will enter through it.
118:21	I will give thanks to You, for You have answered me,
	and You have become for me deliverance.
118:22	A stone which the builders rejected
	has become the head corner[stone].
118:23	From Yahweh has this come about;
	it is wonderful in our eyes.
118:24	This is the day which Yahweh has made;
	let us jubilate and be joyful in it.
118:25	O Yahweh, please deliver;
	O Yahweh, please grant success.

118:26 Blessed is the one coming in the name of Yahweh;
    we have blessed you from the house of Yahweh.
118:27 Yahweh is God, and He has shone [light] on us;
    bind the festival [offering] with ropes unto the horns of the altar.
118:28 You are my God, and I will give thanks to You;
    my God, I will exalt You.
118:29 Give thanks to Yahweh, for He is good;
    for His lovingkindness is forever.

Structure

A topographical division of the psalm may be intentional, starting in the temple, moving to battlefield and to the gates of the temple and, thence, into it:[3]

118:1	INTRODUCTION	
118:2–4	Call	*Temple* ("house of Aaron," 118:3a)
118:5–13	Confidence	*Battlefield*
118:14–20	Confession	*Gates*
118:21–28	Celebration	*Temple* ("house of Yahweh," 118:26b)
118:29	CONCLUSION	

Theological Focus

God who, in his goodness and eternal lovingkindness, grants his people and their leader—those who fear him and fearlessly trust him—victory over their foes, because he is on their side and they are in his presence, motivates the divine community to give corporate thanks to their deity.

Commentary

Introduction; Call (118:1–4)

The first word of the *Introduction* is הוֹדוּ, *hodu*, "give thanks" (118:1a), and the last word, חַסְדּוֹ, *chasdo*, "His lovingkindness" (118:2b), separated by a patterned set of words beginning, in sequence, with לְ, כִּי, כִּי, and לְ (*l, ki, ki,* and *l*; see below).

---

3. Modified from Reed, "Thanksgiving," 61. Significant repeats of phrases/sentences within the psalm include: 118:1b = 2b = 3b = 4b; 118:6aα = 7aα; 118:8a = 9a; 118:8bα = 9bα; 118:10b = 11b = 12c; 118:15c = 118:16b; 118:25aα = 25bα; and 118:1 = 29.

הוֹדוּ ("give thanks")
לַיהוָה, *layhwh* ("to Yahweh")
כִּי־טוֹב, *ki-tov* ("for He [is] good")
כִּי ("for")
לְעוֹלָם, *l'olam* ("forever [is]")
חַסְדּוֹ ("His lovingkindness")

It is likely that the first four verses of Psalm 118 were antiphonally uttered (and probably in the temple precincts: "house of Aaron" shows up in 118:3a), alternating lines between leader (118:1a, 2a, 3a, 4a) and congregation (118:1b, 2b, 3b, 4b), and addressed as a whole to "Israel," to "the house of Aaron," and to all "those who fear Yahweh." It is a call to thanksgiving for the everlasting lovingkindness of God.

Confidence (118:5–13)

In 118:5, a new voice enters, speaking in the first person; in a series of contrasts,[4] it outlines how divine lovingkindness operated in the past experience(s) of deliverance and gave him confidence to face all crises, present and future. A battlefield appears to be the arena in this section, with all the martial "surrounding" and "cutting off" and "extinguishing" going on (118:10–12).

The speaker was in "distress," מֵצַר, *metsar* (118:5a)—that can mean a narrow, constrained place—but he was brought out into "a broad place," מֶרְחָב, *merchav* (118:5b) by deity. So if Yahweh is "for me [לִי, *li*]," then what can mortal humans do "to me [לִי]" (118:6)? Thus, for those who "fear" Yahweh (118:4a), there is no cause for "fear" (118:6a), a reassuring paradox. This verse, 118:6, is chiastically structured, making the contrast stark:

יְהוָה, *yhwh* ("Yahweh")	Noun
לִי ("for me")	Prepositional phrase
לֹא אִירָא, *lo' 'ira'* ("I do not fear")	Verb
מַה־יַּעֲשֶׂה, *mah-ya'aseh* ("What can he do")	Verb
לִי ("to me")	Prepositional phrase
אָדָם, *'adam* ("a human")	Noun

Since Yahweh is for me as a helper (118:7a), one can gaze upon the haters in triumph (118:7b). So, "I do not fear [אִירָא, *'ira'*]" (118:6a); instead, "I—I look upon [אֶרְאֶה, *'er'eh*]" my enemies (notice the emphatic first-person pronoun; 118:7b). And this is the confidence of the people of God: it is better to seek refuge in this great God than to trust in humans, and even high-powered, top-level, upper-class humans ("nobles," 118:9). Because Yahweh is "good [טוֹב]" (118:1a), he is a "better [טוֹב]" refuge than anyone else (118:8a, 9a): he alone is worthy of trust; he alone makes one confident.

---

4. "Distress" vs. "broad place" (118:5); "Yahweh" vs. "a human" (118:6, 8); "one helping me" vs. "ones hating me" (118:7); "Yahweh" vs. "nobles" (118:9).

Then follows a further detailing of the consequences that befell the enemies of this leader of God's people (118:10–12), again employing martial terms: foes may have "surrounded" him (×4; 118:10–12), but "in the name of Yahweh," i.e., in his presence (118:12c), they were destroyed by the supplicant. In a sudden switch—an "apostrophe" in rhetorical terms—the speaker turns to address the "nations" as a singular person, as though present before him (118:13): they ("you") did their best to fell him, but Yahweh helped him, thus retaining the trust of God's people in their God. They can surely be confident, taking refuge in him. And it is deity who helps this leader, this person of God (118:6–9), to be victorious in his battles (118:10–12).[5]

Confession (118:14–20)

The *Confession* seems to be occurring at the gates of the temple: the supplicant requests that the "gates" be opened so that he may "enter" (118:19–20). In any case, the leader continues his first-person affirmation of Yahweh in this confession of deity as his "strength and song," extolling the "right hand of Yahweh" (118:14b, 15c–16), "employing time-honored language of the song of victory."[6] As a result, he will not die but live to recite the great things Yahweh has done (118:17), including God's acts of divine "discipline" (118:18).[7]

In sum, the confession of this redeemed individual is that "his renewed lease on life means opportunity to give this report of Yahweh's intervention on his behalf. He can even incorporate the crisis positively into his praise, as evidence of Yahweh's painful but loving discipline."[8] So here he is, the leader (perhaps with his entourage), at the gates of the temple, seeking entry (118:19–20) to give thanks for Yahweh's marvelous deeds of deliverance, the proper response of the "righteous" (118:20b, i.e., the people of God) to their liberation.[9] What is being praised are the "works" of Yahweh (from עשׂה, 'sh; 118:17b), because Yahweh "does" powerfully (also from עשׂה; 118:15c, 16b): it is for that reason that the psalmist had earlier asked rhetorically, "What can he *do* to me—a human?" (again from עשׂה; 118:6b).

Literally, the "gates" are positioned on either side of the leader promising to "give thanks to Yah" (see below).[10]

---

5. For preaching purposes, since hardly anyone in any congregation is involved in martial endeavors, the "battle" motif may be extended to other situations of conflict, perhaps even spiritual warfare.

6. Allen, *Psalms 101–150*, 124. See Exod 15:2, 12 for Yahweh as "strength and song" and for his "right hand" working powerfully. The "tents" in Ps 118:15b may indicate the barracks of the army supporting this leader. Also, 118:15 is the only tricolon in this psalm, serving to emphasize what is said therein.

7. All other instances of this verb, יסר, *ysr*, "discipline," in the Psalter deal with punishment for sinful acts (see 2:10; 6:2; 38:1; 39:11; 94:10, 12; perhaps 16:7 is an exception, but even here the correction that the psalmist's "innards" are applying to himself may indicate a waywardness on the part of the pleader). It is likely that the notion of some sort of personal failure is operating in 118:18a, too, at least in the background (not uncommon in the psalms of supplication) rendering this poem unlikely to be prophetically applicable *en masse* to Jesus Christ. Besides, the psalm's emphatic focus on personal deliverance of the supplicant (118:21; etc.) seems rather unlike Christ's approach to his passion. And, needless to add, the Savior did die (118:18b). On the application of 118:22–24, see below.

8. Allen, *Psalms 101–150*, 124.

9. The "gates *of righteousness*" (118:19) may indicate the portal of entry of the "righteous" (118:20).

10. Girard, *Les Psaumes Redécouverts*, 232.

118:19abα	"gates"; "righteousness"; "enter"
118:19bβ	"I will give thanks to Yah"
118:20	"gate"; "righteous"; "enter"

And with that a celebration in the temple commences.

Celebration; Conclusion (118:21–29)

The celebration begins with the leader invoking a thanksgiving (118:21) after entering the temple through its gates (118:19–20). It is the people's turn now and they respond with words of celebration (118:22–27). It is likely that the utterance of 118:22 is a proverb or an aphorism borrowed from construction work.

> This aspect of building then provides a figure of speech. Something dismissed for one purpose might turn out to be exactly what was needed for another purpose, possibly a more exalted one than that for which it was rejected. That is what has happened here, the congregation comments. This leader of little Israel, or little Israel itself [or perhaps both seen together as a singular unity], seemed useless and was dismissed contemptuously by the nations. But he or it turns out to occupy a more exalted position than anyone would have dreamed.[11]

It was the grace of God that made this turnaround possible—and it is "wonderful in our eyes," therefore the people of God celebrate (118:23–24). In all likelihood, a contrast is being drawn between the builders' rejection of the leader as worthless (118:22), and their own recognition of their leader as wonderful (118:24):[12]

118:22	"A stone which the builders rejected 　　has become [הָיְתָה, haytah] the head corner[stone]. **From Yahweh**
118:23	has this come about [הָיְתָה]; it is wonderful in our eyes."

---

11. Goldingay, *Psalms*, 3:362. Whether this "head corner[stone]" was a cornerstone (the stone in the foundation, positioned at a corner and installed at the initiation of construction) or a capstone (the crowning stone at top of edifice and put in last of all) is unclear. In fact, Luke 20:18 (with 20:17 citing Ps 118:22) seems to give such a structure *both* senses: people fall over this stone and the stone also falls on them! In any case, the distinction does not affect the thrust of our text.

12. From Auffret, *Merveilles à nos yeux*, 167. Also, conceptually, 118:23a is similar to 118:24a (the work of Yahweh), and 118:23b to 118:24b (the response of God's people to his wonderful work). What Yahweh has "made" (from עשׂה) is the day of deliverance (118:24a; for "deliverance" wrought by Yahweh, see 118:14b, 15a, 21b, 25a; other uses of עשׂה, "do"/"works," are found in 118:6b, 15c, 16b, 17b).

Indeed, this "becoming" and "coming about" (118:22b, 23a; both from the root היה, *hyh*)—the establishment by Yahweh of the leader as the "head corner[stone]"—is equivalent to God "becoming" for his people deliverance (also from the same root 118:21; היה). Yes, celebration is in order!

But in 118:25, amidst all this celebration, there appears a plea for deliverance. It looks to future victory by this once-rejected-but-now-chosen rock/leader: may he continue to be the agent of Yahweh's deliverance, and may God grant him success and victory. The sentence of 118:25 reads: אָנָּא יְהוָה הוֹשִׁיעָה נָּא / אָנָּא יְהוָה הַצְלִיחָה נָּא (*'anna yhwh hatslichah na* / *'anna yhwh hoshi'ah na*). With a parallelism involving two *hiphil* imperatives, it is quite assonant and has eight long "ah" sounds (excluding יְהוָה), "creating an open-throated chant that in our modern culture we might almost call a 'cheer.'"[13] So, even a plea for future triumph is part of present celebration, as the leader, this chosen one, is labeled "blessed"—and the people proceed to "bless" him (118:26). Notice the parallels between 118:26a and 118:26b that clarify that the blessedness of the coming one who represents Yahweh (= "in the name of Yahweh") is the blessing uttered upon him by his people, belonging to Yahweh (= "from the house of Yahweh").

118:26a	"Blessed is	the one coming	in the name of Yahweh;
118:26b	we have blessed	you	from the house of Yahweh."

One can tell that there is a sense of close identification between leader and the led. And, interestingly enough, the picture of the leader "entering through" the gate (–בָא־בָ, *vo'-va–*; 118:19b), and of the righteous "entering through" the same threshold (–בֹאוּ בּ, *bo'u b–*; 118:20b), is reflected in the leader (current/future/Messianic) "coming in" the name of Yahweh (–בָּא בְּ, *ba' b–*; 118:26a), suggesting the equivalence of these depictions: the leader *and* his people are coming victoriously into the presence of their deity![14] At any rate, a cultic sacrifice is called for (118:27b),[15] for "Yahweh is God," the one who has shone upon his people (118:27a). Indeed, the leader echoes this affirmation with a more personal one, "You are *my* God" (118:28a), as he resolves to thank and exalt this deity. Whereas the right hand of Yahweh was "exalted" in his victory (118:16), here it is his leader who "exalts" him (118:28b). The psalm then concludes by repeating its introductory sentence (118:29 = 118:1). God is good . . . all the time!

---

13. Tackmier, "Role of Psalm 118," 247. As for the origin of ὡσαννά, *hosanna*, the Hebrew הוֹשִׁיעָה נָּא was likely rendered in the Aramaic as הוֹשַׁע נָא, *hosha' na*; and, in Greek, without a "sh" sound, the sibilant became an "s." Additionally, the repetition of "indeed/please [נָּא]" in 118:2a, 3a, 4a, 25a, 25b links this plea to the preceding calls to praise.

14. This makes sense for, after all, in Scripture, what is applicable to God's leaders is always applicable to God's people.

15. "As far as we know animals were not tied *to* the altar; the form of expression rather implies an ellipse: 'tie the festal offering with cords [until it comes] up to the horns of the altar'" (Goldingay, *Psalms*, 3:364).

PSALM 118:1-29

Sermon Map

I. Goodness and Grace
   The eternal goodness and lovingkindness of God (118:1–4)
   Move-to-relevance: God's goodness and grace at all times
II. Presence and Power
   God on his people's side in battle (118:5–13)
   Move-to-relevance: God's presence and power in crises
III. Exultation and Exaltation
   God's people rejoicing and thanking (118:14–29)
   Move-to-relevance: The necessity of celebration
IV. *Gratitude for the Grace and Goodness of God*
   Specifics on corporate thanks

PSALM 119:1–176

Psalm of Orientation

God's Servant and God's Word

That Psalm 119 is a Torah-psalm is obvious:[1] it has one of the two instances of תּוֹרַת יְהוָה, *torah yhwh* ("law of Yahweh") in the Psalter (1:2; 119:1), and twenty-five of the thirty-six instances of תּוֹרָה in the psalms.[2] The eight synonyms for God's word found in Psalm 119 are: תּוֹרָה ("law"), עֵדָה, *'edah* ("decree"), פִּקּוּד, *piqqud* ("precept"), חֹק, *choq* ("statute"), מִצְוָה, *mitswah* ("commandment"), מִשְׁפָּט, *mishpat* ("judgment"), דָּבָר, *davar* ("word"), and אִמְרָה, *'imrah* ("utterance").[3] But curiously enough, explicit imperatives to obey the Torah are lacking; instead the psalmist is portrayed as one who obeys the law, a model for readers—not as one who grimly follows a divine diktat, but as one who treasures, loves, longs for, rejoices, and delights in the law.[4] One clearly gets the impression that the psalmist has a committed and abiding relationship with the author of the Torah! That, of course, is not to deny the *implied* emphasis of the psalmist, that his readers are to observe, keep, cleave to, obey, do, and walk in the law, fulfilling its legal requirements, as he himself yearns to do.[5] After all, relationship

---

1. Though the psalm is, overall, one of orientation, individual segments within may be otherwise (as labeled).

2. There are twenty-four instances of "Yahweh," that along with the single instance of *elohim* (119:115), makes for a total of twenty-five references to God—equal to the number of instances of *torah*. The two occur together in the same segment only four times—these sections are symmetric in the entirety of the psalm: in the first (א *Aleph*: 119:1), the seventh (ו *Waw*: 119:41, 44); the sixteenth (ע *Ayin*: 119:126); and the twenty-second (ת *Taw*: 119:174) (Freedman, *Psalm 119*, 34–35).

3. There are few other less specific, and less frequent, terms like "way," "wonders," "discernment," "knowledge," etc. The only verses without a synonym indicating the law of God are 119:3, 37, 90, 122. Two synonyms in a single verse are found in 119:16, 43, 48, 160, 168, 172 (even though "word" occurs twice in 119:42, the first of these instances deals with the "word" of an accuser; however, "word" in the vicinity, in 119:43, 49, does refer to God's "word"). All eight synonyms are found in four segments: 119:57–64 (ח *Cheth*); 119:73–80 (י *Yodh*); 119:81–88 (כ *Kaph*); and 119:129–136 (פ *Pe*). According to Freedman (*Psalm 119*, 35), eighty-eight instances of the synonyms are found in the first half of the psalm (119:1–88) and eighty-nine in the second (119:89–176).

4. See 119:11, 14, 16, 20, 24, 35, 40, 47, 48, 70, 77, 81, 82, 92, 97, 111, 113, 119, 127, 131, 140, 143, 159, 162, 163, 167, 174.

5. See 119:1, 3, 4, 5, 8, 9, 17, 22, 31, 33, 34, 44, 55, 56, 57, 59, 63, 67, 69, 88, 100, 102, 106, 107, 110, 112, 115, 129, 134, 145, 167, 168.

with God mandates responsibility to God.⁶ And, in the end, it is God himself who teaches, instructs, and gives understanding to the psalmist.⁷

Despite the numerous instances of "law" and its synonyms, there is no explicit mention of the specific contents of scriptural instruction. Nor are there any affirmations of Israelite rituals, the covenant, the temple, the Davidic dynasty, Yahweh's work in history, etc. The notion of תּוֹרָה is thus not limited to the Pentateuch, but is broad enough to encompass the universal laws of God that govern the cosmos (119:89–91) and every instruction for how humankind should live in the kingdom of God. That being said, the bulk of the psalm addresses God in the form of petitions of one suffering, praises of one succeeding, and promises of one submitting.⁸

It is quite striking that in Psalm 119, descriptors of God and actions relating to deity are ascribed to the word of God, almost a "theosis" of Scripture: appeal for the word not to be hidden (119:19b; for God, 27:9; 69:17; 102:2; 143:7); setting the word before oneself (119:30b; of God, 16:8); cleaving to the word (119:31a; to God, 63:8); trusting the word (119:42b; trusting God, 4:5; 9:10; 21:7; 22:4–5; 25:2; 26:1; etc.); seeking the word (119:45, 94, 155; seeking God, 9:10; 14:2; 22:26; 24:6; 34:4, 10; etc.); lifting one's hands to the word (119:48; to God, 44:20; 63:4; 88:10; 141:2); waiting/hoping in the word (119:43, 49, 74, 81, 114, 147; upon God, 38:15; 130:5, 7; 147:11); the word as life-giver (119:50; of God, 119:25, 37, 40, 88, 93, 107; etc.); believing in the word (119:66; in God, 106:7–12); loving the word (119:47, 48, 97, 113, 119, 127, 140, 159, 163, 165, 167; loving God, 18:1; 31:23; 97:10; 116:1; 122:6; 145:20); fearing the word (119:120; fearing God, 15:4; 22:23, 25; 25:12, 14; 31:19; etc.); the word as helper (119:175; of God, 10:14; 20:2; 28:7; 30:10; 33:20; 119:86, 173; etc.); and the word as righteous (119:144; of God, 7:9, 11; 11:7; 112:4; 116:5; 119:137; etc.). All that to say, while deification of the word is not at all intended (or corroborated anywhere in Scripture), the association of the word of God with the giver of that word is extremely strong: God's law is God's intention for mankind and to abide by his law is to be loyal to him, to serve him, to walk with him. That is the goal of the psalmist in Psalm 119. And that ought to be the goal of every child of God.

The א *Aleph*-to-ת *Taw* acrostic that Psalm 119 is gives it a sense of exhaustiveness and comprehensiveness. The thrust of each segment is nuanced and differs from those of all the others. However, there is considerable overlap of thrusts that would make the preaching of the psalm in its entirety (or even sequentially by segments) quite redundant. "[The Psalm] looks more like a compendium of things one might say to God at different times than a prayer for someone to pray as a whole at the same time with the same immediacy."⁹ In sum, "Ps 119 uses traditional religious language to construct an acrostic poem with a striking message. The message, which the speaker models throughout the psalm, is that the righteous should internalize Torah to the point that it forms one's character."¹⁰

---

6. For the concept of relationship with God preceding and mandating responsibility to God, see Kuruvilla, *Vision for Preaching*, 123–26. Reynolds, Kent Aaron, *Torah as Teacher*, 58, considers the psalm as comprising "numerous snapshots" of the psalmist as a persona of the model Torah observer, all created for rhetorical purposes, and with a suasive goal.

7. See 119:7, 12, 26, 27, 33, 34, 64, 66, 68, 71, 73, 102, 108, 124, 125, 130, 135, 144, 169, 171.

8. Reynolds, Kent Aaron, *Torah as Teacher*, 70.

9. Goldingay, *Psalms*, 3:380. Notwithstanding the fact that each segment has a specific thrust (pericopal theology) unlike that of any other segment, the broader thematic commonalities and sharing of motifs among the twenty-two segments make Psalm 119 not very suitable for *lectio continua*, segment by segment. I suggest preachers choose a particular segment, or two, that are similar, for a sermon, based on the specific thrust and upon the needs of the flock.

10. Reynolds, Kent Aaron, *Torah as Teacher*, 181.

Theological Focus Of Psalm 119[11]

Those following the law of God, to walk in his ways and keep his commands even when in dire straits, are blessed by divine benevolence and enjoy true life, for their yearning is for the counsel of God's word that they love, fear, and trust, enabling them to thrive with delight, honor, and righteousness, resulting in even more courageous and unceasing commitment to God's word, as they serve God wholeheartedly and unashamedly, and with wisdom beyond that of their peers—all aided by the sovereign grace of a God who is near to his devout.

Psalm 119:1–8 [א ALEPH]

Orientation

Translation

119:1	Blessing [upon] those whose way is blameless,
	the ones who walk in the law of Yahweh.
119:2	Blessing [upon] the ones who observe His decrees;
	they seek Him with all [their] heart.
119:3	Indeed, they have done no unrighteousness;
	in His ways they have walked.
119:4	You—You have commanded Your precepts
	to be kept diligently.
119:5	O that my ways may be established
	to keep Your statutes.
119:6	Then I will not be ashamed
	as I regard all Your commandments.
119:7	I will give thanks to You in uprightness of heart,
	as I learn Your righteous judgments.
119:8	Your statutes I shall keep;
	do not abandon me utterly.

---

11. This is a suggested conflation of the theological foci of all the individual segments of the psalm.

Psalm 119:1–176

Theological Focus

The blessedness of those following the law of God, walking in his way and keeping his commands, motivates God's people to become members of that divinely favored group.

Commentary

The first four verses describe the blessedness of the Torah-keeper in general;[12] the last four address the issue from a personal vantage point. The ones whose "way" is blameless, because they walk in God's ways—"in the law [תּוֹרָה] of Yahweh" (119:1b)—are blessed (119:1a, 3b);[13] the psalmist yearns that his "ways" may be established in such a fashion (119:5). These blessed ones follow God's "command" to "keep" his precepts (119:4a), and the psalmist is not ashamed as he follows all God's "commandments" (119:6)[14] and "keeps" his statutes (119:5b, 8a). The psalmist is confident that divine blessing will be upon on the one who keeps God's precepts "diligently [מְאֹד, *m'od*]" (119:4b); reciprocally, this one will not be abandoned by deity "utterly [מְאֹד]" (or "at all," 119:8b).[15] God's blessings rest upon those who seek him with all their "heart" (119:2); and the psalmist claims to have such a "heart," an upright one (119:7). In sum, 119:1–4 commends the state of those walking in God's law, with the psalmist yearning to be one of those blessed ones (119:5–8)—an appropriate doorway into this exceptional Torah psalm.

Sermon Map[16]

I. Resolution to Keep God's Way (119:5–8)
II. Result of Keeping God's Way (119:1–4)
III. *Commit to the Commandments!*

---

12. The first two verses link the inward attitude of the heart (119:2b) with the walk of blamelessness (119:1–2a)—a matter of integrity. "Behavior without attitude would not be enough; attitude without behavior would not be enough" (Goldingay, *Psalms*, 3:382).

13. The *qatal* verbs of 119:3 are translated with the past tense, but they indicate what happens in general: the ones referred to "do no unrighteousness" and "in His ways they walk"—all the time!

14. Being "ashamed" here likely indicates that sense of guilt for *not* having abided by divine demand.

15. Each of the two halves of the *Aleph* section thus end with the same word.

16. The Sermon Maps in this chapter will uniformly have a bare minimum of moves, usually two (plus one for application). There's nothing magical about this number, but the thrust of the text should be curated in *at least* two moves; of course, there should be one for application. Neither is there anything remarkable about alliterations (except the delight I get out of it them—YMMV!).

Psalm 119:9–16 [ב *BETH*]

Orientation

Translation

119:9   In what [manner] can a young man maintain his path pure?
          By keeping [it] according to Your word.
119:10   With all my heart I have sought You;
          let me not stray from Your commandments.
119:11   In my heart I have treasured Your utterance
          in order that I may not sin against You.
119:12   Blessed are You, Yahweh;
          make me learn Your statutes.
119:13   With my lips I have recounted
          all the judgments of Your mouth.
119:14   In the way of Your decrees I have exulted,
          as [being] over all wealth.
119:15   Upon Your precepts I will muse
          and I will regard Your paths.
119:16   In Your statutes I will be delighted;
          I will not forget Your word.

Theological Focus

The constant and joyful focus upon the word of God, including its recounting and its meditation, is the means by which lives are kept pure, as God, through his word, graciously instructs his people and keeps them from sin.

Commentary

Yahweh is celebrated—and "blessed" (119:12a)[17]—for being the guide of life through his word. The first verse, 119:9, stands separate as a sort of introduction, but all the verses address God directly.[18]

     Purity results from keeping God's law (119:9–11; see below).[19]

---

17. The only other blessing of Yahweh in the second person in the OT is in 1 Chr 29:10 (elsewhere it is in the third person).
18. As also do the rest of the segments of this psalm.
19. Modified from Auffret, *Voyez de vos yeux*, 325.

119:9a	"maintain his path pure"
119:9b	"Your word"
119:10a	"with all my *heart* I have sought …"
119:10b	**"let me not stray"**
119:11aα	"in my *heart* I have treasured …"
119:11aβ	"Your utterance"
119:11b	"that I may not sin against You"

The subsequent blessedness creates joy for the law-keeper (119:14, 16a), further motivating this one to continue in the way of God and be blessed thereby. And may this deity continue to teach him divine "statutes," he prays (119:12b), "statutes" that will be his delight (119:16a). Because one can maintain a pure "path" only by keeping it according to God's "word" (119:9), the psalmist declares that he will focus on those "paths" and not forget God's "word" (119:15b, 16b).[20] It is Yahweh's "utterance" (119:11a) from Yahweh's "mouth" (119:13b), but it is with "my lips" that these divine utterances are "recounted" (119:13a), likely indicating a form of "musing" (119:15a).

The child of God has a responsibility to "keep," "seek," "treasure," "recount," "exult" in, "muse" upon, "regard," "delight" in, and "not forget" God and his word (119:9b, 10a, 11a, 13a, 14a, 15a, 15b, 16a, 16b), but all of that is contingent upon Yahweh "making me learn" his word and, thereby, "not letting me stray" from it (119:10b, 12b). It is only by the grace of God that one can assimilate and act upon God's word. And the desired result is that "I may not sin against You" (119:11b).

Sermon Map

I. Posture towards God's Word (119:9b, 10a, 11a, 13–16)
II. Purity of a Godly Life (119:9a, 10a, 11a, 12)
III. *Ponder Precepts for Purity!*

Psalm 119:17–24 [ג *GIMEL*]

Disorientation

Translation

119:17 Deal [well] with Your servant;
 I will live and I will keep Your word.

---

20. Incidentally, this segment does not employ "law." Also, note that 119:15 and 119:16 are chiastically structured, each following this scheme: synonym for God's word / action of the psalmist // action of the psalmist / synonym for God's word.

> 119:18 Uncover my eyes, and I will regard
> wonderful things from Your law.
> 119:19 A sojourner am I on the earth;
> do not hide from me Your commandments.
> 119:20 My soul has wasted away with longing
> for Your judgments all the time.
> 119:21 You rebuke the arrogant, the ones who are cursed,
> the ones who stray from Your commandments.
> 119:22 Uncover from me reproach and contempt,
> for I observe Your decrees.
> 119:23 Although princes have sat [and] spoken against me,
> Your servant muses on Your statutes.
> 119:24 Even Your decrees are my delight;
> my counselors.

Theological Focus

Even though the people of God may be in dire straits, harassed and oppressed, alienated in the world, their deep desire is for the counsel of God's word, resulting in his benevolence unto them.

Commentary

With the ג *Gimel* segment, the first negative notes in the psalm are sounded and the suffering of the supplicant is in full view. Incidentally, 119:21, 23 also introduce enemies into this psalm for the first time. The psalmist's distressing circumstances include danger to life (119:17b), alienation in the world (119:19a), and the reproach and contempt of high-powered oppressors (119:22–23a). This segment, then, appears to be a lament, in which the psalmist "prays out of a strong sense of religious and moral values and a deep love of Yahweh's revelation, but is conscious of the gap between his faith and his spiritual ambition. His life is threatened and weakened, and he craves that fullness of life which is one of the psalm's heartbeats of desire."[21]

But he still is loyal to God and calls himself "Your servant," beseeching God to "deal [well]" with him (119:17a; perhaps in light of the trials he is facing, 119:21–23). In return he promises to keep God's word (119:17b) and he, "Your servant" (119:23b), does so, meditating on divine statutes, delighting in God's decrees (119:23b–24a). After all, they are "my counselors" (119:24b).

His focus is on the divine "word [דָּבָר, *davar*]" (119:17b) and so, even if rulers have "spoken [דבר, *dvr*]" against him (119:23a), he remains steadfastly committed to God and

---

21. Allen, *Psalms 101–150*, 142.

his word. So much so, even though the psalmist is one without rights and without place in this world, a "sojourner" (119:19a), he desires nothing more than to be intimately related to God's commandments ("do not hide . . . ," 119:19b). Likewise, he pleads with God that deity may "uncover" his eyes that he may learn more of God's law (119:18a);[22] the result would be the "uncovering" (i.e., removal) of the effects of vile words directed against him (119:22a), as his upright life in accordance with God's word puts enemies and opponents to shame, silencing them.

The "arrogant," "the ones who are cursed," and "the ones who stray from *Your commandments*" (119:21) are likely to be the same "princes" pitted against the supplicant (119:23a). But unlike these evildoers, all the psalmist wants to do is follow "Your commandments" (119:19b). Those divine words are his delightful guides to life (119:24b); in fact, the structure of the first half of the psalm literarily depicts the divine word as directing his eyes and his soul/throat:[23]

119:17b	"Your word"	
119:18a		"my eyes"
119:18b	"Your law"	
119:19b	"Your commandments"	
119:20a		"my soul" (נֶפֶשׁ, *nephesh*, also "throat")
119:20b	"Your judgments"	

Sermon Map

I. Lament of Browbeaten People (119:19, 21, 22a, 23a)
II. Loyalty to a Blessing God (119:17–18, 20, 22b, 23b–24)
III. *Be Counseled by Commandments; Be Carried by Commander!*

Psalm 119:25-32 [ד DALETH]

Disorientation

Translation

119:25 My soul cleaves to the dust;
make me live according to Your word.

---

22. The "wonderful things [נִפְלָאוֹת, *niphlaʾot*]" (119:18b) are likely to be an acknowledgment of the exemplary and supreme nature of God's commands, law, judgments, and decrees (rather than referring to acts of God in history, as do its other instances in the Psalter; 107:8, 15, 21, 24, 31; 118:23; etc.; but also see 119:27 that parallels "precepts" with "Your wonderful things"; see on 111:4).

23. Auffret, *Voyez de vos yeux*, 330.

119:26   My ways I recounted, and You answered me;
            make me learn Your statutes.
119:27   The way of Your precepts make me understand,
            so I will muse on Your wonderful things.
119:28   My soul has wept from sorrow;
            establish me according to Your word.
119:29   The way of falsehood turn aside from me,
            and Your law graciously grant me.
119:30   The way of faithfulness I have chosen;
            Your judgments I have placed [before me].
119:31   I have cleaved to Your decrees;
            Yahweh, do not shame me.
119:32   In the way of Your commandments I run,
            for You broaden my heart.

Theological Focus

The enthusiastic choice by the people of God to follow God's ways enables them to thrive with joy, honor, and righteousness, resulting in even more commitment to God's word.

Commentary

The lament that began in the ג *Gimel* segment continues in this one:[24] the life of the supplicant is under threat (119:25), he is sorrowful (119:28a), potentially shamed (119:31b), and wary of deceitful ways (119:29). Whether these distresses are externally sourced is unclear; they might well be describing the tribulations that befall a life lived *apart* from the word of God. So the supplicant promises to turn a new leaf: his soul that once "cleaved" to the dust (119:25a) now only "cleaves" to God's law (119:31a). He abandons the "way of falsehood" (119:29a), adopts the "way of faithfulness" (119:30a), and runs in the "way of Your commandments" (119:32a).[25]

The psalmist is confident: of rescue from death, for God could "make me live according to Your word" (119:25b); of rejoicing when sorrowful, when "established . . . according to Your word" (119:28b); of righteousness "graciously granted" through the law when straying into deceit (119:29b); and of not being ashamed when he "cleaves to Your decrees" (and departs from the sin that shamed him; 119:31a).[26] And with that assurance about, and al-

---

24. The two sections share "live" (119:17b, 25b); "wonderful things" (119:18b, 27b); "my soul" (119:20a, 25a, 28a); and "muse" (119:23b, 27b).

25. Perhaps it is the acrostic constraint that necessitated דֶּרֶךְ, *derek*, "way," being employed at the beginning of five of the eight verses of this section (119:26, 27, 29, 30, 32).

26. The danger of being shamed by God is here likely the consequence of sin.

legiance to, God's word and God's way, the sufferer's "soul" that was "cleaving to the dust" (119:25a) now becomes a "heart" that is "broadened" (119:32b; in the sense of being "relieved," 4:1c; or of attaining liberty, 119:45a).

At any rate, here, too, divine sovereignty is essential: it is deity who "makes me live" (119:25b), "makes me learn" (119:26b),[27] "makes me understand" (119:27a),[28] "establishes me" (119:28b), "turns aside" "the way of falsehood" (119:29a), "graciously grants" the law (119:29b), and "broadens my heart" (119:32b). That being said, there is still a need for human responsibility: "I will muse" (119:27b), "I have chosen" (119:30a), "I have cleaved" (119:31a), and "I run" (119:32a). "Usually we simply walk in the way . . . of Yhwh's commands . . . [119:1b]; running in the way of them is another way of suggesting not mere compliance with Yhwh's expectations but living by them enthusiastically and energetically."[29]

Sermon Map

I. Languishing: Leaving God's Word (119:25a, 26a, 28a, 29a, 31b)
II. Flourishing: Cleaving to God's Word (119:25b, 26b, 27, 28b, 29b–31a, 32)
III. *Flourish, Don't Languish!*

Psalm 119:33–40 [ה HE]

Orientation

Translation

119:33 Instruct me, Yahweh, [in] the way of Your statutes,
and I shall observe it to the end.
119:34 Make me understand, that I may observe Your law,
and keep it with all [my] heart.
119:35 Make me tread the path of Your commandments,
for in it I take pleasure.
119:36 Incline my heart to Your decrees
and not to illicit gain.
119:37 Make my eyes turn away from looking at worthlessness;
in Your ways make me live.

---

27. An "answer" from God (119:26a) is usually deity's response to a cry for help (e.g., 102:2; 108:6; 119:145; etc.); one should probably take "my ways I recounted" (119:26a) to cohere with that sense—it is a recital of the woes of the supplicant, the impious and dolorous "ways" of the sufferer, a confession.

28. The parallel between "Your precepts" and "Your wonderful things" in 119:27 makes the latter point to God's word (and not to God's acts), as also in 119:18b. And, remarkably, the "understanding" of divine precepts leads to "musing" on the marvels of Scriptures (119:27): a circular (spiral?) process: comprehension leading to contemplation, that leads to further comprehension and more contemplation . . . .

29. Goldingay, *Psalms*, 3:396.

119:38   Establish Your utterance to Your servant,
            which is for the fearing of You.
119:39   Make my reproach, which I dread, turn away,
            for Your judgments are good.
119:40   Behold, I long for Your precepts;
            in Your righteousness make me live.

Theological Focus

The sovereign grace of God enables the people of God to exercise their responsibility to walk wholeheartedly in his ways, resulting in joy in God and fear of God—true life, indeed—rather than to succumb to the worthlessness of sin, resulting in divine reproach.

Commentary

Every line in this ה *He* segment (except for 119:40) begins with a *hiphil* imperative, no doubt acceding to the demands of an acrostic. But that does produce the unique effect of a petition-heavy stanza; and since the imperatives are addressed to Yahweh, the segment has a strong emphasis on Yahweh as instructor (119:33a), explainer (119:34a), guide (119:35a), prompter (119:36a), director (119:37a), commander (119:38a), and protector (119:39a).[30] With the repeat of the root דרך, *drk*, the emphasis is on seeking God's help to keep the psalmist on the "way" of God: "instruct me [in] the *way* [דֶּרֶךְ] of Your statutes" (119:33a); "make me *tread* [דָּרַךְ, *darak*] the path of Your commandments" (119:35a), "in Your *ways* [דְּרָכֶיךָ] make me live" (119:37b). The intertwining of דרך and "heart" are enlightening:

119:33a	"way"	
119:34b		"heart"
119:35a	"tread"	
119:36a		"heart"
119:37b	"ways"	

That is to say, may God work in my "heart"—"make me . . . keep it [Your law] with all [my] heart" (119:34b) and "incline my *heart* to Your decrees" (119:36a)—that one may walk in his way, "observing" God's law "to the end" (119:33b, 34a). That involves God's aid in "making my eyes *turn away*" from sin (119:37a), the result of which will be that the supplicant's "reproach"

---

30. In addition to these seven *hiphil* imperatives at the commencement of verses, there are two identical *piel* imperatives in 119:37b, 40b, "make me live"—making a total of nine imperatives in this ה *He* segment of Psalm 119.

(likely from God, the result of "Your judgments" against sin, 119:39b) will also "turn away" (119:39a). No rambling off the way of God means no reproach from the wrath of God. The "fear" of God (119:38b) inculcated by God's word is a reverential awe, which is not at all incompatible with "pleasure" generated by the word of God (119:35b). On the other hand, what is to be "dreaded" is divine reproach for sin (119:39a):[31]

119:37	"turn away"; "make me live"
119:38	"which is for the fearing of You"
119:39aα	"which I dread"
119:39aβ, 40b	"turn away"; "make me live"

Again, as in the earlier ג *Gimel* segment, here also there is an interplay of divine sovereignty in the imperatives addressed to God. As well, there is human responsibility in "observing" and "keeping" God's law (119:33b, 34b). And thus, God "makes [the psalmist] live" (119:37b, 40b), in divine righteousness (119:40b), with "pleasure" (119:35b) and "longing" for God's word (119:40a), for the "fearing" of God (119:38b)—a life lived with God!

Sermon Map

I. Divine Sovereignty (119:33a, 34aα, 35a, 36a, 37, 38a, 39, 40b)
II. Human Responsibility (119:33b, 34aβb, 36b, 38b, 40a)
III. *Look to Law for Life!*

Psalm 119:41–48 [ו *WAW*]

Orientation

Translation

119:41 May Your lovingkindnesses also come to me, Yahweh,
    Your deliverance according to Your utterance,
119:42 so I may answer the one who reproaches me with a word,
    for I trust in Your word.
119:43 And do not utterly take away from my mouth the word of truth,
    for I have waited on Your judgments.
119:44 And I keep Your law continually,
    forever and always.
119:45 And I will walk about in a broad place,
    for Your precepts I seek.

---

31. Mensah, *I Turned Back My Feet*, 134.

119:46   And I will also speak of Your decrees before kings,
         and I will not be ashamed.
119:47   And I will delight in Your commandments,
         which I have loved.
119:48   So I will lift my hands to Your commandments, which I have loved;
         and I will muse on Your statutes.

Theological Focus

The courageous people of God, committed to obeying God's law unceasingly, and expecting the operations of his grace in their lives and of his deliverance from their foes, are unashamed to speak of God's word, even before the highest and mightiest, for this word they intensely love, trust, and keep.

Commentary

The ו *Waw* segment emphasizes the public testimony of the psalmist to God (and God's gracious enabling of that to happen).[32] He beseeches God for his lovingkindness and deliverance (119:41), so that he may answer harassers with a "word [דָּבָר, *davar*]" (119:42a). The parallel statement that the supplicant trusts in God's "word [דְּבָרְ]" (119:42b) indicates that the "word" of answer to a calumniator is from the "word" of God. Earnestly awaiting the law of God—specifically, divine justice ("judgments," 119:43b), perhaps against enemies oppressing him—he asks that the truthful "word [דְּבַר]" not be withheld from his own mouth (119:43a). It will be the divine word that he "speaks [דבר, *dvr*]" of, even in the presence of nobility; and that he will do, he declares, without any shame (119:46a). And why not? He is "walking about in a broad place," untrammeled, unrestricted, unconstrained by any force of evil, for he seeks God's precepts (119:45a). This is the expected courage of one who "keeps Your law *continually, forever* and *always*" (119:44)—the stress on the never-ending nature of the psalmist's commitment is unmistakable and remarkable. And this bold testifier delights in God's "commandments, which I have loved" and will lift his hands to those "commandments, which I have loved," even meditating on them, no doubt unceasingly as well (119:47b, 48a).

Sermon Map

I. Commitment to Word (119:42b, 43b, 44, 45b, 47–48)
II. Courage to Witness (119:41, 42a, 43a, 45a, 46)
III. *Witness to the Word!*

---

32. Except for 119:41, all the other verses commence with words that have an א, ʾ, following the expected initial ו, *w*.

Psalm 119:49-56 [ז ZAYIN]

Disorientation

Translation

119:49   Remember the word to Your servant,
             by which You have made me hope.
119:50   This is my comfort in my affliction,
             that Your utterance has made me live.
119:51   The arrogant have utterly derided me;
             from Your law I have not deviated.
119:52   I have remembered Your judgments
             from forever, Yahweh, and I find comfort.
119:53   Rage—it has seized me because of the wicked,
             the ones abandoning Your law.
119:54   Your statutes have been to me songs
             in the house of my sojourning.
119:55   I have remembered Your name in the night, Yahweh,
             and I keep Your law.
119:56   This has become [a practice] for me,
             that Your precepts I have observed.

Theological Focus

Acknowledging that God's word is a source of hope and comfort and, indeed, of life, the people of God seek to make the remembrance and the keeping of God's law a paramount practice of their lives, in contrast to the wicked who have abandoned God's law.

Commentary

The ז *Zayin* segment appears to be set in a context of "affliction" (119:50a), but the psalmist focuses on the "comfort" of, and "hope" in, God's word that gave him life amidst that distress (119:49b–50a): it has "made me live" (119:50b). Asking God to "remember" his word (119:49a) indicates the supplicant's appeal to deity not to forget his promises therein of divine presence that generate "comfort" and "hope" and "life" (119:49b–50). The psalmist, in turn, has "remembered" forever God's judgments (119:52a). These are likely to be statements of ultimate divine justice against the "wicked" (119:53a), those derisive "arrogant" ones who vilify him for his commitment to God's word (119:51a); these judgments, too, have given him "comfort" (119:52b)—vindicated at last!

God's word is a delight to the psalmist, "songs in the house of my sojourning," alleviating the woe of his alienated existence (119:54). But he is angered at the wicked for their "abandoning Your law" (119:53b), and that draws a sharp contrast with his own "keeping Your law" (119:55b).[33] He concludes by declaring that he has "remembered" the name of Yahweh (i.e., divine presence) in the night (119:55a), and that the keeping of the law is the preeminent praxis of his life (119:56). The intricate layout in 119:50–56[34] of the synonyms for the word of God and for the commitment of the psalmist to it depicts the absolute fealty of supplicant to divine discourse:[35]

119:50	"this [זֹאת, zo't]"; "that [כִּי, kī]"; "Your utterance"	
119:51bα	**"Your law"**	
119:51bβ		"I have not deviated"
119:52aα		"I have remembered"
119:52aβ	**"Your judgments"**	
119:53b	**"Your law"**	
119:54a	**"Your statutes"**	
119:55a		"I have remembered"
119:55bα		"I keep"
119:55bβ	**"Your law"**	
119:56	"this [זֹאת]"; "that [כִּי]"; "Your precepts"	

Sermon Map

I. Comfort from the Law (119:49–50a, 52b, 54–55a)

II. Commitment for Life (119:50b, 51–52a; 53, 55b–56)

III. *Zone of Comfort from the Zeal of Commitment!*

Psalm 119:57–64 [ח CHETH]

Disorientation

Translation

119:57 My portion is Yahweh;

I have said I would keep Your words.

---

33. Even the psalmist's "rage" (119:53a) shows the depth of his commitment to God's word!

34. Notice the juxtaposition of two chiastic structures (119:51–55), encompassed by parallel opening and closing statements (119:50, 56).

35. Modified from Auffret, *Voyez de vos yeux*, 348.

119:58 I have appeased Your face with all [my] heart;
    be gracious to me according to Your utterance.
119:59 I have considered my ways,
    and I turned my feet to Your decrees.
119:60 I hastened, and I did not delay
    to keep Your commandments.
119:61 The ropes of the wicked, they have encircled me;
    Your law I have not forgotten.
119:62 [In] the middle of the night I rise to give thanks to You
    because of Your righteous judgments.
119:63 A companion I am, of all those who fear You,
    and of those who keep Your precepts.
119:64 Your lovingkindness, Yahweh, fills the earth;
    Your statutes—make me learn [them].

Theological Focus

For the people of God, God is all they need, and they, as a company of God fearers, assiduously, expeditiously, wholeheartedly, and gratefully keep his word—despite opposition from the wicked—seeking to learn even more of God's grace and his word.

Commentary

Every line in this segment begins with a different word, providing an unusual variety, and the whole set is bounded by "Yahweh" (119:57a, 64a; these are the only two instances of the name in this segment).

The "wicked" are continuing to give the psalmist trouble (119:61a). In the midst of this tribulation, the psalmist wants nothing more than Yahweh, his "portion," lot, and very possession (119:57a). And obtaining that blessing from God, in response he promises that all he wants to do is "keep" God's words (119:57b), "keep" God's commandments (119:60b), and "keep" God's precepts (119:63b)—and that with haste and fervor (119:60a). He has pledged ("said [אמר, *'mr*]") to obey (119:57b); and doing so, he has "appeased Your face" with his heart (i.e., sought and won God's favor; 119:58a). Would that God reciprocate with grace according to his divine "utterance [אִמְרָה]" (119:58b).[36] So this alignment with divine demand is with both "heart" (119:58a) and "feet" (119:59b): the entirety of the supplicant is dedicated for this purpose.[37]

---

36. I.e., that God would speak words of grace to him, verbally extending his lovingkindness.
37. Mensah, *I Turned Back My Feet*, 155.

119:57b	"keep Your words"
119:58a	"heart"
119:59aα	"I have considered"
119:59aβ	"my ways"
119:59bα	"I turned"
119:59bβ	"feet"
119:60b	"keep Your commandments"

Even though the ropes of the wicked have snared him, he does not forget the law of God (119:61), rising even in the middle of the night to praise God for the gift of Scripture (119:62). Thus he can claim to be a member of the group comprising "all those who fear You," and of "those who keep Your precepts" (119:63), in contrast with the "wicked" who do neither (119:61a). Though the lovingkindness of Yahweh fills the earth, not many are keen on learning about it or assimilating his word (119:64a), so the supplicant concludes with his personal desire to be an ongoing student whose consumption and comprehension of the law of God may be empowered by God's grace (119:64b).

Sermon Map

I. God's Person, Our Apportionment (119:57a, 58a, 62a, 63a, 64a)
II. God's Precepts, Our Aspiration (119:57b, 58b–61, 62b, 63b, 64b)
III. *All We Need; All We Do!*

Psalm 119:65–72 [ט *TETH*]

Disorientation

Translation

119:65 Good You have done with Your servant,
    Yahweh, according to Your word.
119:66 Good discernment and knowledge—do make me learn,
    for on Your commandments I have believed.
119:67 Before I became afflicted I went astray,
    but now Your utterance I have kept.
119:68 Good You are, and the One doing good;
    make me learn Your statutes.
119:69 The arrogant have smeared falsehood against me;
    I—with all [my] heart—I observe Your precepts.

119:70 Their heart is insensitive with fat;
   I—in Your law, I have taken delight.
119:71 Good for me [it was], that I was afflicted,
   in order that I might learn Your statutes.
119:72 Good for me is the law of Your mouth,
   more [so] than thousands of gold and silver [pieces].

Theological Focus

The goodness of God, his deeds, his law, and even his divinely ordained affliction—that corrects the straying of the people of God—help them assimilate his word with greater delight, and practice it with greater enthusiasm, in contrast to the arrogant wicked who are insensitive to divine utterance.

Commentary

The goodness of God (and of his word) takes center stage in the ט *Teth* segment (and bounds it: 119:65a, 72a), perhaps constrained by acrostic needs ("good," טוֹב, *tov*, occurs five times).[38] This "goodness" is centered upon God's person, "the one doing *good*" (119:68a; see below), but "good" also describes God's deeds (119:65a), God's law, specifically its "discernment" and "knowledge," i.e., its wisdom for life (119:66a), and its immense value to the supplicant (119:72a). Even divinely ordained "affliction," sovereignly brought about, and prior to which the psalmist was straying (119:67a), is deemed "good" (119:71a): for with affliction comes course correction.[39]

119:65	"**good**": God's doing (its beneficence)	
119:66		"**good**": God's law (its wisdom)
		"make me *learn ... Your commandments*"
119:68		"**good**": God's person, "the one doing **good**" (his essence)
		"make me *learn Your statutes*"
119:71		"**good**": God's affliction (its correction)
		"that I might *learn Your statutes*"
119:72	"**good**": God's law (its worth)	

---

38. Six, if you count the verb יטב, *ytv*, "do good," in 119:68aβ; the others are nouns.

39. Whether the affliction continued or not is unclear; that it was ongoing is suggested by 119:69–70. Thus far in the Psalter, "straying" (שׁגה, *shgh*; 119:10, 21) was a reprehensible action, a deviation from God's commandments. The word here in 119:67a, however, is שׁגג, *shgg*, that "suggests accidental straying." So this "straying" of the supplicant was not entirely a sinful act, though it displaced him from the straight-and-narrow (Goldingay, *Psalms*, 3:407).

The resounding refrain in the center regarding learning God's law (119:66a, 68b, 71b) underscores the importance of such comprehension to the recognition and experience of God's goodness. Only with the knowledge of the word of God comes an intimate relationship with the goodness of God (no doubt via obedience to the word of God).

The affliction takes a couple more verses to describe, making a contrast between the behavior of oppressors and that of the psalmist in those days of trauma (119:69a vs. 69b; 119:70a vs. 70b). Facing the wiles of deceit from arrogant aggressors, the "heart" of the supplicant is still focused on God's word (119:69b), whereas the "heart" of opposers are laden with fat and impermeable to the word of God in which the psalmist takes great delight (119:70). The emphatic lines in 119:69b, 70b, each with a redundant first-person singular pronoun ("I—. . . I observe . . ."; and "I—. . . I have taken delight"), make the case for the psalmist's total commitment to divine law.

Sermon Map

I. Goodness of God: His Work (119:65a, 67a, 68a, 71a)
II. Goodness of God: His Word (119:65b, 66b, 67b–70, 71b–72)
III. *Perceive the Good; Practice the Good!*

Psalm 119:73–80 [י YOD]

Disorientation

Translation

119:73 Your hands made me, and they founded me;
    make me understand, that I might learn Your commandments.
119:74 May those who fear You see me and be joyful,
    for I have waited on Your word.
119:75 I know, Yahweh, that Your judgments are righteous,
    and in faithfulness You have afflicted me.
119:76 O may Your lovingkindness become my comfort,
    according to Your utterance to Your servant.
119:77 May Your compassion come to me that I may live,
    for Your law is my delight.
119:78 May the arrogant be ashamed, for with falsehood they have subverted me;
    I—I muse on Your precepts.
119:79 May they turn to me—those who fear You
    and those knowing Your decrees.
119:80 May my heart be blameless in Your statutes,
    in order that I will not be ashamed.

PSALM 119:1–176

Theological Focus

The people of God, created by him to follow his will, abide in and await his word with delight, so that even in seasons of distress, God's grace and mercy comfort and revive them, resulting in their honor, to the joy and encouragement of fellow God-fearers, while non-God-fearers gain only dishonor.

Commentary

The י *Yod* segment commences with a reference to creation: God it was who made the psalmist, therefore would that he continue his creative work and bring it to consummation by making the supplicant understand and learn (and obey) God's commandments (119:73). Only the Creator's aid can help him accomplish this goal, as God graciously guides his people to align their lives to his demand. This commitment to God's word—"I have waited on Your word" (119:74b)—is cause for encouragement to the community, "those who fear You," perhaps motivating them also to adhere to divine law with joy (119:74a). This notion of 119:73–74 is also echoed in 119:79–80: may that same group of "those who fear You" renew their kinship and community with the supplicant (119:79), recognizing him as one who, like them, is a God-fearer, blameless in the keeping of divine statutes (119:80).

What it means to "learn Your commandments" (119:73b), "wait on Your word" (119:74b), "know Your decrees" (119:79b), and "be blameless in Your statutes" (119:80a) is explained in 119:75–78. At least in this segment, such a cognition of the divine word involves "knowing" that God's judgments are righteous (119:75a), and therefore trusting God's sovereignty and faithfulness as one is led through affliction, even if the reasons for such distress are inscrutable (119:75b).[40] And the supplicant prays that, in the midst of such crises, divine lovingkindness would comfort him, as God had promised (119:76), and that divine compassion would revive him because of his delight in the law of God (119:77a). Only such trust in God's grace and mercy—comprehended through God's word and grounded in a commitment to God's word—would help the supplicant survive the predicament he was in.

On the other hand, the supplicant asks that the arrogant (the agents of his distress, ostensibly) would be "ashamed" before God as a result of all their deceitful workings (119:78a): these are the ones who care not for God's word, in stark contrast to the psalmist who meditates on God's precepts (note the extra first-person singular pronoun in 119:78b: "I—I muse . . ."); it is he who will end up "not being ashamed" (119:80b).

Sermon Map

I. Created for Abiding (119:73, 74b, 79b, 80)
II. Comforted in Adversity (119:75–78)
III. Cheered for Allegiance (119:74a, 79a)
IV. *Strengthen the Saints by Sticking to the Statutes When Suffering!*

---

40. These verses appear to be hinting at some sort of crisis, perhaps of divine discipline, though there is no suggestion of sin or disobedience on the supplicant's part.

Psalm 119:81–88 [כ *KAPH*]

Disorientation

Translation

119:81 My soul has been destroyed [while longing] for Your deliverance;
        on Your word I have waited.

119:82 My eyes have become destroyed [while longing] for Your utterance,
        as I say, "When will You comfort me?"

119:83 Though I have become like a wineskin [dried] in smoke,
        Your statutes I do not forget.

119:84 How many are the days of Your servant?
        When will You make a judgment on those pursuing me?

119:85 The arrogant have dug pits for me—
        [those] who are not in accordance with Your law.

119:86 All Your commandments are faithful,
        [but] with falsehood they have pursued me—help me.

119:87 They almost destroyed me on earth,
        but I—I have not abandoned Your precepts.

119:88 According to Your lovingkindness make me live,
        so that I may keep the decree of Your mouth.

Theological Focus

In desperate straits from enemy attack, even to the point of death, the people of God, convinced of the faithfulness of his word, remain committed to it, even as they beseech him for his gracious deliverance.

Commentary

The כ *Kaph* segment, 119:81–88, is dominated by the distress of the supplicant, with despair dripping from every verse. This is "by far the most desperate" of the segments, and "recalls most vividly the passionate laments of earlier psalmody."[41] It appears that the psalmist is near death, with his very existence under threat (119:81a, 82–83a, 84–85, 86b–87a), to a great extent due to the operations of aggressors (119:85, 86b). The "destroying" of his soul and the "destroying" of his eyes, as he longs for deliverance and for the divine utterance (119:81a, 82a), may be priming the reader to the "destroying" of the psalmist's being that is being executed by his enemies

---

41. Soll, *Psalm 119*, 100.

(119:87a). So the supplicant asks God "how many [מָה, *mah*]" his days would be (119:84a), seeing that he is almost dying, and "when [מָתַי, *matay*]" he might be comforted (119:82b), and "when [מָתַי]" his pursuing enemies would get their recompense (119:84b). Longing for God's "utterance [אִמְרָה]," the psalmist "says [אמר, *'mr*]" that he needs solace (119:82).[42]

119:83b	"Your statutes I do not forget"
119:84a	"how many are the days of Your servant?"
119:84bα	"when will You make a judgment …?"
119:84bβ–85a	"those *pursuing* me;" "dug pits for me"
119:86a	**"all Your commandments are faithful"**
119:86bα	"with falsehood they have *pursued* me"
119:86bβ	"help me"
119:87a	"they almost destroyed me on earth"
119:87b	"I have not abandoned Your precepts"

In the literary and textual center of all of this—and no doubt, in the middle of such an afflicted life as well—God's word remains faithful (119:86a). So, despite distresses, doubts, and desperation, the sufferer remains loyal to the word of God (119:81b, 83b, 87b): the enemies might be destroyers, "but I—I have not abandoned Your precepts" (119:87b, with an emphatic repeat of the first-person singular pronoun). Indeed, the psalmist argues in 119:86 that since God's commandments are "faithful" in their promises of a serene life, it is incongruous that the foes are pursuing him "with falsehood" (119:86b). So, would God help him out of this predicament, the supplicant pleads. Here, the characteristics of God's word and the psalmist's foes are diametrically opposed: "faithful" precepts vs. "falsehood" purveyors (119:86). The psalmist concludes with a reference to divine lovingkindness and a request that he might be revived (119:88) in order that he may continue to be faithful to the word of God (119:88b).

Sermon Map

I. Adversity from the Wicked (119:81a, 82–83a, 84–85, 86b, 87a)
II. Inflexibility for the Word (119:81b, 83b, 86a, 87b–88)
III. *Determination Even in Destruction.*

---

42. Figure is modified from Auffret, *Voyez de vos yeux*, 363.

Psalm 119:89–96 [ל LAMED]

Orientation

Translation

119:89 Forever, Yahweh,
    Your word stands in the heavens.
119:90 To generation after generation is Your faithfulness;
    You established the earth, and it stands.
119:91 By Your ordinances they have stood this day,
    for all things are Your servants.
119:92 Had Your law not been my delight,
    then I would have perished in my affliction.
119:93 Forever I will not forget Your precepts,
    for by them You have made me live.
119:94 I am Yours, deliver me;
    for Your precepts I have sought.
119:95 For me the wicked have hoped, to cause me to perish;
    Your decrees I [consider with] understand[ing].
119:96 I have seen a limit to all perfection;
    exceedingly broad is Your commandment.

Theological Focus

In contrast with humanity that perishes, particularly under affliction, God's word—and by it, God's world—is permanent, and therefore the people of God commit themselves to it, finding in it deliverance and life.

Commentary

While the ל *Lamed* segment continues to deal with dangerous opposition from the wicked (119:92b, 95a), the unique notion here is the contrast between what "stands" and what "perishes."[43] God's word "stands" (119:89b) and God's cosmos "stands" (119:90b). In fact, it is by "Your ordinances" that the universe has "stood" until now (119:91a): the steadfast word of

---

43. This ל *Lamed* segment appears to be the turning point of the psalm: "Before it came the most desperate strophe, [כ] *Kaph*; now, after it, comes the [מ] *Mem* strophe, the most ebullient" (Soll, *Psalm 119*, 103).

God makes everything stable. After all, "all things are Your servants" (119:91b), whether time or space or anything therein:[44]

119:89a	"forever"	TIME
119:89b	"heavens"	SPACE
119:90a	"generation after generation"	TIME
119:90b	"earth"	SPACE
119:91a	"day"	TIME
119:91b	**"all things are Your servants"**	

On the other hand, what is in danger of "perishing" is humanity under threat from the wicked who lie in wait for the righteous, causing them to "perish" in affliction (119:95a; also 119:92b). But the people of God, the psalmist is implying, can avoid that fate if they cleave to the agent of steadfastness, God, and his instrument of steadfastness, his word (119:92a, 93–94): Scripture, the psalmist declares again in 119:96b, is "exceedingly broad," i.e., limitless in space, and presumably timeless in standing, in contrast to all (humanly derived) "perfection" that is restricted in space and time (119:96a). Therefore, "forever" will the psalmist cling to God's word, the source of life (119:93a), because "forever" is God's word established steadfastly throughout creation (119:89a). Both the consolidating nature of God's word and the committed nature of God's servant are demonstrated in the structure of the whole ל *Lamed* segment:[45]

119:89	"forever ... Your word"
119:91b	"*all* things"
119:92a	**"Your law ... my delight"**
119:92b	"I would have *perished*"
119:93aα	**"I will not forget"**
119:93aβ	"Your precepts"
119:93bα	"for"
119:93bβ	"You have made me live"
119:94aα	**"I am Yours"**
119:94aβ	"deliver me"
119:94bα	"for"
119:94bβ	"Your precepts"
119:94bγ	**"I have sought"**
119:95a	"cause me to *perish*"
119:95b	**"Your decrees I [consider with] understand[ing]"**
119:96a	"*all* perfection"
119:96b	"exceedingly broad ... Your commandment"

---

44. Mensah, *I Turned Back My Feet*, 193.
45. Modified from Auffret, *Voyez de vos yeux*, 368–69; and Auffret, *Mais tu élargiras mon cœur*, 33.

Sermon Map

I. Permanent: God's Word, God's World (119:89–91, 96)
II. Perishing: Humanity's Walk (119:92b, 95a)
III. *Persist with the Perennial!* (119:92a, 93–94)

Psalm 119:97–104 [מ MEM]

Orientation

Translation

119:97 How I have loved Your law;
    all the day it is my musing.
119:98 More than my enemies, I am made wiser by Your commandments,
    for forever it is mine.
119:99 More than all who make me learn, I have insight,
    for Your decrees are my musing.
119:100 More than the aged, I gain understanding,
    for Your precepts I have observed.
119:101 From every evil path I have withheld my feet,
    in order that I may keep Your word.
119:102 From Your judgments I have not turned aside,
    for You—You have instructed me.
119:103 How smooth to my palate is Your utterance,
    more than honey [is] to my mouth.
119:104 From Your precepts I gain understanding;
    therefore I hate every path of falsehood.

Theological Focus

Insight imparted by God's word, that becomes the incessant focus of, and illimitable sweetness to, the people of God, leads them to avoid paths of evil and to adopt ways of righteousness, thus making them wiser than everyone else.

Commentary

As was noted earlier, after the doleful and distressful כ *Kaph* segment, the מ *Mem* segment is serene and (literally) sweet (119:103)! It has no petitions or signs of distress, only assertions: four of its verses begin with "more than/from" (employing the prefixed form of the preposition מִן, 119:98a, 100a, 102a, 104a), and two begin with "more than all/from every [מִכָּל, *mikal*]" (119:99a, 101a).[46] Two verses, 119:97a, 103a, commence with the interrogative particle מָה, *mah*, "how." The segment is also uniquely bookended by "love" (of God's law, 119:97a) and "hate" (of ways of falsehood, 119:104b).

"Yahweh is acclaimed as wisdom teacher via his Torah. [Psalm 119:102b] makes clear that it is not do-it-yourself manual which God has handed over to man to use as best as he can. It is the written part of a lifelong teach-in."[47] In other words the word of God inscripturated (once in history) has to be accompanied by the wisdom of God instructing (constantly in life), no doubt by means of the very Spirit that inspired Scripture.

The first half of this segment extols God's law and the resulting understanding when one dwells in it (119:97–100).[48] The psalmist has loved it and made it his "musing" all the day (119:97b, 99b). Indeed, he has made God's law his own ("forever it is *mine*," 119:98b; and "*my* musing," 119:97b, 99b),[49] assertions made all the more emphatic by the structure of 119:98–99:[50]

119:98
"More than ..."
"I am made wiser"
"Your commandments"
"it is mine [לִי, *li*]"

119:99
"More than ..."
"I have insight"
"Your decrees"
"my [לִי] musing"

Therefore, the one abiding in God's word is wiser than his enemies (119:98a), wiser than his teachers (119:99a), and wiser than the aged (119:100a). Needless to add, this meditation is to be integrated with praxis: "Your precepts I have observed" (119:100b).

---

46. That is, no doubt, another acrostic constraint. In that same vein, מִן, *min*, shows up seven times in eight verses.

47. Allen, *Psalms 101–150*, 143.

48. This Torah-dwelling (i.e., "loving," "musing," and "possessing" it; 119:97, 98b, 99b) also implies alignment thereunto, in the form of obedience (i.e., "observing" God's law; 119:100b, 101a). Yes, doing does improve knowing (119:100) and feeling (119:97a, 103, 104b). Neuroscience and behavioral psychology research confirm that actions do affect cognition and emotion.

49. The assertions in 119:97b, 98b employ the third-person feminine singular pronoun, הִיא, *hi'*, "it," to reflect the feminine "law" and "commandments"; in 119:98b "it" stands for the plural "commandments" considered as a singular unity.

50. From Auffret, *Mais tu élargiras mon cœur*, 35.

The rest of the מ *Mem* segment takes off on 119:100b, detailing what this practice of observing God's word looks like. Subjectively, the smoothness and sweetness of God's law to the psalmist is noted (119:103). No doubt, this is an affective consequence of the Torah-keeper's commitment to the law, his withholding his feet from "every evil path," as he hates "every path of falsehood" (119:101a, 104b) and does "not turn aside" from God's judgments (119:102a).

All of these undertakings are governed by divine demand that shows up in every verse. The keeping of God's word then clearly involves rational elements (119:97b, 98a, 99a, 100a, 104a), emotional elements (119:97a, 103, 104b), and volitional elements (119:101, 102).

119:101a	"From every evil *path* I have withheld my feet"
119:102b	"You—You have instructed me"
119:103aα	"to [לְ, /] my palate"
119:103aβ	"Your utterance"
119:103bα	"honey"
119:103bβ	"to [לְ] my mouth"
119:104a	"I gain understanding"
119:104b	"I hate every *path* of falsehood"

All of these allude to the metaphor of a walk, a way of life, a conduct that has become more than praxis, even a passion, as this eminent student and observer of God's word is constantly instructed by God himself: "You—You have instructed me" (119:102b), made all the more emphatic with its redundant pronoun (119:102b). Thus cognition, via God, the wisdom teacher, produces emotion, and leads to (or should lead to) action which further affects cognition and emotion, producing more action . . . .

Sermon Map

I. Word of God: God's Wisdom, Our Wisdom (119:97–99a)
II. Walk of God's People: God's Holiness, Our Holiness (119:99b–104)
III. *Walk in the Wisdom of the Word!*

Psalm 119:105-112 [נ *NUN*]

Orientation

Translation

119:105 A lamp to my feet is Your word,
    and a light to my pathway.
119:106 I have sworn—and I establish it—
    to keep Your righteous judgments.

119:107 I have become utterly afflicted;
>   Yahweh, make me live according to Your word.
119:108 The freewill offerings of my mouth, please accept, Yahweh,
>   and Your judgments, do make me learn.
119:109 My life is in my palm continually,
>   but Your law I have not forgotten.
119:110 The wicked have set a trap for me,
>   yet from Your precepts I have not wandered away.
119:111 I have inherited Your decrees forever,
>   for they are the joy of my heart.
119:112 I have inclined my heart to do Your statutes,
>   forever, to the end.

Theological Focus

The people of God may go through distresses that put their lives at risk, but they are, nevertheless, intensely committed to keeping God's word, their portion and their joy, forever.

Commentary

Psalm 119:105–112 esteems the Torah (119:105–106, 108, 111–112) but, in a return to the world of dangers, toils, and snares, it also rehearses complaints in between (119:107, 109–110). It is characterized by the mention of several body parts, together telling the "story" of the נ *Nun* segment: "Feet" follow the word that lights the way (119:105a), and "mouth" praises God for his law (119:108a), but life is carried on a "palm"—i.e., exposed and risk-prone (119:109a; as in 1 Sam 19:5; 28:21). Yet when all is said and done, the "heart" is joyful and that "heart" is inclined to obey the will of God (Ps 119:111b, 112a). That, in a nutshell, is the focus of this segment.

The commitment of the psalmist to God's word, that lights his feet and illumines his path (119:105), is laudable. In fact, he takes an oath to emphasize his allegiance to deity's law (119:106). The reason for that swearing here is probably related to his state of being "utterly afflicted" (119:107a). A request to God for the alleviation of "utter" affliction is bolstered by evidence of the supplicant's total commitment to Scripture: he promises that not even trials and tribulation will make him turn away from God's word. He is confident that this "word" which is a beacon of light in the darkness of pain (119:105a)—this selfsame "word" will enable him through those crises and, by God's grace, will "make [him] live" (119:107b). And so he engages in praise, "the freewill offerings" of his mouth, again beseeching God to help him learn divine "judgments" (119:108b).[51] One cannot but notice how, in the first half of

---

51. Likely the expected divine justice against enemies that would relieve his woes.

the segment (119:105-108), affliction is bounded and kept in check on either side by "Your word" and "Your . . . judgments":

119:105a	"Your word"
119:106b	"Your ... judgments"
119:107a	**"utterly afflicted"**
119:107b	"Your word"
119:108b	"Your judgments"

The second half, 119:109-112, continues the same theme, expanding on the "utter affliction" of 119:107a: the sufferer's life is at risk and the wicked are hunting him (119:109a, 110a). But he is confident: God's law he has not forgotten and God's precepts he has not neglected (119:109b, 110b): that commitment to God would stand him in good stead. Indeed, God's law is his "inheritance," his allotment, his portion, and the "joy of my heart"—there is nothing better for him in this life (119:111). So this joy-filled "heart" (109:111b) is inclined to obey from the "heart" (109:112a),[52] not once, not a few times, but "forever, to the end" (109:112b).

119:111a	"Your decrees *forever*"
119:111b	"they are the joy of my *heart*"
119:112a	"I have inclined my *heart*"
119:112b	"Your statutes *forever*"

Would that that were true for all God's people, everywhere . . . forever!

Sermon Map

I. Distresses of the World (119:107a, 109a, 110a)

II. Devotion to the Word (119:105–106, 107b, 108, 109b, 110b, 111–112)

III. *Thank for the Truth Even in Trials!*

---

52. While in 119:36a, it was Yahweh who was expected to "incline my heart" to his decrees, here it is the psalmist himself resolving to "incline my [i.e., his own] heart" to God's statutes. Both are necessary—divine sovereignty and human responsibility.

Psalm 119:113–120 [ס *SAMEKH*]

Disorientation

Translation

119:113 The ones divided [in loyalty] I have hated,
    but Your law I have loved.
119:114 My hiding place and my shield You are;
    on Your word I wait.
119:115 Turn aside from me, evil ones,
    that I may observe the commandments of my God.
119:116 Sustain me according to Your utterance, so that I will live;
    and let me not be ashamed of my hope.
119:117 Uphold me so that I will be delivered,
    that I may have regard for Your statutes continually.
119:118 You have rejected all those who stray from Your statutes,
    for their falsehood is deceitfulness.
119:119 [Like] dross You have made disappear all the wicked of the earth;
    therefore I have loved Your decrees.
119:120 My flesh trembles from terror of You,
    and Your judgments I fear.

Theological Focus

Commitment to God's word involves a love for it and a fear of it—and a simultaneous hatred of those not inclined towards it thus—recognizing God as the sustainer of the lives of those committed to his word, and the spoiler of the lives of those circumventing it.

Commentary

The ס *Samekh* segment is marked by contrasts between the psalmist's commitment to God's word (119:113b, 114b, 115b, 116a, 117b, 119b, 120b)[53] and his deprecation of evildoers for their circumventing of God's word (119:113a, 115a,[54] 118–119a).

---

53. As was noted in the introduction to Psalm 119, the attitude demonstrated towards the word of God—here fear (119:120)—is also manifested towards the person of God (15:4; 22:23, 25; etc.). This equivalence is a striking characteristic of this Torah-composition.

54. Psalm 119:115 is the only place in the song that the psalmist's opponents are addressed directly.

The first verse avers that God's word is "loved" (119:113b; also 119:119b); the last verse, that God's word is "feared" (119:120b). That is not a contradiction: God, himself, is to be both loved and feared.[55] In other words, both the notion of love (which essentially indicates commitment, loyalty, and fidelity)[56] and that of fear point to the devotion of the supplicant to the law of God and to God himself—the terms are not essentially different.[57]

This is the antithesis of the stance of the wicked toward God's law: those nefarious ones are divided in loyalty, not wholeheartedly and singularly committed to God, and are therefore "hated" by the psalmist, who "loves" the law of God (119:113); these are explicitly labeled "evil ones" and turning aside from these baleful corrupters enables one to observe God's commands (119:115a);[58] they are the maleficent who "stray from Your statutes" and operate in deceitful treachery towards others (119:118a). Their fate is sure (119:119a), but the psalmist is confident of a rosier future for himself, the one who "has regard for Your statutes continually" (119:117b) and who "loves Your decrees" (119:119b). Indeed, the supplicant is in reverential awe of God and of his word (119:120). God is to him a "hiding place" and "shield," upon whose word he waits (119:114a), confident that he will be "sustained" and "upheld" by God, and ultimately, that he will be delivered without shame, unlike those straying from Scripture who are rejected by God (119:116–117). The love of God's word (119:113b, 119b) is directly linked to the supplicant's being sustained and upheld (119:116a, 117a):[59]

119:113b	"I have loved"
119:116a	"sustain me … so that I will live"
119:117a	"uphold me so that I will be delivered"
119:119b	"I have loved"

May the people of God, who love and fear God, also love and fear the word of God!

Sermon Map

I. Committed towards God's Word (119:113b–114, 115b–117, 120)
II. Circumvention of God's Word (119:113a, 115a, 118–119a)
III. *Commit, not Circumvent!*

---

55. Deuteronomy 6:2 and 13 command fear, while the Shema calls for love (6:5); both elements are found in 10:12 and 13:3–4. Also see 10:20 with 11:1; as well as Pss 31:19, 23; and 145:19–20.

56. See Levenson, *Love of God*, for an extensive treatise on this notion.

57. One may also see them as almost synonymous, as also does the narrative of Gen 22:1–19 (22:2, 12). See Kuruvilla, "*Aqedah*," 489–508.

58. Perhaps it is the temptation to compromise that is hinted at here, or the direct intervention of the wicked in the psalmist's attempts to be aligned to divine demand.

59. Girard, *Les Psaumes Redécouverts*, 248.

Psalm 119:121-128 [ע AYIN]

Disorientation

Translation

119:121 I have done justice and righteousness;
    do not leave me to my oppressors.
119:122 Stand surety for Your servant for good;
    let not the arrogant oppress me.
119:123 My eyes, they have become destroyed[, longing] for Your deliverance,
    and for the utterance of Your righteousness.
119:124 Do with Your servant according to Your lovingkindness,
    and make me learn Your statutes.
119:125 Your servant I am; make me understand,
    that I may know Your decrees.
119:126 It is time for Yahweh to act:
    they have broken Your law.
119:127 Therefore I love Your commandments
    more than gold, even more than refined gold.
119:128 Therefore all [Your] precepts, concerning all [things], I esteem as upright;
    all the path[s] of falsehood I hate.

Theological Focus

When oppressed by the wicked, the people of God focus on doing God's law, confident that God, in turn, will do lovingkindness, while doing justice to the wicked who break God's law—all of which cause God's people to commit further to God's word, being instructed in it by his grace.

Commentary

The ע *Ayin* segment appears to be returning to a lament of sorts: the psalmist has encountered enemies and pleads with God not to leave him to those "oppressors" (119:121b), or to let those arrogant wicked "oppress" him (119:122b). In fact, while waiting for God's "deliverance" from this crisis, the supplicant's eyes have been destroyed with longing (119:123a). His ground for this plea for rescue is that he has "done [עשׂה, 'sh] justice and *righteousness*" himself, i.e., he has walked with God (119:121a), and he therefore expects a reciprocal utterance of "righteousness" from God (119:123b)[60] and a reciprocal "doing [עשה]," i.e., dealing, with him in divine lovingkindness (119:124a). These hint that a mutual relationship exists between them, obliging God to stand surety and be responsible for the supplicant "for good" (119:122a): a divine guarantee and warranty that good will be done to the psalmist.

But the supplicant goes further, boldly stating that "it is time for Yahweh to act [עשה]" against those evildoers who, in contrast to the sufferer, have broken God's law (119:126a). Thus the three "doings/acts" are, respectively, that of the psalmist unto Yahweh (119:121a), of Yahweh unto the psalmist (119:124a), and of Yahweh unto the wicked oppressors (119:126a). These "doings" and "acts" of supplicant and deity scaffold the ע *Ayin* segment, supported by an interstitium—interwoven reminders to God that he, the psalmist, is "Your servant" (119:122a, 124a, 125aα):[61]

119:121a	"I have done [עשה]"	Psalmist to Yahweh
119:121b	"do not leave me to my oppressors"	
119:122a	"Your servant"	
119:122b	"let not the arrogant oppress me"	
119:124a	"do [עשה]"; "Your servant"	Yahweh to Psalmist
119:124b	"make me learn Your statutes"	
119:125aα	"Your servant"	
119:125aβ–b	"make me understand … Your decrees"	
119:126a	"act [עשה]"	Yahweh to Wicked

With another contrast between "love" and "hate," the psalmist concludes: he intensely "loves" and values God's law (119:127), far more than wealth, esteeming "all [Your] precepts, concerning all [things]" as upright (119:128a); but hating the ways of falsity (119:128b). In furtherance of the divine word and its praxis, God himself instructs this loyal vassal (119:124b, 125), for without that gracious divine illumination, alignment to divine demand is impossible.

Sermon Map

I. Righteous Doing unto God (119:121a, 122aβ, 123, 125, 127–128)
II. God Doing unto Righteous (119:121b–122aα, 122b, 124)
III. God Doing unto Wicked (119:121b, 122b, 126)
IV. *Doing, Doing, Done!*

---

60. Likely God's righteous words declaring the liberation of the supplicant, since "deliverance" is paralleled with "utterance of Your righteousness" (119:123).

61. Modified from Auffret, *Voyez de vos yeux*, 386.

Psalm 119:129–136 [פ *PE*]

Orientation

Translation

119:129 Wonderful are Your decrees,
    therefore my soul has observed them.
119:130 The disclosure of Your words gives light,
    making the simple understand.
119:131 My mouth I opened wide and I panted,
    for I longed for Your commandments.
119:132 Turn [Your face] to me and be gracious to me,
    in accordance with Your judgment for those loving Your name.
119:133 Establish my steps in Your utterance,
    and let not any iniquity gain mastery over me.
119:134 Redeem me from human oppression,
    that I may keep Your precepts.
119:135 Your face—make it shine upon Your servant,
    and make me learn Your statutes.
119:136 Streams of water have gone down [from] my eyes,
    because they do not keep Your law.

Theological Focus

God's people yearn to abide in God's ineffable and enlightening word, and this keeping of God's law, in loving allegiance to him, results in divine favor and grace that enables them to apply Scripture even more, and with such an intensity of commitment that it grieves them that some do not abide in God's word.

Commentary

Oppression continues to be in the background here in 119:129–136 (see 119:134), and it grieves the psalmist that these wicked do not keep God's law (119:136). But the emphasis in this segment is on the wonders of God's enlightening word that motivates the supplicant to abide in it with the yearning of one dying of thirst (119:129–131).[62] Because he loves God's name (i.e., God's person), he expects God's favor and grace, commensurate with his promises

---

62. God's word as containing "wonderful things" was seen in 119:18, 27 (as participles; as a noun here in 119:129a).

("in accordance with Your judgment," 119:132).⁶³ This divine favor and grace includes the ongoing and increasing establishment of the psalmist's steps in God's word (119:133a): God's law and its application is to be the master of one's life, not iniquity (119:133b).

Yet there is evil operating through the agency of others, and often directed towards the people of God; therefore God's favor and grace also involves redemption from "human oppression" (119:134). The purpose of such liberation, too, is more obedience and enhanced keeping of God's law (119:134b)—freed from evil masters to serve the good Master. Emphasizing this again is 119:135, returning to an appeal for divine favor, which is once more said to involve instruction of the supplicant in the statutes of God. It all seems circular, and rightly so: the people of God abide in God's word; God's favor is upon them (the "shining" of God's face, 119:135a); they learn God's word and abide in it even more (for the word gives "light," 119:130a). Thus, the potential cascade of favor upon favor from God is enabled, that leads to even more instruction and, thereby, even more application of divine law; and so on. So committed is the psalmist to God's law that he is grieved by those who "do not keep" it (119:136b; and presumably these non-compliant ones are the human oppressors of 119:134), in contrast to the loyal individual who "keeps" God's precepts (119:134b).

Sermon Map

I. Fidelity to Scripture 1 (119:129–131); Favor of God 1 (119:132)
II. Fidelity to Scripture 2 (119:133–134); Favor of God 2 (119:135a)
III. Fidelity to Scripture 3 (119:135b–136); . . .
IV. *Coast on the Cycle!*

Psalm 119:137–144 [צ TSADE]

Orientation

Translation

119:137 Righteous are You, Yahweh,
      and upright Your judgments.
119:138 You have commanded Your decrees in righteousness
      and exceeding faithfulness.
119:139 My zeal has consumed me,
      for my adversaries have forgotten Your words.

---

63. There is no contradiction here between the appeal for God's graciousness and its basis, the psalmist's love for God (and his word). Grace is not being earned here in a contractual manner. Yes, the psalmist has been loyal to God, and that invites God's blessing, but God's response (and the magnitude of his blessing) to the loyal one is entirely of his grace—incalculable, unconditional, non-enforceable, providential, and sovereign. Perhaps the most we can say is that God's grace (like all of his other blessings, including his love) is unconditional, but the experience thereof is not (see John 14:21; Jude 21; etc.).

119:140 Your utterance is very refined,
    and Your servant loves it.
119:141 Small I am and despised;
    Your precepts I have not forgotten.
119:142 Your righteousness is righteousness forever,
    and Your law truth.
119:143 Distress and trouble have reached me,
    [yet] Your commandments are my delight.
119:144 Righteous are Your decrees forever;
    make me understand that I may live.

Theological Focus

The devotion of God's people to his righteous word leads them to never forget God's law but to delight in it zealously, even when despised and in distress, for only by God's word may one truly live, enabled by God's grace.

Commentary

Constrained by the acrostic, the צ *Tsade* segment echoes with "righteous" and "righteousness": God is "righteous" (119:137a), his word he has proffered in his "righteousness" (119:138a), which "righteousness is righteousness forever" (119:142a); finally, God's Scripture is itself "righteous" and also "forever" (119:144a).

Extolling God's law is an integral part of 119:137–144, for its "uprightness," "refined" nature, "truth[fulness]," the "delight" it is, and for its standing "forever" (119:137b, 140a, 142b, 143b, 144a). In fact, this segment opens with a celebration of Yahweh and his word—the "righteousness" of his person and the "uprightness" of his word (119:137). It ends with another celebration of Yahweh's word—the "righteousness" of his "decrees" (119:144a). Clearly the two are linked: God and his law—both are "righteous" (119:137a, 144a). And God demonstrates "exceeding [מְאֹד, *mʾod*]" faithfulness in his giving of the law (119:138b), and the psalmist confesses that God's utterance is "very [מְאֹד]" refined (119:140a). Thus both God and his word are extolled.[64]

Since deity and his word are seemingly being considered equivalent, how could anyone disregard Scripture? But that is exactly what the adversaries have done (119:139b), while the psalmist so burns with zeal for God's word that he is consumed by it (119:139a). These opponents may neglect God's words, but the refined, divine utterance is "loved" by the devout one,

---

64. As has already been noted, such a tendency to equate the word of God to the person of God is not new to this segment; the entire psalm considers the law a personified substitute for the divine giver thereof. Also characteristic of the צ *Tsade* segment are the doublets: "righteous . . . and upright" (119:137); "righteousness and . . . faithfulness" (119:138); "small . . . and despised" (119:141a); "righteousness" (×2) and "truth" (119:142); and "distress and trouble" (119:143a).

"Your servant" (119:140b). No, this one may not be a reputed noble or a big-shot—in fact, he confesses he is "small" and "despised" (119:141a)—but that is immaterial: unlike the adversaries who have "forgotten" God's words (119:139b), this self-abnegating supplicant declares he has not "forgotten" God's precepts (119:141b). And that is all that matters, because God's righteousness is forever, and his law is "truth," ostensibly also forever (119:142a). Those Scripture-denying "adversaries [צָר, tsar]" (119:139b) may cause "distress [צַר]" and "trouble" (119:143a), but that does not worry the supplicant, for whom God's commands are his "delight" (119:143b).

The segment closes with a reiteration of the everlasting nature of God's righteous decrees and an appeal to God to instruct him in them, that he might live an abundant life. In sum, the psalmist is committed to God and his word; and this allegiance is structurally depicted:[65]

119:137–138	"righteous," "righteousness" "You have commanded"; "Your decrees"
119:139bα	"my adversaries have forgotten"
119:139bβ	"Your words"
119:140	**"Your utterance is very refined"** **"Your servant loves it"**
119:141bα	"Your precepts"
119:141bβ	"I have not forgotten"
119:142–144	"righteousness" (×2); "righteous" "Your commandments"; "Your decrees"

Sermon Map

I. Deity Exalted (119:137a, 138, 142a)

II. Decrees Extolled (119:137b, 140a, 142b, 144a)

III. Devotion Exercised (119:139, 140b, 141, 143)

IV. *Devotion to Deity's Decree!*

Psalm 119:145–152 [ק QOPH]

Disorientation

Translation

119:145 I have called with all [my] heart; answer me, Yahweh;
  Your statutes I will observe.
119:146 I have called to You; deliver me;
  and I will keep Your decrees.

---

65. Girard, *Les Psaumes Redécouverts*, 270.

119:147 I have been [up] early before dawn and I cried for help;
>   on Your word I have waited.
119:148 My eyes have been [up] early, [in] the night watches,
>   to muse on Your utterance.
119:149 Hear my voice according to Your lovingkindness;
>   Yahweh, according to Your judgments, make me live.
119:150 They draw near, those pursuing plots;
>   from Your law, they are far.
119:151 Near are You, Yahweh,
>   and all Your commandments are truth.
119:152 [From] early on I have known, from Your decrees,
>   that forever You have appointed them.

Theological Focus

God's people, often in distress, appeal incessantly to God for aid and deliverance, as they continue to keep God's word, confident of the nearness of God to those demonstrating long-lasting loyalty to his law, unlike evildoers who are distant from deity and his demands.

Commentary

This segment, 119:145–152, commences with an address to Yahweh ("call," in 119:145a, 146a; and "cry for help," in 119:147a) that is more direct than in other segments. It continues for the first five verses, appealing for his aid: "answer me" (119:145a); "deliver me" (119:146a); "hear my voice" (119:149a); and "make me live" (119:149b).[66] Thus the ק Qoph segment is, overall, a lament. It is "with all [my] heart" that Yahweh is called upon (119:145a), for deliverance (119:146a). The psalmist has been pleading for aid "before dawn" (119:147a) and, indeed, even earlier, in "the night watches" (119:148a)—i.e., he has not been sleeping at all. And in each of the first four verses his calling upon God is paralleled to a response to God's word. Both the response and the labeling of God's word are different in each of these four lines: observing his statutes (119:145b), keeping his decrees (119:146b), awaiting his word (119:147b), and musing upon his utterance (119:148b).[67] These responses to divine law are the grounds for Yahweh hearing the call of the supplicant, the bases for why Yahweh ought

---

66. Besides, there is also the unique phenomenon of pairs of verses commencing with the same verb in the Hebrew: 119:145 and 146 (קרא, qr', "call"); 119:147 and 148 (קדם, qdm, "be [up] early"); and 119:150 and 151 (קרב, qrb, "near"; noun and adjective, respectively). The last verse, 119:152, begins with a noun form of the initial verb of 119:147, 148, קֶדֶם, qedem, "early." That makes 119:145 and 146 begin with קְרָ-, qr–, 119:147 and 148 with קְדָ-, qd–, 119:150 and 151 reverting to קְרָ-, and 119:152 closing with קְרָ.

67. Besides, the first lines, 119:145a, 146a, 147a, commence with a first-person verb and offer additional information (two add imperatives directed to Yahweh, 119:145a, 146a). Carefully constructed, indeed!

to render aid in this time of crisis. He should, because the psalmist has been loyal to God and his word, and God is loyal to his devout.

The first four verses of the psalm emphasize, in one way or another, the psalmist's entreaty to God: both 119:145, 146 begin with the call for help; 119:148 begins with the dramatic rendering of the psalmist's insomnia, as he cries for aid—his "eyes" have been [up] early. "My eyes" is עֵינַי, 'enay (119:148a), an obvious wordplay with עֲנֵנִי, 'aneni, "answer me" (119:145a). And 119:147 is chiastically structured, poignantly centering upon the appeal for aid:[68]

"I have been [up] early	piel perfect first-person singular
before dawn	preposition + noun
and I cried for help;	ו (w) + piel imperfect first-person singular
on Your word	preposition + noun
I have waited."	piel perfect first-person singular

Also note that "I will keep" in 119:146b is אֶשְׁמְרָה, 'eshmrah, and "night watches" in 119:148 is אַשְׁמֻרוֹת, 'ashmurot. Even at nighttime, the psalmist's thoughts are pervaded by God's word and the keeping thereof![69]

The next four verses reiterate the psalmist's appeal to God to hear him and enable him to live, according to promises of justice in God's word (119:149). This is followed by a keen sense of divine presence in the hour of crisis (119:150–151): the supplicant's opponents draw "near" to their prey, but they are "far" from God's law (119:150). In stark contrast, Yahweh is "near" to the psalmist, the one who considers God's law to be truth (119:151a).

The second half of the ק Qoph segment then concludes in 119:152 with a statement of the supplicant's commitment to God's eternal word, reinforcing the grounds for seeking God's help—his loyalty to deity's law, "[from] early on."[70] Thus, not only has the psalmist been calling upon God "early" (119:147a; to muse on God's words, 119:148b), he has been faithful to God's eternal law from "early on" (119:152a) i.e., from his former days. It is God and his word, all day long, all life long!

Sermon Map

I. Constant Call upon God (119:145a, 146a, 147a, 148a, 149)

II. Continual Compliance to God's Word (119:145b, 146b, 147b, 148b, 152)

III. Comforting Closeness of God (119:150–151)

IV. *Call, Comply, and Be Close!*

---

68. From Mensah, *I Turned Back My Feet*, 244.

69. As well, there is אֶצֹּרָה, 'etstsorah, "I will observe," in 119:145b, and אֲשַׁוֵּעָה, 'ashawwe'ah, "I cried for help," 119:147a.

70. And thus, further contrasting the neglect thereof by evildoers (119:150b). "I have known, from Your decrees" (119:152a) is מֵעֵדֹתֶיךָ יָדַעְתִּי, me'edoteka yada'tti, a neatly assonant phrase, with three consonants ע ד, and ת (', d, and t) echoing in both words.

Psalm 119:153-160 [ר *RESH*]

Disorientation

Translation

119:153 See my affliction and rescue me,
    for Your law I have not forgotten.
119:154 Dispute my dispute and redeem me;
    with Your utterance make me live.
119:155 Far from the wicked is Your deliverance,
    for Your statutes they have not sought.
119:156 Your mercies are many, Yahweh;
    according to Your judgments make me live.
119:157 Many are my pursuers and my adversaries,
    [yet] from Your decrees I have not deviated.
119:158 I see the traitors and I loathe [them]
    who did not keep Your utterance.
119:159 See how I have loved Your precepts;
    Yahweh, according to Your lovingkindness, make me live.
119:160 The sum of Your word is truth,
    and forever is every judgment of Your righteousness.

Theological Focus

Even as distressing adversities abound, the people of God seek his deliverance, confident that he, in his lovingkindness and as the divine judge, will hear their pleas, for they, unlike their wicked oppressors, have unremittingly sought, loved, and abided by God's truthful, righteous, and eternal word.

Commentary

The first two verses of the ר *Resh* segment have five entreaties: "see," "rescue," "dispute," "redeem," and "make me live" (119:153-154); the last is repeated twice more, in 119:156b, 159b, so the psalmist's life appears to be at stake. Notably, it is on the grounds of both God's "utterance"/"judgments" (i.e., God's word: 119:154b, 156b) and God's "lovingkindness" (i.e., God's person/attributes: 119:159b) that the supplicant requests God to revive him. But the rest of the segment is composed of assured affirmations of the psalmist about his adherence to God's word (119:153b, 157b, 159a) or decisive deprecations of the wicked who do *not* do so (119:155, 158), concluding with a summary assertion of the truthfulness and eternality of God's righteous law (119:160).

God's mercies are "many" (119:156a), but so are the opponents—"many" (119:157a). But this distressed individual "sees" the wicked and loathes them, the ones who did not abide by God's word (119:158a). Therefore, he implores Yahweh to "see" his distress (119:153a; and his commitment to Scripture, 119:159a) and rescue him. The contrasts are pungent: the wicked "have not sought" God's law (119:155b), but the psalmist has "not deviated" from it (119:157b); the supplicant "loathes" evildoers (119:158a) and "loves" God's word (119:159a). Surely God will heed his plea and "redeem" him (119:154a).[71] As for the evildoers: "far from the wicked is Your deliverance" (119:155a)!

Sermon Map

I. Adversity from the Lawless (119:153a, 154a, 157a, 158a)
II. Adherence to the Law (119:153b, 155, 157b, 158b, 159a)
III. Appeal to the Law-Giver (119:153, 154, 156, 159b–160)
IV. Adherence + Appeal in Adversity = Aid!

Psalm 119:161–168 [שׁ SHIN]

Disorientation

Translation

119:161 Princes, they pursue me without cause,
   but at Your words my heart is awed.
119:162 I [am] one exulting at Your utterance
   as one finding great spoil.
119:163 Falsehood I hate and I loathe;
   Your law I have loved.
119:164 Seven times a day I have praised You
   for the judgments of Your righteousness.
119:165 Great peace [is] to those loving Your law,
   and there is nothing that can make them stumble.
119:166 I have hoped for Your deliverance, Yahweh,
   and I do Your commandments.
119:167 My soul has kept Your decrees,
   and I love them exceedingly.

---

71. This involves God "disputing my dispute" (119:154a), i.e., "pleading my cause." That is symbolic, of course: the divine advocate is also the divine judge and can dispose of the opposition summarily.

119:168 I have kept Your precepts and Your decrees,
      for all my ways are before You.

Theological Focus

The love of God's word, that awes, rejoices, and comforts God's people, motivates their praise of deity and their hope for his deliverance from adversity into peace abundant, as they continue to abide unshakably in God's law in all their ways.

Commentary

While the "pursuit" of the psalmist by the powerful persists in the שׁ *Shin* segment (119:161a), there is a great deal more confidence here than in previous iterations of distress. Yes, this undeserved oppression ("without cause," 119:161a) is enough to cause dread, but "at Your words my heart is awed" (119:161b).[72] In fact, one's experience of the comfort of God's word is like that of discovering "great spoil," cause for "exulting" (119:162). Note the chiastic structuring of 119:161b–162a, emphasizing simultaneous awe and joy at God's word:

"at Your words"	*preposition + noun (second-person singular suffix)*
"my heart is awed"	*verb (finite) + noun (first-person singular suffix)*
"I [am] one exulting"	*verb (participle) + pronoun (first-person singular)*
"at Your utterance"	*preposition + noun (second-person singular suffix)*

What the psalmist "loves"—God's law—is contrasted in 119:163 with what he "hates" and "loathes"—all false, i.e., lawless, undertakings. Enamored of God's word (and the suppliant's "love" of God's law is mentioned again in 119:165a, 167b, the last an "exceeding" love), the psalmist cannot but praise God for it, and often: "seven times" (i.e., "umpteen" times; 119:164a). The result is *"great* peace" for "those loving Your law" (119:165a)—after all, they have found *"great* spoil" (119:162b), and so they are steadfast and "nothing . . . can make them stumble" (119:165b), not even their pursuit by the mighty in the land (119:161a). The final three verses reaffirm the supplicant's hope of deliverance from the current adversity (119:166a) and reiterate his faithfulness to God's words (119:166b–168a). But, of course, God knows that, for "all my ways are before You" (119:168). The people of God can be confident that all their life is before him, and therefore "exultation" is their heartfelt response (119:162a) and "great peace" their blessed lot (119:165a).

---

72. That פחד, *pchd* ("awe") is often used of actual fear (31:11; 53:5; 64:1) and is employed in parallel with ירא, *yr'*, "fear" (27:1; 119:120) demonstrates a deliberate poetic connection between 119:161a and 161b, with פחד serving double duty—indicating both the "dread" of pursuers and the "awe" of God's word.

Sermon Map

I. Commitment to God's Law (119:161, 163–164, 167–168)
II. Comfort of God's Law (119:162, 165, 166)
III. *Persistence in Precepts Brings Peace!*

Psalm 119:169-176 [ת *TAW*]

Disorientation

Translation

119:169 May my lament come near to Your face, Yahweh;
    according to Your word, make me understand.
119:170 May my supplication [for grace] come before Your face;
    according to Your utterance, rescue me.
119:171 May my lips pour forth praise,
    for You make me learn Your statutes.
119:172 May my tongue sing of Your utterance,
    for all Your commandments are righteous.
119:173 May Your hand become my help,
    for Your precepts I have chosen.
119:174 I long for Your deliverance, Yahweh,
    and Your law is my delight.
119:175 May my soul live that it may praise You,
    and may Your judgments help me.
119:176 I have wandered away like a sheep that has become lost;
    seek Your servant,
    for Your commandments I have not forgotten.

Theological Focus

The deliverance by God of his lost sheep motivates his praise by the people of God, his flock, who choose to live life God's way, by God's word, delighting and finding succor in it.

Commentary

This grand Torah psalm concludes with the ת *Taw* segment bringing together a final "lament" and "supplication [for grace]" (119:169a, 170a), not to mention "praise" (119:171a).[73] Twice in the first half of this segment, the poet entreats God for understanding and that he may learn the divine word (119:169b, 171b). In the first case, the "understanding" sought may have to do with the circumstances of the lament; perhaps the psalmist wanted a greater comprehension of God's promises in his word regarding the distresses and agonies of the human condition (119:169b). In the second, he is seeking to praise deity for enabling him to learn God's will (119:171).

The last four verses seek Yahweh's help for the supplicant (119:173a, 174a, 175a, 175b, 176b) who has abided by God's word (119:173b, 174b, 176c). In fact, it is only with the deliverance of the psalmist that more praise to God will ensue (119:175); that appears to be an attempt to motivate God to respond positively. The divine "utterance" that is the basis for the supplicant's "rescue" (119:170b) is the "utterance" that his tongue will sing of (119:172a)—likely the promises of deliverance. The lips that pour forth "praise" (119:171a) will continue to "praise" God for the reviving of his soul (119:175a).[74]

And it will be, in the final estimate, God's law that helps him (119:175b), the one who tends to wander away "like a sheep that has become lost" but nevertheless remains "Your servant" (119:176ab). The poignancy of this final self-description and plea, and the assertion of allegiance to God's word, expresses itself in the only definite tricolon of the entire psalm (119:176). Yes, God's word will keep the psalmist from straying; and may it do so for all of God's people.

This is a rather surprising ending for this monumental psalm, sounding a rather somber and sorrowful tone, as well as a confession of the wandering and lost sheep (119:176a). Perhaps it emphasizes the tendencies of the human condition, beset by sin since the fall, to be "prone to wander." And, Lord, we feel it! But we still remain his "servants" and we can trust God's shepherdly instincts to "seek" us, his servants (119:176b).

Sermon Map

I. Serving the Shepherd (119:169b, 171b, 172b, 173b, 174b, 175b, 176c)
II. Searching for Sheep (119:169a, 170, 173a, 174a, 176ab)
III. Saluting the Savior (119:171a, 172a, 175a)
IV. *Saved Sheep, Sing and Serve the Shepherd!*

In sum, "the psalm comprises a manual of moral and religious spirituality. Life is a walk along a way, path, or track. What counts is not (for instance) the development of our thinking, our self-understanding, our prayer life, or our profession, but our walk. But the whole

---

73. There is no obvious external threat to the psalmist in this lament; it is likely a drawing together of various similar strands of plaints from the entirety of the psalm. Also, a series of parallelisms, taking up two verses at a time, makes up the *Taw* section: 119:169 = 119:170; 119:171 = 119:172; 119:173 = 119:174; and 119:175 = 119:176.

74. Note that while it is Yahweh ("Your hand") that "helps" the psalmist in 119:173a, it is God's law that "helps" him in 119:175b, returning to the oft-sounded motif in this psalm equating deity with his word.

person is involved in this walk, heart or spirit and mouth or lips, as well as feet."[75] It is a walk guided entirely by Yahweh's instruction through his law, his word, his demands. Thus, for one in relationship to this God (the particular focus in Psalm 119 is an intense, intimate, and *personal* relationship of the individual and deity),[76] there is a responsibility to abide in the divine will. In the power of the Holy Spirit, we will!

---

75. Goldingay, *Psalms*, 3:443.
76. There are only a few scattered references to community in the composition.

PSALM 120:1–7

Psalm of Disorientation

Life Among Enemies

THE NEXT FIFTEEN PSALMS (Psalms 120–134) are commonly labeled the "Song of Ascents," perhaps because of the references to Jerusalem and Zion (at a geographic elevation): 122:3, 6; 125:1, 2; 126:1; 128:5; 129:5; 132:13; 133:3; 134:3.[1] Prinsloo shows convincingly how a movement may be traced, a narrative ascent so to speak, from Psalm 120–134.[2] Others think the designation reflects the very structure of the psalms in the collection, for every member has a linguistic "step" movement, repetitions that occur between certain verses or within a single one, generating an ascent of sorts, some repetitions even forming *inclusios*.[3]

 1. These psalms also have quasi-liturgical formulas: 121:2; 124:8; 125:5; 128:6; 130:7; 131:3.

 2. Prinsloo narrates the "story" of the Songs of the Ascents thus: The Songs begin in desperate straits with the protagonist living among wicked people (Psalm 120). He cries for help and begins his move to a new destination, trusting Yahweh (Psalm 121). He arrives in Jerusalem/Zion and finds peace (Psalm 122). But the tale isn't told yet: he and his compatriots are still ridiculed and condemned, so they appeal to God for grace (Psalm 123). And had it not been for the grace of God, they would have been in big trouble (Psalm 124). But they, who trusted God, were protected by him, just as the mountains barricaded Jerusalem (Psalm 125). Now God is restoring them, and they are awaiting the consummation of his restoration (Psalm 126). The blessing of Yahweh and his peace is upon them (Psalm 128). Between these two psalms, Psalms 126 and 128, "forming the protective 'arms' around the small individual performing his mundane tasks of sowing and reaping, building a house and raising a family," is Psalm 127. The protection of the righteous God destroys the yoke of the wicked (Psalm 129). But now it is the sinfulness of humankind, their own failures, that sinks them into depths that only God can extricate them from, forgiving, remitting, and redeeming (Psalm 130). And that brings the psalmist to rest, in the arms of a tender God, content and satisfied (Psalm 131). Now on to worship. A commitment to worship by the people of God relates them to God intimately (Psalm 132). This commitment, manifested in unified worship, further enables blessing (Psalm 133). And then they live happily forever in the presence of God, continually engaged in his worship (Psalm 134). What a story—"an ascent into the arms of YHWH"! (See Prinsloo, Gert T. M., "Role of Space," 472–73; and this commentary on the other psalms in this series of Ascent Songs).

 3. These "step" repetitions in these psalms are: "deceitful tongue" (120:2, 3); "abide/abode" (120:5, 6); "peace" (120:6, 7); "my soul" (*inclusio*; 120:2, 6); "my help" (121:1, 2); "not slumber" (121:3, 4); "the one who keeps" (121:4, 5); "He will keep" (121:7 [×2], 8); "come/coming" (*inclusio*; 121:1, 8); "Jerusalem" (122:2, 3); "there" (122:4, 5); "thrones" (122:5a, 5b); "peace" (122:6, 7, 8); "for the sake of" (122:8, 9); "house of Yahweh" (*inclusio*; 122:1, 9); "eyes" (123:1, 2 [×3]); "is/be gracious" (123:2, 3 [×2]); "greatly [. . .] filled . . . contempt" (123:3, 4); "were it not Yahweh who was for us" (124:1, 2); "then" (124:3, 4, 5); "waters" (124:4, 5); "soul" (124:4, 5, 7); "gone over" (124:4, 5); "snare" (124:7a, 7b), "escaped" (124:7a, 7b); "Yahweh" (125:1, 2); "surround" (125;2a, 2b); "the righteous" (125:3b, 3c); "great things Yahweh has done" (126:2, 3); "joyful exclamation" (126:2, 5, 6); "if" (127:1a, 1c); "worthless[ness]" (127:1b, 1d, 2); "keep[ing]" (127:1c, 1d); "sons"

Translation

120:1 To Yahweh—in the distress I was in—
      I called, and He answered me.
120:2 Yahweh, rescue my soul from the false lip,
      from the deceitful tongue.
120:3 What will He give to you, and what will He add to you,
      deceitful tongue?
120:4 Arrows of the warrior that are sharpened,
      with coals of the broom shrub.
120:5 Woe to me, for I sojourn in Meshek,
      I abide among the tents of Kedar.
120:6 Too long my soul has had its abode
      with those hating peace.
120:7 I am [for] peace,
      but when I speak, they are for war.

Structure

The understanding of Psalm 120 demands an interpretive decision: Is 120:2–7 an expansion of the prayer referred to in 120:1, or is it a prayer in a current situation of distress, recalling a *past* answer to prayer in 120:1? Or to put it simply, are there two prayers here (120:1 [past], and 120:2–7 [present]), or is there only one, 120:2–7 explicating 120:1? Goldingay thinks this composition "follows a recurrent pattern in the psalms whereby a suppliant recalls a past answer to prayer . . . [120:1] and then builds on that with a new prayer . . . [120:2], a confrontation of the foes to whom the prayer refers . . . [120:3–4], and a lament at the situation, supporting the prayer and designed for Yhwh's hearing . . . [120:5–7]."[4]

(127:3, 4); "mighty one" (127:4, 5); "blessing [upon]" (128:1, 2); "many a time they have persecuted me from my youth" (129:1, 2); "bless[ing]" (129:8b, 8c); "voice" (130:2a, 2c); "hope" (130:5aα, 5aβ); "my soul" (130:5, 6); "wait" (130:5, 7); "redemption/redeem" (130:7, 8); "not" (131:1a, 1b); "my soul" (131:2a, 2c); "like a just-nursed one" (131:2b, 2c); "with" (131:2b, 2c); "abodes" (132:5, 7); "David . . . turn back" (132:10, 11); "upon your throne" (132:11, 12); "good" (133:1, 2); "beard" (133:2a, 2c); "going down" (133:2, 3); "bless" (134:1, 2, 3); and "Yahweh" (134:1 [×2], 2, 3) (from deClaissé-Walford et al., *Book of Psalms*, 888–90).

4. Goldingay, *Psalms*, 3:448.

Following that line of interpretation, the psalm may be divided into utterances of *Confidence*, *Call*, and *Condemnation* (120:1–4), followed by a *Cry* (120:5–7) that carries repetitions from all three previous sections:[5]

Confidence (120:1)
    ה ִ-, לִי, *–ah li*, "[dist]ress I was in" (120:1a)
Call (120:2)
    "my soul" (120:2a)
Condemnation (120:3–4)
        weapons (120:4a)
        "with [עִם, *'im*]" (120:4b)
        plural construct: "coals of the broom shrub" (120:4b)

Cry (120:5–7)
    אוֹיָה־לִי, "[w]oe to me" (120:5a)
    "my soul" (120:6a)
    "war" (120:7b)
    "among [עִם]" (120:5b)
    plural construct: "tents of Kedar" (120:5b)

Theological Focus

Living as exiles among the hostile, and unjustly slandered and calumniated, the people of God, made confident by their God's deliverance of them in the past, seek his deliverance of them in the future, which includes execution of divine justice.

Commentary

Confidence, Call, Condemnation (120:1–4)

The psalm begins with a recollection of the poet's past distress: he called Yahweh and Yahweh answered (*Confidence*; 120:1)—a statement made to the community. Therefore, he is confident about God's answer in the present (*Call*; 120:2)—appeal is directed to God. Whether the same kind of "distress" (120:1a) is operating in the current crisis of the supplicant is unclear. In any case, the attack from opponents is verbal: "false lip" and "deceitful tongue" is what the psalmist desires rescue from. "He was the victim of lying and misrepresentation. . . . He had doubtless come to the sanctuary cowed and dispirited by these attacks."[6] By recollecting his prior liberation the supplicant appears to be encouraged and emboldened enough to address his opponents personified by their nefarious organs of spoken attacks— the tongue (*Condemnation*; 120:3–4). The implied subject of the verbs, "he," is Yahweh, and 120:3–4 describes deity's judgment on evil-speakers. The formula is an interrogative variant

---

5. From Allen, *Psalms 101–150*, 148–49.
6. Allen, *Psalms 101–150*, 149.

on a malediction called down on oneself or upon others, should there be a failure to do what was promised: "may God do [this]/give [this] to me/you, and may he add more of [that] to me/you" (see 2 Sam 3:9, 35). It almost becomes a rhetorical query: "What will God *not* do to you . . . ?" But the question is answered in Ps 120:4: What Yahweh will give to these wicked ones are sharp, burning arrows.[7] This is likely to be metaphorical, but in any case, severe punishment is hereby assured these maledictors—perhaps in kind, in words.

Cry (120:5–7)

The psalmist's lament takes up the remainder of the psalm, a woeful description of his oppressive situation.[8] Whom he is addressing is uncertain, but it is likely to be directed to his compatriots, his community. The supplicant dwelt as a foreigner, encountering hostility far from the homeland (120:5).[9] The opposition "hated peace" (120:6b), whereas the psalmist was "[for] peace" (120:7a); indeed, his enemies were "for war" (120:7b). Surely Yahweh would hear the prayer and deliver the "soul" (120:2a) of one whose peace-seeking "soul" was surrounded by those war-mongering slanderers (120:6).[10]

As "a vehicle for the homesickness of devout expatriate Jews," especially those being persecuted, it is understandable how this psalm was eventually incorporated into the Song of Ascents. "A dove among hawks, he [the supplicant] has had no success in restoring harmony, but only suffered unmitigated aggression. He has done what he could . . . . God alone can change the situation. Bolstered and armed with the divine word of support [or a history of God's deliverance in the past], he would go back hoping and trusting that the situation would be resolved to the glory of God."[11] This does not counter the psalmist's condemnation of the enemy calling for arrows to be fired against them: such recrimination is acknowledged to be part of the work of God . . . for the purpose of restoring peace!

In sum,

> The psalm hovers between divine promise and fulfilment, like so much of the Bible. Joy and sorrow are poignantly intermingled, equally valid and as yet unresolved. The virtues of truth and honor within God's community and the outworking of justice as God's will for his people are the ideals which this psalm celebrates. The divine pledge of support for the victimized, which characterizes so much of the law and prophets, shines out afresh over the life of an individual believer.[12]

And there is always hope of deliverance from woes temporal!

---

7. Firewood from the broom shrub was used to make charcoal, likely capable of generating quite a sustained incendiary eruption.

8. The כִּי, *ki* ("for"/"but") in 120:5a, 7b forms an *inclusio* for this last section of the psalm.

9. Meshek is likely to be in Turkey; Kedar was a nomadic group of sheepherders in the deserts of Arabia, hence their temporary dwellings, "tents." Again, whether the psalmist actually dwelt in these locations or whether these were co-opted symbolically and rhetorically is unclear.

10. "I abide among" is שָׁכַנְתִּי עִם, *shakantti ʿim* (120:5b); "its abode with" is שָׁכְנָה . . . עִם, *shaknah . . . ʿim* (120:6).

11. Allen, *Psalms 101–150*, 148–49.

12. Allen, *Psalms 101–150*, 150.

Sermon Map

I. Excoriation of the Diaspora
    The foreignness of the people of God (120:5)
    The belligerence of the world (120:6–7)
    Move-to-relevance: Presence of evil

II. Expectation of the Devout
    The experience of the past (120:1)
    The expectation of the present/future (120:2)
    Move-to-relevance: Deliverance from evil

III. Execution of Doom
    The operation of divine justice (120:3–4)
    Move-to-relevance: Response to evil

IV. *Rest in the Redress of the Ruler!*
    Specifics on seeking God in times of trial

PSALM 121:1–8

Psalm of Orientation

Journeying with the Divine Keeper

PSALM 121 IS A poignant engagement with the truth of divine protection.[1] Based on some of its characteristics, Psalm 121 might be considered a wisdom poem: question and answer (121:1–2);[2] application to an individual (121:3–8);[3] employment of a creation theme (121:2b);[4] and Yahweh as keeper (121:3b, 4b, 5a, 7a, 7b, 8a).[5] But who the "I" in 121:1–2 and the "you" in 121:3–8 are is unclear. It might well be an initial personal witness of a pilgrim or even a king (121:1–2 has "*my* help" ×2) that stimulates a subsequent benediction or a wish, from a liturgical leader or priest to that individual (121:3–8 has "keep" ×6 in two different forms; see below).

Translation

121:1   I lift my eyes towards the mountains.
           From where comes my help?

121:2   My help [comes] from Yahweh,
           the One who made the heavens and the earth.

121:3   May He not give your foot to tottering;
           may He not slumber—the One who keeps you.

121:4   Behold, He will not slumber and He will not sleep—
           the One who keeps Israel.

---

1. As also is Psalm 91; like it, Psalm 121 does not address God directly. This theme of our psalm becomes obvious simply by scanning the words that constitute repeats in the composition: "Yahweh" ×5 (121:2a, 5a, 5b, 7a, 8a); "keep" ×6 (121:3b, 4b, 5a [participles], 7a, 7b, 8a [finite verbs]); and second person masculine singular suffixes, "you/your," ×10 (121:3a, 3b, 5a, 5bα, 5bβ, 7a, 7b, 8aα, 8aβ) (see Barker, "'Lord Watches over You,'" 169).

2. See Prov 5:15–23; 23:29–30; etc.

3. See Prov 3:21–30; 23:1–8, 22–28; etc.

4. See Prov 3:19–20; 8:22–26; etc.

5. See Prov 2:8; 3:26; 4:6; 7:5; etc. See Willis, "Psalm 121," 443–47.

121:5		Yahweh [is] the One who keeps you;
		Yahweh [is] your shade on your right hand.
121:6		By day, the sun, it will not strike you,
		or the moon by night.
121:7		Yahweh, He will keep you from all evil;
		He will keep your soul.
121:8		Yahweh, He will keep your going and your coming
		from now unto forever.

Structure

One may structure the psalm as a *Witness* to God's guardianship uttered *by* the supplicant (121:1–2), and a *Wish* for God's guardianship uttered *to* the supplicant (121:3–8):

Witness	121:1–2	"from" (121:1b, 2a); "come" (121:1b)
Wish	121:3–6	**"Yahweh [is] the one who keeps you"** (121:5a)
	121:7–8	"from" (121:7a, 8b); "coming" (121:8a)

The assertion that "Yahweh [is] the one who keeps you" is at the center of the psalm (121:5a): Ceresko notes that in the Hebrew, 58 syllables precede that declaration (יְהוָה שֹׁמְרֶךָ, *yhwh shimreka*; 121:5a), and 58 syllables follow it.[6] A number of word pairs also are found in the poem: "the heavens and the earth" (121:2b); "sun ... moon" and "day ... night" (121:6); "your going and your coming" (121:8a); and "from now unto forever" (121:8b). With the extremes in each pair, a sense of comprehensiveness pervades the ideas of the psalm. Indeed, the whole poem is composed of four couplets (in eight verses) and each couplet is linked by repeats or wordplays—"help" (121:1b, 2a); "He ... not slumber" (121:3b, 4a); יָמִין, *yamin* ("right hand"; 121:5b) and יוֹמָם, *yomam* ("by day"; 121:6a); "He will keep" (121:7b, 8a). One notices that each couplet of verses has a body part in its first verse: "eyes" (121:1a); "foot" (121:3a); "right hand" (121:5a); and "soul" (נֶפֶשׁ, *nephesh*, that also means "throat/neck"; 121:7b). Thus, even the supplicant's body is "kept" and secured by God! The "tight unity and ... the 'totalizing' rhetoric of the psalm ... conjures up in the space of its eight verses a miniature universe ruled and controlled by the benevolent Guardian [Keeper] ... and Creator God ... , a universe from which 'all evil' ... has been banished and into which the reader or hearer is invited to enter and live day by day"—God's ideal world![7]

---

6. Ceresko, "Psalm 121," 499.
7. Ceresko, "Psalm 121," 497.

Theological Focus

> God's people rest confident in the knowledge that deity is their keeper in their spiritual pilgrimages, constantly working for them, protecting them from every evil, and guarding their lives, unto all eternity, so that they need seek no other help from any other resource.

Commentary

Witness (121:1–2)

The *Witness* of the psalmist is carefully structured, with wordplays and repetitions in 121:1–2:

> "I lift [אֶשָּׂא, *'essa'*] my eyes toward the mountains.
>   From [מִן, *min*] where comes
>   **my help?**
>   **My help**
>   [comes] from [מִן] Yahweh,
> the one who made [עֹשֵׂה, *'oseh*] the heavens and the earth."

Usually mountains are positive in connotation (46:2–3; 65:6; 97:5), but the question that is posed in 121:1b suggests a less than salubrious view of these ranges. Indeed, "mountains" might be alluding to illegitimate and insufficient sources of help, for mountains are also the places of worship of Baal and other anti-God entities (Deut 12:2; Isa 57:7; 65:7; Jer 3:6, 23; etc.). Indeed, Yahweh is never designated as inhabiting a plurality of "mountains" (as in Ps 121:1a) only a singular "mountain," Mount Zion. The assertion that Yahweh is the one who made not only the mountains but the entirety of "the heavens and the earth" (121:2b) also suggests that this is the line of thought offered here. Elsewhere in the Psalter, Yahweh's might in creation impels his people to seek his help alone, not that of false deities or of mortal humankind (115:15 with 115:3–14; 124:8 with 124:1–7; 146:5–6 with 146:3–4).[8] Why look to mountains, or for that matter, any other source in the created universe for help, when the Creator of the universe himself is at hand? And that is exactly what the people of God testify and bear witness to: "My help [comes] from Yahweh!" (121:2a).

Wish (121:3–8)

Perhaps it is because the one witnessing to Yahweh's guardianship is a pilgrim (a king on a pilgrimage?) that the metaphors in 121:3–8 are related to travel: "foot" (121:3a), "shade" (121:5b), "day" and "night" and "sun" and "moon" (121:6), and "going and . . . coming" (121:8a). That

---

8. The use of the preposition אֶל, *'el*, "toward" (121:1a), hints that the one lifting up his eyes might have been potentially seeking help in the wrong place (as in Ezek 18:6, 12).

would be appropriate for *all* of God's people, "pilgrim[s] through this barren land."[9] But this section is not just wishful thinking: it "carries the stronger tones of certain promise of such blessing. . . . He [the pilgrim] is graciously given a powerful word to take home in confirmation of his personal faith," and thus we have the shift here to the second person: the pilgrim is being addressed (perhaps by a liturgical leader/priest).[10] The negations of 121:3–4 coupled with the positive declarations of God as "the one who keeps you/Israel" are telling, with the jussives in 121:3 taken over by the imperfects in 121:4:

> *Jussives expecting what* might *happen*
> **121:3** "may He not" (×2)   **"the one who keeps you"**
>
> *Imperfects explaining what* will *happen*
> **121:4** "He will not" (×2)   **"the one who keeps Israel"**

The emphatic shift, in 121:3 to 121:4, from what *might* happen, to what *will* happen, is further underscored by the introductory "behold" in 121:4a, as well as by the change of the negative particle from אַל, 'al, in 121:3 to the stronger לֹא, lo', in 121:4, and the shift from Yahweh's keeping "you" to keeping "Israel"—not just one individual, but *all* his people are kept by this faithful deity! God's "keeping" and care are, thereby, assured and guaranteed.

The emphasis continues with the placement of "Yahweh" at the opening of both lines of 121:5 in verbless clauses, and it is further reinforced by the placement of God at the right hand of the supplicant (121:5b), in the position of a champion and sponsor. It is Yahweh who is the keeper, the protector, of his people. Indeed, in the entirety of the *Wish* section, the verb "keep" occurs six times, each time referring to Yahweh: thrice as a participle in 121:3–5 ("the one who keeps") balanced by three more instances as an imperfect in 121:7–8 ("He will keep"). So much so, the pilgrim is kept safe both by day and by night (121:6)—all the time, no matter what the vicissitudes and vagaries of daily life.

> "By day
>   the sun,
>   it will not strike you,
>   or the moon
> by night."

The structure once again emphasizes divinely granted safety for the pilgrim, and this "from all evil" (121:7a). All throughout the journey of this weary traveler, his "going" and his "coming," God will "keep" that individual, not only now, but also forever (121:8), leading one to gather, quite rightly, that this is not just an isolated trip, but the journey of life itself. Once again, "Yahweh" at the beginning of 121:7a and 121:8a fortifies the certainty of God "keeping" his human supplicant. *How* deity will protect is not detailed, only that he *will!*

> Life is so full of dangers, but Yahweh's help is a match for them all. He is well able to
> keep his own safe in his loving care. As the believer walks in step with the rhythms

---

9. From "Guide Me, O Thou Great Jehovah" (William Williams, 1745; trans. Peter Williams, 1771).
10. Allen, *Psalms 101–150*, 154.

which make up daily life and represent the providential ordering of human existence . . . , he may do so with the assurance that God is with him in his daily toil and rest, ever helping and protecting. So the pilgrim is bidden Godspeed and leaves with the repeated drumbeats of the message, "Yahweh [keeps]," resounding in his ears. He leaves the sacred place of Yahweh's special presence, assured nevertheless that Yahweh goes with him.[11]

And for the pilgrim on the journey of life, amidst "many dangers toils and snares," "grace will lead me home," kept by God![12]

Sermon Map

I. Pilgrimage of Danger
    Source of help in times of trouble (121:1)
    Move-to-relevance: Presence of evil in our world

II. Person of Deity
    Creator of the cosmos (121:2)
    Consistency of his care (121:3–4)
    Move-to-relevance: God's watch over us in the past

III. Protection of the Devout
    From all danger at all times (121:5–6)
    From all evil (121:7–8)

IV. *Know That the King Keeps!*
    Specifics on finding succor in God

---

11. Allen, *Psalms 101–150*, 154.
12. From "Amazing Grace" (John Newton, 1779).

PSALM 122:1–9

Psalm of Orientation

The City of God at Peace

As in Psalm 121, in this psalm also Yahweh is never directly addressed. "Jerusalem," however, is mentioned thrice (122:2b, 3a, 6a), and the city itself is spoken to in 122:2, 7–9, in a rhetorical figure called an apostrophe. It is, of course, understood that the significance of Jerusalem is exclusively related to the deity who resides therein; but in this composition, the focus is squarely upon that capital city of God.

Translation

122:1	I rejoiced with those who said to me,	
	"To the house of Yahweh we will go."	
122:2	Our feet have come to be standing	
	within your gates, Jerusalem:	
122:3	Jerusalem, that has been built	
	as a city that has a community all together;	
122:4	there where the tribes went up,	
	the tribes of Yah,	
	[in accordance with] a decree for Israel,	
	to give thanks to the name of Yahweh;	
122:5	for there thrones were sat [upon] for judgment,	
	thrones of the house of David.	
122:6	Pray for the peace of Jerusalem:	
	"May they be secure, those who love you.	
122:7	May there be peace within your walls,	
	security within your palaces."	
122:8	For the sake of my kindred and my friends,	
	I will indeed speak, "May peace be within you."	
122:9	For the sake of the house of Yahweh our God,	
	I will seek good for you.	

Structure

In addition to the threefold naming of Jerusalem that keeps the focus of this psalm on the city, the verbs of motion, "go" (122:1b), "standing" (122:2a), "went up" (122:4a), and "sat" (122:5a), relate to goings on within that locus. All in all, there is a clear emphasis in Psalm 122 upon the place, Jerusalem, where things are happening. Though the temple therein is mentioned, with the "house of Yahweh" forming a bookend for the psalm (122:1b, 9a), "Jerusalem points more to an earthly city, the capital of Israel, a city of stone and brick, inhabited by people. Zion points more to a religious entity, the place where the temple is, the abode of Yhwh."[1] To that temporal city, Jerusalem, all pilgrims come, at least on the major festival days—Passover, the Feast of Weeks, and the Feast of Tabernacles. Psalm 122 is then perhaps the most apposite of the set of poems bearing the title "Song of the Ascents." One might conceive of a pilgrimage undertaken literarily, with: *Passage* to Jerusalem (122:1–2); *Place* of Jerusalem (122:3–5); and *Prayer* for Jerusalem (122:6–9):[2]

PASSAGE First person Direct address to Jerusalem	122:1aα	"I rejoiced"
	122:1aβ–b	"those who said" "house of Yahweh"
	122:2	"have [היה, *hyh*]" "within your gates" "Jerusalem"
PLACE	122:3–5	"Jerusalem": worship, rulership "house of David" (122:5b)
PRAYER First person Direct address to Jerusalem	122:6–7	"may there be [היה]" (122:7a) "within your walls/palaces" (122:7b) "Jerusalem" (122:6a)
	122:8–9a	"I will indeed speak" (122:8b) "house of Yahweh" (122:9a)
	122:9b	"I will seek good"

So the psalm explicitly focuses upon, and emphasizes, the importance of the city to the people of God as a place of worship (122:1, 4, 9) and locus of rulership (122:5). The theological thrust should, in turn, concentrate upon the worship and rule of God in that same location in the new heavens and new earth, an eschatological state of affairs.

Theological Focus

> The central locus of the worship of Yahweh and of the rulership of his regent is their capital city, where God's people look forward to arriving, and which they ardently yearn for, anticipating the establishment of its peace.

---

1. Goldingay, *Psalms*, 3:462.
2. Or "To Jerusalem," "In Jerusalem," and "From Jerusalem," the last forming a departing wish for the welfare of the city. See Kim, "Reading the Songs of Ascents," 102; and Auffret, *Là montent les tribus*, 28.

Commentary

Passage (122:1–2)

The joy of corporate pilgrimage to the city of God is emphasized in the mention of the destination coming first in exclamation of 122:1b: "*To the house of Yahweh* we will go." While, no doubt, there would be rejoicing in that the pilgrimage is undertaken with fellow believers, here the gladness is in the acknowledgment of where they are all headed: to Jerusalem, God's capital city. This locus was the epicenter of the worship of Yahweh and the site from which Yahweh's regent would reign (see below), making it a location unlike any on earth.

Almost instantly, in 122:2, the psalmist and his cohort appear to have arrived at Jerusalem, teleported as it were. "We will go" (122:1b) is immediately linked to where their "feet" have landed (122:2a). No mention is made of the pilgrimage itself, or of its "many dangers, toils, and snares"; now the people of God "have already come."[3] So the thrust of the psalm is not the pilgrimage per se, but the destination of the pilgrims' passage. And that endpoint is not a nebulous abstraction in the vague then-and-there, but a substantive station in the real here-and-now, for there are pilgrims with "feet" arriving at a city with "gates" (122:2). And so real is this experience, that the psalmist addresses the city directly (122:2, and again in 122:6–9).

Place (122:3–5)

The place where the pilgrims have arrived at is now the focus of attention. The fact that "Jerusalem" is the last word of 122:2 and the first word of 122:3 (both in the Hebrew and in my translation), forming a juxtaposed repetition, is indicative of the joy and awe of the travelers upon arriving at this venue.

It is not exactly clear what the "community [or 'joining,' חבר, *chbr*] all together" means (122:3). It is commonly thought that it describes the town jam-packed with buildings, all crammed together.[4] But Donner notes that the verb חבר is never used in biblical Hebrew, in post-biblical Hebrew writings, or in other Semitic languages as an architectonic term to describe constructions. Neither, apparently, did the LXX or the Vulgate see it that way, both choosing to apply this to people: ἡ μετοχή, *hē metochē* (LXX A has οἱ μέτοχοι, *hoi metochoi*), "partakers of a community," and *participatio*, "sharing," respectively. That is to say, it is the people of the city who are so connected, not the structures thereof.[5] This is likely to be the case especially in light of 122:4 that explicitly describes the people of God in the city.

In 122:4–5 we see this "community all together" (of 122:3b) performing the worship of Yahweh (as commanded by God, 122:4c),[6] and Yahweh's regent exercising his rulership upon the throne of David. The duality of this function of Jerusalem, worship and rulership, is paralleled in the double employment of "there," in 122:4a in connection with worship, and in 122:5a

---

3. From "Amazing Grace" (John Newton, 1779).

4. Quite typical of Jerusalem even today, as is also the case with many contemporary Asian cities.

5. Donner, "Psalm 122," 85. The other uses of the Hebrew root in the OT refer to alliances (forming a community) between people (Gen 14:3; 2 Chr 20:35–37; Dan 11:6; Hos 4:17) or the joining of pieces of drapery or wood (Exod 26:3; 28:7).

6. For e.g., in Exod 23:14–17, delineating the three major occasions for coming before Yahweh in Jerusalem to worship. Note the paronomasia: the pilgrims came to be "standing," עֹמְדוֹת, *'omdot*, in Jerusalem (Ps 122:2a), in accordance with a "decree," עֵדוּת, *'edut* (122:4c), "to give thanks," לְהֹדוֹת, *lhodot*, to Yahweh (122:4d). This wordplay also links the pilgrimage to Jerusalem with the worship of Yahweh in that city.

in connection with rulership. The plural "thrones" in 122:5a, 5b likely indicates that while there would be only one king, there would also be vice-regents and viceroys or other subordinates and subalterns ruling nations, resolving disputes, refereeing negotiations.

Once again, as in 122:1–2, here in 122:3–5 the reader is struck by how concretely these realities are described. This is a real place with real people living real lives! And above all, the worship of Yahweh and the rulership of his king are occurring here. What shall we post-resurrection people of God do with this pre-resurrection prophetic text? For the purposes of preaching in our new dispensation, what must be sermonically offered is this actuality of the people of God arriving at the place where God's King, the Lord Jesus Christ, rules, and where the worship of the Godhead occurs. There will be an eternal (divine) King, and incessant worship of a great God, in a *new* Jerusalem.[7] That will be a distinct, material, corporeal, and objective reality, one that is coming to be ... soon, and very soon!

Prayer (122:6–9)

Each verse of this final section of the psalm closes with "you/your" (the suffix ךְ-, *–k*), referring to the city of Jerusalem personified (as also in 122:2). Each pair of verses depicts parallel repeats, appropriate for a Song of the Ascents:[8] "peace" and "secure/security" in 122:6, 7; "for the sake of" in 122:8, 9. "Peace" itself shows up thrice, in 122:6a, 7a, 8b. What began with "rejoicing" as the pilgrim left for Jerusalem (122:1) ends with "speaking" a prayer of blessing and "seeking [its] good" (122:8–9), i.e., for the sake of the city's inhabitants, as the pilgrim ostensibly departs Jerusalem.

---

7. The earthly city of Jerusalem will also be the capital city of the millennial reign of Christ, prior to the establishment of the new heavens and the new earth, including the new Jerusalem (see Isaiah 25–27; Revelation 21–22; as well as Isa 2:1–4; 62:1–12; 65:17–25; Rev 2:26–27; 3:12; etc.). One might therefore also conceive of all these various iterations of "Jerusalem" as falling within the purview of this text.

8. See the introduction to Psalm 120.

Reinforcing the reality of יְרוּשָׁלִַם, *yrushalaim* ("Jerusalem"), the city—the focus of this psalm—and the yearning for its שָׁלוֹם, *shlom*, its "peace," the letters שׁ, ל, and מ (*sh*, *l*, and *m*), resound in 122:6–8:[9]

122:6
שַׁאֲלוּ שְׁלוֹם יְרוּשָׁלִָם יִשְׁלָיוּ אֹהֲבָיִךְ
shalu shlom yrushalaim yishlayu 'ohavayik
"Pray for the peace of Jerusalem:
  'May they be secure, those who love you.'"

122:7
יְהִי־שָׁלוֹם בְּחֵילֵךְ שַׁלְוָה בְּאַרְמְנוֹתָיִךְ
yhi-shalom bkhelek shalwah b'armnotayik
"'May there be peace within your walls,
  security within your palaces.'"

122:8
לְמַעַן אַחַי וְרֵעָי אֲדַבְּרָה־נָּא שָׁלוֹם בָּךְ
lma'an 'akhi wre'ay 'adabrah-na shalom bak
"For the sake of my kindred and friends,
  I will indeed speak, 'May peace be within you.'"

Such a prayer underscores the current (that is, from Davidic years even unto now) instability of that city, much in need of the שָׁלוֹם implied by its very name. That peace is coming, one day not far hence, when Yahweh's Messianic regent (the Lord Jesus Christ) reigns and God is worshiped by one and all.[10] For that eternal day, God's people yearn; for from יְרוּשָׁלִַם there will be שָׁלוֹם for the world and for the cosmos!

Sermon Map

I. Pilgrimage

  Life of the people of God, a communal pilgrimage (122:1–3)

  Move-to-relevance: Our pilgrimage of life

II. Place

  Jerusalem, the place of the worship of God (122:4)

  Jerusalem, the place of the rulership of God (122:5)

  Move-to-relevance: The less-than-ideal situation of worship/rule today

III. Prayer

  Peace yearned for (122:6–9)

  Move-to-relevance: The absence of peace in the world today

IV. *Pray for the Peace of the Place of God!*

  Specifics on meditating upon, and praying for, the future Jerusalem

---

9. Indeed, eight of the ten words of 122:6–7 contain one or more of these three consonants.

10. Goldingay perspicuously observes that "peace" and "walls" are masculine (122:7a), and "security" and "palaces" are feminine (122:7b), a balanced literary and textual depiction of "the harmony the psalm prays for" (*Psalms*, 3:467).

PSALM 123:1–4

Psalm of Disorientation

Utter Dependence of Servant upon Master

A PSALM OF DISORIENTATION, Psalm 123 appears to have no direct link with the other pilgrimage songs; Goldingay thinks the dire situation described in 123:3b–4 reflects "the circumstances of the postexilic community that collected the psalms of ascent."[1] Yet, as was noted in the introduction to Psalm 120, there are "staircase" parallelisms here, too, that render it a worthy member of the pilgrimage songs: "eyes" (123:1, 2); "is/be gracious" (123:2, 3 [×2]); and "greatly [. . .] filled . . . contempt" (123:3, 4).

Translation

123:1 To You I have lifted up my eyes—
    the one who sits [enthroned] in the heavens.
123:2 Behold, as the eyes of servants [are] to the hand of their masters,
    as the eyes of a maidservant [are] to the hand of her mistress,
so our eyes [are] to Yahweh, our God,
    until He is gracious to us.
123:3 Be gracious to us, Yahweh, be gracious to us,
    for we are greatly filled with contempt.
123:4 Greatly our soul—it is filled
    with the derision of the ones at ease,
    with the contempt of the proud.

---

1. Goldingay, *Psalms*, 3:470.

Structure

The psalm may be structured as follows:

> **123:1–2c**   Reliance on Grace
> **123:2d–3a** Request for Grace
> **123:3b–4**   Reason for Grace

One notices the first-person singular, "I" and "my," in 123:1, as opposed to the plural forms, "our" and "us" in 123:2–4. Perhaps the individual involved is a leader who is speaking both on his personal behalf (123:1) as well as on behalf of the community (123:2–4).

Theological Focus

> With a posture of total humility and utter dependence upon God, the King of the universe, his people earnestly seek his grace in times of crisis and distress.

Commentary

Reliance on Grace (123:1–2c)

With an emphatic "to You," the psalmist/leader affirms that it is to *God* that he is appealing, the one who is enthroned in the heavens (123:1). He who was described as Creator in 121:2 is now depicted as the King of the cosmos. And no one else can render aid in time of need, and so the reliance of the supplicant upon the grace of God is stressed with the first word: אֵלֶיךָ, *'eleka*, "to You."[2] To further underscore the dependent relationship of vassal to suzerain—of the one needing help to the one who is the helper—an analogy is made between servants/maidservants and masters/mistresses (123:2). While there is mutual commitment between the individuals named, clearly it is an act of grace from the superior to rescue the inferior from distress. This relationship between superior and inferior is emphasized in the use of "behold" to introduce the analogy (123:2a).

In detailing the gazes of various protagonists in the example of 123:2, the employment of both first-person singulars and plurals, as well as both masculine plurals and feminine singulars (below), together encompass all individuals and the entirety of the community—a holistic depiction of God's people everywhere appealing to their sovereign in humility.

---

2. While the verb in 123:1a is *qatal*, it is likely to be reflecting an ongoing attitude towards, and approach to, the God-King.

123:1	"*my* [singular] eyes"
123:2a	"eyes of *servants* ... *masters* [masculine plurals]"
123:2b	"eyes of a *maidservant* ... *mistress* [feminine singulars]"
123:2cd	"*our* [plural] eyes"

Everyone—*everyone!*—is dependent on this gracious God-King who alone can offer aid in times of need. And therefore, the thrust of this psalm is upon petitioners' posture of dependence upon the provider.

And with 123:2c, the song moves into a plurality of supplicants (from the individual supplicant, the psalmist, of 123:1a).

> [The leader's] personal avowal of trust sets the tone for the communal words which follow. He leads his fellow-worshipers into a declaration of their own reliance upon Yahweh by means of a double simile [123:2ab]. . . . The community acknowledges, and pleads, that the covenant relationship ("our God") places them in the position of slaves before their divine master. They are utterly reliant upon him. The corollary of his relationship is that he has committed himself to support them as his protégés. For this help they have been waiting and will wait on expectantly, conscious that they have no other help save his.[3]

Request for Grace (123:2d–3a)

Curiously enough the verb, "he is gracious," in 123:2 comes late, only in its last line (123:2d), perhaps to underscore the depth of the need and the humility of the entreaty. And prior to that there was a threefold mention of the direction of eyes in that verse (with the sequence of preposition "to" + "eyes" in 123:1a inverted in 123:2a, 2b, 2c), once again marking the intensity of the plea. Correspondingly, there is a threefold mention of, or a request for, God's grace here (123:2d–3a):

123:1a	"to ... eyes ..."
123:2a	"eyes ... to ..."
123:2b	"eyes ... to ..."
123:2c	"eyes ... to ..."
123:2d	"gracious to us"
123:3aα	"gracious to us"
123:3aβ	"gracious to us"

God alone, through his grace alone, can rescue one from all one's woes.

---

3. Allen, *Psalms 101–150*, 161.

Reason for Grace (123:3b–4)

The psalm concludes with a lament outlining the reason why God's grace is necessary: the supplicant and his cohort are in some sort of undisclosed distress, troubled by the derision and contempt of outsiders, particularly from those who are "at ease" and "proud" (123:4bc)—the well-off, the affluent, and the prospering wicked. What exactly prompted the jeering of these enemies is not mentioned, though it might be fair to attribute the mocking to the minority status of the people of God (perhaps in exile?), uninfluential, weak, disenfranchised, and suffering. The repetitions of "greatly," "filled," and "contempt" (123:3b, 4a, 4c) depict with pathos the plight of the people of God, pilgrims in a foreign land.

Their plight may be fearful, their pain may be grievous, their ridicule agonizing, but those believers got it right—their posture of utter dependence and humility upon the King of the universe, the only one who can render aid!

Sermon Map

I. Persecution
   Constant pressure and oppression from outsiders (123:3b–4)
   Move-to-relevance: Oppression we might be facing

II. Posture
   Utter dependence in humility upon God the universal ruler (123:1–2)
   Move-to-relevance: Our failure to be humbly dependent upon God

III. Plea
   Seeking God's grace in distress (123:3a)

IV. *Supplicate in Subjection to the Sovereign!*
   Specifics on the proper posture of humble dependence in prayer

PSALM 124:1–8

Psalm of Disorientation

But for God . . .

THIS IS ANOTHER PSALM that has no direct address to God; rather, it is testimony to, thanks for, and a declaration of trust in, the help rendered by God. "It is sung for Israel's hearing, because testimony gives the testifier opportunity to articulate what has happened and thus to know what has happened and to be built up by it. The testifier is thus able to recognize future situations that resemble this one and to react in light of this experience."[1]

Translation

124:1	"Were it not Yahweh who was for us"—
	let Israel now say—
124:2	"Were it not Yahweh who was for us,
	when people rose up against us,
124:3	then alive—they would have swallowed us,
	when their anger burned at us;
124:4	then the waters—they would have swept us away;
	the stream would have gone over our soul;
124:5	then it would have gone over our soul,
	the raging waters."
124:6	Blessed be Yahweh,
	who has not given us as prey to their teeth.
124:7	Our soul [is] like a bird that has escaped from the snare of a hunter:
	the snare was broken and we—we escaped.
124:8	Our help is in the name of Yahweh,
	the One who made the heavens and the earth.

---

1. Goldingay, *Psalms*, 3:477. He also suspects "the psalm is sung for the nations' hearing . . . because Yhwh's deeds for Israel are also good news for the nations" (*Psalms*, 3:477). However, the text of Psalm 124 gives no indication of this intention.

Structure

The structure of Psalm 124 is straightforward, with *Testimony* (1234:1–5) and *Thanksgiving and Trust* (124:6–8):

> **Testimony (124:1–5)**
> *Past Deliverance Remembered* (**124:1–5**)
>   Protasis (124:1–2)
>   Apodosis (124:3–5)
>   "Yahweh" (124:1a, 2a)
>   Metaphors (124:3–5)
>   Negation (124:1a, 2a)
>
> **Thanksgiving and Trust (124:6–8)**
> *Past Deliverance Praised* (**124:6–7**)
> *Future Deliverance Trusted* (**124:8**)
>   "Yahweh" (124:8a)
>   Negation (124:6a)
>   Metaphors (124:6b–7)

In its eight verses, the first-person plural suffix נוּ-, *-nu*, "us/our/we," echoes thirteen times (124:1a, 2a, 2b, 3a, 3b, 4a, 4b, 5a, 6b, 7a, 7b [×2], 8a), making this unmistakably a psalm of the community. Of these thirteen plural self-references only one is a suffix to the verbal form (in 124:7bβ, נִמְלָטְנוּ, *nimlatnu*, "we escaped"); the rest are pronominal suffixes and a single free-standing pronoun (אֲנַחְנוּ, *'anachnu*, "we," in 124:7bα). In other words, God's people are not doing a whole lot (with verbs referring to their actions) in this poem, except for escaping.[2] Things are being done *to* them (or *for* them) by the protagonist, Yahweh (124:1a, 2a, 6b, 7bα [divine passive], 8b),[3] and the collective antagonist, the enemy (124:2b, 3a, 3b, 4a, 4b, 5, 6b, 7a). They were given grief by what the latter had done to them, but now the community is filled with gratitude for what the former has done for them. Surely they can face the future with confidence!

Theological Focus

> Testifying to the wondrous deliverance of God, the Creator of the cosmos, from threatening dangers in the past, motivates the people of God to acknowledge their thanks in the present and to continue placing their trust in him for deliverance in the future.

---

2. They are also urged to "say" (124:1b).

3. One might also add 124:6b, for what God has actively not permitted to happen against his people. And indirectly, deity is also responsible for their escape (124:7a). Of course, that Yahweh is his people's "help" is explicitly noted (124:8a).

Commentary

Testimony (124:1–5)

The testimony is posed in its entirety as a counterfactual: what might have transpired had Yahweh not been for his people.[4] With a series of striking metaphors—people rising, animals (?) swallowing, anger burning, waters overwhelming, streams overflowing, and torrents raging—the potentially dire circumstances of the community of God are depicted symbolically, though we are not told what exactly the situation was. The looming disaster is neatly pictured in the assonant parallelism of 124:3a and 124:4a:

	Particle	Noun	Verb
124:3a	אֲזַי 'azay "then	חַיִּים khayyim alive—	בְּלָעוּנוּ bla'unu they would have swallowed us"
124:4a	אֲזַי 'azay "then	הַמַּיִם hammayim the waters—	שְׁטָפוּנוּ shtaphunu they would have swept us away"

Calamity threatened them: their lives were being drowned by waters. "Talk of waters and torrent suggests forces of more than natural significance, the forces of chaos that assert themselves against order and against God and/or the forces of death."[5]

But Yahweh was "for us" (לָנוּ, *lanu*; 124:1a, 2a), despite enemies rising "against us" (עָלֵינוּ, *'alenu*; 124:2b) and their wrath burning "at us" (בָּנוּ, *banu*; 124:3b). One also notices that, with the "staircase" parallelism of 124:2a repeating 124:1a,[6] and with the exhortation to Israel in 124:1b, the people of God are palisaded on either side by their deity who is for them, with the opponents isolated outside:

124:1a	"Yahweh ... for us"	
124:1b	"Israel"	
124:2a	"Yahweh ... for us"	
124:2b		"people ... against us"

A literary depiction of what had actually happened! This expression of relief at Yahweh's protection portrays a community that is "acutely conscious that but for the grace of God they have no existence."[7] The intensity of the threat (124:2b–5) only magnifies the wonder of their supernatural deliverance.

---

4. The suspense is increased with the incomplete nature of 124:1 and the repetition in 124:2—a long protasis (the "if"-clause) before the apodosis (the "then"-clause) in 124:3–5.

5. Goldingay, *Psalms*, 3:480. Raging waters, these fermenting and truculent fluids, are commonly deployed in the Psalter as being anti-God and pro-chaos (18:16; 29:3; 32:6; 33:7; 46:3; 69:1–2, 14–15; 74:13; 77:16, 19; 78:13, 16; etc.).

6. Another such parallelism occurs with the repetition of "would have gone over our soul" (124:4b, 5a).

7. Allen, *Psalms 101–150*, 165.

The result of the counterfactual (the apodosis following the protasis) is also depicted in like fashion, the repetitions making the "waters" surround, literally and actually, "our soul"—overwhelmed, drowned, sunk!

124:4abα	"waters," "stream"
124:4bβ	"our soul"
124:5a	"our soul"
124:5b	"waters"

If it weren't for the first structure (God's people surrounded by Yahweh), the second structure (God's people surrounded by the waters) would have doomed them to perish. Instead they are saved by the grace of God!

Thanksgiving and Trust (124:6–8)

So, thanksgiving is in order, for it was Yahweh who had not given them as feed to the beasts of prey that the opponents resembled (124:6); it was he who had engineered their escape (124:7). Therefore he deserves the worship, blessing, and gratitude of his people for his aid and his protection. Once again, the repetitions create a structure that textually depicts what happened: but this time, it is "our soul" that is outside the "snare"—they have escaped!

124:7aα	"our soul … escaped"
124:7aβ	"snare"
124:7bα	"snare"
124:7bβ	"we—we escaped"

All by the help of Yahweh, the Creator of the cosmos (124:8). People may rise in opposition to God's people (124:2b), but the Almighty Lord is "our help" (124:8). The last verse is thus a declaration of ongoing trust, confident in the deliverance that Yahweh will provide even for the future. Curiously enough, no specific deliverance is sought (or received), making 124:8 simply point to a future that is as yet uncertain. But the paradigm is clear: testimony regarding the past leads to thanks in the present, and thanks in the present leads to trust for the future. God is indeed "our help"!

Sermon Map

I. Ruin
   Threats to life and peace (124:2b–5)
   Move-to-relevance: Oppression in our lives
II. Rescue
   God's rescue from oppression (124:6–7)
   Move-to-relevance: How God has rescued us in the past
III. Recognition
   Testifying to God's past deliverance (124:1–2a)
   Move-to-relevance: How God has rescued us in the past
IV. *Rely on the Rescuer from Ruin!*
   Trusting in God's deliverance for the future (124:8)

PSALM 125:1–5

Psalm of Orientation

Trust, Don't Totter

PSALM 125 APPEARS TO commence where Psalm 124 concluded: with a declaration of confidence (125:1). And it continues in that vein, concluding with a call to God for his blessing upon the righteous (and his bane upon the unrighteous).

Translation

125:1 The ones trusting in Yahweh are like Mount Zion—
    it will not totter; forever it remains.
125:2 [Like] Jerusalem: mountains surround it;
    so Yahweh surrounds His people
    from now and unto forever.
125:3 For it will not rest, the scepter of wickedness,
    upon the portion of the righteous,
    so that they will not send [forth]—the righteous—
    their hands for perversity.
125:4 Do good, Yahweh, to those good
    and to the upright in their hearts.
125:5 But the ones turning aside [to] their crookednesses,
    may Yahweh make them go with the doers of iniquity.
    Peace be upon Israel.

Structure

The declaration of *Confidence in Yahweh* at the psalm's beginning (125:1–3) has both positive (125:1–2) and negative (125:3) assertions. The song ends with a *Calling upon Yahweh* (125:4–5), also stated positively (125:4) and negatively (125:5).[1]

Confidence in Yahweh (**125:1–3**)

125:1	"Yahweh" הַבֹּטְחִים, *habbotchim*, "the ones trusting" יִמּוֹט, *yimmot*, "totter"	+
125:2	"Yahweh"	
125:3a	"wickedness"	
125:3b	"righteous"	−
125:3c	"righteous"	
125:3d	"perversity"	

Calling upon Yahweh (**125:4–5**)

125:4	"Yahweh"	+
125:5	"Yahweh" הַמַּטִּים, *hammattim*, "the ones turning aside"	−

Theological Focus

Because Yahweh, the King of the cosmos, surrounds his people—like mountains do a city—rendering the latter unshakable and unwavering, believers walking with God are secure from nefarious, anti-God forces, and instead experience goodness and peace from the hand of God, unlike the wicked who are subject to the divine punishment.

Commentary

Confidence in Yahweh (125:1–3)

Mountains are solid and stable, and therefore, to compare those who trust in Yahweh to mountains is to consider these faith-filled ones equally solid and stable, unshakable and unwavering. But this is no ordinary mountain the people of God are compared with: this is Mount Zion, the abode of God, their deity. "It is Yhwh's holy mountain, the place where Yhwh lives, the place Yhwh is dedicated to" (2:6; 74:2; 78:68).[2] That gives this simile a whole new dimension. In fact, the use of יָשַׁב, *yshv*, "to remain" or "to sit," in 125:1b, also suggests Yahweh's "sitting" *enthroned* in Zion for which the same verb is employed often in

---

1. "Yahweh" occurs in both sections in the same textual locus: in the first line of the first verse of each section (125:1a, 4a), and in the second line of the second verse of each (125:2b, 5b).
2. Goldingay, *Psalms*, 3:484.

the Psalter.³ It is therefore the King of the cosmos who is his people's patron. How can they ever "totter" (125:1b)? For just as the mountains surround Jerusalem, Yahweh surrounds his people: and thus, "forever" they will not totter but "remain" (also יֵשֵׁב; 125:1b), simply because Yahweh, who "sits [יֵשֵׁב]" on the throne of the cosmos, surrounds them "from now and unto *forever*" (125:2c). All of space is God's; all of time is God's. That is why his people remain unshakable—because of their enthroned King.

What is literarily asserted is also textually depicted, with Jerusalem (metonym for the people of God who trust him) surrounded by mountains and by Yahweh.

125:1aα	"Yahweh"
125:1aβ	"Mount [הַר, *har*] Zion"
125:2aα	"Jerusalem"
125:2aβ	"Mountains [הָרִים, *harim*]"
125:2b	"Yahweh"

The result of Yahweh's surrounding his people (besides their immovable, unassailable status) is given in 125:3. The "portion" of the righteous (125:3b) likely indicates Yahweh's allotment of land for his people. Thus the "scepter of wickedness" would point to enemies and their rulers attempting to thwart this donation of land to the Israelites by God. In other words, the protection of God in 125:1–2 concerns foreign domination for extended periods of time as implied by the word "rest" (125:3a).⁴ This subjugation of God's people by evildoers will be thwarted.

On the other hand, if such a takeover by foes were to occur, it could potentially result in the compromise of the faith of the devout. So much so, it was very likely that they would themselves be involved in evil ("sending [forth] . . . their hands for perversity," 125:3cd). Thus, "the faith of the righteous is at risk. If the wicked are allowed to prevail . . . , then what is to prevent the righteous from concluding that there is no reward for their faithfulness? What is to stop them from doubting God's justice" and concluding that it would be better to join the evildoers?⁵ This lamentable possibility is textually portrayed in 125:3 with the "righteous" ensconced by "wickedness" and "perversity" (see below)—of course, that possibility is explicitly negated twice (125:3aα, 3cα) because of the divine protection of the righteous that is the import of this section, *Confidence in Yahweh*.

"*not rest ...*" (125:3aα)	
125:3aβ	"wickedness"
125:3b	"righteous"
"*not send [forth] ...*" (125:3cα)	
125:3cβ	"righteous"
125:3d	"perversity"

---

3. See 2:4; 9:4, 7; 22:3; 29:10–11; 55:19; 80:1; 99:1; 110:1; 113:5; 123:1.

4. For sermonic purposes, it will suffice to make a connection to evil governments or institutions harassing and oppressing God's people.

5. Reynolds, Carol Bechtel, "Psalm 125," 274. Perhaps the untrammeled success and prosperity of these nefarious agents also tempts God's people to abandon their faith.

All that to say, the confidence of the people of God in their deity is repaid by their protection from the advances of evil.

Calling upon Yahweh (125:4–5)

In their plea for the justice of God to prevail, it is very clear that when deity judges, the outcome for the righteous is diametrically opposed to that for the wicked. Unlike in 125:3, where the wicked potentially surrounded the righteous, here in 125:4–5, the two parties (and their respective fates) are kept distinct (+ vs. –; below):[6]

125:4aα	"Do good, Yahweh,	+
125:4aβ–b	to those good and to the *upright* in heart.	
125:5a	But the ones turning aside [to] their *crookednesses*,	–
125:5b	may Yahweh make them go with the doers of iniquity."	

In sum, "the ones trusting," הַבֹּטְחִים, *habotchim*, who "will not totter," לֹא־יִמּוֹט, *lo'-yimmot* (125:1b), are secure in Yahweh's protection and judgment. But "the ones turning aside," הַמַּטִּים, *hammattim* (125:5a) will receive their just deserts from deity (the assonances are striking). Such is the confidence of the people of God, "from now and unto forever" (125:2b)! No wonder, then, that there is "peace" upon the people of God (125:5c).

Sermon Map

I. Reign of Evil
   Possibility of takeover by wickedness (125:3)
   Move-to-relevance: The ever-present danger of compromise
II. Rule of God
   God's protection of his people (125:1–2)
   Move-to-relevance: God's protection today
III. Recompense from God
   Reward for the righteous (125:4)
   Repayment for the wicked (125:5)
   Move-to-relevance: God's recompense in real life
IV. *Rest in the Rock! Revel in His Reward!*
   Trusting God's protection and his justice

---

6. Goldingay, *Psalms*, 3:487, notes that the word עֲקַלְקַלּוֹתָם, *'aqalqallotam*, "crookednesses," is very strong: not only is the root rare (elsewhere in the OT it is found only in Jdg 5:6 to describe winding paths), it is reduplicated (doubling of the syllable קַל, *qal*), and it is in the plural. It forms an appropriate negative counterpart to the "upright," the root of which, ישׁר, *yshr*, means "straight."

PSALM 126:1–6

Psalm of Reorientation

The Joy of Divine Restoration

PSALM 126 CONFIDENTLY EXPECTS restoration from some sort of communal calamity. Perhaps historically it was the return of the Israelites from exile and the rebuilding of the city, Jerusalem, and the temple therein. But the actual event precipitating this song is not explicitly detailed, rendering it usable by all of God's people in all places, in all times, as they await divine restoration and reorientation.

Translation

126:1	When Yahweh restored the restoration of Zion,
	we became like dreamers.
126:2	Then it was filled with laughter—our mouth,
	and our tongue with joyful exclamation.
	Then they said among the nations,
	"Great things Yahweh has done for them."
126:3	Great things Yahweh has done for us;
	we became rejoicers.
126:4	Restore, Yahweh, our restoration,
	like streams in the South.
126:5	The ones sowing in tears,
	in joyful exclamation they will reap.
126:6	He goes, going and weeping—
	the one carrying a bag of seed;
	he shall come, coming with a joyful exclamation—
	the one carrying his sheaves.

Structure

The first three verses of Psalm 126 provide the grounds for the plea that follows in the last three verses: past experience resulting in future expectation.

> **Experience of the Past (126:1–3)**
> *First verse* (126:1): "restored," "restoration" (126:1a); "like" (126:1b)
> *Second verse* (126:2ab): chiastic
>   "laughter" (126:2a); "joyful exclamation" (126:2b)
>   "when"/"among" (בְּ, b; 126:1a, 2c)

> **Expectation for the Future (126:4–6)**
> *First verse* (126:4): "restore," "restoration" (126:4a); "like" (126:4b)
> *Second verse* (126:5): chiastic
>   "tears" (126:5a); "joyful exclamation" (126:5b, 6c)
>   "in" (בְּ; 126:4b, 5a, 5b)

It is obvious that the composition is structured with much poetic attention. For one, parallel repetitions (including those of the "staircase" variety) are very evident: "restore . . . restoration" (126:1a, 4a); "we became like dreamers/rejoicers" (126:1b, 3b); "great things Yahweh has done" (126:2d, 3a); "joyful exclamation" (126:2b, 5b, 6c); and 126:6ab, 6cd with the parallel between the carrier of seeds and the carrier of sheaves.

Theological Focus

> The experience of past remarkable restorations of God's people by their deity, resulting in their joy and delight, strengthen their expectation of continuing future and even greater restoration, also accompanied by gladness and exultation.

Commentary

Experience of the Past (126:1–3)

The *qatal* verbs in 126:1b, 3a, 3b ("restored," "has done," and "became," respectively) indicate that the first three verses likely deal with an experience of the past. With a careful scrutiny of the twenty-seven occurrences of שׁוּב שְׁבוּת, *shuv shvut*, "restored/restore the restoration," in the OT (here, in 126:1a, 4a), Bracke shows that the phrase "is associated with promises which indicate Yahweh's reversal of his judgment and the restoration of a condition of well-being. Additionally, the vision of restoration . . . often includes Yahweh's correction of that which led to his judgment."[1] Essentially, it is a removal of God's wrath and a return of God's favor upon his people (14:7; 53:6; 85:1).

---

1. Bracke, "*šûb šebût*: Reappraisal," 243.

Notice the parallels in 126:1–4a, centering on the "great things" done by Yahweh (126:2d, 3a), and surrounded by his "restoration" (126:1a, 4a):[2]

126:1a	שׁוּב יְהוָה אֶת־שִׁיבַת, *shuv yhwh 'et-shivat* "**Yahweh** restored the restoration"
126:1b	"we became … dreamers" *(plural participle)*
126:2d	"'Great things **Yahweh** has done for them'"
126:3a	"Great things **Yahweh** has done for us"
123:3b	"we became rejoicers" *(plural participle)*
126:4a	שׁוּבָה יְהוָה אֶת־שְׁבוּתֵנוּ, *shuvah yhwh 'et-shvutenu* "restore, **Yahweh**, our restoration"

While the giving of dreams in the OT was usually a means of revelation, in light of these parallel statements in 126:1–4a, "we became like dreamers" (126:1b; parallel to "we became rejoicers," 126:3b) is likely to be indicating the wonder and near-disbelief at the restoration God had accomplished in the past. The amazement is conveyed in the chiastic structure of the organs of vocalization erupting with a thrill in 126:2:

126:2aα	"laughter"
126:2aβ	"our mouth"
126:2bα	"our tongue"
123:2bβ	"joyful exclamation"

That restoration was so remarkable, even surrounding nations marveled (126:2cd).[3] So all's well that ends well? Not quite.

Expectation for the Future (126:4–6)

The switch of the verb שׁוּב, "restore," from the infinitive in 126:1a to imperative in 126:4a presumes that that earlier restoration was only partial: there was yet more restoration needed. The story, therefore, was not over yet. Even historically in the fifth century BCE, there were waves of repatriation of the exiles back into Israel and it is conceivable that this psalm could have been uttered between some of those remarkable events. And for contemporary audiences, surely the same situation applies. Partially restored we are, but full restoration we await.

Psalm 126 is notable for the absence of any finger-pointing. "The psalmist does not lament the current situation, provide a confession of sin, attack enemies, or accuse God of not paying attention—all of which are typical for a lament psalm (e.g., Psalms 51, 69, and 89). There is no focus on the negative, only an emphasis on the positive hope that God will once

---

2. In the Hebrew, "Yahweh" occurs in the center of the phrase "restore[d] the restoration," in both 126:1a and 126:4a (as shown). I accept the *Kethiv* of the latter (שְׁבוּתֵנוּ, *shvutenu*), and see it as a variant of what is in the former (שִׁיבַת, *shivat*) adding the first-person plural suffix.

3. Perhaps the historical turning point that generated this awe was the post-exilic reestablishment of worship in Jerusalem.

again restore the community's fortunes."[4] That hope is grounded in the experience of the past. Once God restored; God can restore again.

And what a restoration that will be! Like "streams in the South [נֶגֶב, *negev*]," i.e., the Negev, the dry desert area that sees rain only in winter when its streambeds are transformed into torrents of water. Once again, the delight of that restoration breaks out into a marvelous poesy.

126:5aα	"The ones sowing
126:5aβ	in tears,
126:6bα	in joyful shouting
123:6bβ	they will reap."

The reversal is textually depicted by juxtaposing "tears" with "joyful exclamation."[5] As well, the synonymity between 126:6ab and 126:6cd attests to the ecstasy of these restored souls, with 126:6 essentially restating 126:5. This is not just hope, but also an utterance that serves as an inducement to Yahweh to act and to re-restore.

Goldingay is right: "Like life, the psalm is full of weeping and laughter."[6] Or, perhaps better, like the psalm, life is full of tears and joy. The people of God, redeemed from sin—a restoration still to be consummated—continue to wait for that final day for the work of God to be complete: full restoration and life eternal in the kingdom of God in the presence of God and of his Christ, who shall reign forever and ever. And for that day we hope, confident in our God who has already begun to accomplish restoration.[7] "Great things Yahweh has done for us!"

Sermon Map

I. Restoration Experienced
   Restoration in the past accomplished (126:1a)
   Response of rejoicing (126:1b–3)
   Move-to-relevance: What God has done to reorient us
II. Restoration Expected
   Restoration in the future awaited (126:4a)
   Response of rejoicing (126:4b–6)
   Move-to-relevance: What a day that will be!
III. *Confident in the Coming Consummation!*
   Specifics on awaiting God's reorientation

---

4. Flesher, "Psalm 126," 435.

5. While it might well be that the people were dealing with a failure of crops (in light of the agricultural motifs of 126:4–6), these are more likely to be part of an extended simile, with "sowing" relating to what seems to be almost a burial, accompanied by "tears."

6. Goldingay, *Psalms*, 3:495.

7. Because the last state is far better than the first, for then God's people will have been delivered from the very presence of sin, I label this psalm one of reorientation.

PSALM 127:1–5

Psalm of Orientation

Worthlessness without God; Blessing with God

IT APPEARS THAT PSALM 127 is the link between Psalm 126 (that focused on the rebuilding and restoration of the temple and Zion, corresponding to 127:1–2, that deals with construction projects) and Psalm 128 (that focuses on domestic issues, corresponding to 127:3–5, that deals with progeny).[1] Thus, the thrust of Psalm 127 is that the failure to rebuild the city and temple (the issue of Psalm 126) ought not to be a major discouragement because, after all, exertions on behalf of God in cultic and civic matters are "worthless" without the sovereign providence and acquiescence of God. Rather, the people of God should focus primarily on building up the home (the issue that is expatiated on in Psalm 128), for therein lies fulfillment, the "blessing" of God.

Translation

127:1   If Yahweh himself does not build a house,
             in worthlessness the ones building labor on it.
         If Yahweh himself does not keep the city,
             in worthlessness the one keeping [watch] stays vigilant.
127:2   Worthless [it is] for you—
             the early ones to rise, the late ones to sit,
         the ones eating the bread of very painful toil;
             thus He gives to His beloved—[in] sleep.

---

1. A number of similarities link Psalms 127 and 128: "house" (127:1a and 128:3b); בָּנִים, *banim* ("sons" in 127:3a, 4a; and "children" in 128:3c, 6a [×2]); "[mighty] one" [גֶּבֶר, *gever*]" (127:4a, 5a and 128:4b); "blessing" (127:5a and 128:1a, 2b); "fruit" (127:3b and 128:3a); "eating" of one's labors (127:2c and 128:2a); "behold" (127:3a and 128:4a)—and in both psalms the interjection commences a new section; and "city" (127:1c) and "Zion," "Jerusalem" (128:5ab). Besides, there are similes describing the reward of children in both, employing כְּ, "like"—"*like* arrows" (127:4a) and "*like* a fruit-producing vine," "*like* cuttings of olive trees" (128:3a, 3c); as well as כְּ . . . -כְּ, *k-* . . . *ken*, "like . . . thus" (127:4) and כִּי־כֵן, *ki-ken*, "for thus" (128:4a)—and in both psalms the construction concludes the section dealing with Yahweh's reward.

127:3	Behold, sons are a heritage of Yahweh;
	the fruit of the womb is a reward.
127:4	Like arrows in the hand of a mighty one,
	thus are the sons of youth.
127:5	Blessing [upon] the mighty one
	whose quiver He has filled with them;
	they will not be ashamed
	when they speak with their enemies in the gate.

Structure

Psalm 127 comprises two eight-line pieces of poetry (127:1–2 and 127:3–5) that are carefully designed:

Admonition (127:1–2)

Begins with "Yahweh" (127:1a, 1c)
Negation (127:1a, 1c)
What Yahweh gives (127:2d)

    "house" (127:1a); "city" (127:1c)
    בּוֹנָיו, *bonayw*, "the ones building" (127:1b); "thus" (127:2d)
    "worthlessness" (127:1b, 1d); "worthless" (127:2a)

Assurance (127:3–5)

Begins with "Yahweh" (127:3a)
Negation (127:5c)
What Yahweh gives (127:3a)

    "sons [in the house]" (127:3a); "gate [in the city]" (127:5d)
    בָּנִים (127:3a); "thus" (127:4a)
    "reward" (127:3b); "blessing" (127:5a)

There is also a chiastic patterning of the emphasis on certain letters of the alphabet in the opening and closing verses of the psalm (highlighted below):

127:1ab	בּ *emphasis:*	לֹא־יִבְנֶה בַיִת שָׁוְא עָמְלוּ בוֹנָיו בּוֹ *lo'-yivneh bayit shaw' 'amlu bonayw bo* "… [He] does not build a house, in worthlessness the ones building labor on it"
127:1cd	שׁ *emphasis:*	לֹא־יִשְׁמָר־עִיר שָׁוְא שָׁקַד שׁוֹמֵר *lo'-yishmar-'ir shaw' shaqar shomer* "… [He] does not keep the city, in worthlessness the one keeping [watch] stays vigilant"
127:5ab	שׁ *emphasis:*	אַשְׁרֵי הַגֶּבֶר אֲשֶׁר מִלֵּא אֶת־אַשְׁפָּתוֹ מֵהֶם *'ashre haggever 'asher mille' 'et-'ashpato mehem* "blessing [upon] the mighty one whose quiver He has filled with them"
127:5cd	בּ *emphasis:*	לֹא־יֵבֹשׁוּ כִּי־יְדַבְּרוּ אֶת־אוֹיְבִים בַּשָּׁעַר *lo'-yevoshu ki-ydabru 'et-'oyvim bashsha'ar* "they will not be ashamed, when they speak with their enemies in the gate"

On a casual reading, the issues of the first section (*Admonition*) seem unrelated to those of the second (*Assurance*). But, interestingly enough, an ancient Sumerian hymn to the goddess Nisaba also deals with the same combination of these issues, focusing on that deity's sovereignty and providence:[2]

> Nisaba, where you do not ordain it,
> man does not build a (house), he does not build a city,
> he does not build a palace, he does not appoint a king.
> …
> You are the Mistress who gives the heart's joy:
> you put good seed in the womb,
> permit the fruit to grow in the womb,
> give the mother the love for the child.

This suggests that the juxtaposition of these notions of architecture and parenting was not necessarily new to Psalm 127.

In a sense, then, Psalm 127 is a reflection on what Yahweh gives (127:2d and 127:3a), thus recommending how one should not attempt to obtain for oneself what deity does *not* grant. Rather, one should accept what he does.

---

2. From Falkenstein and Von Soden, "Nisaba-Lied," 66–67 (my translation from the German).

It appears, therefore, that 127:1–2c is an expansion of 127:2d; and 127:3b–5 an expansion of 127:3a:

127:1–2c	Expansion:	*Worthless it is to attempt gifting to oneself*
127:2d	What Yahweh gives:	sleep
127:3a	What Yahweh gives:	sons
127:3b–5	Expansion:	*Blessing it is to accept gifting of God*

Theological Focus

Instead of engaging in futility and frustration, and expending energy and agony, in activities that God, in his sovereign prerogative, may not be directly involved in, the people of God focus diligently upon undertaking their responsibilities towards their children—blessings granted by God—an endeavor that potentially yields much fruit.

Commentary

Admonition (127:1–2)

The first eight lines (127:1–2) deal with the "worthlessness" of building house and keeping city if they are exclusively human endeavors. What exactly might these activities entail?

In light of the hinge function of Psalm 127 between Psalms 126 and 128 (as noted earlier), it makes sense to see these undertakings in 127:1–2 as the rebuilding of the temple and of Jerusalem. The "house" + "city" combination (127:1a, 1c) often refers to these entities in the OT.[3] Thus, the *Admonition* in 127:1–2 is being directed against the post-exilic rebuilding of the temple/house and Jerusalem/city with merely human energies and creaturely contrivances, and without the involvement of Yahweh in those endeavors. It is likely that even the unique mention of Solomon in the superscription of this psalm ("Solomon's [לִשְׁלֹמֹה, *lishlomoh*]."; untranslated here), unique for the Songs of Ascents, was because the psalm was understood to involve the building of the temple, Solomon's greatest achievement.[4]

The failure to rebuild the temple in the days of King Cyrus (Ezra 3:8—4:5) and of King Darius (Ezra 5:1—6:18; Hag 1:1—2:9) in the fifth century BCE was, no doubt, an extreme disappointment for the returnees from the exile. The *Admonition* of our psalm declares that if God is not in such an undertaking—for whatever reason in his sovereign prerogative, and we are not

---

3. See 1 Kgs 8:44, 48; 2 Kgs 23:27; 2 Chr 6:34, 38; Jer 26:6, 9, 12. "House [בַּיִת, *bayit*]" referring to the temple is also found in 2 Sam 7:13; 1 Kgs 5:5; 6:1; 8:6, 29; 1 Chr 17:12; Ps 42:4; etc.

4. Other reasons for considering this a Solomonic composition include: the psalm has the feel of a wisdom song, Solomon's forte; that regent not only built God's "house" (1 Kings 5–8; 2 Chronicles 2–7), he also dealt with "worthlessness" (Ecclesiastes, though a different Hebrew word is employed there); and was himself called "Jedidiah" (יְדִידְיָה, *ydidyah*, "beloved of Yah," in 2 Sam 12:25; and the title יְדִידוֹ, *ydido*, "His beloved," occurs in Ps 127:2d). The "sleep" that this "beloved" received (127:2d) may also be an allusion to Solomon's sleep and dream, the defining moment in his life when God granted him wisdom (1 Kgs 3:3–15).

told why—it is worthless for his people to fret, worry, and strain themselves in that endeavor. There was no reason for them to be driven to desperation for an operation that Yahweh did not concur with: "worthless [it is] for you" (Ps 127:2a).[5] That is not to promote laziness or to downplay hard work, but to remind the people of God that unless God is involved in their enterprises, all exertions are futile. They might rise early and sit down only late (127:2b), an "artificial lengthening of the day on both ends,"[6] consuming only the food of drudgery and the drink of agonizing industry (127:2c),[7] but it would all be in vain *sans* God. This, of course, has been, and always is, the case with every human activity, however noble: exclusively human efforts are utterly "worthless," futile, and effete, originating in, and powered by, the flesh.

On the other hand, if God wills it, if he is involved, he can make anything happen. In his providence and sovereignty, he can give to his beloved ones those very things they vainly toil for. Indeed, he gives to them even when they are totally at a standstill and utterly inactive, even in their sleep (127:2d)![8] Notice the contrast:

127:2a	שָׁוְא, *shaw'* ("worthless")
	לְ, *l* ("for [you]")
	לְ ("to [His beloved]")
127:2d	שֵׁנָא, *shena'* ("sleep")

All the spinning of wheels and burning of midnight oil and eating the fruit of "very painful toil" is for naught (127:2c), for God does not need our frenetic activities. That would have been quite an encouragement amidst the failure that God's people were staring at in the historical circumstances of the psalm. But it is equally true today. "We can never know whether the efforts we expend in what we are trying to do will lead anywhere. Yhwh may cause or allow them to be frustrated by events we could never have predicated and made allowance for. But that aspect of Yhwh's involvement in our lives is counterbalanced by the fact that Yhwh loves us [127:2d]. Even the disappointments, frustrations, and reversals can be embraced by that."[9]

And so, in days of futility and failure, God would rather have his people turn their focus elsewhere, and that is dealt with in the *Assurance* section of this psalm.

Assurance (127:3–5)

What God would have his people do, instead of engaging in inutile "very painful toil," is to concentrate upon constructing and strengthening households, family units. And in this

---

5. In light of the contrast later with what is "blessing" (127:5a), Fokkelman considers "worthless [it is] for you" in 127:2a as a "swearword," a "near-exclamation and a near-curse" (*Major Poems*, 3:284). Both terms, "worthless" and "blessing," come emphatically at the beginning of their respective lines, and both are part of verbless clauses.

6. Ross, *Psalms*, 3:682.

7. The "very" in "very painful toil" (127:2c) reflects the intensity of the plural, הָעֲצָבִים, *ha'atsavim*.

8. The "thus" in 127:2d (= those things that are eagerly and frantically sought in these undertakings of hard labor) signifies that the very aims of their once fruitless missions could be fulfilled by God, and that without any input on their part, even as they slumbered. Again, that is not a promotion of indolence, of course.

9. Goldingay, *Psalms*, 3:503.

connection, the psalmist affirms that "sons" are divinely given (127:3), a "heritage" (inheritance) and a "reward."[10] It is a "blessing" (127:5a) to have a quiver-full of those arrows (127:4a, 5b) for security and for protection, particularly when confronting "enemies" at the public square (127:5cd).[11] In fact, the father is called the "mighty one" (127:4a, 5a) precisely because of his sons—the "sons of youth" (127:4b) that this parent has had ample time to develop, mold, and train. This progeny enables him to "not be ashamed" (127:5c)[12] before his enemies, for those "arrows" and the "quiver" filled with those implements of warfare protect this parent ("mighty one"), cocooning him in their care, as is textually depicted:

127:4a	"arrows"
	"mighty one"
127:5ab	"mighty one"
	"quiver"

Perhaps the martial imagery is metaphorical here and not intended to be taken literally as sons going into battle for their fathers. In the sermon application and moves to relevance it certainly should be expanded to indicate the positive influence of any kind upon society by children who are well-raised and well-trained by their parents and who bring their forbears honor.

> As a warrior launches arrows in his long-range offensive, so one is able to propel prepared children into places of societal interchange to make a predetermined impact.... The disorientation of human futility in toil apart from Yahweh is answered by the new orientation of the permanent effect possible through the nurture of children. The pain of vanity is assuaged by the prospect of lasting impact upon human society. As the arrow is employed to accomplish the long-range offensive objective of the warrior, so a form of social immortality is achieved as children steadfastly communicate the parental values in new social contexts.[13]

In sum, we are to engage in activities of "blessing," not those of "worthlessness," primarily on the domestic and personal front.

---

10. So are daughters, too, of course. While בָּנִים in 127:3a, 4b can be translated "children," it appears that "sons" are primarily the focus here, bastions of security and defense, as the subsequent verses show. However, for preaching purposes, application can, and should, extend "sons" to children of both genders (just as the endeavors of house-building and city-keeping can be extended in application to any other activity, particularly those that involve ministry or work for God of some sort). However, what exactly "sons" are a "reward" for (127:3b) is unclear, unless it is means that they are simply gifts of God as are all children (and not necessarily seen as a recompense for some good work).

11. In the ancient Near East, the "gate" of a city was its public square, the locus for the gathering of elders for the settling of disputes and for the making of major decisions involving the community.

12. The "they" who will not be ashamed (127:5c) could indicate either fathers collectively, or perhaps even the sons, unashamed as they are of their parent and willing to defend him in public. Or both.

13. Estes, "Like Arrows," 311.

Sermon Map

I. Futility
   - Activities without God are worthless (127:1–2c)
   - God does not need our frenetic activity (127:2d)
   - Move-to-relevance: Futile activities in our lives, perhaps even ministry

II. Utility
   - Responsibilities urged by God are a blessing (127:3–5b)
   - God blesses the fruit of domestic care (127:5cd)
   - Move-to-relevance: Our familial responsibilities

III. *Don't Be Futile, Be Utile!*
   - Specifics on keeping our priorities straight

PSALM 128:1–6

Psalm of Orientation

Blessing upon God-Fearers

LIKE PSALM 127, PSALM 128 is also a wisdom psalm, with a blessing, a saying about the flourishing of the family, an aphorism about fearing God, and a pronouncement of peace.

Translation

128:1	Blessing [upon] everyone who fears Yahweh,
	who is walking in His ways.
128:2	The labor of your hands you will surely eat—
	blessing [upon] you, and goodness with you:
128:3	your wife like a fruit-producing vine
	in the inner parts of your house;
	your children like cuttings of olive trees
	surrounding your table.
128:4	Behold, for thus he will be blessed,
	the [mighty] one who fears Yahweh.
128:5	May Yahweh bless you from Zion,
	that you may see the goodness of Jerusalem all the days of your life;
128:6	that you may see your children's children.
	Peace be upon Israel.

Structure

The psalm comprises two sections, *Blessing* and a more formal re-declaration of blessing, the *Benediction*:[1]

Blessing (128:1–3)
- 128:1   "blessing ... who fears Yahweh"
- 128:2bα   "blessing"
- 128:2bβ   "goodness"
- 128:3c   "children"

Benediction (128:4–6)
- 128:4   "blessed ... who fears Yahweh"
- 128:5a   "bless"
- 128:5b   "goodness"
- 128:6a   "children" (×2)

The sections, however, run in parallel: each begins with a verse that indicates a general blessing for the God-fearing person in the third person (128:1, 4); two subsequent verses follow, that indicate specific blessings for that one, directly addressing that individual in the second person (128:2–3, 5–6).

Theological Focus

> The fear of God, walking in his ways, brings about abundant blessing, vocational and domestic, that extends from the home to the society and even beyond, unto many generations, and for all of life.

Commentary

Blessing (128:1–3)

The God-fearing one is blessed (128:1a)! And what it means to "fear Yahweh" is spelled out in 128:1b: it is to "walk in His ways": a call to obedience and to align one's life to divine demand. Following this general statement (in the third person), specifics are adduced (in the second person)—what this blessing of God upon the God-fearer looks like, relating primarily to vocational and domestic environments (128:2–3). Psalm 127 warned of the possibility of God not being involved in the "painful toil" of our enterprises (127:2c). Now Psalm 128 exhorts us to fear God, for then God *does* become involved in our lives, making our "labor" fruitful

---

1. From Auffret, *Là montent les tribus*, 64. As shown, "blessing" in the first section is אַשְׁרֵי, *'ashre*; in the second section, "blessed" and "bless" are from the root ברך, *brk*. All throughout the Psalter, I've kept the translations of these words consistent. "Blessing [אַשְׁרֵי]" "describes a state or an experience and does not comment on the agency that brings it about, while 'bless' [and 'blessed': both from ברך] refers to the personal [here, divine] action that generates that state or experience" (Goldingay, *Psalms*, 3:511).

(128:2a): "blessing" and "goodness" will be upon us and with us (128:2b). And even in the matter of fertility, God-fearers are blessed (128:3).[2] If one looks at the first four verses of the psalm (the *Blessing* section + the first verse of the *Benediction* section), one sees the emphases on fearing Yahweh: that endorsement surrounds the blessings that ensue as a result:[3]

128:1a	"everyone who fears Yahweh"
128:2a	"you will surely eat"
128:2bα	"blessing [upon] you"
128:2bβ	"goodness with you"
128:3d	"surrounding your table"
128:4b	"the [mighty] one who fears"

Of course, the rest of Scripture shows how God-fearers can expect divine blessing upon every facet of their lives, not just in the domestic sphere and in one's vocation. But here, continuing the theme of Psalm 127, the focus is limited to the arena of family life and function (including provision for family).

Benediction (128:4–6)

The reminder about fearing Yahweh and the blessing that results (128:4) echoes 128:1: "thus" (128:4a)—i.e., as was detailed in 128:2–3[4]—will such a God-fearer be blessed. But not only that, this individual can expect blessing for the conceivable future, too, spanning generations, and expanding to the rest of the city, all the result of a God-fearing life that benefits not only one's descendants but even one's fellow citizens (128:5). "Seeing the goodness of Jerusalem" is also equated to "seeing your children's children" (128:5b, 6a), ostensibly seeing *their* goodness and welfare and thriving too, in parallel to the prosperity of the city. Notice how "your children" (128:3b) and "your children's children" (128:6a) surround divine blessing (128:4, 5a), textually depicting them as participants of Yahweh's blessings themselves:[5]

---

2. It is possible that "the inner parts of your house" (128:3b) hints at sexual activity, intended to be enjoyed as divine blessing. The emphasis on wives' reproductive capacity in this verse is not to downplay the importance of women in other arenas of life, of course: "Other parts of the OT emphasize the role the woman of the house plays outside the house itself (see especially Prov 31:10–13); because of the psalm's topic of concern, this line [Ps 128:3ab] emphasizes her role inside the house, in the private life of the family in its inner rooms" (Goldingay, *Psalms*, 3:509–10). In 128:3cd, the "olive trees" stand for the parents and the "cuttings" for the children. Goldingay comments on how 128:3ab is a "is a stumbling block to ancient commentators for whom celibacy was a key value," including Augustine and Jerome, who are quick to spiritualize "wife" and "children" (see Augustine, *Exposition on the Psalms* [*NPNF¹*, 609–10]; and Jerome, *Homilies*, 321–22). "Amusingly, it can also be a stumbling block to modern commentators" who mistakenly see this text as endorsing a view of wives as sexual chattel or mere wombs (see Goldingay, *Psalms* 3:513, 513n8). Needless to add, both parties are mistaken!

3. From Auffret, *Là montent les tribus*, 71.

4. That it is this backward glance that is intended in 128:4 is clear in the usage of "for [כִּי, *ki*]" in 128:4a that links with "surely [כִּי]" in 128:2a.

5. From Auffret, *Là montent les tribus*, 71.

128:3b	"your children"
128:4	"blessed ... Yahweh"
128:5a	"Yahweh bless"
128:6a	"your children's children"

And thus the "goodness" that would be with God-fearers (128:2c) is the "goodness" upon the city in which they dwell (128:5b) and, apparently, upon their grandchildren as well (128:6a), and ultimately upon the whole nation: "Peace be upon Israel!" (128:6b). That the blessing comes from Zion (128:5a) denotes that God's dwelling, in the temple, is the direct source of God's blessing that will be upon his people, upon those who fear him.[6] And thus, "Jerusalem [יְרוּשָׁלָםִ, *yrushalaim*]" becomes the source of "peace [שָׁלוֹם, *shalom*]" (128:5–6). The ripple effect of divine blessing for "God-fearing-ness" has extended from home to city to entire nation!

It is quite appropriate that the one who "fears [יָרֵא, *yre'*]" Yahweh (128:1a, 4ab) will "see [רָאָה, *r'h*]" tangible blessing (128:5b, 6a). Indeed, "everyone [כֹּל, *kol*]" who is a God-fearer (128:1a) will enjoy these blessings "all [כֹּל]" their days (128:5b). The relationship between 128:4 and 128:5 bears an implicit exhortation: God-fearers will be blessed thus (128:4), and so, "may you fall into this category so that you are blessed."[7] Calvin is right:

> The maxim "that those are blessed who fear God, especially in the present life," is so much with variance with the common opinion of [people], that very few will give it their assent.... To the sentiment that those are blessed who fear the Lord, [mankind] has an entire aversion.... So much the more requisite then is it to dwell upon the consideration of this truth.... What is here laid down is the chief point of happiness.[8]

Indeed!

Sermon Map

I. Fear of God

  Fearing God and walking in his ways (128:1, 4)

  Move-to-relevance: How we fail to fear God and walk with him

II. Favor of God

  Consequent blessings (128:2–3, 5–6)

  Move-to-relevance: Our failure to experience divine blessings

III. *Fearfully Find Favor!*

  Specifics on walking in God's ways

---

6. "People gathered in Zion/Jerusalem as an expression of their reverence for Yhwh and their commitment to walking in Yhwh's ways, and there they sought blessing on their family life from the God who had agreed to make a permanent home in Zion/Jerusalem" (Goldingay, *Psalms*, 3:511).

7. Allen, *Psalms 101–150*, 184.

8. Calvin, *Commentary on the Book of Psalms*, 5:113–14.

PSALM 129:1–8

Psalm of Disorientation

Unblessedness of Enemies

PSALM 129, TOO, LIKE the couple of compositions preceding it, sounds more like a wisdom composition; it is more *about* God, than being addressed *to* God. And, like Psalms 127 and 128, this song concludes with a blessing statement (though it is about a benediction that is *not* pronounced upon the ungodly; 129:8).

Translation

129:1	"Many a time they have persecuted me from my youth"—
	let Israel now say—
129:2	"Many a time they have persecuted me from my youth;
	but they have not prevailed over me."
129:3	Upon my back the ones plowing plowed;
	they lengthened their furrows.
129:4	Yahweh [is] righteous;
	He cut the ropes of the wicked.
129:5	May they be shamed and turned back,
	all who hate Zion.
129:6	May they be like grass upon roofs;
	that, before it is [even] pulled up, withers:
129:7	with which he does not fill his hand—the one reaping,
	or his bosom—the one gathering [grain].
129:8	And those passing by do not say,
	"The blessing of Yahweh be on you;
	we bless upon you in the name of Yahweh."

Structure

The first four verses of Psalm 129 are a celebration of Yahweh's past deliverance from adversaries; the next four, a wish for adversaries to be punished. Marked by a series of direct speeches, doublings, agricultural motifs, and mentions of enemies, the psalm is structured chiastically, reflecting structural, notional, and linguistic parallels:[1]

Rejoicing of the Righteous (129:1–4)	
129:1–2	Hypothetical direct speech of Israel ("say")
	Doubling (129:1a = 129:2a)
129:3	Agricultural motif
	Metaphorical laborers (participle in 129:3a)
	Doubling ("the ones plowing," "plowed")
129:4	Israel's adversaries ("wicked")

Recrimination of the Wicked (129:5–8)	
129:5	Israel's adversaries ("all who hate Zion")
129:6–7	Agricultural motif
	Metaphorical laborers (participles in 129:7a, 7b)
	Doubling (יֵבֹשׁוּ, yevoshu, "may they be ashamed" and יָבֵשׁ, yavesh, "it withers")
129:8	Hypothetical direct speech of Israel ("say")
	Doubling ("blessing" and "bless"; "Yahweh" [×2])

Theological Focus

God's people recollect and recount his past deliverance of them from constant oppression and await the overthrow of their current oppressors who—unlike the former who are blessed by God—are destined to remain far from divine blessing.

Commentary

Rejoicing of the Righteous (129:1–4)

After the repetitive 129:1–2a, the sentence concludes with 129:2b: enemies have not prevailed against the people of God. We are told the oppressors persecuted the latter "from my youth" (129:1a, 2a). This reference to Israel's "youth" likely deals with the history of the nation from Egypt and onwards,[2] and "many a time" (129:1a, 2a) suggests an innumerable series of hostile undertakings inimical to the people of God.

---

1. See Girard, *Les Psaumes Redécouverts*, 355, 356. There is also a doubling of the relative particle, שׁ, *sha*, ("that," "with which") in 129:6b, 7a. As well, "Israel" and "Zion" make their respective appearances in the first verses of each section (129:1b, 5b), and Yahweh shows up in the last verse of each section (129:4a, 8b, 8c).

2. See Jer 2:2; 32:30; Hos 2:15; etc.

But those adversaries failed to overcome Israel. And to that, God's people, the psalmist recommends, are to testify (129:1–2), even though those foes, like farmers plowing land, had lacerated and savaged the back of the nation (129:3). We are not told how this deliverance came about . . . until we get to 129:4.

There suddenly, God comes into the picture! He is the one who severed the ropes (securing the metaphorical oxen to the plow, as in Job 39:10, perhaps) of the wicked (Ps 129:4). With a clever wordplay the psalmist equates "the ones plowing [חֹרְשִׁים, *chorshim*]" (129:3a) with the "wicked [רְשָׁעִים, *rshaʿim*]" (129:4b). And with that, God, the righteous (129:4a), is shown directly opposed to the wicked and their evildoing. Thus we see a repetitive pattern of persecution followed by preservation in this first section of the psalm:

129:1–2a	Persecution	
129:2b		Preservation
129:3	Persecution	
129:4		Preservation

Recrimination of the Wicked (129:5–8)

If Israel's persecutions happened "many a time," and that from her "youth" (129:1a, 2a), the wicked were, no doubt, many and innumerable, too, and afflicting the nation for centuries. Their punishment is wished for—would that "all who hate Zion" (129:5b), everyone who has colluded with the opposition against Israel, be shamed, for these are the "wicked" (129:4b), anti-God and anti-God's-people in stance and action. Another agricultural motif, as in 129:3–4, shows up in 129:6–7. Flat roofs of the ancient Near East were made with packed mud and branches; the rains would cause the seeds in the mud to sprout but, of course, those seedlings were short-lived. So also would be the end of the wicked: they might grow for a brief moment, but would generate no grain to be "gathered" (129:7b)—their attempts to flourish (at the expense of their victims) would be rendered fruitless and abortive. They who would be thus "shamed [יֵבֹשׁוּ]" (129:5a) would "wither [יָבֵשׁ]" and perish (129:6b). Thereby you have the irony of the enemy plowing, but themselves ending up as a failed harvest! The fate of these evildoers is depicted chiastically in 129:5–6:

129:5a	"may they be shamed [יֵבֹשׁוּ]"
129:5b	"all who hate Zion"
129:6b	"[it] withers [יָבֵשׁ]"

Such is the fate of these wicked and the wretchedness of their outcome that no one even so much as utters a blessing upon them, let alone God actually blessing them (129:8)! They are only objects of a desire that they be rendered sterile, spent, and shriveled (129:5–7). It is because the enemies of God's people are God's enemies that the devout can pray that their deity will have his way with the wicked, in his time and in his fashion.

God's people "sang this song in the night, as it were. By faith rather than sight they clung to God's past revelation of himself as [their] champion . . . . With the courage that sprang from a real faith they dared to assert that their divine help in ages past was their hope for years to come.³" So, what began with a "say" (129:1b) and a doubled lament (129:1a, 2a) ends with another "say" (129:8a) and a doubled (but negated) blessing (129:8b, 8c). All that to say (!), the ones constantly persecuting the people of God remain chronically and forever unblessed!

Sermon Map

I. Persecution by the Wicked: Unprevailing
   Persecution (129:1–2a, 3)
   God's deliverance in the past (129:2b, 4)
   Move-to-relevance: God's deliverance of us in the past
II. Punishment of the Wicked: Unblessing
   Waiting upon God to work (129:5–8)
III. *Wait upon God to Work His Way with the Wicked!*
   Waiting in prayerful hope, recollecting and recounting the past

---

3. Allen, *Psalms 101–150*, 190.

PSALM 130:1–8

Psalm of Disorientation

The Lovingkindness of Being Forgiven

PSALM 130 IS ONE of the seven traditional penitential psalms (along with Psalms 6; 32; 38; 51; 102; and 143). It is clearly a prayer psalm but without any indication of external threats.[1] Instead, the use of such words as "iniquity," "forgiveness," "feared," "lovingkindness," and "redemption" in the psalm (130:3a, 4a, 4b, 7b, 7c) indicate the presence of dangers internal, rather than threats external—one's own sin (as suggested in 130:3–4, 8). "[T]he fearful depths from which the cry goes up to God are not the threat of external or hostile forces but the mental, emotional, and spiritual dark night of the soul that finds itself plunged into sin and guilt, the broken relationship with God and neighbor, and is powerless to extricate itself from that predicament."[2]

But, on the other hand, there is no direct plea for help (beyond an appeal to be heard, 130:2). Perhaps this indicates "a sense of the gulf that lies between the psalmist and Yahweh because of his sin," and the conviction that only God can bridge that gulf.[3] All that the people of God need is that God pay attention; the rest will follow as they wait upon him, the psalm exhorts. Indeed, "Yahweh," "Yah," and "Lord" occur eight times (130:1a, 2a, 3a, 3b, 5a, 6a, 7a, 7b): there is no doubt who the main protagonist is.[4] Also, words relating to salvation and grace occur five times: "supplications [for grace]" (103:2c); "forgiveness" (130:4a); "lovingkindness" (130:7b); "redemption" (130:7c); "redeem" (130:8a). The mending of broken relationships is clearly the theme here.

---

1. Psalm 51 also makes no mention of any opponents; but following the lead of the superscription ("David's. When Nathan the prophet came to him, as he had gone in to Bathsheba."—untranslated in this work), a particular sin of David has been postulated to be the issue there. Also, while "rebellions" is in the plural (51:1), "iniquity" and "sin" in that psalm are in the singular (51:2). The plural is likely to be a generic statement of the sinfulness of the confessor, with the singular nouns indicating a specific sin being repented of. However, in 130:3a, 8b, "iniquities" is in the plural; no particular sin is in focus in this song.

2. Miller, "Psalm 130," 177.

3. Allen, *Psalms 101–150*, 193.

4. Prinsloo notes that the alternation between the more formal "Yahweh" and the more personal "Lord" suggests "the poet's awareness of sinfulness and distance between him and Yahweh on the one hand and the grace and forgiveness granted by the same God on the other hand" (Prinsloo, Gert T. M., "Psalm 130," 458).

Translation

130:1   From the depths I cry to You, Yahweh.
130:2   Lord, hear my voice.
           May Your ears be attentive
               to the voice of my supplications [for grace].
130:3   If You keep [track of] iniquities, Yah,
           Lord, who may stand?
130:4   But with You [is] forgiveness,
           in order that You may be feared.
130:5   I hope for Yahweh, my soul hopes,
           and on His word I wait.
130:6   My soul [hopes] for the Lord
           more than the watchmen for the morning;
           [than] the watchmen for the morning.
130:7   Wait, Israel, on Yahweh;
           for with Yahweh [is] lovingkindness,
           and abundantly with Him [is] redemption.
130:8   And He—He will redeem Israel
           from all his iniquities.

Structure

Based on how Yahweh and the psalmist are depicted (as well as on the content of the verses and repetitions therein), Psalm 130 falls into four two-verse sections:

Exclamation (130:1–2)   *Addressed to Yahweh*
Yahweh in second person; psalmist in first person
    "Yahweh" and "Lord" (juxtaposed, 130:1a, 2a)
Repetition: "voice" (130:2a, 2c)

Expiation (130:3–4)   *Addressed to Yahweh*
Yahweh in second person; no first person
    "Yah" and "Lord" (juxtaposed, 130:3a, 3b)

Expectation (130:5–6)   *Addressed to self*
Yahweh in third person; psalmist in first person
    "Yahweh" and "Lord" (second words in first lines, 130:5a, 6a)
Repetition: "hope" ([×2] 130:5a); "my soul" (130:5a, 6a)
        "the watchmen for the morning" (130:6b, 6c)

Exhortation (130:7–8)   *Addressed to community*
Yahweh in third person; no first person
    "Yahweh" (juxtaposed: "on-Yahweh"; "for-with-Yahweh"; 130:7a, 7b)

Whether the "I" in the psalm is an individual speaking for himself or a leader speaking on behalf of the people is unclear. Either way, its application for the modern day is obvious.

Theological Focus

> The grace and lovingkindness of God enable his sinful people to stand before him forgiven, yet they await the consummation of his redemption, as they continue to conduct their lives in the fear of God.

Commentary

Exclamation and Expiation (130:1–4)

"Depths" (130:1) is found four other times in the OT. In those instances the word is co-located with "sea" (Isa 51:10) or "waters" (Ps 69:2, 14; Ezek 27:34). In Ps 130:1, without any qualifier, "depths" is metaphorical, connoting a dangerous situation that is imminent, a catastrophe that is impending. "The psalmist is praying as from the dead."[5] The alternation between the psalmist's groaning and his plea for God's hearing makes the exclamation poignant:

130:1	"I cry"
130:2aα	"hear"
130:2aβ	"my voice"
130:2b	"may Your ears be attentive"
130:2c	"the voice of my supplications [for grace]"

Indeed, the psalmist's "cry" and "voice" surround God in 130:1–2a:

130:1α	"I cry"
130:1β	"Yahweh"
130:2aα	"Lord"
130:2aβ	"my voice"

The supplicant's request for grace (130:2c) is immediately followed by the mention of the potential of Yahweh keeping track of sin (130:3a). If deity were to do so, no one would withstand the blast of his righteous wrath against evil (130:3b). No wonder the psalmist is crying out to God from the "depths" (130:1). This is a deserved distress that is being felt by the psalmist. There is no protestation of innocence here; the guilt is accepted, with the acknowledgment

---

5. Goldingay, *Psalms*, 3:525. This is an ongoing distress the psalmist has been bemoaning: the *qatal* form of the verb translated "cry" (130:1a) is best taken as an iterative present, in congruence with the imperatives that follow in subsequent verses.

that it is impossible for anyone to claim a stance of innocence before God (130:3b). The sinfulness of humanity is inescapable; the judgment of God is inevitable.

Oddly enough, the supplicant does not request forgiveness, only declaring how terrible it would be if God were *not* to forgive (130:3). Here he appears to be confident that God is a pardoning deity (130:4a). Thus 130:3a is a conditional clause (a counterfactual, contrary to fact)—how Yahweh *could* act (but does not), and 130:4a is an assertion—how Yahweh *does* act.[6]

There is an unusual conclusion that the psalmist then draws: there is forgiveness with Yahweh "in order that You may be feared" (130:4b). But this is not a new notion in Scripture; at the dedication of his temple, Solomon prayed to Yahweh in like fashion. Whenever prayer is made by God's people, the king asserted, "You hear from heaven, the place of Your dwelling, and You forgive ... so that they may fear You, to walk in Your ways" (2 Chr 6:30–31; and 1 Kgs 8:38–40).[7] This "fear" is not merely an emotion or state of mind; clearly, it includes obedience to deity as the parallels in the Solomonic prayer indicate. The connection between fear and obedience is explicitly made in Deut 4:10; 10:12, 20; 28:58; 2 Kgs 17:36–39. Yet, one might ask why forgiveness here ought to lead to the fear of God. Coakley notes "the central insistence of Exodus 34:6–7 on the absolute metaphysical inseparability of divine mercy and judgment. . . . This idea of simultaneous divine threat and divine forgiveness" is at the core of the identity of God and ought to evoke fear.[8] Or perhaps it is the fearful incomprehensibility of the greatness of God, the Creator of the universe forgiving mortal humans, that ought to provoke reverential awe towards deity, impelling humankind to mend their ways in the future, in alignment to God's divine demand. Fear (and obedience) of God is thus to be a consequence of the forgiveness God's people experience.

Expectation and Exhortation (130:5–8)

After the *Exclamation* and desire for *Expiation*, the psalmist addresses himself (Ps 130:5–6), expressing his expectant hope in the Lord's pardon (130:5–6). Perhaps this was a "word" from God (130:5b) assuring the supplicant that his exclamation had been heard, an affirmation that expiation had been accomplished. Indeed, God's "word" is paralleled to "Yahweh" in 130:5 (also see 130:6a, 7a).

---

6. Marrs, "*Šyry-hmʿlwt* (Psalms 120–134)," 179.

7. As another example of "fear" following forgiveness, one might add the experience of Joseph's brothers when their ill-treated sibling forgave them (Gen 50:16–20). In 50:17, the verb translated "forgive" comes from the root נשא, *nsʾ*, not סלח, *slch*, as does the noun "forgiveness" in Ps 130:4a. The latter is never used in the OT of interhuman forgiveness, but only of that offered by God. Indeed, the noun in 130:4a has an article: "*the* forgiveness." "In classical Hebrew abstract nouns have the article more often than is usual in modern languages; in poetry, however, the article is generally left out where it would add a syllable. So its use in Psalm 130:4 appears to be significant. *The* forgiveness is really meant" (Booij, "Psalm 130:3–4," 238).

8. Coakley, "On the Fearfulness of Forgiveness," 36.

> "I hope
>   for Yahweh,
>   my soul hopes,
>   and on His word
>   I wait."

There is—there can be—no other hope of expiating sin, except in Yahweh. And eagerly does the psalmist therefore hope, as keenly as one waits for the light of dawn to dispel the darkness of night (130:6abc). It is because God does not "keep [track of]" (שמר, *shmr*; 130:3a) iniquities, that the psalmist can be like "watchmen" (שֹׁמְרִים, *shomrim*, from the same root; 130:6b, 6c) awaiting Yahweh's renewal of this individual beset by sin.[9]

The hoping and waiting is thus an eager expectation for the arrival of what the psalmist appears to be sure of: pardon. And so he also urges the members of his community to "wait" on Yahweh (130:7a) just as he himself has "waited" (130:5b). All of God's people are thus exhorted to place their hope in, and to wait upon, God with whom alone is lovingkindness and redemption (130:7bc)—indeed, "abundant" redemption, the lavishness of which is also expressed textually in the doubling of that particular element in the otherwise balanced structure of 130:3–8 (note the differences between 130:4a and 130:7bc).[10]

130:3a	"iniquities"
130:4a	"but [כִּי] with You [is] forgiveness"
130:5a	"I hope for Yahweh"
130:6a	"the watchmen for the morning"
130:6b	"the watchmen for the morning"
130:7a	"Hope, Israel, in Yahweh"
130:7bc	"for [כִּי] with Yahweh [is] lovingkindness **and abundantly with Him [is] redemption**"
130:8b	"iniquities"

The verse 130:7–8a is itself structured to center upon the attributes of Yahweh that provide release from sin (see below).

---

9. This wordplay with שמר in 130:4 and 6 also warns his people that Yahweh keeps a close eye on their iniquities.

10. The first כִּי, *ki*, in these elements (130:4a) is adversative, translated "but" in light of the preceding clause of 130:3b ("who may stand?"); the second כִּי (130:7b) is causal and explicative, translated "for" in light of its preceding clause in 130:7a ("hope in Yahweh") (see Marrs, "Cry from the Depths," 89n31). Notably, 130:4a, 7b, 7c are verbless clauses, and 130:4a, 7b have nouns ("forgiveness" and "lovingkindness," respectively) that bear definite articles.

130:7aα	"wait"; "Israel"
130:7aβ	"Yahweh"
130:7b	"with Yahweh [is] **lovingkindness**"
130:7c	"abundantly with Him [is] **redemption**"
130:8aα	"He"
130:8aβ	"redeem"; "Israel"

The emphatic use of the third-person masculine pronoun, "He," in 130:8a, emphasizes that only Yahweh can provide redemption from iniquity. Also notice the similarity of the repetitions of the preposition "with" in the psalm, linked to forgiveness, lovingkindness, and redemption: "with You" (130:4a); "with Yahweh" (130:7b); and "with Him" (130:7c), respectively. Thus, "Yahweh and grace intimately belong together.... Any encounter with Yahweh is also an encounter with his grace!"[11] In 130:2c, תַּחֲנוּן, *tachanun*, "supplication," derived from חַנּוּן, *channun*, "gracious," hinted quite early in the song that this was a gracious deity, keen to extend חֵן, *chen*, "grace."

So what begins in the "depths" (130:1) ends in "redemption" (130:7b). And the psalmist's opening "I cry" (130:1) becomes transformed to "I hope" (130:5b), with an exhortation to all Israel also to "hope" (130:7a)—all because of the "lovingkindness" of Yahweh (130:7b), which makes the supplicant sure of divine redemption: "And He—He will redeem" (130:8a). This dramatic shift in the composition is especially manifested in the closing verse of the psalm: the divine object of the phrases "on Yahweh," "with Yahweh," and "with Him" (all in 130:7) becomes the emphatic subject "He" in 130:8a; the direct object "redemption" in 130:7c becomes a confident verb, "He will redeem" in 130:8a; and the vocative יִשְׂרָאֵל, *yisra'el* ("Israel") in 130:7a becomes a direct object אֶת־יִשְׂרָאֵל, *'et-yisra'el* ("Israel") in 130:8a.[12] Redemption is nigh: Israel will be forgiven from *all* its iniquities (130:8c). The amazing grace of God!

Even though we, unlike the psalmist and his cohort, live in a post-atonement dispensation, our salvation is yet to reach its terminus. We, too, like the psalmist, "wait" and "hope" for the "salvation ready to be revealed in the last time" (1 Pet 1:5).[13] Thus, in a sense, believers live between Ps 130:4 and 130:5, between salvation begun and salvation consummated, between the "already" and the "not yet" (not entirely different from the case of the psalmist who, no doubt, had the privilege of temple sacrifices).[14] Our voice has been heard, forgiveness has been extended, Jesus Christ has atoned for our sinfulness (and for *all* our sins). Yet we are constantly aware of our inherent sinfulness, and we continually seek God's forgiveness based on Christ's atoning work (to maintain our filial relationship with God, not for a forensic purpose—that was once for all settled on the cross), and we walk in his ways, obeying him in "fear" (130:4). Grace will surely see us through!

---

11. Prinsloo, Gert T. M., "Psalm 130," 459.

12. Marrs, "Cry from the Depths," 88n29.

13. And Rom 13:11.

14. The people of God in OT history are placed in the same locus as are those in the current dispensation—between "already" and "not yet"—for the atoning sacrifices instituted by God in the OT were evidence of salvation begun. In fact, one could affirm that the divine promise of Gen 3:15 was when the salvation-clock began to tick—the grace of God in operation right after the fall, with salvation to be consummated in glory one day.

Sermon Map

I. Failure
   Sinfulness (130:1–3)
   Move-to-relevance: Our sinfulness

II. Forgiveness
   God's lovingkindness and redemption (130:4a, 7bc)
   Consummation of salvation awaited (130:5–6, 7a, 8)

III. Fear
   God's mercy causing our reverential awe (130:4b)

IV. *Walk While Waiting!*
   Awaiting, in obedience, the consummation of salvation

PSALM 131:1–3

Psalm of Disorientation

Resting Humbly and Contentedly in God

PSALM 131 IS THE second shortest psalm in the Psalter (after Psalm 117). It shares with Psalm 130 a movement from the testimony of the individual psalmist or leader (131:1–2; see 130:1–2, 5–6) to an address to the community (131:3; see 130:7–8), even concluding with a similar exhortation to Israel to wait upon Yahweh (131:3; see 130:7). It is a song of confidence and contentment in Yahweh, testified to by the psalmist and recommended by him to the rest of the community.

Translation

131:1 Yahweh, my heart has not been lofty,
    and my eyes have not been haughty;
  and I have not gone about in great matters,
    or in wonders beyond me.
131:2 If I have not soothed and quieted my soul,
    like a just-nursed one with his mother . . . .
  Like a just-nursed one with[in] me [is] my soul.
131:3 Wait, Israel, on Yahweh,
    from now unto forever.

Structure

The three verses of the psalm may categorized directionally:[1]

131:1	Gazing Downward in Humility
131:2	Gratified Inward for Hunger
131:3	Going Godward with Hope

Theological Focus

God's people do not manifest boundless ambition to desire, consider, or engage in matters that are solely in the domain of a sovereign God and beyond their knowledge or ability to handle—self-glorifying aspirations worthy of utter deprecation—but remain content in humility, resting upon God who alone provides, cares, and rules.

Commentary

Gazing Downward in Humility (131:1)

Both "lofty" and "haughty" (131:1ab) refer to heights, and thus the heart and eyes of the psalmist, in his confession to God, are directed downward in humility, acknowledging that these elevated concerns, "great matters," and "wonders," are "beyond me" (131:1cd).[2] He does not look to these upwardly mobile agendas, he does not ponder about them, and he does not engage himself in them.[3] The three explicit negations thus are emphatic (131:1abc; and there is an implied negation in 131:1d): these are not interests that the psalmist, in humility, gets involved in.

What exactly are these heightened affairs that the psalmist is distancing himself from? A hint may be caught from the other co-locations of "great [גָּדוֹל, *gadol*]" and "wonders [נִפְלָאוֹת, *niphla'ot*]" in Pss 86:10; 136:4; and 145:5–6. All deal with acts of God. Indeed, the other thirty-eight instances of "wonders" in the Psalter relate to God and his work, making it very likely that "wonders" in 131:1d also relates to divine doings.[4] In other words, no human should ever be interfering with (or poking one's nose into) the domain that is God's alone, including, no doubt, events beyond human control, schemes outside of mankind's prerogative. These are, effectively, desires for the glorification of oneself, even a deification.[5]

---

1. That directional division was stimulated by the notions of height in 131:1 (see below).

2. The many *qatal* verbs in the composition likely indicate the past (as translated) that continues into the present.

3. "Heart" in 131:1a is best understood as standing for the mind (or thought).

4. Several verses in the Psalms also attribute רוּם, *rwm* (translated "be haughty" here, but elsewhere as "exalt"), as a characteristic of God and what he deserves—exaltation: 18:46; 21:13; 34:3; etc.

5. Which, of course, was the age-old temptation that felled Adam and Eve, the suggestion by the serpent

One then concludes that these sky-high agendas rightly belong only to the one dwelling in the skies: he is the sovereign who ordains all things for his own glory (and for his people's good). This then is a subtle put-down of the self-aggrandizing one, who bothers with matters beyond one's allotted portfolio, a making of god in one's own image. It is the description of one possessed by a god-complex, an affliction that comes in various grades of self-pomposity. Indeed, this danger is one that can take over the whole being of the proud person: "heart," "eyes," and "soul" (131:1a, 1b, 2a, 2c; note that נֶפֶשׁ, nephesh, "soul," is also a synonym for "throat"/"neck").⁶ The hubris knows no bounds and is all-consuming; the totality of the individual is at risk for this thralldom. "Subjectively it is almost impossible to be lofty and high without becoming people who see themselves as impressive and important, as godlets. The difference between God and us is that God never thinks he is us. So the wise person flees becoming important, knowing it is almost certain to mean peril and downfall."⁷

Thus, 131:1 depicts the psalmist as one who has been emancipated from such fantasies. His determination to avoid such imaginations of conceit and castles in the stratosphere is textually displayed by the first-person-suffixed verb and preposition surrounding those "great matters" and "wonders" (131:1cd):

"I have not gone about"	verb + first-person suffix
"in great matters"	preposition [בְּ, b] + noun
"in wonders"	preposition [בְּ] + noun
"beyond me"	preposition + first-person suffix

The supplicant knows what is "beyond" him (131:1d); he knows his own limits, and he knows that many things in life are the prerogatives of God alone, and therefore best left to God alone.

Gratified Inward for Hunger (131:2)

"Great matters" and "wonders" were not to be dabbled in (131:1cd); instead, the psalmist had "soothed and quieted" his soul (131:2a)—the two pairs matching each other. And that statement in 131:2a is also a negation, in line with the three negations already seen in 131:1a, 1b, 1c (all with the particle לֹא, lo'). But here it is an elliptical utterance, left incomplete—"if I have not soothed and quieted my soul . . ." (131:2a)—functioning essentially as a curse formula, implying the unstated conclusion: ". . . then may I be cursed." Thus the attitude of hubris is strongly deprecated with a malediction upon one who would dare to adopt such illegitimate aspirations of self-exaltation. Such wrongful attitudes are serious enough to be renounced with an oath!

---

that "you [plural] will become like God" (Gen 3:5).

6. With the "going about" in 131:1c, one might add feet as a body part incriminated in this delusion.
7. Goldingay, *Psalms*, 3:535. Well said!

The comparison with a "just-nursed" child in 131:2b, 2c is apposite.[8] The satiety of the baby after a breastfeed is a strong image of contentment and rest. And that is exactly how the "soul" of the psalmist is within him (131:2c): satiated, contented, and resting, as he refrains from involving himself "in great matters or in wonders beyond me" (131:1cd). It is made clear later in 131:3 why the psalmist is at peace, but even here in 131:2 the picture of a mother hints at the person of God: indeed, the OT has many comparisons of God as a mother: Deut 32:18; Isa 42:14; 46:3; 49:5; 66:13; Hos 11:3–4; 13:8. The contrast is also made clear with the wordplay: אִם־לֹא, 'im-lo', "if . . . not" (Ps 131:2a) and אִמּוֹ, 'immo, "his mother" (131:2b). It is one or the other: one can either be driven by boundless ambition or one can relax with contentment upon one's parent (God).

Going Godward with Hope (131:3)

And with the final verse, we learn the direction of hope that one actually should have: not upward in hubris, but Godward, with a contentment born out of a hopeful waiting upon deity (131:3a). And this, not for a moment or even for an era, but "from now unto forever" (131:3b)! Quite a countercultural assertion!

> Individual believers are fond of the idea that they should seek to make a difference, and the church is fond of the idea that it should seek to bring in or further or extend the kingdom of God. The psalm suggests that the task of the people of God is rather to wait for the kingdom of God . . . . Instead of being lofty and looking high and going about thinking that we can do wonders that are actually too great for us, the suppliant invites us to relax like a child in its mother's arms. This is a statement that will infuriate readers, which as usual shows how important it is.[9]

God does not call his people to take his role; his throne he has not abdicated. Instead, he calls them to rest in him, as he personally and directly takes care of "great matters" and of "wonders beyond me"—deity exercising his parental responsibility towards his children. This is an encouragement to abandon self-glorifying and self-gratifying ambition that does not know its place, an exhortation to humility and a prompt to eschew hubris. For God, and God alone, is the one who provides, the one who cares, the one who rules. He, and no one else!

---

8. It is best to see גָּמֻל, gamul, as connoting "just-nursed" (or "having been fed," a past participle) rather than "weaned," as in most translations. The latter, implying a child that is no longer breastfed, does not make much sense in the verse. On the other hand, "just-nursed" indicates a child still in the nursing phase of its life, but stopping feeding temporarily, as here, when it is sated. So Goldingay, Psalms, 3:537. Labuschagne, "Metaphor," 114–17, also suggests that the unusual preposition עַל, "with," in 131:2b, 2c indicates not the location of the child on the breast, but on the back, carried in a sling (see Deut 33:12; Isa 49:22), freeing the mother's arms for work, but also facilitating nursing as necessary.

9. Goldingay, Psalms, 3:538–39.

PSALM 131:1–3

Sermon Map

I. Humility
   The hubris of mankind (131:1)
   Move-to-relevance: Arenas and areas outside our portfolio
II. Hope
   One's hope is in God (131:3a)
   One hopes in God forever, because God rules forever (131:3b)
III. Hunger
   Satiated and content, as a result of hoping in God (131:2bc)
   The dangers of not being content (131:2a)
   Moves-to-relevance: How we are discontent and the dangers
IV. *Hope in Humility and without Hunger!*
   Abandoning our god-complex and desires for self-exaltation

PSALM 132:1–18

Psalm of Orientation

Worship, Faithful Obedience, and the Presence of God

PSALM 132 IS A prayer psalm concerning the dwelling of Yahweh.[1] What exactly the current exigency was, that called for this prayer psalm, is not evident, though the mention of David's "affliction" and later of his "enemies" (132:1b, 18a), as well as the description of Yahweh as "the Mighty One of Jacob" (132:2b, 5b) who will provide "deliverance" (132:16a), hints that something akin to David's bane may have been crippling the psalmist's generation; they, too, desired that their mighty God would liberate them.[2] Of course, God's people of all time often dwell in a vale of tears, and are desirous of that same preservation and benefaction from their deity, making Psalm 132 worthy of being prayed (and preached) in every age.

Translation

132:1   Remember, Yahweh, for David['s sake],
          all his affliction—
132:2   how he swore to Yahweh,
          and vowed to the Mighty One of Jacob:
132:3   "If I enter into the tent of my house,
          if I ascend into the bed of my couch,
132:4   if I give sleep to my eyes
          [or] to my eyelids slumber,
132:5   until I find a place for Yahweh,
          abodes for the Mighty One of Jacob, ..."

---

1. The identity of the psalmist/speaker is unclear; the first-person plural in 132:6–7 might indicate a leader speaking on behalf of the community.

2. "Remember" (132:1a) is often urged of God in times of crisis (see 25:6–7; 89:47, 50; 106:4, 45), and "horn" (132:17a), symbolic of power, is closely associated with God's deliverance (see 18:2; 75:10; 89:17). As well, the potential of Yahweh "turning back" (132:10–11b) also suggests some ongoing difficulty in the relationship of God's people with deity. First Chronicles 22:14 explicitly notes that David's "affliction" was in relation to his extravagance in preparing for the Solomonic temple, as the king himself confesses to his son.

132:6	Behold, we heard [of] it in Ephratah,	
	we found it in the lands of Jaar.	
132:7	Let us enter into His abodes;	
	let us worship at the stool of His feet.	
132:8	Arise, Yahweh, to Your resting place,	
	You and the ark of Your strength.	
132:9	Your priests, let them clothe [themselves] with righteousness,	
	and Your devout ones, let them shout for joy.	
132:10	For the sake of David Your servant,	
	do not turn back the face of Your anointed.	
132:11	Yahweh has sworn to David [in] truth,	
	He will not turn back from it:	
	"From the fruit of your body	
	I will set upon your throne.	
132:12	If your sons keep My covenant	
	and My decrees which I will teach them,	
	their sons also until always shall sit	
	upon your throne."	
132:13	For He has chosen—Yahweh—Zion;	
	He has desired her for His dwelling.	
132:14	"She is My resting place until always;	
	Here I will dwell, for I have desired her.	
132:15	Her provision I will greatly bless;	
	her needy I will satiate with bread.	
132:16	And her priests I will clothe with deliverance,	
	and her devout ones will vigorously shout for joy.	
132:17	There I will cause to prosper the horn of David;	
	I have prepared a lamp for My anointed.	
132:18	His enemies I will clothe with shame,	
	but upon him his crown will shine."	

Structure

The psalm comprises a pair of direct speeches: *Request of David* (in the form an oath; 132:1–6) and a *Request of the People* (132:7–10), forming the first half, followed by a *Response of God* (also in the form of an oath; 132:11–18, forming the second half). The symmetry between the two halves is easily visible: each section has ten pairs of lines (each verse comprising two lines; 132:11 and 132:12 have two pairs of lines each), and both sections begin and end with references to "David" (132:1a, 10a; and 132:11a, 17a). Each half deals with an oath uttered by the protagonists (132:2, 11); locations are involved in both (132:6, 13); and garments and sounds of worship are mentioned (132:9, 16). Also, each section concludes with a statement about the "anointed" (132:10, 17–18). Thus, "Psalm 132 involves a conversation [of leader and people with deity] and reminds us that this is an aspect of the nature of worship."[3]

The poem is tightly structured and balanced, both in terms of content and in literary art. The first half (*Request of David; Request of the People*) has affirmations from David and from the people, followed by an appeal to Yahweh; the second half (*Response of God*) has an affirmation from Yahweh, followed by his acceptance of his people's appeal:[4]

Request of David (132:1–6); Request of the People (132:7–10)

Affirmation of David (**132:1–5**): frame—"Mighty One of Jacob" (132:2b, 5b)
"Yahweh … for David['s sake] [לְדָוִד, *ldawid*]" (132:1a) "swore" (132:2a)
"if" (132:3a, 3b, 4a); "until" (132:5a)
Affirmation of the People (**132:6–7**)
Appeal to Yahweh (**132:8–10**)
  Abode: "Your resting place" (132:8a)
  Adoration: "Your" (132:9a, 9b); "let them clothe [themselves]" (132:9a)
    "devout ones," "shout for joy" (132:9b)
  Anointed: "Your anointed" (132:10b)

Response of God (132:11–18)

Affirmation of God (**132:11–12**): frame—"upon your throne" (132:11d, 12d)
"Yahweh … to David [לְדָוִד]," "sworn" (132:11a)
"if" (132:12a); "until always" (132:12c)
Acceptance by Yahweh (**132:13–18**)
  Abode: "My resting place" (132:14a)
  Adoration: "her" (132:15a, 15b, 16a, 16b); "I will clothe" (132:16a)
    "devout ones," "vigorously shout for joy" (132:16b)
  Anointed: "My anointed" (132:17b)

Thus each of the psalm's two sections almost form a mirror image of the other, with God's response being "an artistic echo" of the requests of David and of his people. However, his answer is unexpectedly and incommensurately generous and gracious, liberal and lavish.[5]

Theological Focus

> The enthusiastic commitment on the part of God's people to worship and to be faithful to him is reciprocated lavishly by God with abundant blessing as he raises up for his devout leaders who abide by divine demand; as he brings about the advent of his Messiah-King to rule his people in glory, bringing them into the very presence of God; and as he grants prosperity and peace to all, while punishing evildoers.

3. Goldingay, *Psalms*, 3:559.

4. See deClaissé-Walford et al., *Book of Psalms*, 933; Nel, "Psalm 132," 184–85; and Barbiero, "Psalm 132," 240–43.

5. Allen, *Psalms 101–150*, 210. In 2 Samuel 7, when God answers David's affirmation to build a house, deity's response is: "Okay, but . . . ." On the other hand, here in Psalm 132 it is: "Yes, and what's more . . . ." (from Knowles, "To Sanction and to Subvert," 194–95).

Commentary

Request of David; Request of the People (132:1–10)

David's affirmation (132:1–5; the direct quote of the king by the psalmist/speaker is in 132:3–5)[6] contains a number of first-person singulars. The argument is that the merit of David should accrue to future generations of leaders and to the people of God as a whole.

The oath David swore, adduced as evidence of the king's sufficient worthiness for future credit that ought to be applicable to God's leaders and his people, is in the form of an elliptical curse formula (as also in 131:2), beginning with three "if"-conditions (132:3–4) and leaving the malediction itself unstated (132:5). The entirety of the utterance is also delightfully pictured in the text: *if* the "tent" and "bed" that belonged to David (132:3) were to be separated from the "place" and "abodes" of Yahweh (132:5)—i.e., if David possesses the former pair when Yahweh does *not* have the latter, because of the king's negligent dozing and indolent napping (132:4: with "sleep" and "slumber" blanketing "eyes" and "eyelids" in a clever chiasm; see below)—may the oath-taker be accursed (the unspoken self-directed anathema):[7]

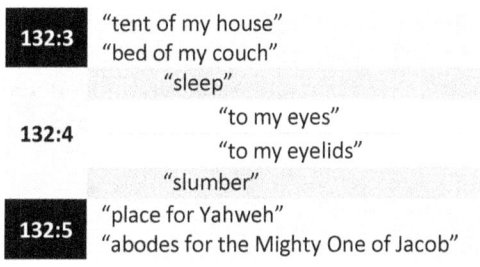

The people's affirmation employs first-person plurals in 132:6–7: the entire community is now making utterance—all God's people are involved in a seeming reenactment of the past. Cultic history is recited in précis here, collapsing a number of historical events without providing a sense of intervening periods of time. Psalm 132:6a has the "hearing" about the ark (and likely about David's oath) in Ephratah;[8] 132:6b has the "finding" of the ark in Kiriath-Jearim ("Jaar," 132:6b);[9] 132:7 deals with the worship of the people in the presence of the ark.[10]

Then comes the appeal to Yahweh (132:8–10), comprising three specific requests.

---

6. This psalmist/speaker is perhaps a leader representing the community himself.

7. The plural "abodes" (132:5b, 7a) likely denotes the many temporary locations of the ark/tent. Or it might denote the majestic nature of the dwelling of Yahweh, a plural of dignity (as in 43:3; 46:4; 84:1). Every single noun in the structure of 132:3–5 (shown above) is a different word, though the parallelisms are unmistakable—another skillful artistic touch (with a little help from the Holy Spirit, no doubt!).

8. This "hearing" is not attested anywhere else in Scripture. It apparently occurred in "Ephratah," another name for Bethlehem, David's city: Gen 35:19; Ruth 4:11; Mic 5:2. Incidentally, Psalm 132 has the only mention of the "ark" in the Psalter (132:8b).

9. The account is found in 1 Sam 6:1—7:2. The "it" of Ps 132:6a, 6b, a feminine singular suffix to the verbs "heard" and "found," refers to the "ark" (132:8).

10. Perhaps it refers to the gathering of the people before Yahweh at Mizpah, related to the ark's discovery: 1 Sam 7:5; 10:17. "Stool of his feet" could also refer to the ark, as in 1 Chr 28:2 and perhaps in Ps 99:5.

Abode: 132:8 leaps forward to the post-construction time-period of the temple, as Yahweh is invited, with the ark, to dwell therein.[11]

Adoration: 132:9 appeals that the leaders of God's people ("priests") may be made righteous and the devotees rendered joyous by God as they worship in the temple.

Anointed: 132:10 pleads that for the sake of David (proven worthy by his oath cited in 132:3–5) Yahweh would not spurn the face of "Your anointed" (132:10).[12] While historically these words (or almost similar ones) were uttered at the inauguration of the temple by Solomon (compare 132:8–10 and 2 Chr 6:41–42), who referred to himself as the "anointed," in the plausible post-exilic setting of Psalm 132 the label, "Your anointed," likely refers to the leader during that later era.[13]

One notices that the goal in the affirmations of David (135:1–5) and of the people (132:6–7) appears to be not so much the construction of the temple to house ark and deity as much as it is the worship of God. They found the ark (132:6), and they worship (132:7); they invoke Yahweh to enter the temple with the ark (132:8), and they worship (132:9)! And no wonder, for "abodes" (132:5a, 7a) and "resting place" (132:8a, 14a), "dwelling" (132:13b), and "dwell" (132:14b), bring to mind "the promise and ultimate fulfillment of God's enduring presence in the midst of the children of Israel."[14]

In sum, in the first half of the psalm, the people of God and their leader(s), enthusiastic in their devotion to God and to his worship, are appealing to God for his presence with them (abode), for their enablement to worship him passionately (adoration), and that he not turn his face from their leader (anointed) and, by extension, from them.[15]

Response of God (132:11–18)

The *Response of God* is remarkable for the fact that it extensively reuses vocabulary from the prior section, *Request of David* and *Request of the People*: "David" (132:1a, 10a, 11a, 17a);[16] "swore" (132:2a, 11a); "if" (132:3a, 3b, 4a, 12a); "until" (132:5a, 12c, 14a); "resting place"

---

11. "Resting place" here (later identified as Zion, in 132:13–14), is opposed to the earlier "place" or "abodes" (132:5, 7a), and suggests a more stable location, as in Deut 12:9; Isa 66:1. See especially 1 Chr 28:2, that has David intending to build for God a "house of rest" for the "ark" and for the "stool of the feet of our God." See Barbiero, "Psalm 132," 246–49. This "rest" of God is not a place where deity is loafing and lollygagging. Rather it depicts his active ruling function in the divine temple (as in Gen 2:1–2, where he takes his "rest" in the cosmos-Temple) (see Kuruvilla, *Genesis*, 41–49).

12. "David['s sake]" is also adduced in 132:1a.

13. As also does the "anointed" in Pss 18:50; 20:6; 28:8; 84:9; 89:20, 38, 51. It must be noted that "anointed" in the Psalter can have a variety of referents, some of which can be identified only by a process of elimination and from the context: besides the ones noted above referring to a leader, 92:10 and 105:15 point to the people of God as "anointed"; other instances, primarily 2:2 and 45:7, refer to the messianic leader (later revealed as Jesus Christ). Indeed, some of the ruling prophecies pertaining to the "anointed" of 2:2 are applied even to the followers of this Messiah (see Rev 2:26–27, citing Ps 2:8), by extension/association with him or because of a similar "anointing" by the Holy Spirit (these are, no doubt, two integrally related factors).

14. deClaissé-Walford et al., *Book of Psalms*, 935.

15. David swore he would *not* "enter" his house (132:3a) without "finding" (132:5a) "abodes" for Yahweh (132:5b); later, the people "find" the ark (132:6b) and "enter" (132:7aα) Yahweh's "abodes" (132:7aβ) to worship. In that same vein of fulfillment, David promises a "place [מָקוֹם, *maqom*]" for Yahweh's house (132:5a) and, subsequently, the people bid Yahweh "arise [קוּמָה, *qumah*]" to his habitation (132:8a). All indicate a close identity between the ruler and the ruled.

16. With "for/to/of David [לְדָוִד]" repeated in 132:1a, 11a, 17a.

(132:8a, 14a); "clothed/clothe" (132:9a, 16a, 18a); "priests" (132:9a, 16a); "devout ones... shout for joy" (132:9b, 16b); "turn back" (132:10b, 11b); and "anointed" (132:10b, 17b). That makes the *Response of God* almost a verbatim echo of the *Request of David* and the *Request of the People*: God enthusiastically adopts the ideas proffered by his leader and his people. That is how pleased God is with the eagerness of his people for his worship and for his glory!

But while there are correspondences between the requests of leader and people and the response of their God, the extent and scope of the latter is of a different dimension—there is a significant intensifying in the divine response to the human requests: it is not just a straightforward acquiescence and answer. David promised a "place"/"abodes" for Yahweh (132:5); deity reciprocates with a "throne" and an everlasting lineage of rulers and leadership for his people (132:11–12). The king was keen on a house "for [ל, *l*]" Yahweh and "for [ל]" the Mighty One of Jacob (132:5); God promises "to [ל]" David (132:11a) that he would provide a ruler "upon [ל]" David's throne (132:11d, 12d). Corresponding to David's "if" (132:3a, 3b, 4a), God also issues an "if" (132:12), but noticeably wider in breadth: divine blessing goes beyond the king who made those original promises, extending even to the sons of David. However, the blessing upon the sons of David would be contingent upon their abiding by the covenant of God (132:12ab).[17] If they abided by God's word, then God would not "turn back from it," his truthful word.[18] That is to say, God promises Davidides on the throne who would be blessed if these future rulers remained faithful to divine demand. The reciprocity of this blessing is visible in the structure of 132:11c–12:[19]

132:11cd	"from the fruit of your body	**I will set upon your throne.**
132:12aα	if your sons keep	
132:12aβ	my covenant	
132:12bα	and My decrees	
132:12bβ	which I will teach them,	
132:12cd	their sons also shall until always	**sit upon your throne."**

David's oath not to sleep was "until" he located a site for the temple (132:5a), but God's oath to bless David's line and his station of rest in Zion extended eternally, "*until* always" (132:12c, 14a).

---

17. Also see 2 Sam 7:14; 1 Kgs 2:4; 8:25; 9:4–5; 11:38–39; and Ps 89:30–31 for this qualification. The parallel of "My covenant" with "My decrees" in 132:12ab indicates that the former term is not referring to an established covenant, but is pointing to divine demand in general, the way of God that mankind is called to walk upon. Such covenant-/divine demand-keeping resulting in the blessing of reward is applicable not only for God's leaders but for all God's people: 25:10; 44:17; 103:18. This conditionality is also reflected in the sequence of events in Psalm 132: the choice of David and his ruling descendants by Yahweh (132:11–12) comes *after* David's vow and its execution (132:1–10). That is not to say that God's actions are entirely conditional; rather, an unconditional vow on his part can always be expanded by conditional elements—bonuses based on how the human actors have responded to deity (see, for instance, God's expanded promises to Abraham subsequent to the latter's passing a "test": Gen 22:15–18). That "bonus" is, of course, grace, granted by a gracious God, but not necessarily in any predetermined proportion to deeds performed, and thus it can never be contractual.

18. The feminine suffix of "from *it* [מִמֶּנָּה, *mimmennah*]" refers to the nearest feminine antecedent, "truth."

19. Auffret, *Là montent les tribus*, 101.

While the *Response of God* is marked by intensification throughout, one should especially note that each of the elements of the appeal to Yahweh took up only a single verse in the first half of the psalm (132:8–10; one verse for each of the items: abode, adoration, and anointed). However, in the second half of the psalm, the response of Yahweh to those requests (132:13–18) allocates two verses for each of those same elements, an obvious enhancement and augmentation of the divine answers to human appeals.

Abode: Whereas Yahweh had been requested to enter into his resting place (132:8), Yahweh goes even further in his response: He, *Yahweh*, chose Zion (note the emphasis in 132:13a); in fact, he "desired her" for his "dwelling" (132:13b, 14b).[20] This is sounding almost as if Yahweh has fallen in love! Perhaps he has. Yahweh's choice of Zion is emphatically depicted in 132:13–14:

"He has desired her"
"His dwelling"
    "She is My resting place until always"
"I will dwell"
"I have desired her"

Adoration: Whereas Yahweh had been requested to enable the enthusiastic worship of his people, led by their leaders in the temple in Zion (132:9), deity, in response, raises the ante. He would abundantly bless the entire city with provision, satiating the needy and caring for his own (132:15). And whereas the celebration in the temple involved the priests clothing themselves with "righteousness" and God's people "shouting for joy" (132:9), Yahweh's abiding in his eternal resting place would generate a far more extravagant exultation, with priests being clothed by God himself with "deliverance" and God's people "*vigorously* shouting for joy" (132:16). Gladness all around, pointedly depicted in 132:15–16 (particularly with the *piel* infinitive absolutes in 132:15a, 16b), overflowing from the very presence of God with his people![21]

"Her provision   I shall greatly bless [בָּרֵךְ אֲבָרֵךְ, *barek 'avarek*];
    her needy   I will satiate   with bread.
    And her priests   I will clothe   with deliverance,
and her devout ones will vigorously shout for joy [רַנֵּן יְרַנֵּנוּ, *rannen yrannenu*]."

Anointed: To the appeal that God not "turn back" from his current leader, "Your anointed" (132:10), God had promised "not [to] turn back" (132:11b) from his promise (see above). But that divine promise moves rapidly forward in time from that current leader, through a whole array of future leaders (132:11–12), to alight upon a specific person, "My anointed"—a single individual (note "his," "him," in 132:18). There are a number of reasons to discern a

---

20. "Dwelling" is from ישׁב, *yshv*; that root is often used in the Psalter to depict a ruler "sitting" enthroned: see 2:4; 9:4, 7; 22:3; 29:10–11; 55:19; 80:1; 99:1; 110:1; 113:5; 123:1. What was "abodes" and a "resting place" in the human *Requests* (132:8) has been magnified into the palace of the king in the divine *Response*.

21. From Auffret, *Là montent les tribus*, 102.

considerable heightening of language in 132:17–18 that points to the remarkable operations, success, and glory of this unique (final?) Davidide.

Firstly, while "turn back" and the "anointed" showed up in the *Request of the People* (13:10b) and was reciprocated immediately in the *Response of God* (13:11b), God does not employ "anointed" in his *Response* at that point in the composition. Instead, deity waits till the end of the psalm to do so (132:17b), timing this unique one's arrival on the scene only *after* a series of other leaders, the Davidides, had occupied the throne (132:11c–12) . . . and presumably failed (see below). This suggests a shift in referent, as well as a shift in time/era. Secondly, the contrast between "there" in 132:17a and "here" in 132:14b suggests a change in the point of view in 132:17–18. Particularly since these two verses continue the first-person speech of deity from the preceding verses of 132:14–16, one would have expected an unchanged perspective across 132:14–18. But with "there" in the emphatic initial position of the sentence in 132:17a, the reader is now placed at a distance from all the goings on far away in the day of "My anointed."[22] Thirdly, 132:17–18 has a sustained focus on the "anointed," with every one of its four lines mentioning this individual: "horn,"[23] "My anointed," "*his* enemies," "upon *him*," and "*his* crown." In contrast, thus far, in 132:13–16, God's *Response* had kept its focus on Zion: "Zion," "desired *her*" (132:13b, 14b), "she" (132:14a), "*her* provision" and "*her* needy" (132:15), and "*her* priests" and "*her* devout ones" (132:16). This makes the shift in focus in 132:17–18 quite special. Fourthly, there is an unexpected introduction of agricultural metaphors in 132:17–18. "Prosper [from צמח, *tsmch*]" (132:17a) elsewhere in the Psalter concerns growth of vegetation;[24] in prophetic literature, one also notes the messianic connotation of the noun צֶמַח, *tsemach*, "Branch,"[25] and the eschatological understanding of the verb צמח.[26] Likewise, "shine [from צוץ, *tswts*]" (132:18b) is also exclusively used in the Psalms of the flourishing of vegetation.[27] This unusual shift in language to metaphors with messianic connotations, as this inimitable individual is described, is significant. Fifthly, as opposed to 2 Sam 21:17; 1 Kgs 11:36; 15:4; 2 Kgs 8:19; and 2 Chr 21:7 that state that there "always" would be a lamp for David, here in Ps 132:17b the lamp has to be "prepared" by God, a rekindling of the flame that had apparently gone out.[28] This divine reignition seems to be reflecting the reestablishment of the Davidic monarchy in the person of "My anointed" (132:17b). In fact, 2 Kgs 8:19 parallels "Judah" with "lamp." Zion, the residence of God in Judah is, thus, the realm of the anointed. Sixthly, the unusual perfect verb "I have prepared [עָרַכְתִּי, *'araktti*]" in Ps 132:17b stands out amidst seven imperfect verbs in 132:15–18. The last set of perfect verbs before this was in 132:13: "He has chosen" and "He has desired." Relating these two perfect verbs in 132:13 with the one in 132:17a, we suspect that the choice of Zion as divine dwelling (132:13) is being equated with the preparation of the dominion and reign of the anointed (132:17). That makes good sense, for where Yahweh dwells is the principal domain and center of operations of this anointed regent. Seventhly: Needless to say, all

---

22. Leow, "Changing One's Tune," 43.

23. Usually indicating the might and power of its bearer. Also see Ps 18:2; 75:4–5, 10; 89:17, 24; 92:10; 112:9; 148:14.

24. See Pss 65:10; 85:11 (metaphorical, but very much related to sprouting, particularly in light of 85:12); 104:14; 147:8.

25. See Isa 4:2; Jer 23:5; 33:15; Zech 3:8; 6:12.

26. See Isa 42:9; 43:19; 44:4; 45:8; 55:10; 58:8; 61:11; Jer 33:15; Ezek 29:21.

27. Pss 72:16; 90:6; 92:7; 103:15.

28. The disobedience of the Davidides, warned about in 132:12, must have significantly contributed to that extinction (see Prov 24:20).

of this king's foes will be vanquished. Whereas the regent's priests, the leaders of God's people, are "clothed" with righteousness and deliverance (132:9a, 16a), the enemies of the "anointed" will be "clothed" with shame (132:18a); at the same time, the outfit of the "anointed," particularly the mark of his kingship, his crown, will blazon forth brilliant and bright (132:18b). Very kingly, indeed! But "crown" in Ps 132:18b is נֵזֶר, *nezer*, related to נזר, *nzr*, "to dedicate/consecrate," with sacral significance (unlike the generally more secular word for crown, עֲטֶרֶת, *'ateret*).[29] Likewise, "prepared" and "lamp" (132:17b) coalesce in the work of the priesthood in Lev 24:3–4. Very priestly, indeed! This is quite an unusual description for a ruler, who seems to be displaying both regal and religious character, wielding a scepter that is also sacred, and wearing a crown that is also cultic.[30]

All that to say, something new is happening here and someone new is being introduced here, in a new place, "there," and in a new time, the eschaton. Following the lead of God's tremendous expansion and intensification in his *Response* to his people's *Request*, this unique individual at the close of the psalm can surely be identified with *the* messianic figure, Jesus Christ, the Son of David, the Davidide *par excellence*.[31] Thus the grandeur of all that pertains to "My anointed" moves the arena of activity from the current age into the eschaton, when divine presence is forever established with his people, and the divine ruler, the messianic anointed, Jesus Christ, the God-King, is forever enthroned in his capital and in his Capitol. God, then, will finally be with his people—עִמָּנוּ אֵל, *'immanu 'el*, "with us [is] God" (Isa 7:14; 8:8)!

No wonder the presence of deity is extremely significant in this psalm that has a number of synonyms for the locus of God's presence: "place" (Ps 132:5a); "abodes" (132:5b, 7a); "stool of his feet" (132:7b); "resting place" (132:8a, 14a); "ark" (132:8b); "Zion" (132:13a); Yahweh's "dwelling" (132:13b);[32] "here" (132:14b); and "there" (132:17a); as well, the third-person feminine singular adjective or pronominal suffixes denoting Zion: "she" (132:14a) and "her" (132:13b, 14b, 15a, 15b, 16a, 16b).

Thus, what started with a building project has culminated in the very presence of God and his Messiah-King with his people, in the temple and upon the throne, forever. Goldingay is right: "It is said that 'if you build it, they will come.' But this psalm says, 'If you build it, he will come.'"[33] Amen, and amen! *Maranatha!*

---

29. See, for instance, Num 6:1–21 for the employment of this root to describe the status of a "Nazirite" (נָזִיר, *nazir*).

30. It is also surely odd, at first reading, that while the disobedience of David's sons to divine demand is anticipated (132:12a), of David, their progenitor, no such potential is envisaged, though this king was considerably wayward himself. Perhaps the reason for this whitewashing is to enable the close linkage of David, the historic king, with *the* anointed Davidide, the eschatological King—the sinless and impeccable Messiah, the Lord Jesus.

31. Not explicitly identified, of course, but described with enough detail to generate hope in readers/listeners in OT days for a time of future glory. That is not very different from the circumstances of God's people today: even though the person referred to is clear to us in this current dispensation, we, too, hope for a new age under this soon-coming God-King!

32. And "sit" (132:12d), "dwell" (132:14b)—all ישׁב.

33. Goldingay, *Psalms*, 3:560.

Sermon Map

I. People's Commitment to Worship and Walk
   Enthusiasm for worship of God (132:1–10)
   Faithfulness to walk with God (132:12)
   Move-to-relevance: Heartfelt worship of, and faithfulness to, God

II. God's Commitment to Bestow and Bless
   Granting of Leaders, including the Messiah (132:11–12, 17)
   Abundance of divine blessing (132:13–16, 18)
   Move-to-relevance: the bliss of God's presence and God's rule forever

III. *Revere God and Be Ruled by God!*
   Worshiping and walking with God, actualizing his rule in Christ now

PSALM 133:1–3

Psalm of Orientation

Human Worship and Divine Blessing

THIS SHORT PSALM EXHAUSTS its punch line at the start in 133:1.[1] However, it is the description in the rest of the psalm of "how good and how pleasant" (133:1a) it is for the people of God to dwell in unity that adds zest to the punch, so to speak. "Psalm 133 is a psalm that starts but never really ends. Its point ... is made in the first verse, and then it chases a chain of similes into a verbal whirlpool and stops, never really clarifying itself. Like a passenger after the jerking halt at the end of a roller-coaster ride, the reader of Ps 133 asks, 'How did I get to ... ["life unto forever"] from the apogee of ... ["kinfolk ... dwelling even as one"]?'"[2] Though it has the feel of a wisdom composition, it appears to relate to the gathering of pilgrims in Jerusalem, making it appropriate for the Songs of Ascents. The long and short of it is that this psalm serves to exhort the people of God to live "even as one."

Translation

133:1 Behold, how good and how pleasant
    for kinfolk to dwell even as one;
133:2 like good oil upon the head,
    going down upon the beard—
the beard of Aaron—which [oil] is going down
    upon the collar of his robes;
133:3 like the dew of Hermon which is going down
    upon the mountains of Zion;
for there Yahweh commanded the blessing—
    life unto forever.

---

1. In my translation all three verses together are construed as generating a single sentence.
2. Zevit, "Psalms at the Poetic Precipice," 356.

Structure

The song has an expression of blessing at either end, with the middle portion taken up by picturing the blessing with an image of abundance:[3]

133:1	**Expression of Blessing 1** *Deictic particle opener:* "behold" *Paired element:* "good" and "pleasant" *Heightened ending:* "even as one" *Assonance:* נְעִים, *na'im*; אַחִים, *'achim*
133:2	**Equation of Blessing 1** ("like") "going down upon" (133:2b, 2c)
133:3ab	**Equation of Blessing 2** ("like") "going down upon"
133:3cd	**Expression of Blessing 2** *Deictic particle opener:* "for there" *Paired element:* "blessing" and "life" *Heightened ending:* "unto forever" *Assonance:* חַיִּים, *chayim*

Theological Focus

The united communal worship of the people of God as one joint entity is not only good and pleasant, it also receives the blessing of abundant life from God.

Commentary

Expression of Blessing 1 (133:1)

The *Expression of Blessing* at the psalm's opening asserts "how good" and "how pleasant" it is for "kinfolk" (literally, "siblings/brothers," but extendable beyond families to entire communities) to live in unity (133:1). In this psalm, one of the Songs of the Ascents, a liturgical or festal community engaged in joint worship of Yahweh is likely to be in view.

Equation of Blessing 1 (133:2)

How "good" and how "pleasant" is this unity? It is like the pouring or anointing of "good oil" (133:2a)—of high quality, and exuding a delightful fragrance—upon a person, not just in minute quantities, but in such a lavish abundance that it flows down the beard of the one so christened (133:2bcd). It is "a high sign of richness, sufficiency, superabundance, and, above

---

3. From Ross, *Psalms*, 3:747; and Allen, *Psalms 101–150*, 214–15.

all, enjoyable pleasure . . . the gesture of drenching the head with a superfluity of this fine oil, a literal image of over-the-topness, superabundance."[4]

And this unction does not drench just any beard, but Aaron's, indicating again the focus upon the worshiper who is implicitly included with that priestly official: the people of God are, after all, a "kingdom of priests" (Exod 19:6; and Ps 135:19 with its parallel between "house of Israel" and "house of Aaron"). The formal anointing of the high priest alluded to in our psalm (see Exod 29:7; Lev 8:12) supplements the sense of a divine dedication of all God's people for the worship of Yahweh. Thus there is a sense of luxuriance and plenty, of joy and gladness, and of the beatific and God-approved nature of worship in joint community, that is akin to this plenitude of "good oil" that inundates beard and collar (and, no doubt, spills even further down the garment; Ps 133:2).[5] "One might have thought this would all get rather messy and unpleasant; that is not the psalm's perspective. The abundance of oil suggests abundance of sacred festivity and thus a powerful image for the wonder of a community living as one," engaged in the worship of their great deity.[6]

Equation of Blessing 2 (133:3ab)

A second simile follows, that of dew from Mount Hermon flowing down the mountains of Zion. This, too, is indicative of the bounty of divine blessing, for dew was critical in an agrarian society, particularly in those summer months lacking rain.[7]

Clearly, and in keeping with Psalm 132 as well, the focus here in 133:2–3b is on the beauty and blessing of worship undertaken as a unified community. After noting the luxuriance of "good oil" (an agricultural product; 133:2), the listing of dew (essential for agricultural produce) as a blessing is apropos.[8] Somehow the dew on Hermon pours into Zion far away.

> We now feel the force of the earlier image of oil running down over head and beard, as well as the general association of the Lebanon and Anti-Lebanon mountains as a source of flowing water . . .—the runoff from the Hermon actually feeds the headwaters of the Jordan. Having the dew spill down onto Zion some hundreds of kilometers to the south is a fabulous image. It accentuates the already high hyperbole and at the same time concretizes the image of superfluity, measures it, makes it graspable, imaginable to the mind's eye.[9]

---

4. Dobbs-Allsopp, "Psalm 133," 10.
5. This "beard" is likely to be the long sidelocks, the adornment of a priest (Lev 19:27; 21:5).
6. Goldingay, *Psalms*, 3:567.
7. See Gen 27:28; Deut 33:13, 28; Prov 3:20; 19:12; Hos 14:5; Mic 5:7; Zech 8:12.
8. Though I did wonder how "oil" and "water" (aka "dew"; 133:3a) could dwell together in unity "even as one" (133:1b). Perhaps that is the point!
9. Dobbs-Allsopp, "Psalm 133," 16.

Expression of Blessing 2 (133:3cd)

This extravagance of all good things thus naturally leads to an acknowledgment of God's blessing, equally bountiful and profuse, gracious and generous. Indeed, the parallelism between oil, dew, and divine blessing is textually portrayed:[10]

132:2a	"like good oil upon the head,	
132:2b–cα	*going down* upon the **beard**—the beard of Aaron—	*verb* + **locus**
132:2cβ–d	which [oil] is *going down* upon the **collar** of his	*verb* + **locus**
133:3aα	like the dew of Hermon	
133:3aβ–b	which is *going down* upon the **mountains** of Zion;	*verb* + **locus**
133:3cα	for **there** Yahweh *commanded*	*verb* + **locus**
133:3cβ–d	the blessing—life unto forever."	

Thus, communality of kinfolk is equated to oil and to dew, which in turn becomes an outlet of expression for divine blessing. In other words, the result of the unity of God's people in worship results in an abundance of blessing from deity, even life forever in his presence, ostensibly continuing the worship begun on this side of eternity. However, the focus remains on the start of a life here with God, worshiping him corporately and enjoying his blessings as a result, a life that will carry on "unto forever"![11]

Sermon Map

I. Worship in Community
   Worship background of the Songs of Ascent
   Corporality of worship (133:1b)
   Liturgical hint (133:2cd)
   Move-to-relevance: Our lack of committed communal worship

II. Weal from Deity
   Goodness and pleasantness of communal worship (133:1a, 2ab, 3ab)
   God's blessing (133:3cd)
   Move-to-relevance: The delight of God in our united worship

III. *Worship Wins Weal!*
   Specifics on sustaining communal worship

---

10. "There" in 133:3c indicates Zion, the place of the gathering of the people of God for worship and the zip code for blessing. One might consider Zion both as the place *of* blessing (9:14; 48:2, 9; 51:18; 65:1, 4; etc.) and the place *from which* blessing flows to the rest of the world, because of its divine resident (14:7; 20:2; 53:6; 128:5; 134:3; etc.).

11. Thus the theme of corporate worship and its resultant blessing is continued in this psalm from the previous one.

PSALM 134:1–3

Psalm of Orientation

Blessers Blessed

PSALM 134 IS THE final member in the Songs of the Ascents; it is also the shortest of the collection (by word count). Though "Yahweh" shows up four times in its three verses (134:1a [×2], 2b, 3a), the song is *about* God, not addressed *to* God. The worship theme of the previous two psalms continues here, and Psalm 134 likely functions as a doxology to the group of ascent songs. The parallels with Psalm 133 are obvious: this one, too, begins with a "behold" (134:1a; and 133:1a) and ends with "blessing" (134:3a; and 133:3c). Unlike other psalms of this nature, its opening summons to praise does not provide explanations for praising. Perhaps none is required at the end of the Songs of Ascents—worship is a self-evident, essential, and incontrovertible response of humanity to deity.

Translation

134:1	Behold, bless Yahweh, all servants of Yahweh,
	those standing in the house of Yahweh in the nights.
134:2	Lift your hands to the holy place
	and bless Yahweh.
134:3	May Yahweh bless you from Zion—
	the One who made the heavens and the earth.

Structure

The "blessing" motif resounds in each of the three verses (134:1a, 2b, 3a), with locations where the blessing by humans is to be performed and whence the blessing by Yahweh proceeds:

> **Blessing *of* Yahweh (134:1–2)**
> "bless Yahweh" (134:1a, 2b)
> Locations: "house of Yahweh" (134:1b); "holy place" (134:2a)
>
> **Blessing *from* Yahweh (134:3)**
> "May Yahweh bless you" (134:3a)
> Locations: "Zion" (134:3a); "heavens and the earth" (134:3b)

It is conceivable that 134:1–2 is uttered by a leader or a priest calling the people of God to praise, and that 134:3 is antiphonally uttered by the people, blessing their leader/priest. On the other hand, 134:1–2 may be the people's exhortation to those serving in the house of Yahweh "in the nights" (134:1b),[1] with the leader/priest wishing blessing upon them in turn, in 134:3. In either case, the thrust of the psalm is not affected.

Theological Focus

> The blessed worship of God by the people of God in all places, at all times, with all of one's being, brings reciprocal, but asymmetrically greater, blessing from God the Creator of the universe.

Commentary

Blessing of Yahweh (134:1–2)

Here, and in the Songs of Ascents, the motif of worship is the predominant call of God to his people. As was noted, it is quite possible this psalm was employed as a doxological song of pilgrims at the end of their journey of worship, perhaps sung the night (see Ps 134:1b) before they departed Jerusalem. The bidding is to "bless Yahweh" (134:1a, 2b), as is appropriate for "all servants of Yahweh" (134:1a). Whether these are officials in the temple ("those standing in the house of Yahweh in the nights," 134:1b) or people in general (113:1; 135:1; Isa 54:17), the blessing of deity is a critical aspect of worship, equally applicable to all God's people.

Goldingay notes the ironic call to "bless [בָּרֵךְ, *barak*]"—the word is derived from the action of bending the "knee [בֶּרֶךְ, *berek*]"—while "standing" (134:1b). One can bend the knee before deity, even if one's posture is otherwise! He also notes that bending of knee and "lifting of hands" indicates the importance of bodily motion in the worship of God: this is a blessing

---

1. Guards (as in 130:6)? Levites (1 Chr 9:27, 33; 23:30; Ps 92:2)?

of God that involves all of a human being as an integral unity. All that to say, "standing is the posture of people who are present, alert, and ready to do whatever their master wants done."[2]

132:1a	"bless Yahweh"	
132:1bα	"house of Yahweh"	[*place*]
132:1bβ	"nights"	[*time*]
132:2a	"holy place"	[*place*]
132:2b	"bless Yahweh"	

The imperative for the people of God to praise/worship him—equivalent to blessing him—is clear everywhere in Scripture; perhaps this psalm stresses the importance of worshiping him *even at nights*, or in other words, at all times. The location of worship, at least in this psalm and in these verses, appears to be restricted to the "house of Yahweh" and the "holy place," perhaps by the historical and contextual constraint of this psalm being a member of the Songs of Ascent, but see below, on 134:3. In sum, such blessing of deity is to be performed by "servants of Yahweh" in every place and in every time.

Blessing from Yahweh (134:3)

The blessing from Yahweh is directed to the congregation (even though the suffix "you" is singular in 134:3a, as also in the Aaronic benediction of Num 6:24–26).[3] And with that Yahweh, who is blessed by his people, in turn blesses them.

One notices that there are two locations in Ps 134:1–2, "house of Yahweh" and "holy place," where God is blessed. Likewise there are two locations in 134:3 that indicate whence God blesses: "Zion" and its parallel, "the heavens and the earth." In creation history, the entire cosmos is a temple that has Yahweh as its deity (Isa 66:1–2), with the temple in "Zion" serving as a visible token, a microcosm, of that paradigmatic cosmic sanctuary (Ps 78:69).[4] This is the response of a gracious God: he blesses those who worship (bless) him. This reciprocity is also depicted in the text with the parallel between the work of the "hands" of God's people (134:2a) and the work of God's hands—creation (often depicted in the Psalter as his handiwork) (see below).[5]

---

2. Goldingay, *Psalms*, 3:572.

3. The possibility of 134:3 being addressed by the people to the leader/priest was mentioned earlier. In any case, what is obvious is that the God, the "blessee" of his people, reciprocates by being the blesser of his people.

4. In fact, the building of the temple by Yahweh (in Ps 78:69) is said to *precede* even the selection of David as God's regent (78:70; likewise in Psalm 132). Following that lead, Yahweh had built his temple, the "heavens and the earth," and therefore the Solomonic temple simply reflected what Yahweh had already created. The expansion of temple precincts to the rest of the cosmos, that will take place one day in the eschaton to reflect what it was in the cosmos pre-fall, is "the infinite extension of sacred space, the elimination of the 'profane,' that which stands *pro fano*, 'in front of the temple.' The world in its fullness is the Temple" (Levenson, "Temple," 296). One day, there will be no part of creation that is "profane"—all will be part of the divine sanctuary, filled with the worship of deity. So all of cosmos is (or will be) God's Temple, and all of cosmos is therefore a sanctified station, and it is from this cosmic arena that God blesses his people. See Kuruvilla, *Genesis*, 39–49.

5. See 8:3, 6; 19:1; 28:5; 92:4; 102:25; 111:7; 138:8; 143:5.

134:2aα	"Lift your hands	**Human handiwork**
134:2aβ	to the holy place	
134:2b	and bless Yahweh.	
134:3aα	May Yahweh bless you	
134:3aβ	from Zion—	
134:3b	the one who made the heavens and the earth."	**Divine handiwork**

And with that the cycle of mutual blessing is begun. Of course, the reciprocal blessing by Yahweh of mankind far exceeds any kind of blessing by humans of God.

> It is a lopsided duality.... Dynamic potential is given to those who give Yahweh sincere acknowledgment of his power. Essentially it is unsought and comes as a gracious byproduct of worship. In keeping with this attribute of power the divine object of blessing becomes an active subject. He generously shares with his devoted followers from his own resources of omnipotence so that abundant life may be theirs.[6]

Worshipers (blessers) of the divine are divinely blessed, indeed!

Sermon Map

I. Blessing of Yahweh
    Worship background of the Songs of Ascent
    Worship in all places, at all times, with all of one's being (134:1–2)
    Move-to-relevance: Our weak worship

II. Blessed by Yahweh
    Worshipers blessed by the Creator of the cosmos (134:3)
    Move-to-relevance: The asymmetry of divine blessing

III. *Bless, and Be Blessed!*
    Specifics on communal praise, and enjoying God's blessings

---

6. Allen, *Psalms 101–150*, 218.

PSALM 135:1–21

Psalm of Orientation

Praising the Sovereign and Unique God

RIGHT AFTER THE PRAISE-AND-WORSHIP call of the previous psalms (Psalms 132–134), and following the Songs of Ascents, Psalm 135 presents another call to praise God.

Translation

135:1	Praise Yah:
	praise the name of Yahweh;
	praise, servants of Yahweh,
135:2	the ones who are standing in the house of Yahweh,
	in the courts of the house of our God.
135:3	Praise Yah, for Yahweh [is] good;
	make music to His name, for it is pleasant.
135:4	For Jacob, Yah has chosen for Himself,
	Israel, for His own possession.
135:5	For I—I know that Yahweh [is] great,
	and that our Lord [is greater] than all gods.
135:6	All that which Yahweh pleases, He has done,
	in the heavens and in the earth,
	in the seas and in all the depths:
135:7	the One causing the clouds to ascend from the ends of the earth;
	lightnings for the rain He made,
	the One bringing out the wind from His storehouses.
135:8	He who struck the firstborn of Egypt,
	from humans unto cattle,
135:9	He sent signs and portents into your midst, Egypt,
	against Pharaoh and against all his servants.

135:10 He who struck many nations
    and He [who] slew mighty kings—
135:11 Sihon, king of the Amorites,
    and Og, king of Bashan,
    and all the kingdoms of Canaan—
135:12 He also gave their land as an inheritance,
    an inheritance to Israel, His people.
135:13 Yahweh, Your name [is] forever,
    Yahweh, Your remembrance, from generation to generation.
135:14 For Yahweh will govern His people
    and in His servants He gets himself relieved [from His concern].
135:15 The idols of the nations [are] silver and gold,
    the work of human hands.
135:16 Mouths they have, but they do not speak;
    eyes they have, but they do not see;
135:17 ears they have, but they do not [use the] ear,
    indeed, [there is] no existence of breath in their mouths.
135:18 Like them will be the ones making them,
    all the ones who trust in them.
135:19 House of Israel, bless Yahweh;
    house of Aaron, bless Yahweh;
135:20 house of Levi, bless Yahweh;
    those who fear Yahweh, bless Yahweh.
135:21 Blessed be Yahweh from Zion,
    the One who abides [in] Jerusalem.
Praise Yah.

Structure

Psalm 135 begins and ends with *Exhortations to Praise*, and provides extensive reasons for doing so (*Explanation for Praise*), primarily dealing with the relationship between God and Israel and the superiority of God over idols:[1]

Exhortation to Praise 1 (135:1–2)
"Praise Yah" (135:1a); Seven references to God
"house" (135:2a, 2b); cultic language
Vocatives for those praising
Object marker for "name" (אֶת, *'et*; 135:1b)

Explanation for Praise (135:3–18)
Explanation Summarized (135:3–7)
God and Israel (135:3–4)
God and Idols (135:5–7):
(8 lines; "done/made [עשׂה, *'sh*]"; "wind [רוּחַ, *ruach*]")
Explanation Supplemented (135:8–18)
God and Israel (135:8–14)
God and Idols (135:15–18):
(8 lines; "work/making [עשׂה]"; "breath [רוּחַ]")

Exhortation to Praise 2 (135:19–21)
"Praise Yah" (135:21c); Seven references to God
"house" (132:19a, 19b, 20a); cultic language
Vocatives for those praising (135:19a, 19b, 20a, 20b)
Object marker for "Yahweh," the blessed (אֶת, 135:19a, 19b, 20a, 20b)

Theological Focus

There is only one true God worthy of being served, the One who is absolutely sovereign in the cosmos, and who, out of his gracious concern for his servants, works wonders of deliverance, preservation, and blessing for them, unlike lifeless non-gods, the service of which only causes deadly deprivation for devotees.

---

1. The psalm looks like "a conglomeration of snatches of other parts of the OT" (Allen, *Psalms 101–150*, 224): for instance, 135:5 = Exod 18:11; Ps 135:6 = 115:3; Ps 135:7 = Jer 10:13 (and 51:16); Ps 135:9 = Deut 34:11; Ps 135:10–12 = 136:17–22; Ps 135:13 = Exod 3:15; Ps 135:14 = Deut 32:36; Ps 135:19–20 = 115:9–11; etc.

Commentary

Exhortation to Praise 1 (135:1–2)

The exhortation to praise that opens the psalm deals with the *person* who is to be praised ("Yah" and "the name of Yahweh," i.e., his person; 135:1a, 1b); the *people* who are to praise ("servants of Yahweh," "the ones who are standing . . ."; 135:1c, 2a); the *place* where praise is primarily to be uttered ("house of Yahweh," "house of our God"; 135:2a, 2b); and the *palace*, the specific locus of praise-making ("the courts . . ."; 135:2b).[2] All that to say, God's people in God's presence must praise God! For those people of God in the current dispensation, with the Holy Spirit indwelling them, that means deity must be praised everywhere by his gathered saints![3]

Explanation for Praise (135:3–18)

The *Explanation* section forms the bulk of the psalm.[4] It begins with a summary (135:3–7) of the reasons for praising God, relating to Israel (135:3–4)—"for Yahweh [is] good [כִּי־טוֹב יְהוָה, *ki-tov yhwh*]" (135:3a)—and relating to idols, i.e., false gods[5] (135:5–7)—"that Yahweh [is] great [כִּי־גָדוֹל יְהוָה, *ki-gadol yhwh*]" (135:5a).

This personal and covenantal God of Israel, Yahweh, is "good" and his name, i.e., his person, is "pleasant" (135:3). These two descriptors were also applied to worshipers conducting their praise in community, united as one: "how good and how pleasant . . ." (133:1). It is because Yahweh is "good" and "pleasant" that the unified corporate worship of him is also "good" and "pleasant."[6] This benevolent deity, whose worship is delightful, has chosen Israel for himself, making them his people, his own possession (135:4).

But this Israelite God is also the universal God, greater than all false gods (idols) (135:5)[7] because he, unlike them, is utterly sovereign in the cosmos (135:6), and able to control its elements at his will and pleasure (135:7). The "all" in 135:6a forms a bracket with "all" in 135:6c, making the sovereignty of deity comprehensive—God's dominion is absolute—and that in contrast to "all" gods (135:5b). The verses, 135:6–7, perform a number of literary acrobatics to demonstrate the totality of God's control. That control extends over all the earth, which is hemmed in by the "doings" and "makings" of Yahweh (below).

---

2. The value of this kind of dissection of the text that I have just done is doubtful, especially for preaching purposes (except that it gives me yet another chance to alliterate!).

3. I would argue that this psalm still exhorts corporate praise (because of the temple context) rather than individual praise; the corporate indwelling of the Holy Spirit is also the impetus for such praise also (see Eph 3:19–21; 1 Cor 3:16; etc.).

4. I have placed the praise exhortations of 135:3 in the *Explanation*, since: it appears to be a resumptive beginning (this is the only place in the Psalter where "praise Yah" occurs in the middle of a psalm); also, the two "for"-clauses (135:3a, 3b) give reasons for praising God—these clauses clearly link 135:3 with 135:4, 5 (each of which also begin with similar "for"-clauses).

5. Which might well be demonic, anti-God entities.

6. "Pleasant" in the Psalter is associated with God (135:3), with his praise (81:2; 133:1; 147:1), and with his blessings to his people (16:6, 11). In the parallelism of 135:3, "pleasant" is synonymous with "good."

7. The "I" in 135:5a, the only first-person singular in the psalm, is likely to be the leader of the congregation in worship; God, on the other hand, is "*our* Lord" (135:5b).

135:6a	"done [עשה]"
135:6b	"earth"
135:7a	"earth"
135:7b	"made [עשה]"

Furthermore, that control is also exercised over all the elements of the earth, with the causative agent, God (described with participles) surrounding the active "makings" (or "doings"; perfect verb) of Yahweh:

135:7a	"the one causing ... to ascend [*participle*] from ..."
135:7b	"He made" [*perfect*]
135:7c	"the one bringing out [*participle*] ... from ..."

As well, a number of wordplays lends assonance to 135:7, adding to the poetic sense of completeness, logic, and beauty, all of which characterize deity:

135:7a	מִקְצֵה הָאָרֶץ *miqtseh ha'arets* "from the ends of the earth"
135:7cα	מוֹצֵא־רוּחַ *motse'-ruakh* "the one bringing out the wind"
135:7cβ	מֵאוֹצְרוֹתָיו *me'otsrotayw* "from His storehouses"

On 135:7, Goldingay notes:

> The psalm utilizes three different models for the divine causality involved in the event. The first colon [135:7a] suggests Yhwh working through natural processes. The second [135:7b] has Yhwh specially bringing into being each natural phenomenon [lightings and rain], without there being any link between them; the different aspects of a storm are all discrete phenomena. The third [135:7c] uses a metaphor, Yhwh as the householder who keeps a multiplicity of resources in storage already in being, and available for use whenever they are needed.[8]

Yahweh is truly supreme in the cosmos—who is like our God? And this supreme one cares for his people, so much so, as the psalmist suggests in 135:14b, he worries about them!

After these summarizing declarations of God's loyalty to Israel and his greatness over idols, the same affirmations are supplemented and expanded upon, in 135:8–14 (regarding Israel) and 135:15–18 (regarding idols).[9] The relative particle, שֶׁ, *sha*, that opens 135:8a, 10a

---

8. Goldingay, *Psalms*, 3:581.

9. After the participles of 135:7a, 7c, a new section is begun with a series of perfect verbs: "He ... struck" (135:8a); "He sent" (135:9a); "He struck" (135:10a); "He slew" (135:10b); and "He ... gave" (135:12a).

("He *who* struck"), separate 135:8–9 (dealing with the Exodus) from 135:10–14 (dealing with the conquest of the promised land). Here again, the literary structure is illuminating:

135:8aα	"He *who* struck"
135:8aβ–b	"Egypt"; "from humans unto cattle"
135:9	"Egypt"; "against Pharaoh and against all his servants"
135:10a	"He *who* struck"

Thus, again, the theme of divine sovereignty predominates. While the "*servants* of Yahweh" worship him (135:1c), and Yahweh is "relieved [from his concern]" in "His *servants*" (135:14b), "all his [Pharaoh's] *servants*" are doomed (135:9b). Just as God rules over "*all* gods" (135:5b) and "*all* the depths" (135:6c), doing "*all* that Yahweh pleases" (135:6a), so also he controls "*all* his [Pharaoh's] servants" (135:9b), and decimates "*all* the kingdoms of Canaan" (135:11c).[10] Whether they be false gods, cosmic elements, antagonistic kingdoms, or individual enemies, God is indubitably, incalculably, and incomparably greater than them all!

The cascade of increasing instances of the ending םי-, -[y]im, within each verse from 135:8 to 135:10, figuratively demonstrates the "many" nations, "mighty" kings, and "all" the kingdoms of Canaan that were subjugated by Yahweh:[11] one occurrence in 135:8 (מִצְרָיִם, *mitsrayim*, "Egypt"); two in 135:9[12] (מֹפְתִים, *miphtim*, "portents"; and מִצְרָיִם; and four in 135:10 (גּוֹיִם, רַבִּים, מְלָכִים, and עֲצוּמִים; *goyim*, *rabbim*, *mlakim*, and *'atsumim*; "nations," "many," "kings," and "mighty"). Here, too, the text depicts the "nations" and "kingdoms," with their "kings" embedded in the middle, defeated by this great God who struck those kings (135:10aα) and divvied up their kingdoms (135:12):

135:10aα	"He who struck"
135:10aβ	"nations"
135:10b	"kings"
135:11ab	"Sihon, king ..."; Og, king ..."
135:11c	"kingdoms"
135:12	"He also gave their land ... to Israel"

"*All* his servants," i.e., of the enemy king Pharaoh (135:9b) and "*all* the kingdoms" of the foes (135:11c) are subjugated—nothing and nobody is exempt from the reach of God's mighty hand! And these conquering operations of God accrue to the benefit of his people: notice, below, how the transfer of land is textually pictured, from Canaan to Israel—"*their* land" goes to "*His* people."[13]

---

10. See Num 32:33; Deut 1:4; 29:7; etc.

11. Usually that ending designates a plural noun, though that is not the case of "Egypt [מִצְרָיִם]," of course. Still the literary art is suggestive.

12. This verse is also remarkable for direct address to Egypt in the second person, making the narrative come alive in a rhetorical figure (apostrophe), as if it were actually happening to the current generation of God's people.

13. Of course, God can transfer rights to "land" (אֶרֶץ, *'erets*; 135:12a) to whomever he pleases; after all his rulership includes the "earth" (אֶרֶץ, 135:6b, 7a) in its entirety.

135:11c–12aα	"Canaan—... *their land*"
135:12aβ	"inheritance"
135:12bα	"inheritance"
135:12bβ	"Israel, *His people*"

The only direct address to Yahweh in this psalm, in 135:13, brings this section, 135:8–14, to a close. While 135:8–12 dealt with the past, 135:13–14 deals with the future: God's name, which remains forever, would be remembered for generations to come, because God would govern his people (forever, implied) and would be "relieved [from His concern]" regarding them (ostensibly also forever; 135:14b). "Yhwh is moved by the needs of Israel as 'his people,' 'his servants,' and gets relief in connection with those feelings by acting on Israel's behalf in relation to its foes. In the parallelism, then, 'governs' is an action word and 'gets himself relief' is a feelings word; the action implements the feelings, and the feelings impel the action."[14] Divine superintendence over, and divine benevolence for, his own surround his "people," his "servants":

135:14aα	"Yahweh will govern"	verb
135:14aβ	"His people"	noun
135:14bα	"His servants"	noun
135:14bβ	"He gets himself relieved"	verb

To his people, who remember him forever, his faithfulness and lovingkindness, his care and his concern, are extended ... forever (135:13)!

Then it is the turn of the God-and-idols theme to get supplemented (135:15–18). These eight lines parallel the eight lines of the summarization of God and idols (135:5–7): each has two instances of עשה ("done/made," 135:6a, 7b, and "work/making," 135:15b, 18a) and one of רוּחַ ("wind/breath," 135:7c and 135:17b). Stunningly, coming right after the exalted description of Yahweh, the first word of this section is עֲצַבֵּי, *'atsabbe*, "idols" (135:15a)—what a contrast! Also, there is no "Yahweh" in 135:15–18, only the speechless mouths, sightless eyes, and soundless ears of non-gods (135:16–17)! And a description of their equally effete devotees: "like them will be the ones making them, all the ones who trust them" (135:18).[15]

---

14. Goldingay, *Psalms*, 3:582. Adding to the emphasis of 135:14 is an unusual alliteration in Hebrew: excluding כִּי, *ki*, "for," 135:14a begins with two י-initial words (יָדִין, *yadin*, "[He] will govern"; and יהוה, *yhwh*, "Yahweh") and ends with a single ע-initial word (עַמּוֹ, *'ammo*, "His people"); whereas, excluding וְ, *w*, "and," 135:14b begins with two ע-initial words (עַל, *'al*, "in"; and עֲבָדָיו, *'avadayw*, "His servants") and ends with a single י-initial word (יִתְנֶחָם, *yitnecham*, "He gets himself relieved") (Todd, "Poetic and Contextual Analysis," 77).

15. This is quite a derogatory aspersion, for gods that one makes are no gods at all! The figure is modified from Todd, "Poetic and Contextual Analysis," 86.

135:15a	"the idols of the nations"
135:15b	"the work [עשׂה] of human hands"
135:16a	speechless "mouths"
135:16b	sightless "eyes" [*dual*]
135:17a	soundless "ears" [*dual*]
134:17b	breathless "mouths"
134:18a	"the ones making [עשׂה] them"
134:18b	"all the ones who trust in them"

Indeed, the structure is bracketed by "idols" on one side and "the ones who trust in them" on the other—both equally moribund![16] Indeed the phrase כֹּל אֲשֶׁר, *kol 'asher*, "all that which"/"all the ones who," is cleverly deployed only in 135:6a and 135:18b in the psalm: "In the former, the Lord does . . . ['all that which'] he desires. In the latter, . . . ['all the ones who'] trust in idols become like them. Thus, the Lord's ability to enact all of his desires contrasts the idols' ability to bring death upon all who trust in them."[17] And again, note the pungent opposition: God forever governs his servants and finds comfort in them (135:14), but as for idols and their servants . . . .

Exhortation to Praise 2 (135:19–21)

And with that lethal proclamation of the lifelessness of idols and their devotees, the psalm reaches its obvious conclusion: What else can we do after the eighteen verses of this song, but to fall on our knees and "praise Yah"—the immanent "one who abides [in] Jerusalem" (135:21bc)? That is exactly the exhortation of the psalmist to the "house of Israel," to the "house of Aaron," to the "house of Levi," and indeed, to all "those who fear Yahweh" (135:19–20)—all of God's "servants" (135:1c, 14b), his people of all time and in all places, in Zion, Jerusalem, and every other location: "bless Yahweh"![18]

---

16. In another powerful literary contrast and affirmation, there are only two nominal phrases in this section: in 135:13a that proclaims the true God's nature, and in 135:15a that ridicules false gods' natures: *Yahweh is great; idols are dead!* The reuse of "mouths" in 135:17b is also clearly deliberate, for one would have expected "noses" here (as in 115:6). Wait, we do have אַף, *'aph*, "nose" in 135:17b—but, alas, it is only a homonym of the word, meaning "indeed." Why this prestidigitation and misdirection? It appears that the psalmist wants to force the reader to focus on 135:17b, rendered different from the preceding three lines by its emphatic particle ("indeed" = "nose" in camouflage!), its superfluous use of "existence" ("no [. . .] breath in their mouths" would have been sufficient), and its verbless structure. Todd, "Poetic and Contextual Analysis," 81–82, draws attention to the fact that 135:5a is similar: it, too, begins with an emphatic particle ("for"), has a redundant pronoun ("I"), and is verbless. Putting the two lines together we get, again: *Yahweh is great; idols are dead!* Enough said!

17. Todd, "Poetic and Contextual Analysis," 87.

18. That this final exhortation parallels the initial exhortation (135:1–2) is clear from the similarities between these two sections (as noted in the figure of the psalm's structure). Of note, the object marker, אֵת, occurs only in 135:1b, 19a, 19b, 20a, 20b in Psalm 135; likewise, "praise," only in 135:1a, 1b, 1c, 3a, 21c.

Sermon Map

I. False Gods
- Character of those non-gods (135:15–17)
- The fate of the servants of non-gods (135:18)
- Move-to-relevance: The non-gods we serve

II. True God
- Character of God (135:3–12)
- The bliss of the servants of God (135:13–14)
- Move-to-relevance: What God has done for us

III. *Worship only the Worthy!*
- Praising God (135:1–2, 19–21)
- Specifics on serving God and abandoning gods

PSALM 136:1–26

Psalm of Orientation

Lovingkindness unto Forever

THE PECULIARITY OF THE consistent refrain of this unique psalm makes it impossible to consider the person and acts of God—upon which the composition focuses in its non-refrain lines—apart from his eternal lovingkindness.[1] Every act of God, both in creation and in history, thus becomes a manifestation of God's forever-lovingkindness. In a sense, then, this psalm defines the otherwise rather undefinable חֶסֶד, *chesed*, of God!

Translation

136:1 Give thanks to Yahweh, for [He is] good,
          for unto forever is His lovingkindness.
136:2 Give thanks to the God of gods,
          for unto forever is His lovingkindness.
136:3 Give thanks to the Lord of lords,
          for unto forever is His lovingkindness.
136:4 To the One who alone does great wonders,
          for unto forever is His lovingkindness;
136:5 to the One who made the heavens with skill,
          for unto forever is His lovingkindness;
136:6 to the One who spread out the earth over the waters,
          for unto forever is His lovingkindness;
136:7 to the One who made the great lights,
          for unto forever is His lovingkindness:

---

1. The only alteration in the refrain is the shift in 136:3b to לְעֹלָם, *l'olam* (all the others have לְעוֹלָם, the plene form, with an extra ו, *w*). The same refrain is found in the OT in 1 Chr 16:34; 2 Chr 20:21; Ezra 3:11; Pss 106:1; 107:1; 118:1–4. It is possible that the recitation of the psalm was conducted antiphonally, with the congregation taking up the repeating lines.

136:8	the sun for dominion in the day,
	for unto forever is His lovingkindness,
136:9	the moon and stars for dominions in the night,
	for unto forever is His lovingkindness;
136:10	to the One who struck Egypt in their firstborns,
	for unto forever is His lovingkindness,
136:11	and He brought Israel out from their midst,
	for unto forever is His lovingkindness,
136:12	with a strong hand and with an outstretched arm,
	for unto forever is His lovingkindness;
136:13	to the One who divided the Reed Sea into divisions,
	for unto forever is His lovingkindness,
136:14	and He made Israel pass through its midst,
	for unto forever is His lovingkindness,
136:15	but He shook off Pharaoh and his army into the Reed Sea,
	for unto forever is His lovingkindness;
136:16	to the One who caused His people to go through the wilderness,
	for unto forever is His lovingkindness,
136:17	to the One who struck great kings,
	for unto forever is His lovingkindness,
136:18	and He slew majestic kings,
	for unto forever is His lovingkindness:
136:19	Sihon, king of the Amorites,
	for unto forever is His lovingkindness,
136:20	and Og, king of Bashan,
	for unto forever is His lovingkindness,
136:21	and He gave their land as an inheritance,
	for unto forever is His lovingkindness,
136:22	an inheritance to Israel His servant,
	for unto forever is His lovingkindness;
136:23	who in our low estate remembered us,
	for unto forever is His lovingkindness,
136:24	and He snatched us from our adversaries,
	for unto forever is His lovingkindness;
136:25	the One who gives food to all flesh,
	for unto forever is His lovingkindness.
136:26	Give thanks to the God of heavens,
	for unto forever is His lovingkindness.

Structure

Psalm 136 begins and ends with *Exhortations* to give thanks to Yahweh (136:1–3, 26); the *Explanation* for these exhortations forms the remainder of the composition (136:4–25). This middle chunk, that has twenty-two verses, the number of the letters of the Hebrew alphabet (though not in acrostic form), expands upon the references to God in 136:1–3.[2]

Exhortation 1 (136:1–3)
  "Give thanks to" + divine name/title (136:1a, 2a, 3a)

Explanation (136:4–25)

  Creation 1 (**136:4–9**): God in Creation
  Universality of God
    Heaven and earth (136:4–6)
    Day and night (136:7–9)

  History Sketched (**136:10–22**): God in Redemption
  Particularity of God: "Israel" (136:11a, 14a, 22a); "His people' (136:16a)
    Israel in Egypt (136:10–15): "to the one who struck" (136:10a)
      Land (136:10–12): "Egypt"; "Israel"; "midst"
      Sea (136:13–15): "Israel"; "midst"; "Pharaoh"
    Israel in the Wilderness (136:16)
    Israel in Canaan (136:17–22): "to the one who struck" (136:17a)
      Kings (136:17–20): "king(s)" (×4)
      Land (136:21–22): "inheritance" (×2); "Israel"

  History Summarized (**136:23–24**): God in Compassion
  Particularity of God: "us" (×2); "our" (×2)

  Creation 2 (**136:25**): God in Provision
  Universality of God

Exhortation 2 (136:26)
  "Give thanks to" + divine title (136:26a)

Theological Focus

The forever-lovingkindness of God—manifest in his wondrous creative activity, in his historical redemptive work towards his people as he overwhelmed all their enemies, and in his compassionate deeds on behalf of his creation—is constantly and continuously extolled with gratitude by its human beneficiaries, the people of God.

---

2. Those twenty-two verses form enjambments based on 136:1–3, expansions of that syntactic unit with no pause in between. The figure is modified from Allen, *Psalms 101–150*, 232–33; Auffret, "Note sur la structure littéraire du Psaume CXXXVI," 1–12; and deClaissé-Walford et al., *Book of Psalms*, 949.

Commentary

Exhortation 1 (136:1–3)

Yahweh (136:1a)—described as "God of gods" and "Lord of lords" (136:2a, 3a)—is the one to be thanked, because he is "good." In effect, the subsequent extended explanation of divine goodness, i.e., the rationale for the exhortation to give thanks, is what takes up most of the psalm (136:4–25). Indeed, 136:4–25 is, in effect, a description of the deity whom the psalmist exhorts people to praise.[3] The imperative to "give thanks" in the first three verses is implied in the following twenty-two verses, explicitly resuming only in the closing verse, 136:26. This giving of thanks is not merely an expression of gratitude but an engagement with public praise of, and proclamation about, this awesome God. With the refrain, each of the first three verses (and the entirety of *Exhortation 1*) begins with "give thanks [הוֹדוּ, *hodu*]" and ends with "His lovingkindness [חַסְדּוֹ, *chasdu*]." That is the beginning and end of the whole story!

Explanation: Creation 1 (136:4–9)

Unlike the first three verses that have three-word first lines in Hebrew (136:1a, 2a, 3a), this section begins and ends with four-word first lines (136:4a, 9a). The creation of the heavens and earth takes up 136:4–6,[4] and that of the "great lights," 136:7–9. One might consider "great wonders" in 136:4a as encompassing the creation of the "heavens" and of the "earth" (136:5–6), and "great lights" in 136:7 covering the creation of "day" and of "night" (136:8–9). In any case, this section is focused on God's operations and doings, indicated by עשׂה, *'sh*—all acts of God's "greatness":

136:4a	"does [עשׂה]"; "great"
136:5–6	"made [עשׂה]" (136:5a)
136:7–9	"made [עשׂה]"; "great" (136:7a)

God's creative work, a manifestation of his forever-lovingkindness, is worthy of thanksgiving.

Explanation: History Sketched and History Summarized (136:10–24)

The explanation for the exhortation to give thanks continues in 136:10–22, divided into a sketched history (136:10–22) and a summarized history (136:23–24).

---

3. This is evident in the repetition of the preposition לְ, *l* ("to") in 136:4a, 5a, 6a, 7a, 10a, 13a, 16a, 17a, and the relative pronoun שׁ, *sha*, in 136:23a. The conjunctions and the prepositions of 136:1 make it a chiastic structure: הוֹדוּ / לַיהוָה, *layhwh* / כִּי־טוֹב, *ki-tov* // כִּי / לְעוֹלָם / חַסְדּוֹ ("give thanks / to Yahweh, / for [He is] good, // for / unto forever / is His lovingkindness") (Todd, "Poetic and Contextual Analysis," 96, 98).

4. The "waters" over which the earth is spread (136:6a) likely indicates subterranean masses of liquid.

The history sketched deals with the various phases of Israel's journey from exile in Egypt (136:10–15), through the wilderness (136:16), and into Canaan (136:17–22). It all begins with Israel decamping from Egypt with supernatural, divine aid:[5]

136:10	God strikes "Egypt"	
136:11	God brings out "Israel ... from their midst"	
136:12	God's "hand" and "arm" secures safety	
136:13	God divides the "Reed Sea"	
136:14	God passes "Israel ... through its midst"	
136:15	God shakes off "Pharaoh and his army"	

While the exodus proper takes six verses (136:10–15), the wilderness experience is boiled down to one, 136:16, the only verse in the psalm that has "His people." The takeover of Canaan quickly follows (136:17–22): thanks is due "to the one who caused his people to go [מוֹלִיךְ, *molik*]" through the wilderness (136:16a), "to the one who struck [לְמַכֵּה, *lmakkeh*]" great "kings [מְלָכִים, *mlakim*]" (136:17a) and slew majestic "kings [מְלָכִים]" (136:18a)—the wordplay is patent. And there is also Sihon, a "king [מֶלֶךְ, *melek*]," and Og, another "king [מֶלֶךְ]" (136:19–20). All together it is a resounding echo of the root מלך, *mlk* (or its consonants), to highlight the true King, God, the divine ruler for whom the "greatness" or "majesty" of earthly rulers (136:16a, 17a) is no obstacle to his purposes. As if to emphasize the might of these regents, "king(s)" is the middle word in each of the five lines—136:17a, 18a, 19a, 20a (in the Hebrew). But they are no match for "the one who struck" Egypt (136:10a: in the *exo*dus, as Israel exits Egypt): now God is "the one who struck" all these despots (136:17a: in the "*eis*odus," so to speak, as Israel enters Canaan). Strikingly enough (pun intended!), while the two Canaanite kings, Sihon and Og, are named in 136:19–20, no Israelite is referred to by name anywhere in Psalm 136—it is all God's work![6] And it culminated in the people of God obtaining their "inheritance" of land (136:21–22), even at the cost of their deity engaging in violence for their liberty: "The psalm assumes that love [God's forever-lovingkindness] issues in action. God's love can be terrifying."[7]

This history is summarized in 136:23–24 with a remarkable deployment of first-person plural suffixes ("our" and "us," 136:23a [×2], 24a [×2], the only instances of the first person in the psalm), effectively making God's people of all time "present" in those particular historical events and partaking the benefits of God's mighty redemptive work.[8] And no wonder, God's lovingkindness is "forever," extending to his people, one and all, in every space and in every time. This summary of history in 136:23–24 is marked by a sense of divine compassion.

---

5. See Auffret, "Note sur la structure littéraire du Psaume CXXXVI," 6; and Girard, *Les Psaumes Redécouverts*, 408.

6. Sihon and Og are the stereotypical sovereigns often mentioned in the OT in connection with Israel's takeover of Canaan: Num 21:21–35; 32:33; Deut 1:4; 4:46–47; 31:4; Josh 2:10; 9:10; 12:2–5; 13:10–12; 1 Kgs 4:19; Neh 9:22; Ps 135:11.

7. Goldingay, *Psalms*, 3:597.

8. As well, 136:23a has the only instance in the song of the relative pronoun שׁ.

God remembered his people in their "low estate" and dramatically "snatched" them from their adversaries. The first lines of this duo of verses are chiastically organized:[9]

136:23aα	"who in *our* low estate"
136:23aβ	"remembered *us*"
136:24aα	"and He snatched *us*"
136:24aβ	"from *our* adversaries"

On the outside "we" have "our" deplorable situations: "low estate" and "adversaries" (136:23aα, 24aβ) But inside "we" are cocooned and ensconced in the protective care of the God who "remembered us" and "snatched us" (136:23aβ, 24aα)!

Explanation: Creation 2 (136:25)

With a return to the motif of creation in 136:25 (that forms an *inclusio* with 136:4–9), related to his activity in Gen 1:29–30, the explanation section of the psalm concludes: God's forever-lovingkindness is manifest in his provision of food to all living beings—a matter of thanks, praise, and worship. "It would be no use if Yhwh were inherently good but not committed to us; it would be frightening if Yhwh were supreme God and supreme Lord but not committed to us. But Yhwh's being good *and* supreme God, supreme Lord, is something to confess."[10]

Exhortation 2 (136:26)

And so the psalm ends as it began: "Give thanks to the God of heavens, for unto forever is His lovingkindness"!

Sermon Map

I. God in Creation; God in Provision
   God's creative work; his provision for life (136:4–9, 25)
   Move-to-relevance: Our experience of God's magnificent creation
   Thank God, the Designer!
   Specifics on thankfulness for his forever-lovingkindness in creation
II. God in Redemption; God in Compassion
   God's historical work; his compassion for his own (136:10–22, 23–24)
   Move-to-relevance: Our experience of God's amazing redemption
   Thank God, the Deliverer!
   Specifics on thankfulness for his forever-lovingkindness in history[11]

---

9. See Prinsloo, W. S., *Die Psalms leef*, 98.
10. Goldingay, *Psalms*, 3:597.
11. I have incorporated applications into each of the moves of this Map.

PSALM 137:1–9

Psalm of Disorientation

Justice for the Infliction of Terror

PSALM 137 APPEARS TO be set in the background of the exiles residing in Babylon—after the destruction of Jerusalem in 587 BCE, but before the fall of the former in 539 BCE to the Persians. Though the composition seems to point to a particular period and set of events in Israel's history, the notion of "exile" is valid for all of God's people everywhere in all times, this side of the eschaton: "Exile is thus primarily not a geographical issue, but it is a social, moral, cultural, liturgical and spiritual issue; an understanding that one is in a hostile, alien situation."[1] And thus, the exiles constitute not only the first generation of those who directly experienced that trauma, but all generations following, vicariously being exiled once (in the lives of their ancestors in the community of God) and actually experiencing the exiled state now (in their own lives). And all of them remember: either they remember their past situation of orientation (pre-exile), or they "remember" what their future state of reorientation is going to be (post-exile),[2] or they remember both (remembrance is a key motif of Psalm 137). For most of God's people, such a trans-generational memory is directed to the future, towards the eschaton, when God's presence will be manifest in a new Temple in a New Jerusalem—it is a remembrance of God and his interests.

Translation

137:1 By the rivers of Babylon,
    there we dwelt, but we wept
    when we remembered Zion.
137:2 Upon the poplars in her midst
    we hung our lyres.

---

1. Maré, "Psalm 137," 116.
2. This is, of course, essentially a remembrance of God's promises for the future.

137:3 For there our captors asked us [for] songs with words,
           and our tormentors [for] joy[fulness]:
        "Sing to us one of the songs of Zion."
137:4 How can we sing the song of Yahweh
           on foreign ground?
137:5 If I forget you, Jerusalem,
           may my right hand be crippled;
137:6 may my tongue cleave to my palate
           if I do not remember you,
        if I do not exalt Jerusalem
           over my chief joy.
137:7 Remember, Yahweh, against the children of Edom,
           [regarding] the day of Jerusalem,
        the ones who said, "Lay [it] bare, lay [it] bare,
           unto her foundation."
137:8 Daughter of Babylon, the one devastated,
           blessing [upon] the one who repays to you
        with your recompense which you have recompensed to us.
137:9 Blessing [upon] the one who seizes
           and smashes your babies on the rock.

Structure

Goldingay calls Psalm 137 "an ironically inverted version" of a Song of Zion. Whereas the typical form of such a composition celebrated Yahweh's victory, Zion's blessing, and enemies' defeat, here this trio is replaced by a victorious enemy, beaten Zion, and an almost-absent Yahweh.[3]

---

3. See Goldingay, *Psalms*, 3:601; and Allen, *Psalms 101–150*, 241.

In any case, the psalm is carefully organized in three stanzas, dealing with the *Past*, *Present*, and *Future*, respectively):[4]

> **PAST (137:1–4): Distress**
> *Addressed to reader*
> *Direct quote of Babylonian enemy with plural imperatives* (137:3c)
>   **"Remembered"** (137:1c)
>   **"Zion"** (137:1c, 3c)
>   137:1, tricolon with "Babylon" in its first line (137:1a)
>   Preposition (בְּ, *b*) + third-person feminine suffixes: "in her midst" (137:2b)
>   לָנוּ, *lanu*, "to us," in the penultimate verse of the section (137:3c)
>   אֲדָמָה, *'adamah*, "ground" (137:4b)
>   Section ends with "Yahweh" (137:4a)

> **PRESENT (137:5–6): Determination**
> *Addressed to Jerusalem*
> *No direct quote, but first-person speech* (137:5–6)
>   **"Remember"** (137:6b)
>   **"Jerusalem"** (137:5a, 6c)

> **FUTURE (137:7–9): Denunciation**
> *Addressed to Yahweh (137:7), and to Babylon (137:8–9)*
> *Direct quote of Edomite enemy with plural imperatives* (137:7cd)
>   **"Remember"** (137:7a)
>   **"Jerusalem"** (137:7b)
>   137:8, tricolon with "Babylon" in its first line (137:8a)
>   Preposition (בְּ) + third-person feminine suffixes: "unto her" (137:7d)
>   לָנוּ, "to us," in the penultimate verse of the section (137:8c)
>   אֱדוֹם, *'edom*, "Edom" (137:7a)
>   Section begins with "Yahweh" (137:7a)

Theological Focus

In the face of abysmal evil and wickedness directed against them, the people of God pledge their utmost commitment to remember him and his interests, and appeal to their deity to take retributive action against evildoers and the wicked.

---

4. Modified from Goldingay, *Psalms*, 3:602–8; Bar-Efrat, "Love of Zion," 4; and Allen, *Psalms 101–150*, 240–41. The first and third sections share the most features, as shown.

Commentary

Past: Distress (137:1–4)

The psalm begins with a dolorous view of the past, with the tears of the exiles (137:1b),[5] but it is an expression of mirth that is commanded by their captors (137:3b). The misery of the afflicted is evident even in the structure of the first verse, with the first-person plural declaration of mourning in the center, highlighting the dire state of the exiles, with Babylon and Zion opposed to each other at the ends:[6]

> "Babylon"
> "we dwelt"
> **"we wept"**
> "we remembered"
> "Zion"

Indeed, the first-person plural ending נוּ-, *nu*-, echoes nine times in the first three verses (eight times referring to the Israelites, and once to the "tormentors" in their own quoted speech): "we dwelt," "we wept," "we remembered" (137:1); "we hung," "our lyres" (137:2); "our captors," "asked us," "our tormentors," and "'to us'" (137:3)—adding to the pathos of recounting the past.

The first verse begins with an adverbial phrase of place, "by the rivers of Babylon" (137:1a), a rare occurrence in the OT, and indicating emphasis. No longer in Zion, God's people dwelt in Babylon, of all places. The importance of place is also underscored with named locales in this first section that are linked to the preposition, עַל: Zion is literally hemmed in by "Babylon" and "foreign ground" and the "poplars" growing there:[7]

137:1a	"by [עַל, '*al*] the rivers of Babylon"
137:1c	"Zion"
137:2–3b	"upon [עַל] the poplars in her midst"
137:3c	"Zion"
137:4b	"on [עַל] foreign ground"

The disparagement engaged in by the exiles' "captors" and "tormentors" (137:3ab) involved getting their captives to render "songs of Zion," ones with words (137:3c), intended to elicit ridicule from the powerful and evoke despair from the powerless.[8] The exiles them-

---

5. Ezekiel 3:15 also describes the exiled Israelites in Babylon as "the ones dwelling [יֹשֵׁב, *yshv*] at the river [נָהָר, *nahar*] Kebar," employing words used in Ps 137:1. The plural "rivers" in 137:1a may indicate "great river," the Euphrates, or the many irrigation canals/streams in Babylon.

6. Auffret, "Essai sur la structure littéraire du Psaume 137," 348. The three first-person plural middle terms are preceded by an adverb (שָׁם יָשַׁבְנוּ, *sham yashavnu*, "there we dwelt"), a conjunction (גַּם־בָּכִינוּ, *gam-bakinu*, "but we wept"), and a preposition (בְּזָכְרֵנוּ, *bzakrenu*, "when we remembered"), respectively, giving the run-on trio a rhythmic assonance.

7. Auffret, "Essai sur la structure littéraire du Psaume 137," 348.

8. Perhaps these "songs of Zion" included Psalms 46; 48; 76; or 84. The "joy[fulness]" (137:3b) could be

selves must have felt that God, the one they were to sing about, had abandoned them: "The problem lies not merely in what the captors are saying, but in what the captives' own hearts are saying."[9] They were "by [עַל] ... Babylon" (136:1a), their lyres were retired "upon [עַל] the poplars" (137:2a).[10] How then could they be joyful "on [עַל] foreign ground?" (137:4b). The despair is foregrounded by the assonance of "we hung [תָּלִינוּ, talinu]" and "our tormentors [תּוֹלָלֵינוּ, tolalenu]" (137:2b, 3b). Though it seems likely that the exiles' material condition was better in fertile Babylon, their remembrance of Zion, not to mention the derision directed against them, evoked only anguish.

And so the response of the exiles is poignant: "How can we sing the song of Yahweh on foreign ground?" (137:4). How (and why) should they sing songs of triumph when there was no victory in sight, only abject defeat and abysmal evil? How (and why) would they sing about a powerful God when there was no indication of his power operating on their behalf? "We remembered Zion," they claim in 137:1c, and they would continue to do so in 137:5–6, but what about Yahweh? Does he remember them?

Present: Determination (137:5–6)

In what is entirely a first-person utterance—the first and only such in this psalm—the psalmist utters a self-imprecation. Perhaps this reflects his intense desire to demonstrate to God that he has been loyal to Jerusalem/Zion all along by "remembering" and not "forgetting" her (137:5a, 6b) despite dire and baleful circumstances. No doubt, it is also a self-resolution that, no matter what, he would always be loyal to God and to God's interests. In either case, it is persuasive rhetoric, intended to prod God into action; at the foundation of such an utterance is, of course, a rock-solid trust in deity's will and ability to engage in action on behalf of the pleader.[11] At any rate, the imploring poet grants, via a counterfactual, that if he were to forget Jerusalem and not make it his greatest joy and his primary concern (137:6cd), it would be justifiable, permissible, and appropriate to be afflicted by the crippling of his right hand and the immobilizing of his tongue (137:5b–6a).[12] Very possibly, the mention of these organs relate to their primary importance in the performance of "songs with words" (137:3a) accompanied by lyres. There is also the mention of "chief [רֹאשׁ, rʾosh]" joy (137:6d); רֹאשׁ can also mean "head," adding, via a pun, yet another body part, and generating a clever double chiasm (below).

---

that of the scoffers or the singers, but in either case this is nothing but hazing of a severe order.

9. Goldingay, *Psalms*, 3:604.

10. The cessation of music-making on the lyre is particularly noted as a form of mourning in Ezek 26:13.

11. Thus, these are not very different from the standard elements of a lament psalm that employs all manner of rhetorical ingredients to motivate Yahweh to act decisively for his people.

12. As written, the MT has "may my right hand forget [תִּשְׁכַּח, tishkach] ..." (137:5b). It is best to take תִּשְׁכַּח as a metathesis of תִּכְשַׁה, *tikshah*, an older form of the verb כָּשַׁה, *kashah*, "to be crippled" (as also in Arabic cognates). See Eitan, "Identification," 193–95.

	137:5a	"If I forget you, Jerusalem,		
CHIASM 1	137:5b	may *my right hand* be crippled;		
	137:6a	may *my tongue* cleave to my palate	137:6a	CHIASM 2
	137:6b	if I do not remember you,	137:6b	
		if I do not exalt Jerusalem	137:6c	
		over *my* chief [*head*] joy."	137:6d	

This is, in sum, an intense personal commitment to be loyal to Yahweh and to his center of operations (i.e., to God and his interests). The psalmist, presumably along with his cohort, "remembered" Zion (137:1c); now he utters a maledictory self-curse should he ever "forget" Jerusalem (137:5a) and not "remember" her (137:6a). *He has/they* have been faithful to God; would that God reciprocate. To that end, the final section of the psalm begins with a direct appeal to God to "remember" (137:7a)!

Future: Denunciation (137:7–9)

This is the first address to Yahweh in this psalm (137:7), and what the psalmist desires of Yahweh is in keeping with the recurring motif in the rest of the poem: remembrance, primarily of the dastardly deeds of Israel's enemies against her. Those denunciated against are the "children of Edom" (137:7a) and the "daughter of Babylon" (137:8a). The latter, of course, were the "captors" and "tormentors" of 137:3ab. The former engaged in anti-Israelite activity during the Babylonian siege and overthrow of Jerusalem (as indicated in Lam 4:21–22; Ezek 25:12–14; 35:1–15; Obadiah 10–15). Even after the destruction of Judah, the Edomites continued their incursions into and colonizations of Israelite land (Ezek 35:10; 36:5). Denunciations of both entities are parallel in structure and in paronomasia:[13]

Ps 137:7	Ps 137:8–9
"children of Edom"	"daughter of Babylon"
"Jerusalem [יְרוּשָׁלַםִ, *yrushalaim*]"	"repays [יְשַׁלֶּם, *yshallem*]"
"'lay [it] bare'" (×2)	"blessing [upon] the one who ..." (×2)

Of course, there were other states that participated in the fall of Jerusalem, among whom were Ammon, Moab, and Philistia (see Ezek 25:1–7, 8–11, 15–17). But the construal of Edom's actions as particularly heinous stemmed from the Israelite conception that their enmity with that nation reflected the struggle between their respective progenitors, the twin brothers Esau and Jacob.[14] Therefore, what Edom had done here was a fraternal stab in the back! And perhaps there was also a lingering fear that God had abandoned the children of

---

13. From Girard, *Les Psaumes Redécouverts*, 417. That the Edomite treachery was linked to the Babylonian violence seems to be suggested in that Ps 137:7 ends with בָּהּ, *bah*, "her," and 137:8 begins with בַּת־בָּבֶל, *bat-babel*, "daughter of Babylon." It is also conceivable that the wordplay of אֲדָמָה (the "foreign ground" of Babylon, 137:4b) and אֱדוֹם (137:7a) led to the psalmist's introduction of Edom into this otherwise Babylon-focused composition.

14. See Gen 25:19–34; 27:1–46; Num 20:14–22; Deut 2:2–5, 8; Amos 1:11; Obad 10, 12; Mal 1:2–4.

Jacob (Isa 40:27; 41:8-9; Jer 33:24-26; Lam 3:6, 8; Ezek 37:11-12) and had decided to sponsor the children of Esau henceforth.[15]

A number of linguistic parallels link the first section (Ps 137:1-4, *Past: Distress*) with the last one (137:7-9, *Future: Denunciation*; see the psalm structure above). The only instances in the psalm of a root that is repeated in both verb and object forms occur in these sections: 137:3c (שִׁירוּ לָנוּ מִשִּׁיר, *shiru lanu mishshir*, "sing to us one of the songs"); 137:4a (אֵיךְ נָשִׁיר אֶת־שִׁיר־יְהוָה, *'ek nashir 'et-shir-yhwh*, "how can we sing the song of Yahweh"); and 137:8c (גְּמוּלֵךְ שֶׁגָּמַלְתְּ, *gmulek sheggamalt*, "recompense which you have recompensed"). Besides, the fivefold occurrence of the root שִׁיר (137:3a, 3c [×2], 4a [×2]) is assonant with the twofold אַשְׁרֵי, *'ashrey*, "blessing" (137:8b, 9a); also לָנוּ, "to us," in 137:3c (the enemies referring to themselves) is repeated in 137:8c (the exiles referring to themselves). All of this ties the various parts of the poem together, suggesting that the denunciation of the enemies by the exiles is commensurate with the distress inflicted by enemies upon those exiles.

The execution of the desired retribution is left to God. All the victims ask for is that deity "remember" (137:7ab), reciprocating to the loyal exiles what they had done (being faithful to God and his interests) and to the wicked captors and tormentors what they had done (oppressing the people of God). And, while recrimination for Edom is pled for, Babylon's reprisal is taken for granted—it is even assumed to have already occurred: that nation is called "the one devastated" (137:8a).[16] All that underscores a fact the Bible makes quite clear: vengeance is not the prerogative of the people of God, but of the deity in whom they put their trust.[17] Besides, Yahweh is explicitly noted to be the agent of retribution in the psalms preceding this one: 135:8-11; 136:10-20, 24. Though there may be human agents wittingly or unwittingly involved in the execution of God's sentence, "recompense" and "repayment" (137:8) is ultimately from God, and sometimes it is delivered in kind, tit for tat.[18] The balanced structure of 137:8-9 validates this like-for-like punitive arrangement (see below).[19]

---

15. See Assis, "Why Edom?," 14-15.

16. "The one devastated" is from the root שדד, *shdd*; and שד, *shd*, "destruction," is related to שַׁדַּי, *shadday*, the "Almighty," the one who destroys. Indeed, in Isaiah's oracle against Babylon, שד is deployed in 13:6. "Daughter of Babylon" elsewhere in the OT also assumes judgment from the hand of God (Isa 47:1; Jer 50:42; 51:33; Zech 2:7). Jeremiah also issued a call for a divine curse upon Babylon: Lam 3:64-66.

17. See Lev 19:18 (the verse that also promotes love of neighbor as oneself!); Deut 32:41; etc.

18. See, for instance, Jer 51:24 that has "repayment"; and 51:56 has "recompense"—both in relation to the vengeance of Yahweh against Babylon (also see 51:6). It is notable that though Assyrian and Babylonian takeovers of Israel were accomplished by God's human agents acting according to his sovereign plan to execute his justice upon Israel, those conquering nations were themselves condemned for their evil actions (Isa 10:5-34; 13:1—14:27; 21:1-10; 33:1-24; 46-47; Jeremiah 50-51; Zeph 2:13-15).

19. Modified from Auffret, "'Souviens-toi YHWH!,'" 251. This is, of course, commensurate with *lex talionis* described in Exod 21:22-25; Lev 24:17-22; Deut 19:16-21, which essentially was a guard against the excesses of revenge (Day, "Imprecatory Psalms," 174). Needless to say, God is a God who requires justice: sin has to be punished; the cross is ample evidence of that divine disposition.

137:8a	"*daughter* of Babylon"
137:8bα	"blessing [upon] the one who [שֶׁ] repays"
137:8bβ	"to you [לָךְ, *lak*]"
137:8cα	"with your *recompense*"
137:8cβ	"which you have *recompensed*"
137:8cγ	"to us [לָנוּ]"
137:9a	"blessing [upon] the one who [שֶׁ] seizes"
137:9b	"and smashes your *babies*"

The enemies were once the exiles' "tormentors" (from תּוֹלָל, *tolal*; 137:3b); now the "babies" (from עוֹלָל, *'olal*; 137:9b) of the latter are duly imprecated against.[20]

Excursus

Violence Against Children in Wartime

The last verse of the psalm has been a crux for the longest time. The vengeful nature of the words, particularly the violence directed against innocent children, inspires horror. But the harming of babies in wartime was (and still is) not an unusual occurrence: see Lam 2:11, 20; 4:4, 10 for what happened to the children of the Israelites during the Babylonian siege.[21] Quite similar to the destruction of "babies" in Ps 137:9b are the following OT texts that also depict "babies" being "dashed" (employing רטשׁ, *rtsh*, not נפץ, *nphts*, "smashed," as in 137:9b)[22] in the atrocities of military hostility: 2 Kgs 8:12 (against Israel); Hos 13:16 (against Samaria; LXX Hos 13:16 uses the same verb as in LXX Ps 137:9b, ἐδαφίζω, *edaphizō*; and see Hos 10:14, also with ἐδαφίζω, but depicting "children," not "babies"); Nah 3:9–10 (against Nineveh; also with ἐδαφίζω in the LXX); and Isa 13:16, 18 (against Babylon). Thus, in our text, the psalmist appears to be echoing a prior divine oracle against Babylon, not creating an imprecation *de novo*.[23] Even the joy resulting from Babylon's doom was prescribed (Jer 51:48).[24]

Indeed, the same verb, ἐδαφίζω, "dash" (Ps 137:9b LXX) is used by Jesus in Luke 19:44 in relation to children ("they will raze [ἐδαφίζω] to the ground—you and your children"). Josephus, the first-century historian, also describes "children ... dashed to the ground" (*Jewish Wars* 5.3.433–34; my translation). The verb here is also different, but "ground" is ἔδαφος,

---

20. The "babies" of 137:9b balances the "*children* [or 'sons,' from בֵּן, *ben*] of Edom" (137:7a) and the "*daughter* [בַּת, *bat*] of Babylon" (137:8a).

21. Another violent wartime action involved "ripping open pregnant women," killing both mother and child (Amos 1:13, and also in 2 Kgs 8:12; Hos 13:16). Elsewhere it is found in a seventh-century BCE ancient Near Eastern dirge (translated in Lambert, "Neo-Babylonian Tammuz Lament," 212).

22. But Jeremiah's oracle against Babylon, 51:20–24, employs the same verb נפץ nine times in relation to that ungodly regime—God promises to use his agent, King Cyrus, to "smash" various groups of people and animals and implements, including "youths." The prophecy concludes, "I [Yahweh] will repay [שׁלם, *shlm*, as also in Ps 137:8b] Babylon ... for all their wickedness which they have done to Zion" (Jer 51:24; also see 13:14 that has fathers and sons being 'smashed' together) (see Bar-Efrat, "Love of Zion," 9).

23. "Every word in this chilling declaration takes up Yhwh's promises ... and envisages them being fulfilled. Then justice will have been done" (Goldingay, *Psalms*, 3:610).

24. For a NT example of such a bidding to rejoice at the judgment of enemies, see Rev 18:20.

edaphos (one can see how ἐδαφίζω came to mean "dash to the ground").²⁵ And such notions of brutality extend back several millennia. *The Admonitions of Ipuwer* 4.3 (an Egyptian document ca. 1900–1800 BCE) employs a dirge that has this line: "Forsooth, the children of princes are dashed against the walls."²⁶ In the eighth century BCE, Homer (*Iliad* 22.63–64; my translation) also describes "little children hurled to the ground in the grim battle." It is apparent, from this compilation of maledictions from varying times and divergent spaces across the Levant, Greece, and Rome, that the description of violence perpetrated on children during wartime was at least a trope, an idiom, a *topoi*, if not actually reflections of historical reality.²⁷ "Since the motif of children being smashed against walls or on the streets is encountered in cultural areas that are far apart in terms of time and geography, we are dealing more with a conventional [and perhaps stereotypical] depiction of wartime experiences than with the depiction of a concrete historical event."²⁸

Such a trope deployed in Psalm 137, then, is "designed more to express the outrage and pain than to spell out the penalties the psalmist desired."²⁹ Yet, the use of אַשְׁרֵי to introduce an imprecation is unique in the Psalter and does raise some uncomfortable questions. How can the human agent of such violence be considered blessed?³⁰ But, as was noted, God frequently co-opts human agents in the execution of divine vengeance. And that executor—and the psalmist in Psalm 137 is agnostic about who that individual or nation might be—is labeled "blessed," simply because they are a tool in the hands of a holy God to further his holy purposes. Such an attitude, betokening the utter hatred by God's people of evil (a theme common in Scripture—in 139:20–21, for instance), ought not to be considered out of place in a broken world. "God is both sovereign and righteous; he possesses the unquestionable

---

25. Also, Lucian in the second century CE (*On Funerals* 12; my translation) has mourners grieving: "heads they dash against the floor [ἔδαφος]."

26. Translation from Gardiner, *Admonitions*, 36.

27. For other kinds of violence perpetrated against children in enemy action, see 2 Kgs 6:24–30; 25:7 (the slaughtering of Zedekiah's sons by the Babylonians); Isa 14:21; 2 Macc 6:10; and 4 Macc 4:25.

28. Lux, "Die Kinder auf der Gasse," 205n41 (my translation from the German). "They seem to function in our sources as images reflecting a vision of a world without limits or structure or morality" (Kern, *Ancient Siege Warfare*, 85). Of Jeremiah's account of the vicious enemy approaching Israel from the north, Kalmanofsky observes: "The prophets adopt a rhetoric of horror to maintain an audience. They use language and construct images to attract an audience and effect change.... If the prophets were simply predicting the grim future, what is the purpose of their message for their own and for subsequent generations?... If scared Israel simply runs away, the prophet would not have achieved his ultimate goal of reform" (*Terror All Around*, 10 [emphases removed]). Such texts, particularly poetry, are not employing the language of information; instead, they utilize the language of transformation. Of course, that is not to deny that such abominable acts may have occurred. But one must bear in mind the rhetorical nature of such incendiary literature.

29. Ross, *Psalms*, 3:794. Of relevance is the hyperbolic utterance frequently encountered in the Middle East that wishes death upon some individual or party. In Iran, for instance, in past years the populace often chanted "Death to America!" In the 2022 uprising against the ruling theocracy the protesters were chanting "Death to the Ayatollah!" In both cases, these imprecations did not necessarily carry literal force or intent, but were to be taken metaphorically, indicating the intensity of outrage against the particular nation or individual imprecated against. So much so, Keel thinks the mention of "babies" in Ps 137:9b simply indicates the generational continuation of ungodly Babylon: "In this vein, one might translate: 'Happy is he who puts an end to your self-renewing domination!'" (Keel, *Symbolism of the Biblical World*, 9). Or: "May Babylon have no descendants, no future, and may the reign of this oppressor come to an end" (Versluis, "'Knock the Little Bastards' Brains Out,'" 389).

30. For more on imprecations in the Psalms, and on praying them, see the Introduction to this work in *Psalms 1–44*.

right to destroy all evil in his universe; if it is right for God to plan and effect this destruction, then it is also right for the saints to pray for the same."[31]

But here, let me make a distinction between praying these prayers, i.e., doing what the psalmist did, and *preaching* these prayers, i.e., expositing what the psalmist wrote, for the purpose of catching the thrust of the inspired word of God. This latter undertaking must be performed on every text of Scripture, for "every [text of] Scripture [is] God-breathed and profitable for teaching, for reproof, for correction, for training in righteousness so that the person of God may be capable, fully equipped for every good work" (2 Tim 3:16–17). Comprehending (experiencing) the theology of this "pericope," Psalm 137, is therefore essential. Granted, the application of that theological thrust in the lives of the people of God may involve actually praying such prayers (as the Sermon Map, below, recommends), but that may not, and perhaps should not, be the only specific application possible from the pericopal theology of Psalm 137. Indeed, it might be advisable not to default to an application that simply copies what the psalmist is doing, for that would make the preaching and application of the contents of the Psalter tedious, repetitive, and wearisome. Rather, I would urge preachers to employ their pastoral love, wisdom, and authority to derive and propose applications that are not only concrete, but also creative and compelling.[32]

Sermon Map

I. Past: Distress

   Evil leading to distress of exiles (137:1–4: "remember," 137:1c)

   Move-to-relevance: Our experience of abysmal evil

II. Present: Determination

   Evil reinforcing determination to loyalty (137:5–6: "remember," 137:6b)

   Move-to-relevance: Our lack of faithfulness in the face of attack

III. Future: Denunciation

   Evil inspiring denunciation of evildoers (137:7–9: "remember, 137:7a)

   Move-to-relevance: Our pleas to God

IV. *Promise to Commit! Pray for Consequences!*

   Specifics on the undertaking of imprecatory prayers by the faithful

---

31. Vos, "Ethical Problem," 136. He notes that these are cases of "execution," not "murder." Again, for my take on the appropriateness of praying in the fashion of the psalmist in these imprecatory prayers, see the Introduction (in *Psalms 1–44*).

32. See Kuruvilla, *Manual for Preaching*, 57–86.

PSALM 138:1–8

Psalm of Orientation

Thanksgiving to the One on High Who Delivers the Lowly

THIS PSALM OF GRATITUDE may well have been the composition of a leader of the community or king of the nation, in light of the recommendations in 138:4–5 to "kings of the earth" to thank and praise Yahweh.

Translation

138:1	I will give You thanks with all my heart;
	before the gods I will make music to You.
138:2	I will worship toward Your holy temple
	and I will give thanks to Your name
	for Your lovingkindness and for Your truth;
	for You have made great above all [things] Your name, Your utterance.
138:3	On the day I called, You answered me;
	You emboldened me in my soul with strength.
138:4	May all the kings of the earth give You thanks, Yahweh,
	for they have heard the utterances of Your mouth.
138:5	And may they sing of the paths of Yahweh,
	for great is the glory of Yahweh.
138:6	For Yahweh is the One on high,
	yet He sees the lowly,
	and the haughty from a distance, He knows.
138:7	Though I walk in the midst of distress, You will keep me alive;
	against the wrath of my enemies You will send forth Your hand,
	and Your right hand will deliver me.

138:8   Yahweh—He will requite [enemies] on my behalf.
    Yahweh, Your lovingkindness is forever;
        the works of Your hands do not forsake.

Structure

An *Exaltation* section (138:1–3) begins the psalm, which then leads to an *Exhortation* section (138:4–6); the psalm concludes with an *Expectation* section (138:7–8):[1]

Exaltation (138:1–3)
"**gods**" (138:1b)
  "give You thanks" (138:1a, 2b)
  "for You have *made great* ... Your name, Your utterance" (138:2d)
  "Your *utterance*" (138:2d; feminine singular noun in כִּי- (*ki-*) clause)
  "*all*" (138:1a [in construct: כָּל־לִבִּי, *kal-libbi*, "*all* my heart"])
    "Your lovingkindness" (138:2c)

Exhortation (138:4–6)
"**kings**" (138:4a)
  "give You thanks" (138:4a)
  "for *great* is the glory of Yahweh" (138:5b)
  "*utterances* of Your mouth" (138:4b; masculine plural noun in כִּי-clause)
  "*all*" (138:4a [in construct: כָּל־מַלְכֵי, *kal-malke,* "*all* the kings"])
    Vocative "Yahweh" (138:4a)

Expectation (138:7–8)
"**enemies**" (138:7b)
  "Your lovingkindness" (138:8b)
    Vocative "Yahweh" (138:8b)

Theological Focus

God's people, exalting their heavenly deity for their past deliverance—and exhorting all earthly rulers also to glorify God as they acknowledge deity's words and salvific deeds, especially his condescension to the lowly and his confrontation of the lofty—expect future deliverance from their enemies (and the requital of the latter) to be accomplished by God because of his forever-lovingkindness towards them.

---

1. From Allen, *Psalms 101–150*, 247; Singer, "Literary Context," 171–73; and Auffret, "Tu me feras vivre," 479.

Commentary

Exaltation (138:1–3)

The psalmist's heartfelt gratitude to God is obvious: in words (138:1a, 2b), in music (138:1b), and in posture (138:2aα),[2] God is worshiped and thanked (138:1aα, 2aα, 2b), "before the gods" and "toward Your holy temple" (138:1bα, 2aβ). Or one could put it this way: by liturgical utterance (words), in sacred space (location), and through ritual action (music making and bowing/worshiping), the psalmist is going all out ("with all my heart," 138:1a) in formal praise of God:[3]

138:1a	"I will give You thanks"	*Liturgical utterance*
138:1bα	"before the gods"	*Sacred space*
138:1bβ	"I will make music"	*Ritual action*
138:2aα	"I will worship"	*Ritual action*
138:2aβ	"toward Your holy temple"	*Sacred space*
138:2b	"I will give thanks to Your name"	*Liturgical utterance*

In the realm of the sacred—in the presence of the "gods" (138:1b) and in relation to God's "holy temple" (138:2aβ)—there is no one like Yahweh. All that to say, worshipers' hearts, mouths, and bodies are involved in this giving of thanks and exaltation of this supreme, unique, Almighty God. The reason for the psalmist's thanksgiving is specifically because of God's lovingkindness and truth (i.e., the truthful keeping of divine promises), and because thereby God has made himself—his "name" and his "utterance"—great (138:2d), glorifying himself. How this lovingkindness and truth was manifest is explained in 138:3. Thus, the psalmist's exaltation has a more concrete reason for his gratitude—his answered prayer and his emboldening and strengthening, presumably in a day of distress (138:3). This God is worthy to be praised!

Exhortation (138:4–6)

Uniquely for the Psalter, foreign rulers are exhorted to "give thanks to Yahweh," and "sing of the paths of Yahweh" (138:4a, 5a).[4] Such worship of Yahweh is to be undertaken by earthly kings after their hearing the "utterances of Your mouth" (138:4b). Of course, it is not enough to have auditioned the utterances of Yahweh—after all, these regents are singing of the "paths" of Yahweh. So, in all likelihood, they probably have seen Yahweh in action, too (particularized in 138:6), especially as he keeps his word to his people (see below). Thus, the words and deeds of Yahweh, his declarations and his doings, the psalmist exhorts, ought

---

2. "Worship," חוה, *chwh*, is also synonymous with "bow down" (see 5:7; 72:11; 86:9; 96:9; 99:5; 132:7).
3. Modified from Girard, *Les Psaumes Redécouverts*, 427.
4. And with "singing" (138:5a) yet another modality of thanksgiving is added to the ones already seen in 138:1–3 (vocal utterances, making of music, and physical posture). Of course, it was highly unlikely that leaders of nations would attend to these words; thus, the authorial *doing* in this psalm is for the people of God to attend, that they may acknowledge the greatness of their deity who, one day, will be worshiped even by those nobles who wield worldly power.

to convince all human potentates ("all the kings of the earth," 138:4a) to acknowledge the greatness of this heavenly King.

The thanking and singing by the rulers of earth acknowledge that this ruler of the heavens, the "one on high," paradoxically, sees "the lowly" and, ostensibly, rescues them (138:6ab; evidenced in 138:3). Besides, this "one on high" also knows the "haughty" and, presumably, gives these conceited ones their just deserts (138:6c; see 138:8a).[5] "Yhwh's honor thus lies . . . in fulfilling the ideal of any kingship, that the king does not sit in his palace in comfort enjoying his position of prestige and authority far away from ordinary people in their need. Even though his position means he is far away from them in their everyday lives, he sees the lowly in their need and acknowledges them," and he knows the arrogant in their evil audacity and afflicts them.[6] An exemplary King indeed! And so, the words and deeds of Yahweh, the psalmist exhorts, should cause every ruler in every nation on earth to fall on their face in worship of this heavenly regent *par excellence*. Just as in the realm of the sacred (in the heavens—"before the gods," 138:1b) there is no one like Yahweh, so also, in the realm of the secular (on the earth—among the "kings"; 138:4a) there is no one like this deity. And the final outcome? "Great is the glory of Yahweh" (138:5b).

Expectation (138:7–8)

The result of the psalmist's heartfelt *Exaltation* (for the past), and his well-grounded *Exhortation* (in the present) to all earthly rulers that they should bow before Yahweh, leads the psalmist to a trustful *Expectation* (for the future) even when assailed and assaulted by enemies. If the foreign kings can sing of the "paths" of Yahweh (138:5a), surely the people of God can safely "walk" (on those same paths?) with God even in the midst of distress, for he sustains them (138:7a): his "hand" and his "right hand" doing all the work (138:7bc) to succor the "work of his hands" (138:8c)—his people, called and created as a divine community, perhaps referring specifically to the deliverance he had accomplished for them in the past (138:3).

Enemies might rage (138:7b), but God's hands, accomplishing deliverance in the current distress, will not be thrust away. And equally certain, divine retribution will be the lot of those wrathful foes (138:8a). All of this proves that the lovingkindness of Yahweh is forever upon his people (138:8b). "The suppliant knows that one experience of divine deliverance does not mean that life will be smooth forever. God's people are not immune from trouble . . . , but neither are they overwhelmed by trouble . . . ; they live by the dynamic of trouble and deliverance. This is what the psalm expects for the future," and thus God continues to be glorified, more and more, more and more![7]

---

5. "Haughty," גָּבֹהַּ, *gavoah*, is also translated "lofty" in 103:11; 104:18; 113:5. This makes a clever contrast with Yahweh being the "one on *high*" who "sees the *lowly*," and . . . he "knows the *haughty/lofty*" (138:6).

6. Goldingay, *Psalms*, 3:620.

7. Goldingay, *Psalms*, 3:620–21.

PSALM 138:1–8

Sermon Map

I. Exaltation

    Past deliverance from God produces praise that glorifies him (138:1–3)

    Move-to-relevance: Our experience of past deliverance

II. Exhortation

    God, the King of kings, deserves praise from earthly kings (138:4a)

    His words and his deeds bring glory to God (138:4b–6)

    Move-to-relevance: Our witness to God's words and deeds

III. Expectation

    Future deliverance from enemies (and their requital) (138:7–8a)

    God's lovingkindness towards his people brings confidence (138:8bc)

    Move-to-relevance: Our current distresses

IV. *Thank and Testify and . . . Trust!*

    Specifics on the undertaking of corporate thanks and witness

PSALM 139:1–24

Psalm of Disorientation

God's Attributes and God's Aid

PSALM 139 IS A popular psalm, but at the outset of its interpretation it is important to note that 139:19–24—distinct from the far more utilized section, 139:1–18—serves to provide the context of the entire prayer: the psalmist and his cohort are being assaulted by enemies, bloodthirsty foes and God-haters. It is in this setting that the supplicant presents his case, in the preceding eighteen verses of the psalm, for vindication before a God who knows everything, is everywhere, and spans all time. Such an omniscient, omnipresent, and omnitemporal deity, the supplicant claims, can surely see that the afflicted one is innocent; therefore, God ought to take action to clear him (as well as, presumably, to deliver him and destroy his enemies).[1] Indeed, terms that open and close the composition, "examine" (139:1, 23a), and "know" (139:1, 2a, 23a, 23b), are employed metaphorically and forensically to urge God to act as judge, exculpating supplicant and inculpating sinners. All that to say, "the psalmist is not engaged in quiet reverie on a divine attribute [or two or three], but pleading for justice to be done."[2] And with that, he is also implicitly declaring his submissive trust in a mighty God who, he expects, will take appropriate action for him and against his foes (139:19) and in whose paths he promises to walk (139:24). In sum, since God knows (139:1–6), God sees (139:7–12), and God creates (139:13–18), it is to this deity that the psalmist appeals in the face of opposition that is quite deadly (139:19–24).

Translation

139:1   Yahweh, You have examined me and You know;
139:2   You—You have known my sitting and my rising;
        You have understood my thought from afar.
139:3   My wayfaring and my lying down You have measured,
        and [with] all my paths You are familiar.

---

1. It is striking that there is no specific deliverance explicitly sought; even the imprecation uttered against adversaries occupies but half a verse (139:19a).

2. Allen, *Psalms 101–150*, 261.

139:4	For there is not an utterance on my tongue,
	[and] behold, Yahweh, You have known it all.
139:5	Behind and in front You have enclosed me,
	and You set upon me Your palm.
139:6	Too wonderful [is this] knowledge for me;
	it is too high, I am incapable of [grasping] it.
139:7	Where can I go from Your Spirit,
	and where from Your face can I flee?
139:8	If I climb the heavens, You are there;
	and [if] I spread out a bed in Sheol, behold, You [are there].
139:9	[If] I am lifted high [with] the wings of the dawn,
	[if] I abide in the farthest [side of the] sea,
139:10	even there Your hand—it will lead me,
	and it will seize me—Your right hand.
139:11	And [if] I say, "Surely the darkness will cover me,
	and [it will be] night—the light around me,"
139:12	even the darkness is not dark to You,
	and the night, like day, gives light;
	like darkness [is to You, it is] like light.
139:13	For You—You formed my innards;
	You wove me in my mother's womb.
139:14	I will give thanks to You, because I am awesomely set apart;
	wonderful are Your works.
	And my soul is one knowing very well:
139:15	it was not hidden, my bone, from You,
	when I was made in secret,
	knit in the depths of the earth.
139:16	My unshaped form Your eyes saw,
	and on Your scroll all of them were written—
	the days that were created [for me],
	even [when there was] not one of them.
139:17	So, for me, how difficult are Your thoughts, God,
	how vast is their totality.
139:18	[Should] I count them, they would outnumber the sand;
	I have awoken, and I am still with You.
139:19	If You, God, would [only] kill the wicked.
	So, men of bloodshed, depart from me,
139:20	who are speaking against You deceitfully,
	and Your foes [who] lift up [Your name] in worthlessness.
139:21	Is it not [so] that the ones hating you, Yahweh, I hate,
	and those who rise up against You, I loathe?

139:22   With utter hatred, I hate them;
         enemies they have become to me.
139:23   Examine me, God, and know my heart;
         try me, and know my disquieted mind;
139:24   and see if there is a path of idolatry way in me,
         and lead me in the path of antiquity.

Structure

With the argument of Psalm 139 in mind (see above), the composition may essentially be structured as comprising a *Declaration* section that praises God (139:1–18) and a *Disputation* section that has the psalmist explicitly seeking to motivate God to take action in what is almost a defiant protest, while implicitly trusting in God's forthcoming aid (139:19–24):[3]

> **Declaration (139:1–18)**
>
> *Divine Omniscience* (**139:1–6**): subject "You"
>   Merisms: "sitting"/"rising" (139:2a); "wayfaring"/"lying down" (139:3a)
>   "behind"/"in front" (139:5a)
>
> *Divine Omnipresence* (**139:7–12**): subject "I"
>   Merisms: "heavens"/"Sheol" (139:8)
>   "wings of the dawn"/"farthest [side of the] sea" (139:9)
>   "darkness"/"light" (139:11); "night"/"day" (139:11b, 12b)
>
> *Divine Omnitemporality* (**139:13–18**): subject "You"
>
> **Disputation (139:19–24)**
>
> *Wish for Enemies* (**139:19–20**): "Hold them guilty!"
>   **Deity**: "God [אֱלוֹהַּ, *'eloha*]" (139:19a)
> *Commitment to Yahweh's Interests* (**139:21–22**): "I'm for You!"
>   **Deity**: "Yahweh" (139:21a)
> *Wish for Self* (**139:23–24**): "Find me guiltless!"
>   **Deity**: "God [אֵל, *'el*]" (139:23a)
>   Recap of key verbs from the *Declaration*:
>   "know" (139:23a and 139:1, 2a, 4b, 6a)
>   "lead" (139:24b and 139:10a); "see" (139:24a and 139:16a)

---

3. See Goldingay, *Psalms*, 3:627–28, 636; Holman, "Structure of Psalm CXXXIX," 308; and Allen, *Psalms 101–150*, 256. Notice also that the three attributes of deity in the *Declaration* is balanced by three mentions of deity (all in the vocative) in the *Disputation*. As well, see the figure for recap in the *Disputation* of key words from the *Declaration*.

That 139:1–18 is a unified section (with a distinct caesura between 139:18 and 139:19) is further underscored by an inverted parallelism of structure between its beginning and ending (almost chiastic if not for the intervening verses, 139:6b–14a):[4]

139:2b	"my thought"
139:3–4b	"all" (×2); negative clause (139:4a)
139:6a	"wonderful"; "knowledge"
139:14bc	"wonderful"; "knowing"
139:16bcd	"all"; negative clause (139:16d)
139:17a	"Your thoughts"

Theological Focus

In light of God's omniscience, omnipresence, and omnitemporality—wonders too marvelous for humans to comprehend and which demonstrate the care of God for his people—they look to him for aid when assailed by enemies (hating those God-haters), expecting him to take action, while affirming their continued commitment to him and submitting to his ways.

Commentary

Declaration: Divine Omniscience (139:1–6)

Besides "Yahweh" (139:1a, 4b), reference to God in this subsection is made with eleven second-person elements—verbs, pronouns, and pronominal suffixes (139:1 [×2], 2a [×2], 2b, 3a, 3b, 4b, 5a, 5b [×2]). As well, there are ten self-references to the psalmist (139:1, 2a [×2], 2b, 3a [×2], 3b, 4a, 5a, 5b). All this emphasizes the "I–Thou" relationship of deity and supplicant. Such a relationship is "the unifying thread of the whole texture of the discourse."[5]

The assertion that Yahweh has "examined" and that he "knows" (139:1) is basically a claim of innocence:[6] judicially Yahweh has scrutinized the supplicant and, it is implied, found him guiltless in every facet of living: "my sitting," "my rising," "my wayfaring," and "my lying down" (139:2–3a).[7]

---

4. From Holman, "Structure of Psalm CXXXIX," 305; and Allen, *Psalms 101–150*, 256.

5. Holman, "Semiotic Analysis," 99.

6. "Examine" comes from the root חקר, *chqr* (139:1a); "afar" is רָחוֹק, *rachoq* (139:2b). The assonance poetically depicts that Yahweh is hardly near-sighted. This judge sees everything, knows everything, and is everywhere—the heavenly examiner!

7. Of course, this claim does not mean that the psalmist is claiming sinlessness. In the Psalms (and in the rest of the OT) such assertions simply mark one who is generally walking with God in righteousness and is a member of the community of God.

An intriguing interweaving of two chiastic structures within the space of just two verses (139:2–3; surrounded at either end by affirmations that "Yahweh" "knows," in 139:1a, 4b) creates a literary portrayal of God's omniscience permeating every circumstance of the psalmist, percolating through every arena of human undertaking:[8]

139:1a	**"Yahweh ... You know"**			
139:2aα	"You have known"			
139:2aβ	"my sitting"			
139:2aγ	"my rising"			
		"You have understood"		139:2bα
		"my thought"		139:2bβ
139:3aα	"my wayfaring"			
139:3aβ	"my lying down"			
139:3aγ	"You have measured"			
		"my paths"		139:3bβ
		"You are familiar"		139:3bγ
		"Yahweh, You have known"		**139:4b**

And, thus, when the supplicant adds in the next verse, 139:5a, "Behind and in front You have enclosed me," he has textually depicted Yahweh doing exactly that (in the structure of 139:1–4; above)! All over and all around, inside and outside, above and below, God encloses and covers his people. This, as the psalmist avers, is "too wonderful" and "too high" (139:6a) for him to grasp; such overwhelming and all-encompassing knowledge of what we do (139:2a, 3), what we say (139:4), and even what we think (139:2b) is incredible and, to our human ken, incomprehensible. We can only confess with the supplicant: "I am incapable of [grasping] it" (139:6b).[9]

Declaration: Divine Omnipresence (139:7–12)

The psalmist then affirms God's omnipresence with two rhetorical questions (139:7a, 7b) and five hypothetical situations (139:8a, 8b, 9a, 9b, 11). With these questions and these hypotheticals the psalmist affirms that there is no place he can escape from the presence of God, the merisms (see the psalm's structure above) underscoring that even extremes of location and of circumstance can never obviate the presence of deity.[10] Wherever the supplicant goes he is divinely "led" and divinely held ("seized," 139:10). Darkness might abound, night may never cease, but Yahweh is always there and everywhere: he is the one for whom darkness

---

8. Modified from Auffret, *La sagesse*, 326. These portions dealing with divine omniscience contain some clever assonances: in 139:3a, אָרְחִי, *'archi* ("my wayfaring"—the first word of the verse) and זרה, *zrh* ("lie down") are paralleled in 139:5a by אָחוֹר, *'achor* ("behind"—the first word of that verse) and צוּר, *tswr* ("enclose") (also, "farthest" is אַחֲרִית, *'acharit*; 139:9b; modified from Auffret, "O Dieu, connais mon coeur," 7).

9. That sense of wonder and amazement is found both in this declaration of omniscience and in the next of omnipresence—notice the exclamatory sequence both share: "You [אַתָּה, *'attah*]" (139:2a, 8a), followed by the interjection "behold" (139:4b, 8b), relating to God's knowledge and God's presence, respectively.

10. And, of course, the one who is aware of "my lying down" (139:3a) would be present with me even if I were to "spread out a *bed* in Sheol" (139:8b).

is like light—there is no difference (139:11–12). Thus Psalm 139 has the people of God "set upon . . . Your *palm*" (139:5b), led by "Your *hand*" (139:10a), and held by "Your *right hand*" (139:10b)—a close relationship with deity, indeed.

Once again, the "I-Thou" dialectic is visible in the psalmist's declarations in 139:7 and 139:10, those verses with "Your Spirit," "Your face," "Your hand," and "Your right hand":

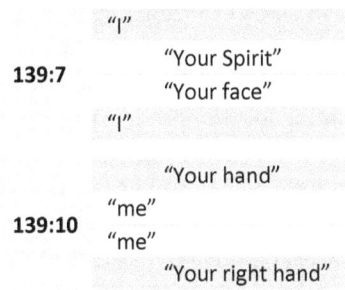

In the first, 139:7, the psalmist ("I") is without and God (his "Spirit"/"face") is within. But that situation quickly gets transformed with the stunning realization in 139:10 that no matter where the supplicant is, he ("me," i.e., the psalmist) is within and God (his "hand"/"right hand") is without, surrounding and enfolding and holding his devout. One just cannot get away from "The Hound of Heaven"—what a blessed privilege![11]

Declaration: Divine Omnitemporality (139:13–18)

The outline and trajectory of human life are detailed in this subsection, but the focus is ultimately on God's knowledge of the supplicant at all times, from conception on. The first part, 139:13–16, deals with embryology, the development of a human being: the plaiting, weaving, and knitting together of the person from one cell to over thirty trillion of them! The structure of 139:13–16, not surprisingly then, centers upon the fact that such embryogenetic acts of divine creation "awesomely sets apart" the person. Therefore, "wonderful" are God's works (139:14ab):[12]

139:13	"formed" and "wove"; "innards"; "mother's womb"
139:14aα	"I will give thanks" (from ידה, *ydh*)
139:14aβ	"awesomely *set apart*" (from פלא, *pl'*)
139:14b	"wonderful [פָּלָא, *pala'*]"
139:14c	"knowing" (from ידע, *yd'*)
139:15–16	"made" and "knit"; "unshaped form"; "depths of the earth"

---

11. The title of a poem by Francis Thompson (1890).

12. From Girard, *Les Psaumes Redécouverts*, 450. Both 139:13 and 139:15–16, at either end of the chiastic structure, contain a pair of verbs denoting creation, a noun for the inchoate shape of the individual, and a phrase denoting the locus of such formation (see figure above). Also "works" in 139:14b is likely referring to what follows, the "making" of the human being by God (139:15b): both "work" and "make" translate עשה, *'sh*.

"Set apart" (139:14a, from the root פלא) hints at God's choice of the person for himself.[13] That verb, נִפְלֵיתִי, niphleti, niphal first-person singular ("I am . . . set apart"), is immediately followed by נִפְלָאִים, niphla'im, "wonderful," niphal participle plural from the same root (139:14b), adding to the poignancy of what is being stated: this divinely ordained "setting apart" is nothing but "wonderful"!

At this magnificent, "awesome" work of God, the psalmist can muster only more incredulous amazement (139:17-18). God's thoughts are so much greater (and more "difficult," 139:17a)[14] than ours: the wisdom of one who knows "my bone [עָצְמִי, 'atsmi]" (139:15a) is surely "vast [עָצְמוּ, 'atsmu]" in its totality (139:17b). One could count and count and count, and never come to an end of accounting for the wisdom and knowledge of Yahweh (139:18a). In fact, God's omnitemporality entails that his spanning of time extends far beyond the embryonic fashioning and gestational developing of a person. God is there even after the psalmist has "awoken" (139:18b), i.e., after he has been birthed.[15] God's presence covers obstetrics and geriatrics and every age (and medical specialty) in between. No wonder the psalmist declares, "I am still with You" (139:18b). God's omnipresence entails his being with his people, but in his omnitemporality it seems it is *we* who are with him!

Disputation (139:19-24)

This last portion of the psalm directs the interpreter to the life-setting and context of the composition as a whole: "all this material [139:1-18] proves to be the prelude to a more direct protestation of innocence [139:19-24]."[16] The *Disputation* section has three parts, each with two verses, and each deploying a different vocative for God. There is a wish for enemies that basically pleads: "Hold them guilty!" (139:19-20, with "God [אֱלוֹהַּ]" in 139:19a); a central part concerning the psalmist's commitment to Yahweh's interests that essentially declares: "I am for You!" (139:21-22, with "Yahweh" in 139:21a); and an urging of God, "Find me guiltless!" (139:23-24, with "God [אֵל]" in 139:23a).

While the wish for the wicked is their removal from his presence one way or another (139:19-20), the psalmist grounds this appeal in his own commitment to the interests of Yahweh (139:21-22). He utterly hates those who hate God (139:21-22); i.e., he is on Yahweh's side. Goldingay notes the paradox of "the parallelism of a plea for God to kill them with an exhortation to them to go away" (139:19; God is directly addressed in 139:19a, and the wicked are directly addressed in 139:19b). He suggests, therefore, that neither verb should be taken too woodenly or literally. "The point of both is to indicate that the suppliant will have nothing to do with them and totally repudiates what they stand for," further explicated in 139:21-22.[17] What the wicked ones are lifting up in "worthlessness" (empty, vain speech; 139:20b) is, apparently,

---

13. The verb is used this way in Exod 33:16; Ps 4:3 (employing the variant root פלה, plh).

14. Notice the wordplay: 139:16d has וְלֹא, wlo', "even [when there was] not"; 139:17a begins with וְלִי, wli, "so for me." An individual is known by God in the womb "even [when there was] not" yet a single day experienced by that one, "so for [that person]" how insurmountably difficult it is to even begin a reciprocal knowing of the works of God!

15. The metaphorical sense of "waking" is not elsewhere in the OT applied to birth, nonetheless it could conceivably mark the transition from embryo/fetus to neonate (or perhaps even denote the imparting of life by God's hand).

16. Allen, *Psalms 101-150*, 262.

17. Goldingay, *Psalms*, 3:637.

the divine name, as the parallel with 139:20a—the deceitful anti-God speech of these pernicious ones—seems to suggest. Appropriately enough, those who so "*lift up* [נשׂא, *nsʾ*]" (139:20b) are God-*haters* [from שׂנא, *snʾ*] who are *hated* [שׂנא] by the psalmist—and by God himself, no doubt (139:21a, 22a; the two verbs are anagrams of each other).[18]

Finally, and belatedly, comes the psalmist's wish for himself. His "disquieted mind" (139:23b) may have been a symptom of his enemies' attacks and his dire need for divine aid. Recalling verbs that commenced the psalm, the supplicant seeks a judicial reckoning for vindication (139:23-24; see figure of the psalm's structure above for those repetitions). Surely the all-knowing, everywhere-present, and all-time-encompassing deity is aware of the psalmist's innocence. The psalmist here is making a claim of guiltlessness (in a limited, not absolute, sense, of course), asserting that God ought to know this for a fact (139:23).[19] So the implicit suggestion is that God should intervene and remove the current spate of evil besetting the people of God. "You," the psalmist appeals, "who understand my '*thought*' [139:2b], and whose own '*thoughts*' are far beyond us [139:17a]—surely You 'know my disquieted *mind*' [139:23b] affrighted by all the evil and the abounding of evildoers. The God who knows 'my rising' (139:2a) certainly sees the wicked 'rising up' against me (139:2b). Surely You appreciate my concurring with Your views on the matter of evil and evildoers. So wouldn't You, God, do something about it?" Thus there is a movement here from the wickedness of enemies (139:19-20), through commitment to God (139:21-22), to the guiltlessness of self (139:23-24a)—all creating a spirited appeal to God to take action, pro-righteous and anti-wicked.

At the same time the psalmist (and the people of God) promises to walk in divine "paths" (139:24). The "path of idolatry" is contrasted here with the "path of antiquity" (139:24). Though the meaning of both phrases is vague, the thrust is clear: the psalmist walks on the path established by God from of old (see Jer 6:16; 18:15), i.e., in God's service, under God's care, and zealous for God's interests—unlike those treading the path of idolatry. After all, this deity knows "all my paths" (Ps 139:3b; and "my wayfaring," 139:3a); would that this God now lead his people on the "paths" of righteousness he has established in ages past.

In all the psalm, the request for an explicit action by God, that he *do* something about the current distress, takes up only half a verse (139:19a), and that expressed as a wish and likely to be metaphorical. No doubt, the psalmist and his cohort desire God's deliverance and the removal of their attackers, but in this prayer, after the awe-inspiring declarations of God's attributes in 139:1-18 (evidence of his care for them), they are simply expecting God to do the right thing, whatever it may be, and however he chooses to visit punishment upon evildoers. And so in him they continue to trust, and in his paths they continue to walk. And so should we!

---

18. Elsewhere in the Psalter, too, the psalmist's hatred aligns him with the interests of God: see 26:5; 31:6; 97:10; 101:2-4; 119:104, 113, 128, 163; as well, see Prov 8:13; Amos 5:15; Mic 3:2; etc. After all, God, too, hates such evildoers: Pss 5:5; 11:5.

19. "Know" is an ongoing motif in this composition: 139:1a, 1b, 2a, 4b, 6a, 14c, 23a, 23b.

Sermon Map

I. Declarations about Deity
   God's omniscience, omnipresence, omnitemporality (139:1–18)
   Care of God for his people: the wonder of it all!
   Move-to-relevance: God's care for his people
II. Disputation for Deliverance
   Crushed by enemies: plea for deliverance (139:19–20)
   Move-to-relevance: Assaults on our lives
   Commitment of God's people to God and his interests (139:21–22)
   Compliance of God's people to his guidance (139:23–24)
III. *You Care! They Crush! We Commit! We Comply!*
   Specifics on commitment and submission to God and his care

PSALM 140:1–13

Psalm of Disorientation

Prayer for Preservation

PSALM 140 LAUNCHES INTO a plea for deliverance with its first word. Essentially, the poem is addressed to Yahweh, including a direct quote of what the psalmist had once said (140:6), and a single verse that talks about, and not to, Yahweh (in the third person; 140:12). In a sense, this psalm may be continuing where Psalm 139 left off: that song had concluded with a mere half-verse plea for deliverance, 139:19a. Here, it is all request for rescue.

Translation

140:1   Rescue me, Yahweh, from the evil one;
          from the person of violences preserve me—
140:2   who have devised evils in [their] heart;
          all the day they stir up wars;
140:3   they sharpen their tongues like a serpent;
          the poison of a viper is under their lips.
140:4   Keep me, Yahweh, from the hands of the wicked [one];
          from the person of violences preserve me—
          who have devised to upend my feet.
140:5   The proud have hidden a trap for me, and ropes;
          they have spread a net at the side of the track;
          snares they have set for me.
140:6   I said to Yahweh, "My God You are;
          give ear, Yahweh, to the voice of my supplications [for grace]."
140:7   Yahweh, Lord, the strength of my deliverance,
          You have covered my head in the day of [battle] armor.
140:8   Do not grant, Yahweh, the desires of the wicked [one];
          his scheme, do not promote, [lest] they are exalted.

140:9   The head of those surrounding me,
          the trouble from their lips, may it cover them.
140:10 May it be brought down upon them—[burning] coals;
          into fire may they be caused to fall,
          into miry pits [from which] they cannot rise.
140:11 A person of [evil] tongue, may he not be established in the earth;
          a person of violence, may evil hunt him to blows.
140:12 I know that Yahweh will make a verdict [for the] afflicted,
          a judgment for the needy.
140:13 Surely the righteous, they will give thanks to Your name;
          they will dwell, the upright, in Your presence.

Structure

In the first section of Psalm 140 the dire *Circumstances* of the psalmist is detailed (140:1–5);[1] in the second he proceeds with a *Call* for help (140:6–11); and in the third he exudes *Confidence* in Yahweh's vindication and the safety of God's people (140:12–13), evidenced by the absence of those elements repeated in the first and second sections:

Circumstances (140:1–5)
Address: vocative "Yahweh" (140:1a, 4a)
Antagonists: singular (140:1b, 4ab); plural (140:2–3, 4c, 5)
          "person" (140:1b, 4b); "wicked [one]" (140:4a)
Amorality: "evil" (140:1a, 2a); "violences" (140:1b, 4b)
          "day ... wars" (140:2b)
Appendages: "heart" (140:2a) "tongues" (140:3a)
          "their lips" (140:3b); "hands" (140:4a)
          "*my* feet" (140:4c)

Call (140:6–11)
Address: vocative "Yahweh" (140:6b, 7a, 8a); "Lord" (140:7a)
Antagonists: singular (140:8abα, 11); plural (140:8bβ, 9–10)
          "person" (140:11a, 11b); "wicked [one]" (140:8a)
Amorality: "evil" (140:11b); "violence" (140:11b)
          "day of [battle] armor" (140:7b)
Appendages: "tongue" (140:11a);
          "their lips" (140:9b); "head" (140:9a)
          "*my* head" (140:7b)

Confidence (140:12–13)
No address
No antagonists
No amorality
No appendages

---

1. Even though there are pleas for deliverance ("rescue me," 140:1a; "keep me," 140:4a), 140:1–5 is mostly lament, describing the ruinous state of affairs.

Psalm 140:1-13

Theological Focus

Circumstances may be dire, with foes on the assault and wickedness on the ascend, but the people of God, in ardent supplication to him for their own protection and their enemies' retribution, rest confident in the knowledge that they can praise God for his deliverance, and dwell in his presence always.

Commentary

Circumstances (140:1-5)

This section is mostly a lament, as noted above, despite "rescue me, Yahweh" and "keep me, Yahweh" (140:1a, 4a).[2] The bulk of 140:1-5 describes the dire situation of the psalmist, and it does so in a repeated pattern (140:1-2a = 140:4):[3]

140:1a	"rescue me, Yahweh, from the evil one"	
140:1b	"from the person of violences preserve me"	
140:2a	"who have devised ..."; "heart"	
140:4a	"keep me, Yahweh, from the hands of the wicked [one]"	
140:4b	"from the person of violences preserve me"	
140:4c	"who have devised ..."; "feet"	

The structure of 140:2 emphasizes the depth of the wickedness: it comes from the heart of the wicked and they plan on performing their nefarious acts throughout the day, devising evils and even stirring up wars!

> "... who have devised evils
> in [their] heart;
> all the day
> they stir up wars."

Goldingay thinks the descriptions are "too varied to take them all as literal descriptions of actual opponents,"[4] but there is no reason to suspect such enemies to be non-existent; conceivably they are conflations of a number of foes over a period of time. The appendages of these malefactors indicate that the violence is both verbal and physical: "heart" (140:2a), "tongues"

---

2. Only two vocatives in *Circumstances*; the next section, *Call*, has four. Also this section has four appendages, bespeaking the holistic involvement of the wicked in their evil; the next has only three (see figure above).

3. The first verse, 140:1, is itself chiastic: "rescue me" / "from the evil man" // "from the person of violences" / "preserve me." Likewise, 140:4ab: "keep me" / "from the hands of the wicked" // "from the person of violences" / "preserve me."

4. Goldingay, *Psalms*, 3:644-45.

(140:3a), "lips" (140:3b), and "hands" (140:4a) apparently stretched out to seize the hapless supplicant. The third verse, 140:3, describing the reptilian nature of the enemies, literally hisses with the multiple sibilants:[5]

> שָׁנְנוּ לְשׁוֹנָם כְּמוֹ־נָחָשׁ חֲמַת עַכְשׁוּב תַּחַת שְׂפָתֵימוֹ
> *shananu lshonam kmo-nachash chamat 'akshuv tachat sphatemo*
> "They sharpen their tongues like a serpent;
>   the poison of a viper is under their lips."

With four appendages listed (see above), the evildoers are in earnest about their heinous deeds. The sole appendage of the supplicant listed in this section, "feet" are successfully "upended" by his opponents (140:4c). Not tripped by the *feet* of foes as one might have expected, it is the "hands" of the wicked ones (140:4a) that topple the psalmist. And then, like a trapped animal, he is netted in ropes (140:5). Pointedly, "side" in 140:5b is יָד, *yad*, also translated "hand" in 140:4a: it is the "hands" of the wicked that net the psalmist by the "side [hand]" of the road. Dire circumstances indeed!

Call (140:6–11)

Unlike the previous section with two vocatives addressing deity, here there are four: "Yahweh" (140:6b, 7a, 8a) and "Lord" (140:7a)—supplication is clearly the focus.[6] And there are fewer appendages of the antagonists mentioned here (three, instead of the four in the first section): the lament of circumstances is not necessarily being emphasized here. So, in this *Call* section, the psalmist proceeds with his supplication proper. While his "feet" had been upended in 140:4a, here his "head" is "covered" "in the day of [battle] armor" (140:7b). God—"the strength of my deliverance" (140:7a, i.e., the strength that delivers him)—is working on his behalf already. And in a stunning reversal, the supplicant prays that the "head" of his enemies may be "covered" by all the trouble they have generated (140:9). Not only is he asking for fire to drop on them, he hopes they themselves fall into fire, too, into nether regions that are, inexplicably, also "miry pits" from which there is no rescue (140:10c; likely a mixing of metaphors generated in the throes of emotion).[7]

The divinely distributed deserts are just: they, who were seeking to be exalted (יָרוּמוּ, *yarumu*; 140:8b) will not be able to "rise" (יָקוּמוּ, *yaqumu*; 140:10c). And the ones who trapped the psalmist in "ropes" (חֲבָלִים, *chavalim*; 140:5a, a masculine plural noun) are now themselves trapped in "coals" (גֶּחָלִים, *gechalim*; 140:10a, another masculine plural noun):[8]

---

5. Add the "selah" to the end of 140:3 (untranslated) and you have yet another word with a sibilant. Also, another chiasm shows up in 140:3: "their tongues" / "serpent" // "viper" / "their lips."

6. With regard to the direct speech beginning in 140:6, I've chosen to end the quote with that verse because 140:7 begins with another vocative (actually two of them) signaling a fresh start.

7. It is possible that the "[burning] coals" (140:10a) wished for are flaming arrows (as also in 120:4). That the psalmist is still thinking of those snakes in 140:3 is evident: "serpent" there is נָחָשׁ, *nachash*; and "[battle] armor" in 140:7b is נֶשֶׁק, *nasheq*. Also of note is the assonance in this section of the potential fate that befalls the wicked: "head" is רֹאשׁ, *ro'sh* (140:9a), "fire" is אֵשׁ, *'esh* (140:10b), and "person" is אִישׁ, *'ish* (140:11a, 11b), almost wishing for the evil person to fall headlong into the furnace!

8. Figure below is modified from Girard, *Les Psaumes Redécouverts*, 461.

140:8a	"wicked"
140:8b	"[lest] they are exalted [רום, rwm]"
140:10aα	"may it be brought down upon them"
140:10aβ	"[burning] coals"
140:10bα	"fire"
140:10bβ	"may they be caused to fall"
140:10c	"they cannot rise [קום, qwm]"
140:11b	"evil"

There is a moral law at work in the world whereby evil wreaks its own nemesis. It is by no means separate from Yahweh's own activity: he works through it, grinding steadily away with his mills of providential judgment. By contrast with the psalmist's own head being covered [140:8], he asks that theirs may be—with disaster earned by their own slander [140:9]. He has suffered the heat (or poison) of their attacks [140:3], so their just desserts are the heat of divine judgment [140:10ab] . . . . They have tried to get him to fall into traps they set for him 140:5a], so they too should be plunged into pits of destruction [140:10c]. They have hunted him with their snares [140:5bc], and they should be hounded in their turn [140:11].[9]

Confidence (140:12–13)

The confidence section is remarkable for the absence of any direct address to Yahweh with a vocative (no pleas here), the lack of any mention of antagonists (they have disappeared!), or of amorality (that too has vanished for God has already worked—no wonder the psalmist is confident); and what is more, there are no appendages on display here either (no wicked body parts that create trouble—they have vanished along with their owners; besides, there are no limbs of the supplicant here that need protection)!

God has answered prayer in the past, and he will do so, now, too; 140:12–13 is an unambiguous declaration of faith. Yet, "it does not actually say that Yhwh will make a judgment or a decision for *me* as a weak or needy person, even though those terms are surely ones designed to apply to the suppliant. Faith knows what God *can* do, but not what God *will* do."[10] Precisely! God's people can rest assured he will take action in his own way, in his own time; so then and now and always, the righteous will praise him and dwell in his presence (140:13). Who would want anything more?

---

9. Allen, *Psalms 101–150*, 268.
10. Goldingay, *Psalms*, 3:650.

Sermon Map

I. Circumstances
   Belligerent enemies (140:1–5)
   Move-to-relevance: Dire circumstances in our lives
II. Call
   Beseeching saints (140:6–11)
   Move-to-relevance: Supplication and imprecation are valid prayers
III. Confidence
   Believable God (140:12–13)
IV. *Circumstances Cannot Curtail Confidence!*
   Specifics on remaining prayerfully confident in crises

PSALM 141:1–10

Psalm of Disorientation

Maintaining Integrity in Distressing Times

PSALM 141, LIKE THE previous psalm, also presumes that the psalmist is under attack from foes. Indeed, it might not just be the psalmist who is under siege; a first-person plural in 141:7b shows that the community, too, has been intensely oppressed. In any case, a number of similarities in vocabulary evidence the linkage between Psalms 140 and 141.[1] However, the response to being assailed is quite different in this composition: besides the two verses asking God to give an ear to his plea (141:1–2), the first section has several verses requesting preservation of the supplicant's integrity (141:3–6). Whereas in 140:1 the supplicant sought protection from "evil," here that individual does not want to be engaging in "evil," himself (141:4a); whereas the malefactors were employing their poisoned "lips" in 140:3, here the psalmist wants God to keep his own "lips" from unrighteous utterances (141:3b). All in all, this psalm makes a different sort of request in the middle of distress.

Translation

141:1 Yahweh, I cry to You; hurry to me;
          give ear to my voice when I cry to You.
141:2 May my prayer be established as incense before Your face,
          the lifting up of my hands as an evening offering.
141:3 Set a keep, Yahweh, at my mouth;
          preserve the door of my lips.
141:4 Do not incline my heart to an evil matter,
          to engage in engagements of wickedness
          with people—the ones doing iniquity—
          and I will not dine of their pleasant [edibles].

---

1. For instance, "keep" (141:3a, 9a and 140:4a); "lip" (141:3b and 140:3b, 9b); "evil" (141:4a and 140:1a, 2a, 11b); "wicked" (141:4b, 10a and 140:4a, 8a); "righteous" (141:5a and 140:13a); "Yahweh, Lord" (141:8a and 140:7a); "trap" (141:9a and 140:5a); and "snare" (141:9a, 9b and 140:5c).

141:5   May the righteous smite me in lovingkindness and may they reprove me;
           it is oil upon the head; may my head not thwart it,
           for even my prayer is still against their evil deeds.
141:6   Their judges have been thrown by the sides of the rock,
           and they have heard my utterances, for they are pleasant.
141:7   Like when one is plowing and one is breaking open the earth,
           our bones have been scattered at the mouth of Sheol.
141:8   For toward You, Yahweh, Lord, are my eyes;
           in You I seek refuge; do not lay bare my soul.
141:9   Keep me from the sides of the trap they have snared for me,
           and from the snares of the ones doing iniquity.
141:10 May they fall into their own nets—the wicked together,
           until I—I pass by.

Structure

The composition may broadly be organized in two sections, 141:1–6 (*Preservation of Integrity*), as noted above, and 141:7–10 (*Protection of Individuals*), closing with pleas for protection of the supplicating individual(s) (and for the punishment of the wicked). The two parts are constructed with similar verbiage:[2]

Preservation of Integrity (141:1–6): "Keep me from them!"
"to me [לִי, *lî*]" (141:1a); "keep" (141:3a); "at my mouth" (141:3a)
"not [אַל, *'al*]" (141:4a, 5b); "wickedness" (141:4b)
"the ones doing iniquity" (141:4c)
"still [עַד, *'ad*]" (141:5c); "sides" (141:6a)

   Enemies "thrown down" (141:6a)
   Body parts: Yahweh's "ear" (141:1b); "Your face" (141:2a)
                  "my hands" (141:2b); "my mouth," "my lips" (141:3)
                  "my heart" (141:4a); "[my] head" (141:5b [×2]

Protection of Individuals (141:7–10): "Keep them from me!"
"for me [לִי]" (141:9a); "keep" (141:9a); "at the mouth" (141:7b)
"not [אַל]" (141:8b); "wicked" (141:10a)
"the ones doing iniquity" (141:9b)
"until [עַד]" (141:10b); "sides" (141:9a)

   Enemies "fall" (141:10a)
   Body parts: "our bones," "mouth of Sheol" (141:7b)
                  "my eyes," "my soul" (or "throat"/"neck"; 141:8)

---

2. Modified from Allen, *Psalms 101–150*, 273–74.

PSALM 141:1–10

Theological Focus

When assailed by evildoers, the people of God, conscious of the dangers of being tempted by the lifestyles and ways of the wicked, seek God's help in preserving the integrity of their speech, attitudes, and actions, and in being accountable to the reprimand of their fellow-righteous, as they continue to look to him in faith for protection from havoc wrought by malefactors, who will receive their just deserts.

Commentary

Preservation of Integrity (141:1–6)

The first two verses are standard appeals for Yahweh to listen, each carefully organized:

141:1
"Yahweh, I *cry* to You;
hurry to *me*;
give ear to *my voice*
when I *cry* to You."

141:2
"May my *prayer* be established
as incense before Your *face,*
the lifting up on my *hands*
as an evening *offering.*"

The relationship in 141:1 appears to be that of child and parent; in 141:2 it is between devotee and deity. Thus the psalmist approaches Yahweh as a child/devotee would a parent/deity with the rights and privileges appertaining to those affiliations: a response from God is therefore expected.

But rather than plead for a typical divine rescue mission (as in Psalm 140), quite unusually 141:3–6 goes elsewhere. The four verses are focused on words and locutions: 141:3a, 3b, 4a (where "matter" is דָּבָר, *davar*, elsewhere translated "word," suggesting that the inclination of the psalmist's heart was towards evil speech), 5a, 5c, 6b. Yes, victims of assailants and attackers need protection from their foes' violence, but they also need protection from the malign and corrupting influence emanating from these malefactors that potentially entangle their victims. Evildoers seem to be winning in this world, so the temptation to join them (or to employ the same deceptive and maleficent tactics against them, or even with them, on their side), thus jettisoning one's commitment to probity and to God, is often a strong one. And this, no doubt, starts manifesting in words spoken. In sum the main request in the first half of this psalm is the *Preservation of Integrity* of the psalmist, particularly in his speech, for the obvious first slip and slide in this regard is in the matter of utterances. Therefore, would that God place a "keep" (guard) at the supplicant's mouth and an impassable door at his lips (141:3a).

But of course, speech does not come out of one's lungs, larynx, and lips without first being conceived in the mind/heart. And so the psalmist also beseeches God to watch his heart (141:4a) which, undisciplined, can lead to sinning in deeds—"engaging in engagements [לְהִתְעוֹלֵל עֲלִלוֹת, lhit'olel 'alilot] of wickedness"—with the evil ones (141:4bc). So while words get prime billing in these verses, attitudes and actions are not neglected: the supplicant wants his locution, his cognition, and his volition to be subject to divine standards and godly guidelines. The tempting attraction of participating in wickedness is spelled out in 141:4d: the psalmist is seduced by the titillations of fine food, likely standing for all the good things those bad folks enjoy in their depraved lives.[3]

Not only does the psalmist seek divine protection for mouth (and heart and hands), he also wants to be open to the rebuke of his fellow-righteous in the congregation of God's people (perhaps recognizing that the requested divine protection is often granted through other members of the community of God; 141:5ab). The supplicant exults about such reprimand: it is as valuable and luxurious as scented oil on the head with which one might welcome a dear guest. May God prevent him from resisting these corrections.[4] After all, he is still praying "against their [i.e., the wicked's] evil deeds" (141:5d), i.e., he has not—yet—been taken in hook, line, and sinker, by the evildoers' bait: he is still on the side of God.[5] If he is praying *anti*-wickedness, he argues, he should be, and is, *pro*-rebuke from his fellow-faithful for any failure to demonstrate integrity or even for any inclination to dabble in wickedness. All that to say, he rejects the allure of the reprobates, but accepts the admonition of the righteous. A good move, indeed, and may God help us also to develop that same teachability and accountability.

This prayer of the supplicant against the evil of the wicked appears to have been answered already:[6] the "judges" (i.e., the nobles and rulers) of these mobsters have been "thrown down by the sides of the rock" (probably cliffs; 141:6a).[7] But then we have 141:6b with its rather incongruous "they have heard"—who, these evil judges? The solution to this unclarity is to link 141:5a ("righteous," "they") with 141:6b ("they," i.e., the righteous), and to connect 141:5c ("their," i.e., the wicked's) with 141:6a ("their," also pertaining the wicked):

141:5ab	"Let the *righteous* smite me, and may *they* reprove …"	Righteous
141:5c	"my prayer is against *their* evil deeds."	Wicked
141:6a	"*Their* judges have been thrown by the sides …"	Wicked
141:6b	"*they* have heard my utterances, for they are pleasant"	Righteous

Thus, 141:5ab, 6b talk of the righteous reprimanding the psalmist and the effect thereof; and they, the righteous, now hear the pleasant utterances of the one they had corrected earlier, who was in danger of transgressing by way of speech (141:3). He who was tempted to introduce

---

3. The metaphor employed in the consumption of delicacies also involves the mouth, the organ of speech that needed divine guarding (141:3).

4. That the psalmist is praying that he may not repulse the rebuke of the righteous suggests that that disregard of deserved censure in such circumstances was a distinct possibility: as if the allurements of the wicked actors were not bad enough, the supplicant was also in danger of staving off reprimand from godly associates.

5. Perhaps this "prayer" (141:5c) refers to the "prayer" that commenced the psalm (141:2a) that he wished would be, like incense, acceptable before God.

6. Or perhaps the perfect verb, "they have been thrown" (141:6a), is prophetic—describing what is yet to happen, but of the certainty of which there is no doubt.

7. The assonance of "judges [שפט, shpht]" and "thrown [שמט, shmt]" hints that their punishment fits their crimes.

the evildoers' "pleasant" gourmet cuisine into his mouth (141:4d) is now producing "pleasant" utterances out of that same organ (141:6b). And, in 141:5c–6a, the psalmist's prayer against the evil deeds of the wicked appears to have been fulfilled: the wicked generation's leaders have been overthrown. All that to say, God is keenly interested in preserving the integrity of his people and does take appropriate action against evildoers, hearing the prayers of his devout.

Protecting the Individuals (141:7–10)

For the first time in this psalm we encounter a first-person plural, "our" (141:7b), representing the psalmist and his cohort, the people of God. Yes, the "mouth" of the psalmist was no doubt a danger to his integrity (141:3), but the greater danger was the "mouth" of Sheol (141:7b) waiting to devour God's people as their foes did away with them. This danger is not minimized: they are being slaughtered with their remains ("bones," 141:7b) dispersed on the plains. It is as if Sheol the monster had feasted on God's people with its "mouth" and spat out their "bones": their very souls were being laid bare, exposed to die (141:8b). Would that God—to whom alone the supplicant approaches for refuge, and upon whom alone the supplicant gazes for favor[8]—step in (141:8). Thus the praying people of God have their "hands" lifted to him (141:2b), their "lips" and "mouths" guarded by him (141:3), their "hearts" set on the straight and narrow by him (141:4ab), and their "heads" accepting the correction of the righteous (141:5b). Now—despite their "bones" being scattered and their "souls" (נֶפֶשׁ, *nephesh*, "soul," also means "throat"/"neck") being laid bare (141:7b, 8b)—their "eyes" are set on God, and on God alone (141:8a)![9]

And what is deity requested to do? Would that he protect his people (represented by the psalmist) and prevent them from being caught in the "sides" of the trap (141:9),[10] unlike those judges defenestrated by the "sides" of the rock (141:6a). On the other hand, God should turn the tables on the wicked, "the ones doing iniquity" (141:9b; these were the psalmist's erstwhile or potential fellow-perpetrators of evil, also labeled "the ones doing iniquity," 141:4c)—all of them (141:10a), not just their leaders already prosecuted in 141:6a—that they may "fall into their own nets" (141:10). And thus the psalmist and his community "pass by" in safety, integrity preserved, soul and body protected and delivered by their great God (141:10b).

---

8. The emphatic "toward You, Yahweh, Lord" (141:8a) asserts that this God is the supplicant's only God and his only recourse in times of deathly distress. Also see the equally emphatic "I—I pass by," confidently envisaging the safety with which this God surrounds him.

9. See Goldingay, *Psalms*, 3:659.

10. While setting a "keep" at the psalmist's mouth was indeed something important he was imploring Yahweh to do (141:3a), "keeping" him from being annihilated by the wicked was even more crucial (141:9a).

Sermon Map

I. Preservation of Integrity
   Hazard of being attracted by the lifestyles of evildoers (141:1–4)
   Happiness of being admonished by the fellow-righteous (141:5–6)
   Move-to-relevance: Allure of evil; accountability to the righteous
II. Protection of Individuals
   Dire circumstances (141:7–8)
   Punishment of evildoers; protection of individuals (141:9–10)
   Move-to-relevance: God's protection of us in the past
III. *Avoid Attraction; Accept Admonition!*
   Specifics on maintaining one's integrity, with God's help

PSALM 142:1–7

Psalm of Disorientation

Revived, Restored, Recompensed

PSALM 142 PORTRAYS A supplicant on the edge of survival, appealing to God for intervention and grace (142:1), with no one to notice, let alone help, him (142:4). There are a number of voice-related endeavors towards Yahweh reported here: the psalmist "wails" (142:1a, 5a); he "makes supplication [for grace]" (142:1b); he "pours out" his musings of pain (142:2a); he "announces" his distress (142:2b); he "says" (142:5b); he makes a "lament" (142:6a); and later he "gives thanks" (142:7b). The entire psalm is therefore a prayer for attention and deliverance—indirectly to Yahweh (142:1–2; Yahweh spoken of in the third person), as well as directly to him (142:3–7: Yahweh spoken to in the second person).

Translation

142:1   With my voice to Yahweh I wail;
            with my voice to Yahweh I make supplication [for grace].

142:2   I pour out before His face my musing [of pain];
            my distress before His face I announce.

142:3   When my spirit is faint within me,
            You—You know my pathway.
        On this way [that] I walk
            they have hidden a trap for me.

142:4   Look to [my] right hand and see;
            for there is no one who is taking notice of me;
        escape has perished from me;
            there is no one who is seeking [good] for my soul.

142:5   I wailed to You, Yahweh;
            I said, "You are my refuge,
            my share in the land of the living."

142:6   Be attentive to my lament,
            for I have become very low;
        rescue me from my pursuers,
            for they are too strong for me.
142:7   Bring out my soul from the dungeon,
            to give thanks to Your name;
        me, the righteous will encircle,
            for You will recompense [bountifully] upon me.

Structure

The parallelism of structure within the psalm shows it organized in two halves, each with similar moves—*Plea to Listen, Protection of the Lord,* and *Plight of Loneliness* (first section)/ *Plight of Lethality* (second section):[1]

> **Plea 1 (142:1–2)** to Listen
> "I wail" (141:1a); "to Yahweh" (141:1a, 1b)
>
> > **Protection 1 (142:3ab)** of the Lord
> > "You [אַתָּה, *'attah*]" (142:3b)
> >
> > > **Plight 1 (142:3c–4)** of Loneliness
> > > "trap" (142:3d); "my soul" (142:4d)
> > > "from me [מִמֶּנִּי, *mimmeni*]" (142:4c)
> > > *Repetition*:
> > > "there is no one [אֵין, *'en*]" (142:4b, 4d)
>
> **Plea 2 (142:5a)** to Listen
> "I wail" (141:5a); "to You, Yahweh" (141:5a)
>
> > **Protection 2 (142:5bc)** of the Lord
> > "You [אַתָּה]" (142:5b)
> >
> > > **Plight 2 (142:6–7)** of Lethality
> > > "dungeon" (142:7a); "my soul" (142:7a)
> > > "too ... for me [מִמֶּנִּי]" (142:6d)
> > > *Repetitions*:
> > > Hiphil imperatives (142:6a, 6c, 7a)
> > > "for [כִּי, *ki*]" (142:6b, 6d, 7d)

At the end of the psalm, reversals appear to be taking place: plight drifts towards praise: the earlier vocal initiatives of torment amidst distress are now transformed into verbal intimations of thanks upon deliverance (142:7b). Besides, now the supplicant is no longer alone

---

1. Modified from Girard, *Les Psaumes Redécouverts*, 475. Besides what is shown below, the last three verses are also tied together by "I wailed" (142:5a) linking with "my lament" (142:6a); the need for "refuge" (142:5b) with "my pursuers" (142:6c); departing from "the land of the living" (142:5c) with the allusion to Sheol, "dungeon" (142:7a), which the psalmist fears will be his destination.

(as he was earlier: 142:4b, 4d)—the righteous encircle him (142:7c), and the dangers of the past (will) become bountiful "recompense" from God himself (142:7d). Yes, God hears the prayers of his people.

Theological Focus

In dire and distressing circumstances, particularly in light of their abandonment by one and all, the people of God continue to seek him as their only refuge and protection, the one who rescues and revives, giving cause for the delivered community of saints to praise him for his bounteous blessing.

Commentary

Plea 1; Protection 1; Plight 1 (142:1–4)

These first couple of verses do not address Yahweh directly, as do the remaining verses of the psalm. So, in all likelihood 142:1–2 are meant for the community (and/or the readers/hearers of this poem).

In a synonymously parallel duo of lines in the first verse (142:1a, 1b), and a chiastically arranged subsequent verse (142:2), the psalmist launches into his plea. Each line of those verses identifies the direction of the pleas: "to Yahweh" and "before His face" (in italics and unshaded, below):

| 142:1a | "With my voice | *to Yahweh* | I wail; |
| 142:1b | with my voice | *to Yahweh* | I make supplication [for grace]." |

142:2aα	"I pour out		
142:2aβ		*before His face*	
142:2aγ			my musing [of pain];
142:2bα			my distress
142:2bβ		*before His face*	
142:2bγ	I announce."		

As was noted there are a number of verbs relating to speech in the entirety of the psalm: the supplicant is calling out to God, appealing to him in considerable distress, though the details of the suffering are not yet forthcoming, apart from the woes being given the generic label "distress" (142:2b).[2]

Yet the supplicant affirms in 142:3ab that his trust in the protection and care of God, the one who "knows" (an emphatic assertion: "You—You know . . .") the dangers he is facing. If God knows the "pathway" (142:3b), the "way" the psalmist is "walking" on (142:3c), as he

---

2. And in the employment of שִׂיחַ, *siach*, in 142:2a, that implies some pain: the "musing [of pain]" is thus a complaint or a lament. Whatever the situation, the supplicant's "spirit is faint" (142:3a).

makes the dangerous trek of life amidst distresses and dangers, what more could one want? For divine knowledge is not just intellectual cognition, but an active and intimate knowledge that ensures that God will act.

In the next *Plight 1* subsection (142:3c–4) also, though a "trap" is mentioned, set up by a yet-unidentified "they" (142:3d), the focus is not upon what exactly the dire circumstances are, but upon the unfortunate lot of the psalmist: he appears to be all alone on "this way I walk" (142:3c; also see 142:4b).[3] And that presumably is what causes his spirit to be "faint within me" (142:3a). "Look," the psalmist pleads to Yahweh, and "see": there is no one at his right hand (142:4ab), where one might expect a powerful patron supporting and sustaining him on this dreadful road. In fact, "there is no one who is taking notice of me" (142:4b)—nobody even sees. "So would you, God, 'look . . . and see'" (142:4a). Every avenue of escape has been shut off, and no human seeks his good (142:4d).[4] A trio of echoing references to himself (prepositions with suffixes at the ends of 142:4b, 4c, 4d) makes the agony almost palpable:[5]

142:4b	"there is no one taking notice	of me"
142:4c	"escape has perished	from me"
142:4d	"there is no one …	for my soul"

But has not the psalmist just talked about his protection? He had confessed that God was the one who knew his "pathway," the "way" that was nothing but a minefield of traps (142:3bcd). Surely he can "walk" in peace aware that God "knows" (142:3bc)? Perhaps the supplicant's angst continues because he has not seen Yahweh act yet and, in the midst of his loneliness, that seeming inaction has only further enervated and paralyzed him, rendering his "spirit . . . faint" (142:3a). All that to say, the "story" of the psalm is not over in its first round (142:1–4), and so the psalmist engages in a second round of *Plea 2*, *Protection 2*, and *Plight 2* (but with a shift: the plight is now being transformed to praise).

Plea 2; Protection 2; Plight 2 (142:5–7)

With *Plea 2*, "wailing" begins all over again (142:5a, as in 142:1a), with the supplicant citing himself in 142:5bc. The direct (self-)quote of the psalmist appears to conclude after 142:5c because 142:6 moves into *Plight 2*.

---

3. In contrast with the later scene of his being surrounded by a righteous cohort (142:7c).

4. It is conceivable that even friends had abandoned him, not wanting anything to do with this "loser" going through disaster.

5. From Auffret, *Merveilles à nos yeux*, 238.

Also, as was noted, 142:5a is expanded upon in 142:6ab; 142:5b is extended in 142:6cd; and 142:5c in 142:7a—thus 142:5 is a sort of heading that is explicated in the subsequent two verses:[6]

142:5a	*"I wailed to You, Yahweh"*	
142:6a	"be attentive to my lament"	
142:5b	*"I said, 'You are my refuge'"*	
142:6c	"rescue me from my pursuers"	
142:5c	*"'my share in the land of the living'"*	
142:7a	"bring out my soul from the dungeon"	

Notice how *Plight 2* is expressed in 142:6–7, with three *hiphil* imperatives, each calling for God's intervention, and each followed by a motivational כִּי- (*ki*-) clause that has a different subject each time:

142:6a	"be attentive"	*Hiphil* imperative
142:6b	"for [כִּי] **I** have become very low"	Subject: **supplicant**
142:6c	"rescue me"	*Hiphil* imperative
142:6d	"for [כִּי] **they** are too strong for me"	Subject: **enemies**
142:7a	"bring out"	*Hiphil* imperative
142:7d	"for [כִּי] **You** will recompense"	Subject: **God**

Though the plight continues to be prominent in this second section of the psalm, the tone of the psalm is moving rapidly into a confident assertion of the protection that Yahweh is: "my refuge" (142:5b) and "my share in the land of the living" as opposed to the realm of Sheol (142:5c; "dungeon" in 142:7a suggests Sheol). Allocation and possession of land was always symbolic of, and essential to, the security of family, clan, and tribe. But here it is even more emphatic, intense, and expansive: the psalmist's portion is not just land, but God himself, in the metaphysical "land of the living"—deity now belonged to the supplicant. One cannot get any more secure!

That the tide is shifting is clear from the reversals of distress. Whereas there was "no one" caring for the psalmist, and "no one" seeking his good (142:4b, 4d), now Yahweh is acknowledged to be his "refuge" (142:5b). Whereas once the supplicant could only make a plaintive "musing [of pain] [שִׂיחִי, *sichi*]" (142:2a), now he recognizes God, with an assonant wordplay, as his "refuge [מַחְסִי, *machsi*]" (142:5b). Whereas once his spirit was faint "within me [עָלַי, *'alay*]" (142:3a), now he experiences God's bounteous recompense "upon me [עָלָי]" (142:7d). Whereas even "escape had perished" from him earlier (142:4c), Yahweh is now his portion in "the land of the living" (142:5c): no longer "perishing," he is going to be "living."

---

6. From Auffret, *Merveilles à nos yeux*, 239.

Yes, the sufferer is still "very low"[7] and he is still "lamenting" (142:6ab), but rescue is nigh! No one else can perform that deliverance from these "strong" foes, except God (142:6cd) who, the psalmist is certain, will bring his "soul" out of the dungeon (142:7a)—that same "soul" that was being afflicted (142:4d). And then he will give praise to God, he promises. The contrast between "I wailed to You" (142:5a) and "give thanks to Your name" (142:7b) is not just in content: these contain the only two instances in the psalm of the second-person masculine singular pronominal suffix, ךָ-, -ka (shaded): אֵלֶיךָ ('eleka, "to You") and אֶת־שְׁמֶךָ ('et-shemka, "to Your name").

Unlike the preceding psalms, this one makes no mention of the baneful fate of the wicked and the enemy;[8] rather, 142:7cd proclaims the beatific fate of the supplicant as he is encircled by his righteous companions (in contrast to the situation of aloneness in 142:4),[9] and he is "recompensed [bountifully]" by God! All's well that ends well!

Sermon Map

I. Plight and Plea

    Plight (142:3cd–4, 6b, 6d)

    Plea (142:1–2, 5a, 6a, 6c, 7a)

    Move-to-relevance: Distresses of our lives that cause us to plead

II. Protection and Praise

    Protection (142:3ab, 5bc)

    Praise (142:7bcd)

    Move-to-relevance: Deliverances of our lives that cause us to praise

III. *Exclaim! Expect! Express!*

    Exclaiming pleas, expecting protection, expressing praise

---

7. Perhaps again alluding to the nether depths of Sheol.
8. See 137:8–9; 138:7b–8a; 139:19; 140:8–12a; 141:6a, 10a.
9. "Solitary confinement . . . will make way for communal solidarity" (Basson, "Image Schemata," 266).

PSALM 143:1–12

Psalm of Disorientation

Spiritual Pursuit of God by His Servants in Distress

Psalm 143 is one of the seven traditional penitential psalms, perhaps because of 143:2 that appears to confess unrighteousness.[1]

Translation

143:1   Yahweh, hear my prayer,
        give ear to my supplications [for grace] in Your faithfulness;
        answer me in Your righteousness.

143:2   And do not enter into judgment with Your servant,
        for in Your presence no person [among] all the living is righteous.

143:3   For the enemy has pursued my soul;
        he has crushed to the ground my life;
        he has made me dwell in dark places like those long dead.

143:4   Therefore it is faint within me—my spirit;
        in my midst it is desolated—my heart.

143:5   I have remembered the days from before;
        I have meditated on all Your doings;
        on the work of Your hands I muse.

143:6   I have stretched out my hands to You;
        my soul, like parched ground, [longs] for You.

143:7   Hasten, answer me, Yahweh,
        my spirit has wasted away;
    do not hide Your presence from me,
        [lest] I become similar to those going down to the pit.

---

1. The others are Psalms 6; 32; 38; 51; 102; and 130. Extrapolating from 143:8, this prayer may have been recited at night or before dawn, anticipating an answer "in the morning."

143:8 Cause me to hear, in the morning, Your lovingkindness,
           for in You I trust;
       cause me to know the path that I should go,
           for to You I lift up my soul.
143:9 Rescue me from my enemies, Yahweh;
           in You I find cover.
143:10 Teach me to do [what is according to] Your favor,
           for You [are] my God;
       Your good Spirit, may He lead me on level ground.
143:11 For the sake of Your name, Yahweh, make me live;
           in Your righteousness bring out of distress—my soul.
143:12 And in Your lovingkindness, destroy my enemies,
           and cause them to perish—all who are distressing my soul,
           for I [am] Your servant.

Structure

The structure of Psalm 143 is somewhat hard to pin down (and the various elements are not organized in a precise chiasm, though the linguistic parallels suggest such a layout; see below). Pleas for deliverance weave their way through the poem (143:1–2, 7, 9, 11–12b). Despite there being enmity directed against the supplicant (143:3, 9, 12), for most of the psalm one finds him confessing his unrighteousness (143:2) and resolving to follow God (143:5–6, 8, 10), as he affirms his position as God's "servant" (143:2a, 12c). All these utterances are likely intended motivate God to take action to relieve him of his distress; nonetheless, they make Psalm 143 stand out from its neighbors.

Plea 1 (143:1–2)
"Your faithfulness" and "Your righteousness"; "Your servant"
"supplications [for grace] [תַּחֲנוּנַי, *tachanunay*]"
"*all* the living [from חַי, *chay*]"

    Plight (143:3–4)
    "enemy"; "ground"; "spirit"

        Pursuit (143:5–6)
        "Your hands" and "my hands"

        Plea 2 + Profession (143:7–8)
        "my spirit" and "my soul"

    Plea 3 + Pledge (143:9–10)
    "enemies"; "ground"; "Spirit"

Plea 4 + Position (143:11–12)
"Your righteousness" and "Your lovingkindness"; "Your servant"
"make me live [תְּחַיֵּנִי, *tchayyeni*, from חיה, *chyh*]"
"*all* who are distressing my soul"

Theological Focus

Even in times of distress and enemy assault, while pleading for relief from foes and retribution for them, the servants of God pursue him, acknowledging his past actions on their behalf; they profess their ongoing faith in deity, desiring to walk with him; and they promise their commitment to him, seeking to follow the leading of God's Spirit in their lives.

Commentary

Plea 1 (143:1–2)

The psalmist pleads for God to hear his "supplications [for grace]" because of divine "faithfulness" and because God favors "righteousness" (143:1). Yet that raises an immediate issue for the psalmist: If God is righteous and utterly so, then how can he countenance anyone less than fully righteous? So the psalmist pleads that God would refrain from judging him based on his human righteousness.[2] Obviously, the only way one can approach Yahweh is on the grounds of his grace, and so the psalmist makes "supplications [for *grace*]" (תַּחֲנוּן, *tachanun*, from חֵן, *chen*, "grace," 143:1b). This motif of the supplicant's righteousness (or potential lack thereof) and his desire to move towards a righteous walk with God propels the entirety of the psalm (see 143:8c, 10a, 10c); the danger is that, otherwise, personal guilt may jeopardize access to divine aid.

Plight (143:3–4)

After the plea for God's attention, the psalmist launches into the distress at hand in 143:3, continuing from 143:1 (with 143:2 almost parenthetical), and describing his *Plight*: enemies are hunting him down, crushing his life to the ground, making him dwell in dark, deathly places (an allusion to Sheol) (143:3c; also see "pit" in 143:7d). So much so, the supplicant's spirit is faint, his heart desolated (143:4): psychologically he has been traumatized and rendered shocked. Yet, no request for rescue is uttered yet.[3] After 143:3 with the enemy as subject, and after 143:4 with the psalmist's spirit and heart as subjects, it is time to bring deity into the picture of current distress.

Pursuit (143:5–6)

This section, the *Pursuit* of God by the psalmist, extends 143:2. Yes, no one is righteous, but "I have remembered" the past of God's activity, "I have meditated" on God's doings, "I

---

2. That 143:2, pleading for divine mercy, is immediately followed by an account of the enemies implies that the distress suffered by psalmist at their hands is aggravated by Yahweh's displeasure at his unrighteousness, perhaps causing deity to refrain from delivering the supplicant.

3. Such an explicit entreaty for aid comes only more than halfway through the psalm, in 143:9a, but, as we will see, even that entreaty is part of the psalmist's affirmation of his trust in Yahweh(143:9b).

muse" on God's handiwork (143:5). Likely the psalmist is offering these reflections of God's operations as evidence of his relative righteousness and his commitment to God and God's interests.[4] And as he remembers, meditates, and muses on how God has delivered in the past, he "stretches out [his] hands" to God, pursuing him, panting for deity like one in a parched land (143:6). The suffering one is in dire need of God. It is quite appropriate that the remembrance of the "work of *Your hands*" (143:5c) prompts the supplicant to stretch out "*my hands* to You" (143:6a).

The parallel structure of 143:4 and 143:6, with the chiasm of 143:5bc intervening (see below), add to the poignance of the psalmist's pursuit and seeking after God. In 143:4, the central textual elements of the psalmist's innards ("within me" and "in my midst"; dark-shaded column, below) signified the intensity of his feelings and the depth of his despair. But, after remembering God's work in the past (143:5; literally centered on God's operations; see below), the supplicant is impelled to stretch out "my hands" and even "my soul" (the central textual elements in 143:6; dark-shaded column, below), yearning for, and thirsting for, God—a relocation from a place of instability of "spirit" and "heart" (143:4) to a locus of stability that is with deity alone—"to You" and "for You" (143:6):[5]

143:4
"it is faint"	"within me"	"my spirit"
	"in my midst"	
"it is desolated"		"my heart"

143:5bc
"I have meditated"
　　"on all Your doings"
　　"on the work of Your hands"
"I muse"

143:6
"I have stretched out"	"my hands"	"to You"
	"my soul"	
"like parched ground"		"for You"

Thus a shift in the sufferer's perspective is apparent in 143:5–6, the *Pursuit* section, after the despair of the *Plea* and the *Plight* sections: the supplicant is now focusing on Yahweh, longing for him.[6]

---

4. Though the psalmist is not absolutely righteous, in the general terms that the Psalter (and the OT) employs for God's people this relative righteousness simply describes an individual walking with God in the community of God; the supplicant here claims to fall into that category.

5. Modified from Auffret, *Merveilles à nos yeux*, 252.

6. Also notice that "to/in You [אֵלֶיךָ, 'ēleka]" occurs only in 143:6a, 8d, 9b in this psalm, each time in the context of a movement towards God (and away from enemies and their distressing actions).

Plea 2 + Profession (143:7–8)

This section, 143:7–8, is made up of four parallel sequences of two lines each. Each pair of lines commences with verbal clause (143:7a, 7c, 8a, 8c) followed by a rationale for the request (143:7b, 7d, 8b, 8d).

Plea 2 for God to hear him commences the section, for the supplicant is in dire distress—the wasting away of his "spirit" and his descent into the "pit" (143:7). Similar to 143:4 (the fainting of his "spirit" and his dwelling among the "long dead"), 143:7 is also likely to be dealing with the consequences of enemy oppression. But the next verse, 143:8, is clearly a *Profession* of faith in God: "in You I trust" (143:8b). And he wants to experience God's lovingkindness and learn how to live (to "know the path that I should go"; 1143:8c), and so to God he "lifts up [his] soul," putting himself entirely in God's care (143:8d). Presumably, such a commitment to righteous living will dispose Yahweh to helping him in times of distress.

Whereas he was being made to dwell in "dark places" by evildoers (143:3c), here the psalmist expects God's lovingkindness in the "morning" (143:8a): brighter times ahead! Whereas the enemies had pursued "my soul" (143:3a) and "my soul" was once parched (143:6b), now "my soul" is lifted up to God, as he deposits himself into the care of God (143:8d). Whereas when he began the psalm "Your presence" was fearful (in light of God's righteousness and humanity's lack thereof, 143:2b), here he implores God not to hide "Your presence" from him (143:7c). Again, the perspective has shifted towards hope and stability with this *Profession* of faith.

Plea 3 + Pledge (143:9–10)

Finally, in the last third of the psalm, an explicit *Plea 3* is made regarding his oppressors: "rescue me from my enemies, Yahweh" (143:9a), but even this entreaty is scaffolded by faith: "in You I find cover" (143:9b). Yes, fear is certainly giving way to faith!

And such a change of attitude bespeaks a change in action, too, as the psalmist makes an implicit *Pledge* to "do [what is according to] Your favor" (143:10a), i.e., what is acceptable to God.[7] His goal is to please God (and find his "favor"), and so he prays that God teach him how to do so (143:10a) and that God's good Spirit would lead him on that unshakable path, walking with God (143:10c). Whereas once his life had been "crushed to the *ground*" (143:3b), so much so his soul was a "parched *ground*" (143:6b), here he is confident that he will be traversing a "level *ground*" (143:10c). And earlier he had been "going down to the pit" (143:7d). No more "slip slidin' away"[8] into the depths of the underworld; the path of the people of God is now fixed, firm, and fast—"on level ground!" So whereas once "my spirit" was faint in the supplicant (143:4a), and "my spirit" was wasting away (143:7b), now it is no longer "my spirit" that is running the show, but "Your good Spirit" (143:10c), sustaining, supporting, and stabilizing "my spirit."

---

7. "Teach me to *do* [from עשׂה, *'sh*]" (143:10a) is a response to what *God* has done—the "*work* [also from עשׂה] of Your hands" (143:5c).

8. The title of a song by Paul Simon, 1977.

Centered upon God and his Spirit, 143:10 has the psalmist implicitly promising to submit to divine guidance in his life, resulting in the maintenance of righteousness by the grace of God—no longer will there be the dread of being unrighteous (143:2):

> "Teach me to do [what is according to] Your favor,
>   for You are my God;
>   Your good Spirit,
> may He lead me on level ground."

"The suppliant knows that only as people walk in Yhwh's way can they expect Yhwh to rescue them."[9] The psalmist, therefore, is committing his ways to Yahweh, hoping for divine deliverance from deity, for "You are my God!" Things are, altogether, looking up!

Plea 4 + Position (143:11–12)

The psalm concludes with the summarizing *Plea 4* directly related to the agony the supplicant was going through: he wants to be revived and his soul brought out of distress (143:11), an act of a righteous God ("in Your righteousness," 143:11b; repeating in effect, 143:1c: "answer me *in Your righteousness*").[10] Whereas once he was apprehensive, rightly, about the absolute righteousness of God that could jeopardize "living" (143:2; חָיָה), here he has regained his confidence: "make me live" (חיה; 143:11a). Earlier it was "*all* the living" who, in the presence of God, could potentially suffer the consequences of unrighteousness (143:2b); here the ones whom God will cause to perish are "*all* who are distressing my soul" (143:12b)—the enemies of the people of God. Such retribution, too, is an act of a gracious God for his people's sake ("in Your lovingkindness," 143:12a). Divine deliverance of the devout in God's lovingkindness also means divine destruction of the distressors in God's legislatorship. Those who are unjust towards God's people will meet their just deserts from God.

That intimate relationship between deity and subject is emphasized in the verbless clause of the last three words of the poem (*Position*; 143:12c): "for I [am] Your-servant [כִּי אֲנִי עַבְדֶּךָ, *ki 'ani 'avdeka*]." This, of course, has come right after another three-word asseveration of relationship, also verbless, in 143:10b: "for You [are] my-God [כִּי־אַתָּה אֱלוֹהָי, *ki-'attah 'elohay*]. "It is on this ground that he enlists God's aid to fight his battle against those who, unlike himself, have not pledged their lives to Yahweh and stand outside the covenant circle. Like an attacked vassal appealing to his overlord, he seeks vindication at God's hands, which in turn will prove a vindication of God's own pledges and power," i.e., by demonstrating "Your righteousness" (143:11b).[11] And for the furthering of this end, the people of God, in the exalted position as deity's servants, submit themselves to this righteous and faithful overlord, placing their trust in him and pledging their commitment to him, no matter what.

---

9. Goldingay, *Psalms*, 3:676.

10. This divine righteousness generates righteous divine decisions and righteous divine actions for the benefit of his (righteous) people.

11. Allen, *Psalms 101–150*, 285.

PSALM 143:1–12

Sermon Map

I. Plight and Plea
   Plight (143:3–4)
   Plea (143:1–2, 7, 9, 11–12b)
   Move-to-relevance: Plights and pleas of our lives
II. Pursuit, Profession, and Pledge
   Pursuit of God (143:5–6)
   Profession of faith in God (143:8)
   Promise to walk with God (143:10, 12c)
III. *Pursue! Profess! Pledge!*
   Specifics on pursuing God, professing faith, promising a walk with him

PSALM 144:1–15

Psalm of Reorientation

Prosperity Under the Hand of God Who Does It All

PSALM 144 HAS TWO voices, that of a leader/king (*Commander* in the structure below) in 144:1–11, and that of the people of God (*Community* in the structure) in 144:12–15. The first articulates the call for deliverance from Yahweh and the second expresses the confidence that Yahweh will bless. The psalm begins with a blessing pronounced upon Yahweh (144:1a) and ends with another blessing upon the people of Yahweh—those "for whom Yahweh is God" (144:15b).

Translation

144:1 Blessed be Yahweh, my rock,
    the One teaching my hands for war,
    my fingers for battle;
144:2 my lovingkindness and my steadfastness,
    my stronghold and the one saving me,
    my shield and in whom I seek refuge,
    the One subduing my people under me.
144:3 Yahweh, what is a human, that You acknowledge him,
    [or] the child of a mortal, that You consider him?
144:4 A human is like a breath,
    his days like a shadow—one that is passing.
144:5 Yahweh, incline Your heavens and come down;
    touch the mountains that they may smoke.
144:6 [Do] light lightning and scatter them;
    send out Your arrows and confuse them.
144:7 Send Your hands from on high;
    free me and rescue me from great waters,
    from the hand of the children of foreignness,

144:8	whose mouth speaks worthlessness,
	and whose right hand is a right hand of falsehood.
144:9	God, a new song I will sing to You,
	upon a harp of ten [strings] I will make music to You,
144:10	the One giving deliverance to kings,
	the One freeing David, His servant, from the evil sword.
144:11	Free me and rescue me from the hand of the children of foreignness,
	whose mouth speaks worthlessness,
	and their right hand is a right hand of falsehood.
144:12	Then may our sons, in their youth, [be] as shoots, ones that are grown,
	our daughters as corner pillars, ones that are being carved,
	[as after] the pattern of a palace;
144:13	may our granaries [be] full, providing kind after kind [of food],
	our flocks generating thousands,
	becoming ten thousands, in our [fields] outside;
144:14	may our cattle [be] ones that are laden;
	and [may there be] no breach [of walls], and no going out [in exile],
	and no cry of distress in our squares.
144:15	Blessing [upon] the people to whom [it] is thus;
	blessing [upon] the people for whom Yahweh is God.

Structure

The voices in the psalm divide the composition into its two sections: *Call of the Commander* (144:1–11; marked by the first-person singular in 144:1–2, 7, 9, 11),[1] and *Confidence of the Community* (144:12–15; marked by the first-person plural in 144:12–14):[2]

Call of the Commander (144:1–11)

Praise (**144:1–2**): Yahweh in third-person singular
  "people" (144:2d); Yahweh "blessed [ברך, *brk*]" (144:1a)
    God, in two articulated participles:
      "the One teaching," "the One subduing" (144:1b, 2b, 2d)

Perishability (**144:3–4**): "Yahweh" in second person (vocative; 144:3a)

Petitions (**144:5–8**): "Yahweh" in second person (vocative; 144:5a)
  Refrain (144:7b–8)

Praise (**144:9–11**): "God" in second person (vocative; 144:9)
  Refrain (144:11)
    God, in two articulated participles:
      "the One giving," "the One freeing" (144:10a, 10b)

Confidence of the Community (144:12–15)

Prosperity (**144:12–15**): Yahweh in third-person singular
  "people" (144:15a, 15b); people's "blessing [אַשְׁרֵי, *'ashre*]" (144:15a, 15b)

Theological Focus

The leader of God's people, representing them, acknowledging with amazement that it is God who accomplishes all victories on behalf of his people—humans with limited lifespans—confidently petitions God for deliverance from evildoers, and anticipates divine blessing of generational thriving, economic prosperity, and social stability upon the community that recognizes God as its deity.

---

1. In 144:2d, his people are said to be subdued under the *Commander*; and in 144:10, this leader praises God for his deliverance of kings.

2. Figure below modified from Goldingay, *Psalms*, 3:683; and deClaissé-Walford et al., *Book of Psalms*, 985.

Commentary

Call of the Commander (144:1–11)

The call to God actually commences with praise because God is "my rock" (144:1a); "my lovingkindness";[3] "my steadfastness"[4] (144:2a); "my stronghold"; "the one saving me" (144:2b); "my shield"; the one "in whom I seek refuge" (144:2c); and "the one subduing my people under me"[5] (144:2d). Thus the first two verses are peppered with first-person suffixes, translated "my," "me," and "I" (×11).[6] Yet they uniformly point to God as the main actor on the stage. All that God is doing (and all that he does to aid his people's doing—for instance, his training of the hands and fingers of his leaders to engage in battle) is worthy of praise.[7]

And that leads the speaker to an expression of wonder and amazement: God is doing all these things . . . for perishable humans (144:3)? "Why should Yhwh be training his [the leader's] fingers when Yhwh's own fingers have undertaken a much bigger project than this leader could ever dream of"—creation (see 8:3)?[8] Why this co-opting of human doings when divine doings are more than sufficient for all things? After all, transient, ephemeral, perishable mortals are but a "breath," and their days but "shadows," never permanent, always "passing" (144:4).[9]

It is best to see 144:1–8 as adducing an argument to move God to deliver: "Lord, you do everything for me [*praise*: 144:1–2]. And that is a wonder: after all I am only a mortal human [*perishability*: 144:3–4]. Therefore, in light of my transience, would you keep doing . . . [*petitions*: 144:5–8; see below]?" Clearly there is persuasive rhetoric being transacted, an attempt to motivate God, as the voice of the commander finally arrives at his petitions in 144:5–8.

The request of this commander in 144:5–8 is that he wants God to rescue him. The verbiage here is reminiscent of descriptions of the Canaanite god Baal, the god of storms.[10] Here, Yahweh, bending the heavens, makes a theophany (144:5a)—"the breaking into time and space of a colossal energy with devastating effect"[11]—causing the mountains to smoke (144:5b), and

---

3. God's lovingkindness forms the basis for all of his actions on behalf of this leader. It is because God is "my lovingkindness," חַסְדִּי, *chasdi* (144:2a), that in that same God "I seek refuge [חָסִית, *chasit*]" (144:2c).

4. It is God who gives one stability. In 31:2d, "house of *steadfastness*" may indicate a fortress. Given that the word מְצוּדָה, *mtsudah*, "steadfastness," when used of God is always employed in connection with military terms such as "rock," "cliff," "refuge," "shield," "haven," "stronghold," etc. (see 18:2 = 2 Sam 22:2; Pss 31:2, 3; 71:3; 91:2), such a martial context may well be the case here, too: God is, thus, the fortress of the commander here.

5. Some have emended עַמִּי, *'ammi* ("my people") to עַמִּים, *'ammim* ("peoples"), but that is not necessary: God is also the one who helps the commander govern his own people in respectful submission to their leader.

6. See 144:1a, 1b, 1c, 2a (×2), 2b (×2), 2c (×2), 2d (×2).

7. That is to say that human actors are not absolved from discharging the responsibilities of their own roles. After all, God is "the one teaching my hands for battle, my fingers for battle" (144:1bc). The hands and fingers of the people of God—or here, of the commander—need to be actively engaged. Of course, these actions of humans are subject to the sovereignty and control of the divine protagonist, but the tension between one's responsibility towards God to act and God's actions on behalf of his people must not be dispelled or dissolved.

8. Goldingay, *Psalms*, 3:685.

9. "A human . . . is like" translates אָדָם . . . דָּמָה, *'adam . . . damah* (144:4a).

10. See on Psalm 29.

11. Allen, *Psalms 101–150*, 291.

hurling bolts of lightning (144:6; the "arrows" of 144:6b likely refer to forked lightning).[12] And an unidentified "they" ("them" [×2] in 144:6, ostensibly the enemies) are "scattered" and "confused." This awesome power of theophany is visible in the fourfold action–effect patterning of the clauses in 144:5–6:

	Action	Effect
144:5aα	"Yahweh,	
144:5aβ	incline Your heavens	and come down;
144:5b	touch the mountains	that they may smoke.
144:6a	[Do] light lightning	and scatter them;
144:6b	send out Your arrows	and confuse them."

As if this were not enough, Yahweh is asked to intervene directly in the crisis of this commander and to "send Your hands from on high" (144:7a) to aid the supplicant.

This description of a martial deity is followed by a refrain picturing in more detail the adversaries of the psalmist (144:7b–8, repeated almost verbatim in 144:11; both sets of verses serve as a sort of refrain in the psalm). These foes are like "great waters" (144:7b), turbulent, chaotic, and overwhelming; and they are foreigners (144:7c; "children of foreignness"). Their mouths emit false words and their hands engage false deeds (144:8).[13] Notice that God's "hands" are requested to act (144:7a); earlier it was the leader's "hands" that God was educating about warfare (144:1b). Therefore, putting these two factoids together, in all likelihood God's "hands" are working through human "hands" . . . to rescue him from the "right hand" of the enemies, which is a "right hand" of evil (144:8b). This spectacular intervention by the *hands* of God against the (right) *hand* of the enemy, by the indirect agency of the *hands* of his people, moves the commander to praise.[14]

Because of all that God is doing on his behalf, this leader promises, "a new song I will sing to You" and "make music to You" (144:9). The intensity of his commitment is clear in 144:9, directed to deity ("God," "to You," "to You"), who alone is worthy of this "new song" (see below).[15]

---

12. By the way, these "arrows" (144:6b) and, later, a "sword" (144:10b) are the only weapons mentioned in this psalm: the first is wielded by God and the second, by the enemies. The people of God who are being trained for battle and war (144:1bc) are apparently being educated in warfare *sans* weapons! (Their artillery and ammunition must be their prayers to this awesome deity who will do all the fighting for them!)

13. "Right hand of falsehood" (144:8b) indicates the fraudulent activities of the enemies. The "scattering [פוץ, *pwts*]" of the evildoers (144:6a) is rendered equivalent, in a pun, to the "freeing [פצה, *ptsh*]" of the supplicant (144:7b; also in 144:10b, 11a).

14. "Right hand" is יָמִין, *yamin*; "hand" is יָד, *yad*.

15. Modified from Auffret, "O bonheurs du peuple," 510. It is possible to see this "new song" as comprising 144:12–15—a trailer, if you will, for a novel aria, one that will be sung once the deliverance from enemies is accomplished (which is not consummated in this psalm). This "new song," then pictures an ideal world, filled with the blessings of God upon the people of God.

> "God,
>   a new song   I will sing
> to You,
>   upon a harp ...   I will make music
> to You."

God is worthy of praise because he is the one who delivers kings, especially the Davidide, his special "servant" and the leader of his people, from the "evil sword" (a metonym for the evildoers wielding that weapon; 144:10). Therefore, this particular leader, too, can beseech God to duplicate his past deliverances of regents, as the parallel structure of 144:10–11 shows (equating "kings" and "David" to "me," the current chieftain):[16]

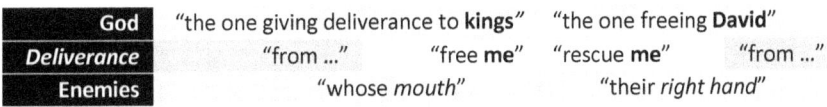

God	"the one giving deliverance to **kings**"		"the one freeing **David**"	
Deliverance	"from ..."	"free **me**"	"rescue **me**"	"from ..."
Enemies	"whose *mouth*"		"their *right hand*"	

And with that petition of confidence (and the refrain), the *Call of the Commander* closes. The psalm is now in the community's court.[17]

Confidence of the Community (144:12–15)

Perhaps it is still the leader speaking, now on behalf of the people of God (there is a predominance of first-person plurals in this section), but the scene has seemingly shifted into the future (or is on the brink thereof).[18] Grammatically 144:12–14 comprises a series of verbless clauses, creating a beatific vision for the future, involving the welfare of the next generation (144:12), as well as agrarian prosperity (144:13–14a), and social stability (144:14bc).[19] Though

---

16. From Auffret, "O bonheurs du peuple," 510.

17. Singer, "Literary Context," 216, notes that in this psalm there are two pairs of participles that are articulated and that also commence clauses: "the one teaching" (144:1b) and "the one subduing" (144:2d); and "the one giving" (144:10a) and "the one freeing" (144:10b). These two pairs, that describe the work of Yahweh for the supplicant, effectively begin and close out this section of the psalm, the *Call of the Commander* (144:1–11).

18. The *Confidence of the Community* section "contrasts the fates of the foreigner enemies ['children of foreignness,' 144:7c, 11a] (at the hand of Yahweh) and the children of the nation of faith" (Singer, "Literary Context," 218). Goldingay, *Psalms*, 3:689, takes 144:12–14 as "an extensive extraposed clause" that anticipates the "thus" of 144:15; i.e., the "thus" points to blessings outlined in 144:12–14. One also observes that there are several correspondences in 144:12–14 with the divine promises of Deut 28:3–8, especially of 28:4 that deals with offspring of humans (as also in Ps 144:12), with the produce of the land (as also in 144:13a), and with animals (as also in 144:13b–14a)—in fact, they appear in the same sequence there as they do in 144:12–14.

19. Hence, my categorizing of this psalm as one of reorientation. Note that 144:14ab poses serious translational problems. Both אַלּוּפֵינוּ, *'alluphenu*, "our cattle," and מְסֻבָּלִים, *msubbalim*, "ones that are laden," are in the masculine plural; the root of the latter, סבל, *sbl*, is never used elsewhere in the OT or in contemporary Semitic languages to signify pregnancy. It is best, therefore, to take "laden" cattle (144:14a)—i.e., laden with goods and produce—as a sign of agricultural prosperity. As well, in 144:14b, פרץ, *prts*, root of פֶּרֶץ, *perets*, "breach," is not used of reproductive failure, but rather of disruption of walls (as in Neh 1:3; 2:13; 4:3, 7; 6:1).

the "child [בֵּן, ben] of a mortal" is temporary and perishing (144:3b), suffering the bane of those "children [בְּנֵי] of foreignness" (144:7c, 11a), yet the "sons [from בֵּן]" of the people of God (and their "daughters"; 144:12ab) enjoy the blessing of their God, Yahweh (144:12–15).

All this is the result of Yahweh's work for and on behalf of his people, the consequence of deity's answering the petitions voiced earlier. And so, while 144:12 began with אֲשֶׁר, 'asher, "then,"[20] 144:15a and 15b each begin with אַשְׁרֵי, "blessing [upon]." In other words, the consequence of God's work for his people, the result of which is depicted in 144:12–14 ("then . . ."), *is* the "blessing [of God] upon the people for whom Yahweh is God" (144:15). Blessed, indeed, are they!

Sermon Map

I. Praise
 Praise for all that God is for his people (144:1–3)
 Perishability of humans (144:3–4)
 Move-to-relevance: Our transience and our great God's works for us
II. Petitions
 Potency of theophany (144:5–6)
 Petition for rescue (144:7–8, 11)
 Praise for deliverance (144:9–10)
 Move-to-relevance: Our distresses and God's past rescues
III. Prosperity
 Prosperity across generations (144:12)
 Prosperity in economy (144:13–14a)
 Prosperity for society (144:14bc)
 Prosperity for the people of God (144:15)
IV. *Praise for Preservation and Prospering of Perishable People!*
 Specifics on praising God, in anticipation of future thriving

---

Thus, in Ps 144:14bc, the unbreached walls, the safety of the populace (not being exiled), and the absence of distressing cries in public squares all betoken social stability and *shalom* (see Makujina, "Interpretation of Ps 144,14," 487).

20. I have taken אֲשֶׁר as indicating result, "then . . ." (as in Gen 13:16; Deut 4:40 [its second use in this verse]; Ruth 2:2; etc.).

PSALM 145:1–21

Psalm of Reorientation

Praise of the God-King by All Flesh

PSALM 145 IS AN incomplete acrostic in the MT lacking the נ *Nun* segment. As is true of the other seven acrostics in the Psalter,[1] here in Psalm 145, "the entire alphabet [or at least 95.45 percent of it], the source of all words, is marshalled in praise of God."[2]

Translation

145:1	[א ALEPH]	I will exalt You, my God, the King,
		and I will bless Your name forever and always.
145:2	[ב BETH]	Every day I will bless You,
		and I will praise Your name forever and always.
145:3	[ג GIMEL]	Great is Yahweh, and much to be praised,
		and His greatness is unsearchable.
145:4	[ד DALETH]	Generation to generation will laud Your works,
		and Your mighty acts they will announce.
145:5	[ה HE]	The splendid glory of Your majesty
		and the matters of Your wonders, I will muse [on],
145:6	[ו WAV]	and [of] the strength of Your awesome [doings], they will say,
		and Your greatness, I will recount.
145:7	[ז ZAYIN]	The remembrance of Your abundant goodness, they will pour out,
		and at Your righteousness, they will shout for joy.
145:8	[ח CHETH]	Gracious and merciful is Yahweh,
		slow to anger and great in lovingkindness.

---

1. Psalms 9; 10; 34; 37; 111; 112; and 119.
2. Berlin, "Rhetoric of Psalm 145," 18. In a biblical book titled תְהִלִּים, *thillim*, Psalm 145 is the only one with the superscription תְהִלָּה, *thillah* (untranslated here).

145:9 [ט TETH]	Good is Yahweh to all,	
	and His mercies are over all His works.	
145:10 [י YODH]	They will give You thanks, Yahweh, all Your works,	
	and Your devout ones—they will bless You.	
145:11 [כ KAPH]	Of the glory of Your Kingdom, they will say,	
	and of Your mighty acts, they will speak,	
145:12 [ל LAMED]	to make known to the children of humanity His mighty acts	
	and the glorious splendor of His Kingdom.	
145:13 [מ MEM]	Your Kingdom is a Kingdom [for] all [time,] forever,	
	and Your dominion for every generation after generation.	
145:14 [ס SAMEKH]	Yahweh [is] the One sustaining all those who are fallen,	
	and the One raising up all those who have been bowed down.	
145:15 [ע AYIN]	The eyes of all, upon You they hope,	
	and You are the One giving them their food in its season;	
145:16 [פ PE]	the One opening Your hand,	
	and the One satiating the desire of every living being.	
145:17 [צ TSADE]	Yahweh [is] righteous in all His ways,	
	and [showing] lovingkindness in all His works.	
145:18 [ק QOPH]	Yahweh [is] near to all those who are crying to Him,	
	to all who cry to Him in truth.	
145:19 [ר RESH]	The desire of those who fear Him He works [out];	
	and their cry for help He hears, and He delivers them.	
145:20 [ש SHIN]	Yahweh [is] the One keeping all those who love Him,	
	but all the wicked He will exterminate.	
145:21 [ת TAW]	The praise of Yahweh my mouth will speak,	
	and all flesh will bless His holy name forever and always.	

Structure

The poem is essentially split into two by means of an interlude (145:10), that is one of a piece with the prelude (145:1–2) and the postlude (145:21).

Each of the two halves comprises a section on God's transcendence and immanence, shown below as *Transcendence 1* and *Transcendence 2* (145:3–6, 11–13), and *Immanence 1* and *Immanence 2* (145:7–9, 14–20):[3]

PRELUDE (145:1–2): Blessing by the Composer

First of two *vocatives* to deity: "My God" (145:1a)
First of two pairs of *second-person verbal suffixes*: 145:1a, 2a
  "praise [הלל, *hll*]" (145:2b)
  four *piel/polel* imperfect verbs: "exalt"; "bless" (×2); "praise"
    "**I will bless** Your *name forever and always*" (145:1b)
    "**I will bless** You" (145:2a)

Transcendence 1 (145:3–6): *God as he is*
  Bounded by "great," "greatness" (145:3) and "greatness" (145:6b)
  "mighty" (145:4b); "splendid" (145:5a); "glory" (145:5a)
  Begins with "generation to generation" (145:4a)

Immanence 1 (145:7–9): *God as he relates to humanity*
  Bounded by "goodness" (145:7a) and "good" (145:9a)
  "merciful," "mercies" (145:8a, 9b)

INTERLUDE (145:10): Blessing by the Congregation

Second of two *vocatives* to deity: "Yahweh" (145:10a)
Second of two pairs of *second-person verbal suffixes*: 145:10a, 10b
  "**Your devout ones—they will bless** You" (145:10b)

Transcendence 2 (145:11–13): *God as he is*
  Bounded by "Kingdom" (145:11a) and "Kingdom" (145:12b, 13a [×2])
  "glory/ious" (145:11a, 12b); "mighty" (145:11b, 12a); "splendor" (145:12b)
  Ends with "generation after generation" (145:13b)

Immanence 2 (145:14–20): *God as he relates to humanity*
  Bounded: participial clauses: "Yahweh is the one ... all" (145:14a, 20a)
  Mercies of God explicated (145:14–20)

POSTLUDE (145:21): Blessing by the Cosmos

"praise [תְּהִלַּת, *thillat*]" (145:21a)
two *piel* imperfect verbs: "speak"; "bless"
  "**all flesh will bless** His holy *name forever and always*" (145:21b)

By tracking the prelude, interlude, and postlude, one can discern the trajectory of the psalm: it moves from praise of God by the psalmist ("*I* will bless" in 145:1b, 2a), to praise of God by God's people ("*Your devout ones . . .* will bless," 145:10b), to praise of God by humankind as a whole ("*all flesh* will bless," 145:21b). This momentum from composer's praise, via congregation's praise, to cosmopolitan praise is the motivating dynamo of the entire psalm.

An unusually high number of instances of כֹּל, *kol* ("all"/"every") lends credence to this notion: "Its virtual ubiquity highlights the unending universal chorus of praise to a God whose

---

3. Modified from Kimelman, "Psalm 145," 38–53; deClaissé-Walford, "Psalm 145," 62–63; Goldingay, *Psalms*, 3:696; Jung, "Davidic Persona," 207; and Singer, "Literary Context," 222, 228–31.

sovereignty and solicitude are not only eternal but everywhere breaking through both temporal and spatial frontiers."[4] God: is righteous in "all" his ways and shows lovingkindness to "all" his works (145:17); is near to "all" who call upon him—to "all" who cry to him (145:18); is the keeper of "all" who love him" and the exterminator of "all" the wicked (145:20); is good to "all" and his mercies are over "all" his works" (145:9); is the sustainer of "all" the fallen and "all" the bowed down (145:14), and satiates the needs of "every" living being (145:16b); is the one upon whom "all" hope (145:15a), and who will be blessed "every" day (145:2a) and thanked by "all" his works (145:10a), and whose kingdom will be for "all" time, and his dominion for "every" generation (145:13).[5] No wonder "all" flesh will bless this amazing God (145:21b). And thus Psalm 145 opens the portal to the final series of songs in the Psalter that praise God (Psalms 146–150).

Theological Focus

The great and good God—whose glorious kingdom is forever, and whose loving-kindness is manifest in his serving, satiating, and succoring those faithful to him—is worthy of being praised forever by individuals, by multiple generations of God's people who make him known to all humankind, and thus by every living being.

Commentary

Prelude (145:1–2)

In the very first verse of the prelude the theme of God's sovereignty is declared: "my God, the King." Other psalms label God (or his Messianic agent) as King,[6] but only here and in 98:6 is God designated *the* King." He, and he alone, is King and this motif of Yahweh's exclusive dominion kicks off the psalm. It is with the dynamic of this powerful royal acclamation that the vector of the psalm proceeds from the blessing of this great deity by an individual, to blessing by God's people, and ultimately to blessing by all humans—and that "forever and always" (145:1b, 2b, 21b).

With 145:1b–2, a clever double chiasm is created:

CHIASM 1	145:1bα	"I will bless Your name		
	145:1bβ	forever and always.		
	145:2aα	Every day	145:2aα	CHIASM 2
	145:2aβ	I will bless You,	145:2aβ	
		and I will praise Your name	145:2bα	
		forever and always."	145:2bβ	

---

4. Kimelman, "Psalm 145," 51.

5. Singer, "Literary Context," 222n56, notes that only Psalm 119 has more occurrences of כֹּל (twenty-six times in 176 verses), but the frequency of the word is far higher in Psalm 145 (fifteen times in twenty-one verses). This overwhelming comprehensiveness is also reflected in the many temporal terms: "forever and always" (145:1b, 2b, 21b), "forever" (145:13a), and "generation to/after generation" (145:4a, 13b).

6. Pss 2:6; 5:2; 10:16; 24:7–10; 29:10; 44:4; 47:2, 6–7; 48:2; 68:24; 74:12; 84:3; 95:3; 99:4; 149:2.

And, appropriately enough, their twin cores declare the expression of performance of God's praise ("I will bless" and "I will praise") and the temporal extent thereof ("forever and always" and "every day"): this divine sovereign deserves never-ending praise! Or: *God, the sovereign deity, is worthy of being praised forever by individuals!*[7]

Transcendence 1 (145:3–6)

The theme of transcendence is set by 145:3 that describes the worthiness of this great God to be praised, and by 145:4–6 that describes the actual performance of praise ("[they] will laud," "they will announce," "I will muse [on]," "they will say," and "I will recount." Though the psalm had commenced with the praise of an individual (145:1–2), here it becomes obvious that a single voice is insufficiently worthy of a great God: a chorus of many that resounds from "generation to generation" is required to effect adequate praise (145:4a).[8] Besides, "the sheer magnificence and glory of God elicit a thesaurus of adulation that seeks to be exhaustive":[9] not only is God "exalted," "blessed," "praised . . . forever," and "much to be praised" (145:1–3a), he and his works are to be "lauded," "announced" (145:4), "mused" upon (145:5), "said" of, and "recounted" (145:6).

What exactly is praised also undergoes an augmentation by the piling on of synonyms, all bookended by the quality of deity, his being "great" and his "greatness" (145:3a, 3b, 6b):

145:3	**"Great is Yahweh"; "His greatness"**
145:4a	"Your works"
145:4b	"Your mighty acts"
145:5a	"the splendid glory of Your majesty"
145:5b	"the matters of Your wonders"
145:6a	"the strength of Your awesome [doings]"
145:6b	**"Your greatness"**

"Such a compounding of synonyms, found only here in the whole Psalter, indicates a structure of intensification, not simply a juggling of semantic equivalents. Through such a structure, the psalmist would have us believe that the loftiest encomium proves to be an understatement."[10] Indeed: *God, the sovereign deity, is so splendidly great, he is not only worthy of being praised forever by individuals, but also by multiple generations!*[11]

---

7. At the end of each section of this psalm, I will attempt to create a synthetic reduction of all the authorial *doings* up to that point, in a cumulative fashion (see italicized sentences).

8. Another chiasm pops up in 145:4: "Generation to generation will laud / Your works, // and Your mighty acts / they will announce."

9. Kimelman, "Psalm 145," 43.

10. Kimelman, "Psalm 145," 43.

11. These reductions, henceforth, denote what has already been said in previous sections by a "not only . . ."; what is being added in the current section is designated by "but also . . ."

Immanence 1 (145:7–9)

Bounded by "goodness" and "good" (145:7a, 9a), *Immanence 1* acclaims the goodness of the God who was announced earlier as being great. This goodness, as 145:9b notes briefly, comprises divine mercies directed to all his creation, and thus what is celebrated here is the immanence of God. This great, transcendent God (pictured in *Transcendence 1*) is a good and immanent God! Unlike the previous section (145:3–6) that added layer upon layer of synonyms for intensification, this section, particularly in 145:8, is fueled by liturgical echoes of earlier texts, especially Exod 34:6.[12]

By having *Transcendence 1* (Ps 145:3–6) and *Immanence 1* (145:7–9) in tandem, these two sections "converge to make the point that praise is generated by appreciating the link between divine greatness and goodness."[13] All that to say, *God, the sovereign deity, is not only splendidly great and worthy of being praised forever by individuals and in multiple generations, but he is also abundantly good to all his creation!*

Interlude (145:10)

Chiastically structured,[14] 145:10 connects both with what preceded ("all His works" in 145:9b is reflected in "all Your works" in 145:10a)[15] and with what the prelude had begun: "*I will bless Your name*" in 145:1b, and "*I will bless You*" in 145:2a. But the latter with an individual focus have now transformed into "*Your devout ones—they will bless You*" in 145:10b, with a communal focus. Thus it rightly serves as the hinge between the two halves of the composition. Thus, *God, the sovereign deity, splendidly great and abundantly good to his creation, is not only worthy of being praised forever by individuals and in multiple generations, but also by all of God's people!*

Transcendence 2 (145:11–13)

The following two sections, *Transcendence 2* (145:11–13) and *Immanence 2* (145:14–20), especially the latter, make explicit what was implicit in their corresponding elements in the first half of the psalm.

Here, 145:11–13 resounds with the word "Kingdom" (145:11a, 12b, 13a [×2]; also note "dominion," in 145:13b), giving further meaning to, and amplifying, the theme of, God's greatness from *Transcendence 1* (145:3–6). This is in addition to the terms of majesty and power shared between those two sections, as well as the temporal phrase "generation to/after generation" found in both (145:4a, 13b; and see the psalm's structure above).

---

12. Kimelman, "Psalm 145," 43. One might notice that here we have "great" in lovingkindness (145:8b), rather than an "abounding [רב, *rav*]" of that attribute as in Exod 34:6. That is perhaps because "abundant [רב]" had already been employed in Ps 145:7a; but there is also the switch from "merciful and gracious" in Exod 34:6 to "gracious and merciful" in Ps 145:8a (as also in 111:4; 112:4), no doubt called for by the constraint of the acrostic. In any case, these tweaks do catch the reader's attention.

13. Kimelman, "Psalm 145," 41.

14. "They will give You thanks, Yahweh, / all Your works, // and Your devout ones /—they will bless You."

15. And that is appropriate: God's mercies are over "all His works" (145:9b), so "all Your works" give him thanks (145:10a).

Kingship is the overriding (and unique) motif in this section that is praised by his people (the third-person plural verbs, "they will say" and "they will speak" in 145:11 have as their subjects "Your devout ones" from 145:10b). But the receivers of this proclamation are also noted: "the children of humanity," i.e., all humankind (145:12a): this is an announcement being made to one and all.

There is also the intriguing "reverse acrostic" of 145:11–13: the first letters of 145:13, 12, 11 (i.e., read backwards), are מ, ל, and ך, respectively (*m, l,* and *k*)—spelling מלך, *mlk*, "king," the root of "Kingdom [מַלְכוּת, *malkut*]" (145:11a). In fact, if one were to add to this trio the first letter of 145:10, י, *y*, the word spelled by the four initials (read again in reverse) is מלכי, *mlky*, "my king"—taking us right back to how the psalm began: "my God, the King" (145:1a).[16] Further hammering home the theme of divine regency, "Kingdom [מַלְכוּת]" occurs four times in 145:11–13, with a cascade of three instances in back-to-back staccato (in the Hebrew of 145:12b–13a):

הֲדַר מַלְכוּתוֹ׃ מַלְכוּתְךָ מַלְכוּת כָּל־עֹלָמִים ... (... *hadar malkuto. malkutka malkut kal-'olamim*)
... splendor of His Kingdom. Your Kingdom is a Kingdom [for] all [time,] forever.

As if that were not enough, the psalm seeks to etch the message of deity's rulership indelibly on readers' minds with a chiasm in 145:11–12:

145:11a	"Of the *glory* of **Your Kingdom**, they will say,
145:11b	and of *Your mighty acts,* they will speak,
145:12a	to make known ... *His mighty acts*
145:12b	and the *glorious* splendor of **His Kingdom**."

It should also be noted that 145:11 is the middle verse of this twenty-one-verse psalm, its content appropriate for the centerpiece that it is: the declaration of the glory of the divine kingdom and of divine acts of might. In other words, *God, the sovereign deity—worthy of being praised forever by individuals, by multiple generations, and by all of God's people who make him known to all humankind—is not only splendidly great and abundantly good to all his creation, but he is also the divine ruler whose glorious kingdom is forever!*

Immanence 2 (145:14–20)[17]

As with *Transcendence 2* that made more explicit the theme of its counterpart in the first half of the psalm (God's greatness, expanded to his everlasting reign), so also *Immanence 2*

---

16. Watson, "Reversed Rootplay," 101–2. The first words of those four verses are (in reverse order): מַלְכוּתְךָ, *malkutka,* "Your kingdom" (145:13a); לְהוֹדִיעַ, *lhodia',* "to make known" (145:12a); כְּבוֹד, *kvod,* "of the glory" (145:11a); and יוֹדוּךָ, *yoduka,* "they will give You thanks" (145:10a).

17. The interpolation of a נ *Nun* segment verse between 145:13 and 145:14 is found in 11QPs[a], Kennicott MS 142, and the LXX (but not in Aquila, Symmachus, or Theodotion), Syriac and Ethiopic versions, and the Vulgate. The Qumran version of this added verse is quite similar to 145:17, with their second colons being exactly the same. This would make it a member of the section 145:14–20 but would thereby destroy the framing functions of the participial phrases in 145:14a, 20a ("the one sustaining" and "the one

(145:14-20) proceeds to describe in much more detail and at greater length the goodness and mercies of God outlined in *Immanence 1* (145:7-9). That this section takes seven verses orients the reader to the significance of divine immanence and spells out several facets of this relationship of God to mankind.

The section is bounded by "Yahweh" and descriptions of his needy devout ("all ...") in *qal* participles (145:14, 20a). The assonance is quite striking between the description of Yahweh in 145:14aα (סוֹמֵךְ, *somek*, "the one sustaining") and that in 145:20a (שׁוֹמֵר, *shomer*, "the one keeping"):[18]

	Yahweh (participles)	Devout (masculine plural participles)
145:14	"the one sustaining"	*all* those who have fallen"
	"the one raising up"	*all* those who have been bowed down"
145:20a	"the one keeping"	*all* those who love Him"

In this last major section of the psalm, the God-King's relationship to humankind is detailed. Related to the immanence of deity, God's lovingkindness was declared to be great in 145:8b (part of *Immanence 1*). Here, though, details are fleshed out, and "the shift from divine reign [*Transcendence 2*] to divine regard [*Immanence 2*] is as dramatic as it is intentional."[19] It is a case of regal power being mustered and deployed for the benefit of those who are needy—to sustain the falling, feed the hungry, succor the suffering, satisfy the reverent, and preserve the faithful (145:14-20a). The generosity of Yahweh is also amply evident in the liberality of his provision. "Yhwh gives with an open hand [145:16a] . . . , like a person feeding animals who allows them to take as much as they like. Yhwh does not dispense in small, measured amounts."[20]

The attention of this divine regent sharpens its focus from common beneficence to all to specific grace for the devout: note the progression from "every living being" (145:16b), to "all who are crying to Him" (145:18a), to "all who cry to Him in truth" (145:18b), to "those who fear Him" (145:19a), and finally to "all who love Him" (145:20a). The kingly lovingkindness of

---

keeping"). Kimelman, "Psalm 145," 50, suspects that "the absence of the *nun* line is part of the message; namely, as all human praise of God is theologically inadequate, so the psalm is alphabetically imperfect." That poetic perfection was never sought as the overarching goal is evident in the fact that of the twenty-one verses in the psalm, nineteen commence their respective second lines with ו, "and/but"; two verses do not: 145:8b, 18b. The reason for this "discrepancy" in those two verses is because of the demands of content that override artistic perfection and uniformity: "Consistency is not allowed to straitjacket poetic felicity" (Kimelman, "Psalm 145," 51). Indeed, the omission of the נ *Nun* segment may also have been in deference to content, particularly to maintain 145:11, with its magnificent affirmations, as the middle verse in a composition *sans* the נ *Nun* segment verse. In any case, the paucity of ancient manuscript witnesses makes the more difficult MT reading preferable.

18. "Yahweh" occurs four times in 145:14-20: the first and last are in verbal (participial) clauses as noted (145:14a, 20a). The two middle ones are in verbless adjectival clauses: "Yahweh [is] righteous [צַדִּיק יְהוָה, *tsaddiq yhwh*]" and "Yahweh [is] near [קָרוֹב יְהוָה, *qarov yhwh*]" (145:17a, 18a) (see Kimelman, "Psalm 145," 46n44). Other participles describing Yahweh occur in 145:15b, 16a; as well one describing the devout in 145:18a.

19. Kimelman, "Psalm 145," 46.

20. Goldingay, *Psalms*, 3:703.

this deity towards his suffering faithful is also manifest in the punishment of the wicked who oppress his people (145:20b).[21] That, too, is a manifestation of divine immanence!

In sum, "this recital of God's benefactions confirms the faith of hearers in his power and his commitment to protect those who are loyal to him."[22] Thus far, then, we see that *God, the sovereign deity—worthy of being praised forever by individuals, by multiple generations, and by all of God's people who make him known to all humankind—is not only splendidly great, abundantly good to all his creation, and the divine ruler whose glorious kingdom is forever, but he is also the one whose righteous lovingkindness is exhibited in all his doings, as he serves, satiates, and succors those faithful to him, and punishes those who are not!*

Postlude (145:21)

In 145:19–20, there are six words that have a ש, *sh*, and a ם, *m*, in close proximity, literally priming the reader and hearer for God's holy "name [שֵׁם, *shem*]" to sound in 145:21:

145:19b	שַׁוְעָתָם יִשְׁמַע וְיוֹשִׁיעֵם (*shaw'atam yishma' wyoshi'em*)	"their cry for help He hears, and He delivers them"
145:20a	שׁוֹמֵר (*shomer*)	"the one keeping"
145:20b	הָרְשָׁעִים יַשְׁמִיד (*harsha'im yashmid*)	"the wicked He will exterminate"
145:21b	שֵׁם (*shem*)	"name"

Yes, indeed, "all flesh"—every living being *will* bless the name of God forever and always (145:21).[23] And so the psalm concludes in its *Postlude* as it began in its *Prelude*, with similar *piel* imperfect verbs, direct objects, and an indicator of time:

	Subject	Piel *imperfect*	Direct object	Time
145:1b	"I	will bless	Your name	forever and always"
145:21b	"all flesh	will bless	His holy name	forever and always"

But there is a major difference between the beginning and the end: the expansion of the subject doing the blessing from the singularity of the "I" (145:1) to the plurality of "all flesh,"

---

21. This verse, 145:20, is also chiastic: "Yahweh is the One keeping / all who love Him, // but all the wicked / He will exterminate."
22. Kimelman, "Psalm 145," 46.
23. This verse, 145:21, too, is chiastic: "The praise of Yahweh / my mouth will speak, // and all flesh will bless / His holy name forever and always."

all living beings (145:21)—via the blessing engaged in by God's community of the "devout" (145:10b)—from composer to congregation to the cosmos, as it were.[24]

To sum up: *This sovereign God—splendidly great, abundantly good to all his creation, the divine ruler whose glorious kingdom is forever, and the one whose righteous lovingkindness, exhibited in all he does, serving, satiating, and succoring those faithful to him, and punishing those who are not—is worthy of being praised forever not only by individuals, multiple generations, and by all of God's people who make him known to all humankind, but also by every living being!*[25]

Each section, thus, has progressively contributed more information to the thrust of the psalm, accumulating reasons to sing the praises of God and recommending who those singers of praises ought to be, impelling them to change their lives according to the call of Psalm 145, for the glory of "my God, the King."

Sermon Map

I. God is . . .
  Great (145:1, 3, 5–6, 11–13)
  Good (145:7–9, 14–20)
  Move-to-relevance: The greatness and goodness of God in our lives

II. . . . worthy of praise by . . .
  Individuals (145:1–2)
  Generations (145:4)
  Devout (145:10)
  Everyone (145:21)
  Move-to-relevance: The neglect of our praise of God

III. *Glorify the Great and Good God!*
  Specifics on praising God for his greatness and goodness

---

24. Or: From a solo performer, to a chamber ensemble, to a symphony orchestra!

25. This long (and unwieldy) sentence is only for demonstration of the "narrative" or "storying" of the psalm. The Theological Focus is a condensed version of this final reduction of pericopal theology. Neither specimen of reduction has much utility for the sermon-*listener* and does not necessarily need to be explicitly stated within a sermon. However, the product of reduction, i.e., the Theological Focus, does have value for the sermon-*preparer*, for maintaining focus, for creating maps, and for deriving application. See Kuruvilla, *Manual for Preaching*, 57–112, 263–68.

PSALM 146:1–10

Psalm of Reorientation

Trusting in God, the Patron and Ruler

THE LAST FIVE PSALMS of the Psalter are linked by "Praise Yah" that begins and ends each of them (146:1a, 10c; 147:1a, 20c; 148:1a, 14d; 149:1a, 9c; 150:1a, 6b). It is as if the promise of Psalm 145—particularly in its closing, 145:21: "the praise of Yahweh my mouth will speak"—to utter praises to/of Yahweh, and the urging of "all flesh" to "bless his name forever," is being literally carried out in Psalms 146–150. Yet, in this first member of the quintet, Yahweh is never addressed directly. In light of the self-address ("my soul") and individualistic tone of 146:1–2 (as opposed to the communal stance of 146:10: "your God, Zion"), it is likely that the composer, the "I" of the psalm, is a leader/king in the community.

Translation

146:1	Praise Yah.
	Praise Yahweh, my soul.
146:2	I will praise Yahweh for [all] my life;
	I will make music to my God for always.
146:3	Do not trust in nobles, in the son of a human,
	with whom there is no deliverance:
146:4	his spirit goes out, he returns to the ground;
	in that day his thoughts perish.
146:5	Blessing [upon] the one for whom the God of Jacob is his help,
	whose hope is in Yahweh, his God,
146:6	One who made heaven and earth,
	the sea and all that which is in them;
	the One keeping truth unto forever;
146:7	One doing justice for the oppressed;
	One giving food to the hungry.
	Yahweh is [the] One setting free those who are prisoners;

146:8	Yahweh is One opening [the eyes of] the blind;
	Yahweh is One raising up ones who are bowed down.
	Yahweh is One loving the righteous;
146:9	Yahweh is One keeping the sojourners.
	The fatherless and the widow He helps,
	but the path of the wicked He subverts.
146:10	Yahweh will reign unto forever,
	your God, Zion, from generation to generation.
	Praise Yah.

Structure

The psalm begins and ends with *Expressions of Praise* (146:1–2, 10), sandwiching *Exhortations* regarding whom God's people must *not* trust (146:3–4) and whom they should (146:5–9):

Expression of Praise: Psalmist (146:1–2)
"Praise Yah!" (146:1a)
"my soul" (psalmist); "to my God"; "praise" (146:1a, 1b, 2a)
Preposition + time: "for [בְּ, b] [all] my life"
"for [בְּ] always"

Exhortation *not* to Trust Humanity (146:3–4)
Preposition + time: "in [בְּ] that day" (146:4b)
Perishing of wicked humanity (146:4)

Exhortation to Trust Deity (146:5–9)
Preposition + time: "unto [לְ, l] forever" (146:6c)
Punishment of wicked humanity (146:9b)

Expression of Praise: People (146:10)
"Praise Yah!" (146:10c)
"Zion" (people); "your God"; "praise" (146:10c)
Preposition + time: "unto [לְ] forever"
"from [לְ] generation to generation"

The time indicators (preposition + time) in each section demonstrate the trajectory of the thrust: praise is forever (146:2), God protects forever (146:6), and God reigns forever (146:10); on the other hand, the wicked perish in a moment, "in that day" of judgment (146:4b).

Theological Focus

The patronage of his people by God the Creator, their helper and protector—leading them to trust in him rather than in temporal powers and entities—render them blessed and motivate them to praise God forever.

Commentary

Expression of Praise: Psalmist (146:1–2)

This expression of praise is a rhetorical urging by the psalmist/leader to his own self ("my soul") to engage in praise (146:1b), as well as an assertion of intent to praise and make music to Yahweh always (146:2).

Exhortation not to Trust Humanity (146:3–4)

The larger exhortation section (146:3–9) commences with a negative (146:3–4): whom God's people should not trust (and therefore not praise, ostensibly). These untrustworthy folks are the "nobles," equated to "the son of a human"—a collective singular, indicating the powerful ones, with influence, say-so, and know-how (146:3a). These are not necessarily leaders outside the community of Israel; the section simply makes the point that "it is unwise to rely on imperial authorities, the leaders of other local peoples, or leaders within Israel or Judah."[1] The reason is clear, triply stated, in an asyndetic construction: "his spirit goes out, he returns to the ground; in that day his thoughts perish" (146:4). The fate is fitting: בֶן־אָדָם, ben-'adam, "the son of a human," returns to אֲדָמָה, 'adamah, "the ground" (146:3a, 4a). Clearly mortal humans can never be everlasting champions in whom one may place one's trust. All their proposals and programs and productions are in vain—indeed, even their "thoughts perish." How can one rely upon such transient, ephemeral entities? Hill's words are wise:

> In every country there are men in power, there are politicians, and what the psalmist said about princes in his day and country can surely be applied to politicians in ours. Don't trust them an inch, he says; don't rely on them for any sort of political, social, national or individual salvation. Not because they are more treacherous or fickle than other men, but simply because they are just like other men—they will die, and their plans and policies and panaceas with them. It is not only the politicians you must be wary of; it is anything on two legs whenever it claims and exercises power.[2]

---

1. Goldingay, *Psalms*, 3:709.
2. If I were cynical, I would add "and promises beneficences, support, security, and prosperity, in exchange for your votes" (Hill, *Prayer, Praise and Politics*, 70–71) (Goldingay, *Psalms*, 3:713, using part of this quotation, pointed me to Hill's work).

Exhortation to Trust Deity (146:5–9)

Instead, there is only one who is worthy of trust: God the patron (146:5). Unlike the vanishing breath that humanity is (146:4), this God is a helper and truth-keeper "forever" (146:6c), because he reigns "forever," and "from generation to generation" (146:10ab). And so, appropriately enough, this section on trusting deity takes up the largest chunk of the psalm (146:5–9): eight of the fifteen references to "Yah/Yahweh" and "God" in the psalm are found in these five verses. God is the champion of his people, their help, their hope (146:5). In fact, the chiastic structure of this verse has deity safely enclosing the "help" and "hope" of his people:

> "Blessing [upon] the one for whom
> the God of Jacob
> is his help,
> whose hope is in
> Yahweh, his God."

Upon such a one, whose help and hope is in God, comes "blessing." After all, one is not to trust potentates and powers or regents and rajahs, but the Creator of the universe and of all that is in the heavens and the earth (he is the producer, if you will; 146:6ab): God.[3]

After the assertion of this creative activity encompassing the cosmos, there is a leap towards earth, its inhabitants and their lives: "the oppressed," "the hungry," and "prisoners" (146:7); "the blind," "the ones . . . bowed down," and "the righteous" (146:8); "the sojourners," "the fatherless," and "the widow" (146:9). And God relieves them all of all their woes![4] Thus this deity is also his people's protector, described in a series of participles (146:6c–9a),[5] as well as his enemies' punisher (146:9b). As champion of his devout and faithful, this protector's work also includes retribution for those who trouble his people.

In sum, this God the patron, because he is God the producer, becomes God the protector (and God the punisher) rendering his people, those who trust him, blessed!

Expression of Praise: People (146:10)

The introduction of "Zion," the congregation of God's people, completes the move from praise by the individual (146:1) to praise by the community (146:10). Earthly nobles and other petty officials are temporary (146:3), but the patron God, producer, protector, and punisher, rules "forever," "from generation to generation" (146:10).[6] And thus, the one who "reigns forever," "from generation to generation," is worthy of the praise of his people!

3. Later, we find that this deity is also King (146:10ab).

4. "Politicians do none of these things, either because they cannot, or because they do not make it their priority. But how does God do these same things? Paradoxically, it is usually through people who are willing to be involved in politics, or leadership, but who do it as God's servants and agents" (Goldingay, *Psalms*, 3:713–14). True, but ultimately it is through the sovereignty of God (and the agents he providentially deigns to use for his purposes) that he accomplishes the protective care of his people.

5. An articular participle, "*the* one keeping truth," commences 146:6c, demarking a new subsection here. Nonetheless, there are nine participles, all *qal*, that refer to God: 146:6a, 6c (the only articulated one in the series), 7a, 7b, 7c, 8a, 8b, 8c, 9a.

6. The change in structure of 146:10 renders it a unique section, *Expression of Praise: People*. In 146:10a,

PSALM 146:1–10

Sermon Map

I. Humanity: Untrustworthy

    The transience of human rulers (146:3–4)

    Move-to-relevance: Untrustworthy leaders of our times

II. Deity: Trustworthy

    God the Patron (146:5)

    God the Producer (146:6ab)

    God the Protector (146:6c–9)

    Move-to-relevance: God's trustworthiness evidenced in our lives

III. *Acclaim the Almighty Always!*

    Praise the patron, producer, and protector, reigning forever (146:1–2, 10)

---

the verb, "He-will-reign," begins the line in Hebrew; in the preceding lines, in 146:9b, 9c, the verbs, "He-helps" and "He-subverts," are at the end of their clauses. Besides, the *inclusio* that 146:10 makes with 146:1 signals that this final verse is distinct from the ones immediately before it.

PSALM 147:1–20

Psalm of Reorientation

Pleasing God by Obedience

PRAISE CONTINUES IN PSALM 147, and it is clear from a cursory scan of the psalm that God is at the center of it all—primarily his actions: twelve of the twenty verses begin with a masculine singular participle referring to Yahweh (147:2, 3, 4, 6, 8, 9, 11, 14, 15, 16, 17, 19),[1] all predicates of nominal clauses that have deity as subject. And, commencing the sentence, the assertions of these verbal forms are being emphasized. Thus it is God's actions that achieve prominence in this composition.[2]

Translation

147:1 Praise Yah,
    for it is good to make music to our God;
    for it is pleasant, praise is fitting.
147:2 The One building Jerusalem is Yahweh,
    the ones who are cast out of Israel, He gathers;

---

1. I have rendered these Hebrew participles somewhat artificially as English gerunds ("the One [. . .]ing . . .") to make them discernible in translation (note that in the Hebrew of 147:11 also, the participle commences the verse, though I have placed the subject first in the translation).

2. Brodersen, *End of the Psalter*, 174. A repetition of vocabulary in adjacent lines or verses, hook-words, so to speak, link the verses of the poem together: "number[ing]" (147:4a, 5b); "take pleasure" (147:10b, 11a); "casting [שלך, *shlk*]" and "sending [forth] [שלח, *shlch*]" (147:17a, 18a); "ice[-coldness]" (147:17a, 17b); "His word(s)" (147:18a, 19a); "His judgments" (147:19b, 20b). Besides, there are assonant words in close proximity: בְּרִיחֵי, *briche* ("bars," 147:13a), בֵּרַךְ, *berak* ("He has blessed," 147:13bα), and בְּקִרְבֵּךְ, *bqirbek* ("in your midst," 147:13bβ); and כְּפוֹר כָּאֵפֶר, *kphor ka'epher* ("frost, like ashes," 147:16b). Allen (*Psalms 101–150*, 308) also notes the assonance of a number of words in 147:12–18, particularly with the juxtaposition of שׁ and ל (*sh* and *l*; shaded): there is, of course, יְרוּשָׁלָם, *yrushalaim* ("Jerusalem," 147:12a) and the related שָׁלוֹם, *shalom* ("peace," 147:14a). But one also sees (or is it "hears"?) other terms that bear the same sequence of letters: הַשֹּׁלֵחַ, *hashsholeach* ("the one sending [forth]," 147:15a), שֶׁלֶג, *sheleg* ("snow," 147:16a), מַשְׁלִיךְ, *mashlik* ("the one casting [forth]," 147:17a), and יִשְׁלַח, *yishlach* ("he sends [forth]," 147:18a). Perhaps all of these hint at deity's capital city, the base of operations for God's actions.

147:3	the One healing the brokenhearted,
	and the One binding their wounds;
147:4	the One counting the number of the stars:
	all of them [by] names He calls.
147:5	Great is our Lord and abundant in power;
	[as] to His understanding, there is no number[ing of it].
147:6	The One helping up the afflicted is Yahweh;
	the One bringing low the wicked unto the ground.
147:7	Sing to Yahweh with thanksgiving;
	make music to our God on the lyre;
147:8	the One covering the heavens with clouds,
	the One establishing for the earth rain,
	the One causing to grow on the mountains—grass;
147:9	the One giving to the animal its food,
	to the young of the ravens which cry.
147:10	Not in the might of the horse does He delight;
	not in the legs of a man does He take pleasure.
147:11	Yahweh is the One taking pleasure in those who fear Him,
	the ones hoping for His lovingkindness.
147:12	Laud Yahweh, Jerusalem;
	praise your God, Zion.
147:13	For He has strengthened the bars of your gates;
	He has blessed your children in your midst;
147:14	the One setting [within] your borders peace;
	with the best of the wheat He satiates you;
147:15	the One sending [forth] His utterance [to the] earth—
	very quickly His word runs;
147:16	the One giving snow like wool,
	frost, like ashes, He scatters;
147:17	the One casting [forth] His ice like fragments—
	before the face of His ice-coldness who can stand?
147:18	He sends [forth] His word and makes them melt;
	He makes His wind to blow, and the waters flow—
147:19	the One announcing His words to Jacob,
	His statutes and His judgments to Israel.
147:20	He has not done thus with any nation;
	and His judgments, they have not known them.
	Praise Yah.

Structure

Psalm 147 is organized in three pairs of *Exhortation-Explanation* sequences (147:1 and 147:2–6; 147:7 and 147:8–11; 147:12 and 147:13–20):[3]

Exhortation 1 (147:1)
"praise" (×2) and "make music"; "Yah ... our God"

Explanation 1 (147:2–6)
God's Care for the City (147:2–3: constructing)
God's Control over the Cosmos (147:4–5: creating)
God's Cherishing of the Community (147:6: choice +/–)

"Jerusalem" and "Israel" (147:2)
"building" (from בנה, *bnh*; 147:2a)
"ground [אֶרֶץ, *'erets*]" (147:6b)

Exhortation 2 (147:7)
"sing" and "make music"; "Yahweh ... our God"

Explanation 2 (147:8–11)
God's Control over the Cosmos (147:8–9: catering)
God's Cherishing of the Community (147:10–11: choice +/–)

"the young" (from בֵּן, *ben*; 147:9b)
"earth [אֶרֶץ]" (147:8b)

Exhortation 3 (147:12)
"laud" and "praise"; "Yahweh ... your God"

Explanation 3 (147:13–20)
God's Care for the City (147:13–14: championing)
God's Control over the Cosmos (147:15–18: commanding)
God's Cherishing of the Community (147:19–20: choice +/–)

"Jacob" and "Israel" (147:19)
"children" (from בֵּן, 147:13b)
"earth [אֶרֶץ]" (147:15a)

The *Exhortations* are quite uniform; the *Explanations*—God's relationship with city (which is missing in *Explanation 2*), cosmos, and community—undergo some change as they move from the first section of the psalm to the third. In *Explanation 1*, there is the formation of the city in parallel with the creation of the cosmos (147:2–3, 4–5);[4] God's cherishing of the community is depicted in his raising them high and bringing the wicked to their downfall (147:6: facets of divine choice, both positive and negative). In *Explanation 2*, God's control over the

---

3. From Goldingay, *Psalms*, 3:717; Allen, *Psalms 101–150*, 307–8; Ross, *Psalms*, 3:932; Girard, *Les Psaumes Redécouverts*, 518–19; and Auffret, *Hymnes d'Égypte*, 129.

4. As Goldingay (*Psalms*, 3:718) noted, a city is more than the sum total of its citizens, most certainly more than the faithful believers inhabiting it. Thus God's care for the city is his *general* grace to all. This is probably why there is no element describing God's care for the city in *Explanation 2* that focuses at its end (148:11) on those who fear him (those who experience his *special* grace)—the ones pleasing God.

cosmos is manifested in his catering food for living beings (147:8–9), and his favor upon his people—"those who fear him"—is explicitly noted (147:10–11: a choice between what does and does not please God). In the last section of Psalm 147, *Explanation 3* returns to deity's care for the city in its protection and provision (147:13–14); God controls the cosmos by his commanding "word" (147:15–18), and the patronage of his community is depicted in his giving his "word" only to them and not to others (147:19–20, another facet of divine choice, also both positive and negative).

If we attend to the *Explanation* sections, a "narratival" flow of the psalm may be discerned. *Explanation 1*: God, the one who cares for the city, controlling the cosmos, and cherishing his community by aiding the needy (and putting down the wicked) is worthy of praise: *Let's* praise *God! Explanation 2*: God, the controller of the cosmos who provides for all living beings, cherishes those who fear him (there is nothing else in the cosmos that gives him that kind of pleasure): *Let's praise and* please *God! Explanation 3*: God continues to care for the city, championing it with protection and provision, but now the control of the cosmos and the cherishing of his community are related to God's "word" and "statutes" and "judgments"—obedience and alignment to which are what it means to fear God: *Let's praise and please God by* performing *God's word!*

Theological Focus

In response to God's concerned care for his city (his general grace), to his comprehensive control over the cosmos, and especially, to his championed cherishing of his community (his specific grace), not only do God's people praise their deity, they also seek to please God by obediently aligning themselves to the call of his word.

Commentary

Exhortation 1 and Explanation 1 (147:1–6)

Praising Yahweh is "good," "pleasant," and "fitting" (147:1). It is the fittingness of praise that is the focus of the three *Explanation* sections that follow—why praise is fitting and how the lives of those praising God contribute to make that praise fitting.

The care of deity for his city—its building (147:2a)—is further explicated in 147:2b: God's city is made up of outcasts (likely exiles, now returning), the brokenhearted, and the wounded! Thus is the re-creation of God's people begun.[5] This city construction is being done by the cosmos controller (147:4–5), so there need be no doubt about God's capability to undertake the former task.

---

5. This might make the psalm a post-exilic composition.

Note the chiasm of 147:4, expressing how God manages all the astronomical elements (at the center, below), surrounded by his enumeration and classification of them:

> "the one counting
>   the number
>   of the stars:
>   all of them
>   [by] names
>   He calls."

If he can count the heavenly bodies (countless from a human perspective), and even address them individually by name, then surely the reconstitution of an earthly city will be no problem for God. The contrast is between deity's counting the "number" of the stars (147:4a) and the impossibility of humans "numbering" (or measuring) God's understanding (147:5b). God's transcendent and awesome power and understanding is working on behalf of his people, especially the downtrodden among them. And that leads the psalmist to God's cherishing of his community (147:6)—God's choice, so to speak, with a discrimination between "the afflicted" (equivalent to the "righteous")[6] and "the wicked."[7] Implicit is a warning to those who might rebel: they face retribution from God (this also hints at where the psalm is heading in the next section). In any case: *Let's* praise *God!*

Exhortation 2 and Explanation 2 (147:7–11)

After an exhortation to praise ("sing" and "make music," 147:7), God's control over the cosmos is outlined, predominantly in the form of his catering to the needs of life therein, by means of clouds, rain, growth of grass, and provision of food (147:8–9).[8] *Explanation 2* closes with an explicit statement of how God cherishes his community (147:10–11): a choice is made between the things mankind may trust (for security and preservation) and the one whom humanity *should* trust and fear: God. Those who do the latter please him. The verses, 147:10–11, cleverly portray the antithesis (below).[9]

---

6. See the parallelism in 14:5b, 6a; also in 18:24–27; 37:11–12; 69:28–29; 73:13–14. Note, as well, the parallelism of "afflicted" with "those who fear Him" in 34:6–7, and with "the devout one . . . Your servant" in 86:1–2.

7. These evildoers are brought "unto the ground" in 147:6b, likely an allusion to their final destination—death and Sheol.

8. God "calls [קרא, *qrʾ*]" stars by names (147:4b), and he feeds the young ravens who "cry [קרא]" (147:9b)—both facets of God's cosmic control. Deity is transcendent *and* immanent.

9. Modified from Auffret, "L'étude structurelle des Psaumes réponses et complements II," 58.

	False Trust	God's Displeasure
147:10a	"might of the horse"	"not … delight"
147:10b	"legs of a man"	"not … pleasure"

	God's Pleasure	True Trust	
	"those who fear"	"Him"	147:11a
	"the ones hoping"	"His lovingkindness"	147:11b

The urging is clear: *Let's praise and* please *God* (by fearing him).

Exhortation 3 and Explanation 3 (147:12–20)

In this section the exhortation is to "laud" and "praise" Yahweh (147:12), directed to "Jerusalem" and "Zion," likely synecdoche for the people of God. And so, the city and God's care for it show up again (147:13–14): he defends it (147:13a), blesses its citizens (147:13b), establishes peace (147:14a), and provisions his people (147:14b).[10] God's control of the cosmos is here viewed as the efficacy of the "word" "cast [שׁלך]"/"sent forth [שׁלח]" by God (147:15a, 17a, 18a). And this divine "word," broadcast to the very ends of the earth, accomplishes its work rapidly (147:15): snow falls,[11] frost scatters, ice forms (147:16–17a). And equally efficiently, at God's "word," ice melts, winds blow, waters flow (147:18). In between 146:16–17a and 147:18 is 147:17b that raises a rhetorical question at the center of it all: "Before the face of his ice-coldness who can stand?"

147:16	producing "snow"
	scattering "frost"
147:17	casting "ice"
	"Who can stand?"
	melting "them" (ice)
147:18	blowing "wind"
	flowing "waters"

This is not a statement about the frigidity of elements or of precipitation; rather the "ice-coldness" symbolically stands for the power of God's word (or for God's word, itself): its righteousness is incomparable, and no human can withstand its glorious might. Nature obeys, so should not humans? And the psalmist makes that argument quite clearly as he closes out with a final expression of God cherishing his community, choosing them to bear his oracles (147:19–20): his "words" were given to "Jacob" and "Israel," his people, and to no one else. No one else knows them. Perhaps the nations' "not knowing" God's word (147:20b) implies that

---

10. See 81:16 for the motif of God filling his people with "the best of wheat," as here in 147:14b.
11. God who "gives" snow (147:16a) is also the one who "gives" animals their food (147:9a); both are aspects of God's control over the cosmos—again deity's transcendence and immanence on display.

God's people *do* (or *should*) "know" them—in an intimate, life-transforming, God-glorifying way.[12] That is to say, *Let's praise and please God by* performing *God's word!*

Sermon Map

I. God's Care for the City
   Constructing and championing (147:2–3, 13–14)
   Move-to-relevance: God's calling us as his people and his protection

II. God's Control over the Cosmos
   Creating, catering, and commanding (147:4–5, 8–9, 15–18)
   Move-to-relevance: God's caring control over the universe

III. God's Cherishing of the Community
   God's choosing: positive and negative (147:6, 10–11, 19–20)
   Move-to-relevance: Consequences of God's and our choices

IV. *Praise and Please God by Performing God's Word!*
   Specifics on worshipful obedience to please God

---

12. The word ידע, *yd'*, "know," has that comprehensive connotation in the OT.

PSALM 148:1–14

Psalm of Reorientation

Joining Praise with All Creation

THIS PSALM EXHORTS THE praise of Yahweh and lists the various actants executing that praise, those in the heavens and those on the earth. The entire psalm is bounded by "Praise Yah" (148:1a, 14d).[1]

Translation

148:1 Praise Yah.
       Praise Yahweh from the heavens;
          praise Him in the heights.
148:2 Praise Him, all His angels;
          praise Him, all His armies.
148:3 Praise Him, sun and moon;
          praise Him, all stars of light.
148:4 Praise Him, heaven of heavens,
          and the waters that are above the heavens.
148:5 Let them praise the name of Yahweh,
          for He—He commanded and they were created;
148:6 and He stood them for always, forever;
          He has given a statute, and it will not pass away.
148:7 Praise Yahweh from the earth,
          sea monsters and all depths;
148:8 fire and hail, snow and smoke[-like fog];
          stormy wind, doing His word;
148:9 mountains and all heights;
          fruit trees and all cedars;

---

1. And also by "heights [מָרוֹם, *marom*]" (from רום, *rwm*; 148:1c) and "raised high [רוּם]" (148:14a).

148:10	the animal and all cattle;
	the creeping thing and winged bird;
148:11	kings of the earth and all peoples;
	princes and all judges of the earth;
148:12	young men and also virgins;
	old men with young men.
148:13	Let them praise the name of Yahweh
	for exalted is His name alone;
	His splendor is above the earth and the heavens,
148:14	and He raised high a horn for His people,
	[resulting in] praise for all His devout,
	for the children of Israel, a people near Him.
	Praise Yah.

Structure

That everything in the cosmos is involved in the praise of Yahweh is signified in Psalm 148 by the "exuberant word," "all" (148:2a, 2b, 3b, 7b, 9a, 9b, 10a, 11a, 11b, 14b) that "rings out in a striving for totality of praise."[2] Though there are two כִּי- (ki-) clauses in the psalm (148:5b, 13b), there is hardly any explanation of why praise is necessary: it is taken for granted, rightly, that Yahweh will—and should—be praised. The focus is thus on the object of praise and the ones performing his praise.

Praise by All in the Heavens (148:1–6)
"from the heavens" (148:1b)
  Executors of Praise who are God's: "His angels"; "His armies" (148:2)
    Recommendation: "let them praise the name of Yahweh" (148:5a)
    Reason: "for [כִּי] ..." (148:5b): Submission to God
    Result: "and He stood ..." (148:6a): Stabilization by God

Praise by All on the Earth (148:7–14)
"from the earth" (148:7a)
  Executors of Praise who are God's: "His people"; "His devout" (148:14ab)
    Recommendation: "let them praise the name of Yahweh" (148:13a)
    Reason: "for [כִּי] ..." (148:13b): Sublimity of God
    Result: "and He raised high ..." (148:14a): Success from God

---

2. Allen, *Psalms 101–150*, 316.

Psalm 148:1–14

Theological Focus

That all things in the cosmos—obedient and eloquent, though silent, witnesses to the praise of the sublime God (who alone is to be exalted)—are firmly established forever motivates humankind, and particularly the people of God, to be equally enthusiastic in its praise of God's supreme majesty, resulting in success in every endeavor.

Commentary

Praise by All in the Heavens (148:1–6)

That the exhortation is to praise God is obvious: "praise" occurs nine times in this section (148:1a, 1b, 1c, 2a, 2b, 3a, 3b, 4a, 5a). The location of the actants executing praise in the first section are all in the "heavens" (148:1b), though even the "heaven of heavens" (148:4a) itself, as well as the "waters that are above the heavens" (148:4b) are recommended—nay, commanded!—to praise.[3] Whatever might be the constituents of the universe and their arrangements, the rhetorical thrust is that *all* of them are to be involved in praising Yahweh. "By fulfilling their divinely allotted functions, the works of celestial creation exist as eloquent witnesses to [God's] self-revelation through them."[4] The assonance in 148:3–5 compounds the sense of a comprehensive involvement of the praise of God: שֶׁמֶשׁ, *shemesh*; "sun" (148:3a); שְׁמֵי הַשָּׁמַיִם, *shme hashshamayim*, "heaven of heavens" (148:4a), הַשָּׁמַיִם, "heavens" (148:4b; also in 148:1b); and שֵׁם, *shem*, "name" (148:5a). Also notable is a pair of praise performers that are labeled "His"—"His angels" and "His armies" (148:2)—the only two worshiping entities in this section that are rational. They are God's. They praise him.

The reason for the praise by these heavenly inhabitants is simply because God is their Creator. These always-obeying beings are firmly established, made stable by the statute of God, and that forever (148:6). And, in mute obedience, producing only the sounds of silence,[5] they give praise to the one who made them (148:5).

Praise by All on the Earth (148:7–14)

Another exhortation introduces a new series of protagonists executing praise to Yahweh "from the earth" (148:7a). This list includes water-dwelling creatures and the depths themselves (148:7b),[6] atmospheric elements (148:8—particularly noted to be "doing His word"),

---

3. The cosmological sequencing of the various stations, going from below upwards, seems to be earth, heavens, waters above the heavens, and the heaven of heavens. The heavens and the waters above the heavens constitute what today would be called the atmosphere.

4. Allen, *Psalms 101–150*, 316.

5. Even if the angels and armies of God can produce sounds, the fact is that we earthlings are unable to hear them. So, too, perhaps the sounds of the planets. Are their sonic frequencies, if there are any, outside of the 20–20,000 Hz bandwidth audible to the human ear? I wouldn't be surprised....

6. If the "heights" can be a source of God's praise (148:1c), so can the "depths" (148:7b). The fact that it is "in the heights" that God is praised suggests that these terms stand for the denizens of those respective

topographical landmarks (148:9a), flora (148:9b), fauna (148:10), and humans: rulers and powers-that-be, as well as "all peoples" (148:11), young and old, married and single (148:12). The reason for their praise is the sublimity, preeminence, and absolute superiority of Yahweh—"exalted is His name alone" (148:13). This verse appears to be summing up the psalm: 148:1 had praise "from the heavens"; 148:7a had praise "from the earth"; now, in 148:13c, the psalm moves to its conclusion with praise from "the earth and the heavens"!

The result of the praise, particularly the consequence for humans—for the first time listed as actants executing praise in 148:11–12—is that they become victorious in battle ("the raising of their horn" by God, 148:14a),[7] and win acclaim (they are themselves praised, 148:14bc).[8] The layered (staircase?) structuring of 148:14 emphasizes the magnificent consequences for human praise-producers:

Verb	Object	Beneficiaries
"and He raised high	a horn	for His people,
	[resulting in] praise	for all His devout,
		for the sons of Israel"

The collocation of rational and non-rational actants of praise in this psalm is intriguing. Fretheim calls it a "symbiosis of human and natural orders" for the purpose of the praise and glory of God.[9] He argues that there needs to be both sets of actants to execute plenary praise to God, mutually supporting one another. "The natural order provides raw material for human praise. Without the natural order the praising metaphors . . . would be fewer in number, . . . that is, we would be without much [of the] praise-full painting, music, and literature inspired by nature" that has been undertaken by humankind, divinely appointed scribes attesting to nature's praise of God.[10] Without this writing species, nonhuman praise would have no language, no voice, no articulation: "It is up to human beings to give it clear voice."[11] Fretheim concludes: "The integration of heavenly, human, and nonhuman language in Psalm 148 may well recognize this interconnectedness of praise possibilities. That is, it

---

spaces, not that the locations themselves are praising God.

7. After all, they are God's devout, the children of Israel, a people near to God (148:14bc)—so of course, God will aid his faithful in their battles, signified by his "raising high of a horn" for them. The martial connotations of lifted horns are also seen in 18:2; 75:4–5, 10; 89:17–18, 23–25; 92:9–11; 112:8–9; etc.

8. The nature of the battle is not described; that is beyond the scope of this psalm which simply urges praise. In its Theological Focus, I mention "success in every endeavor." The direction this might take in the homiletical undertaking is left to the preacher. On the people of God themselves deserving praise (148:14b), also see: Deut 26:19; Isa 62:7; Jer 13:11; 33:9; Zeph 3:20. Are there entities/elements praising them, or is this simply a statement of honor? Probably both.

9. Fretheim, "Nature's Praise," 28.

10. Or, as George Herbert (1593–1633) put it in "Praise":

"Of all the creatures both in sea and land
Only to man Thou hast made known Thy ways,
And put the pen alone into his hand,
And made him secretary of Thy praise."

11. Fretheim, "Nature's Praise," 28. Unfortunately, post-fall, humankind's sinfulness has muffled the full-throated praise of nature: "The heavens proclaim the glory of God with less clarity on a smoggy day in Los Angeles than on other days" (Fretheim, "Nature's Praise," 29).

is only as all creatures of God together join in the chorus of praise that the elements of the natural order or human beings witness to God as they ought."[12]

And so there is an implicit polemic in this composition against the potential non-execution of praise on the part of humankind, and the neglect thereof by God's people. If every other kind of created entity, rational and otherwise, heavenly and earthly, moving and immobile, can be effective executors of the praise of God in obedience to their sublime Creator, why cannot humans, too, "join with all nature in manifold witness," with exultant and exuberant glorification of God?[13]

Sermon Map

I. Praising God Above

    All entities in the heavenlies praise God (148:1–4) . . .

    . . . because they submit to God's creative intent for them (148:5) . . .

    . . . and therefore, are established forever by God (148:6)

    Move-to-relevance: Obedience of nature in God's praise

II. Praising God Below

    All entities on earth praise God (148:7–10) . . .

    . . . including humankind (148:11–12) . . .

    . . . because he alone is worthy of praise (148:13) . . .

    . . . and, therefore, God's people find success in every endeavor (148:14)

    Move-to-relevance: If nature can . . . shouldn't we . . . ?

III. *Magnify the Maker's Majesty with the Macrocosm . . . and Be Magnified!*

    Specifics on how to partner with nature in the proclamation of God's glory

---

12. Fretheim, "Nature's Praise," 29.
13. From "Great Is Thy Faithfulness," Thomas O. Chisholm (1923).

PSALM 149:1–9

Psalm of Reorientation

Praise for Justice Executed

PSALM 149 LOOKS AHEAD to a time when Yahweh reigns, with his people undertaking royal service on his behalf. So of course, there is praise to the God-King, the one who reigns. Along with that, however, is a depiction of God's people also executing justice on behalf of the cosmic regent against evildoers. Thus, in Psalm 149, there is an odd combination of the community of God engaging in both worshipful and warlike activities.

Translation

149:1   Praise Yah.
        Sing to Yahweh a new song,
            His praise in the congregation of the devout.
149:2   Let Israel rejoice in the One who made them;
            the children of Zion, let them jubilate in their King.
149:3   Let them praise His name in dance;
            with timbrel and lyre let them make music to Him.
149:4   For Yahweh takes pleasure in His people;
            He will adorn those afflicted with deliverance.
149:5   Let the devout exult in glory;
            let them shout for joy upon their beds,
149:6   the exaltation of God in their throat,
            and a sword of two edges in their hand,
149:7   to do vengeance on the nations,
            and punishment on the peoples;
149:8   to imprison their kings in chains,
            and their glorious ones in fetters of iron;
149:9   to do to them the judgment that has been written;
            this is splendor[-filled honor] for all His devout.
        Praise Yah.

Structure

One sees in this psalm the devout looking to "their King" with praise (149:2b; *Devout Engaging Praise*: 149:1–4) and the devout looking at "their [i.e., foreigners'] kings" with pugnacity (149:8a; *Devout Exercising Power*: 149:5–9):[1]

Devout Engaging Praise (149:1–4)

Exhortation (149:1–3)
Explanation (149:4): Why?

"Praise Yah"; "devout" (149:1)
"Israel"; "sons of Zion" (149:2)
"Yahweh" (149:1b, 4a); "their King" (149:2b)
"... the one who made [עשׂה, 'sh] them" (149:2a)
"in [בְּ, b] dance; with [בְּ] timbrel and lyre" (149:3)

Devout Exercising Power (149:6–9)

Exhortation (149:5–6a)
Explanation (149:6b–9): How?

"Praise Yah"; "devout" (149:9)
"nations"; "peoples" (149:7)
"their kings"; "their glorious ones" (149:8)
"to do [עשׂה]" (149:7a)
"in [בְּ] chains"; "in [בְּ] fetters" (149:8)

Walter Brueggemann wryly observes that "this psalm is exceedingly problematic because ... it combines 'praise the Lord' with 'pass the ammunition.'"[2] Yes, that is a strange nexus of two aspects of the (future) life of the devout, but one cannot separate the prophesied triumph of the divine King and his people from the promised tribulation of godless kings and their people. Divine justice demands both and sees to both, and humans may be deployed as agents of God's retribution. That also leads to God's praise.

Theological Focus

> God, the King of the universe, is worthy of exuberant corporate praise employing body and voice, because he delivers those whom he delights in, his people, those he created, and deploys them as his agents for the retribution of enemies, godless kings and their people, all redounding to the honor of the godly and devout.

---

1. Each of the two parts has an exhortation and an explanation section. Also of interest in the structuring of this poem is the occurrence of the preposition בְּ, *b*, "in/with/on/to," in every one of its lines (and twice in 149:2, 3, 4, 6, 7, 8).

2. Brueggemann, *Psalms and the Life of Faith*, 124.

Commentary

Devout Engaging Praise (149:1–4)

The section begins with an exhortation to "praise" Yahweh (149:1–3) and to "sing," "rejoice," "jubilate," "praise," and "make music" to him. The "new song" (149:1b)[3] need not be a fresh creation, with new words or a new tune; rather, it might broadly indicate praise for "the coming dynamic intervention of Yahweh into history in a new, unprecedented and final manner."[4] Thus every new deliverance or rescue effected by God results in a "new song," renewed praise directed to deity. At any rate this praise is to be engaged in community ("in the congregation of the devout," 149:1c), and is not only music-making (verbally and instrumentally, 149:1b, 149:3b), but also movement-manifesting ("dance," 149:3a).[5] The entirety of one's being is to be devoted to the praise of Yahweh by the devout, in the worship of their Creator and their King.

The exhortation to praise (149:1–3) is then followed by an explanation for praise (149:4): Yahweh is praiseworthy because he delights in the devout and will bless ("adorn") them with his deliverance. The relationships between "the children of Zion" and "their King" (149:2b), and that between "Yahweh" and "His people" (149:4a), are mutual and reciprocal. In the former statement, God's people are to "jubilate" in their regent; in the latter, God "takes pleasure" in his people. These affirmations are neatly laid out, all united with the preposition בְּ.[6]

149:2b	"children of Zion, let them jubilate in [בְּ] their King"
149:3aα	"let them praise His name"
149:3aβ	"in [בְּ] dance"
149:3bα	"with [בְּ] timbrel and lyre"
149:3bβ	"let them make music to Him"
149:4a	"Yahweh takes pleasure in [בְּ] His people"

There is also the assonance of בְּעֹשָׂיו, *b'osayw*, "in the one who made them" (149:2a) and בִּישׁוּעָה, *bishu'ah*, "with deliverance" (149:4b). Their Maker is also their Deliverer! The deliverance of God's people will be accomplished (149:4), and the devout will no longer be the "afflicted" (149:4b) but agents of God in his justice (see below). The eschaton is likely to be the time-space arena where the praise of the godly (and the retribution of the godless) transpires.

Devout Exercising Power (149:5–9)

The exhortation to praise in 149:5a is to be directed to Yahweh, of course, but the people of God are exultant and shouting for joy because of "glory," likely the honor invested in them

---

3. Also in 33:3; 40:3; 96:1; 98:1; and 144:9.

4. Allen, *Psalms 101–150*, 319. Or this psalm itself might be the "new song" referred to. "The *One* who made them" (149:2a) is actually a plural participle, "the *Ones* . . . ," likely a plural of majesty for the singular deity.

5. Note that 149:3 is chiastic: "Let them praise His name / in [בְּ] dance; // with [בְּ] timbrel and lyre / let them make music to Him."

6. Modified from Auffret, *Merveilles à nos yeux*, 278–79.

as part of Yahweh's deliverance of them (likewise the "splendor[-filled honor] for all His devout" in 149:9b).[7]

The explanation, here in 149:6b–9, is more an answer to *how* the devout are to exercise power (unlike *why* the devout are to engage praise, as in 149:4). The subjects of 149:5b–9 continue to be the "devout" of 149:5a, 9b, though the infinitives ("to do vengeance," "to imprison," and "to do to them"; 149:7a, 8a, 9a) create a degree of ambiguity: Is this about the devout exercising power, or is it God himself doing so? Most likely it is the former, but the equivocalness is likely to be deliberate, indicating *God's* work through human hands. That "the one who made [עשׂה] them" (God; 149:2a) and "to do [עשׂה]" (administer retribution; 149:7a, 9a) share the same verb underscores this notion: the one who "made" is the one who is "doing . . . ." After all, vengeance is God's prerogative (and so is his choice of human agents to deliver reprisals).[8] Thus, what is depicted here is "judgment that has been written" (149:9a). God has judged; God has passed sentence; and God is executing his decree. In no uncertain terms, 149:7–9 paints a sadly tormented—but spectacularly textual—picture of the godless in their dire predicament:[9]

	"to [לְ, /] do"
149:7a	"vengeance"
	"on [בְּ] the nations"
	"punishment"
149:7b	"on [בְּ] the peoples"
	"to [לְ] imprison"
149:8a	"their kings"
	"in [בְּ] chains"
	"their glorious ones"
149:8b	"in [בְּ] fetters"
149:9a	**"to [לְ] do"**

The rulers and their peoples are trapped between retribution ("vengeance" and "punishment"; 149:7) and restraint ("in chains" and "in fetters"; 149:8), all because of the actions of God and those of his agents, his devout ("to do" [×2] and "to imprison"; 149:7a, 8a, 9a). Davis's words are appropriate:

> There is a clear marker that distinguishes the violence that takes hold of God's kingdom from that which wreaks destruction in our world—a difference between the saints' violence, always conjoined with God's high praise, and the unholy

---

7. In fact, we have just seen an earlier instance of praise redounding upon the "devout," in 148:14. The location where God's people are shouting for joy, "upon their beds" (149:5b), is cryptic; perhaps it indicates their joy in private, while the exultation and exaltation (149:5a, 6a) are public expressions of their gladness. There is also the possibility that all of this, including the rather violent weapon-wielding that follows, is to be done in the mind, on a couch, *in camera*. In that case, 149:6b–9a is not intended to be taken literally. But the people of God should not be surprised if this is an actual description of divine retribution upon the godless, with God's people as the agents of this exaction of penalty (see the Introduction in *Psalms 1–44* for my take on imprecations, as well as the commentary on Psalm 137). That would not be a notion foreign to Scripture, or even to the Psalter. The triumph granted to tremulous underdogs (149:4b) is always accompanied by the trouncing of tyrannical overlords. Thus is justice done and deserts disbursed in the divine economy.

8. See Deut 32:35–36; Pss 18:47; 94:1; 99:8; 137:8–9; Jer 46:10.

9. Modified from Auffret, *Merveilles à nos yeux*, 280n22, 281.

violence that rings as shrill mockery in God's ears. The difference is this: every kind of godless violence is directed at getting something or holding on to it—power, oil, satisfaction, vengeance, personal or national security. But the battle of the saint is always fundamentally directed toward giving, giving praise to God.[10]

Whereas in the first half of the psalm (*Devout Engaging Praise*) it was the divine King and his relationship with his people that were in focus (and the pleasure of God that they experience), here (in *Devout Exercising Power*) it is the earthly kings and their peoples who are highlighted (and their suffering grievous loss):[11]

149:2b	"their King"
149:4a	"in His people [בְּעַמּוֹ, b'ammo]"
49:7b	"on the peoples [בַלְאֻמִּים, bal'ummim]"
149:8a	"their kings"

And while the devout exult in "glory [כָּבוֹד, kavod]" (149:5a), the "glorious ones [נִכְבְּדֵיהֶם, nikbdehem]" of the ungodly are excommunicated (149:8b). Thus the potential fate of the nations in the second psalm of the Psalter (2:5, 9) is depicted again in the penultimate psalm of the book (149:6b–9). Both texts have shared references to "nations," "peoples," "kings," "judges/judgment," "fetters," and "iron,"[12] all contributing to the first and last portrayals of God as a regal figure in the Psalter, and the first and last portrayals of foreign nations as well, but here as ruined foes. Thus it is established conclusively that there is no king but Yahweh! And, as was intimated in 149:5a, so it is reiterated in 149:9b: the victory of God through his agents is a "splendor[-filled honor]" for them, his people, the devout! "Praise Yah," indeed!

---

10. Davis, "Self-Inflicted Violence," 296. She is quick to add that the exercising of such power by the people of God also involves a "lifelong work of self-inflicted, surgical violence which tradition calls repentance." Without that, godly violence relapses into sheer ungodliness.

11. From Auffret, *Merveilles à nos yeux*, 283n31. The MT has בַּל־אֻמִּים, bal-'ummim, in 149:7b, but the negative particle בַּל never occurs with a substantive elsewhere in the OT; so it is best to read it as בַלְאֻמִּים, "on the peoples," that also then creates a parallel with "on the nations [בַגּוֹיִם, baggoyim]" in 149:7a. See Barbiero and Pavan, "Ps 44,15; 57,10; 108,4; 149,7," 599.

12. See 149:2b, 4a, 8a, 8b, 9a; and 2:1a, 1b, 2a, 3a, 6a, 10a, 10b.

Sermon Map

I. The Favor of God toward the Godly
    God's pleasure in the godly (149:4a)
    God's deliverance of his people (149:4b)
    Move-to-relevance: The triumph of the godly, coming soon

II. The Fierceness of God against the Ungodly
    God's displeasure with the ungodly (149:6b–9a)
    God's agency of retribution: his people (149:5–6a, 9b)
    Move-to-relevance: The trouncing of the ungodly, coming soon

III. *Enjoy God's Pleasure, Engaging God's Praise, Exercising God's Power!*
    Engagement of praise right now (149:1–3, 9c)
    Specifics on engaging praise with responsibility for exercising power

PSALM 150:1–6

Psalm of Reorientation

Self-Abandoning Praise

AND FINALLY, THE PSALTER comes to a grand close with Psalm 150, the response of all living beings to the magnificence of God (and to all that has been declared about him and about his actions in the preceding psalms). The root הלל, *hll*, "praise," occurs at least twice in every verse—thrice in 150:1—for a total of thirteen instances. The main goal of the psalm is clear: to exhort the praise of God. But unlike in Psalm 148, no non-rational beings are urged to do so; indeed, 150:6a seems to restrict this call to praise to voice-employing, instrument-wielding, and body-engaging beings (i.e., rational entities).[1] So, "this Psalm is a determined, enthusiastic, uninterrupted, relentless, unrelieved summons which will not be content until all creatures, all of life, are 'ready and willing' to participate in an unending song of praise that is sung without reserve or qualification."[2]

Translation

150:1   Praise Yah.
        Praise God in His holy place;
            praise Him in the sky of His strength.
150:2   Praise Him for His mighty deeds;
            praise Him according to His abundant greatness.

---

1. And also unlike the closing Hallel Psalms (Psalms 146–149), no reference is made in this psalm to Israel or Zion. God, after all, and at the end of it all, is universal, the God-King of the cosmos. See Cha, "Psalms 146–150," 103. "Every [thing with] breath" (150:6a) is not likely to include non-humans of the animal kingdom: the praise seems to be reasoned (150:2), performed with appurtenances (150:3, 4aα, 4b–5), and involving kinetic exertions (150:4a). However, one cannot rule out non-human, angelic beings in this symphony of praise: they are rational and employ both voices and instruments (see Job 38:7; Ps 148:2; Isa 14:11 [?]; Matt 24:31; 1 Thess 4:16; Rev 5:8; 8:2; 14:2), though the musical equipment seems to be restricted to harps and trumpets. (No pipe organ?)

2. Brueggemann, "Bounded by Obedience," 67. Brueggemann's essay is worth reading in its entirety; I am grateful for his thoughtful scholarship as I borrow liberally from his work here.

150:3	Praise Him with the blast of the horn;
	praise Him with harp and lyre.
150:4	Praise Him with timbrel and dance;
	praise Him with strings and pipe.
150:5	Praise Him with the sound of cymbals;
	praise Him with the joyful shout of cymbals.
150:6	Every [thing with] breath, praise Yah.
	Praise Yah.

Structure

The structure of Psalm 150 is straightforward, answering a number of implied questions:[3]

150:1a	Exclamation of Praise ("Praise Yah")	*What?*
150:1bc	Exhortation to Praise "God"	*Who in Heaven?*
150:2	Exhortation to Praise	*Why?*
150:3–5	Exhortation to Praise	*How?*
150:6a	Exhortation to Praise "Yah"	*Who on Earth?*
150:6b	Exclamation of Praise ("Praise Yah")	*What?*

Thus the Psalter commenced with a summons to obedience unto God (Psalm 1) and concludes with a summons to praise God (Psalm 150). Brueggemann observes that only the obedient can praise God, with obedience being the qualifying criterion for rendering praise to God. "Only those who willingly begin in Psalm 1 can honestly and gladly end in Psalm 150."[4] Not only does one need to walk with God in obedience, but as one does so, one can abandon oneself to enthusiastic, exuberant, euphoric, and ecstatic praise.

But the notion of walking with God in obedience is completely absent in Psalm 150;[5] that, however, should not be surprising, for "obedience has been overcome, transcended and superseded in the unfettered yielding of Psalm 150" to the praise of this great deity. The gravity of duty has been overridden by the gaiety of doxology![6] Not that obedience is abandoned, of course; it is simply assumed in Psalm 150.

All that to say, within the bounds of the Psalter, life is a move from responsible diligence in performance to rapturous delight in praise. There is a sense that when the one is integrated into one's being the other will follow, and indeed become prominent. Life, with all its joys and sorrows, certainties and doubts, thrills and desperations, is lived between these two psalms at the boundaries of the song book, between absolute obedience and ecstatic worship. And

---

3. While this dissected structure with questions may be helpful for sermon-*preparers* to visualize the psalm, the utility of such an atomization is extremely doubtful for sermon-*listeners* seeking to catch the thrust (pericopal theology) for application.

4. Brueggemann, "Bounded by Obedience," 69.

5. Just as praise is absent from its counterpart at the start, Psalm 1.

6. Brueggemann, "Bounded by Obedience," 69–70.

throughout this journey in the Psalter, from its introduction of blessing to its conclusion of praise, the people of God are conducted, carried, and even cushioned, by God's lovingkindness which is unto forever! Needless to add, the ultimate fulfillment of Psalm 150's self-abandoning, all-encompassing, overwhelming praise, the culmination of the journey of life, is yet to come. But it will. One day, soon and very soon. And then . . . it will be Psalm 150 forever!

Theological Focus

> Everyone, everywhere (in the heavens and on the earth), and with everything (voice, music, and movement) engages in the praise of God with enthusiasm and exuberance, manifesting an elemental simplicity of praise, expressed in self-abandonment unto deity.

Commentary

After the opening exclamation of praise ("Praise Yah"; *What?* in 150:1a) comes an exhortation to praise "God" that lists the praise-performing ones as being located in "His holy place" and in "the sky of His strength" (*Who in Heaven?* in 150:1bc). But the identity of these glory-givers is not revealed, though it is likely that they are delegates to the divine council, or those in a heavenly sanctuary, or even members of God's army.[7] A heavenly host, no less, is to praise God!

And the reason for this acclaim is given in the second round of exhortation (*Why?* in 150:2): praise is due this deity because of what he has done and because of his intrinsic and incomparable greatness.

Then follows six lines (three verses; *How?* in 150:3–5) specifically dealing with the music of this praise (150:3, 4aα, 4b, 5) and the movements of this praise (150:4aβ). Apparently the scene has now shifted earthwards, with humankind's contrivances for, and choreography of, worship. All manner of instruments are employed: strings, wind, and percussion. "Together with the visual and mobile art of the sacred dance, they [these instruments] create a loud symphony of praise, as a response to the glory of God, and rise to a crescendo in the clashing cymbals."[8]

---

7. The parallelism of "His holy place" and "the sky of His strength" suggests they are the same locus—a heavenly station, as opposed to the earthly station implied in 150:6a, with its exhortation to "every [thing with] breath" to praise.

8. Allen, *Psalms 101–150*, 324.

Notice the construction of this section that links exhortations to praise with the preposition בְּ, *b*, "with," and creates pairs of instruments (and instrument + dance) with the conjunction וְ, *w*, "and," adding an extra set of clangorous percussion in the last element (150:5b):[9]

150:3	"praise Him with [בְּ] the blast of the horn"
	"praise Him with [בְּ] harp and [וְ] lyre"
150:4	"praise Him with [בְּ] timbrel and [וְ] **dance**"
	"praise Him with [בְּ] strings and [וְ] pipe"
150:5	"praise Him with [בְּ] the sound of cymbals"
	"praise Him with [בְּ] the joyful shout of cymbals"

This repetitive sequence gives the solicitation to praise God a sense of totality and comprehensiveness: nothing is to be left out of this clamorous and vigorous praising of God (not even the movements of dance, that come right in the middle of the pattern).[10] But the fact is that there *is* something left out, made noticeable by its absence: there is no notation in the psalm of these worshipers' thoughts or feelings: the emphasis is exclusively on noise and dance (bodily movement directed by the euphonic melodies and percussive rhythms). Goldingay may well be right in positing that this omission is deliberate:

> The enthusiasm about noise in worship that dominates this psalm issues the Psalter's closing piece of advice to intellectual and socially activist readers of the Psalms. It ignores the possible anti-intellectual or escapist implications of its enthusiasm to fulfill this function. It is prepared to take that risk in order to remind us that sharp thinking and social function are not the only important things in the world. Indeed, it makes no reference to intelligent content, sincerity of heart, integrity of life, feelings of joy, or commitment of love. It closes with simple enthusiasm.[11]

As Brueggemann declares, Psalm 150 brazenly and baldly expresses "lyrical self-abandonment, an utter yielding of self, without vested interest, calculation, desire, or hidden agenda."[12] Perhaps right thinking and feeling are assumed, the state of mind and heart that these worshipers possess having been already established, for these devout walk with God as they traverse the Psalter, from Psalm 1 to Psalm 150. Only music and movement prevail in praise in this final song, not mind or brain, not guts or heart, but hands (making music) and feet (making movement). And as if to make that even more clear, the psalmist concludes with another exhortation to praise God, this time likely addressing earthbound denizens: "every [thing with] breath" (*Who?* in 150:6a), and following up with another exclamation: "Praise Yah" (*What?* in 150:6b). If heavenly beings are to praise (150:1bc), surely earthly creatures are equally obligated to praise, too. And only as they do so will God's people fulfill their highest

---

9. Modified from Auffret, *Merveilles à nos yeux*, 286. The last verse of the trio, 150:5, has only one pair of identical instruments, that are not conjoined with וְ.

10. Emphasizing the noise-making, ringing and rattling cymbals are repeated in 150:5b. Thus the first instrument, horn (150:3a), and the last, cymbals (150:5a, 5b), are qualified by "the blast" and "the sound/the joyful shout," respectively, unlike the other means of celebration listed.

11. Goldingay, *Psalms*, 3:749–50.

12. Brueggemann, "Bounded by Obedience," 67.

function, praise, for which they were created and redeemed. May that be the case, with God's people proclaiming God's praise, now and forever. Amen!

Sermon Map

I. Praising God: By Everyone
   Heavenly beings (150:1)
   Earthly beings (150:6)
   Move-to-relevance: Even heavenly beings praise God

II. Praising God: With Everything
   Music- and movement-making (150:3–5)
   Move-to-relevance: Praise with all our being

III. Praising God: In Enthusiasm
   The simplicity of praise that ought not to be analyzed

IV. *Everyone, Everywhere, Exalt with Enthusiasm!*
   Specifics on exalting God in the simplicity of enthusiasm

CONCLUSION

> *Blessing [upon] those whose way is blameless,*
> *the ones who walk in the law of Yahweh.*
> *Blessing [upon] the ones who observe His decrees;*
> *they seek Him with all [their] heart.*
>
> Psalm 119:1–2

AT THE CORE OF the Psalter is God's desire to bless his people. This blessing is experienced by "those whose way is blameless," "[those] who walk in the Law of Yahweh," "[those] who observe His decrees," and who "seek Him with all [their] heart" (119:1–2)—all synonymous terms. How this is achieved by people broken by the fall, and what this blessed life looks like in a world equally ruined by that calamitous event, is the burden of the book of Psalms. Their lives, with all of its ups and downs, zeniths and nadirs, triumphs and turmoils, and delights and desperations, is depicted with candor and without whitewash, as God's people seek to walk with him, in his ways and in his laws, yearning for him with the entirety of their beings.

That the thrust of the book inclines in the direction of human alignment to divine will is seen right at the start:

> Psalm 1 is usually labeled a Torah psalm. The Hebrew word *tôrâ* occurs twice in verse 2 . . . . The effect, in part, is to orient the reader and pray-er of the Psalms to expect to learn something about God and God's will from the psalms themselves, as one might expect more readily to do from the Torah (Genesis—Deuteronomy). In short, the psalms, which originated as liturgical materials, have become *tôrâ*, "instruction." While the word *tôrâ* is reminiscent of the material in the Torah, it can also mean God's will in the broadest sense. Thus, what is commended from the very beginning of the Psalter is a life fundamentally oriented to God and lived in conformity to God's will.[1]

Perhaps it is therefore not accidental that the first book (Psalms 1–41) and last book (Psalms 107–150) of the Psalter have a Torah-Psalm (Psalms 19 and 119, both with a variety of terms for God's divine demand, the latter having one or more of these synonyms in almost every one of its verses). Also of note is that Psalm 119 is an acrostic, and the third Torah-Psalm, Psalm 1, though not an acrostic, has its first word begin with א, ' (אַשְׁרֵי, *ashre*, "blessing"), and its last with ת, *t* (תֹּאבֵד, *to'ved*, "[it] perishes"). "By using every letter of the alphabet the poet was trying to ensure that his treatment of a particular topic was complete," approaching it

---

1. McCann, "Shape and Shaping of the Psalter," 351–52.

from every angle, apparently.[2] And this topic is what it means to walk in the blameless way of God's Torah, seeking deity with all their hearts and minds and souls, and enjoying divine blessing as they do so.

Note also how Psalms 19 and 119 could conceivably be the centers of a seemingly deliberate arrangement of the sequence of psalms that precede and follow each of them:[3]

PSALMS 15–24
- **A** Psalm 15 (entrance liturgy psalm: "Who may abide?" [15:1])
  - **B** Psalm 16 (psalm of trust: "Yahweh ... my cup" [16:5])
    - **C** Psalm 17 (lament psalm)
      - **D** Psalm 18 (royal psalm: context of battle)
        - **E** **Psalm 19 (Torah psalm)**
      - **D'** Psalms 20–21 (royal psalms: context of battle)
    - **C'** Psalm 22 (lament psalm)
  - **B'** Psalm 23 (psalm of trust: "My cup overflows" [23:5])
- **A'** Psalm 24 (entrance liturgy psalm: "Who may ascend?" [24:3])

PSALMS 107–150
- **A** Psalm 107 (call to praise in every circumstance)
  - **B** Psalms 108–110 (Davidic psalms)
    - **C** Psalms 111–112 (Prelude to the "Egyptian Hallel")
      - **D** Psalms 113–118 ("Egyptian Hallel")
        - **E** **Psalm 119 (Torah psalm)**
      - **D'** Psalms 120–134 ("Songs of Ascents")
    - **C'** Psalms 135–136 (Postlude to the "Songs of Ascents")
- **Psalm 137 (Lament)**
  - **B'** Psalms 138–145 (Davidic psalms)
- **A'** Psalms 146–150 (call to praise by every being)

Sa'adiah ben Yosef Gaon (ca. 882/892–942), the Jewish rabbi and philosopher active during the Abbasid Caliphate, declared that the Psalms were to be considered like the Torah, intended for instruction. All of it was God's word to God's people, despite the presence of voices addressing deity.

> It is incumbent upon anyone who reads this book to realize that the purpose to be derived from its entire contents, however they are literarily expressed, reverts to the word of God, whence it was revealed. I mean, for instance, that if one hears the book say: "O Lord, my heart is not proud nor my look haughty" [Ps 131:1] he should realize that He, blessed and exalted, intended [thereby] to command His servants to be neither haughty nor supercilious, nor to behave arrogantly. . . . Similarly, if he hears: "Hear my prayer, O Lord, give ear to my cry" [Ps 39:12], he must realize that God desires us to know that He hears the prayers of His servants and their supplications, and will not ignore their tears. Likewise the entire book,

---

2. Watson, *Classical Hebrew Poetry*, 198. For more on the didactic function of Psalm 119 see that chapter.

3. Psalm 137 appears to be oddly thrust into an otherwise reasonable structure of Psalms 107–150; perhaps it reminds the reader, as the end of the Psalter is being arrived at, that life is still not perfect, and that the people of God are still in exile.

including those portions of it which are commands or prohibitions, promises or threats, narratives of past or future, shares this description as do [the portions] containing intercession or words of caution, etc. All have to be referred back to the word of God as we have described.[4]

This scholar adduced Deut 31:30—32:47, among other texts, for support. That Torah text contains the Song of Moses delivered by the leader shortly before his demise. Notably God himself introduces this composition by enjoining the people of Israel to write down "this song [הַשִּׁירָה הַזֹּאת, *hashshirah hazzo't*]" and "teach it to the children of Israel," so that it would be "a witness ... against the children of Israel" (31:19). Accordingly, Moses wrote down "this *song* [הַשִּׁירָה הַזֹּאת]" and "taught it to the children of Israel" (31:22). But then in 31:24, we have Moses completing the writing of "this *law* [הַתּוֹרָה־הַזֹּאת, *hattorah-hazzo't*]" in a book and commanding the Levites to place the book of "this law [הַתּוֹרָה הַזֶּה, *hattorah hazzeh*]" in the ark of Yahweh, so that it would be "a witness against you." The similarities in phrasing are obvious. At the very least "song" would have been encompassed by "law," making the former an integral part of the latter. All that to say, to call "songs" the Torah may not be way off track.

There is also the curious phenomenon in Moses' Song of the oft-unannounced alterations between speaker and scribe. The Song begins with Moses speaking (Deut 32:1-19), switches to God (32:20-27; though with an introduction "then He said ...," 32:20), and back to Moses (32:28-33; but with no warning about a change of speaker). It returns to the voice of God (32:34-35; again without notice), jumps back to Moses (32:36; without any signal), then returns to God's voice (32:37-42; introduced by "and He will say ...," 32:37), to finally close with Moses (32:43; without any obvious switch in speaker). In sum, the Song of Moses is the voice of God, one way or another. One must consider the Psalter in that sense, too.[5]

In any case, the Torah-centeredness of the Psalter is obvious. The eight synonyms (or derivatives from the roots of those terms) for God's word found in the Grand Torah Psalm, Psalm 119, are also found elsewhere in the Psalter (below).[6]

---

4. Sokolow, "Saadiah Gaon's Prolegomenon," 166-67 (translated from the Arabic by Sokolow).

5. Even if one does not accept the extremes proposed by the venerable sage.

6. The figure excludes instances of the eight terms (or their cognates) that occur in the three Torah psalms (Psalms 1; 19; and 119). In addition, "covenant," בְּרִית, *brit*, is found in 25:10, 14; 44:17; 50:5, 16; 55:20; 74:20; 78:10, 37; 83:5; 89:3, 28, 34, 39; 103:18; 105:8, 10; 106:45; 111:5, 9; 132:12; the term does not occur in the three Torah psalms.

TERMS	REFERENCES in Psalms (excluding Psalms 1; 19; 119)
"Law" תּוֹרָה, torah	37:31; 40:8; 78:1, 5, 10; 89:30; 94:12; 105:45
"Decree" עֵדָה, 'edah	25:10; 78:5, 56; 81:5; 93:5; 99:7; 122:4; 132:12
"Precept" פִּקּוּד, piqqud	103:18; 111:7
"Statute" חֹק, choq	2:7; 50:16; 81:4; 94:20; 99:7; 105:10, 45; 147:19; 148:6 (and חֻקָּה, chuqqah, in 18:22; 89:31)
"Commandment" מִצְוָה, mitswah	78:7; 89:31; 112:1 (and צָוָה, tsawah, in 7:6; 33:9; 42:8; 44:4; 68:28; 78:5, 23; 91:11; 105:8; 111:9; 133:3; 148:5)
"Judgment" מִשְׁפָּט, mishpat	7:6; 9:5 (×2), 8, 16; 10:5; 17:2; 18:23; 25:9; 33:5; 35:23; 36:7; 37:6, 28, 30; 48:12; 72:1, 2; 76:10; 81:5; 89:14, 30; 94:15; 97:2, 8; 99:4 (×2); 101:1; 103:6; 105:5, 7; 106:3; 111:7; 112:5; 122:5; 140:12; 143:2; 146:7; 147:19, 20; 149:9
"Word" דָּבָר, davar	17:4; 33:4, 6; 50:17; 56:4, 10; 103:20 (×2); 105:8, 27, 28, 42; 106:12, 24; 107:20; 130:5; 147:15, 18, 19; 148:8 (and as a verb, "speak," in 2:5; 50:1, 7; 51:4; 60:6; 62:11; 85:8 (×2); 89:19; 99:7; 108:7)
"Utterance" אִמְרָה, 'imrah (also "saying")	12:6 (×2); 18:30; 68:11; 77:8; 105:19; 107:11; 138:2, 4; 147:15 (and as a verb, "speak" or "say," in 2:7; 12:5; 33:9; 35:3; 50:12, 16; 68:22; 87:5; 89:19; 90:3; 95:10; 105:11, 31, 34; 106:23, 34)

Thus it is right to declare that "*Todah* [תּוֹדָה, 'thanksgiving'] is *Torah*," i.e., "praise of God is instruction for the fellow-faithful."[7]

Yet the Psalter is different. Unlike the other books of Scripture, this one unremittingly depicts the struggles and successes of the people of God as they seek to become better *Torah*-pursuers and *Todah*-producers. The edification of the people of God living in a fallen world (soon to be set right as all things in the cosmos are consummated in Christ)[8] by faith, through grace, in Christ, and in the power of the Holy Spirit, is the burden of all preaching of Scripture, and in this endeavor the Psalms plays a particularly critical role with its gritty realism. Not only is God speaking to his people through the Psalter, the Psalter speaks for God's people to him.

So the Psalms, like other books of the Bible, but in a remarkably different way, is designed to induce (seduce?) its readers to change their lives in thought, in feeling, and in action, to comply with the precepts, priorities, and practices of God's world (i.e., the theology of each psalm) that is displayed in, with, and through the inspired script.[9] And all the emotion and pathos, and

---

7. Modified from Beuken, "Psalm 16," 378.

8. See Eph 1:8–10. Thus the overarching interpretative arc of biblical history that I espouse is a "consummative-theological" hermeneutic. "Consummative" pertaining to God's ultimate goal; "theological" pertaining to how a christiconic theology is assimilated and Christ manifested in the lives of Christians (Rom 8:29) when the thrust of each pericope—pericopal theology—is discerned, curated, and applied in preaching.

9. I want to underscore here that the child of God is never to attempt a self-glorifying, flesh-driven, merit-seeking, grace-denying, faith-negating obedience to God's demands. That is legalism. Rather, with

pains and pleasures, as this walk in God's way is undertaken, is demonstrated herein, inviting us to use its words ourselves, in preaching about God and in praying to God. When all is said and done, the Psalter, psalm by psalm (as do other books pericope by pericope), nudges God's people towards Christlikeness—a christiconic mode of interpreting Scripture.[10]

That is to say—again!—that the A/author of each psalms is *doing* something with what he is saying. This theological agenda of the writer mandates that interpreters, particularly those who interpret for preaching purposes, attend not only to what is being said, but also to what is being *done* with what is said. In attempting to aid the preacher to arrive at this goal, my commentary has approached the Psalter in a unique fashion, undertaking a form of exegesis geared towards discerning the theological thrust of each psalm (pericopal theology)—*theological* exegesis.[11] It is a foundational conviction of this work that valid application of a pericope (here psalm) of Scripture may be arrived at only via this critical intermediary between text and praxis, pericopal theology.[12] The hermeneutical philosophy behind this commentary also holds that such valid application to change lives for the glory of God is the appropriate endpoint of every sermon. Thus the task of the preacher with a pastoral heart ought to include the delineation of specific ways in which the theological focus of the pericope may be translated into the real life of real people.

Inasmuch as the application propounded by homileticians in each sermon is faithfully assimilated into listeners' lives, creating Christian dispositions and forming Christlike character, the people of God will have aligned themselves to the will of God for the glory of God. Text will have become praxis, the people of God will have experienced and enjoyed divine blessings, and Christlikeness will have been inculcated in God's children: the economy of God furthered. As shepherds preach particular psalms to the flock as they see fit, those preachers fulfill the solemn responsibility, aided by the Holy Spirit, to align the people of God to the will of God, to walk in the ways of God, and thus to be blessed by God. And thus God's mission is being promoted, and the microcosmic scope of God's world instantiated in the here-and-now is gradually expanding into the macrocosm of God's world to be consummated soon: "thy Kingdom come!"

---

a faith-filled dependence upon the work of Christ and upon the power of the Spirit, the flesh is defeated, obedience to divine will is achieved, and God is glorified. So obedience to God is a God-glorifying, Spirit-driven, merit-excluding, grace-accepting, faith-exercising endeavor: a walk with God in the ways of God.

10. See Kuruvilla, *Privilege the Text!*, 238–69; Kuruvilla, *Vision for Preaching*, 131–48; and Kuruvilla, "Christiconic Interpretation."

11. See Introduction; Kuruvilla, *Privilege the Text!*, 33–65; and Kuruvilla, "Pericopal Theology," 265–83.

12. In the commentary, a crystallization of pericopal theology shows up as the "Theological Focus."

Bibliography

Alden, Robert L. "Chiastic Psalms (III): A Study in the Mechanics of Semitic Poetry in Psalms 101–150." *Journal of the Evangelical Theological Society* 21 (1978) 199–210.

Allen, Leslie C. *Psalms 101–150*. Word Biblical Commentary 21. Dallas: Word, 1983.

Aloisi, John. "Who Is David's Lord? Another Look at Psalm 110:1." *Detroit Baptist Seminary Journal* 10 (2005) 103–23.

Assis, Elie. "Why Edom? On the Hostility Towards Jacob's Brother in Prophetic Sources." *Vetus Testamentum* 56 (2006) 1–20.

Auffret, Pierre. "En mémoire éternelle sera le juste: Étude structurelle du Psaume CXII." *Vetus Testamentum* 48 (1998) 2–14.

———. *Essai sur la structure littéraire du Psaume 105*. Biblische Notizen Beiheft 3. Munich: Manfred Görg, 1985.

———. "Essai sur la structure littéraire du Psaume 137." *Zeitschrift für de alttestamentliche Wissenschaft* 92 (1980) 346–77.

———. "Et toi, tu béniras: Nouvelle étude structurelle du Psaume 109." *Rivista Biblica* 59 (2011) 331–52.

———. "Grandes sont les œuvres de YHWH: Étude structurelle du Psaume 111." *Journal of Near Eastern Studies* 56 (1997) 183–96.

———. *Hymnes d'Égypte et d'Israël: Études de structures littéraire*. Orbis Biblicus et Orientalis 34. Göttingen: Vandenhoeck & Ruprecht, 1981.

———. "Il est seigneur sur les nations: Étude structurelle du Psaume 110." *Biblische Notizen* 123 (2004) 65–73.

———. "'Je marcherai à la face de YHWH': Étude structurelle du Psaume 116 (suite)." *Old Testament Essays* 10 (1997) 161–77.

———. *Là montent les tribus: Étude structurelle de la collection des Psaumes des Montées, d'Ex 15, 1–18 et des rapports entre eux*. Berlin: de Gruyter, 1999.

———. *La sagesse a bati sa maison: Études de structures littéraires dans l'Ancien Testament et spécialement dans les Psaumes*. Orbis Biblicus et Orientalis 49. Göttingen: Vandenhoeck & Ruprecht, 1982.

———. "L'étude structurelle des Psaumes réponses et complements II (Pss. 61, 77, 82, 100, 138, 147)." *Science et Esprit* 49 (1997) 39–61.

———. "Louez YHWH, toutes les Nations! Étude structurelle du Psaume 117." *Biblische Notizen* 74 (1994) 5–9.

———. *Mais tu élargiras mon cœur: Nouvelle étude structurelle du Psaume 119*. Beihefte zur Zeitschrift für die alttestamentliche Wissenschaft 359. Berlin: de Gruyter, 2006.

———. *Merveilles à nos yeux: Étude structurelle de vingt psaumes dont celui de 1Ch 16,8–36*. Beihefte zur Zeitschrift für die alttestamentliche Wissenschaft 235. Berlin: de Gruyter, 1995.

———. "Note sur la structure littéraire du Psaume CXXXVI." *Vetus Testamentum* 27 (1977) 1–12.

———. "O bonheurs du peuple dont Yhwh est le Dieu: Nouvelle étude structurelle du psaume 144." *Vetus Testamentum* 60 (2010) 505–17.

———. "O Dieu, connais mon coeur: Étude Structurelle du Psaume CXXXIX." *Vetus Testamentum* 47 (1997) 1–22.

———. *Que seulement de tes yeux tu regardes . . . Étude structurelle de treize psaumes*. Beihefte zur Zeitschrift für die alttestamentliche Wissenschaft 330. Berlin: de Gruyter, 2003.

———. "'Souviens-toi YHWH!' Étude structurelle du Psaume 137: Réponses et complements." *Biblizche Zeitschrift* 41 (1997) 250–52.

———. "Tu me feras vivre—Étude structurelle du psaume 138." *Old Testament Essays* 18 (2005) 472–81.

———. *Voyez de vos yeux: Étude structurelle de vingt psaumes, dont le psaume 119*. Vetus Testamentum Supplement 48. Leiden: Brill, 1993.

Augustine. *Exposition on the Psalms: The Nicene and Post-Nicene Fathers, Series 1, Volume 8*. Edited by Philip Schaff. New York: Christian Literature Co., 1888.

Barbiero, Gianni, and Marco Pavan. "The Non-Violent Messiah of Psalm 110." *Biblische Zeitschrift* 58 (2014) 1–20.

———. "Ps 44,15; 57,10; 108,4; 149,7: בלאמים or בל־אמים?" *Zeitschrift für de alttestamentliche Wissenschaft* 124 (2012) 598–605.

———. "Psalm 132: A Prayer of 'Solomon.'" *Catholic Bible Quarterly* 75 (2013) 239–58.

———. "The Structure of Psalm 111." In *Wisdom for Life: Essays Offered to Honor Prof. Maurice Gilbert, SJ on the Occasion of His Eightieth Birthday*, edited by Nuria Calduch-Benages, 321–39. Berlin: de Gruyter, 2014.

Bar-Efrat, Shimon. "Love of Zion: A Literary Interpretation of Psalm 137." In *Tehillah le-Moshe: Biblical and Judaic Studies in Honor of Moshe Greenberg*, edited by Mordechai Cogan et al., 3–11. Winona Lake, IN: Eisenbrauns, 1997.

Barker, David G. "'The Lord Watches over You': A Pilgrimage Reading of Psalm 121." *Bibliotheca Sacra* 152 (1995) 163–81.

Barré, Michael L. "Psalm 116: Its Structure and Its Enigmas." *Journal of Biblical Literature* 109 (1990) 61–79.

Basson, Alec. "Image Schemata of Containment and Path as Underlying Structures for Core Metaphors in Psalm 142." *Old Testament Essays* 21 (2008) 261–72.

Berlin, Adele. "The Message of Psalm 114." In *Birkat Shalom: Studies in the Bible, Ancient Near Eastern Literature, and Post-Biblical Judaism Presented to Shalom M. Paul on the Occasion of His Seventieth Birthday*, edited by Chaim Cohen et al., 347–63. Winona Lake, IN: Eisenbrauns, 2008.

———. "Myth and Meaning in Psalm 114." In *Diachronic and Synchronic: Reading the Psalms in Real Time: Proceedings of the Baylor Symposium on the Book of Psalms*, edited by Joel S. Burnett et al., 67–80. Library of Hebrew Bible/Old Testament Studies 488. London: T. & T. Clark, 2007.

———. "The Rhetoric of Psalm 145." In *Biblical and Related Studies Presented to Samuel Iwry*, edited by Ann Kort and Scott Morschauser, 17–22. Winona Lake, IN: Eisenbrauns, 1985.

Beuken, W. A. M. "Psalm 16: The Path to Life." *Bijdragen* 41 (2013) 368–85.

Booij, Thijs. "Psalm 109:6–19 as a Quotation: A Review of Evidence." In *Give Ear to My Words: Psalms and Other Poetry in and around the Hebrew Bible: Essays in Honour of Professor N. A. van Uchelen*, edited by Janet Dyk, 92–106. Amsterdam: Societas Hebraica Amstelodamensis, 1996.

———. "Psalm 130:3–4: The Words and Their Context." In *"Unless Someone Guide Me . . . ": Festschrift for Karel A. Deurloo*, edited by J. W. Dyk et al., 237–45. Maastricht, Netherlands: Uitgeverji Shaker, 2001.

———. "The Role of Darkness in Psalm CV 28." *Vetus Testamentum* 39 (1989) 209–14.

Botha, P. J. "Psalm 101: A Supplication for the Restoration of Society in the Late Post-exilic Age." *HTS/Theological Studies* 72 (2016) 1–8.

Bracke, John M. "*šûb šebût*: A Reappraisal." *Zeitschrift für de alttestamentliche Wissenschaft* 97 (1985) 233–44.

Brodersen, Alma. *The End of the Psalter: Psalms 146–150 in the Masoretic Text, the Dead Sea Scrolls, and the Septuagint*. Beihefte zur Zeitschrift für die alttestamentliche Wissenschaft 505. Berlin: de Gruyter, 2017.

Brueggemann, Walter. "Bounded by Obedience and Praise: The Psalms as Canon." *Journal for the Study of the Old Testament* 50 (1991) 63–92.

———. *The Message of the Psalms: A Theological Commentary*. Augsburg Old Testament Studies. Minneapolis: Augsburg, 1984.

———. *The Psalms and the Life of Faith*. Edited by Patrick D. Miller. Minneapolis: Fortress, 1995.

———. *Theology of the Old Testament: Testimony, Dispute, Advocacy*. Minneapolis: Fortress, 1997.

Calvin, John. *Commentary on the Book of Psalms*. 5 vols. Translated by James Anderson. Grand Rapids: Eerdmans, 1949.

Ceresko, Anthony R. "A Poetic Analysis of Ps 105, with Attention to Its Use of Irony." *Biblica* 64 (1983) 20–46.

———. "Psalm 121: A Prayer of a Warrior?" *Biblica* 70 (1989) 496–510.

Cha, Kilnam. "Psalms 146–150: The Final Hallelujah Psalms as a Fivefold Doxology to the Hebrew Psalter." PhD diss., Baylor University, 2006.

Clifford, Richard J. "Style and Purpose in Psalm 105." *Biblica* 60 (1979) 420–27.

Coakley, Sarah. "On the Fearfulness of Forgiveness: Psalm 130.4 and Its Theological Implications." In *Meditations of the Heart: The Psalms in Early Christian Thought and Practice. Essays in Honour of Andrew Louth*, edited by Andreas Andreopoulos et al., 33–51. Turnhout: Brepols, 2011.

Davis, Ellen F. "Self-Inflicted Violence." In *The Art of Reading Scripture*, edited by Ellen F. Davis and Richard B. Hays, 294–99. Grand Rapids: Eerdmans, 2003.

Day, John N. "The Imprecatory Psalms and Christian Ethics." *Bibliotheca Sacra* 159 (2002) 166–86.

deClaissé-Walford, Nancy, et al. *The Book of Psalms*. New International Commentary on the Old Testament. Grand Rapids: Eerdmans, 2014.

Dobbs-Allsopp, F. W. "Psalm 133: A (Close) Reading." *Journal of Hebrew Scriptures* 8 (2008) 1–30.

Donner, Herbert. "Psalm 122." In *Text and Context: Old Testament and Semitic Studies for F. C. Fensham*, edited by W. Claasen, 81–91. Sheffield: JSOT, 1988.

Egwim, Stephen C. *A Contextual and Cross-Cultural Study of Psalm 109*. Biblical Tools and Studies 12. Leuven: Peeters, 2011.

Eitan, Israel. "An Identification of *tiškaḥ yěmīnī*, Ps 137." *Journal of Biblical Literature* 47 (1928) 193–95.

Estes, Daniel J. "Like Arrows in the Hand of a Warrior (Psalm CXXVII)." *Vetus Testamentum* 41 (1991) 304–11.

Falkenstein, A., and W. von Soden, eds. "Nisaba-Lied." In *Sumerische und akkadische Hymnen und Gebete*, 65–67. Zurich: Artemis, 1953.

Flesher, LeAnn Snow. "Psalm 126." *Interpretation* 60 (2006) 434–36.

Fokkelman, J. P. *Major Poems of the Hebrew Bible at the Interface of Prosody and Structural Analysis: Volume III: The Remaining 65 Psalms*. Assen: Van Gorcum, 2003.

Freedman, David Noel, et al. *Psalm 119: The Exaltation of Torah*. Biblical and Judaic Studies 6. Winona Lake, IN: Eisenbrauns, 1999.

Fretheim, Terence E. "Nature's Praise of God in the Psalms." *Ex Auditu* 3 (1987) 16–30.

Gardiner, Alan H. *The Admonitions of an Egyptian Sage from a Hieratic Papyrus in Leiden (Pap. Leiden 344 recto)*. Hildesheim: Olms, 1969.

Girard, Marc. *Les Psaumes Redécouverts: De la Structure au Sens: 101–150*. Montreal: Bellarmin, 1994.

Goldingay, John. *Psalms. Volume 3: Psalms 90–150*. Baker Commentary on the Old Testament. Grand Rapids: Baker, 2008.

Hill, Edmund. *Prayer, Praise and Politics: Reflections on 32 Psalms*. London: Sheed & Ward, 1973.

Holman, Jan. "A Semiotic Analysis of Psalm CXXXVIII (LXX)." In *In Quest of the Past: Studies on Israelite Religion, Literature and Prophetism*, edited by A. S. van der Woude, 84–100. Oudtestamentische Studiën 26. Leiden: Brill, 1990.

———. "The Structure of Psalm CXXXIX." *Vetus Testamentum* 21 (1971) 302–10.

Jarick, John. "The Four Corners of Psalm 107." *Catholic Bible Quarterly* 59 (1997) 270–87.

Jenkins, Steffen G. "A Quotation in Psalm 109 as Defence Exhibit A." *Tyndale Bulletin* 71.1 (2020) 115–35.

Jerome. *The Homilies of Saint Jerome 1 (1–59 On the Psalms)*. In The Fathers of the Church 48, translated by Marie Liguori Ewald, 79–89. Washington, DC: Catholic University of America Press, 1964.

Jung, Won-Seok. "The Davidic Persona in Psalms 138–145 (MT): The Movement and Development of the Portrait of David in the Psalter." PhD diss., Trinity Evangelical Divinity School, 2016.

Kalmanofsky, Amy. *Terror All Around: The Rhetoric of Horror in the Book of Jeremiah*. Library of Hebrew Bible/Old Testament Studies 390. London: T. & T. Clark, 2008.

Keel, Othmar. *The Symbolism of the Biblical World: Ancient Near Eastern Iconography and the Book of Psalms*. Translated by Timothy J. Hallett. Winona Lake, IN: Eisenbrauns, 1997.

Kern, Paul Bentley. *Ancient Siege Warfare*. Bloomington: Indiana University Press, 1999.

Kimelman, Reuven. "Psalm 145: Theme, Structure, and Impact." *Journal of Biblical Literature* 113.1 (1994) 37–58.

Kim, Sung-Soo. "Reading the Songs of Ascents (Psalms 120–134) in Context." PhD diss., Luther Seminary, 2003.

Kitz, Anne Marie. "An Oath, Its Curse and Anointing Ritual." *Journal of the American Oriental Society* 124 (2004) 315–21.

Knowles, Melody D. "To Sanction and to Subvert: The Reuses of Psalm 132 in the Hebrew Bible." In *Prayers and the Construction of Israelite Identity*, edited by Susanne Gillmayr-Bucher and Maria Häusl, 189–202. Atlanta: SBL, 2019.

Kselman, John S. "Psalm 101: Royal Confession and Divine Oracle." *Journal for the Study of the Old Testament* 33 (1985) 45–62.

Kuruvilla, Abraham. "The *Aqedah*: What Is the Author *Doing* with What He Is *Saying*?" *Journal of the Evangelical Theological Society* 55 (2012) 489–508.

———. "Christiconic Interpretation." *Bibliotheca Sacra* 173 (2016) 131–46.

———. *Genesis: A Theological Commentary for Preachers*. Eugene, OR: Resource Publications, 2017.

———. *A Manual for Preaching: The Journey from Text to Sermon*. Grand Rapids: Baker, 2019.

———. "Pericopal Theology." *Bibliotheca Sacra* 173 (2016) 3–17.

———. *Privilege the Text! A Theological Hermeneutic for Preaching*. Chicago: Moody, 2013.

———. *A Vision for Preaching: Understanding the Heart of Pastoral Ministry*. Grand Rapids: Baker, 2015.

Labuschagne, C. J. "The Metaphor of the So-Called 'Weaned Child' in Psalm cxxxi." *Vetus Testamentum* 57 (2007) 114–18.

Lambert, W. G. "A Neo-Babylonian Tammuz Lament." *Journal of the American Oriental Society* 103 (1983) 211–15.

Lee, Archie C. C. "Genesis I and the Plagues Tradition in Psalm CV." *Vetus Testamentum* 40 (1990) 257–63.

Leow, Wen-Pin. "Changing One's Tune: Re-reading the Structure of Psalm 132 as Complex Antiphony." *Old Testament Essays* 32 (2019) 32–57.

Levenson, Jon D. *The Love of God: Divine Gift, Human Gratitude, and Mutual Faithfulness in Judaism*. Library of Jewish Ideas 8. Princeton: Princeton University Press, 2015.

———. "The Temple and the World." *Journal of Religion* 64 (1984) 275–98.

Lux, Rüdiger. "Die Kinder auf der Gasse: Ein Kindheitsmotiv in der prophetischen Gerichts- und Heilsverkündigung." In *"Schaffe mir Kinder . . ." Beiträge zur Kindheit im alten Israel und in seinen Nachbarkulturen*, edited by Andreas Kunz-Lübcke and Rüdiger Lux, 197–221. Leipzig: Evangelische Verlagsanstalt, 2006.

Makujina, John. "The Interpretation of Ps 144,14: Applying a Pluralistic Approach to a Manifold Difficulty." *Biblica* 92 (2011) 481–502.

Maré, Leonard P. "Psalm 137: Exile—Not the Time for Singing the Lord's Song." *Old Testament Essays* 23 (2010) 116–28.

Marrs, Rick Roy. "A Cry from the Depths (Ps 130)." *Zeitschrift für de alttestamentliche Wissenschaft* 100 (1988) 81–90.

———. "The *Šyry-hm'lwt* (Psalms 120–134): A Philological and Stylistic Analysis." PhD diss., Johns Hopkins University, 1983.

Martin, Lee Roy. "The Chiastic Structure of Psalm 106." *Old Testament Essays* 31.3 (2018) 506–21.

———. "An Embedded Chiasm in the Narrative Structure of Psalm 105." *Journal for Semitics* 28.1 (2019) 1–14.

———. "'Oh Give Thanks to the Lord for He Is Good': Affective Hermeneutics, Psalm 107, and Pentecostal Spirituality." *Pneuma* 36 (2014) 355–78.

McCann, J. Clinton, Jr. "The Shape and Shaping of the Psalter: Psalms in Their Literary Context." In *The Oxford Handbook of the Psalms*, edited by William P. Brown, 350–62. Oxford Handbooks. Oxford: Oxford University Press, 2014.

Mensah, Michael Kodzo. *I Turned Back My Feet to Your Decrees (Psalm 119,59): Torah in the Fifth Book of the Psalter*. Österreichische Biblische Studien 45. New York: Lang, 2016.

Merrill, Eugene H. "Royal Priesthood: An Old Testament Messianic Motif." *Bibliotheca Sacra* 150 (1993) 50–61.

Miller, Patrick D. "The Poetry of Creation: Psalm 104." In *God Who Creates: Essays in Honor of W. Sibley Towner*, edited by William P. Brown and S. Dean McBride Jr., 87–103. Grand Rapids: Eerdmans, 2000.

———. "Psalm 130." *Interpretation* 33 (1979) 176–81.

Nel, Philip. "Psalm 132 and Covenant Theology." In *Text and Context: Old Testament and Semitic Studies for F. C. Fensham*, edited by W. Claassen, 183–91. Journal for the Study of the Old Testament Supplement Series 48. Sheffield: JSOT, 1988.

Prinsloo, Gert T. M. "Psalm 130: Poetic Patterns and Social Significance." *Old Testament Essays* 15 (2002) 453–69.

———. "Reading Psalm 112 as a 'Midrash' on Psalm 111." *Old Testament Essays* 32 (2019) 636–68.
———. "The Role of Space in the שירי המעלות (Psalms 120–134)." *Biblica* 8 (2005) 457–77.
Prinsloo, W. S. *Die Psalms leef: 'N Eksegetiese Studie van Psalm 3, 15, 23, 112, 126, 131, 136, 148*. Pretoria, South Africa: NG Kerk Boekhandel, 1988.
Purcell, Richard Anthony. "The King as Priest? Royal Imagery in Psalm 110 and Ancient Near Eastern Iconography." *Journal of Biblical Literature* 139 (2020) 275–300.
Reed, Gregory. "The Thanksgiving of YHWH's King: A Canonical Reading of Psalm 118." ThM thesis, Baptist Bible Seminary, 2020.
Reynolds, Carol Bechtel. "Psalm 125." *Interpretation* 8 (1994) 272–75.
Reynolds, Kent Aaron. *Torah as Teacher: The Exemplary Torah Student in Psalm 119*. Vetus Testamentum Supplement 137. Leiden: Brill, 2010.
Ross, Allen P. *A Commentary on the Psalms: Volume 3 (90–150)*. Grand Rapids: Kregel, 2016.
Singer, Dwight Charles. "The Literary Context of the Fourth Davidic Grouping in the Psalter (Psalms 138–145)." PhD diss., Westminster Theological Seminary, 2013.
Snyman, Fanie. "Reading Psalm 117 Against an Exilic Context." *Vetus Testamentum* 61 (2011) 109–18.
Sokolow, Moshe. "Saadiah Gaon's Prolegomenon to Psalms." *Proceedings of the American Academy for Jewish Research* 51 (1984) 131–74.
Soll, Will. *Psalm 119: Matrix, Form, and Setting*. Catholic Bible Quarterly Monograph Series 23. Washington, DC: Catholic Biblical Association of America, 199.
Tackmier, Bill J. "The Role of Psalm 118 in Worshiping Jesus the Messiah." *Wisconsin Lutheran Quarterly* 113 (2016) 243–51.
Todd, James M., III. "A Poetic and Contextual Analysis of Psalms 135–137." PhD diss., Southeastern Baptist Theological Seminary, 2010.
Tucker, W. Dennis, Jr. "Revisiting the Plagues in Psalm CV." *Vetus Testamentum* 55 (2005) 401–11.
Versluis, Arie. "'Knock the Little Bastards' Brains Out': Reception History and Theological Interpretation of Psalm 137:9." In *Violence in the Hebrew Bible: Between Text and Reception*, edited by Jacques van Ruiten and Koert van Bekkum, 373–96. Oudtestamentische Studiën 79. Leiden: Brill, 2020.
Vos, Johannes G. "The Ethical Problem of the Imprecatory Psalms." *Westminster Theological Journal* 4 (1942) 123–38.
Watson, W. G. E. *Classical Hebrew Poetry: A Guide to Its Techniques*. Journal for the Study of the Old Testament Supplement Series 26. Sheffield: JSOT Press, 1986.
———. "Reversed Rootplay in Ps 145." *Biblica* 62 (1981) 101–2.
Weinfeld, Moshe. "A Comparison of a Passage from the Šamaš Hymn (Lines 65–78) with Psalm 107." In *Vorträge gehalten auf der 28. Rencontre Assyriologique Internationale in Wien, 6–10 July 1981*, edited by H. Hirsch and H. Hunger, 275–79. Beiheft Archiv für Orientforschung. Horn, Austria: Berger, 1982.
Whitekettle, Richard. "A Communion of Subjects: Zoological Classification and Human/Animal Relations in Psalm 104." *Bulletin for Biblical Research* 21 (2011) 173–88.
Willis, John T. "Psalm 121 as a Wisdom Poem." *Hebrew Annual Review* 11 (1987) 435–51.
Zevit, Ziony. "Psalms at the Poetic Precipice." *Hebrew Annual Review* 10 (1986) 351–66.

Index of Keywords and Selected Topics

(by Psalm)

Aaron, 77, 99, 105, 106, 115, 118, 133, 135
Abandonment, 37
    by God, 9, 10, 13, 16, 22, 27, 37, 42–43, 50, 71, 77, 78, 88, 89, 94, 119
    by others, 31, 38, 69, 88, 142
Abide (and Abode, Lodge, also see Dwell, Inhabit), 15, 16, 26, 37, 43, 46, 49, 55, 65, 68, 74, 78, 84, 85, 87, 94, 102, 104, 120, 132, 135, 139
Abomination, 5, 14, 53, 88, 106, 107, 119
Abraham, 47, 105
Accountability, 141
Acrostic, 9, 10, 25, 34, 37, 111, 112, 119, 145
Adversaries (see Enemies)
Afflicted (also see Humble), 9, 10, 12, 22, 25, 34, 35, 37, 40, 44, 68, 69, 70, 72, 73, 74, 76, 82, 86, 88, 91, 107, 109, 119, 132, 147
Afterlife, hints of, 9, 16, 17, 30, 49, 71, 73, 103, 116
Aging, 37, 55, 71, 74, 77, 78, 92, 119, 148
Aha, 35, 40, 70
Agitated, 2, 55
Agriculture, 65, 67, 68, 72, 85, 92, 104, 129
Almighty, 68, 91
Altar, 26, 43, 51, 84, 118
Amen, 41, 72, 89, 106
Ambition, 131
Ambush, 10, 59
Angel(s), 78, 91, 103, 148
    of Yahweh, 34, 35
Anger, of God, 2, 6, 7, 18, 30, 38, 56, 58, 59, 69, 74, 76, 78, 79, 80, 85, 86, 88, 89, 90, 95, 102, 103, 106, 119, 145
Animals, 7, 8, 11, 17, 18, 20, 22, 29, 32, 33, 36, 42–43, 44, 49, 50, 51, 57, 58, 59, 63, 66, 68, 69, 73, 74, 79, 80, 91, 104, 106, 107, 114, 140, 144, 147, 148
Annihilation, 18, 54

Anointed, 18, 20, 28, 84, 89, 105, 132
Answer, 3, 4, 13, 17, 20, 22, 27, 34, 38, 55, 60, 65, 69, 81, 102, 108, 118, 119, 120, 138, 143
Ark, 132
Armies, 18, 27, 33, 44, 60, 68, 108, 103, 108, 136, 148
    God/Yahweh of, 24, 46, 48, 59, 69, 80, 84, 89, 103, 148
Arrogance, 5, 10, 59, 64, 75, 101, 119
Arrow, 18, 38, 45, 64, 91, 127, 144
Ascend, 24, 47, 68, 74, 132, 135
Ashes, 102, 113
Assembly (and Congregation), 1, 7, 22, 26, 35, 40, 47, 48, 68, 74, 82, 89, 107, 111, 149
Astronomical bodies, 8, 19, 58, 72, 74, 81, 89, 104, 113, 121, 136, 147, 148
Atheism, 10, 14
Attendants, 45
Awesomeness, of God 22, 33, 45, 65, 66, 68, 89, 99, 106, 111, 119, 139, 145

Babies (also see Children, Descendant, Generation), 8, 17, 137
Babylon, 87, 137
Balances, 62
Banner, 60
Barren, 113
Battle (also see War, Weapons), 18, 24, 55, 68, 78, 89, 133, 148
Beard, 133
Beast (also see Animals), 8, 49, 50, 73, 74, 79, 104
Beauty, 16, 48, 50, 68
    of God, 27, 45, 96
    of God's people, 45
Bed (also see Couch, Lying down), 36, 63, 132, 139
Beer, 69

365

Bees, 118
Belial, 41
Beloved, 60, 108, 109, 127
Belt, 109
Besieging, 31, 53
Betrayal, 4, 41, 55, 59, 119
Birds, 8, 11, 50, 55, 68, 78, 79, 84, 102, 103, 104, 105, 147, 148
Birth, 22, 48, 58, 71, 78, 87, 90
Bitterness, 64, 69, 73
Blameless, 18, 19, 37, 51, 64, 119
Blessing, from God, 1, 3, 5, 21, 24, 28, 29, 32, 33, 34, 37, 40, 41, 45, 65, 67, 72, 84, 89, 94, 106, 107, 109, 112, 115, 118, 119, 127, 128, 129, 133, 134, 137, 144
    upon God, 16, 18, 26, 28, 31, 34, 41, 63, 66, 68, 72, 89, 96, 100, 103, 104, 106, 113, 115, 118, 119, 124, 134, 135, 144, 145
    upon God's people, 37
    upon earth, 65, 132
Blind, 146
Blood, 5, 9, 16, 26, 30, 50, 55, 58, 59, 68, 72, 78, 79, 105, 106, 139
Blowing, 1, 68, 81, 147
Blows, 140
Boar (also see Animals), 80
Boasting, 10, 52, 73, 75, 94, 97
    in God, 34
Body parts (also see Bones, Eyes, Face, Feet, Flesh, Hands, Heart, Inner, Lips, Mouth), 3, 5, 7, 10, 17, 18, 21, 22, 23, 24, 26, 27, 37, 38, 40, 41, 44, 56, 57, 58, 60, 63, 64, 66, 68, 69, 71, 73, 74, 75, 77, 79, 81, 83, 88, 89, 94, 98, 105, 108, 109, 110, 112, 115, 118, 119, 124, 132, 133, 135, 136, 137, 139, 140, 141, 144, 145, 147, 149
Bones, 6, 22, 31, 32, 34, 35, 38, 42–43, 51, 53, 102, 109, 139, 141
Book (and Scroll), 40, 69, 139
Bow, 7, 11, 18, 21, 37, 44, 46, 60, 76, 78
Bowing, 5, 10, 20, 22, 45, 57, 72, 95, 107, 145, 146
Branch, 80, 104
Bread (also see Eating, Food), 14, 37, 41, 53, 78, 80, 102, 105, 127, 132
Breath, 18, 27, 33, 39, 62, 94, 135, 144, 150
Brevity of life, 39, 89, 102
Bribery, 15, 26
Bride, God's people as, 45
Brimstone, 11
Building, 127, 147
Burden, 55, 68, 81
Bury, 79

Calamity, 79, 80, 91
Call, 3, 4, 14, 17, 18, 30, 31, 42–43, 49, 50, 53, 55, 56, 61, 72, 79, 80, 81, 88, 91, 99, 102, 105, 116, 118, 119, 120, 138
    by God, 7, 10, 89, 105, 147
Canaan, 105, 106, 135
Captives of God, 68
Captors, 137
Caterpillar, 78
Celebration, 13, 14, 20, 21, 32, 35, 57, 59, 87, 90, 92, 104, 118
Chaff, 1, 35, 83
Chains, 2, 105, 116, 149
Chalice, 75
Chaos (also see Disorder), 9, 10, 24, 29, 46, 65, 74, 77, 89, 93
Chariot, 20, 68, 76, 104
Cherub(im), 18, 80, 99
Children (also see Babies, Descendant, Generation, Sons), 8, 34, 78, 80, 82, 103, 109, 113, 115, 127, 128, 137, 147
Choice, 25, 119
    by God, 33, 65, 78, 89, 105, 106, 132, 135
Citizenship, 87
City, 55, 59, 60, 107, 108, 122, 127
    of God, 46, 48, 87, 101, 122
Clap, 47, 98
Cleansing, 51, 73
Cleaving, 101, 119, 137
    to God, 63
    to the word of God, 119
Climate (and Seasons, Weather), 11, 18, 51, 65, 68, 72, 74, 77, 78, 84, 105, 135, 147, 148
Clothing, 22, 30, 35, 45, 69, 73, 102, 104, 109
Cloud, 18, 57, 68, 77, 78, 87, 97, 99, 104, 105, 108, 135, 147
Coals, 120, 140
Cognition, 119
Collar, 133
Comfort, 23, 69, 71, 86, 119
Commander, God as, 108
Commanding, by God (also see Judge, Law, Utterance, Word), 7, 19, 33, 42–43, 44, 68, 78, 89, 91, 105, 111, 112, 119, 133, 148
Commitment, 17, 18, 37, 40, 45, 50, 119, 132
Community, of God (also see Assembly), 16, 40, 68, 69, 70, 74, 107, 122, 133, 141, 142, 145, 149
Compassion of God (also see Mercies), 25, 40, 51, 69, 72, 78, 79, 102, 103, 106, 111, 112, 116, 119, 136
    of God's people, 112
Complain, 55, 64, 69, 77
Conception, 51
Concern of God, 82

366

INDEX OF KEYWORDS AND SELECTED TOPICS

Condescension of God, 113, 138
Confession, 32, 38, 51, 106
Confidence, 62, 78
Confusion, 55, 57, 107, 144
Congregation (see Assembly)
Conservation by God, 104
Consolation, 94
Conspiracy, 31, 83
Consume (also see Devour), 21, 37, 39, 49, 50, 52, 59, 69, 71, 78, 79, 102, 104, 119
Contemplating (also see Meditating), 27, 48
Contempt, 31, 107, 119, 123
Contentment, 131
Corpses, 79, 110
Corruption, 14, 53
Couch (also see Bed, Lying down), 41, 132
Count, 22, 40, 48, 71, 90, 139, 147
Council, of God's people, 111
    of heaven, 82, 89
Counsel, 2, 13, 14, 64, 71, 83, 107, 107
    of God (also see Instruction, by God), 16, 25, 32, 73, 106, 119
Courage, 27, 31
Courts of God 65, 84, 92, 96, 100, 135
Covenant, 25, 44, 50, 55, 74, 83, 89, 105, 106, 111, 132
Cover (and Uncover), 5, 18, 32, 44, 55, 68, 69, 71, 73, 78, 80, 84, 85, 91, 104, 105, 106, 119, 139, 140, 143, 147
Creation, 8, 24, 33, 50, 74, 93, 94, 95, 96, 98, 100, 102, 104, 115, 119, 121, 124, 134, 136, 139, 146, 148
Creature (also see Animals), 50, 68, 80
Creditor, 109
Crooked, 125
Crowbars, 74
Crowd (and Throng), 35, 42–43, 55, 68, 86
Crown, 8, 21, 89, 103, 132
Crushed, 34, 38, 44, 143
Cursing (also see Imprecation), 10, 59, 62, 109
    by God, 37, 119
Cut, 12, 31, 34, 37, 80, 88, 101, 109, 118, 128, 129

Dancing, 30, 149, 150
Darkness, 11, 18, 35, 38, 42–43, 69, 74, 82, 88, 91, 97, 104, 105, 107, 112, 139, 143
Daughter, 9, 45, 48, 97, 106, 137, 144
David, 18, 72, 78, 89, 122, 132, 144
Dawn, 46, 57, 108, 110, 119, 139
Dead, the (and Deadly), 17, 31, 79, 88, 106, 115, 143
Deafness, 28, 38, 58, 109
Death-shadow, 23, 44, 107

Death (and Dying), 6, 9, 13, 16, 18, 22, 30, 31, 33, 39, 49, 55, 61, 63, 73, 79, 82, 88, 102, 104, 106, 115, 116, 118, 119, 143
    of evildoers, 54, 55, 58, 69, 71, 104, 109
Deceit, 5, 10, 18, 24, 35, 52, 55, 78, 101, 119, 120, 139
Deeds of God, 8, 9, 17, 19, 28, 33, 44, 46, 64, 66, 71, 72, 77, 78, 80, 86, 90, 92, 95, 96, 102, 103, 104, 105, 106, 107, 111, 118, 119, 126, 138, 139, 143, 145, 146, 150
Deep (and Depths), 33, 36, 42–43, 64, 68, 69, 71, 77, 86, 88, 92, 95, 104, 106, 107, 130, 135, 139, 148
Defamation, 31
Delaying (also see Hastening), 22, 38, 39, 40, 70, 119
Delight, 1, 16, 102, 111, 119
    of God, 18
    in God's word, 1, 112, 119
Deliverance (and Rescue, Redemption, also see Save, Savior), 3, 4, 6, 7, 9, 12, 14, 18, 20, 22, 25, 27, 28, 31, 33, 34, 35, 36, 37, 38, 39, 40, 41, 50, 51, 52, 53, 54, 55, 56, 57, 59, 62, 65, 66, 67, 68, 69, 70, 71, 72, 74, 76, 77, 79, 80, 81, 82, 85, 86, 88, 91, 94, 95, 96, 97, 98, 106, 107, 108, 109, 116, 118, 119, 120, 140, 142, 143, 144
Demons, 91, 106
Depression, 42–43, 60, 109
Depths, 69, 88, 130, 135, 148
Descendants (also see Babies, Children, Generation), 21, 22, 25, 37, 112
Desert, 74, 106, 107
Deserts, 7, 35, 140
Desire, 10, 20, 21, 27, 34, 35, 38, 40, 41, 52, 73, 78, 105, 107, 112, 140, 145
    of God (also see Delight, of God, Pleasure, of God), 40, 45, 51, 68, 81, 132
Desolate, 40, 46, 63, 69, 73, 79, 143
Destruction (also see Killing, Perishing), 5, 11, 18, 32, 40, 52, 54, 55, 57, 59, 62, 63, 69, 74, 78, 91, 88, 89, 91, 105, 119
Devour (also see Consume), 18, 27, 57, 106
Devout, 4, 12, 16, 18, 30, 31, 32, 42–43, 50, 52, 79, 85, 86, 89, 91, 97, 116, 132, 145, 148, 149
Dew, 133
Discipline, 6, 32, 38, 39, 42–43, 118
Diseases, 6, 30, 38, 41, 103, 107, 147
Disorder (also see Chaos), 9, 10, 24, 46
Disorientation, psalms of, 3, 4, 6, 7, 9, 10, 11, 12, 13, 14, 17, 18, 22, 25, 26, 27, 28, 31, 35, 38, 39, 40, 41, 42–43, 44, 55, 56, 57, 58, 59, 60, 61, 62, 64, 69, 70, 71, 73, 77, 78, 79, 80, 82, 85, 86, 88, 89, 90, 94, 102, 106, 108, 109, 119, 120, 121, 123, 124, 125, 129, 130, 137, 139, 140, 141, 142, 143

367

INDEX OF KEYWORDS AND SELECTED TOPICS

Distress (and Sorrow, Disturbed, also see Afflicted, Trouble), 4, 6, 13, 18, 20, 25, 31, 34, 35, 37, 39, 40, 46, 50, 54, 59, 69, 71, 77, 86, 88, 89, 91, 102, 106, 107, 109, 116, 118, 119, 120, 124, 125, 126, 129, 138, 141, 142, 143, 144
Dog (also see Animals), 22, 59, 68
Doing (and Deed, Practice, Work), 14, 15, 17, 28, 33, 37, 45, 52, 53, 90, 92, 101, 103, 106, 107, 109, 115, 119, 135, 141, 148
    of God, 8, 9, 17, 19, 28, 33, 44, 46, 62, 64, 66, 71, 72, 77, 78, 86, 92, 95, 96, 102, 103, 104, 106, 107, 111, 118, 119, 138, 139, 143, 145, 146, 150
Door (also see Gate), 24, 78, 107, 141
Doubt, 73, 77
Dread, 14, 27, 53, 78, 119
Dream, 73, 126
Drink, 36, 50, 60, 69, 78, 80, 102, 110
Dry, 32, 63, 66, 95, 105, 107
Dung, 83
Dust (also see Mud, Sand), 7, 18, 22, 30, 44, 72, 78, 102, 103, 104, 113, 119
Dwell (also see Abide, Inhabit), 4, 5, 23, 27, 33, 55, 65, 68, 69, 72, 74, 75, 76, 91, 98, 101, 102, 107, 132, 133, 140, 143

Eagle, 103
Earth (also see Ground, Land, World), 2, 8, 12, 18, 19, 21, 22, 24, 33, 44, 45, 46, 47, 48, 50, 57, 58, 59, 61, 63, 65, 66, 67, 68, 69, 71, 72, 73, 74, 75, 76, 77, 78, 79, 81, 82, 83, 85, 89, 90, 94, 95, 96, 97, 98, 99, 100, 102, 103, 104, 106, 108, 109, 110, 112, 113, 114, 115, 119, 121, 124, 134, 135, 136, 138, 139, 140, 141, 146, 147, 148
Earthquake, 18, 46, 60, 68, 77, 99
East, 48, 75, 78, 103, 107
Eating (also see Bread, Food), 14, 22, 42–43, 44, 50, 53, 59, 63, 69, 73, 74, 78, 79, 102, 104, 106, 107, 111, 127, 128, 136, 141, 144, 145, 146
Egypt, 78, 80, 105, 106, 114
Eighty, 90
Embroidery, 45
Embryology, 139
Emptiness, 18, 24, 41, 89
Encampment, 27, 34, 69
Enemies (and adversaries, foes), 3, 5, 6, 7, 8, 10, 13, 17, 21, 22, 23, 25, 27, 30, 31, 35, 38, 41, 42–43, 44, 54, 56, 59, 60, 61, 62, 64, 66, 69, 70, 71, 72, 74, 78, 80, 81, 83, 87, 89, 91, 92, 93, 94, 97, 102, 105, 106, 107, 108, 110, 112, 118, 119, 123, 124, 127, 136, 138, 139, 143, 144
    conversion of, 2, 6, 7, 40, 46, 59, 64, 68, 71, 83, 109, 138
    defeat of, 3, 6, 18, 21, 35, 37, 40, 41, 45, 48, 55, 56, 59, 60, 68, 81, 83, 89, 94, 106, 108, 110, 118, 119, 136, 143
Enthronement of God (also see King, God as), 9, 11, 22, 29, 45, 47, 55, 61, 80, 89, 93, 97, 99, 103, 110, 113, 122, 123, 132
Envy, 37, 73
Establish, 7, 8, 9, 10, 24, 37, 48, 65, 68, 74, 78, 81, 87, 89, 93, 96, 99, 102, 103, 104, 107, 119, 140, 141, 147
Eternality of God, 90, 93, 102
Eternity (also see Forever), 2, 24, 87, 93, 133
Evening, 17, 55, 65
Evil (also see Harm, Sin), 5, 7, 15, 21, 23, 27, 50, 51, 52, 28, 34, 35, 36, 38, 40, 41, 49, 50, 51, 52, 54, 55, 56, 64, 71, 90, 91, 94, 101, 107, 109, 112, 119, 121, 140, 144
    hatred of, 5, 11, 15, 26, 31, 34, 45, 97, 101, 119, 139
    doers of (also see Sinners), 10, 22, 26, 27, 54, 55, 58, 69, 92, 94, 104, 109, 119, 140
Exaltation (also see Laud), 12, 18, 38, 49, 55, 75, 87, 89, 137, 140
    of God, 18, 21, 30, 34, 46, 47, 57, 92, 99, 107, 108, 118, 145, 148, 149
    by God, 37, 75, 89, 92
    of the righteous, 18, 37, 75, 89, 92, 112, 113
Examination by God, 7, 11, 17, 26, 139
Exodus, 66, 68, 77, 78, 81, 105, 106, 135, 136
Eyes (also see Body parts), 5, 6, 10, 11, 13, 15, 17, 18, 19, 25, 26, 31, 32, 33, 34, 35, 36, 38, 50, 54, 66, 69, 72, 73, 77, 88, 90, 91, 92, 94, 98, 101, 115, 116, 118, 119, 121, 123, 131, 132, 135, 139, 141, 145, 146
Exulting (see Joy, Rejoicing), 5, 9, 19, 25, 28, 35, 40, 60, 68, 7094, 96, 108, 119, 149

Face (also see Body parts), 17, 21, 34, 40, 42–43, 44, 55, 57, 61, 68, 69, 80, 83, 84, 89, 104, 106, 132
    of God, 11, 13, 17, 18, 25, 27, 30, 31, 34, 44, 56, 61, 62, 67, 68, 69, 86, 88, 89, 90, 98, 102, 104, 105, 106, 114, 116, 119, 139, 141, 142, 147
Failure, 60
Faintness, 61, 77, 107, 142, 143
Faithfulness (also see Trust), 37, 89, 102, 137
    of God, 30, 33, 36, 40, 54, 66, 78, 88, 89, 91, 92, 96, 98, 100, 105, 119, 143
    of the word, 111, 119
    to God, 12, 18, 31, 37, 44, 66, 78, 89, 101

Fall, 5, 7, 10, 16, 18, 20, 27, 35, 36, 37, 45, 55, 57, 68, 69, 73, 78, 82, 91, 105, 106, 118, 140, 141, 145
Falsehood (also see Lying), 4, 5, 12, 62, 63, 119, 120
Family, 22, 35, 38, 49, 50, 69, 96, 197, 122, 128
Far (also see Near), 10, 22, 35, 38, 48, 71, 73, 109, 119, 139
Fasting, 35, 69, 109
Fat, 63, 65, 66, 73, 109, 119
Father (see Parents)
Favor of God, 30, 90, 106, 143
Fear (and Terror, Horror, also see Dread), 3, 6, 10, 14, 18, 27, 31, 34, 36, 40, 46, 48, 49, 53, 55, 56, 64, 78, 83, 88, 90, 91, 104, 105, 112, 118, 119
Fearing, 23, 27, 46, 49, 52, 55, 60, 64, 76, 91, 112, 118, 119
   God, 2, 4, 5, 6, 9, 15, 19, 22, 25, 31, 33, 34, 36, 40, 47, 55, 61, 64, 66, 67, 78, 76, 85, 86, 90, 96, 102, 103, 111, 112, 113, 115, 118, 119, 128, 130, 135, 145, 147
   the word, 119
Fearlessness of God's people, 27, 112
Feet (also see Body parts), 8, 9, 17, 18, 22, 25, 26, 31, 36, 37, 38, 40, 47, 56, 58, 66, 68, 69, 73, 74, 77, 85, 89, 91, 94, 99, 105, 110, 115, 116, 118, 119, 121, 122, 132, 140
Fermenting, 75
Festival, 42–43, 81, 118
Fetters, 2, 105, 149
Fingers (also see Body parts), 8, 144
Fire (and Flame, Burning), 11, 18, 21, 29, 37, 38, 39, 46, 50, 51, 58, 66, 68, 69, 74, 76, 78, 79, 80, 83, 85, 88, 89, 97, 104, 105, 106, 118, 124, 140, 148
Firstborn, 78, 89, 105, 135, 136
Fish, 8, 105
Flattery, 5, 36
Fleeing, 11, 31, 39, 55, 68, 104, 114, 139
Flesh (also see Body parts), 16, 27, 38, 50, 56, 63, 65, 73, 78, 79, 84, 102, 109, 119, 136, 145
Flock (also see Pasture, Sheep, Shepherd), 65, 77, 78, 80, 100, 144
Flourishing, 37, 52, 66, 72, 90, 92
Flower (also see Plants), 103
Foes (see Enemies)
Food (also see Bread, Eating), 42–43, 59, 63, 69, 73, 74, 78, 79, 102, 104, 107, 111, 136, 144, 145, 146, 147
Foolishness (and Fool, also see Senseless, Stupid), 14, 39, 53, 69, 74, 107
Footsteps of God, 85, 132
Footstool, 99, 110

Foreign (and Foreigners), 18, 69, 81, 97, 114, 137, 144
Forest, 83, 96
Forever (also see Eternity), 5, 9, 10, 12, 18, 21, 28, 29, 30, 31, 33, 37, 41, 44, 45, 48, 49, 52, 55, 61, 66, 72, 73, 75, 77, 78, 79, 81, 85, 86, 89, 90, 100, 102, 103, 104, 105, 106, 107, 110, 111, 112, 113, 115, 117, 118, 119, 121, 125, 131, 133, 135, 136, 138, 145, 146, 148
Forgetting (also see Remembrance), 9, 10, 13, 31, 42–43, 44, 45, 50, 59, 74, 77, 78, 79, 102, 103, 106, 119, 137
Forgiveness (and Pardon), 25, 32, 51, 65, 85, 86, 90, 99, 103, 130, 143
Forty, 95
Fountain, 68
   of life, 36
Foxes, 63
Free (and Liberate), 22, 41, 89, 91, 102, 105, 107, 108, 116, 144, 146
Friend (and Companion), 31, 35, 38, 41, 45, 55, 69, 119, 122
Fruit (also see Grass, Plants), 1, 58, 72, 104, 105, 107, 127, 128, 132, 148
Futility, 4, 31, 60, 78, 89, 96, 101, 108, 119, 127, 139, 144
Fulfill, 20, 56, 61, 65, 66, 76, 116

Garments (and Clothing), 22, 30, 35, 45, 65, 69, 73, 89, 102, 104, 109, 132
Gate (also see Door), 9, 24, 69, 87, 100, 107, 118, 122, 127, 147
Generation (also see Babies, Children, Descendant), 10, 12, 14, 22, 24, 33, 45, 48, 49, 61, 69, 72, 73, 77, 78, 79, 85, 89, 90, 95, 100, 102, 105, 109, 112, 119, 126, 128, 145, 146
Gift (also see Tribute), 45, 68, 72
Glory, 3, 8, 21, 49, 84, 85, 106, 149
   of God, 8, 19, 24, 26, 29, 57, 63, 66, 67, 72, 76, 79, 85, 86, 87, 96, 102, 104, 107, 113, 115, 138, 145
God as Father, 68, 89
God as Most High, 7, 9, 18, 21, 46, 47, 50, 57, 73, 77, 78, 82, 83, 89, 91, 92, 97, 107
Gods, 82, 86, 95, 96, 97, 135, 136, 138
Gold (also see Silver, Wealth), 19, 21, 45, 68, 72, 105, 119, 135
Good, doing, 14, 34, 37
Goodness, 4, 14, 16, 21, 23, 25, 27, 31, 34, 35, 36, 37, 38, 39, 45, 51, 52, 53, 54, 65, 68, 69, 73, 84, 85, 86, 92, 100, 103, 104, 106, 109, 111, 112, 118, 119, 122, 125, 128, 133, 135, 136, 143, 145, 147
   of the word, 119

INDEX OF KEYWORDS AND SELECTED TOPICS

Grace, of God (also see Lovingkindness, of God), 6, 28, 30, 31, 45, 55, 84, 86, 116, 119, 130, 140, 142, 143
Grain, 4, 20, 65, 72, 78, 81, 129, 144, 147
Grandchildren (also see Babies, Children, Descendant, Generation), 128
Grass (also see Fruit, Plants), 23, 37, 72, 90, 92, 102, 103, 104, 106, 129, 147
Grave (and Pit, Tomb, Hole, also see Sheol), 5, 7, 9, 16, 28, 30, 35, 40, 49, 55, 57, 69, 88, 94, 103, 107, 119, 140, 143
Gray hair, 71
Greatness
   of God, 22, 31, 47, 48, 57, 66, 69, 71, 76, 77, 79, 86, 92, 95, 96, 97, 99, 103, 104, 106, 108, 111, 117, 126, 135, 136, 138, 145, 147, 150
   of God's people, 18, 21, 71
Grieving God, 78
Groaning (also see Sighing, Wailing), 5, 6, 12, 22, 31, 32, 38, 77, 79, 88, 90, 102, 107, 142
Ground (also see Earth, Land, World), 7, 17, 80, 83, 89, 104, 105, 107, 137, 143, 146, 147
Guidance of God, 27, 48, 143
Guilt, 5, 34, 51, 68, 69, 79, 90

Hail (also see Climate), 18, 78, 105, 148
Hair, 40, 68, 69, 71
Hand (and Arm, also see Body parts), of enemies, 10, 22, 26, 28, 31, 36, 37, 44, 55, 58, 71, 82, 76, 78, 82, 83, 89, 97, 106, 107, 115, 125, 129, 135, 140, 144
   of God, 8, 9, 10, 16, 17, 18, 19, 20, 21, 28, 31, 32, 38, 39, 44, 45, 48, 60, 63, 73, 74, 75, 77, 78, 79, 80, 81, 88, 89, 91, 92, 95, 98, 102, 104, 106, 108, 109, 110, 111, 118, 119, 136, 138, 139, 143, 144, 145
   of God's people, 7, 16, 18, 22, 24, 28, 37, 44, 47, 63, 68, 73, 77, 89, 109, 119, 121, 123, 125, 127, 128, 134, 137, 141, 142, 143, 144, 149
   right, 16, 17, 18, 20, 21, 26, 44, 45, 48, 60, 63, 74, 77, 78, 80, 89, 91, 98, 108, 109, 110, 118, 121, 137, 138, 139, 142, 144
Harm (and Hostility, Persecution, also see Evil, Sin), 5, 6, 7, 10, 14, 28, 36, 39, 41, 53, 55, 56, 59, 64, 66, 70, 90, 105, 106, 109
Harvest, 107, 126, 129
Hastening (also see Delaying), 22, 38, 55, 68, 70, 71, 106, 119, 143
Hatred (and Despising, Animosity), 36, 50, 120
   of evil, 5, 11, 15, 26, 31, 45, 97, 101, 119, 139
   of God, 5, 21, 95, 68, 81, 83, 106, 139
   of God's people, 9, 18, 22, 25, 34, 35, 38, 41, 44, 55, 69, 71, 86, 89, 105, 106, 118, 119, 129
   by God, 5, 11, 22, 45, 51, 69, 73, 102
   by God's people, 26, 31
Head (also see Body parts), 3, 7, 18, 21, 22, 23, 24, 27, 38, 40, 44, 60, 64, 66, 68, 69, 71, 74, 83, 108, 109, 110, 118, 133, 140, 141
Healing, 30, 103, 146
Health, 38, 92
Hearing, 18, 19, 31, 34, 38, 44, 48, 49, 50, 51, 58, 59, 62, 66, 69, 78, 85, 92, 97, 106, 115, 132, 138, 141
   by God, 4, 5, 6, 10, 17, 18, 22, 27, 28, 30, 31, 34, 39, 40, 54, 55, 61, 64, 65, 66, 76, 78, 84, 94, 102, 106, 116, 119, 130, 143, 145
Heart (also see Body parts), 4, 7, 9, 10, 11, 12, 13, 14, 15, 16, 17, 19, 20, 21, 22, 24, 25, 26, 27, 28, 31, 32, 33, 34, 35, 36, 37, 38, 39, 40, 41, 44, 45, 46, 48, 49, 51, 53, 55, 57, 58, 61, 62, 64, 66, 69, 73, 74, 76, 77, 78, 81, 83, 84, 86, 90, 94, 95, 97, 101, 102, 104, 105, 107, 108, 109, 111, 112, 119, 125, 131, 138, 139, 140, 141, 143, 147
Heartbroken, 34, 51, 69, 147
Heaven, 2, 8, 11, 14, 18, 19, 20, 29, 33, 36, 50, 53, 57, 68, 69, 71, 73, 76, 78, 79, 809, 85, 89, 96, 97, 102, 103, 104, 105, 107, 108, 113, 115, 119, 121, 123, 124, 134, 135, 136, 139, 144, 146, 147, 148
Heels (also see Body parts), 56
Height (and High, also see God as Most High), 7, 10, 18, 20, 27, 36, 56, 59, 61, 68, 69, 71, 75, 78, 91, 92, 93, 102, 103, 104, 107, 113, 138, 139, 144, 148
Help from God, 5, 10, 18, 20, 22, 27, 28, 39, 31, 33, 34, 35, 37, 39, 40, 44, 46, 54, 59, 60, 63, 70, 71, 72, 79, 86, 88, 89, 94, 102, 108, 109, 115, 118, 119, 121, 124, 145, 146, 147
Heritage (also see Inheritance, Portion, Possession), 127
Hiding (and Concealing), 9, 19, 38, 40, 51, 55, 69, 78, 90, 139, 140, 142
   by God, 10, 13, 17, 22, 27, 31, 32, 40, 44, 51, 55, 64, 69, 88, 89, 102, 104, 119, 143
Highways, 84
Hill (also see Meadow), 24, 50, 65, 72, 114
History of God's people, 22, 44, 78, 105, 136
Holiness related to God, 2, 3, 5, 11, 15, 20, 22, 24, 28, 29, 30, 33, 43, 46, 47, 48, 51, 60, 63, 65, 68, 71, 74, 77, 78, 79, 87, 89, 93, 96, 97, 98, 99, 102, 103, 105, 106, 108, 110, 111, 114, 134, 138, 145, 150
Holy place, 20, 24, 63, 74, 114, 134, 150
Home, 68, 101, 127
Honey, 19, 81, 119
Honored by God, 15, 73, 91, 112
Honoring God, 50

INDEX OF KEYWORDS AND SELECTED TOPICS

Hope (also see Wait), 9, 25, 27, 37, 38, 39, 40, 52, 62, 69, 71, 119, 130, 145, 146
Hopelessness, 25, 88
Hoping on the word, 119
Horn, 18, 22, 75, 89, 92, 112, 132, 148
Horror, 31, 55, 88
Horse, 20, 32, 33, 76, 147
Hounding, 10, 56, 57
House, 101, 127, 128
    of God (also see Temple, Tent), 5, 23, 26, 27, 36, 42–43, 52, 55, 65, 66, 69, 84, 92, 93, 116, 118, 122, 134, 135
Humankind (and Mankind, Mortals), 8, 9, 10, 17, 22, 33, 36, 39, 45, 49, 53, 56, 57, 58, 60, 62, 66, 73, 80, 82, 89, 90, 94, 103, 104, 107, 108, 115, 116, 118, 135, 144, 145, 146
Humble (and Humbling, also see Afflicted), 25, 34, 75, 76, 107
Humiliation (and Disgracing), 4, 35, 40, 44, 69, 70, 71, 74, 83
Hunger, 34, 50, 107, 146

Ice, 147
Idolaters, 16, 31, 44, 78, 96, 97, 106, 115, 135, 139
Illness (and Sickness, also see Plague, Wounds), 6, 31, 35, 38, 41, 69, 103, 109
Image (also see Idolaters), 97, 106
Imagination, 50, 73
Immanence of God, 113, 138, 145
Imprecation (also see Cursing), 7, 35, 58, 59, 69, 83, 109, 137, 139
Imprisonment (also see Captives of God, Prisoner), 68, 69, 79, 88, 102, 105, 146, 149
Incense, 141
Increase, 16, 25, 44, 62, 71, 72, 73, 107
Inhabit (and Habitation, also see Abide, Dwell), 26, 33, 49, 68, 71, 79, 83, 84, 107
Inheritance (also see Heritage, Portion, Possession), 2, 16, 28, 33, 37, 47, 49, 61, 69, 78, 79, 105, 111, 136
    of God (also see Heritage, Portion), 68, 74, 82, 106, 127
    of the word, 119
Injustice, 7, 53, 58, 64, 82
Inner (and Innards, Insides, also see Body parts), 7, 16, 17, 22, 26, 30, 31, 39, 40, 51, 57, 73, 108, 109, 128, 139
Innocence, 6, 7, 10, 15, 17, 18, 24, 25, 26, 40, 59, 69, 73, 78, 79, 94, 106, 130, 139, 143
Insects, 105, 108
Instruction (and Teaching), 34, 45, 51, 105,
    by God (also see Counsel, of God), 16, 25, 27, 32, 50, 86, 94, 119, 132, 143, 144

Instruments, musical (also see Musicmaking, Singing, Song), 33, 42–43, 45, 49, 57, 68, 71, 81, 87, 92, 98, 49, 108, 137, 147, 149, 150
Integrity, 15, 26, 41, 78, 101
    of God, 101
Intercession, 20, 106
Interest, 15
Iron, 2, 105, 107, 149
Isaac, 105
Israel, 14, 22, 25, 41, 50, 53, 59, 68, 69, 71, 72, 73, 76, 78, 80, 81, 83, 89, 98, 103, 1095, 106, 114, 115, 118, 121, 122, 124, 125, 128, 129, 130, 131, 135, 136, 147, 148, 149
Ivory, 45

Jackals, 44
Jacob, 14, 20, 22, 24, 44, 46, 47, 53, 59, 75, 76, 77, 78, 79, 81, 84, 85, 87, 94, 99, 105, 114, 132, 146, 147
Jaw, 3, 58
Jealousy, 106
    of God, 79
Jerusalem (also see Zion), 51, 68, 76, 79, 102, 116, 122, 125, 128, 137, 147
Jordan, 42–43, 114
Joseph, 77, 78, 80, 81, 105
Joy (and Jubilation, also see Exulting, Pleasure, Rejoicing), 2, 4, 5, 9, 13, 14, 16, 19, 20, 21, 27, 30, 31, 32, 33, 34, 35, 28, 40, 41, 42–43, 44, 45, 46, 47, 48, 49, 50, 51, 53, 58, 59, 63, 64, 65, 66, 67, 68, 69, 70, 71, 7, 84, 85, 86, 89, 90, 92, 95, 96, 97, 98, 100, 104, 105, 106, 107, 109, 113, 115, 118, 119, 122, 126, 132, 135, 137, 145, 147, 149, 150
Judah, 48, 60, 68, 69, 76, 78, 97, 108, 114
Judge (and Judging, also see Commanding by God, Law, Utterance, Word), 2, 58, 82, 109, 141, 148
    God as, 1, 7, 9, 10, 11, 17, 19, 26, 33, 35, 36, 37, 48, 50, 51, 54, 58, 64, 67, 68, 72, 75, 76, 82, 89, 94, 96, 97, 98, 99, 101, 103, 105, 110, 111, 140, 143, 146, 149
Justice (also see Injustice), 9, 10, 33, 35, 37, 54, 72, 82, 101, 106, 112, 119, 137, 140

Keeper, God as, 12, 17, 34, 41, 56, 66, 89, 91, 116, 121, 127, 140, 141, 145, 146
Keeping the word, 19, 78, 89, 103, 105, 119, 132
Killing (and Slaying, also see Destruction, Perishing), 10, 17, 34, 37, 44, 59, 79, 88, 94, 109
    by God, 17, 59, 78, 89, 139

371

King, 2, 18, 20, 21, 33, 48, 63, 68, 72, 76, 89, 102, 105, 110, 119, 135, 136, 138, 144, 148, 149
    God as (also see Enthronement of God), 2, 5, 9, 10, 24, 29, 44, 45, 47, 48, 55, 59, 61, 68, 72, 74, 84, 89, 93, 95, 96, 97, 98, 99, 103, 113, 123, 145, 146, 149
        Messiah as, 2, 45, 61, 72, 89, 110, 132
Kingdom, 22, 45, 46, 68, 79, 102, 105, 135, 145
Kiss, 85
Kneeling, 17, 72, 78, 95, 109
Know, 1, 4, 9, 14, 16, 18, 20, 25, 31, 32, 35, 36, 37, 39, 40, 41, 44, 46, 48, 50, 51, 53, 55, 56, 59, 67, 69, 71, 73, 74, 76, 77, 78, 79, 81, 82, 83, 87, 88, 89, 90, 91, 94, 95, 98, 100, 101, 103, 104, 105, 106, 109, 119, 135, 138, 139, 140, 142, 143, 144, 145, 147
Knowledge, 19, 73, 92, 94, 119, 139

Labor, 7, 78, 90, 104, 105, 109, 127, 128
Lack, absence of, 23, 34
Lament, 11, 14, 17, 30, 61, 74, 88, 106, 119, 142
Lamp (also see Light), 18, 105, 119, 132
Land (also see Earth, Ground, World), 10, 16, 25, 27, 35, 37, 41, 42–43, 44, 48, 49, 60, 61, 66, 68, 78, 80, 81, 85, 88, 95, 101, 105, 106, 107, 116, 132, 135, 136, 142
    of the living, 27, 52, 116, 142
Laud (also see Exaltation), 49, 63, 106, 117, 145, 147
Laughter of God, 2, 37, 59,
    of the righteous, 52, 126
Law (and Decree, Lawless, Precept, Saying, Statute, also see Commanding by God, Judge, Utterance, Word), 1, 2, 7, 12, 18, 19, 25, 37, 40, 50, 78, 81, 84, 89, 91, 94, 95, 99, 103, 105, 111, 119, 122, 132, 147, 148
Leader (and Leadership), 20, 21, 63, 101, 118, 132, 141, 146
Lean, 109
Lebanon, 29
Legs, 147
Lending, 15, 37, 112
Levi, 135
Leviathan, 74, 104
Life (also see Soul), 7, 16, 17, 26, 27, 30, 31, 34, 36, 38, 42–43, 49, 59, 63, 64, 66, 71, 74, 78, 88, 103, 104, 128, 143, 146
    book of, 69
    brevity of, 39, 55, 78, 89, 90, 102, 103, 109, 119, 144
    forever, 49, 89, 133
    longevity of, 21, 23, 34, 61, 72, 89, 91, 93, 128, 133

Light (also see Darkness, Lamp), 56, 112, 119, 139
    God, related to, 4, 13, 18, 19, 27, 36, 43, 44, 56, 74, 78, 89, 90, 97, 104, 105, 112, 118, 119, 136, 139, 148
Lightning 18, 77, 78, 97, 135, 144
Lion, 7, 17, 22, 34, 35, 57, 58, 91
Lips (also see Body parts), 12, 16, 17, 21, 22, 31, 34, 40, 45, 51, 59, 63, 66, 71, 81, 89, 90, 106, 116, 119, 120, 140, 141
    of God, 89
Living, 18, 22, 27, 30, 33, 34, 41, 42–43, 49, 52, 55, 56, 58, 72, 84, 89, 116, 118, 119, 124, 138, 142, 143, 145
    God as, 42–43, 84
    by the word, 119
Locusts, 78, 105, 109
Loins, 38, 69
Longing, for deliverance, 119
    for God, 33, 42–43, 63, 84, 119, 143
    for the word, 40, 106, 119
Lots, casting, 16, 22
Love, by God, 11, 33, 37, 47, 60, 78, 87, 99, 108, 127, 146
    for the word, 119
    of evil, 4, 11, 52, 109
    related to God, 5, 18, 26, 31, 40, 45, 69, 70, 84, 97, 116, 119, 122, 145
    unrequited, 109
Lovingkindness, of God, 5, 6, 13, 17, 18, 21, 23, 25, 26, 31, 32, 33, 36, 40, 44, 48, 51, 52, 57, 59, 62, 63, 66, 69, 77, 85, 86, 89, 90, 92, 94, 98, 100, 101, 103, 106, 107, 108, 109, 115, 117, 118, 119, 136, 138, 143, 145, 147
    of God's people, 141
Low, 8, 35, 38, 79, 88, 113, 116, 136, 138, 142, 147
Lying, down (also see Bed, Couch), 4, 23, 41, 57, 68, 88, 104, 139
    in speech (also see Falsehood), 58, 59, 78, 89, 116

Magnify, 34, 35, 40, 41, 69, 70
Maid(en) (also see Virgin), 68: 86, 116, 123
Majesty, of God, 8, 29, 45, 68, 76, 90, 93, 96, 104, 111, 145
Manna, 78
Marriage, 45
Martyrdom, 44
Massah, 95
Meadow (also see Hill), 65
Meaninglessness of life, 49
Meat, 78
Meditating (also see Contemplating), 19, 27, 48, 49, 63, 77, 104, 105, 119, 142, 143, 145
    on the word, 1, 119

INDEX OF KEYWORDS AND SELECTED TOPICS

Melchizedek, 110
Melting, 22, 46, 58, 68, 97, 107, 147
Mercies of God (also see Compassion), 86, 99, 119, 145
Meribah, 81, 95
Messengers of God, 104
Messiah of God, 2, 6, 22, 61, 72, 89, 110, 132
Midday, 55
Ministers of God, 104
Miscarriage, 58
Mistress, 123
Mocking, 2, 22, 35, 69, 73, 80
Moon (also see Astronomical bodies), 8, 72, 81, 89, 104, 121, 136, 148
Money (see Gold, Silver, Wealth)
Morning, 5, 59, 65, 73, 90, 92, 101, 143
Mortal, 8, 9, 56, 103, 144
Moses, 77, 99, 103, 105, 106
Moth, 39
Mother (see Parents)
Mountain (or mount), 2, 3, 11, 15, 18, 30, 36, 42–43, 43, 46, 48, 65, 68, 72, 74, 75, 78, 80, 83, 87, 90, 95, 98, 99, 104, 114, 121, 125, 133, 144, 147, 148
Mouth (also see Body parts), 5, 8, 10, 17, 18, 19, 22, 33, 34, 35, 36, 37, 38, 39, 40, 49, 50, 51, 54, 55, 58, 59, 62, 63, 66, 69, 71, 73, 78, 81, 89, 105, 107, 109, 115, 119, 126, 135, 138, 141, 144, 145, 149
　of God (also see Body parts), 119, 138
Mud (also see Dust, Sand), 18, 69
Murder (also see Killing), 94
Musical instruments (also see Musicmaking, Singing, Song), 33, 42–43, 45, 49, 57, 68, 71, 81, 87, 92, 98, 49, 108, 137, 147, 149, 150
Musicmaking (also see Musical Instruments, Singing, Song), 7, 9, 21, 30, 33, 47, 57, 59, 61, 66, 71, 75, 81, 92, 98, 104, 105, 108, 135, 138, 144, 149, 150
Myrrh, 45
Mystery, 78

Name, 9, 16, 41, 49, 83, 109, 147
　of God, 5, 7, 8, 9, 18, 20, 22, 23, 25, 29, 31, 33, 34, 44, 45, 48, 52, 54, 61, 63, 66, 68, 69, 72, 74, 75, 76, 79, 80, 83, 86, 89, 91, 92, 96, 99, 100, 102, 103, 105, 106, 109, 111, 113, 115, 116, 118, 119, 122, 124, 129, 135, 138, 139, 140, 142, 143, 145, 148, 149
Nations, 2, 7, 9, 18, 22, 33, 44, 45, 46, 47, 59, 67, 78, 79, 82, 86, 96, 97, 98, 102, 105, 106, 108, 110, 113, 115, 117, 118, 135
　worshiping by, 2, 7, 22, 45, 46, 47, 66, 67, 68, 72, 86, 87, 97, 98, 99, 102, 102, 117, 126, 148

Near (also see Far), 22, 32, 34, 65, 69, 73, 75, 85, 91, 119, 145, 148
Necklace, 73
Needy (also see Poor), 9, 12, 35, 37, 40, 69, 70, 72, 74, 82, 86, 107, 109, 112, 113, 132
Neighbor, 15, 28, 88
Net (also see Snare, Trap), 9, 10, 25, 31, 35, 57, 66, 140, 141
Night, 1, 4, 6, 16, 17, 19, 22, 30, 32, 42–43, 55, 59, 63, 74, 77, 88, 90, 91, 92, 104, 105, 119, 121, 134, 136, 139
Nobles, 45, 47, 83, 107, 113, 118, 146
Noontime, 91
North, 89, 107
Numbers, 12, 79, 90, 91, 95, 105, 119, 144
Nursing, 131

Obedience, of angels, 103
　of humans (outside the Torah Psalms, 1, 19, 119, also see Purity, Integrity, Righteousness) 15, 24, 26, 40, 50, 67, 78, 85, 95, 103, 105, 111, 130, 132, 139, 147
　of nature, 148
Offering (also see Sacrifice), 20, 40, 51, 54, 56, 66, 96, 119, 141
Offspring, 21, 89, 78, 105, 135, 136
Oil, 23, 45, 89, 92, 133
Old, 37, 148
Olive, 52, 128
Omnipresence of God, 139
Omniscience of God, 94, 139
Omnitemporality of God, 139
Opponents (also see Enemies), 7, 56, 57, 103, 120
Oppression, 9, 10, 11, 12, 13, 14, 17, 18, 22, 25, 27, 28, 31, 42–43, 44, 53, 55, 56, 58, 59, 61, 62, 64, 69, 71, 72, 73, 74, 76, 83, 86, 94, 106, 109, 119, 137, 140, 141
Order, 9, 10, 24, 46
Orientation, psalms of, 1, 2, 5, 8, 15, 16, 19, 20, 21, 23, 28, 33, 34, 36, 46, 49, 50, 52, 53, 54, 63, 65, 66, 67, 68, 72, 75, 76, 81, 83, 84, 91, 92, 93, 95, 96, 97, 98, 99, 100, 101, 103, 104, 105, 107, 110, 111, 112, 113, 114, 115, 116, 117, 118, 119, 122, 127, 128, 131, 132, 133, 134, 135, 136, 138
Orphan, 10, 68, 82, 94, 109, 146
Outcome of the wicked, 73
Owner, God as, 50

Palace, 45, 122, 144
Palate, 22, 119, 137
Palm (also see Body parts) 26, 98, 119
　of God (also see Body parts), 139
Panting, 42–43, 119
Parable, 80

Parched, 68, 143
Parents, 22, 27, 35, 39, 44, 45, 49, 50, 51, 69, 71, 78, 95, 103, 106, 109, 113, 131, 139, 146
Partiality, 82
Partnering with God, 24, 60
Past, 22, 44, 78, 105, 136
Pasture (also see Flock, Sheep, Shepherd), 23, 37, 65, 74, 79, 83, 95, 100
Path (and Way, Track), 8, 23, 78, 80, 84, 89, 102, 107, 110, 139, 140, 142
    of God, 5, 10, 17, 18, 25, 27, 32, 37, 44, 50, 65, 67, 77, 81, 86, 101, 103, 107, 119, 128, 138, 143, 145
    of the righteous, 1, 16, 18, 37, 39, 50, 85, 95, 119, 139, 142
    of the wicked, 1, 2, 17, 35, 36, 37, 49, 107, 119, 139, 146
Peace, 4, 7, 28, 29, 34, 35, 37, 55, 72, 73, 85, 119, 120, 122, 125, 128, 147
Pen, 45
Peoples (see Nations)
Perfection, 50, 64, 119
Perishing (also see Destruction, Killing) of the wicked, 1, 2, 4, 9, 10, 18, 21, 37, 49, 68, 69, 73, 74, 80, 81, 83, 89, 92, 94, 101, 112, 143, 146
Perishing, eternal, 9, 69, 81
Perversity, 18, 101, 125
Pessimism, 11
Pharaoh (also see Ruler, King), 135
Pilgrimage, 84, 120, 121, 122, 123, 124, 125, 1226, 127, 128, 129, 130, 131, 132, 133, 134
Pillars, 75, 99, 144
Pity, 72, 90,
Plague (also see Illness), 38, 41, 78, 91, 105, 106
Plan (and Intention), 33, 56,
    of God, 24, 33, 40
Planting (and Transplanting), 1, 44, 80, 92, 94, 104, 107
Plants, (also see Flower, Fruit, Grass, Tree, Wheat), 1, 29, 37, 52, 72, 74, 78, 80, 81, 90, 92, 96, 103, 104, 105, 128, 147, 148
Pleasure, of God (also see Delight, of God, Desire of God), 35, 41, 44, 85, 147
    in God, 16
    in the word, 119
Plowing, 129, 141
Plot (and Conspire, Scheme), 2, 10, 21, 31, 37, 83, 119, 140
Plunder, 44, 69, 76, 89, 109
Polemic, 68
Politics, 2, 101
Pomp, 49
Poor (also see Needy), 49, 82, 102, 113

Population, 47, 57, 67
Portent (also see Wonders of God), 78, 105, 135
Portion (also see Heritage, Inheritance, Possession, Share), 16, 60, 63, 68, 73, 108, 119, 125
    God, 16, 73, 119, 142
    of the wicked, 11, 17
Possession (also see Heritage, Inheritance, Portion), 83
    by God, 2, 44, 82, 104, 135
    by God's people, 25, 37, 44, 61, 69, 105
Potter, 2
Power (and Strength, Might), 64, 77, 83, 103, 135, 147
    of God, 6, 8, 18, 20, 21, 22, 24, 28, 29, 30, 43, 46, 59, 61, 62, 63, 65, 66, 68, 71, 73, 74, 77, 78, 80, 81, 84, 86, 89, 93, 96, 99, 106, 105, 108, 111, 118, 132, 140, 145, 147, 150
    of God's people, 10, 18, 22, 29, 33, 38, 68, 71, 78, 88, 89, 90, 102, 112, 118, 127, 128, 138
Purpose, 17, 64
Praise (also see Magnify), 7, 8, 9, 21, 22, 29, 31, 33, 34, 35, 40, 42–43, 44, 45, 46, 48, 51, 53, 56, 63, 64, 65, 66, 68, 69, 70, 71, 76, 79, 86, 92, 96, 98, 99, 100, 101, 102, 103, 105, 106, 109, 111, 112, 113, 115, 117, 119, 135, 142, 145, 146, 147, 148, 149, 150
Prayer (and Request), 4, 6, 17, 20, 21, 35, 37, 39, 42–43, 54, 55, 61, 65, 66, 69, 72, 80, 84, 86, 88, 102, 106, 109, 141, 143
Precious, 17, 36, 72, 116
Presence of God (also see Face of God), 11, 14, 15, 16, 17, 21, 22, 23, 24, 27, 42–43, 51, 65, 68, 69, 73, 84, 92, 102, 131, 132, 140, 143
Presumption, 30
Preservation, 25, 34
    by God, 12, 31, 32, 33, 40, 41, 61, 64, 79, 86, 97, 140, 141
Prey, 124
Pride (and Arrogant, Pride), 5, 10, 12, 17, 18, 31, 36, 40, 47, 59, 73, 86, 89, 90, 94, 101, 119, 123, 131, 138, 140
Priesthood, 78, 99, 110, 132
Prince, 45, 68, 76, 82, 105, 119, 148
Prisoner (also see Captives of God, Imprisonment), 68, 69, 102, 107, 146
Procession, 42–43, 68
Proclaiming, 9, 19, 22, 30, 40, 59, 64, 68, 69, 71, 75, 81, 92, 95, 96, 97, 111, 142, 145, 147
Profaning, 35, 74, 89
Prophet, 74, 105
Prosperity, 10, 30, 37, 49, 72, 73, 85, 144
    of the wicked, 10, 37, 49, 73
Protection, 5, 12, 23, 17, 28, 27, 32, 34, 46, 48, 55, 57, 59, 61, 63, 78, 81, 84, 105, 119, 121, 146

INDEX OF KEYWORDS AND SELECTED TOPICS

Provision of God, 34, 65, 78, 81, 84, 68, 104, 105, 114, 136, 147
Provocation of God, 106
Punishment (also see Recompense), 1, 2, 7, 11, 17, 28, 36, 53, 54, 55, 57, 58, 63, 64, 68, 69, 77, 78, 79, 80, 81, 82, 83, 88, 89, 94, 95, 104, 106, 107, 112, 129, 138, 140, 141, 143, 145, 146, 149
Purity (also see Integrity, Obedience, Righteousness), 18, 19, 24, 73, 101, 119
Pursuit, 7, 18, 23, 31, 34, 35, 38, 69, 71, 83, 119, 142, 143

Quail, 105
Queen, 45
Quiet (also see Silence), 35, 83, 131, 139

Rahab, 87, 89
Rain, 11, 65, 68, 72, 77, 78, 84, 105, 135, 147
Ransom (also see Deliverance, Redemption), 49, 69
Ravens, 147
Razor, 52
Re-creation, 51
Reaping, 107, 126, 129
Rebellion, 2, 25, 32, 36, 37, 39, 51, 59, 65, 66, 78, 103, 106, 107
Rebuke, 6, 9, 18, 38, 39, 68, 73, 76, 80, 94, 104, 106, 119
Recompense (also see Punishment, Reward), 18, 28, 31, 37, 41, 57, 58, 62, 91, 94, 137, 138, 142
Recounting, 22, 48, 50, 66, 71, 73, 75, 78, 79, 88, 96, 102, 107, 118, 119, 145
Redemption (also see Deliverance, Ransom), 19, 25, 26, 31, 33, 34, 44, 49, 55, 69, 71, 72, 74, 77, 78, 103, 106, 107, 111, 119, 130
Reed Sea, 106, 136
Refining, 12, 26, 66, 105, 119
Refuge (also see Stronghold), 5, 7, 9, 11, 14, 16, 17, 18, 25, 31, 34, 37, 46, 55, 57, 59, 61, 62, 64, 71, 73, 91, 94, 118, 141, 142, 144
Regret of God, 90, 106
Reign (see Kingship)
Rejection, 36, 106, 118
 by God, 43, 44, 53, 60, 74, 77, 78, 88, 89, 108, 119
Rejoicing (also see Exulting, Joy), 1, 4, 5, 9, 13, 16, 18, 19, 20, 21, 22, 27, 30, 32, 33, 35, 37, 42–43, 45, 46, 47, 48, 51, 53, 58, 62, 63, 64, 65, 66, 67, 68, 70, 87, 89, 90, 92, 94, 95, 96, 97, 98, 100, 102, 104, 106, 109, 111, 112, 113, 118, 119, 126, 132, 137, 145, 147, 149
 by God, 18, 22, 51, 147
Relenting by God, 106, 110

Remembrance (and Forgetting, Memory), 6, 9, 20, 22, 30, 31, 34, 42–43, 44, 45, 50, 59, 77, 78, 79, 83, 88, 89, 97, 98, 102, 103, 105, 106, 109, 111, 112, 115, 119, 135, 137, 143, 145
 by God, 9, 10, 13, 42–43, 44, 74, 77
Renew, 51, 103, 104
Reorientation, psalms of, 18, 24, 30, 32, 45, 47, 51, 74, 87, 48, 126, 144, 145, 146, 147, 148, 149, 150
Repentance, 7, 25, 39, 41, 119
Reproach (and Accusation, Reviling), 7, 10, 17, 22, 31, 39, 42–43, 44, 55, 69, 71, 74, 78, 79, 89, 102, 109, 119
Reprobate, 15
Reproof, 50, 141
Reptiles (also see Animals), 58, 91, 140, 148
Reputation of God (see Glory)
Rescue (see Deliverance)
Resting (and Rest), 23, 55, 94, 95, 116, 125, 131, 132
Restoration, 14, 19, 23, 35, 53, 60, 80, 85, 116, 126
Revenge, of God, 99
Reward, 19, 95, 127
Riddle, 49
Ridicule (also see Mocking), 3, 10, 22, 42–43, 44, 69, 73, 74, 79, 80, 102, 115, 123
Riding, 45, 66, 68
Right hand, of God, 16, 17, 20, 21, 44, 45, 48, 60, 63, 74, 77, 78, 80, 89, 98, 108, 110, 118, 138, 139
 of the needy, 15, 91, 109, 121, 137, 142
 of the wicked, 26, 89, 144
Righteous, 1, 4, 5, 7, 11, 14, 15, 17, 18, 31, 32, 33, 34, 37, 49, 52, 55, 58, 64, 68, 69, 72, 75, 92, 94, 97, 106, 112, 113, 118, 119, 125, 132, 140, 141, 142, 146
 exaltation of, 18, 75, 113
Righteousness, 17, 106, 112, 132
 of God, 5, 7, 9, 11, 22, 31, 33, 35, 36, 40, 45, 48, 50, 51, 65, 69, 71, 72, 85, 88, 89, 92, 94, 96, 97, 98, 99, 103, 111, 116, 119, 129, 143, 145
 of God's people (also see Integrity, Obedience, Purity), 4, 18, 19, 35
 of the word, 19, 119
Rising (and Raising), 10, 81, 104, 107, 113, 148
 of the wicked, 1, 17, 18, 27, 35, 36, 44, 54, 59, 86, 89, 92, 109, 139, 140
 of the righteous, 20, 41, 78, 88, 119, 127
 of God, 3, 7, 9, 10, 12, 17, 18, 35, 44, 68, 74, 82, 94, 102, 132
Rising sun, 113
River (also see Stream), 24, 36, 46, 66, 72, 74, 78, 80, 89, 93, 98, 104, 105, 107, 114, 137

375

INDEX OF KEYWORDS AND SELECTED TOPICS

Roaring (and Uproar), 22, 39, 46, 65, 74, 83, 96, 98, 104
Rob (and Thief), 35, 50, 62
Robe (also see Garments), 45, 129, 133
Rock (and Cliff), 27, 40, 78, 81, 104, 105, 114, 137, 141
    God as, 18, 19, 28, 31, 42–43, 61, 62, 71, 78, 89, 92, 94, 95, 144
Roof, 129
Root, 9, 52, 80
Rope, 2, 18, 116, 118, 119, 129, 140
Ruin, 9, 14, 18, 38, 53, 74, 79, 89, 91, 94, 102, 109
Ruler (also see King), 2, 8, 10, 32, 45, 47, 58, 72, 76, 82, 83, 89, 102, 105, 107, 110, 113, 119, 122, 135, 138, 141, 146, 148, 149
Running, 19, 59, 78, 119, 147

Sackcloth, 30, 35, 69
Sacrifice (also see Offering), 4, 27, 40, 50, 51, 54, 106, 107, 116
    of children, 106
Safety (also see Stability), 4, 16, 31, 59, 69, 78, 84, 89, 91, 107, 122, 20, 144
Samuel, 99
Sanctuary (also see Temple), 68, 73, 74, 78, 96
Sand (see also Dust, Mud), 78, 139
Sandal, 60, 108
Satan as Belial, 41
Satiated by God, 37, 81, 103, 104, 105, 107, 132, 145
Satisfaction, 17, 22, 36, 37, 59, 63, 65, 73, 81, 90, 91, 103, 104, 105, 107, 132, 145, 147
Save, 6, 7, 17, 18, 22, 31, 33, 34, 37, 43, 50, 60, 71, 82, 91
Savior, 40, 70
Scatter, 18, 44, 53, 68, 89, 92, 106, 112, 141, 144, 147
Scepter, 45, 60, 108, 110, 125
Scoffing, 1, 59
Scroll, 40, 139
Sea, 24, 33, 46, 65, 66, 68, 69, 72, 74, 77, 78, 80, 89, 93, 95, 96, 98, 104, 106, 107, 114, 135, 136, 139, 146, 148
Secrets (and Covert), 44, 61, 64, 101, 102, 107, 122
Seed, 89, 105, 106, 126
Seeking, 4, 35, 37, 38, 40, 63, 70, 71, 109, 122, 142
    by God, 9, 119
    of God, 2, 5, 9, 10, 14, 22, 24, 25, 27, 34, 40, 53, 64, 69, 70, 83, 91, 104, 105, 119, 141, 144
Senseless (also see Foolishness, Stupid), 49, 73, 92, 94
Servant (and Slave), 19, 27, 31, 34, 35, 69, 78, 79, 86, 89, 90, 100, 102, 105, 109, 113, 116, 119, 123, 132, 134, 135, 143, 144

Serving, 2, 18, 22, 72, 97, 100, 101, 102, 103, 106
Seven/seventy, 12, 79, 90, 119
Shade, 121
Shadow, 17, 23, 36, 39, 44, 57, 63, 73, 80, 91, 102, 107, 109, 140, 144
Shame, 6, 25, 31, 35, 40, 44, 53, 69, 70, 71, 83, 86, 109, 119, 129, 132
Share, 16, 78, 105, 142
Sheep (also see Animals, Flock, Pasture, Shepherd), 8, 44, 49, 68, 74, 78, 79, 95, 119
Shelter, God as, 27, 31, 61, 76, 90, 91
Sheol, 6, 9, 16, 18, 30, 31, 49, 55, 86, 88, 89, 116, 139, 141
Shepherd, death as, 49
    God as, 23, 28, 77, 78, 79, 80, 95, 100
Shield, 3, 5, 7, 18, 28, 33, 35, 59, 84, 89, 91, 115, 119, 144
Shining of God, 31, 50, 67, 80, 94, 119, 132
Ships, 48, 107
Shout, 5, 20, 27, 32, 33, 35, 41, 47, 51, 59, 60, 63, 65, 66, 67, 71, 81, 84, 89, 90, 92, 95, 96, 98, 100, 108, 132, 145, 149, 150
Sibling, 50, 69
Sighing (also see Groaning, Wailing), 38
Silence (also see Quiet), 4, 30, 32, 38, 39, 50, 62, 65, 83, 107, 115
    of God, 22, 28, 35, 44, 50, 83
Silver (also see Gold, Wealth), 12, 15, 66, 68, 105, 115, 119, 135
Sin (and Iniquity, Rebellion, also see Evil, Harm), 2, 4, 5, 18, 19, 25, 31, 32, 36, 37, 38, 39, 40, 41, 49, 51, 59, 65, 66, 68, 69, 78, 79, 85, 89, 90, 92, 94, 103, 106, 107, 109, 119, 130
Singing (also see Musical Instruments, Musicmaking, Song, new), 13, 21, 27, 28, 33, 40, 42–43, 57, 59, 65, 68, 69, 77, 87, 89, 95, 96, 98, 101, 104, 105, 106, 108, 118, 119, 137, 138, 144, 147, 149
Single, 68
Sinners (and Doers of iniquity, also see Evil, doers of), 1, 25, 26, 51, 94, 101, 104, 125, 141
Slander, 15, 101
Sleep (and Slumber), 3, 4, 76, 78, 90, 121, 127, 132
    of God, 44, 121
Slip, 35, 37, 66, 73, 90
Smile, 39
Smoke, 18, 37, 66, 74, 102, 104, 119, 144, 148
Snail (also see Animals), 58
Snare (also see Net, Trap), 9, 18, 38, 64, 69, 106, 109, 124, 140, 141
Snakes (also see Animals), 58, 91, 140, 148
Snow, 51, 68, 147, 148
Sojourning, 39, 61, 105, 119, 120, 140, 146
Sold, 105
    by God, 44

Solitary, 68
Son, 45, 89, 106, 127, 132, 144
Song, new, 33, 40, 96, 98, 144, 149
Sorrow, 13, 39, 106, 116, 119
Soul (also see Life), 3, 6, 7, 10, 11, 13, 16, 17, 19, 22, 23, 24, 25, 26, 30, 31, 33, 34, 35, 41, 42–43, 43, 44, 49, 54, 55, 56, 57, 62, 63, 66, 69, 70, 71, 72, 74, 77, 78, 84, 86, 88, 89, 94, 97, 103, 104, 107, 109, 116, 119, 120, 121, 123, 124, 130, 131, 138, 139, 141, 142, 143, 146
Sound, 5, 19, 38, 42–43, 47, 77, 81, 93, 98, 102, 104, 115, 118, 150
South, 78, 89, 126
Sovereignty of God, 8, 29, 33, 66, 74, 75, 82, 97, 105, 108, 109, 115, 127, 131, 135
Sowing, 97, 107, 126
Speech, direct, 2, 16, 29, 30, 31, 32, 35, 38, 39, 40, 41, 42–43, 52, 55, 58, 66, 70, 73, 75, 77, 87, 89, 91, 94, 96, 102, 106, 107, 116, 118, 119, 122, 124, 126, 129, 132, 139, 140, 142, 145
 of God, 2, 12, 19, 27, 32, 35, 46, 50, 60, 68, 75, 81, 82, 85, 87, 89, 90, 91, 95, 105, 106, 108, 110, 132
 of nature, 19
 of the wicked, 3, 4, 10, 11, 12, 13, 14, 22, 35, 40, 41, 42–43, 52, 53, 59, 64, 70, 71, 73, 74, 78, 79, 83, 94, 115, 137
Spices, 75
Spirit, of animals, 104
 of God, 104, 106, 139, 143
 of humankind, 31, 32, 34, 51, 76, 77, 78, 88, 104, 142, 143, 146
Splendor of God, 8, 45, 71, 76, 78, 93, 96, 104, 111, 145, 148
Spurn, 74, 107
Stability (and Shaking, also see Safety, Stumbling, Tottering), 7, 8, 9, 10, 16, 18, 21, 24, 30, 37, 40, 46, 48, 55, 59, 62, 65, 68, 69, 74, 78, 82, 87, 89, 93, 96, 102, 104, 107, 119, 140, 147
Staff (and Rod), 2, 23, 89
Stand, 33, 38, 39, 104, 111, 112, 119
 of the wicked, 2, 5, 76, 89, 101, 109
 of the righteous, 20, 22, 24, 26, 30, 31, 41, 45, 84, 94, 122, 130, 134, 135, 147
 of God, 10, 82, 107, 109, 119
Stars (also see Astronomical bodies), 8, 136, 147, 148
Steps, 17, 18, 37, 40, 44, 57, 73, 74, 85, 89, 119
Stones, 91, 102, 118
Stool (see Footstool)
Stranger, 54, 94, 109
Straying from the word, 119
Stream (also see River), 42–43, 46, 65, 74, 78, 83, 119, 124, 126

Street, 18, 31, 55
Strife, 31, 55
Stronghold (and Steadfastness, also see Refuge), 51, 60, 78, 89, 108, 112
 God as, 18, 27, 28, 31, 37, 46, 48, 52, 59, 62, 71, 91, 94, 144
Stubbornness, 78, 81
Stumbling (also see Stability, Tottering), 9, 17, 27, 31, 35, 38, 56, 64, 73, 105, 107, 116, 119
Stupid (also see Foolishness, Senseless), 49, 73, 92, 94
Success, from God, 20, 21
 of God's people, 1, 20, 21, 118, 148
Summer, 74
Summons of God, 50
Sun (also see Astronomical bodies), 19, 50, 58, 72, 74, 84, 89, 104, 113, 121, 136, 148
 God as, 84
Supplication (for grace), 6, 28, 30, 55, 86, 116, 119, 130, 140, 142, 143
Support, 18, 37, 71, 91, 104
Surround, 5, 17, 18, 22, 32, 40, 49, 88, 89, 97, 109, 118, 1125, 128, 140
Sustainer God as, 54, 55, 145
Sustenance by the word, 119
Swallowed, 124
Swarm, 78, 104, 105
Swear, 102
Swearing (also see Vows), 15, 24, 89, 95, 102, 119, 132
 by God, 110
Sweet, 19, 55
Sword (also see Weapons), 22, 44, 45, 55, 59, 63, 64

Table, 23, 69, 78, 128
Taste, 34
Tears (also see Weeping), 16, 42–43, 56, 126, 139
Teeth (also see Body parts), 3, 57, 58, 112, 124
Temple (also see House of God), 5, 11, 15, 24, 26, 27, 29, 42–43, 48, 52, 63, 65, 66, 68, 69, 73, 74, 78, 79, 83, 84, 92, 93, 96, 118, 122, 132, 134, 135, 138
Temptation, 11, 141
Tempting God, 78
Tent (also see Temple), 27, 52, 69, 78, 83, 84, 118
 of God, 15
Terminate (and Exterminate), 46, 73, 106, 145
Testing, of God, 78, 95
 by God, 17, 66
Testifying to nations (also see Testimony, Witness), 9, 18, 49, 57, 67, 77, 96, 102, 103, 105, 108
Testimony (also see Testifying, Witness), 40, 51, 71, 119, 124, 138

INDEX OF KEYWORDS AND SELECTED TOPICS

Thanksgiving, 6, 7, 9, 18, 26, 28, 30, 31, 33, 35, 42–43, 44, a45, 52, 54, 57, 67, 69, 71, 75, 79, 86, 88, 92, 95, 97, 100, 105, 106, 107, 108, 109, 111, 116, 118, 119, 122, 136, 138, 139, 140, 142, 145, 147
Thirst, 42–43, 63, 69, 104, 107
Thorns, 58, 118
Thoughts, 64, 92, 94, 139, 146
    of God, 139
Thousand (also see Numbers), 3, 50, 68, 84, 90, 91, 105, 119, 144
Thread, 45
Throat (also see Body parts), 5, 69, 115, 149
Throne, 45, 47, 89, 93, 11, 122, 132
    of God (and Enthroned), 9, 11, 22, 29, 45, 47, 55, 61, 80, 89, 93, 97, 99, 103, 110, 113, 123
    of the wicked, 94
Throw, 2, 37, 50, 60, 102, 108, 141
Thunder, 104
Tongue, 5, 12, 22, 31, 34, 45, 50, 51, 52, 55, 57, 64, 68, 119, 120, 137, 140
Topography, 114
Torment, 31
Tottering (also see Stability, Stumbling), 15, 46, 60, 62, 93, 94, 96, 112, 121, 125
Tower, 48, 61
Trample, 7, 44, 60, 68, 91, 108
Transcendence of God, 113, 138, 145
Transience, 62, 89, 90, 103, 144, 146
    of the wicked, 37
Trap (also see Net, Snare), 9, 31, 35, 38, 47, 64, 66, 69, 91, 109, 119, 124, 140, 142
Treachery, 4, 41, 55, 59, 119
Tree (and Forest, also see Plants), 1, 29, 50, 52, 74, 80, 83, 92, 96, 104, 148
Trembling, 48, 55, 96, 114, 119
Tribe, 74, 78, 105, 122
Tribute (also see Gift), 68, 72, 76
Triumph (and Victory), 41, 54, 49, 65, 66, 92, 95, 98, 100, 112
    of God, 45, 60, 108
Trouble (also see Afflicted, Distress), 7, 9, 10, 25, 34, 35, 44, 55, 73, 88, 94, 119, 140
Trust (and Believe, also see Faithfulness), 3, 4, 6, 7, 10, 11, 12, 14, 15, 20, 21, 22, 25, 26, 27, 31, 32, 33, 37, 38, 40, 44, 52, 54, 55, 56, 57, 60, 62, 65, 71, 74, 78, 86, 88, 91, 106, 112, 115, 116, 118, 119, 124, 125, 140, 143, 146
    in idols, 115, 135
    in riches, 49, 52
    in the word, 119
Truth (and truthfulness), 5, 15, 25, 26, 31, 40, 42–43, 45, 51, 57, 61, 69, 71, 85, 86, 89, 108, 111, 115, 117, 119, 132, 138, 145, 145
    of God's word, 119
Tumbleweed, 83

Unclean, 106
Understanding, 14, 32, 47, 49, 50, 53, 64, 73, 82, 92, 94, 106, 107, 119
    of the word, 14, 47, 119, 147
    by God, 33, 132, 147
Ungratefulness of enemies, 35
Unity, 47, 133
Universality, 150
Upholding, 112,
    by God, 9, 18, 41, 111, 119
Upper limb, of God (also see Body parts), 44, 77, 79, 89, 98, 136
    of the wicked (also see Body parts), 10, 37
Uprightness, of God, 25, 45, 67, 75, 92, 96, 98, 99, 111
    of God's people, 7, 11, 25, 32, 33, 36, 37, 49, 64, 84, 94, 97, 107, 112, 119, 125, 140
    of the word, 33, 111, 119
Uproot, 9, 52, 80
Utterance (also see Commanding by God, Judge, Law, Word), 5, 17, 19, 36, 37, 45, 54, 59, 71, 139, 141,
    of God, 18, 68, 778, 105, 107, 119, 138, 147

Valley, 23, 60, 65, 84, 104, 108
Vengeance, 79, 149
    of God, 18, 94
Venom 58
Verdict, 72, 76, 140
Victory (also see Judge, Justice), 20, 21, 27, 45, 47, 68, 76, 81, 95, 110, 118, 149
Vindication, 7, 35, 37, 42–43, 82
Vindictive, 44
Vine (also see Plants), 80, 128
Violence, 3, 7, 17, 18, 25, 27, 35, 37, 54, 55, 58, 59, 68, 72, 73, 74, 86, 140
Virgins (also see Maid[en]), 45, 78, 148
Visiting by God, 17, 65, 106
Voice, 19, 58, 77, 142
    of the afflicted, 3, 5, 6, 18, 26, 27, 28, 31, 55, 64, 66, 77, 86, 116, 119, 130, 140, 141, 142
    of enemies, 44, 55, 74
    of God, 18, 29, 46, 68, 81, 95, 103, 106
Vows (also see Swearing), 22, 50, 61, 65, 66, 76, 105, 116

Wailing (also see Groaning, Sighing), 9, 22, 31, 34, 38, 77, 88, 107, 142
Wait (also see Hope, 130
    upon God, 4, 31, 33, 37, 38, 39, 42–43, 62, 65, 71, 104, 119, 131

INDEX OF KEYWORDS AND SELECTED TOPICS

upon the word, 119, 130, 131
Waking, 17, 35, 44, 57, 59, 73, 102, 108
Walking, 1, 12, 15, 23, 26, 32, 48, 55, 56, 78, 81, 82, 84, 86, 89, 101, 115, 116, 119, 128, 138, 142
Walls, 18, 51, 55, 62, 80, 89, 122, 144
Wandering, 56, 58, 95, 107, 119
War (also see Battle, Weapons), 18, 20, 24, 27, 46, 55, 78, 89, 120, 140, 144
Warrior, 19, 33, 45, 52, 76, 78, 120
    God as, 45, 68
Wasting, 6, 32, 78, 106, 107, 119, 143
Water (and Flood), 1, 6, 18, 22, 23, 29, 32, 33, 42–43, 46, 58, 63, 65, 66, 69, 73, 74, 77, 78, 79, 81, 84, 93, 104, 105, 106, 107, 109, 114, 119, 124, 136, 144, 147, 148
Waterfalls, 42–43
Wax, 22, 68, 97
Weak, 6, 31, 72, 82, 102, 109, 112
Wealth (and Rich), 4, 15, 36, 37, 39, 45, 49, 52, 62, 63, 73, 52, 112, 119
Weapons (also see Arrow, Battle, Bow, Shield, War), 7, 11, 18, 21, 22, 35, 37, 44, 45, 46, 55, 57, 59, 60, 63, 64, 76, 78, 89, 149, 127
Weeping (also see Tears), 6, 30, 69, 80, 84, 102, 119, 126, 137
West, 75, 103, 107
Wheat (also see Plants), 81, 147
Whisper, 41
Wicked, 1, 3, 5, 7, 9, 10, 12, 17, 28, 31, 32, 34, 36, 37, 39, 43, 50, 55, 58, 68, 71, 73, 75, 82, 91, 92, 94, 101, 104, 106, 109, 112, 119, 129, 139, 140, 141, 145, 146, 147
Widow, 68, 78, 94, 109, 146
Wife, 109, 128
Wilderness, 29, 55, 65, 68, 75, 78, 95, 102, 106, 107, 136
Wind, 1, 11, 18, 35, 48, 55, 77, 78, 103, 104, 135, 147, 148
Wine, 4, 60, 75, 78, 104, 119
Wings, 17, 18, 36, 55, 57, 61, 63, 68, 78, 91, 104, 139, 148
    of God, 17, 36, 57, 61, 63, 91
Winter, 74
Wisdom (and Wise), 19, 36, 37, 49, 51, 90, 104, 105, 107, 111, 112, 119

of God, 19, 51, 104, 111
Witness (also see Testifying, Testimony), 27, 35, 50, 89
Womb, 22, 58, 71, 110, 127, 139
Women, 68, 113
Wonderfulness, of the word, 119
Wonders of God, 9, 17, 26, 31, 40, 71, 72, 75, 77, 78, 86, 88, 89, 98, 105, 106, 107, 111, 118, 131, 136, 1139, 145
Wool, 147
Word (also see Commanding by God, Judge, Law, Utterance), 19, 22, 35, 36, 44, 45, 49, 52, 55, 59, 64, 69, 78, 94, 109, 119, 137, 148
    of God, 17, 33, 50, 56, 103, 105, 106, 107, 119, 130, 147
Work (or labor, toil), 7, 78, 90, 104, 105, 109, 127, 128
World (also see Earth, Ground, Land), 9, 17, 18, 19, 24, 33, 49, 50, 77, 89, 90, 93, 96, 97, 98
Worm (also see Animals), 22
Worry, 13
Worship, 2, 22, 26, 27, 42–43, 48, 51, 66, 76, 84, 86, 95, 96, 97, 99, 118, 122, 132, 133, 135, 136, 138, 150
    by leaders, 20
    by nations, 2, 7, 22, 45, 46, 47, 66, 67, 68, 72, 86, 87, 97, 98, 99, 102, 102, 117, 126, 148
    inappropriate, 50
Worthlessness, 4, 31, 60, 78, 89, 96, 101, 108, 119, 127, 139, 144
Wounds (also see Illness), 38, 64, 69, 109, 147
Writing, 40, 45, 102, 139, 149

Yearning, 63, 84
Years, 31, 61, 77, 78, 90, 95, 102
Young, 17, 29, 34, 37, 50, 51, 58, 68, 69, 78, 84, 91, 104, 115, 119, 147, 148
Youth, 25, 37, 71, 88, 89, 103, 110, 119, 127, 129, 144, 148

Zeal, 69, 119
Zion (also see Jerusalem), 2, 9, 14, 20, 50, 51, 53, 65, 69, 74, 76, 78, 84, 87, 97, 99, 102, 110, 125, 126, 128, 129, 132, 133, 134, 135, 137, 146, 147, 149

Index of Authors

Alden, Robert L., 102, 107, 108, 169, 170, 176, 177, 184
Allen, Leslie C., 9, 54, 74, 82, 87, 88, 89, 93, 98, 101, 107, 118, 128, 129, 147, 188, 209, 213, 214, 228, 231, 232, 237, 243, 246, 255, 260, 261, 270, 274, 276, 280, 287, 290, 304, 306, 311, 313, 332, 338, 339, 344, 350
Aloisi, John, 73
Assis, Elie, 265
Auffret, Pierre, 25, 29, 36, 40, 50, 71, 78, 82, 83, 113, 119, 126, 136, 143, 145, 147, 154, 178, 207, 208, 255, 257, 262, 265, 270, 278, 298, 299, 312, 332, 334, 344, 345, 346, 351
Augustine, 208

Bar-Efrat, Shimon, 261, 266
Barbiero, Gianni, 74, 76, 77, 78, 81, 83, 84, 228, 230
Barker, David G., 172
Barré, Michael L., 106, 108
Basson, Alec, 300
Ben Yosef Gaon, Sa'adiah, 354, 355
Berlin, Adele, 97, 315
Beuken, W. A. M., 356
Booij, Thijs, 38, 66, 217
Botha, P. J., 2, 3, 4
Bracke, John M., 196
Broderson, Alma, 330
Brueggemann, Walter, 343, 348, 349, 351

Calvin, John, 209
Ceresko, Anthony R., 34, 40, 173
Cha, Kilnam, 348
Chisholm, Thomas O., 341
Clifford, Richard J., 39
Coakley, Sarah, 217

Davis, Ellen F., 346
Day, John N., 265

deClaissé-Walford, Nancy, et al., 9, 15, 18, 34, 35, 43, 46, 56, 57, 74, 168, 228, 230, 255, 310, 317
Dobbs-Allsopp, F. W. 238
Donner, Herbert, 179

Egwim, Stephen C., 66
Eitan, Israel, 263
Estes, Daniel J., 204

Falkenstein, A., 201
Flesher, LeAnn Snow, 198
Fokkelman, J. P., 203
Freedman, David Noel, 122
Fretheim, Terence E., 340, 341

Gardiner, Alan H., 267
Girard, Marc, 2, 9, 10, 11, 18, 25, 26, 28, 29, 30, 34, 38, 41, 47, 49, 50, 74, 82, 89, 118, 152, 158, 211, 264, 271, 279, 286, 296, 332
Goldingay, John, 3, 4, 5, 12, 13, 14, 19, 21, 26, 27, 30, 41, 70, 81, 85, 88, 92, 94, 95, 97, 99, 108, 109, 110, 112, 113, 119, 123, 125, 131, 139, 166, 168, 178, 181, 182, 186, 188, 192, 194, 198, 203, 207, 208, 209, 216, 223, 224, 228, 234, 238, 242, 248, 250, 257, 258, 260, 261, 263, 272, 276, 280, 285, 287, 293, 306, 311, 313, 317, 322, 327, 328, 332, 351

Herbert, George, 340
Hill, Edmund, 327
Holman, Jan, 276, 277
Homer, 267

Jarick, John, 54
Jenkins, Steffen G., 66
Jerome, 208
Josephus, 266
Jung, Won-Seok, 317

INDEX OF AUTHORS

Kalmanofsky, Amy, 267
Keel, Othmar, 267
Kern, Paul Bentley, 267
Kim, Sung-Soo, 178
Kimelman, 317, 318, 319, 320, 321, 321, 323
Kitz, Anne Marie, 70
Knowles, Melody D., 228
Kselman, John S., 4
Kuruvilla, Abraham, 15, 21, 41, 84, 123, 152, 242, 268, 324, 357

Labuschagne, C. J., 224
Lambert, W. G., 266
Lee, Archie C., 39
Leow, Wen-Pin, 233
Levenson, Jon D., 84, 107, 152, 242
Lucian, 267
Lux, Rüdiger, 267

Makujina, John, 314
Maré, Leonard P., 259,
Marrs, Rick Roy, 217, 218, 219
Martin, Lee Roy, 34, 46, 47, 55
McCann, J. Clinton, Jr., 353
Mensah, Michael Kodzo, 133, 137, 145, 160
Merrill, Eugene H., 75
Miller, Patrick D., 24, 28, 214

Nel, Philip, 228
Newton, John, 176, 179

Pavan, Marco, 346
Prinsloo, Gert T. M., 86, 167, 214, 219
Prinsloo, W. S., 258
Pritchard, James B., 25
Purcell, Richard Anthony, 75
Reed, Gregory, 116
Reynolds, Carol Bechtel, 193
Reynolds, Kent Aaron, 123
Ross, Allen P., 46, 203, 237, 267, 332
Simon, Paul, 305
Singer, Dwight Charles, 270, 313, 317, 318
Snyman, Fanie, 113
Sokolow, Moshe, 354, 355
Soll, Will, 142, 144
Tackmier, Bill J., 120
Tennyson, Alfred, Lord, 27
Thompson, Francis, 279
Todd, James M., III, 250, 251, 256
Tucker, W. Dennis, Jr., 39

Versluis, Arie, 267
Von Soden, W., 201
Vos, Johannes G., 268
Watson, W. G. E., 321, 354
Weinfeld, Moshe, 55
Whitekettle, Richard, 26
Williams, Peter, 175
Williams, William, 175
Zevit, Ziony, 236

Index of Scripture and Apocrypha

OLD TESTAMENT

Genesis

1–3	27
1	27, 39
2:1–2	230n11
2:7	28n15
2:8	28n15
2:19	28n15
3:5	223n5
3:15	219n14
3:17	30
13:16	314n20
14:3	179n5
14:18	75, 75n8
22:15–18	231n17
25:19–34	264n14
27:1–46	264n14
27:28	238n7
35:19	229n8
41:37	38n10
50:16–20	217n7

Exodus

3:8	56n6
3:10–12	57n12
3:15	246n1
5:23	56n6
6:6–7	57n12
6:13	57n12
6:26–27	57n12
7:1—15:21	46
7:14–25	38
7:21	39n14
8:1–15	39
8:16–19	39
8:20–32	39
8:6	39n14
8:16	39n14
8:24	39n14
9:1–7	39n14
9:6	39n14
9:8–12	39n14
9:10	39n14
9:13–35	39
9:23	39n14
10:1–20	39
10:14–15	39n14
10:21–29	38
10:22	39n14
13:21	57n12
14:30	57n8
15:2	118n6
15:12	118n6
15:13	57n12
15:15	30
15:22–25	46
16:1—17:1	46
17:1–5	98n14
18:11	246n1
19:6	97, 238
19:7	84n12
19:18	30n23
20:2–3	84
21:22–25	265n19
23:14–17	179n6
29:7	238
33:13	19
34:6–7	217
34:6	19, 83n5, 320
34:7	19

Leviticus

8:12	238
19:18	265n17
19:27	238n5
21:5	238n5
24:3–4	234
24:17–22	265n19

Numbers

6:1–21	234n29
6:24–26	242
11	46
13:25–29	46
14:3	46
16–17	46
16:40	75n5
17:21	75n5
17:22	75n5
17:23	75n5
17:24	75n5
17:25	75n5
20:1–13	98n14
20:8–13	46
20:14–22	264n14
21:21–35	257n6
25:3–9	46
25:13	75n5
28:6	84
32:33	249n10, 257n6

Deuteronomy

1:4	249n10, 257n6
2:2–5	264n14
2:8	264n14
4:10	217
4:13	83n8
4:40	314n20
4:46–47	257n6
5:6–7	84
6:2	152n55
6:13	152n55
9:7–29	46
10:12	152n55, 217
10:20	217
12:2	174
12:9	230n11
13:3–4	152n55
17:18–20	3n7
19:16–21	265n19
24:18	84
26:19	340n8
28:3–8	313n18
28:4	313n18
28:58	217
29:7	249n10
31:4	257n6
31:19	355
31:22	355
31:24	355
31:30—32:47	355

32:1–19	355
32:18	224
32:20–27	355
32:20	355
32:28–33	355
32:34–35	355
32:35–36	345n8
32:36	246n1, 355
32:37–42	355
32:37	355
32:41	265n17
32:43	355
33:12	224n8
33:13	238n7
33:28	238n7
34:11	246n1

Joshua

2:10	257n6
9:10	257n6
12:2–5	257n6
13:10–12	257n6

Judges

1:18–36	46
2:1–3	46
2:16–19	46
2:18–19	46
3:9	46
5:2	77n13
5:6	194
5:9	77n13

Ruth

2:2	314n20
4:11	229n8

1 Samuel

6:1—7:2	229n9
7:5	229n10

2 Samuel

3:9	170
3:35	170
6	75n5
7:13	202n3
7:14	231n17
8:18	75n5

12:25	202n4
21:17	233
22:2	311n4

1 Kings

1:38–40	78n20
2:4	231n17
3:3–15	202n4
3:3–4	75n5
4:19	257n6
5–8	202n4
5:5	202n3
6:1	202n3
8:5	75n5
8:6	202n3
8:25	231n17
8:29	202n3
8:38–40	217
8:44	202n3
8:48	202n3
8:55	75n5
8:62–63	75n5
9:4–5	231n17
11:36	233
11:38–39	231n17
15:4	233

2 Kings

6:24–30	267n27
8:12	266, 266n21
8:19	233
17:36–39	217
23:27	202n3
25:7	267n27

1 Chronicles

9:27	241n1
9:33	241n1
15	75n5
16:29	74n4
16:34	253n1
17:12	202n3
20:21	74n4
22:14	226n2
23:30	241n1
28:2	75, 229n10, 230n11
29:5–6	77n13
29:10	126n17
29:17	77n13

2 Chronicles

1:3	75n5
1:6	75n5
2–7	202n4
6:30–31	217
6:34	76n9, 202n3
6:38	202n3
6:41–42	230
17:16	77n13
20:21	253n1
20:35–37	179n5
21:7	233
26:16–23	75n5

Ezra

3:8—4:5	202
3:11	253n1
4:1—6:18	202
10:9	30

Nehemiah

1:3	313n19
2:13	313n19
4:3	313n19
4:7	313n19
6:1	313n19
9:22	257n6

Job

3:8	28
20:29	66n9
38:7	348n1
41:1–34	28

Psalms

(Also see within the appropriate psalms for references to verses of those chapters.)

1–41	353
1	349, 351, 353, 355n6, 356
1:2	122
2	353
2:1a	346n12
2:1b	346n12
2:2–3	65n1
2:2	230n13
2:2a	346n12
2:3a	346n12
2:4	193n3, 232n20

Psalms (continued)

2:5	346, 356
2:6	192, 318n6
2:6a	346n12
2:7	356
2:8	230n13
2:9	346
2:10	118n7
2:10a	346n12
2:10b	346n12
3:2	65n1
4:5	123
5:2	318n6
5:7	271n2
6	7, 214
6:2	118n7
7:11	123
7:6	356
7:9	123
8:3	28n17, 242n5
8:6	242n5
9	315n1
9:4	193n3, 232n20
9:5	356
9:7	193n3, 232n20
9:8	356
9:10	123
9:14	239n10
9:16	356
10	315n1
10:5	356
10:14	123
10:16	318n6
11:7	123
12:5	356
12:6	356
13:4	65n1
13:6	265n16
14:2	123
14:5b	334n6
14:6a	334n6
14:7	196, 238n10
15–24	354
15	354
15:4	123
16	354
16:7	118n7
16:8	123
16:9	62n1
17	354
17:2	356
17:4	356
17:10–11	65n2
17:12–13	65n2
18	354
18:1	123
18:2	226n2, 233n23, 311n4, 340n7
18:8–9	30n23
18:16	188n5
18:22	356
18:23	356
18:24–27	334n6
18:30	356
18:46	222n4
18:47	345n8
18:50	230n13
19	354, 355n6, 356
19:1	242n5
20–21	354
20:2	123, 238n10
20:6	230n13
21:7	123
21:13	222n4
22	354
22:3	193n3
22:3	232n20
22:4–5	123
22:19	66
22:23	123
22:25	123
22:26	123
23	354
24	354
24:2	97n9
24:6	123
24:7–10	318n6
25:10	231n17, 355n6, 356
25:12	123
25:14	123, 355n6
25:2	123
25:6–7	226n2
25:9	356
26:1	123
26:5	281n18
27:1	163n72
27:9	123
27:26	78n21
28:5	242n5
28:7	123
28:8	230n13
29:2	74n4
29:3	188n5
29:10	318n6
29:10–11	193n3, 232n20
30:10	123
30:12	62n1

31:2	311n4	44:4	318n6, 356
31:3	311n4	44:17	231n17, 355n6
31:6	281n18	44:20	123
31:11	163n72	46	262n8
31:19	123	46:2–3	174
31:23	123	46:3	188n5
32	7, 214, 301n1	46:4	229n7
32:6	188n5	46:10	66
32:8	66	47	113n6
33:3	344n3	47:2	318n6
33:4	356	47:6–7	318n6
33:5	356	48	262n8
33:6	356	48:2	239n10, 318n6
33:7	188n5	48:9	238n10
33:9	356	48:12	356
33:9	356	49:13	66n9
33:20	123	50:1	356
34	315n1	50:5	37n7, 355n6
34:3	222n4	50:7–15	66
34:4	123	50:7	356
34:10	123	50:12	356
35:3–7	65n2	50:16	355n6, 356
35:3	356	50:17	356
35:8	65n2	51	7, 197, 214, 301n1
35:10	65n2	51:4	356
35:11–13	65n2	51:18	238n10
35:15–17	65n2	53:5	163n72
35:19–21	65n2	53:6	196, 238n10
35:21	65n1	55:5	30
35:23	356	55:19	193n3, 232n20
35:24–26	65n2	55:20	355n6
35:25	65n1	55:23	66
36:7	356	56:10	356
37	315n1	56:14	356
37:6	356	57	113n6
37:11–12	334n6	57:8–12	60
37:20	30n23	57:8	62n1
37:28	356	59:8	66
37:30	356	60:6–12	60
37:31	356	60:6	356
38	7, 214, 301n1	62:11	356
38:1	118n7	63:4	123
38:15	123	63:8	123
39:11	118n7	64:1	163n72
39:12	354	65:1	238n10
40:3	344n3	65:4	238n10
40:8	356	65:6	174
40:15	65n1	65:10	233n24
41:7–8	65n1	67	113n6
41:10	66	68	113n6
41:15	65n1	68:2	30n23
42:4	202n3	68:11	356
42:8	356	68:22	356
43:3	229n7	68:24	318n6

Psalms (continued)

68:28	356	84:3	318n6
69	197	84:9	230n13
69:1–2	188n5	85:1	196
69:2	216	85:8	356
69:14–15	188n5	85:11	233n24
69:14	216	85:12	233n24
69:17	123	86:1–2	334n6
69:28–29	334n6	86:9	271n2
71:3	311n4	86:10	222
72:1	356	86:15	66
72:2	356	87:5	356
72:8	97n9	88:10	123
72:11	271n2	89	197
72:16	233n27	89:3–4	66
72:17	75, 76	89:3	77, 355n6
73:13–14	334n6	89:4	37n7, 356
74:1	30n23	89:17–18	340n7
74:2	192	89:17	226n2, 233n23
74:12	318n6	89:19	356
74:13	188n5	89:20	230n13
74:14	28	89:23–25	340n7
74:20	355n6	89:24	233n23
75:4–5	233n23, 340n7	89:25	97n9
75:10	226n2, 233n23, 340n7	89:28	355n6
76	262n8	89:30	356
76:10	356	89:30	356
77:8	356	89:30–31	231n17
77:16	188n5	89:31	356
77:17–19	97n89	89:34	355n6
77:19	188n5	89:35	77
78:1	356	89:36–37	75, 76
78:5	356	89:38	230n13
78:7	356	89:39	355n6
78:10	355n6, 356	89:47	226n2
78:13	188n5	89:49	77
78:14	57n12	89:50	226n2
78:16	57n12, 188n5	89:51	230n13
78:23	356	90:3	356
78:29–30	90n10	90:6	233n27
78:37	355n6	91:2	311n4
78:53	57n12	91:11	356
78:56	356	92:10	230n13, 233n23
78:68	192	92:2	241n1
78:69	242, 242n4	92:4	242n5
78:72	57n12	92:7	233n27
80:1	193n3, 232n20	92:9–11	340n7
80:4	30n23	93:5	356
81:4	356	94:1	345n8
81:5	356	94:10	118n7
83:5	37n7, 355n6	94:12	118n7, 356
84	262n8	94:15	356
84:1	229n7	94:20	356
		95:3	318n6
		95:10	356

96	111, 113n6	106:43	52n6
96:1	344n3	106:45	226n2, 355n6
96:9	74n4, 271n2	106:47	52, 56
97:10	123, 281n18	107–150	353, 354, 354n3
97:2	356	107	354
97:5	97n8, 174	107:1	253n1
97:8	356	107:8	129n22
98:1	344n3	107:11	356
98:7–8	97n8	107:15	129n22
99	113n6	107:20	356
99:1	193n3, 232n20	107:21	129n22
99:4	318n6, 356	107:24	129n22
99:5	75, 229n10, 271n2	107:31	129n22
99:7	356	108–110	354
99:8	345n8	108:6	131n27
100	111, 113n6	108:7	356
101:1	356	110:1	193n3, 232n20
101:2–4	281n18	111–16	111
102	214, 301n1	111–12	354
102:2	123, 131n27	111	86, 86n1, 315n1
102:25	242n5	111:1–2	86
103:6	356	111:1a	86n1
103:11	272n5	111:1b	86n1
103:15	233n27	111:1c	86n1
103:18	231n17, 355n6, 356	111:2a	86, 86n1
103:20	356	111:2b	86n1
104:18	272n5	111:3b	86n1
105	43	111:4	129n22
105:5	356	111:4a	86n1
105:7	356	111:4b	86n1
105:8	355n6, 356	111:5	355n6
105:10	355n6, 356	111:5a	86n1
105:11	356	111:5b	86n1
105:15	66	111:6b	86n1
105:19	356	111:7	242n5, 356
105:27	356	111:7b–8a	86n1
105:28	356	111:8a	86n1
105:31	356	111:9	355n6, 356
105:34	356	111:9b	86n1
105:37–38	57n12	111:9c	86n1
105:42	356	111:10	86, 86n1
105:43	57n12	111:10b	86n1
105:45	356	111:10c	86n1
106:1	253n1	112	94n6, 315n1
106:3	356	112:1	356
106:4	226n2	112:4	123
106:7–12	123	112:5	356
106:8	57n8	112:8–9	340n7
106:10	57n8	112:9	233n23
106:12	356	113–18	354
106:14	90n10	113:4	272n5
106:23	356	113:5	193n3, 232n20
106:24	356	114	105n2, 111
106:34	356		

Psalms (continued)

115	105n2
115:3–14	174
115:3	246n1
115:9–11	246n1
115:15	174
116:1	123
116:5	123
117	221
118:1–4	253n1
118:23	129n22
119	315n1, 353, 354, 354n2, 355, 356, 355n6
119:1–2	353
119:27	83n10
119:104	281n18
119:113	281n18
119:128	281n18
119:163	281n18
120–134	167
120–124	354
120	180n8
121	167n2
121:1	167n3
121:2	167n1, 167n3
121:3	167n3
121:4	167n3
121:5	167n3
121:7	167n3
121:8	167n3
122	167n2
122:2	167n3
122:3	167, 167n3
122:4	167n3, 356
122:5	167n3, 356
122:5a	167n3
122:5b	167n3
122:6	123, 167, 167n3
122:7	167n3
122:8	167n3
122:9	167n3
123	167n2
123:1	167n3, 193n3, 232n20
123:2	167n3
123:3	167n3
123:4	167n3
124	167n2, 191
124:1–7	174
124:1	167n3
124:2	167n3
124:3	167n3
124:4	167n3
124:5	167n3
124:7	167n3
124:7a	167n3
124:7b	167n3
124:8	167n1, 174
125	167n2
125:1	167, 167n3
125:2	167, 167n3
125:2a	167n3
125:2b	167n3
125:3b	167n3
125:3c	167n3
125:5	167n1
126	167n2, 199
126:1	167
126:2	167n3
126:3	167n3
126:5	167n3
126:6	167n3
127	167n2, 206, 207, 208, 210
127:1a	167n3
127:1b	167n3
127:1c	167n3
127:1d	167n3
127:2	167n3
127:2c	207
127:3	168n3
127:4	168n3
127:5	168n3
128	167n2, 199, 210
128:1	168n3
128:1a	199n1
128:2	168n3
128:2a	199n1
128:2b	199n1
128:3a	199n1
128:3b	199n1
128:3c	199n1
128:4a	199n1
128:4b	199n1
128:5ab	199n1
128:5	238n10
128:6	167, 167n1
128:6a	199n1
129	167n2
129:1	168n3
129:2	168n3
129:5	167
129:8b	168n3
129:8c	168n3
130	7, 167n2, 221, 301n1
130:1–2	221
130:2a	168n3
130:2c	168n3
130:5–6	221

130:5	123, 168n3, 356	140	289, 291
130:5aα	168n3	140:1	289
130:5aβ	168n3	140:1a	289n1
130:6	168n3	140:2a	289n1
130:7–8	221	140:3	289
130:7	123, 167n1, 168n3, 221	140:3b	289n1
130:8	168n3	140:4a	289n1
130:9b	289n1	140:5a	289n1
131	167n2	140:5c	289n1
131:1	354	140:7a	289n1
131:1a	168n3	140:8–12a	300n8
131:1b	168n3	140:8a	289n1
131:2a	168n3	140:11b	289n1
131:2b	168n3	140:12	356
131:2c	168n3	140:13a	289n1
131:3	167n1	141:2	123
132–134	244	141:6a	300n8
132	167n2, 238, 242n4	141:10a	300n8
132:5	168n3	143	7, 214
132:7	75, 95, 168n3, 271n2	143:2	356
132:10	168n3	143:5	242n5
132:11–12	75, 76	143:7	123
132:11	168n3	144:4–7	97n8
132:12	168n3, 355n6, 356	144:5	30
132:13	167	144:9	344n3
133	167n2, 240	145:5–6	222
133:1	168n3	145:20	123
133:1a	240	145:21	325
133:2	168n3	146–150	318, 325, 354
133:2a	168n3	146–149	348n1
133:2c	168n3	146:3–4	174
133:3	167, 168n3, 356	146:5–6	174
133:3c	240	147:1a	325
134	167n2	146:7	356
134:1	168n3	147:11	123
134:2	168n3	147:15	356
134:3	167, 168n3, 238n10	147:18	356
135–136	3354	147:19	356
135:8–11	265	147:20	356
136:10–20	265	147:20c	325
135:11	257n6	148:1a	325
135:19	238	148:2	348n1
136:4	222	148:5	356
136:17–22	246n1	148:6	356
136:24	265	148:8	356
137	345n7, 354, 354n3	148:14	233n23
137:8–9	300n9, 345n8	148:14d	325
138–145	354	149:1a	325
138:2	356	149:2	318n6
138:4	356	149:9	356
138:7b–8a	300n8	149:9c	325
138:8	242n5	150	113n6
139	283	150:1a	325
139:19	300n8	150:6b	325
139:19a	232		

Proverbs

2:8	172n5
3:19–20	172n4
3:20	238n7
3:21–30	172n3
3:26	172n5
4:6	172n5
5:15–23	172n2
7:5	172n5
8:13	281n18
8:22–26	172n4
19:12	238n7
23:1–8	172n3
23:22–28	172n3
23:29–30	172n2
24:20	233n28
31:10–13	208n2

Isaiah

2:1–4	180n7
4:2	233n25
7:14	234
8:8	234
9:17	30n21
10:5–34	265n18
13:1—14:27	265n18
13:16	266
13:18	266
14:11	348n1
14:21	267n28
15:7	69n14
21:1–10	265n18
25–27	180n7
27:1	28
33:1–24	265n18
33:46–47	265n18
40:27	265
41:8–9	265
42:9	233n26
42:14	224
43:19	233n26
44:4	233n26
45:8	233n26
46:3	224
47:1	265n16
49:22	224n8
51:10	216
55:10	233n26
57:7	174
58:8	233n26
61:11	233n26
62:1–12	180n7
62:7	340n8
65:17–25	180n7
66:1–2	242
66:1	75, 230n11
66:13	224

Jeremiah

1:13–14	57n9
2:2	211n2
3:6	174
3:23	176
6:16	281
10:13	246n1
13:11	340n8
13:14	266n22
18:15	281
23:5	233n25
26:6	202n3
26:9	202n3
26:12	202n3
32:30	211n2
33:9	340n8
33:15	233n25, 233n26
33:24–26	265
46:10	345n8
50–51	265n18
50:42	265n16
51:16	246n1
51:20–24	266n22
51:24	265n18, 266n22
51:33	265n16
51:48	266
51:56	265n18

Lamentations

2:1	75
3:6	265
3:8	265
3:64–66	265n16

Ezekiel

9:2	57n9
18:6	174n8
18:12	174n8
25:1–7	264
25:8–11	264
25:15–17	264
26:13	263n10
27:34	216
29:21	233n26
37:11–12	265
47:5–14	78

Daniel

10:11	30
11:6	179n5

Hosea

2:15	211n2
4:17	179n5
10:14	266
11:3–4	224
13:8	224
13:16	266, 266n21
14:5	238n7

Joel

3:18	78

Amos

1:11	264n14
1:13	266n21
5:15	281n18

Obadiah

10	264n14
12	264n14

Micah

3:2	281n18
5:2	229n8
5:7	238n7

Nahum

3:9–10	266

Zephaniah

2:13–15	254n18
3:20	340n8

Haggai

1:1—2:9	202

Zechariah

2:7	265n16
3:8	233n25
6:12	233n25
8:12	238n7
14:8	78

Malachi

1:2–4	264n14

NEW TESTAMENT

Matthew

21:9	114n1
21:42	114n1
22:43–44	73
22:44	73n1
23:39	114n1
24:31	248n1
26:64	73n1

Mark

11:9–10	114n1
12:10	114n1
12:36	73, 73n1
14:62	73n1
16:19	73n1

Luke

13:35	114n1
19:38	114n1
19:44	266
20:17	114n1, 119n11
20:18	119n11
20:42–44	73
20:42–43	73n1
22:69	73n1

John

12:13	114n1
12:34	73n1
14:15	84n11
14:21	84n11, 156n63
14:23	84n11

Acts

2:34–35	73, 73n1

Romans

8:29	356n8
8:34	73n1
13:11	219n13

1 Corinthians

3:16	247n3
15:25	73n1

Ephesians

1:8–10	98, 356n8
1:20	73n1
3:14–21	3n6
3:19–21	247n3

Colossians

3:1	73n1

1 Thessalonians

4:16	348n1

2 Timothy

3:16–17	268

Hebrews

1:3	73n1
1:13	73n1
5:6	73n1
5:10	73n1
6:20	73n1
7:3	73n1
7:17	73n1
7:21	73n1
8:1	73n1
10:12–13	73n1
12:2	73n1

1 Peter

1:5	219

1 John

2:3	84n11
3:24	84n11
5:2–3	84n11

2 John

6	84n11

Jude

21	156n63

Revelation

2:26–27	180n7, 230n13
3:12	180n7
5:8	348n1
8:2	348n1
14:2	348n1
18:20	266n24
21–22	180n7

APOCRYPHA

2 Maccabees

6:10	267n28

4 Maccabees

4:25	267n28

www.ingramcontent.com/pod-product-compliance
Lightning Source LLC
Chambersburg PA
CBHW081533300426
44116CB00015B/2616